新曲綫 | 用心雕刻每一本……
New Curves

http://site.douban.com/110283/
http://weibo.com/nccpub

U0531841

用心字里行间　雕刻名著经典

Essentials of Economics

Eleventh Edition

Bradley R. Schiller
Professor Emeritus, American University

Karen Gebhardt
University of Colorado Boulder

经济学基础

（第 11 版，双语教学通用版）

〔美〕布拉德利·希勒　卡伦·格布哈特　著

王福重　张志超　译注

商务印书馆
2023年·北京

Bradley R. Schiller, Karen Gebhardt

Essentials of Economics, 11e

ISBN: 978-1-260-22533-4

Copyright © 2020 by McGraw-Hill Education.

All Rights reserved. No part of this publication may be reproduced or transmitted in any form or by any means, electronic or mechanical, including without limitation photocopying, recording, taping, or any database, information or retrieval system, without the prior written permission of the publisher.

This authorized Bilingual edition is published by The Commercial Press in arrangement with McGraw-Hill Education (Singapore) Pte. Ltd.. This edition is authorized for sale in the People's Republic of China only, excluding Hong Kong, Macao SAR and Taiwan region.

Translation Copyright © 2023 by McGraw-Hill Education (Singapore) Pte. Ltd and The Commercial Press.

About the Authors 作者介绍

Bradley R. Schiller has over four decades of experience teaching introductory economics at American University, the University of California (Berkeley and Santa Cruz), the University of Maryland, and the University of Nevada (Reno). He has given guest lectures at more than 300 colleges ranging from Fresno, California, to Istanbul, Turkey. Dr. Schiller's unique contribution to teaching is his ability to relate basic principles to current socioeconomic problems, institutions, and public policy decisions. This perspective is evident throughout *Essentials of Economics*.

Dr. Schiller derives this policy focus from his extensive experience as a Washington consultant. He has been a consultant to most major federal agencies, many congressional committees, and political candidates. In addition, he has evaluated scores of government programs and helped design others. His studies of income inequality, poverty, discrimination, training programs, tax reform, pensions, welfare, Social Security, and lifetime wage patterns have appeared in both professional journals and popular media. Dr. Schiller is also a frequent commentator on economic policy for television, radio, and newspapers.

©Bradley R. Schiller

Dr. Schiller received his PhD from Harvard and his BA degree, with great distinction, from the University of California (Berkeley). When not teaching, writing, or consulting, Professor Schiller is typically on a tennis court, schussing down a ski slope, or enjoying the crystal blue waters of Lake Tahoe.

Karen Gebhardt is the Director of the Online Economics Program in the Department of Economics and regularly teaches in the Masters of the Environment program at the University of Colorado Boulder. Dr. Gebhardt has a passion for teaching economics. She has taught online since 2005, and regularly instructs on-campus large introductory courses in macro- and microeconomics; upper-division courses in Public Finance, Microeconomics, Money and Banking, and International Trade; and graduate courses in Public Finance and Environmental Statistics. She is an early adopter of technology in the classroom and advocates strongly for it because she sees the difference it makes in student engagement and learning. Dr. Gebhardt was the recipient of the Water Pik Excellence in Education Award in 2006 and was awarded the Colorado State University Best Teacher Award in 2015.

©Karen Gebhardt

Dr. Gebhardt's research interests, publications, and presentations involve economics education and the economics of human–wildlife interaction. Before joining academia, she worked as an economist at the USDA/APHIS/Wildlife Services/National Wildlife Research Center conducting research on the interactions of humans and wildlife. Her current research focuses on using learning analytics to improve student learning outcomes in economics education with an emphasis on improving grades and completion rates in online courses.

In her free time, Dr. Gebhardt enjoys learning about new teaching methods that integrate technology, as well as rock climbing and camping in the Colorado Rockies and beyond.

Preface 前言

Election campaigns bring out the best and the worst economic ideas. Virtually every candidate promises a "chicken in every pot," without regard to the supply of chickens. They will clean up the environment, fix our schools, put more police on the streets, build more affordable housing, and, of course, guarantee every American access to quality health care. And they'll do this while cutting taxes, subsidizing alternative energy sources, and rebuilding America's infrastructure.

Don't you wish you lived in such a utopia?! I know I do. And our students overwhelmingly embrace these promises.

The problem is, of course, that there is no such thing as a free lunch. Nor free health care, free environmental protection, or free infrastructure development. As economists, we know this; we know that resource scarcity requires us to make difficult choices about competing uses of those resources. We know that politicians can't place a chicken in every pot without allocating more resources to poultry production—and fewer resources to the production of other desired goods and services.

Our first task as instructors is to convince students of this basic fact of life—that every decision about resource use entails opportunity costs. If we can establish that beachhead early on, we have a decent chance of instilling in students a basic appreciation of economic theory.

The other challenge for us as instructors is to instill in students a sense of *why* the economic problems we analyze are important. We know that inflation and unemployment cause serious hardships. But most of our students haven't experienced the income losses that accompany unemployment or seen their retirement savings decimated by inflation. We have to explain and illustrate why the macro problems we seek to solve are politically, socially, and economically important.

The same reference gap exists in micro. Formulas and graphs illustrating externalities or monopoly pricing are meaningless abstractions to most students. If we want them to appreciate these concepts, we have to illustrate them with real-world examples (e.g., the death toll from secondhand smoke; the higher airfares that result on monopoly airplane routes). For most students, this course is their first exposure to economics. If we want them to understand the subject—maybe even pursue it further—we have got to relate our concepts and theories to the world that they live in. This has been the hallmark of *Essentials* from the beginning: introducing the core concepts of economics in a reality-based, policy-driven context. This eleventh edition continues that tradition.

WHAT, HOW, FOR WHOM? 生产什么，如何生产，为谁生产

The core theme that weaves through the entire text is the need to find the best possible answers to the basic questions of WHAT, HOW, and FOR WHOM to produce. Students are confronted early on with the reality that the economy doesn't always operate optimally at either the macro or micro level. In Chapter 1 they learn that markets sometimes fail to generate optimal outcomes, but also that government interventions can fail to improve economic performance. The policy challenge is to find the mix of market reliance and government regulation that generates the best possible outcomes. Every chapter ends with a Policy Perspectives feature that challenges students to apply the economic concepts they have just encountered to real-world policy issues. In Chapter 1 the policy question is, "Is 'Free' Health Care Really Free?"—a question that emphasizes the opportunity costs associated with all economic activity. In Chapter 9 the issue is "Is Another Recession Coming?"—which challenges students to think about the causes and advance indicators of economic downturns. And Chapter 16 is devoted to explaining the perennial contrast between theory and reality, with a mixture of institutional, political, and theoretical factors. Students love that macro capstone.

FOCUS ON CORE CONCEPTS 关注核心概念

It's impossible to squeeze all the content—and the excitement—of both micro and macro economics into a one-semester course, much less an abbreviated intro text. But economics is, after all, the science of choice. Instructors who teach a one-term survey of economics know how hard the content choices can be. There are too many topics, too many economic events, and too little time.

Few textbooks confront this scarcity problem directly. Some one-semester books are nearly as long as full-blown principles texts. The shorter ones tend to condense topics and omit the additional explanations, illustrations, and applications that are especially important in survey courses. Students and teachers alike get frustrated trying to pick out the essentials from abridged principles texts.

Essentials of Economics lives up to its name by making the difficult choices. The standard table of contents has been pruned to the core. The surviving topics are the essence of economic concepts. In microeconomics, for example, the focus is on the polar models of perfect competition and monopoly. These models are represented as the endpoints of a spectrum of market structures. Intermediate market structures—oligopoly, monopolistic competition, and the like—are noted but not analyzed. The goal here is simply to convey the sense that market structure is an important determinant of market outcomes. The contrast between the extremes of monopoly and perfect competition is sufficient to convey this essential message. The omission of other market structures from the outline also leaves more space for explaining and illustrating *how* market structure affects market behavior.

The same commitment to essentials is evident in the section on macroeconomics. Rather than attempt to cover all the salient macro models, the focus here is on a straightforward presentation of the aggregate supply–demand framework. The classical, Keynesian, and monetarist perspectives on aggregate demand (AD) and aggregate supply (AS) are discussed within that common, consistent framework. There is no discussion of neo-Keynesianism, rational expectations, public choice. The level of abstraction required for such models is neither necessary nor appropriate in an introductory survey course. Texts that include such models tend to raise more questions than survey instructors can hope to answer. In *Essentials* students are exposed to only the ideas needed for a basic understand-ing of how macro economies function.

CENTRAL THEME 主旨

The central goal of this text is to convey a sense of how economic *systems* affect economic *outcomes*. When we look back on the twentieth century, we see how some economies flourished while others languished. Even the "winners" had recurrent episodes of slow, or negative, growth. The central analytical issue is how various economic systems influenced those diverse growth records. Was the relatively superior track record of the United States a historical fluke or a by-product of its commitment to market capitalism? Were the long economic expansions of the 1980s and 1990s the result of enlightened macro policy, more efficient markets, or just good luck? What roles did policy, markets, and (bad) luck play in the Great Recession of 2008–2009? What forces deserve credit for the accelerated economic growth of 2016–2019?

In the looming 2020 presidential election, economic issues will again be at the forefront (as Yale economist Ray Fair has been telling us for decades). President Trump will claim credit for the economic expansion of the last few years. Democrats will argue that the expansion started when President Obama was in office. Republicans will say the 2017 tax cuts propelled the economy forward. Democrats will counter that the 2017 tax cuts merely enriched the top 1 percent of U.S. households and ballooned budget deficits. President Trump will hail his trade and tariff policies as sources of economic strength; Democrats will emphasize how those same policies increased the cost of living for middle-class households.

How are students—and voters—supposed to sort out these conflicting claims? *Essentials* offers an analytical foundation for assessing both economic events and political platforms. Students get an initial bird's-eye view of the macro economy that relates macro determinants to macro outcomes. Then they get enough tools to identify cause-and-effect relationships and to sort out competing political claims.

A recurrent theme in *Essentials* is the notion that economic institutions and policies *matter*. Economic prosperity isn't a random occurrence. The right institutions and policies can foster or impede economic progress. The challenge is to know when and how to intervene.

This central theme is the focus of Chapter 1. Our economic accomplishments and insatiable materialism set the stage for a discussion of production possibilities. The role of economic systems and choices is illustrated with the starkly different "guns versus butter" decisions in Russia, and the United States. The potential for both market failure (or success) and government failure (or success) is highlighted. After reading Chapter 1, students should sense that "the economy" is important to their lives and that our collective choices on how the economy is structured are important.

REAL-WORLD EMPHASIS 强调现实世界

Students rarely get interested in stories about the mythical widget manufacturers that inhabit so many economics textbooks. But glimmers of interest—even some enthusiasm—surface when real-world illustrations, not fables, are offered.

Every chapter starts out with real-world applications of core concepts. As the chapters unfold, empirical illustrations continue to enliven the text analysis. The chapters end with a **Policy Perspectives** section that challenges the student to apply new concepts to real-world issues. The Policy Perspective in Chapter 2 ("Cap Water Prices in Natural Disasters?") highlights the challenges that policymakers face when markets shift in the wake of natural disasters.

POLICY PERSPECTIVES

CAP WATER PRICES IN NATURAL DISASTERS?

Hurricane Harvey was the second most costly natural disaster in the United States since 1900. When it slammed into the Houston area in August 2017, it destroyed thousands of homes, forced the evacuation of nearly 40,000 people, and caused massive flooding. It also damaged 10 water systems, temporarily cutting off water to thousands of homes and businesses. Bottled water became the only option for thousands of people.

The real-world approach of *Essentials* is reinforced by the boxed **News Wires** that appear in every chapter. The 67 News Wires offer up-to-date domestic and international applications of economic concepts. Some new examples that will particularly interest your students include:

- The impact of lower gas prices on sales of electric vehicles.
- The diversity in starting pay for various college majors.
- Taylor Swift's use of dynamic pricing for concerts.
- Tesla's new Gigafactory in Shanghai.
- The impact of the 2017 tax cuts on consumer spending.
- The price fixing conspiracy on canned tuna.
- How the strong dollar has made European vacations cheaper.

This is just a sampling of the stream of real-world applications that cascades throughout this text. Thirty-five of the News Wires are new to this edition.

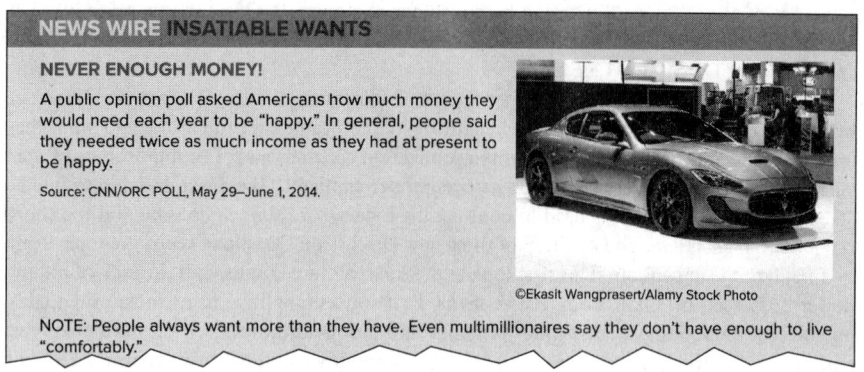

THEORY AND REALITY　理论与现实

In becoming acquainted with the U.S. economy, students will inevitably learn about the woes of the business cycle. As the course progresses, they will not fail to notice a huge gap between the pat solutions of economic theory and the dismal realities of occasional recession. This experience will kindle one of the most persistent and perplexing questions students have. If the theory is so good, why is the economy such a mess?

Economists like to pretend that the theory is perfect but politicians aren't. That's part of the answer, to be sure. But it isn't fair to either politicians or economists. In reality, the design and implementation of economic policy is impeded by incomplete information, changing circumstances, goal trade-offs, and politics. Chapter 16 examines these real-world complications. In this signature chapter, students get a more complete explanation of why the real world doesn't always live up to the promises of economic theory.

NEW IN THIS EDITION　本版的更新

The dedication of *Essentials* to introducing core economic principles in a real-world context requires every edition to focus on trending policies and front-page developments. As in earlier editions, this eleventh edition strives to arouse interest in economic theories by illustrating them in the context of actual institutions, policy debates, and global developments. The following list highlights both the essential focus of each chapter and the new material that enlivens its presentation:

Chapter 1: The Challenge of Economics—The first challenge here is to get students to appreciate the concept of *scarcity* and how it forces us to make difficult choices among desirable, but competing, options. That is really the essence of economic thinking. How we make those choices is also critical. Political campaigns always seem to suggest that we can have it all, without higher taxes or other sacrifices. With the 2020 elections looming on the horizon, we have another chance to emphasize opportunity costs. Chapter 1 includes eight new Problems, two new Discussion Questions, one new News Wire, and new opinion polls about fears of another recession in 2020 and the prospects for the next generation of Americans.

Chapter 2: Supply and Demand—This introduction to the market mechanism explains how markets set both prices and production for various goods. Interesting new News Wires include the shortages that accompany new iPhone launches and the impact of falling gaso-line prices on sales of electric vehicles. Four new Problems and four new Discussion Ques-tions are included, as well as a new Policy Perspective on post-hurricane price gouging.

Micro

Chapter 3: Consumer Demand—This chapter starts by looking at patterns of U.S. consumption, then analyzing the demand factors that shape those patterns. The elasticity of demand gets a lot of attention, as illustrated by consumer responses to iMac prices, price hikes at Starbucks, and higher gasoline prices (all new News Wires). There are four new Problems and three new Discussion Questions.

Chapter 4: Supply Decisions—The key point of this chapter is to highlight the difference between what firms *can* produce (as illustrated by the production function) and what they *want* to produce (as illustrated by profit-maximization calculations). The importance of marginal costs in the production decision gets its proper spotlight. The Tesla decision to build a "Gigafactory" in Shanghai is used to contrast the long-run *investment decision* and the short-run *production decision*. The addition of three new Discussion Questions keeps the topic lively.

Chapter 5: Competition—This first look at market structure emphasizes the lack of pricing power possessed by small, competitive firms. Perfectly competitive firms must relentlessly pursue cost reductions, quality improvements, and product innovation if they are to survive and prosper. Although few firms are perfectly competitive, competitive dynamics keep all firms on their toes. Those dynamics affect even the behavior of such giants as Apple (relentlessly trying to stay ahead of the pack)—not just the small T-shirt vendors on beach boardwalks (both new News Wires). How firms locate the most profitable rate of production with the use of market prices and marginal costs is illustrated. The chapter includes four new Problems and three new Discussion Questions. The chapter-ending Policy Perspective considers how competition helps rather than hurts society.

Chapter 6: Monopoly—As a survey introduction to economics, *Essentials* focuses on the differences in structure, behavior, and outcomes of only two market structures—namely, perfect competition and monopoly. This two-way contrast underscores the importance of market structure for social welfare. The monopoly produces less and charges more than a competitive market with the same cost structure, as illustrated with a step-by-step comparison of market behavior. The various barriers monopolies use to preserve their position and profits are illustrated as well. The chapter includes three new Problems, three new Discussion Questions, and three News Wires on monopoly-like behavior in Big Pharma, canned tuna, and oil.

Chapter 7: The Labor Market—The looming 2020 elections are showcasing very different views about income equality, minimum wages, unions, and mandatory workforce regulations. This chapter delves into these issues by first illustrating how market wages are set and then examining how various interventions alter market outcomes. Highlighted stories include Dale Earnhardt's earnings, Nick Saban's salary and benefits at Alabama, minimum-wage proposals, and Bernie Sanders' critique of CEO pay. Of special interest to students is the latest data on salaries for college grads in various majors. There are three new Problems and four new Discussion Questions.

Chapter 8: Government Intervention—Another focus of every election is the appropriate role for government in a market-driven economy. This chapter identifies the core rationale for government intervention and offers new illustrations of public goods (Israel's "Iron Dome" anti-missile program) and externalities (the Keystone XL Pipeline). There is also new poll data on trust in government. The chapter includes four new Problems and one new Discussion Question.

Macro

Chapter 9: The Business Cycle—This introduction to macro examines the up-and-down history of the economy and then looks at the impact of cyclical instability on unemployment, inflation, and the distribution of income. The goal here is to get students to recognize why macro instability is a foremost societal concern. The latest macro data are incorporated, along with a new News Wire on seasonal unemployment, four new Problems, and one new Discussion Question.

Chapter 10: Aggregate Supply and Demand—This chapter gives students a conceptual overview of the macro economy, highlighting the role that market forces and other factors play in shaping macro outcomes. Aggregate supply (AS) and aggregate demand (AD) are assessed, with an emphasis on the distinction between curve positions and curve shifts (the source of instability). The bottom line is that either AS or AD must shift if macro outcomes are to change. A News Wire on the aftermath of Hurricane Harvey illustrates how an aggregate supply curve can shift. There are five new Problems and three new Discussion Questions. The Policy Perspectives section summarizes the broad policy options that President Trump and other presidents have at their disposal to alter market outcomes.

Chapter 11: Fiscal Policy—This chapter highlights the potential of changes in government spending and taxes to shift the AD curve. The power of the income multiplier is illustrated in the context of the AS/AD framework and operationalized with analysis of the 2017 income tax cuts. The implications of fiscal policy for budget deficits are also examined. Updated budget data are included, along with five new Problems and three new Discussion Questions.

Chapter 12: Money and Banks—ApplePay and Bitcoins are used to illustrate differences between *payment services* and *money*. A News Wire focuses on the methods of payment consumers utilize. The core of the chapter depicts how deposit creation and the money multiplier work, using a step-by-step illustration of each. The Policy Perspectives section assesses why Bitcoins aren't really "money." There are six new Problems and one new Discussion Question. A new News Wire highlights the importance of a stable currency by looking at the resort to barter in inflation-battered Venezuela.

Chapter 13: Monetary Policy—In this chapter, students first get an overview of how the Federal Reserve is organized, including an introduction to Jerome Powell. Then the three basic tools of monetary policy are illustrated, with an emphasis on how open-market operations work. The narrative then focuses on how the use of these monetary tools shifts the AD curve, ultimately affecting both output and prices. News about China's cut in reserve requirements helps illustrate the intended effects. The 2008–2015 spike in excess reserves is also discussed, along with the Fed's new policy targeting. The chapter includes seven new Problems and three new Discussion questions.

Chapter 14: Economic Growth—The challenge of every society is to grow its economy and lift living standards. This chapter reviews the world's growth experience and then highlights the factors that affect growth rates. Of special interest in today's policy context is the role of immigration in spurring growth. The chapter's Policy Perspectives section examines whether economic growth is desirable, a question which students often ask. There are eight new Problems and four new Discussion Questions.

International
Chapter 15: International Trade—Students are first introduced to patterns of global trade, highlighting international differences in export dependence and trade balances. Then the question of "why trade at all?" is explicitly addressed, leading into an illustration of comparative advantage. Of importance is also a discussion of the sources of resistance to free trade and the impact of trade barriers. A News Wire illustrates how some people lost from President Trump's tariff policies and how others won. In addition to updating all data, four new News Wires, five new Problems, and two new Discussion Questions are included.

Capstone
Chapter 16: Theory and Reality—This unique capstone chapter addresses the perennial question of why economies don't function better if economic theory is so perfect. The chapter reviews the major policy tools and their idealized uses. Then it contrasts theoretical expectations with real-world outcomes and asks why macro performance doesn't live up to its promise. Impediments to better outcomes are explored, and the chapter ends by asking students whether they favor more or less policy intervention. Lots of new data are incorporated, along with four new Problems and three new Discussion Questions.

ACKNOWLEDGMENTS 致谢

The eleventh edition continues to benefit from the prodigious contributions of my digital co-author, Karen Gebhardt. Karen is a distinguished teacher who won numerous awards for her pedagogical prowess. As the Director of the Online Economics Program in the Department of Economics at University of Colorado Boulder she continues to share her passion for teaching economics by teaching online, mentoring online instructors, and teaching face-to-face in the Masters of the Environment program. She has assumed responsibility for the digital content of the *Essentials* learning package, including an overhaul of the test bank, the *Connect* program, LearnSmart, and other digital products. She has done a marvelous job not only improving the content of each digital supplement, but also enhancing the symmetry between the text and all dimensions of the digital products. Students and instructors will share my gratitude for Karen's excellent work.

The following manuscript reviewers were generous in sharing their teaching experiences and offering suggestions for the revision:

Ruth Bandzak, *Chaffey College*
Ronald Dunbar, *Madison Area Technical College*
Omar A. Esqueda, *Tarleton State University*
Jack A. Green, *Wentworth Institute of Technology*
Staish Gupta, *Tacoma Community College*
Kosin Isariyawongse, *Edinboro University*
Syed H. Jafri, *Tarleton State University*
David Kisel, *St. Phillip's College*
Riley Moore, *Saint Martin's University*
Lawrence Overlan, *Wentworth Institute of Technology*
Jeffery Phillips, *Colby-Sawyer College*
Kimberly Anne Sims, *University of Tennessee*
Ariuna Taivan, *University of Minnesota-Duluth*

Reviewers and users of past editions of *Essentials* have also contributed to the evolution of this text.

Bob Abadie, *National College*
Vera Adamchik, *University of Houston at Victoria*
Jacqueline Agesa, *Marshall University*
Jeff Ankrom, *Wittenburg University*
J. J. Arias, *Georgia College & State University*
James Q. Aylsworth, *Lakeland Community College*
Mohsen Bahmani-Oskooee, *University of Wisconsin-Milwaukee*
Nina Banks, *Bucknell University*
John S. Banyi, *Central Virginia Community College*
Ruth M. Barney, *Edison State Community College*
Nancy Bertaux, *Xavier University*
John Bockino, *Suffolk County Community College*
T. Homer Bonitsis, *New Jersey Institute of Technology*
Judy Bowman, *Baylor University*
Jeff W. Bruns, *Bacone College*
Douglas N. Bunn, *Western Wyoming Community College*
Ron Burke, *Chadron State College*
Kimberly Burnett, *University of Hawaii-Manoa*
Tim Burson, *Queens University of Charlotte*

Hanas A. Cader, *South Carolina State University*
Raymond E. Chatterton, *Lock Haven University*
Hong-yi Chen, *Soka University of America*
Howard Chernick, *Hunter College*
Porchiung Ben Chou, *New Jersey Institute of Technology*
Jennifer L. Clark, *University of Florida*
Norman R. Cloutier, *University of Wisconsin-Parkside*
Mike Cohick, *Collin County Community College-Plano*
James M. Craven, *Clark College*
Tom Creahan, *Morehead State University*
Kenneth Cross, *Southwest Virginia Community College*
Patrick Cunningham, *Arizona Western College*
Dean Danielson, *San Joaquin Delta College*
Ribhi M. Daoud, *Sinclair Community College*
Amlan Datta, *Cisco College & Texas Tech University*
Susan Doty, *University of Southern Mississippi*
Kevin Dunagan, *Oakton College*
James Dyal, *Indiana University of Pennsylvania*
Angela Dzata, *Alabama State University*
Erick Elder, *University of Arkansas at Little Rock*
Vanessa Enoch, *National College*
Maxwell O. Eseonu, *Virginia State University*
Jose Esteban, *Palomar College*
Bill Everett, *Baton Rouge Community College*
Randall K. Filer, *Hunter College*
John Finley, *Columbus State University*
Daisy Foxx, *Fayetteville Technical Community College*
Scott Freehafer, *University of Findlay*
Arlene Geiger, *John Jay College*
Lisa George, *Hunter College*
Gregory Gilpin, *University of Montana*
Chris Gingrich, *Eastern Mennonite University*
Yong U. Glasure, *University of Houston-Victoria*
Devra Golbe, *Hunter College*
Emilio Gomez, *Palomar College*
Anthony J. Greco, *University of Louisiana-Lafayette*
Cole Gustafson, *North Dakota State University*
Sheryl Hadley, *Johnson County Community College*
Patrick Hafford, *Wentworth Institute of Technology*
John Heywood, *University of Wisconsin-Milwaukee*
Jim Holcomb, *University of Texas at El Paso*
Philip Holleran, *Radford University*
Ward Hooker, *Orangeburg-Calhoun Technical College*
Yu Hsing, *Southeastern Louisiana University*
Syed Hussain, *University of Wisconsin*
Hans Isakson, *University of Northern Iowa*
Allan Jenkins, *University of Nebraska-Kearney*

Bang Nam Jeon, *Drexel University*
Hyojin Jeong, *Lakeland Community College*
Derek M. Johnson, *University of Connecticut*
Dan Jubinski, *St. Joseph's University*
Judy Kamm, *Lindenwood University*
Jimmy Kelsey, *Whatcom Community College*
R.E. Kingery, *Hawkeye Community College*
Allen Klingenberg, *Ottawa University-Milwaukee*
Shon Kraley, *Lower Columbia College*
Sean LaCroix, *Tidewater Community College*
Richard Langlois, *University of Connecticut*
Teresa L. C. Laughlin, *Palomar College*
Willis Lewis Jr., *Lander University*
Joshua Long, *Ivy Tech Community College*
B. Tim Lowder, *Florence-Darlington Technical College*
Kjartan T. Magnusson, *Salt Lake Community College*
Tim Mahoney, *University of Southern Indiana*
Michael L. Marlow, *California Polytechnic State University*
Vincent Marra, *University of Delaware*
Mike Mathea, *Saint Charles Community College*
Richard McIntyre, *University of Rhode Island*
Tom Menendez, *Las Positas College*
Amlan Mitra, *Purdue University-Calumet-Hammond*
Robert Moden, *Central Virginia Community College*
Carl Montano, *Lamar University*
Daniel Morvey, *Piedmont Technical College*
John Mundy, *University of North Florida*
Jamal Nahavandi, *Pfeiffer University*
Diane R. Neylan, *Virginia Commonwealth University*
Henry K. Nishimoto, *Fresno City College*
Gerald Nyambane, *Davenport University*
Diana K. Osborne, *Spokane Community College*
Shawn Osell, *Minnesota State University-Mankato*
William M. Penn, *Belhaven College*
Diana Petersdorf, *University of Wisconsin-Stout*
James Peyton, *Highline Community College*
Ron Presley, *Webster University*
Patrick R. Price, *University of Louisiana at Lafayette*
Janet Ratliff, *Morehead State University*
Mitchell H. Redlo, *Monroe Community College*
David Reed, *Western Technical College*
Terry L. Riddle, *Central Virginia Community College*
Jean Rodgers, *Wenatchee Valley College at Omak*
Vicki D. Rostedt, *University of Akron*
Terry Rotschafer, *Minnesota West Community and Technical College-Worthington*
Matthew Rousu, *Susquehanna University*
Sara Saderion, *Houston Community College-Southwest*

George Samuels, *Sam Houston State University*
Mustafa Sawani, *Truman State University*
Joseph A. Schellings, *Wentworth Institute of Technology*
Lee J. Van Scyoc, *University of Wisconsin-Oshkosh*
Dennis D. Shannon, *Southwestern Illinois College*
William L. Sherrill, *Tidewater Community College*
Gail Shipley, *El Paso Community College*
Johnny Shull, *Central Carolina Community College*
James Smyth, *San Diego Mesa College*
John Somers, *Portland Community College-Sylvania*
Rebecca Stein, *University of Pennsylvania*
Carol Ogden Stivender, *University of North Carolina-Charlotte*
Carolyn Stumph, *Indiana University Purdue University-Fort Wayne*
James Tallant, *Cape Fear Community College*
Frank Tenkorang, *University of Nebraska-Kearney*
Audrey Thompson, *Florida State University*
Ryan Umbeck, *Ivy Tech Community College*
Darlene Voeltz, *Rochester Community & Technical College*
Yongqing Wang, *University of Wisconsin-Waukesha*
Dale W. Warnke, *College of Lake County*
Nissan Wasfie, *Columbia College-Chicago*
Luther G. White, *Central Carolina Community College*
Mary Lois White, *Albright College*
Dave Wilderman, *Wabash Valley College*
Amy Wolaver, *Bucknell University*
King Yik, *Idaho State University*
Yongjing Zhang, *Midwestern State University*
Richard Zuber, *University of North Carolina-Charlotte*

FINAL THOUGHTS 寄语

I am deeply grateful for the enormous success *Essentials* has enjoyed. Since its first publication, it has been the dominant text in the one-semester survey course. I hope that its brevity, content, style, and novel features will keep it at the top of the charts for years to come. The ultimate measure of the book's success, however, will be reflected in student motivation and learning. As the author, I would appreciate hearing how well *Essentials* lives up to that standard.

Bradley R. Schiller

Contents in Brief 简要目录

第一编　基础	**BASICS**
第 1 章　经济学面临的挑战　1	The Challenge of Economics
第 2 章　供给与需求　27	Supply and Demand
第二编　微观经济学	**MICROECONOMICS**
第 3 章　消费者需求　57	Consumer Demand
第 4 章　供给决策　77	Supply Decisions
第 5 章　竞争　97	Competition
第 6 章　垄断　121	Monopoly
第 7 章　劳动力市场　143	The Labor Market
第 8 章　政府干预　163	Government Intervention
第三编　宏观经济学	**MACROECONOMICS**
第 9 章　商业周期　185	The Business Cycle
第 10 章　总供给和总需求　209	Aggregate Supply and Demand
第 11 章　财政政策　231	Fiscal Policy
第 12 章　货币与银行　253	Money and Banks
第 13 章　货币政策　269	Monetary Policy
第 14 章　经济增长　287	Economic Growth
第四编　国际经济学	**INTERNATIONAL**
第 15 章　国际贸易　307	International Trade
第五编　总结	**CAPSTONE**
第 16 章　理论与现实　329	Theory and Reality

Contents 详细目录

第一编 基础

第1章 经济学面临的挑战 1

我们是如何变得如此富有的 2
核心问题——稀缺 4
三个基本经济问题 5
 生产什么 5
 如何生产 11
 为谁生产 12
选择机制 12
 政治过程 13
 市场机制 13
 中央计划 13
 混合经济 14
经济学到底为何物 14
 市场失灵 14
 政府失灵 14
 宏观与微观 15
 理论与现实 15
 政治学与经济学 16
 适度的期望 17
附录：图表的使用 21
 斜率 22
 移动 23
 线性和非线性曲线 24
 因果关系 25

第2章 供给与需求 27

市场参与者 28
 目标 28
 约束 28
 专业化与交换 28
市场中的相互作用 29
 两个市场 30
 货币与交换 30
 供给与需求 31
需求 31
 个体需求 31
 需求的决定因素 34
 其他条件不变 35
 需求的移动 35
 沿着曲线移动与曲线的移动 36
 市场需求 37
 市场需求曲线 37
 需求曲线的应用 39
供给 39
 供给的决定因素 39
 市场供给曲线 40
 供给的移动 41
均衡 42
 市场出清 42
 市场短缺 44
 市场过剩 45
 均衡的变化 46

xvii

非均衡价格 47
   价格上限 47
   价格下限 49
   自由放任 50

第二编 微观经济学

第3章 消费者需求 57

消费模式 58
需求的决定因素 59
   社会精神病学的解释 59
   经济学的解释 60
需求曲线 61
   效用理论 61
   价格与数量 63
价格弹性 63
   需求富有弹性和缺乏弹性 65
   价格弹性和总收益 67
   价格弹性的决定因素 69
   消费者行为的其他变化 71
   收入变化 72

第4章 供给决策 77

产能约束：生产函数 78
   效率 80
   生产能力 80
   边际物质产品 80
   收益递减规律 81
   短期与长期 82
生产成本 83
   总成本 83
   哪个成本重要 85

   平均成本 85
   边际成本 87
供给水平 88
   短期生产决策 89
   长期投资决策 90
经济成本与会计成本 90
   经济成本 91
   经济利润 92

第5章 竞争 97

市场结构 98
完全竞争 99
   没有市场权力 100
   价格接受者 101
   市场需求与企业需求 101
厂商的生产决策 102
   产出与收益 102
   收益与利润 103
利润最大化 104
   价格 104
   边际成本 104
   利润最大化的产出率 104
   总利润 108
供给行为 109
   单个厂商的供给 109
   市场供给 110
行业进入与退出 110
   进入 111
   零经济利润趋势 113
   退出 114
   均衡 114
   低进入壁垒 115
   市场特征 115

第 6 章　垄断　121

垄断结构　122
　　垄断者＝整个行业　122
　　价格与边际收益　122
垄断行为　125
　　利润最大化　125
　　生产决策　125
　　垄断价格　125
　　垄断利润　126
进入壁垒　127
　　进入威胁　127
　　专利保护：宝丽来与柯达之争　128
　　其他进入壁垒　128
比较结果　130
　　竞争与垄断　130
　　近乎垄断　131
　　生产什么　133
　　为谁生产　133
　　如何生产　133
垄断亦有益　133
　　研究和开发　133
　　对企业家的激励　134
　　规模经济　134
　　自然垄断　135
　　可竞争市场　135
　　市场结构与市场行为　136

第 7 章　劳动力市场　143

劳动供给　144
　　收入与闲暇　145
　　市场供给　146
劳动需求　146

派生需求　146
　　边际物质产品　148
　　边际收益产品　149
　　收益递减规律　149
雇用决策　152
　　厂商对劳动的需求　152
市场均衡　154
　　均衡工资　154
　　均衡就业　154
改变市场结果　155
　　生产率的变化　155
　　价格的变化　156
　　法定最低工资　156
　　工会　158

第 8 章　政府干预　163

市场失灵　164
　　市场失灵的本质　164
　　市场失灵的来源　165
公共物品　165
　　共同消费　165
　　搭便车困境　166
外部性　168
　　消费决策　169
　　生产决策　170
　　社会成本与私人成本　172
　　政策选择　173
市场权力　176
　　有限的供给　176
　　反垄断政策　177
不公平　177
宏观不稳定性　178

第三编　宏观经济学

第 9 章　商业周期　185

评估宏观表现　187

GDP 增长　187

　　商业周期　187

　　实际 GDP　188

　　不稳定增长　189

失业　191

　　劳动力　191

　　失业率　192

　　充分就业目标　194

通货膨胀　195

　　相对价格与平均价格　196

　　再分配　197

　　不确定性　202

　　衡量通货膨胀　203

　　价格稳定目标　203

第 10 章　总供给和总需求　209

宏观视角　210

　　宏观经济的结果　210

　　宏观决定因素　210

稳定还是不稳定　211

　　古典理论　211

　　凯恩斯革命　212

总供求模型　213

　　总需求　213

　　总供给　215

　　宏观均衡　215

宏观失灵　217

　　非合意的结果　217

　　不稳定的结果　219

　　移动因素　220

短期不稳定理论的比较　222

　　需求方面的理论　222

　　供给方面的理论　224

　　折衷解释　224

政策选择　224

　　财政政策　224

　　货币政策　225

　　供给学派政策　225

第 11 章　财政政策　231

总需求的构成　232

　　消费　232

　　投资　234

　　政府支出　234

　　净出口　235

　　均衡　235

财政政策的本质　236

财政刺激　237

　　更多的政府支出　238

　　减税　243

　　对通货膨胀的担忧　245

财政紧缩　245

　　缩减预算　246

　　增税　246

　　财政方针　246

第 12 章　货币与银行　253

货币的用途　254

　　货币的许多种类　254

货币供给　255

　　现金与货币　255

　　交易账户　255

基础货币供给　256
　　准货币　257
　　总需求　258
货币创造　258
　　派生存款　258
　　垄断银行　259
　　法定准备金　261
　　超额准备金　261
　　多家银行并存的世界　262
货币乘数　262
　　派生存款的极限　263
　　将超额准备金作为贷款资本　264
银行的宏观角色　264
　　融资总需求　264
　　货币创造的局限　265

第13章　货币政策　269

联邦储备系统　270
　　联邦储备银行　270
　　理事会　271
　　美联储主席　272
货币工具　272
　　法定准备金　272
　　贴现率　274
　　公开市场操作　276
　　强有力的杠杆　279
移动总需求　279
　　扩张性政策　279
　　紧缩性政策　280
　　利率目标　280
价格与产出效应　280
　　总需求　281
　　总供给　281

第14章　经济增长　287

增长的性质　288
　　生产能力利用的短期变化　288
　　生产能力的长期变化　289
　　名义GDP与实际GDP　289
增长指数　290
　　GDP增长率　290
　　人均GDP：生活水平的衡量标准　291
　　单个工人的GDP：生产率的衡量标准　293
生产率提高的源泉　294
　　劳动力的素质　294
　　资本投资　295
　　管理　295
　　研发　296
政策杠杆　296
　　教育和培训　297
　　移民政策　297
　　投资激励政策　298
　　储蓄激励政策　298
　　政府财政　299
　　放松政府监管　299
　　经济自由　301

第四编　国际经济学

第15章　国际贸易　307

美国贸易模式　308
　　进口　308
　　出口　309
　　贸易余额　309
贸易动机　310
　　无贸易时的生产和消费　311
　　贸易促进专业化并增加世界产出　313

比较优势　314
　　机会成本　314
　　不考虑绝对成本　315
贸易条件　315
　　贸易条件的限制　315
　　市场机制　315
来自保护主义者的压力　316
　　微观经济的失败者　316
　　净收益　317
贸易壁垒　317
　　关税　318
　　配额　318
　　非关税壁垒　321
汇率　321
　　全球定价　321
　　升值/贬值　322
　　外汇市场　323

第五编　总结

第16章　理论与现实　329

政策工具　330
　　财政政策　330
　　货币政策　332
　　供给学派的政策　334
理想化的应用　336
　　情形1：衰退　336
　　情形2：通货膨胀　336
　　情形3：滞胀　337
　　微调　338
经济记录　338
为什么办法并不总能起作用　340
　　目标冲突　340
　　衡量问题　341
　　设计问题　342
　　实施问题　343

CHAPTER ONE

The Challenge of Economics　经济学面临的挑战

Source: Library of Congress Prints and Photographs Division [LC-DIG-ppmsca-17563]

LEARNING OBJECTIVES

After reading this chapter, you should be able to:

1. Explain the meaning of scarcity.
2. Define "opportunity cost."
3. Recite society's three core economic questions.
4. Discuss how market and command economies differ.
5. Describe the nature of market and government failures.

It's hard to imagine how much life has changed for the better in a relatively short amount of time. Back in 1900, life was hard and short. Life expectancy in the United States was only 47 years for whites and a shockingly low 33 years for blacks and other minorities. Americans who survived infancy faced substantial risk of early death from tuberculosis, influenza, pneumonia, or gastritis. Measles, syphilis, whooping cough, malaria, typhoid, and smallpox were all life-threatening diseases back then.

Work was a lot harder back then, too. In 1900 one-third of all U.S. families lived on farms, where the workday began before sunrise and lasted all day. Those who lived in cities typically worked 60 hours a week for wages of only 22 cents an hour. Hours were long, jobs were physically demanding, and workplaces were often dirty and unsafe.

Work Then:

Source: Library of Congress, LC-DIG-nclc-01107

---

tuberculosis 肺结核。measles 麻疹。 syphilis 梅毒。 malaria 疟疾，瘴气。 typhoid 伤寒症。 smallpox 天花。

Work Now:

Technology has transformed work.
©Morsa Images/Getty Images

People didn't have much to show for all that work. By today's standards, nearly everyone was poor at that time. The average income per person was less than $4,000 per year (in today's dollars). Very few people had telephones, and even fewer had cars. There were no television sets, no home freezers, no microwaves, no dishwashers or central air conditioning, and no computers. Even indoor plumbing was a luxury. Only a small elite went to college; an eighth-grade education was the norm.

All this, of course, sounds like ancient history. Today most of us take new cars, central air and heat, remote-control TVs, flush toilets, smartphones, college attendance, and even long weekends for granted. We seldom imagine what life would be like without the abundance of goods and services we encounter daily. Nor do we often ponder how hard work might still be had factories, offices, and homes not been transformed by technology. ■

我们是如何变得如此富有的
HOW DID WE GET SO RICH?

然而，我们应该思考，我们何以变得这般富足。现在世界上仍有数十亿人像我们在 1900 年时那样贫困，可我们是如何变得如此富有的？是高尚的道德标准让我们变得富有，还是宗教信仰？政治与之有关吗？是扩大妇女选举权、终止禁酒令或废除征兵制提高了我们的生活水平，还是 20 世纪的多次战争增加了我们的物质财富？是公共部门的大幅扩张刺激了经济增长，还是仅仅因为我们幸运？

We ought to ponder, however, how we got so affluent. Billions of people around the world are still as poor today as we were in 1900. How did we get so rich? Was it our high moral standards that made us rich? Was it our religious convictions? Did politics have anything to do with it? Did extending suffrage to women, ending prohibition, or repealing the military draft raise our living standards? Did the many wars fought in the twentieth century enhance our material well-being? Was the tremendous expansion of the public sector the catalyst for growth? Were we just lucky?

Some people say America has prospered because our nation was blessed with an abundance of natural resources. But other countries are larger. Many nations have more oil, more arable land, more gold, more people, and more math majors. Yet few nations have prospered as much as the United States.

Students of history can't ignore the role that economic *systems* might have played in these developments. Way back in 1776 the English economist Adam Smith asserted that a free market economy would best promote economic growth and raise living standards. As he saw it, people who own a business want to make a profit. To do so, they have to create new products, improve old ones, reduce costs, lower prices, and advance technology. As this happens, the economy grows, more jobs are created, and living standards rise. *Market capitalism*, Adam Smith reasoned, would foster prosperity.

Karl Marx, a German philosopher, had a very different view of market capitalism. Marx predicted that the *capitalist system* of private ownership would eventually self-destruct. The capitalists who owned the land, the factories, and the machinery would keep wages low and their own lifestyles high. They would continue exploiting the working class until it rose up and overthrew the social order. Long-term prosperity would be possible only if the *state* owned the means of production and managed the economy—a *communist system*.

---

market capitalism 市场资本主义。 prosperity 繁荣。

Chapter One: The Challenge of Economics   3

In the United States the quest for greater prosperity continues. As rich as we are, we always want more. Our materialistic desires, it seems, continue to outpace our ever-rising incomes. We need to have the newest iPhone, a larger TV, a bigger home, a faster car, and a more exotic vacation. People today seem to think they need twice as much income as they have to be really happy (see the News Wire "Insatiable Wants"). Even multimillionaires say they need much more money than they already have: People with more than $10 million of net worth say they need at least $18 million to live "comfortably."

How can any economy keep pace with these ever-rising expectations? Will the economy keep churning out more goods and services every year like some perpetual motion machine? Or will we run out of goods, basic resources, and new technologies? Will the future bring *more* goods and services—or *less*?

NEWS WIRE INSATIABLE WANTS

NEVER ENOUGH MONEY!

A public opinion poll asked Americans how much money they would need each year to be "happy." In general, people said they needed twice as much income as they had at present to be happy.

Source: CNN/ORC Poll, May 29–June 1, 2014.

©Ekasit Wangprasert/Alamy Stock Photo

NOTE: People always want more than they have. Even multimillionaires say they don't have enough to live "comfortably."

注：人们想要的总比他们拥有的要多。即使是千万富翁也说他们没有足够的金钱过"舒适的"生活。

The Great Recession of 2008–2009   2008—2009 年的大衰退

Anxiety about the ability of the U.S. economy to crank out more goods every year spiked in 2008–2009. Indeed, the economic system screeched to a halt in September 2008, raising widespread fears about another 1930s-style Great Depression. Things didn't turn out nearly that bad, but millions of Americans lost their jobs, their savings, and even their homes in 2008–2009. As the output of the U.S. economy contracted, people's faith in the capitalist *system* plunged. By the end of 2009, only one of four American adults expected their income to increase in the next year. Ten years later—after years of economic growth—that kind of fear persisted: nearly 60 percent of Americans feared another recession would occur in 2020. Worse yet, one of two Americans also expected their children to have *fewer* goods and services in the future than people now do (see the News Wire "Future Living Standards"). Could that happen?

People worry not only about the resilience of the economic *system* but also about resource limitations. We now depend on oil, water, and other resources to fuel our factories and irrigate our farms. What happens when we run out of these resources? Do the factories shut down? Do the farms dry up? Does economic growth stop?

人们不仅担心美国经济制度的恢复力，也担心资源的有限性。我们现在依赖石油等资源为工厂提供燃料，用水来灌溉农田。如果我们用尽了这些资源怎么办？工厂会倒闭吗？农场会干旱吗？经济增长会停止吗？

An end to world economic growth would devastate people in other nations. Most people in the world have incomes far below American standards. A *billion* of the poorest inhabitants of Earth subsist on less than $3 per day—a tiny fraction of the $75,000 a year the average U.S. family enjoys. Even in some countries where incomes have been rising rapidly, daily living standards are below those that U.S. families experienced in the Great Depression of the 1930s. To attain current U.S. standards of affluence, these nations need economic systems that will foster economic growth for decades to come.

---

insatiable 无法满足的。   churn out 大量生产。

NEWS WIRE FUTURE LIVING STANDARDS?

WILL YOUR KIDS BE BETTER OFF?

Question: Do you think the future of the next generation of Americans will be better, worse, or about the same as life today?

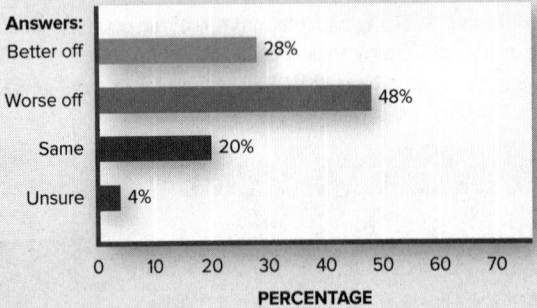

Source: *Children's Financial Future*, Pew Research Center, June–July 2017.

NOTE: Will you be better off than your parents? For living standards to keep rising, the economy must continue to grow. Will that happen? How?
注：你会比你的父母过得更好吗？要不断提高生活水平，经济必须持续增长。经济会持续增长吗？如何才能实现经济持续增长？

Will consumers around the world get the kind of persistent economic growth the United States has enjoyed? Will living standards rise, stagnate, or fall in future years?

To answer this question, we need to know what makes economies "tick." That is the foremost goal of this course. We want to know what kind of system a "market economy" really is. How does it work? Who determines the price of a textbook in a market economy? Who decides how many textbooks will be produced? Will everyone who needs a textbook get one? And why are gasoline prices so high? How about jobs? Who decides how many jobs are available or what wages they pay in a market economy? What keeps an economy growing? Or stops it in its tracks?

为了理解经济如何运行，我们不得不提出并回答许多问题。其中最重要的问题包括：

- 经济制度的基本目标是什么？
- 市场经济如何实现这些目标？
- 在形成经济结果的过程中，政府应扮演什么样的角色？

To understand how an economy works, we have to ask and answer a lot of questions. Among the most important are these:

- What are the basic goals of an economic system?
- How does a market economy address these goals?
- What role should government play in shaping economic outcomes?

We won't answer all of these questions in this first chapter. But we will get a sense of what the study of economics is all about and why the answers to these questions are so important.

核心问题——稀缺
THE CENTRAL PROBLEM OF SCARCITY

The land area of the United States stretches over 3.5 million square miles. We have a population of 340 million people, about half of whom work. We also have over $100 trillion worth of buildings and machinery. With so many resources, the United States produces an enormous volume of output. But it is never enough: Consumers always want more. We want not only faster cars, more clothes, and larger TVs but also more roads, better schools, and more police protection. Why can't we have everything we want?

答案非常简单：我们的欲望超过了我们的资源。虽然我们的资源看起来似乎很充足，但还

The answer is fairly simple: ***Our wants exceed our resources.*** As abundant as our resources might appear, they are not capable of producing everything we want. The same kind of problem makes doing homework so painful. You have only 24 hours in a day. You can spend it watching movies, shopping, hanging out with friends, sleeping, texting, scrolling your Facebook timeline, or doing your homework. With only 24 hours in a day, you can't do everything you want to, however: Your time is *scarce*. So you must choose which activities to pursue—and which to forgo.

Economics offers a framework for explaining how we make such choices. The goal of economic theory is to figure out how we can use our scarce resources in the *best possible* way.

Consider again your decision to read this chapter right now. Hopefully, you'll get some benefit from finishing it. You'll also incur a *cost*, however. The time you spend reading could be spent doing something else. You're probably missing a good show on TV right now. Giving up that show is the *opportunity cost* of reading this chapter. You have sacrificed the opportunity to watch TV in order to finish this homework. In general, whatever you decide to do with your time will entail an **opportunity cost**—that is, the sacrifice of a next-best alternative.

What should you do? The rational thing to do is to weigh the benefits of doing your homework against the implied opportunity cost (watching TV) and then make a choice.

The larger society faces a similar dilemma. For the larger economy, time is also limited. So, too, are the resources needed to produce desired goods and services. To get more houses, more cars, or more movies, we need not only time but also resources to produce these things. These resources—land, labor, capital, and entrepreneurship—are the basic ingredients of production. They are called **factors of production**. The more factors of production we have, the more we can produce in a given period of time.

As we've already noted, our available resources always fall short of our output desires. The central problem here again is **scarcity**, a situation where our desires for goods and services exceed our capacity to produce them.

三个基本经济问题
THREE BASIC ECONOMIC QUESTIONS

The central problem of scarcity forces every society to make difficult choices. Specifically, every nation must resolve three critical questions about the use of its scarce resources:

- **WHAT** to produce.
- **HOW** to produce.
- **FOR WHOM** to produce.

We first examine the nature of each question and then look at how different countries answer these three basic questions.

WHAT to Produce 生产什么

The WHAT question is quite simple. We've already noted that there isn't enough time in the day to do everything you want to. You must decide *what* to do with your time. The economy confronts a similar question: There aren't enough resources in the economy to produce all the goods and services society desires. ***Because wants exceed resources, we have to decide WHAT goods and services we want most, sacrificing less desired products.***

Production Possibilities 生产可能性

Figure 1.1 illustrates this basic dilemma. Suppose there are only two kinds of goods, "consumer goods" and "military goods." In this case, the question of WHAT to produce boils down to finding the most desirable combination of these two goods.

To make that selection, we first need to know how much of each good we *could* produce. That will depend in part on how many resources we have available. The first thing we need to do, then, is count our factors of production.

---

dilemma 进退两难的局面，困难的选择。fall short of 不足，缺乏。

生产要素包括：

- 土地（包括自然资源）
- 劳动力（劳动者的数量和技能）
- 资本（机器、建筑物和网络）
- 企业家精神（开发产品、服务和流程的能力）

The factors of production include the following:

- **Land** (including natural resources).
- **Labor** (number and skills of workers).
- **Capital** (machinery, buildings, networks).
- **Entrepreneurship** (skill in creating products, services, and processes).

The more we have of these factors, the more output we can produce. Technology is also critical. The more advanced our technological and managerial abilities, the more output we will be able to produce with available factors of production. If we inventoried all our resources and technology, we could figure out what the physical *limits* to production are.

To simplify the computation, suppose we wanted to produce only consumer goods. How much *could* we produce? Surely not an infinite amount. With *limited* stocks of land, labor, capital, and technology, output would have a *finite* limit. The *limit* is represented by point *A* in Figure 1.1. That is to say, the vertical distance from the origin (point *O*) to point *A* represents the *maximum* quantity of consumer goods that could be produced this year. To produce the quantity *A* of consumer goods, we would have to use *all* available factors of production. At point *A* no resources would be available for producing military goods. The choice of *maximum* consumer output implies *zero* military output.

We could make other choices about WHAT to produce. Point *B* illustrates another extreme. The horizontal distance from the origin (point *O*) to point *B* represents our *maximum* capacity to produce military goods. To get that much military output, we would have to devote *all* available resources to that single task. At point *B*, we wouldn't be producing *any* consumer goods. We would be well protected but ill nourished and poorly clothed (wearing last year's clothes).

Our choices about WHAT to produce are not limited to the extremes of points *A* and *B*. We could instead produce a *combination* of consumer and military goods. Point *C* represents one such combination. To get to point *C*, we have to forsake maximum consumer goods output (point *A*) and use some of our scarce resources to produce military goods. At point *C* we are producing only *OD* of consumer goods and *OE* of military goods.

C点只是我们能够生产的许多产出组合中的一种。我们可以生产图1.1中曲线上的任意一种产出组合。因此我们称这条曲线为**生产可能性**曲线，它表示在一定时期内、在一定的资源和技术条件下，能够生产出的各种商品和服务的数量组合。实际上，它就像是一个经济菜单，我们必须从中选择某种商品和服务的产出组合。

Point *C* is just one of many combinations we *could* produce. We could produce *any* combination of output represented by points along the curve in Figure 1.1. For this reason we call it the **production possibilities** curve; it represents the alternative combinations of goods and services that *could* be produced in a given time period with all available resources and technology. It is, in effect, an economic menu from which one specific combination of goods and services must be selected.

The production possibilities curve puts the basic issue of WHAT to produce in graphic terms. The same choices can be depicted in numerical terms as well. Table 1.1, for example, illustrates specific trade-offs between missile production and home construction. The output mix *A* allocates all resources to home construction, leaving nothing to produce missiles. If missiles are desired, the level of home construction must be cut back. To produce 50 missiles (mix *B*), home construction activity must be cut back to 90. Output mixes *C* through *F* illustrate other possible choices. Notice that every time we increase missile production (moving from *A* to *F*), house construction must be reduced. The question of WHAT to produce boils down to choosing one specific mix of output—a specific combination of missiles and houses.

The Choices Nations Make   国家的选择

生产可能性曲线上没有哪个点能在任何时间都最适用于所有国家。在美国，"大炮"在总产出中的比重变化很明显。第二次世界大战期间，美国把汽

No single point on the production possibilities curve is best for all nations at all times. In the United States, the share of total output devoted to "guns" has varied greatly. During World War II, we converted auto plants to produce military vehicles. Clothing manufacturers cut way back on consumer clothing in order to produce more uniforms for the army, navy, and air force.

---

vertical 垂直的。   combination 组合。

	Possible Output Combinations					
Output	A	B	C	D	E	F
Missiles	0	50	100	150	200	250
Houses	100	90	75	55	30	0

Table 1.1 Specific Production Possibilities The choice of WHAT to produce eventually boils down to specific goods and services. Here the choices are defined in terms of missiles or houses. More missiles can be produced only if some resources are diverted from home construction. Only one of these output combinations can be produced in a given time period. Selecting that mix is a basic economic issue. ■

The government also drafted 12 million men to bear arms. By shifting resources from the production of consumer goods to the production of military goods, we were able to move down along the production possibilities curve in Figure 1.1 toward point X. By 1944 fully 40 percent of all our output consisted of military goods. Consumer goods were so scarce that everything from butter to golf balls had to be rationed.

车厂改造成生产军用车辆的工厂；服装制造商缩减民用服装产量以生产更多的海陆空三军制服；政府还征募了1 200万人参军。随着资源由消费品生产向军需品生产转移，在图1.1中的产出组合沿着生产可能性曲线向X点移动。到1944年，美国总产出中有40%是军需品。消费品如此匮乏，以至于从黄油到高尔夫球的所有消费品都要配给供应。

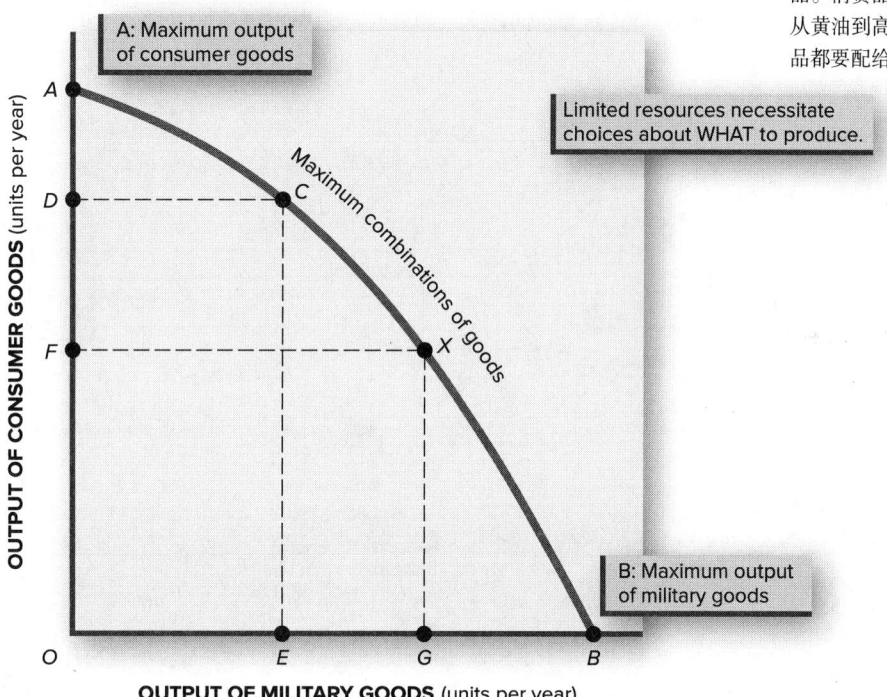

Figure 1.1 A Production Possibilities Curve A production possibilities curve describes the various combinations of final goods or services that could be produced in a given time period with available resources and technology. It represents a menu of output choices.

Point C indicates that we could produce a *combination* of OD units of consumer goods and the quantity OE of military output. To get more military output (e.g., at point G), we have to reduce consumer output (from OD to OF), ending up at point X on the curve.

We must decide WHAT to produce (i.e., pick a single point on the production possibilities curve). Our goal is to select the *best* possible mix of output. ■

Figure 1.2 illustrates that rapid military buildup during World War II. The figure also illustrates how quickly we reallocated factors of production to consumer goods after the war ended. By 1948 less than 4 percent of U.S. output was military goods. We had moved close to point *A* in Figure 1.1.

Peace Dividends 和平红利

为了打朝鲜战争，美国再度大幅调整了产出组合。1953 年，军事产出占美国总产出的比重接近 15%。按现在的美元和产出水平来算，这相当于每年接近 2 万亿美元的国防支出。

We changed the mix of output dramatically again to fight the Korean War. In 1953 military output absorbed nearly 15 percent of America's total production. That would amount to nearly $2 *trillion* of annual defense spending in today's dollars and output levels. We're not spending anywhere near that kind of military money, however. After the Korean War, the share of U.S. output allocated to the military trended sharply downward. Despite the buildup for the Vietnam War (1966–1968), the share of output devoted to "guns" fell from 15 percent in 1953 to a low of 3 percent in 2001. In the process, the U.S. armed forces were reduced by nearly 600,000 personnel. As those personnel found civilian jobs, they increased consumer output. That increase in nonmilitary output is called the *peace dividend*.

The Cost of War 战争的成本

发生在纽约和华盛顿的"9·11"恐怖袭击使产出组合向相反的方向移动。在"9·11"事件之后的三年内，军事支出增加了 50%。伊拉克战争

The 9/11 terrorist attacks on New York City and Washington, DC, moved the mix of output in the opposite direction. Military spending increased by 50 percent in the three years after 9/11. The wars in Iraq and Afghanistan absorbed even more resources. The *economic* cost of those efforts is measured in lost consumer output. The money spent by the government

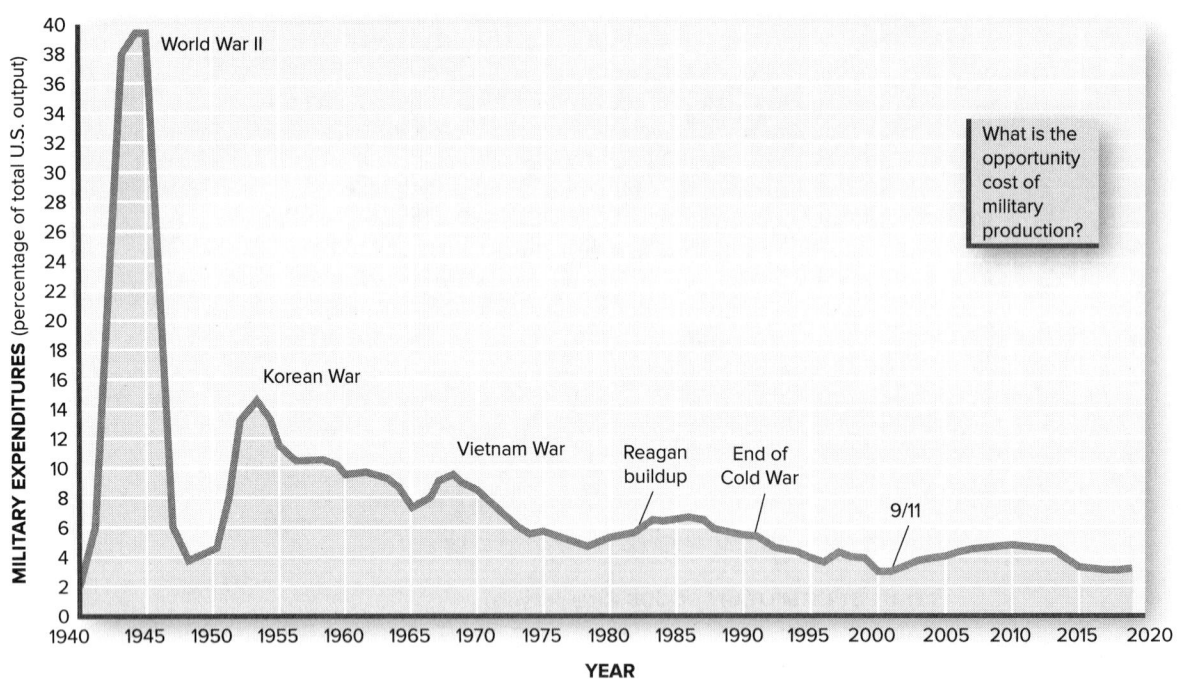

Figure 1.2 Military Share of Total U.S. Output The share of total output devoted to national defense has risen sharply in war years and fallen in times of peace. The defense buildup of the 1980s increased the military share to more than 6 percent of total output. The end of the Cold War reversed that buildup, releasing resources for other uses (the peace dividend). The September 11, 2001, terrorist attacks on New York City and Washington, DC, altered the WHAT choice again, increasing the military's share of total output.

Source: Congressional Research Service.

on war might otherwise have been spent on schools, highways, or other nondefense projects. The National Guard personnel called up for the war would otherwise have stayed home and produced consumer goods (including disaster relief). These costs of war are illustrated in Figure 1.3. Notice how consumer goods output declines (from C_1 to C_2) when military output increases (from M_1 to M_2).

As Figure 1.4 illustrates, in some countries the opportunity cost of military output seems far too high. That compares with a military share of only 3.3 percent in the United States and 2.1 percent in China.

和阿富汗战争消耗了更多的资源。其经济成本可以用消费品产出的减少来衡量。政府花在战争上的钱本可以花在学校、高速公路或其他非军事项目上。为战争而征募的国民警卫队人员也会留下来生产消费品（包括灾难救援）。图1.3展示了这些战争的成本。注意观察当军需品产出增加时（从M_1到M_2），消费品产出是如何减少的（从C_1到C_2）。

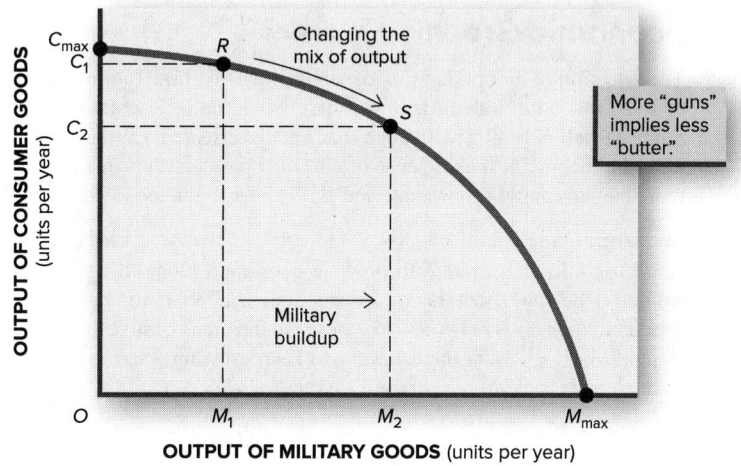

Figure 1.3 The Cost of War An increase in military output absorbs factors of production that could be used to produce consumer goods. The military buildup associated with the move from point R to point S reduces consumption output from C_1 to C_2. The economic cost of war is measured by the implied reduction in nondefense output ("less butter"). ■

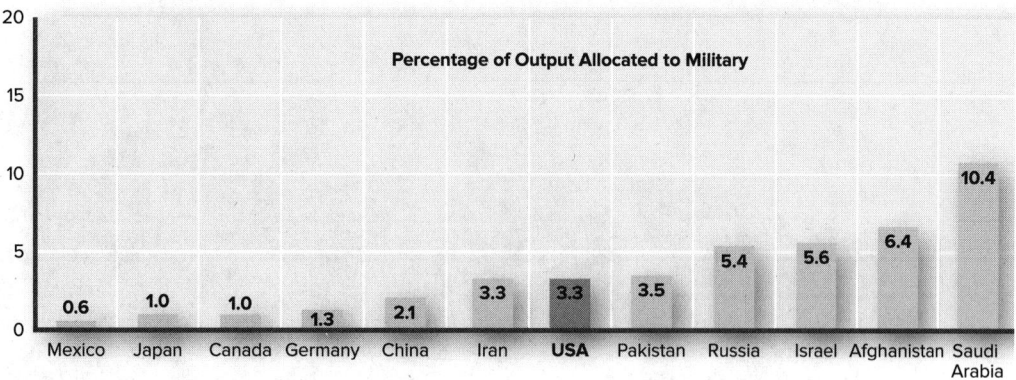

Figure 1.4 The Military Share of Output The share of output allocated to the military indicates the opportunity cost of maintaining an army. ■

Source: *The World FactBook,* Central Intelligence Agency, 2015–2018.

The Best Possible Mix 最优产出组合

Ultimately the designation of any particular mix of output as "best" rests on the value judgments of a society. A militaristic society would prefer a mix of output closer to point *B* in Figure 1.1. By contrast, Iceland has no military and so produces at point *A*. In general, **one specific mix of output is optimal for a country**—that is, a mix that represents the *best* possible allocation of resources across competing uses. Locating and producing that *optimal* mix of output is the essence of the WHAT challenge.

The same desire for an optimal mix of output drives your decisions on the use of scarce time. There is only one *best* way to use your time on any given day. If you use your time in that way, you will maximize your well-being. Other uses won't necessarily kill you, but they won't do you as much good.

Economic Growth 经济增长

The selection of an optimal mix depends in part on how future-oriented one is. If you had no concern for future jobs or income, there would be little point in doing homework now. You might as well play all day if you're that present-oriented. On the other hand, if you value future jobs and income, it makes sense to allocate some present time to studying. Then you'll have more human capital (knowledge and skills) later to pursue job opportunities.

The larger society confronts the same choice between present and future consumption. We *could* use all our resources to produce consumer goods this year. If we did, however, there wouldn't be any factors of production available to build machinery, factories, or telecommunications networks. Yet these are the kinds of **investment** that enhance our capacity to produce. If we want the economy to keep growing—and our living standards to rise—we must allocate some of our scarce resources to investment rather than current consumption. The

resultant **economic growth** will expand our production possibilities outward, allowing us to produce *more* goods in future years. The phenomenon of economic growth is illustrated in Figure 1.5 by the outward *shift* of the production-possibilities curve. Such shifts occur when we acquire *more* resources (e.g., more machinery) or *better* technology. Our decision about WHAT to produce must take future growth into account.

HOW to Produce　　如何生产

The second basic economic question concerns HOW we produce output. Should this class be taught in an auditorium or in small discussion sections? Should it meet twice a week or only once? Should the class be taught online? Should the instructor assign more electronic supplements and homework? Should exams be open book? Should, heaven forbid, this textbook be replaced with online text files? There are numerous ways of teaching a course. Of these many possibilities, one way is presumably best, given the resources and technology available. That best way is HOW we want the course taught. Educational researchers and a good many instructors spend a lot of time trying to figure out the best way of teaching a course.

Should pig farmers be free to breed pigs and to dispose of waste in any way they desire? Or should the government regulate how pigs are produced?
©DN1988/Shutterstock

Pig farmers do the same thing. They know they can fatten pigs up with a lot of different grains and other food. They can also vary breeding patterns, light exposure, and heat. They can use more labor in the feeder process or more machinery. Faced with so many choices, pig farmers try to find the *best* way of raising pigs.

The HOW question isn't just an issue of getting more output from available inputs. It also encompasses our use of the environment. Should the waste from pig farms be allowed to contaminate the air, groundwater, or local waterways? Or do we want to keep the water clean for other uses? Humanitarian concerns may also come into play. Should live pigs be processed without any concern for their welfare? Or should the processing be designed to minimize trauma? The HOW question encompasses all such issues. Although people may hold different views on these questions, everyone shares a common goal: ***to find an optimal method of producing goods and services.*** The best possible answer to the HOW question will entail both efficiency in the use of factors of production and adequate safeguards for the environment and other social concerns. Our goal is to find that answer.

尽管人们对这些问题有不同看法，但所有人都有一个共同目标：找到一种生产商品和服务的最优方式。对如何生产问题的最佳答案既要考虑生产要素的使用效率，又要考虑对环境以及其他社会问题的充分保障。我们的目标就是找到这样的答案。

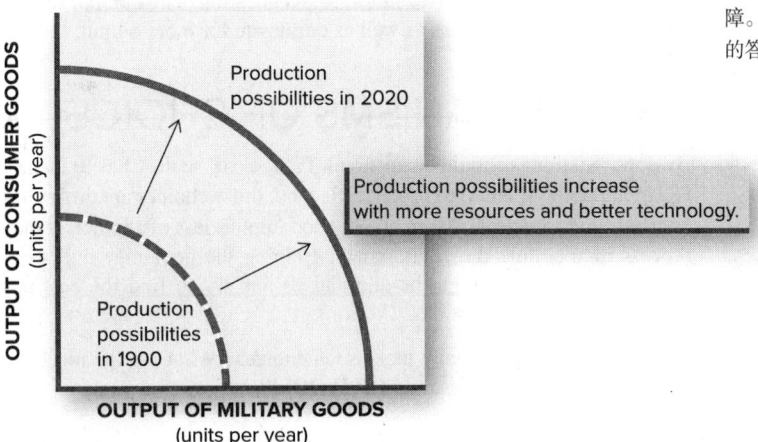

Figure 1.5 Economic Growth Since 1900 the U.S. population has quadrupled. Investment in machinery and buildings has increased our capital stock even faster. These additional factors of production, together with advancing technology, have expanded (shifted outward) our production possibilities. ■

FOR WHOM to Produce   为谁生产

The third basic economic question every society must confront is FOR WHOM? The answers to the WHAT and HOW questions determine how large an economic pie we'll bake and how we'll bake it. Then we have to slice it up. Should everyone get an equal slice of the pie? Or can some people have big pieces of the pie while others get only crumbs? In other words, ***the FOR WHOM question focuses on how an economy's output is distributed across members of society.***

A pie can be divided up in many ways. Personally, I like a distribution that gives me a big slice even if that leaves less for others. Maybe you feel the same way. Whatever your feelings, however, there is likely to be a lot of disagreement about what distribution is best. Maybe we should just give everyone an equal slice. But should everyone get an equal slice even if some people helped bake the pie while others contributed nothing? The Little Red Hen of the children's fable felt perfectly justified eating all the bread she made herself after her friends and neighbors refused to help sow the seeds, harvest the grain, or bake it. Should such a work-based sense of equity determine how all goods are distributed?

Incentives   激励

There is a risk entailed in distributing slices of the pie based on need rather than work effort. People who work hard to bake the pie may feel cheated if non-workers get just as large a slice. Worse still, people may decide to exert less effort if they see no tangible reward to working. If that happens, the size of the pie may shrink, and everyone will be worse off.

This is the kind of problem income transfer programs create. Government-paid income transfers (e.g., welfare, unemployment benefits, Social Security) are intended to provide a slice of the pie to people who don't have enough income to satisfy basic needs. As benefits rise, however, the incentive to work diminishes. If people choose welfare checks over paychecks, total output will decline.

The same problem emerges in the tax system. If Paul is heavily taxed to provide welfare benefits to Peter, Paul may decide that hard work and entrepreneurship don't pay. To the extent that taxes discourage work, production, or investment, they shrink the size of the pie that feeds all of us.

The potential trade-offs between taxes, income transfers, and work don't compel us to dismantle all tax and welfare programs. They do emphasize, however, how difficult it is to select the right answer to the FOR WHOM question. The *optimal* distribution of income must satisfy our sense of fairness as well as our desire for more output.

THE MECHANISMS OF CHOICE   选择机制

By now, two things should be apparent. First, every society has to make choices about WHAT, HOW, and FOR WHOM to produce. Second, those choices are difficult. ***Every choice involves conflicts and trade-offs.*** More of one good implies less of another. A more efficient production process may pollute the environment. Helping the poor may dull work incentives. In every case, society has to weigh the alternatives and try to find the best possible answer to each question.

How does "society" actually make such choices? What are the mechanisms we use to decide WHAT to produce, HOW, and FOR WHOM?

---

optimal 最优的。

The Political Process 政治过程

Many of these basic economic decisions are made through the political process. Consider again the decision to increase the military share of output after 9/11. Who made that decision? Not me. Not you. Not the mass of consumers who were streaming through real and virtual malls. No, the decisions on military buildups and builddowns are made in the political arena: the U.S. Congress makes those decisions. Congress also makes decisions about how many interstate highways to build, how many Head Start classes to offer, and how much space exploration to pursue.

Should *all* decisions about WHAT to produce be made in the political arena? Should Congress also decide how much ice cream will be produced and how many bluetooth earbuds? What about essentials like food and shelter? Should decisions about the production of those goods be made in Washington, DC, or should the mix of output be selected some other way?

这些基本的经济决策很多都是在政治过程中做出的。回想一下美国在 "9·11" 事件之后增加军事产出比重的决策。是谁做出了这个决策？不是我，不是你，也不是穿梭在各个实体或者网店中的大批消费者。决定军事产出收缩还是扩张的决策是在政治舞台上做出的，即美国国会做出了这些决策。国会做出的决策还有修建多少州际公路，开办多少学前班，以及进行多大范围的太空探索。

The Market Mechanism 市场机制

The market mechanism offers an alternative decision-making process. In a market-driven economy the process of selecting a mix of output is as familiar as grocery shopping. If you desire ice cream and have sufficient income, you simply buy ice cream. Your purchases signal to producers that ice cream is desired. By expressing the *ability and willingness to pay* for ice cream, you are telling ice cream producers that their efforts are going to be rewarded. If enough consumers feel the same way you do—and are able and willing to pay the price of ice cream—ice cream producers will churn out more ice cream.

The same kind of interaction helps determine which crops we grow. There is only so much good farmland available. Should we grow corn or beans? If consumers prefer corn, they will buy more corn and shun the beans. Farmers will get the market's message: They will devote more of their land to corn, cutting back on bean production. In the process, the mix of output will change—moving us closer to the choice consumers have made.

The central actor in this reshuffling of resources and outputs is the **market mechanism**. *Market sales and prices send a signal to producers about what mix of output consumers want.* If you want something and have sufficient income, you buy it. If enough people do the same thing, total sales of that product will rise, and perhaps its price will as well. Producers, seeing sales and prices rise, will want to increase production. To do so, they will acquire more resources and use them to change the mix of output. No direct communication between us and the producer is required; we don't need Twitter or Facebook to get our message transmitted. Instead, market sales and prices convey the message and direct the market, much like an "invisible hand."

在资源和产出的重新配置中起核心作用的是**市场机制**。市场上的销售量和价格向生产商传达了消费者想要的产出组合信号。如果你想要某种商品并且有足够的收入，那就去购买。如果有足够多的消费者像你一样这么做，这种商品的销售量就会增加，价格也可能随之上升。生产商看到销售量和价格上升，就会有意愿增加该商品的生产。为了增加生产，生产商会获取更多资源并利用它们来改变产出组合。我们和生产商之间并不需要直接交流。我们不需要 Twitter 或 Facebook 来传递信息。取而代之的是，市场销售量和价格会传递信息并指导市场，就像一只 "看不见的手"。

It was this ability of "the market" to select a desirable mix of output that so impressed the eighteenth-century economist Adam Smith. He argued that nations would prosper with less government interference and more reliance on the invisible hand of the marketplace. As he saw it, markets were efficient mechanisms for deciding what goods to produce, how to produce them, and even what wages to pay. Smith's writings (*The Wealth of Nations,* 1776) urged government to pursue a policy of **laissez faire**—leaving the market alone to make basic economic decisions.

Central Planning 中央计划

Karl Marx saw things differently. In his view, a freewheeling marketplace would cater to the whims of the rich and neglect the needs of the poor. Rich consumers would get all the ice cream, while poor families survived on gruel. Workers would be exploited by industrial barons and great landowners. To "leave it to the market," as Smith had proposed, would encourage exploitation. In the mid-nineteenth century, Karl Marx proposed a radical alternative: Overturn the power of the elite and create a communist state in which everyone's needs would be

---

ability and willingness to pay 支付能力和意愿。　laissez faire 自由放任。

fulfilled. Marx's writings (*Das Kapital,* 1867) encouraged communist revolutions and the development of central planning systems. The (people's) government, not the market, would decide what goods were produced, at what prices they were sold, and even who got them.

Central planning is still the principal mechanism of choice in some countries. In DPRK and Cuba, for example, the central planners decide how many cars and how much bread to produce. They then assign workers and other resources to those industries to implement their decisions. They also decide who will get the bread and the cars that are produced. The government also decides who goes to college and what subjects they can study. Private ownership of land and other resources is discouraged, even forbidden. The WHAT, HOW, and FOR WHOM outcomes are all directed by the central government.

Mixed Economies 混合经济

Few countries still depend so fully on central planners (government) to make basic economic decisions. China, Russia, and other nations have turned over many decisions to the market mechanism. Likewise, no nation relies exclusively on markets to fashion economic outcomes. In the United States, for example, we let the market decide how much ice cream will be produced and how many cars. We use the political process, however, to decide how many highways to construct, how many schools to build, and how much military output to produce.

Because most nations use a combination of government directives and market mechanisms to determine economic outcomes, they are called **mixed economies**. There is huge variation in that mix, however. The government-dominated economic systems in DPRK, Cuba, Laos, and Libya are starkly different from the freewheeling economies of Singapore, Bahrain, New Zealand, and the United States.

经济学到底为何物
WHAT ECONOMICS IS ALL ABOUT

The different economic systems employed around the world are all intended to give the right answers to the WHAT, HOW, and FOR WHOM questions. It is apparent, however, that they don't always succeed. We have too much poverty and too much pollution. There are often too few jobs and pitifully small paychecks. A third of the world's population still lives in abject poverty.

Economists try to explain how these various outcomes emerge. Why are some nations so much more prosperous than others? What forces cause economic downturns in both rich and poor nations? What causes prices to go up and down so often? How can economies grow without destroying the environment?

Market Failure 市场失灵

In studying these questions, economists recognize that neither markets nor governments always have the right answers. On the contrary, we know that a completely private market economy can give us the *wrong* answers to the WHAT, HOW, and FOR WHOM questions on occasion. A completely free market economy might produce too many luxury cars and too few hospitals. Unregulated producers might destroy the environment. A freewheeling market economy might neglect the needs of the poor. When the market mechanism gives us these kinds of suboptimal answers, we say the market has *failed.* **Market failure** occurs when the market mechanism does not generate the best possible (optimal) answers to the WHAT, HOW, and FOR WHOM questions.

Government Failure 政府失灵

When market failure occurs, there is usually a call for the government to "fix" the failure. This may or may not be a good response. Government intervention doesn't always make things better. Indeed, economists warn that government intervention can fail as well. **Government failure** occurs when intervention fails to improve—or actually worsens—economic outcomes.

---

military output 军需品。　intervention 干预。

The possibility of government failure is sufficient warning that *there is no guarantee that the visible hand of government will be any better than the invisible hand of the marketplace.*

Economists try to figure out when markets work well and when they are likely to fail. We also try to predict whether specific government interventions will improve economic outcomes—or make them worse.

Macro versus Micro 宏观与微观

The study of economics is typically divided into two parts: macroeconomics and microeconomics. Macroeconomics focuses on the behavior of an entire economy—the big picture. In macroeconomics we study such national goals as full employment, control of inflation, and economic growth, without worrying about the well-being or behavior of specific individuals or groups. The essential concern of **macroeconomics** is to understand and improve the performance of the economy as a whole.

Microeconomics is concerned with the details of this big picture. In microeconomics we focus on the individuals, firms, and government agencies that actually make up the larger economy. Our interest here is in the behavior of individual economic actors. What are their goals? How can they best achieve these goals with their limited resources? How will they respond to various incentives and opportunities?

A primary concern of macroeconomics, for example, is to determine the impact of aggregate consumer spending on total output, employment, and prices. Very little attention is devoted to the actual content of consumer spending or its determinants. Microeconomics, on the other hand, focuses on the specific expenditure decisions of individual consumers and the forces (tastes, prices, incomes) that influence those decisions.

The distinction between macro- and microeconomics is also reflected in discussions of business investment. In macroeconomics we want to know what determines the aggregate rate of business investment and how those expenditures influence the nation's total output, employment, and prices. In microeconomics we focus on the decisions of individual businesses regarding the rate of production, the choice of factors of production, and the pricing of specific goods.

The distinction between macro- and microeconomics is a matter of convenience. In reality, macroeconomic outcomes depend on micro behavior, and micro behavior is affected by macro outcomes. Hence we cannot fully understand how an economy works until we understand how all the participants behave and why they behave as they do. But just as you can drive a car without knowing how its engine is constructed, you can observe how an economy runs without completely disassembling it. In macroeconomics we observe that the car goes faster when the accelerator is depressed and that it slows when the brake is applied. That is all we need to know in most situations. There are times, however, when the car breaks down. When it does, we have to know something more about how the pedals work. This leads us into micro studies. How does each part work? Which ones can or should be fixed?

Theory versus Reality 理论与现实

The distinction between macroeconomics and microeconomics is one of many simplifications we make in studying economic behavior. The economy is much too vast and complex to describe and explain in one course (or one lifetime). Accordingly, we focus on basic relationships while ignoring unnecessary detail. What this means is that we formulate theories, or *models*, of economic behavior and then use those theories to evaluate and design economic policy.

The economic models that economists use to explain market behavior are like maps. To get from New York to Los Angeles, you don't need to know all the details of topography that lie between those two cities. Knowing where the interstate highways are is probably enough. An interstate route map therefore provides enough information to get you to your destination.

---

participant 参与者。 disassemble 分解，拆解。

The same kind of simplification is used in economic models of consumer behavior. Such models assert that when the price of a good increases, consumers will buy less of it. In reality, however, people *may* buy *more* of a good at increased prices, especially if those high prices create a certain snob appeal or if prices are expected to increase still further. In predicting consumer responses to price increases, we typically ignore such possibilities by *assuming* that the price of the good in question is the *only* thing that changes. This assumption of "other things remaining equal (unchanged)" (in Latin, ***ceteris paribus***) allows us to make straightforward predictions. If instead we described consumer responses to increased prices in any and all circumstances (allowing everything to change at once), every prediction would be accompanied by a book full of exceptions and qualifications. We would look more like lawyers than economists.

Although the assumption of *ceteris paribus* makes it easier to formulate economic theory and policy, it also increases the risk of error. Obviously, if other things do change in significant ways, our predictions (and policies) may fail. But like weather forecasters, we continue to make predictions, knowing that occasional failure is inevitable. In so doing, we are motivated by the conviction that it is better to be approximately right than to be dead wrong.

Politics versus Economics   政治学与经济学

Politicians cannot afford to be quite so complacent about predictions. Policy decisions must be made every day. And a politician's continued tenure in office may depend on being more than approximately right. Economists contribute to those policy decisions by offering measures of economic impact and predictions of economic behavior. But in the real world, those measures and predictions always contain a substantial margin of error.

Even if the future were known, economic policy could not rely completely on economic theory. There are always political choices to be made. The choice of more consumer goods ("butter") or more military hardware ("guns"), for example, is not an economic decision. Rather it is a sociopolitical decision based in part on communal preferences and in part on economic trade-offs (opportunity costs). The "need" for more butter or more guns must be expressed politically—ends versus means again. Political forces (societal preferences) are a necessary ingredient in economic policy decisions.

Both politics and economics are involved in the continuing debate regarding the merits of a laissez faire approach versus government intervention. The pendulum has swung from laissez faire to central government control and to an ill-defined middle ground where the government assumes major responsibilities for economic stability (John Maynard Keynes) and for answers to the WHAT, HOW, and FOR WHOM questions. In the 1980s the Reagan administration pushed the pendulum a bit closer to laissez faire by cutting taxes, reducing government regulation, and encouraging market incentives.

President Clinton thought the government should play a more active role in resolving basic economic issues. His "Vision for America" spelled out a bigger role for government in ensuring health care, providing skills training, protecting the environment, and regulating working conditions. In this vision, well-intentioned government officials could correct market failures. President George W. Bush favored less government intervention and more reliance on the market mechanism. President Obama moved the pendulum back: He made it clear that he believed *more* government intervention and *less* market reliance were needed to attain the right WHAT, HOW, and FOR WHOM answers. The pendulum reversed direction again with the election of Donald Trump in 2016. Trump believed that government interference in market decisions made the economy worse off, not better. He dismantled a slew of government regulations and increased incentives for private investment.

The debate over markets versus government persists in part because of gaps in our economic understanding. For over 200 years economists have been arguing about what makes the economy tick. None of the competing theories have performed spectacularly well. Indeed, few

---

ceteris paribus（拉丁语）其他条件不变。 sociopolitical 社会政治的。 pendulum 钟摆，摇摆不定的事态。

economists have successfully predicted major economic events with any consistency. Even annual forecasts of inflation, unemployment, and output are regularly in error. Worse still, there are never-ending arguments about what caused a major economic event long after it occurred. In fact, economists are still arguing over the causes of not only the Great Recession of 2008–2009 but even the Great Depression of the 1930s! Did government failure or market failure cause and deepen those economic setbacks?

Modest Expectations 适度的期望

In view of all these debates and uncertainties, you should not expect to learn everything there is to know about the economy in this text or course. Our goals are more modest. We want you to develop a fresh perspective on economic behavior and an understanding of basic principles. With this foundation, you should acquire a better view of how the economy works. Daily news reports on economic events should start to make more sense. Political debates on tax, budget, and environmental policies should take on more meaning. You may even develop some insights that you can apply toward running a business or planning a career.

鉴于上述这些争论和不确定性，你应该明白，不能期望在本书或本课程中学到有关经济的所有知识。我们的目标比较适中——我们希望你对经济行为有一个全新的认识并理解基本原理。在此基础上，你应该对经济如何运行获得一个更好的观点。你会对每天关于经济事件的新闻报道有更多的理解。关于税收、预算和环保政策的政治争论对你来说也有了更多意义。如果将理论应用于企业经营或职业规划中，你甚至会获得一些有见地的洞察。

> **POLICY PERSPECTIVES**
>
> **IS "FREE" HEALTH CARE REALLY FREE?**
>
> Everyone wants more and better health care, and nearly everyone agrees that even the poorest members of society need reliable access to doctors and hospitals. That's why President Obama made health care reform such a high priority in his first presidential year.
>
> Although the political debate over health care reform was intense and multidimensional, the economics of health care are fairly simple. In essence, President Obama wanted to *expand* the health care industry. He wanted to increase access for the millions of Americans who didn't have health insurance and raise the level of service for people with low incomes and preexisting illnesses. He wasn't proposing to *reduce* health care for those who already had adequate care. Thus his reform proposals entailed a net increase in health care services.
>
> Were health care a free good, everyone would have welcomed President Obama's reforms. But the most fundamental concept in economics is this: **There is no free lunch.** Resources used to prepare and serve even a "free" lunch could be used to produce something else. So it is with health care. The resources used to expand health care services could be used to produce something else. The **opportunity costs** of expanded health care are the other goods we could have produced (and consumed) with the same resources.
>
> ©Morsa Images/Getty Images
>
> Figure 1.6 illustrates the basic policy dilemma. In 2009 health care services absorbed about 16 percent of total U.S. output. So the *mix* of output resembled point X_1, where H_1 amount of health care is produced and O_1 of other goods. At H_1 millions of Americans had no health insurance and were not receiving adequate care. So, President Obama wanted to *increase* health care access and services. His goal was to increase the quantity of health services from H_1 to H_2.
>
> If health care were a free good, no one would object to raising the quantity of health care from H_1 to H_2. But health care isn't a free good: It absorbs resources that could be used to produce other goods. We can't move the mix of output from X_1 to X_2 (i.e., get more health care without giving up other goods). The production possibilities curve tells us we can get more health care only by reducing the output of other goods (i.e., by moving from the output mix X_1 to the mix X_3). At X_3 we have more health care (H_2) but fewer other goods (O_2) than we had before. That's the policy dilemma. What other goods will be sacrificed and who will absorb the loss?

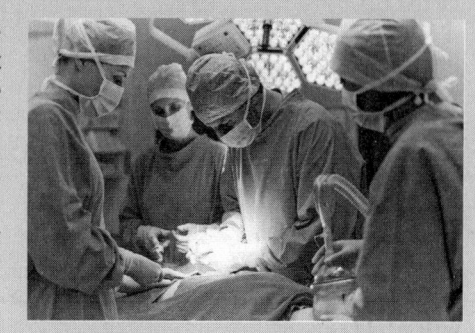

---

multidimensional 多维的，多面的。 sacrifice 牺牲，放弃。

The Affordable Care Act of 2010 imposed taxes and fees that forced consumers to buy more health care (insurance) and left them with less income to purchase "other goods." President Trump sought to eliminate those taxes and mandates, giving consumers more freedom about how to spend their incomes. Here again, it was a debate about markets versus government. The inevitable trade-off (opportunity cost) that accompanies expanded health care is what makes such decisions about WHAT to produce so difficult.

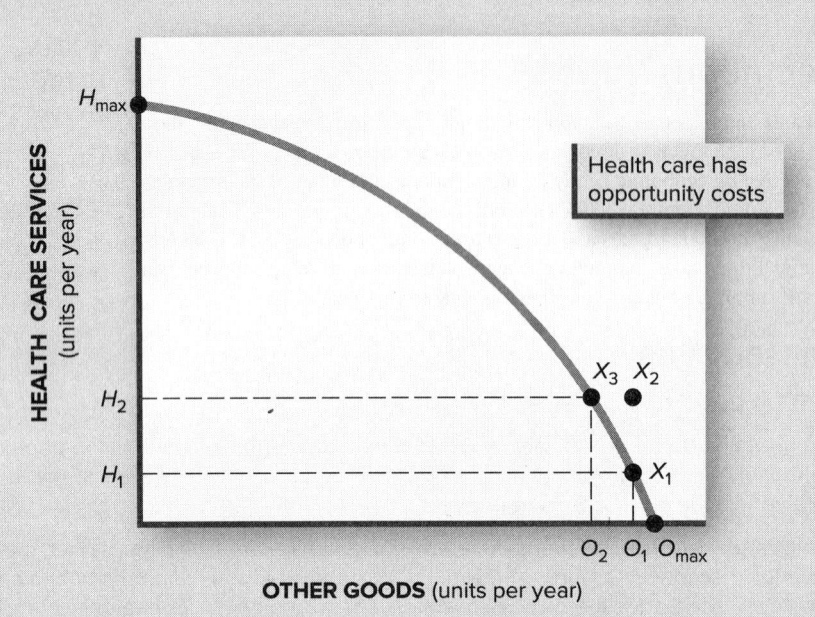

Figure 1.6 No Free Health Care Health care absorbs resources that can be used to produce other goods. Increasing health care services from H_1 to H_2 requires a reduction in the production of other goods from O_1 to O_2.

CHAPTER 1 REVIEW

SUMMARY

- Every nation confronts the three basic economic questions of WHAT to produce, HOW, and FOR WHOM. **LO3**
- The need to select a single mix of output (WHAT) is necessitated by our limited capacity to produce. Scarcity results when our wants exceed our resources. **LO1**
- The production possibilities curve illustrates the limits to output dictated by available factors of production and technology. Points on the curve represent the different output mixes that we may choose. **LO1**
- All production entails an opportunity cost: We can produce more of output A only if we produce less of output B. The implied reduction in output B is the opportunity cost of output A. **LO2**
- The HOW question focuses on the choice of what inputs to use in production. It also encompasses choices made about environmental protection. **LO3**
- The FOR WHOM question concerns the distribution of output among members of society. **LO3**
- The goal of every society is to select the best possible (optimal) answers to the WHAT, HOW, and FOR WHOM questions. The optimal answers will vary with social values and production capabilities. **LO3**
- The three questions can be answered by the market mechanism, by a system of central planning, or by a

mixed system of market signals and government intervention. **LO4**

- Price signals are the key feature of the market mechanism. Consumers signal their desires for specific goods by paying a price for those goods. Producers respond to the price signal by assembling factors of production to produce the desired output. **LO4**
- Market failure occurs when the market mechanism generates the wrong mix of output, undesirable methods of production, or an inequitable distribution of income. Government intervention may fail, too, however, by not improving (or even worsening) economic outcomes. **LO5**
- The study of economics focuses on the broad question of resource allocation. Macroeconomics is concerned with allocating the resources of an entire economy to achieve broad economic goals (e.g., full employment). Microeconomics focuses on the behavior and goals of individual market participants. **LO3**

TERMS TO REMEMBER

Define the following terms:

economics
opportunity cost
factors of production
scarcity
production possibilities
investment
economic growth
market mechanism
laissez faire
mixed economy
market failure
government failure
macroeconomics
microeconomics
ceteris paribus

QUESTIONS FOR DISCUSSION

1. As rich as America is, how can our resources possibly be "scarce"? **LO1**
2. What opportunity costs did you incur in reading this chapter? **LO2**
3. How would you answer the question in the News Wire "Future Living Standards"? Why? **LO3**
4. In a purely private market economy, how is the FOR WHOM question answered? Is that optimal? **LO3**
5. If taxes on the rich were raised to provide more housing for the poor, how would the willingness to work be affected? What would happen to total output? **LO3**
6. What kind of knowledge must central planners possess to manage an economy efficiently? **LO4**
7. **POLICY PERSPECTIVES** Why can't we produce at point X_2 in Figure 1.6? Will we ever get there? **LO5**
8. **POLICY PERSPECTIVES** What was President Obama's goal for the Affordable Care Act? Why didn't President Trump like that policy? **LO2**

PROBLEMS

1. Iceland has no military. (*a*) So, at what point in Figure 1.1 is Iceland producing? (*b*) If Iceland decided to produce the quantity *OE* of military goods, how much consumer output would it have to give up? **LO2**
2. What percentage of total U.S. output consisted of military goods **LO2**
    a. in 1944? (Figure 1.2)
    b. in 2018? (Figure 1.2)

3. Draw a production possibilities curve based on Table 1.1, labeling combinations A–F. What is the opportunity cost of increasing missile production **LO2**
    a. from 50 to 100?
    b. from 100 to 150?
4. Assume that it takes four hours of labor time to paint a room and two hours to sand a floor. If 24 hours were spent painting: (*a*) How many rooms could be painted? (*b*) If a decision were made to sand two floors, how many painted rooms would have be given up? (*c*) Illustrate with a production possibilities curve. **LO1**
5. Assume that it takes four hours of labor time to paint a room and two hours to sand a floor. If two workers each spend 24 hours painting: (*a*) How many rooms could be painted? (*b*) If a decision were made to only sand floors, how many floors could be sanded? (*c*) Illustrate with a production possibilities curve. **LO2**
6. The table below describes the production possibilities confronting an economy. Using that information: **LO3**
    a. Calculate the opportunity costs of building hospitals.
    b. Draw the production possibilities curve.
    c. Why can't more of both outputs be produced?
    d. Which point on the curve is the most desired one?

Potential Output Combinations	Homeless Shelters	Hospitals
A	20	0
B	17	1
C	13	2
D	7	3
E	0	4

7. **POLICY PERSPECTIVES** In Figure 1.6, (*a*) If as much health care as possible is provided, how many other goods will be provided? (*b*) What is the opportunity cost of increasing health care from H_1 to H_2? **LO5**
8. **POLICY PERSPECTIVES** Suppose the following data reflect the production possibilities for providing health care and education: **LO5**

Units per Year

Health care	400	370	330	270	190	100	0
Education	0	20	40	50	60	70	80

   a. Graph the production possibilities curve.
   b. If maximum health care is provided, how much education will be provided?
   c. What is the opportunity cost of increasing health care from 100 to 190 units?

Study Time (Hours per Week)	Grade Point Average
16	4.0 (A)
14	3.5 (B+)
12	3.0 (B)
10	2.5 (C+)
8	2.0 (C)
6	1.5 (D+)
4	1.0 (D)
2	0.5 (F+)
0	0 (F)

Table A.1 Hypothetical Relationship of Grades to Study Time These data suggest that grades improve with increased study time.

APPENDIX–USING GRAPHS 附录：图表的使用

Economists like to draw graphs. In fact, we didn't even make it through the first chapter without a few graphs. The purpose of this appendix is to look more closely at the way graphs are drawn and used.

The basic purpose of a graph is to illustrate a relationship between two *variables*. Consider, for example, the relationship between grades and studying. In general, you expect that additional hours of study time will result in higher grades. If true, you should be able to see a distinct relationship between hours of study time and grade point average. In other words, there should be some empirical evidence that study time matters.

Suppose we actually tracked study times and grades for all the students taking this course. The resulting information might resemble the data in Table A.1.

According to the table, students who don't study at all can expect an F in this course. To get a C, the average student apparently spends eight hours a week studying. All those who study 16 hours a week end up with an A in the course.

These relationships between grades and studying can also be illustrated on a graph. Indeed, the whole purpose of a graph is to summarize numerical relationships in a visual way.

We begin to construct a graph by drawing horizontal and vertical boundaries, as in Figure A.1. These boundaries are called the *axes* of the graph. On the vertical axis we measure one of the variables; the other variable is measured on the horizontal axis.

In this case, we shall measure the grade point average on the vertical axis. We start at the *origin* (the intersection of the two axes) and count upward, letting the distance between horizontal lines represent half (0.5) a grade point. Each horizontal line is numbered, up to the maximum grade point average of 4.0.

The number of hours each week spent doing homework is measured on the horizontal axis. We begin at the origin again, and count to the right. The *scale* (numbering) proceeds in increments of 1 hour, up to 20 hours per week.

When both axes have been labeled and measured, we can begin to illustrate the relationship between study time and grades. Consider the typical student who does eight hours of homework per week and has a 2.0 (C) grade point average. We illustrate this relationship by first locating eight hours on the horizontal axis. We then move up from that point a distance of 2.0 grade points, to point *M*. Point *M* tells us that eight hours of study time per week is typically associated with a 2.0 grade point average.

The rest of the information in Table A.1 is drawn (or *plotted*) on the graph in the same way. To illustrate the average grade for people who study 12 hours per week, we move upward from the number 12 on the horizontal axis until we reach the height of 3.0 on the vertical axis. At that intersection, we draw another point (point *N*).

Once we have plotted the various points describing the relationship of study time to grades, we may connect them with a line or curve. This line (curve) is our summary. In this case, the line slopes upward to the right—that is, it has a *positive* slope. This slope indicates that more hours of study time are associated with *higher* grades. Were higher grades associated with *less* study time, the curve in Figure A.1 would have a *negative* slope (downward from left to right)—a puzzling outcome.

Slopes 斜率

The upward slope of Figure A.1 not only tells us that more studying raises your grade, it also tells us *by how much* grades rise with study time. According to point *M* in Figure A.1, the average student studies eight hours per week and earns a C (2.0 grade point average). In order to earn a B (3.0 grade point average), a student apparently needs to study an average of 12 hours per week (point *N*). Hence an *increase* of four hours of study time per week is associated with a 1-point *increase* in grade point average. This relationship between *changes* in study time and *changes* in grade point average is expressed by the steepness, or *slope*, of the graph.

The slope of any graph is calculated as

$$\text{Slope} = \frac{\text{vertical distance between two points}}{\text{horizontal distance between two points}}$$

Some people simplify this by saying

$$\text{Slope} = \frac{\text{the rise}}{\text{the run}}$$

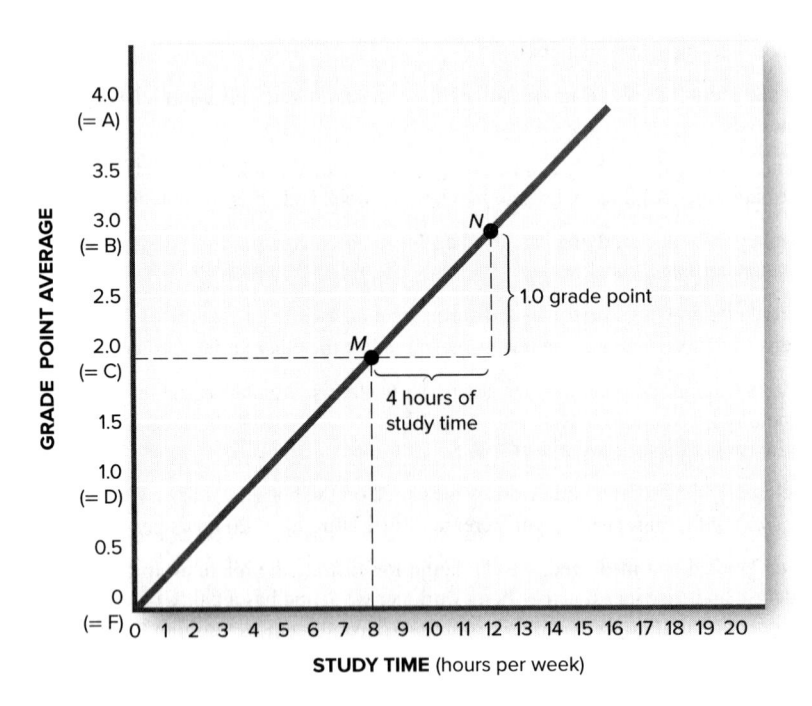

Figure A.1 The Relationship of Grades to Study Time The upward (positive) slope of the curve indicates that additional studying is associated with higher grades. The average student (2.0, or C grade) studies eight hours per week. This is indicated by point *M* on the graph.

In our example, the vertical distance (the "rise") between points *M* and *N* represents a change in grade point average. The horizontal distance (the "run") between these two points represents the change in study time. Hence the slope of the graph between points *M* and *N* is equal to

$$\text{Slope} = \frac{3.0 \text{ grade} - 2.0 \text{ grade}}{12 \text{ hours} - 8 \text{ hours}} = \frac{1 \text{ grade point}}{4 \text{ hours}}$$

In other words, a four-hour increase in study time (from 8 to 12 hours) is associated with a 1-point increase in grade point average (see Figure A.1).

Shifts 移动

The relationship between grades and studying illustrated in Figure A.1 is not inevitable. It is simply a graphical illustration of student experiences, as revealed in our hypothetical survey. The relationship between study time and grades could be quite different.

Suppose that the university decided to raise grading standards, making it more difficult to achieve good grades. To achieve a C, a student now would need to study 12 hours per week, not just 8 (as in Figure A.1). To get a B, you now have to study 16 hours, not the previous norm of only 12 hours per week.

Figure A.2 illustrates the new grading standards. Notice that the new curve lies to the right of the earlier curve. We say that the curve has *shifted* to reflect a change in the relationship between study time and grades. Point *R* indicates that 12 hours of study time now "produces" a C, not a B (point *N* on the old curve). Students who now study only four hours per week (point *S*) will fail. Under the old grading policy, they could have at least gotten a D. ***When a curve shifts, the underlying relationship between the two variables has changed.***

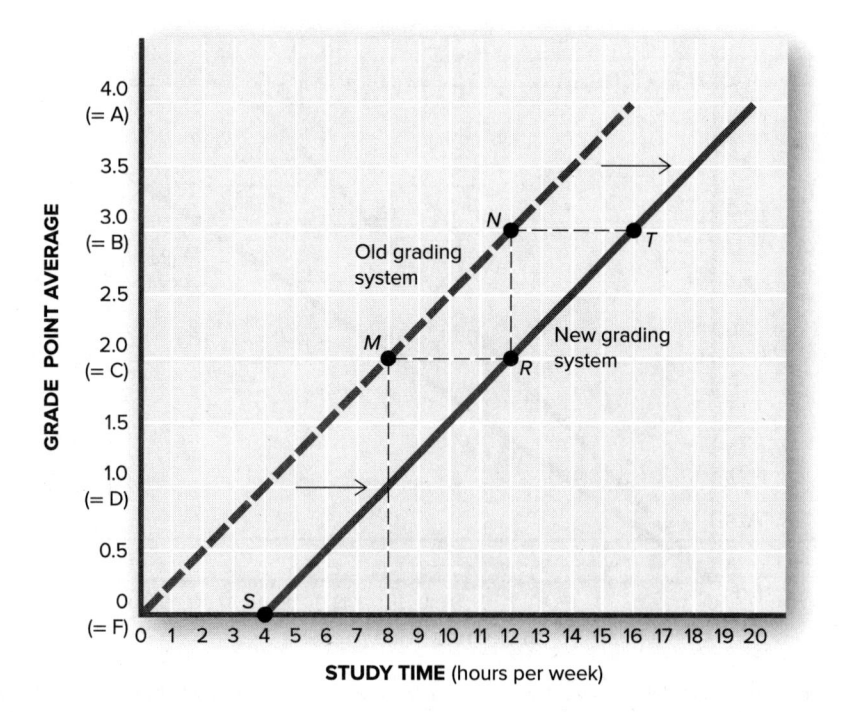

Figure A.2 A Shift When a relationship between two variables changes, the entire curve *shifts*. In this case a tougher grading policy alters the relationship between study time and grades. To get a C, one must now study 12 hours per week (point *R*), not just 8 hours (point *M*). ∎

A shift may also change the slope of the curve. In Figure A.2, the new grading curve is parallel to the old one; it therefore has the same slope. Under either the new grading policy or the old one, a four-hour increase in study time leads to a 1-point increase in grades. Therefore, the slope of both curves in Figure A.2 is

$$\text{Slope} = \frac{\text{vertical change}}{\text{horizontal change}} = \frac{1}{4}$$

This, too, may change, however. Figure A.3 illustrates such a possibility. In this case, zero study time still results in an F. But now the payoff for additional studying is reduced. Now it takes six hours of study time to get a D (1.0 grade point), not four hours as before. Likewise, another four hours of study time (to a total of 10) raises the grade by only two-thirds of a point.

It takes six hours to raise the grade a full point. The slope of the new line is therefore

$$\text{Slope} = \frac{\text{vertical change}}{\text{horizontal change}} = \frac{1}{6}$$

The new curve in Figure A.3 has a smaller slope than the original curve and so lies below it. What all this means is that it now takes a greater effort to *improve* your grade.

Linear versus Nonlinear Curves   线性和非线性曲线

In Figures A.1–A.3, the relationship between grades and studying is represented by a straight line—that is, a *linear* curve. A distinguishing feature of linear curves is that they have the same (constant) slope throughout. In Figure A.1, it appears that *every* four-hour increase in study time is associated with a 1-point increase in average grades. In Figure A.3, it appears that every six-hour increase in study time leads to a 1-point increase in grades.

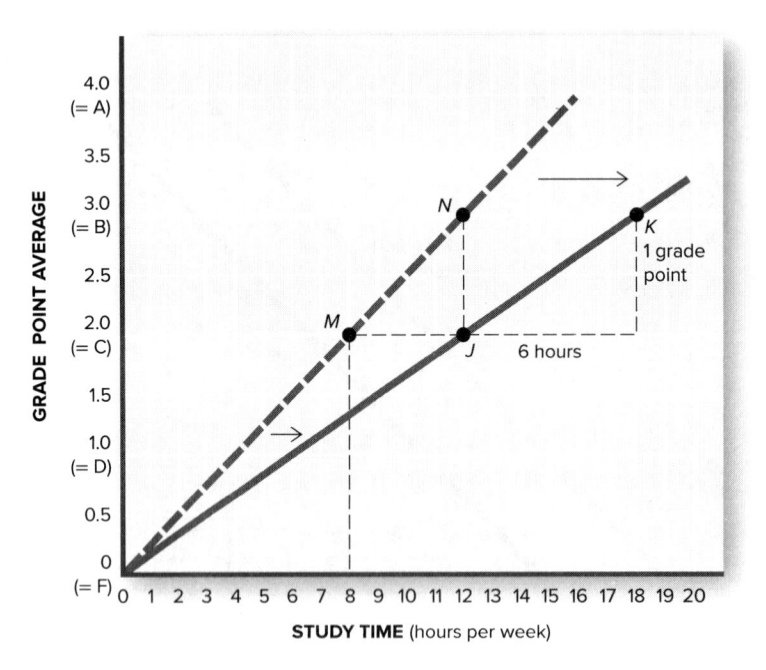

Figure A.3 A Change in Slope When a curve shifts, it may change its slope as well. In this case, a new grading policy makes each higher grade more difficult to achieve. To raise a C to a B, for example, one must study six additional hours (compare points *J* and *K*). Earlier it took only four hours to move up the grade scale a full point. The slope of the line has declined from 0.25 (= 1 ÷ 4) to 0.17 (= 1 ÷ 6). ∎

In reality, the relationship between studying and grades may not be linear. Higher grades may be more difficult to attain. You may be able to raise a C to a B by studying six hours more per week. But it may be harder to raise a B to an A. According to Figure A.4, it takes an additional *eight* hours of studying to raise a B to an A. Thus the relationship between study time and grades is *nonlinear* in Figure A.4; the slope of the curve *changes* as study time increases. In this case, the slope decreases as study time increases. Grades continue to improve, but not so fast, as more and more time is devoted to homework. You may know the feeling.

Causation 因果关系

Figure A.4 does not itself guarantee that your grade point average will rise if you study four more hours per week. In fact, the graph drawn in Figure A.4 does not prove that additional study ever results in higher grades. The graph is only a summary of empirical observations. It says nothing about cause and effect. It could be that students who study a lot are smarter to begin with. If so, then less able students might not get higher grades if they studied harder. In other words, the *cause* of higher grades is debatable. At best, the empirical relationship summarized in the graph may be used to support a particular theory (e.g., that it pays to study more). Graphs, like tables, charts, and other statistical media, rarely tell their own stories; rather, they must be *interpreted* in terms of some underlying theory or expectation. That's when the real fun starts.

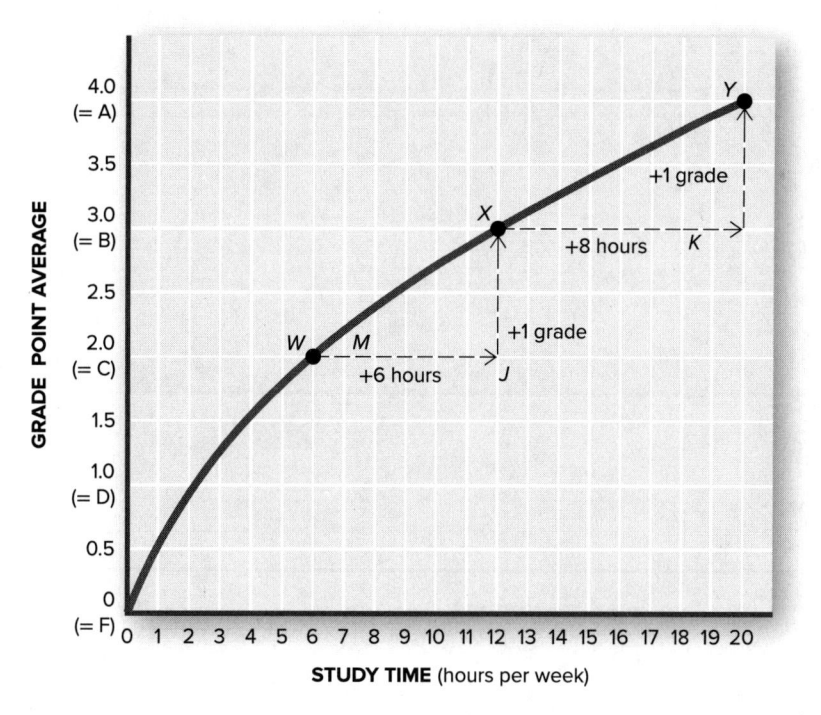

Figure A.4 A Nonlinear Relationship Straight lines have a constant slope, implying a constant relationship between the two variables. But the relationship (and slope) may vary. In this case it takes six extra hours of study to raise a C (point *W*) to a B (point *X*) but eight extra hours to raise a B to an A (point *Y*). The slope is decreasing as we move up the curve.

CHAPTER TWO

Supply and Demand 供给与需求

©Yuen Man Cheung/Alamy Stock Photo

LEARNING OBJECTIVES

After reading this chapter, you should be able to:

1. Explain why people participate in markets.
2. Describe what market demand and supply measure.
3. Depict how and why a market equilibrium is found.
4. Illustrate how and why demand and supply curves sometimes shift.
5. Explain how market shortages and surpluses occur.

A few years ago a Florida man tried to sell one of his kidneys on eBay. As his offer explained, he could supply only one kidney because he needed the other to survive. He wanted the bidding to start out at $25,000, plus expenses for the surgical removal and shipment of his kidney. He felt confident he could get at least that much money since thousands of people have potentially fatal kidney diseases.

He was right. The bids for his kidney quickly surpassed $100,000. Clearly there were lots of people with kidney disease who were willing and able to pay high prices to get a lifesaving transplant.

The seller never got the chance to sell his kidney to the highest bidder. Although organ transplants are perfectly legal in the United States, the purchase or sale of human organs is not. When eBay learned the pending sale was illegal, it shut down the man's advertisement.

Despite its illegality, there is clearly a market for human kidneys. That is to say, there are people who are willing to *sell* kidneys and others who are willing to *buy* kidneys. Those are sufficient conditions for the existence of a market. The market in kidneys happens to be illegal in the United States, but it is still a market, although illegal. The markets for drugs, prostitution, and nuclear warheads are also illegal, but still reflect the intentions of potential buyers and sellers.

Fortunately we don't have to venture into the underworld to see how markets work. You can watch markets work by visiting eBay or other electronic auction sites. Or you can simply go to the mall and watch people shop. In either location you will observe people deciding whether to buy or sell goods at various prices. That's the essence of market activity.

---

kidney 肾。bidding 出价，报价。pending 未成交的，未决的。prostitution 卖淫。nuclear warhead 核弹头。venture into the underworld 闯入黑市。

The goal in this chapter is to assess how markets actually function. How does the invisible hand of the market resolve the competing interests of buyers (who want low prices) and sellers (who want high prices)? Specifically,

- What determines the price of a good or service?
- How does the price of a product affect its production or consumption?
- Why do prices and production levels often change?

MARKET PARTICIPANTS 市场参与者

More than 340 million individual consumers, about 30 million business firms, and thousands of government agencies participate directly in the U.S. economy. Millions of foreigners also participate by buying and selling goods in American markets.

Goals 目标

所有这些经济行为者参与市场都是为了实现特定的目标。消费者努力使自己的幸福感最大化；厂商试图实现利润最大化；政府机构试图实现社会福利的最大化。外国人追求的目标也和消费者、厂商或政府机构相同。在每种情况下，他们都是通过买卖商品、服务或生产要素的最优可能组合来实现这些目标的。

All these economic actors participate in the market to achieve specific goals. Consumers strive to maximize their own happiness; businesses try to maximize profits; government agencies attempt to maximize social welfare. Foreigners pursue the same goals as consumers, producers, or government agencies. In every case, they strive to achieve those goals by buying or selling the best possible mix of goods, services, or factors of production.

Constraints 约束

所有市场参与者使利润、个人满足感或社会福利最大化的愿望并不是他们唯一的共同特征。所有参与者的另一个共性是其有限的资源。你和我都不可能购买所有我们想要的东西，因为我们没有足够的收入。因此，我们必须在可获得的产品中做出选择。我们总是希望能从有限的那点钱中得到尽可能多的满足。同样，厂商和政府机构也必须决定如何最好地利用其有限的资源以实现利润或公共福利的最大化。这就是我们在第 1 章分析过的稀缺问题，它是所有经济决策的核心。

The desire of all market participants to maximize something—profits, private satisfaction, or social welfare—is not their only common trait. Another element common to all participants is their *limited resources*. You and I cannot buy everything we desire; we simply don't have enough income. As a consequence, we must make *choices* among available products. We're always hoping to get as much satisfaction as possible for the few dollars we have to spend. Likewise, business firms and government agencies must decide how *best* to use their limited resources to maximize profits or public welfare. This is the scarcity problem we examined in Chapter 1. It is central to all economic decisions.

Specialization and Exchange 专业化与交换

To maximize the returns on our limited resources, we participate in the **market**, buying and selling various goods and services. Our decision to participate in these exchanges is prompted by two considerations. First, most of us are incapable of producing everything we desire to consume. Second, even if we *could* produce all our own goods and services, it would still make sense to *specialize*, producing only one product and trading it for other desired goods and services.

Suppose you were capable of growing your own food, stitching your own clothes, building your own shelter, and even writing your own economics text. Even in this little utopia, it would still make sense to decide how *best* to expend your limited time and energy and to rely on others to fill in the gaps. If you were *most* proficient at growing food, you would be best off spending your time farming. You could then exchange some of your food output for the clothes, shelter, and books you desired. In the end, you'd be able to consume *more* goods than if you had tried to make everything yourself.

Our economic interactions with others are thus necessitated by two constraints:

- 作为个体，我们没有能力生产所有我们想要的东西。
- 对于我们能够自己生产的东西，我们所拥有的时间、精力和资源也是有限的。

- Our inability as individuals to produce all the things we desire.
- The limited amount of time, energy, and resources we possess for producing those things we could make for ourselves.

Together these constraints lead us to specialize and interact. Most of the interactions that result take place in the market.

---

resolve 化解，解决。 specialize 专业化。 stitch 缝，缝合。 utopia 乌托邦，理想的完美社会。

MARKET INTERACTIONS 市场中的相互作用

Figure 2.1 summarizes the kinds of interactions that occur among market participants. Note, first of all, that we have identified *four separate groups of market participants:*

- *Consumers.*
- *Business firms.*
- *Governments.*
- *Foreigners.*

Domestically, the "consumers" rectangle includes all 340 million consumers in the United States. In the "business firms" box we have grouped all the domestic business enterprises that buy and sell goods and services. The third participant, "governments," includes the many separate agencies of the federal government, as well as state and local governments. Figure 2.1 also illustrates the role of foreigners.

图 2.1 总结了发生在市场参与者之间的各种相互作用。注意，首先我们划分了四个不同的市场参与者：

- 消费者
- 厂商
- 政府
- 外国参与者

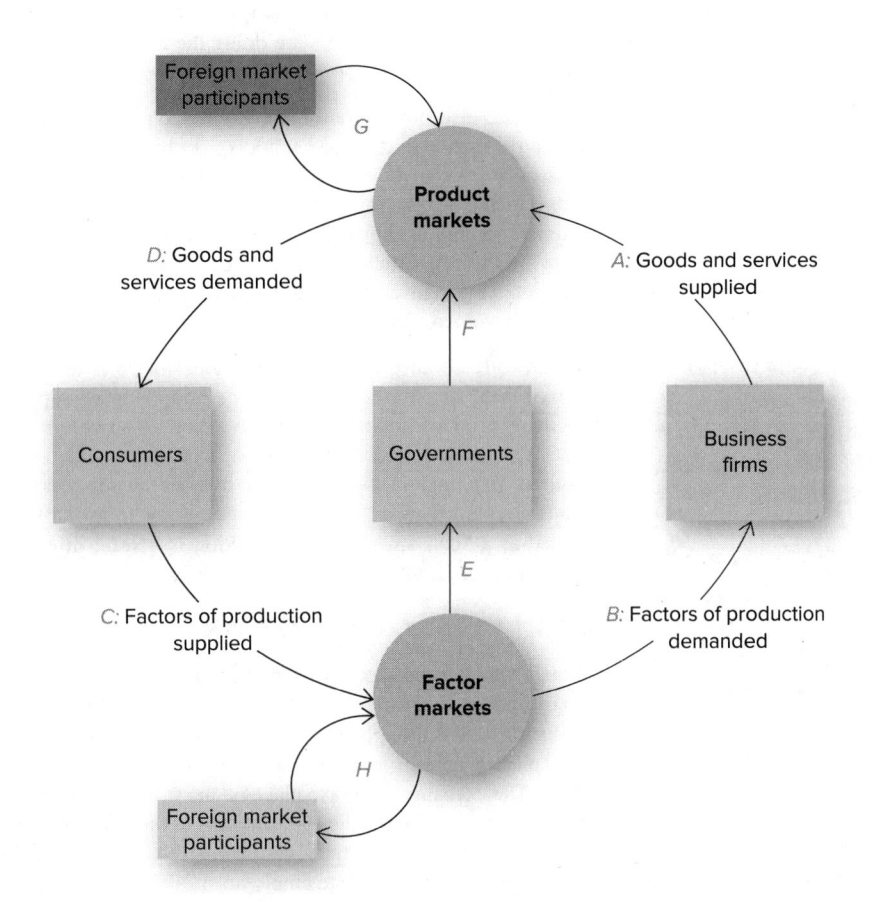

Figure 2.1 Market Interactions Business firms participate in markets by supplying goods and services to product markets (point *A*) and purchasing factors of production in factor markets (*B*).
Individual consumers participate in the marketplace by supplying factors of production such as their own labor (*C*) and purchasing final goods and services (*D*).
Federal, state, and local governments also participate in both factor (*E*) and product markets (*F*).
Foreigners participate by supplying imports, purchasing exports (*G*), and buying and selling resources (*H*). ∎

---

domestically 国内地，就国内而言。rectangle 长方形，矩形。

The Two Markets   两个市场

The easiest way to keep track of all this market activity is to distinguish two basic markets. Figure 2.1 does this by depicting separate circles (in blue) for product markets and factor markets.

Factor Markets   要素市场

在**要素市场**中交换的是生产要素。市场参与者购买或销售生产过程中所使用的土地、劳动或资本。例如，当你找工作时，你就是在向生产者提供生产要素，即你的劳动。你在出售你的时间和才能。如果你以他们愿意支付的价格提供其需要的技能，生产者将雇用你，即在要素市场购买你的服务。

In **factor markets**, factors of production are exchanged. Market participants buy or sell land, labor, or capital that can be used in the production process. When you go looking for work, for example, you are making a factor of production—your labor—available to producers. You are offering to *sell* your time and talent. The producers will hire you—*buy* your services in the factor market—if you are offering the skills they need at a price they are willing to pay.

Product Markets   产品市场

The activity in factor markets is only half the story. At the end of a hard day's work, consumers go to the grocery store, the mall, or the movies to purchase desired goods and services—that is, to buy *products*. In this context, consumers again interact with business firms. This time, however, their roles are reversed: Consumers are doing the *buying*, and businesses are doing the *selling*. This exchange of goods and services occurs in **product markets**.

Governments also supply goods and services to product markets. The consumer rarely buys national defense, schools, or highways directly; instead such purchases are made indirectly through taxes and government expenditure. In Figure 2.1, the arrows running from governments through product markets to consumers remind us, however, that all government output is intended "for the people." In this sense, the government acts as an intermediary, buying factors of production (e.g., government employees) and providing certain goods and services consumers desire (e.g., police protection).

在图 2.1 中连接产品市场和消费者的箭头（*D*）强调了这样一个事实：根据定义，消费者不提供产品。个人想生产商品和服务时，就只有在政府或企业部门内才能做到。作为医生、牙医或者经济顾问的个人在两个部门发挥作用。当一个人在市场上出售服务时，这个人就被视为"厂商"；出了办公室，他（她）就被视为"消费者"了。这种区分有助于突出消费者是生产出来的商品和服务的最终接受者。

In Figure 2.1, the arrow connecting product markets to consumers (point *D*) emphasizes the fact that consumers, by definition, do not supply products. When individuals produce goods and services, they do so within the government or business sector. An individual who is a doctor, a dentist, or an economic consultant functions in two sectors. When selling services in the market, this person is regarded as a "business"; when away from the office, he or she is regarded as a "consumer." This distinction is helpful in emphasizing that ***the consumer is the final recipient of all goods and services produced.***

Locating Markets   寻找市场

虽然我们反复提到两种市场，但如果真的去寻找产品市场和要素市场，就未免有些愚蠢了。要素市场和产品市场都不是单一的、可以辨别出来的机构。市场这个术语就是指发生经济交换的任何地方——买方和卖方在此进行交易。交换可能发生在街上、出租车里、或通过电话、邮件、网络或报纸上的分类广告进行。在有些情况下，市场可能是非常清晰可辨的，例如零售商店、芝加哥商品交易所或国家就业中心。但不管这个地方看起来像什么，任何时候、任何地方，只要有交易发生，就存在市场。

Although we refer repeatedly to two kinds of markets, it would be a little foolish to go off in search of the product and factor markets. Neither a factor market nor a product market is a single, identifiable structure. The term *market* simply refers to any place where an economic exchange occurs—where a buyer and seller interact. The exchange may take place on the street, in a taxicab, over the phone, by mail, online, or through the classified ads of the newspaper. In some cases, the market used may in fact be quite distinguishable, as in the case of a retail store, the Chicago Commodity Exchange, or a state employment office. But whatever it looks like, *a market exists wherever and whenever an exchange takes place.*

Dollars and Exchange   货币与交换

Sometimes people exchange one good for another directly. On eBay, for example, you might persuade a seller to accept some old DVDs in payment for the Xbox One she is selling. Or you might offer to paint someone's house in exchange for "free" rent. Such two-way exchanges are called **barter**.

---

keep track of 了解。 intermediary 中间人。 barter 物物交换。

The problem with bartered exchanges is that you have to find a seller who wants whatever good you are offering in payment. This can make shopping an extremely time-consuming process. Fortunately, most market transactions are facilitated by using money as a form of payment. If you go shopping for an Xbox, you don't have to find a seller craving old DVDs; all you have to do is find a seller willing to accept the dollar price you are willing to pay. Because money facilitates exchanges, **nearly every market transaction involves an exchange of dollars for goods (in product markets) or resources (in factor markets).** Money thus plays a critical role in facilitating market exchanges and the specialization they permit.

Supply and Demand 供给与需求

The two sides of each market transaction are called **supply** and **demand**. As noted earlier, we are *supplying* resources to the market when we look for a job—that is, when we offer our labor in exchange for income. But we are *demanding* goods when we shop in a supermarket—that is, when we are prepared to offer dollars in exchange for something to eat. Business firms may *supply* goods and services in product markets at the same time that they are *demanding* factors of production in factor markets.

Whether one is on the supply side or the demand side of any particular market transaction depends on the nature of the exchange, not on the people or institutions involved.

DEMAND 需求

Although the concepts of supply and demand help explain what's happening in the marketplace, we are not yet ready to summarize the countless transactions that occur daily in both factor and product markets. Recall that *every market transaction involves an exchange and thus some element of both supply and demand.* Then just consider how many exchanges you alone undertake in a single week, not to mention the transactions of the other 340 million or so consumers among us. To keep track of so much action, we need to summarize the activities of a great many individuals.

Individual Demand 个体需求

We can begin to understand how market forces work by looking more closely at the behavior of a single market participant. Let us start with Tom, a senior at Clearview College. Tom has majored in everything from art history to government in his five years at Clearview. He didn't connect with any of those fields and is on the brink of academic dismissal. To make matters worse, his parents have threatened to cut him off financially unless he graduates sometime soon. They want him to take courses that will lead to a job after graduation so they don't have to keep supporting him.

Tom thinks he has found the perfect solution: web design. Everything associated with the Internet pays big bucks. Plus, girls seem to think webbies are "cool." Or at least so Tom thinks. And his parents would definitely approve. So Tom has enrolled in web design courses.

Unfortunately for Tom, he never developed computer skills. Until he got to Clearview College, he thought mastering Sony's latest alien attack video game was the pinnacle of electronic wizardry. His parents gave him a MacBook Pro but he used it only to post on Facebook and to visit gaming message boards. The concept of using his computer for coursework, much less developing some web content, is completely foreign to him. To compound his problems, Tom doesn't have a clue about streaming, interfacing, animation, or the other concepts the web design instructor has outlined in the first lecture.

Given his circumstances, Tom is desperate to find someone who can tutor him in web design. But desperation is not enough to secure the services of a web architect. In a market-based economy, you must also be willing to *pay* for the things you want. Specifically, *a demand*

---

brink 边缘。dismissal 解雇，开除。buck 原意是雄鹿，这里指收益、收入。pinnacle 顶点，尖峰。wizardry 杰作，非凡成就。animation 动画制作。

exists only if someone is willing and able to pay for the good—that is, exchange dollars for a good or service in the marketplace. Is Tom willing and able to pay for the web design tutoring he so obviously needs?

Let us assume that Tom has some income and is willing to spend some of it to get a tutor. Under these assumptions, we can claim that Tom is a participant in the *market* for web design services.

But how much is Tom willing to pay? Surely Tom is not prepared to exchange *all* his income for help in mastering web design. After all, Tom could use his income to buy more desirable goods and services. If he spent all his income on a web tutor, that help would have an extremely high **opportunity cost**. He would be giving up the opportunity to spend that income on other goods and services. He might pass his web design class but have little else. That doesn't sound like a good idea to Tom. Even though he *says* he would be willing to pay *anything* to pass the web design course, he probably has lower prices in mind. Indeed, there are *limits* to the amount Tom is willing to pay for any given quantity of web design tutoring. These limits will be determined by how much income Tom has to spend and how many other goods and services he must forsake to pay for a tutor.

Tom also knows that his grade in web design will depend in part on how much tutoring service he buys. He can pass the course with only a few hours of design help. If he wants a better grade, however, the cost is going to escalate quickly.

Naturally Tom wants it all—an A in web design and a ticket to higher-paying jobs. But here again the distinction between *desire* and *demand* is relevant. He may *desire* to master web design, but his actual proficiency will depend on how many hours of tutoring he is willing to *pay* for.

We assume, then, that when Tom starts looking for a web design tutor he has in mind some sort of **demand schedule**, like that described in Figure 2.2. According to row *A* of this schedule, Tom is willing and able to buy only one hour of tutoring service per semester if he must pay $50 an hour. At such an "outrageous" price he will learn minimal skills and just pass the course. But that's all Tom is willing to buy at that price.

At lower prices, Tom would behave differently. According to Figure 2.2, Tom would purchase *more* tutoring services if the price per hour were *less*. At lower prices, he would not have to give up so many other goods and services for each hour of technical help. The reduced opportunity costs implied by lower service prices increase the attractiveness of professional help. Indeed, we see from row *I* of the demand schedule that Tom is willing to purchase 20 hours per semester—the whole bag of design tricks—if the price of tutoring is as low as $10 per hour.

Notice that the demand schedule doesn't tell us *why* Tom is willing to pay these specific prices for various amounts of tutoring. Tom's expressed willingness to pay for web design tutoring may reflect a desperate need to finish a web design course, a lot of income to spend, or a relatively small desire for other goods and services. All the demand schedule tells us is what this consumer is *willing and able* to buy, for whatever reasons.

Also observe that the demand schedule doesn't tell us how many hours of design help the consumer will *actually* buy. Figure 2.2 simply states that Tom is *willing and able* to pay for one hour of tutoring at $50 per hour, two hours at $45 per hour, and so on. How much service he purchases will depend on the actual price of web services in the market. Until we know that price, we cannot tell how much service will be purchased. Hence **demand is an expression of consumer buying intentions, of a willingness to buy, rather than a statement of actual purchases.**

---

escalate 增加，增长。proficiency 熟练程度。demand schedule 需求表。semester 学期。outrageous 不可接受的，无法容忍的。

	Demand Schedule	
	Price of Tutoring (per Hour)	Quantity of Tutoring Demanded (Hours per Semester)
A	$50	1
B	45	2
C	40	3
D	35	5
E	30	7
F	25	9
G	20	12
H	15	15
I	10	20

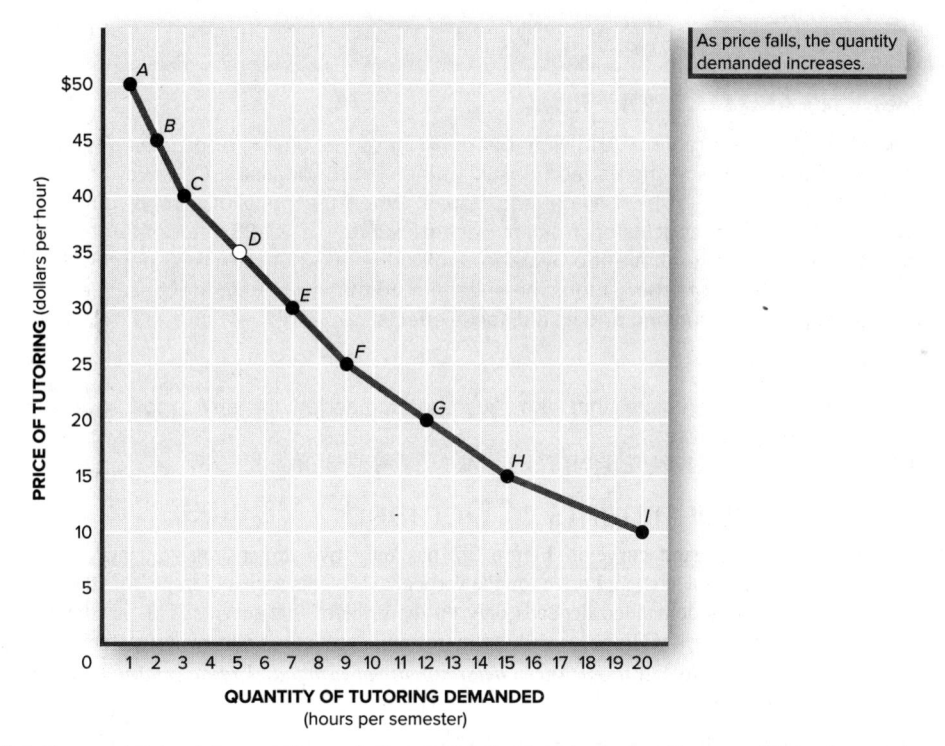

As price falls, the quantity demanded increases.

Figure 2.2 A Demand Schedule and Curve A **demand schedule** indicates the quantities of a good a consumer is able and willing to buy at alternative prices (*ceteris paribus*). The demand schedule indicates that Tom would buy five hours of web design tutoring per semester if the price were $35 per hour (row D). If tutoring were less expensive (rows E–I), Tom would purchase a larger quantity.

A **demand curve** is a graphical illustration of a demand schedule. Each point on the curve refers to a specific quantity that will be demanded at a given price. If the price of tutoring were $35 per hour, this curve tells us that Tom would purchase five hours of tutoring per semester (point D). Each point on the curve corresponds to a row in the above schedule.

A convenient summary of buying intentions is the **demand curve**, a graphical illustration of the demand schedule. The demand curve in Figure 2.2 tells us again that if the price of web design tutoring is $50 per hour (point A), this consumer is willing to pay for only one hour; if the price is $45 per hour (point B), he will pay for two hours; if the price is $40 per hour (point C), he will pay for three hours; and so on. Once we know what the market price of web tutoring actually is, a glance at the demand curve tells us how much service this consumer will buy.

What the notion of *demand* emphasizes is that the amount we buy of a good depends on its price. We seldom if ever decide to buy a certain quantity of a good at whatever price is charged. Instead we enter markets with a set of desires and a limited amount of money to spend. *How much we actually buy of any good will depend on its price.*

A common feature of demand curves is their downward slope. As the price of a good falls, people tend to purchase more of it. In Figure 2.2, the quantity of web tutorial services demanded increases (moves rightward along the horizontal axis) as the price per hour decreases (moves down the vertical axis). This inverse relationship between price and quantity is so common that we refer to it as the **law of demand**.

College administrators think the law of demand could be used to curb student drinking. Low retail prices and bar promotions encourage students to drink more alcohol. As the accompanying News Wire "Law of Demand" explains, higher prices would reduce the quantity of alcohol demanded.

NEWS WIRE LAW OF DEMAND

CAMPUS DRINKING AND ALCOHOL PRICES

Campus drinking is a common problem. And with that drinking comes a slew of problems, including traffic accidents, sexual assault, property crimes, and sexually transmitted diseases. One way to curb campus drinking is to increase the price of beer, wine, and booze. When the price of alcohol goes up, college students drink less. That's the conclusion from a Harvard survey of 22,831 students at 158 colleges. Students faced with a $1 increase above the average drink price of $2.17 will be 33 percent less likely to drink at all or as much. Dozens of other studies have confirmed that higher alcohol prices (e.g., via excise taxes) really do reduce campus drinking and its antisocial effects.

Source: News accounts.

NOTE: The law of demand predicts that the quantity demanded of any good—even beer and liquor—declines as its price increases.
注：需求法则预测，任何商品的需求量都会随其价格的上升而减少，啤酒和其他酒类也不例外。

Determinants of Demand 需求的决定因素

The demand curve in Figure 2.2 has only two dimensions—quantity demanded (on the horizontal axis) and price (on the vertical axis). This seems to imply that the amount of tutorial services demanded depends only on the price of that service. This is surely not the case. A consumer's willingness and ability to buy a product at various prices depend on a variety of forces. We call those forces *determinants of demand*. ***The determinants of market demand include***

- ***Tastes*** (desire for this and other goods).
- ***Income*** (of the consumer).
- ***Other goods*** (their availability and price).
- ***Expectations*** (for income, prices, tastes).
- ***Number of buyers***.

If Tom didn't have to pass a web design course, he would have no taste (desire) for web page tutoring and thus no demand. If he had no income, he would not have the ability to pay and

---

demand curve 需求曲线。graphical 用图形表示的。glance 浏览，匆匆一瞥。tutorial（与）辅导（有关）的。law of demand 需求法则。

thus would still be out of the web design market. The price and availability of other goods affect the opportunity cost of tutoring services—that is, what Tom must give up. Expectations for income, grades, graduation prospects, and parental support also influence his willingness to buy such services.

Ceteris Paribus 其他条件不变

If demand is in fact such a multidimensional decision, how can we reduce it to only the two dimensions of price and quantity? This is the **ceteris paribus** trick we encountered earlier. To simplify their models of the world, economists focus on only one or two forces at a time and *assume* nothing else changes. We know a consumer's tastes, income, other goods, and expectations all affect the decision to buy web design services. But *we focus on the relationship between quantity demanded and price.* That is to say, we want to know what *independent* influence price has on consumption decisions. To find out, we must isolate that one influence, price, and assume that the determinants of demand remain unchanged.

The *ceteris paribus* assumption is not as far-fetched as it may seem. People's tastes (desires) don't change very quickly. Income tends to be fairly stable from week to week. Even expectations for the future are slow to change. Accordingly, the price of a good may be the only thing that changes on any given day. In that case, a change in price may be the only thing that prompts a change in consumer behavior.

Shifts in Demand 需求的移动

The determinants of demand do change, of course, particularly over time. Accordingly, *the demand schedule and curve remain unchanged only so long as the underlying determinants of demand remain constant.* If the *ceteris paribus* assumption is violated—if tastes, income, other goods, or expectations change—the ability or willingness to buy will change. When this happens, the demand curve will shift to a new position. This is referred to as a **shift in demand**.

Suppose, for example, that Tom wins $1,000 in the state lottery. This increase in his income would increase his ability to pay for tutoring services. Figure 2.3 shows the effect of this windfall on Tom's demand. The old demand curve, D_1, is no longer relevant. Tom's lottery winnings enable him to buy more tutoring services at any price. This is illustrated by the new demand curve, D_2. According to this new curve, lucky Tom is now willing and able to buy 11 hours of tutoring per semester at the price of $35 per hour (point d_2). This is a large increase in demand, as previously (before winning the lottery) he demanded only five hours at that price (point d_1).

With his higher income, Tom can buy more tutoring services at *every* price. Thus *the entire demand curve shifts to the right when income goes up.* Both the old (pre-lottery) and the new (post-lottery) demand curves are illustrated in Figure 2.3.

Income is only one of four basic determinants of demand. Changes in any of the other determinants of demand would also cause the demand curve to shift. Tom's taste for web design tutoring might increase dramatically, for example, if his other professors made the quality of personal web pages a critical determinant of course grades. His taste (desire) for web design services might increase even more if his parents promised to buy him a new car if he got an A in the course. Whatever its origins, *an increase in taste (desire) or expectations also shifts the demand curve to the right.*

Other goods can also shift the demand curve. Hybrid vehicles became more popular when gasoline prices rose. The demand for gas-saving hybrids increased, while demand for gas guzzlers declined. The situation reversed itself in 2014–2016, when gasoline prices plummeted. Lower gasoline prices made electric vehicles (EVs) less attractive (see the News Wire "Shifts of Demand"). Sales of EVs declined, while sales of SUVs and trucks increased. The (leftward) shift in demand for EVs was caused by this decrease in the price of a substitute good. EV sales picked up again in 2018 when oil prices started rising.

---

lottery 彩票。windfall 意外之财。hybrid 混合的。gas guzzlers 油耗大的汽车。

如果需求实际上由多维因素所决定，我们怎么能将它简化为价格和数量的二维关系呢？这就是我们之前用过的假设其他条件不变的方法。为了简化经济领域的模型，经济学家们每次仅集中考虑一两个因素，并且假设其他条件都不变。我们知道，消费者的偏好、收入、其他商品和预期都会影响其购买网页设计辅导服务的决定，但我们主要讨论的是需求量和价格之间的关系。也就是说，我们想知道价格对消费决策单独产生的影响。为了弄清这种影响，我们必须将这个影响因素（价格）分离出来，并且假设需求的其他决定因素保持不变。

当然，需求的决定因素都是变化的，尤其是随着时间变化。因此，需求表和需求曲线只有在需求的其他决定因素恒定的情况下才保持不变。如果违反了其他条件不变的假设，即如果偏好、收入、其他商品或预期发生了变化，则购买能力或意愿也将发生改变。当这些变化发生时，需求曲线将移动到一个新位置。这被称为**需求的移动**。

由于收入提高，汤姆在每一价格下都能购买更多的辅导服务。因此，当收入提高时，整个需求曲线向右移动。

不管是何原因，偏好（欲望）或者预期的增加都会使需求曲线向右移动。

NEWS WIRE SHIFTS OF DEMAND

LOW GAS PRICES HURT EV SALES

The price of gasoline is a major consideration for consumers deciding whether to buy an electric vehicle (EV) or a gasoline-fired vehicle. When gasoline prices are low, the lure of the EVs fades quickly. When gas prices fell sharply in 2014–2016, the hybrid share of California auto sales fell from 6.3 percent to 5.8 percent. Nationally, the impact was even more pronounced: EV sales declined by 13 percent while sales of gasoline-guzzling SUVs and pickup trucks rose by 37 and 41 percent, respectively. In 2018 the pattern reversed: Rising oil prices gave a boost to sales of EVs and slowed sales of gas guzzlers.

Source: News accounts of 2016–2018.

NOTE: Demand decreases (shifts left) when tastes diminish, the price of substitute goods declines, or income or expectations worsen. What happened here?
注：当偏好降低，替代品价格下降或收入和预期变差时，需求会减少（需求曲线向左移动）。这里发生了什么？

Movements versus Shifts 沿着曲线移动与曲线的移动

区分需求曲线的移动和沿着需求曲线的移动尤为重要。沿着需求曲线的移动是对该种商品的价格变化作出的反应。这样的移动假设需求的其他决定因素是不变的。相反，当需求的其他决定因素发生变化时，需求曲线将会移动。当偏好、收入、其他商品或预期改变时，价格和需求数量的基本关系发生了改变（需求曲线移动）。

It is important to distinguish shifts of the demand curve from movements along the demand curve. ***Movements along a demand curve are a response to price changes for that good.*** Such movements assume that determinants of demand are unchanged. By contrast, ***shifts of the demand curve occur when the determinants of demand change.*** When tastes, income, other goods, or expectations are altered, the basic relationship between price and quantity demanded is changed (i.e., shifts).

For convenience, the distinction between movements along a demand curve and shifts of the demand curve have their own labels. Specifically, take care to distinguish

- ***Changes in quantity demanded:*** movements along a given demand curve in response to price changes of that good (such as from d_1 to d_2 in Figure 2.3).

- 需求量的变动：沿着既定需求曲线的移动，是对商品价格变化的反应。

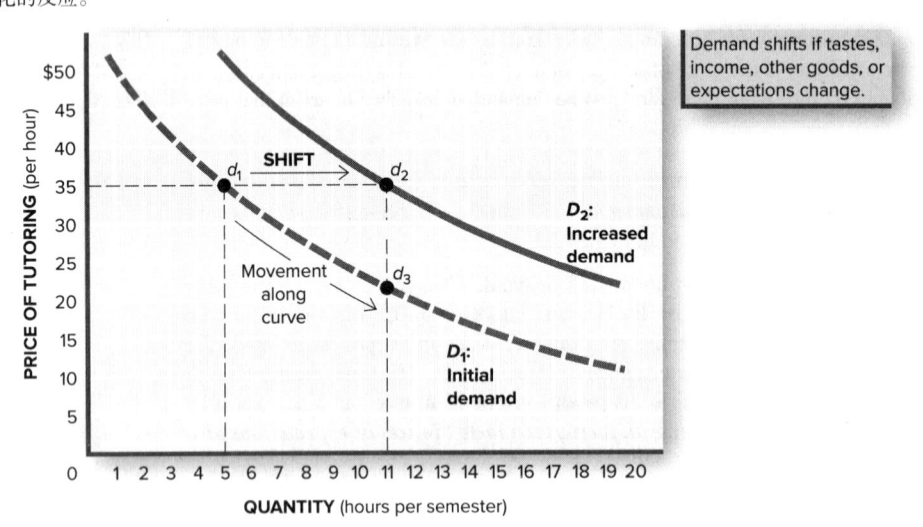

Figure 2.3 A Shift in Demand A demand curve shows how the quantity demanded changes in response to a change in price, *if* all else remains constant. But the determinants of demand may themselves change, causing the demand curve to *shift*.

In this case, an increase in income increases demand from D_1 to D_2. After this shift, Tom demands 11 hours (d_2), rather than 5 (d_1), at the price of $35. The quantity demanded at all other prices increases as well.

- ***Changes in demand:*** shifts of the demand curve due to changes in tastes, income, other goods, or expectations (such as from D_1 to D_2 in Figure 2.3).

The News Wire "Law of Demand" told how higher alcohol prices could reduce college drinking—pushing students up the demand curve to a smaller quantity demanded. College officials might also try to *shift* the entire demand curve leftward: If the penalties for campus drinking were increased, altered expectations might shift the demand curve to the left, causing students to buy less booze at any given price.

Tom's behavior in the web tutoring market is subject to similar influences. A change in the *price* of tutoring will move Tom up or down his demand curve. By contrast, a change in an underlying determinant of demand will shift his entire demand curve to the left or right.

Market Demand   市场需求

The same forces that change an individual's consumption behavior also move entire markets. Suppose you wanted to assess the *market demand* for web tutoring services at Clearview College. To do that, you'd want to identify every student's demand for that service. Some students, of course, have no need or desire for professional web design services and are not willing to pay anything for such tutoring; they do not participate in the web design market. Other students have a desire for such services but not enough income to pay for them; they, too, are excluded from the web design market. A large number of students, however, not only have a need (or desire) for tutoring but also are willing and able to purchase such services.

What we start with in product markets, then, is many individual demand curves. Then we combine all those individual demand curves into a single **market demand**. Suppose you would be willing to buy one hour of tutoring at a price of $80 per hour. George, who is also desperate to learn web design, would buy two hours at that price; and I would buy none, since my publisher (McGraw-Hill) creates a web page for me. What would our combined (market) demand for hours of design services be at that price? Our individual inclinations indicate that we would be willing to buy a total of three hours of tutoring if the price were $80 per hour. Our combined willingness to buy—our collective market demand—is nothing more than the sum of our individual demands. The same kind of aggregation can be performed for all the consumers in a particular market. The resulting ***market demand is determined by the number of potential buyers and their respective tastes, incomes, other goods, and expectations.***

The Market Demand Curve   市场需求曲线

Figure 2.4 provides a market demand schedule and curve for a situation in which only three consumers participate in the market. The three individuals who participate in this market obviously differ greatly, as suggested by their respective demand schedules. Tom *has* to pass his web design classes or confront college and parental rejection. He also has a nice allowance (income), so he can afford to buy a lot of tutorial help. His demand schedule is portrayed in the first column of the table in Figure 2.4 (and is identical to the one we examined in Figure 2.2). George, as we already noted, is also desperate to acquire some job skills and is willing to pay relatively high prices for web design tutoring. His demand is summarized in the second column under "Quantity of Tutoring Demanded."

The third consumer in this market is Lisa. Lisa already knows the nuts and bolts of web design, so she doesn't have much need for tutorial services. She would like to upgrade her skills, however, especially in animation and e-commerce applications. But her limited budget precludes paying a lot for help. She will buy some technical support only if the price falls to $30 per hour. Should tutors cost less, she'd even buy quite a few hours of design services.

The differing personalities and consumption habits of Tom, George, and Lisa are expressed in their individual demand schedules and associated curves, as depicted in Figure 2.4. To determine the *market* demand for tutoring services from this information, we simply add up these three separate demands. The end result of this aggregation is, first, a *market* demand

---

penalty 惩罚。 be excluded from 被排除在……之外。 nuts and bolts 具体细节，基本要点。 preclude 妨碍，阻止。

38　Chapter Two: Supply and Demand

这些市场加总描述了 Clearview 学院的学生在不同价格下，每学期愿意并且有能力购买网页设计辅导服务的数量。

schedule (the last column in the table) and, second, the resultant *market* demand curve (the curve in Figure 2.4*d*). These market summaries describe the various quantities of tutoring services that Clearview College students are *willing and able* to purchase each semester at various prices.

Market Demand Schedule
Quantity of Tutoring Demanded (Hours per Semester)

	Price per Hour	Tom	+	George	+	Lisa	=	Total Quantity Demanded
A	$50	1		4		0		5
B	45	2		6		0		8
C	40	3		8		0		11
D	35	5		11		0		16
E	30	7		14		1		22
F	25	9		18		3		30
G	20	12		22		5		39
H	15	15		26		6		47
I	10	20		30		7		57

(a) Tom's demand curve + *(b)* George's demand curve + *(c)* Lisa's demand curve = *(d)* The market demand curve

PRICE (per hour) / QUANTITY DEMANDED (hours per semester)

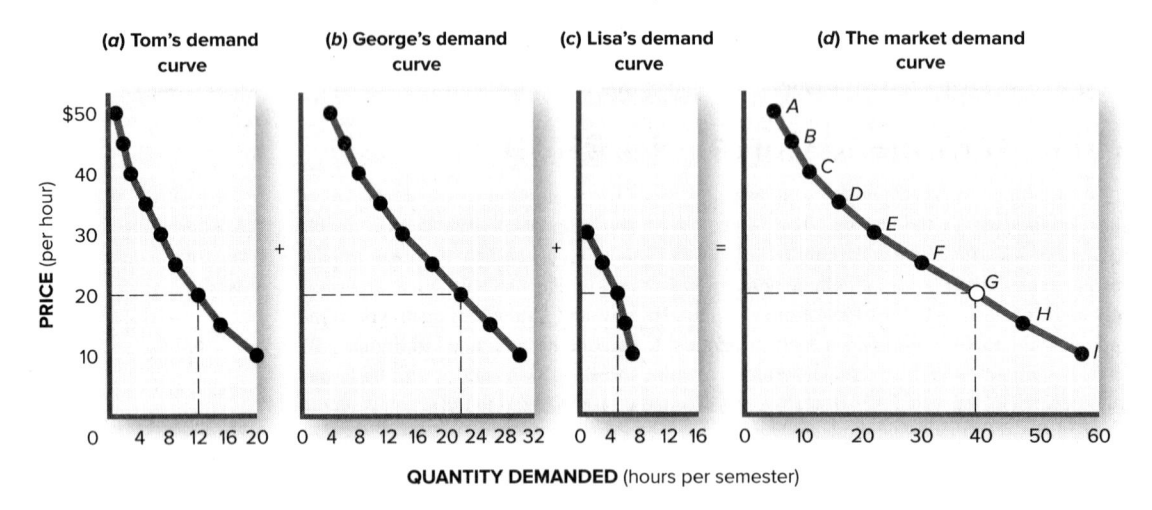

Figure 2.4 The Market Demand Schedule and Construction of the Market Demand Curve Market demand represents the combined demands of all market participants. To determine the total quantity of tutoring demanded at any given price, we add up the separate demands of the individual consumers. Row *G* of this demand schedule indicates that a *total* quantity of 39 hours of service per semester will be demanded at a price of $20 per hour. The market demand curve illustrates the same information. At a price of $20 per hour, the total quantity of web design services demanded would be 39 hours per semester (point *G*): 12 hours demanded by Tom, 22 by George, and 5 by Lisa. As price declines, the quantity demanded increases (the law of demand).

The Use of Demand Curves 需求曲线的应用

So why does anybody care what the market demand curve looks like? What's the point of doing all this arithmetic and drawing so many graphs?

If you were a web designer at Clearview College, you'd certainly like to have the information depicted in Figure 2.4. What the market demand curve tells us is how much tutoring service could be sold at various prices. Suppose you hoped to sell 30 hours at a price of $30 per hour. According to Figure 2.4d (point E), students will buy only 22 hours at that price. Hence, you won't attain your sales goal. You could find that out by posting ads on campus and waiting for a response. It would be a lot easier, however, if you knew in advance what the market demand curve looked like.

Would this many fans show up if concert prices were higher?
©Frank Micelotta/Getty Images

People who promote music concerts need the same kind of information. They want to fill the stadium with screaming fans. But fans have limited income and desires for other goods. Accordingly, the number of fans who will buy concert tickets depends on the price. If the promoter sets the price too high, there will be lots of empty seats at the concert. If the price is set too low, the promoter will confront hoards of frustrated fans and may lose potential sales revenue. What the promoter wants to know is what price will induce the desired quantity demanded. If the promoter could consult a demand curve, the correct price would be evident.

SUPPLY 供给

Even if we knew what the demand for every good looked like, we couldn't predict what quantities would be bought. The demand curve tells us only how much consumers are willing and able to buy at specific prices. We don't know the price yet, however. To find out what price will be charged, we've got to know something about the behavior of people who *sell* goods and services. That is to say, we need to examine the *supply* side of the marketplace. The **market supply** of a good reflects the collective behavior of all firms that are willing and able to sell that good at various prices.

即使我们知道了每种商品大致的需求曲线，也不能预期消费者将要购买的数量。需求曲线仅仅告诉我们在特定价格下消费者愿意而且能够购买的商品数量。但我们还不知道价格。为了弄清价格，我们需要了解销售商品和服务的人的行为。也就是说，我们需要分析一下市场的供给方。某种商品的**市场供给**反映的是不同价格下愿意而且能够销售该商品的所有厂商的整体行为。

Determinants of Supply 供给的决定因素

Let's return to the Clearview campus for a moment. What we need to know now is how much web tutorial services people are willing and able to provide. Web page design can be fun, but it can also be drudge work, especially when you're doing it for someone else. Software programs like PhotoShop, Flash, and Muse have made web page design easier and more creative. But teaching someone else to design web pages is still work. So few people offer to supply web services just for the fun of it. Web designers do it for money. Specifically, they do it to earn income that they, in turn, can spend on goods and services they desire.

How much income must be offered to induce web designers to do a job depends on a variety of things. The ***determinants of market supply include***

- *Technology.*
- *Factor costs.*
- *Other goods.*
- *Taxes and subsidies.*
- *Expectations.*
- *Number of sellers.*

市场供给的决定因素包括：

- 技术
- 要素成本
- 其他商品
- 税收和补贴
- 预期
- 卖方数量

---

arithmetic 算数。in advance 预先，提前。drudge work 苦工，苦差事。

The technology of web design, for example, is always getting easier and more creative. With a program like PageOut, for example, it's very easy to create a basic web page. A continuous stream of new software programs (e.g., Fireworks, Dreamweaver) keeps stretching the possibilities for graphics, animation, interactivity, and content. These technological advances mean that web design services can be supplied more quickly and cheaply. They also make *teaching* web design easier. As a result, they induce people to supply more web design services at every price.

How much tutoring is offered at any given price also depends on the cost of factors of production. If the software programs needed to create web pages are cheap (or, better yet, free!), web designers can afford to charge lower prices. If the required software inputs are expensive, however, they will have to charge more money per hour for their services.

Other goods can also affect the willingness to supply web design services. If you can make more income waiting tables than you can designing web pages, why would you even boot up the computer? As the prices paid for other goods and services change, they will influence people's decisions about whether to offer web services.

In the real world, the decision to supply goods and services is also influenced by the long arm of Uncle Sam. Federal, state, and local governments impose taxes on income earned in the marketplace. When tax rates are high, people get to keep less of the income they earn. Some people may conclude that tutoring is no longer worth the hassle and withdraw from the market.

Expectations are also important on the supply side of the market. If web designers expect higher prices, lower costs, or reduced taxes, they may be more willing to learn new software programs. On the other hand, if they have poor expectations about the future, they may just find something else to do.

Finally, the *number* of available web designers will affect the quantity of service offered for sale at various prices. If there are lots of willing web designers on campus, a large quantity of tutoring services will be available.

The Market Supply Curve 市场供给曲线

Figure 2.5 illustrates the market supply curve of web services at Clearview College. Like market demand, the market supply curve is the sum of all the individual supplier decisions about how much output to produce at any given price. The market supply curve slopes upward to the right, indicating that ***larger quantities will be offered at higher prices.*** This basic **law of supply** reflects the fact that increased output typically entails higher costs and so will be forthcoming only at higher prices. Higher prices may also increase profits and so entice producers to supply greater quantities.

Note that Figure 2.5 illustrates the *market* supply. We have not bothered to construct separate supply curves for each person who is able and willing to supply web services on the Clearview campus. We have skipped that first step and gone right to the *market* supply curve. Like the market demand curve, however, the market supply curve is based on the supply decisions of individual producers. The curve itself is computed by adding up the quantities each producer is willing and able to supply at every given price. Point *f* in Figure 2.5 tells us that those individuals are collectively willing and able to produce 90 hours of tutoring per semester at a price of $30 per hour. The rest of the points on the supply curve tell us how many hours of tutoring will be offered at other prices.

None of the points on the market supply curve (Figure 2.5) tell us how much tutoring service is actually being sold. ***Market supply is an expression of sellers' intentions, of the ability and willingness to sell, not a statement of actual sales.*** My next-door neighbor may be *willing* to sell his 1996 Honda Civic for $6,000, but it is most unlikely that he will ever find a buyer at that price. Nevertheless, his *willingness* to sell his car at that price is part of the *market supply* of used cars.

---

stretch 伸展、拓展。hassle 麻烦、困难，这里的意思是付出、辛苦工作。

Chapter Two: Supply and Demand   41

At higher prices a larger quantity is supplied.

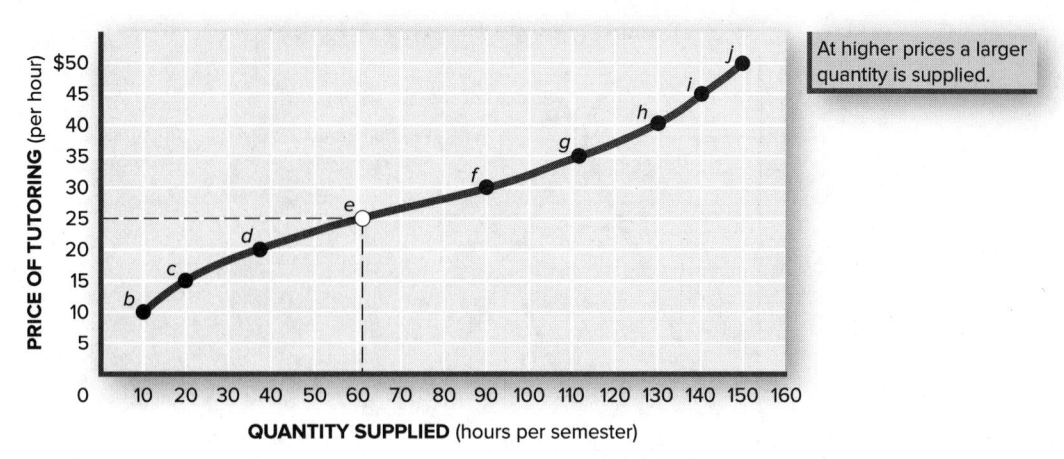

Figure 2.5 The Market Supply Curve The market supply curve indicates the *combined* sales intentions of all market participants. If the price of tutoring were $25 per hour (point e), the *total* quantity of tutoring service supplied would be 62 hours per semester. This quantity is determined by adding together the supply decisions of all individual producers. ■

Shifts in Supply 供给的移动

As with demand, there is nothing sacred about any given set of supply intentions. Supply curves *shift* when the underlying determinants of supply change. Thus we again distinguish

- ***Changes in quantity supplied:*** movements along a given supply curve.
- ***Changes in supply:*** shifts of the supply curve.

Our Latin friend *ceteris paribus* is once again the decisive factor. If the price of tutoring services is the only thing changing, then we can **track changes in quantity supplied along the supply curve** in Figure 2.5. But if *ceteris paribus* is violated—if technology, factor costs, other goods, taxes, or expectations change—then **changes in supply are illustrated by shifts of the supply curve.** The News Wire "Supply Shift" illustrates how Hurricane Harvey caused a leftward shift in the supply of Houston-area apartments, pushing rents higher.

因此我们要再次区分两种移动：

- 供给量的变动：沿着既定供给曲线的移动。
- 供给的变动：供给曲线的移动。

NEWS WIRE SUPPLY SHIFT

RENTS RISING IN HURRICANE'S WAKE

Houston. Hurricane Harvey wiped out a massive chunk of the Houston-area housing stock. FEMA estimates that 203,000 homes were damaged and 12,700 destroyed. Somewhere between 15,000 and 20,000 apartment units suffered a similar fate. That damage created a severe imbalance in the housing market: more people seeking new housing and fewer units available. Local realtors say this imbalance has pushed apartment rents up by 15–20 percent.

©Dieter Spears/Getty Images

---

decisive 决定性的。realtor 房地产经纪人。

MARKET FOR APARTMENTS

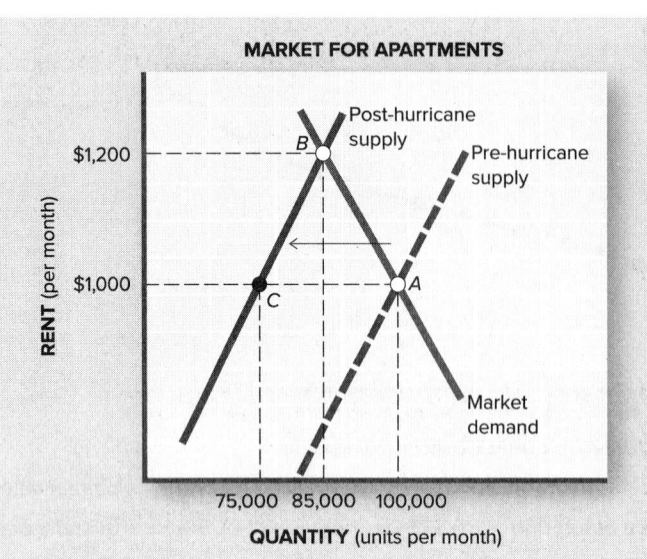

[Figure 2.6: Graph showing Rent (per month) vs Quantity (units per month). Pre-hurricane supply (dashed) and Post-hurricane supply curves intersect Market demand. Point A at $1,000 and 100,000 units (pre-hurricane equilibrium); Point B at $1,200 and 85,000 units (post-hurricane equilibrium); Point C at $1,000 and 75,000 units.]

Source: News accounts of August–September 2017.

NOTE: If an underlying determinant of supply changes, the entire supply curve shifts. A hurricane reduced the available supply of apartments, causing rents to spike.
注：如果供给的潜在决定因素发生变化，整个供给曲线就会发生移动。飓风使公寓的供给减少，导致其价格飙升。

现在我们有工具来确定在 Clearview 学院销售网页设计辅导服务的价格和数量。市场供给曲线表示生产者在不同价格下销售网页设计辅导服务的能力和意愿。而市场需求曲线所描述的是汤姆、乔治和莉莎在那些同样价格下购买网页设计辅导服务的能力和意愿。当把这两条曲线放在一起时，我们发现只有一种价格和数量的组合能同时满足买者和卖者现有的意向。这个**均衡价格**出现在图 2.6 中两条曲线的交点上。均衡价格一旦确定，便表明购买网页设计辅导服务每小时将要花费 20 美元。在该价格下，校园网页设计师每学期将总共销售 39 小时的辅导服务——恰好等于该价格下学生希望购买的数量。

虽然并不是每个人都对市场均衡完全满意，但是这个唯一的结果是有效的。均衡价格和均衡数量反映了买方与卖方之间的妥协。没有其他折衷方案能产生恰好与供给量相等的需求量。

EQUILIBRIUM 均衡

We now have the tools to determine the price and quantity of web tutoring services being sold at Clearview College. The market supply curve expresses the *ability and willingness* of producers to *sell* web services at various prices. The market demand curve illustrates the *ability and willingness* of Tom, George, and Lisa to *buy* web services at those same prices. When we put the two curves together, we see that ***only one price and quantity are compatible with the existing intentions of both buyers and sellers.*** This **equilibrium price** occurs at the intersection of the two curves in Figure 2.6. Once it is established, web tutoring services will cost $20 per hour. At that price, campus web designers will sell a total of 39 hours of tutoring service per semester—exactly the same amount that students wish to buy at that price.

Market Clearing 市场出清

An equilibrium doesn't imply that everyone is happy with the prevailing price or quantity. Notice in Figure 2.6, for example, that some students who want to buy web tutoring don't get any. These would-be buyers are arrayed along the demand curve *below* the equilibrium. Because the price they are *willing* to pay is less than the equilibrium price, they don't get any tutoring.

Likewise, there are would-be sellers in the market who don't sell as much tutoring services as they might like. These people are arrayed along the supply curve *above* the equilibrium. Because they insist on being paid a price that is higher than the equilibrium price, they don't actually sell anything.

Although not everyone gets full satisfaction from the market equilibrium, that unique outcome is efficient. ***The equilibrium price and quantity reflect a compromise between buyers and sellers. No other compromise yields a quantity demanded that is exactly equal to the quantity supplied.***

---

would-be 潜在的、未来的。array 排列。

Chapter Two: Supply and Demand 43

THE INVISIBLE HAND 看不见的手

The equilibrium price is not determined by any single individual. Rather it is determined by the collective behavior of many buyers and sellers, each acting out his or her own demand or supply schedule. It is this kind of impersonal price determination that gave rise to Adam Smith's characterization of the market mechanism as the "invisible hand." In attempting to explain how the market mechanism works, the famed eighteenth-century economist noted a certain feature of market prices. The market behaves as if some unseen force (the invisible hand) were examining each individual's supply or demand schedule, then selecting a price that ensured an equilibrium. In practice, the process of price determination is not so mysterious; rather, it is a simple one of trial and error.

均衡价格不是由任何单个个体决定的，而是由很多买方和卖方的行为共同决定的，这些买方和卖方中的每个人都依各自的需求表或供给表行事。正是这种非个人的价格决定，使亚当·斯密将市场机制描述为一只"看不见的手"。在试图解释市场机制是如何运行的过程中，这位18世纪著名的经济学家注意到了市场定价的这一特征。市场好像是某种看不见的力量（看不见的手）在分析着每个人的供给表或需求表，然后选择一个能够达到均衡的价格。实际上，价格的决定过程并没有那么神秘；相反，它只是一个反复试错的简单过程。

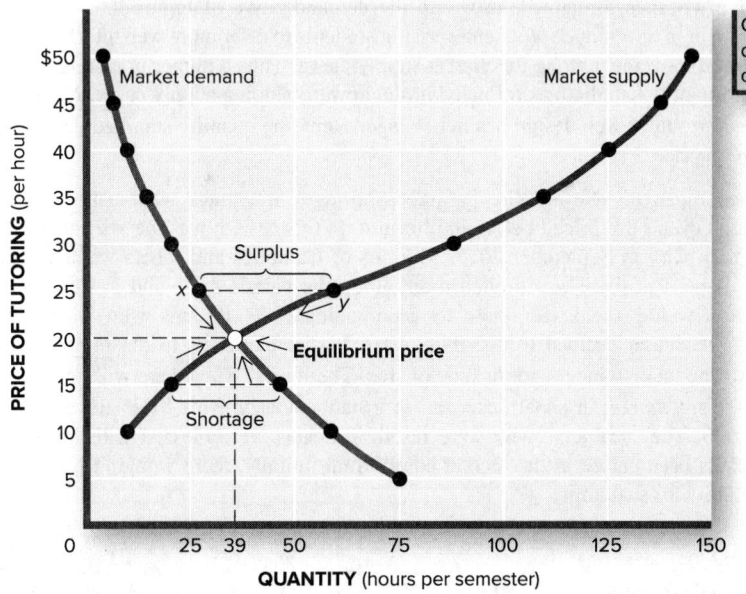

Price per Hour	Quantity Supplied (Hours per Semester)		Quantity Demanded (Hours per Semester)
$50	148		5
45	140		8
40	125	Market	11
35	114	surplus	16
30	90		22
25	62		30
20	39	**Equilibrium**	39
15	20	Market	47
10	10	shortage	57

Figure 2.6 Market Equilibrium Only at equilibrium is the quantity demanded equal to the quantity supplied. In this case, the **equilibrium price** is $20 per hour, and 39 hours is the **equilibrium quantity.**

At above-equilibrium prices, a market surplus exists—the quantity supplied exceeds the quantity demanded. At prices below equilibrium, a market shortage exists.

The intersection of the demand and supply curves determines the equilibrium price and output in this market. ■

---

equilibrium price 均衡价格。equilibrium quantity 均衡数量。

Market Shortage　市场短缺

Suppose for the moment that someone were to spread the word on the Clearview campus that tutors were available at only $15 per hour. At that price Tom, George, and Lisa would be standing in line to get help with their web classes, but campus web designers would not be willing to supply the quantity desired at that price. As Figure 2.6 confirms, at $15 per hour, the quantity demanded (47 hours per semester) would exceed the quantity supplied (20 hours per semester). In this situation, we speak of a **market shortage**—that is, an excess of quantity demanded over quantity supplied. At a price of $15 an hour, the shortage amounts to 27 hours of web service.

现在假设有人在 Clearview 校园里散布消息说：网页设计辅导费每小时仅为 15 美元。在这样的价格下，汤姆、乔治和莉莎就会排队来上他们的网页设计辅导课，但是，在这样的价格下校园里的网页设计师们不愿提供大家所需要的服务数量。正如图 2.6 所证实的那样，在价格为每小时 15 美元时，需求量（47 小时 / 学期）将会超过供给量（20 小时 / 学期）。在这种情况下，我们就说出现了**市场短缺**，即需求量超过供给量。在每小时 15 美元的价格下，网页设计辅导服务短缺的数量为 27 小时。

When a market shortage exists, not all consumer demands can be satisfied. Some people who are *willing* to buy tutoring services at the going price ($15) will not be able to do so. To assure themselves of good grades, Tom, George, Lisa, or some other consumer may offer to pay a *higher* price, thus initiating a move up the demand curve of Figure 2.6. The higher prices offered will in turn induce other enterprising students to offer more web tutoring, thus ensuring an upward movement along the market supply curve. Thus a higher price tends to call forth a greater quantity supplied, as reflected in the upward-sloping supply curve. Notice, again, that the *desire* to tutor web design has not changed: only the quantity supplied has responded to a change in price.

The accompanying News Wire "Market Shortage" illustrates what happens when tickets to special events are priced below equilibrium. In this case, it was the visit of Pope Francis to New York City in September 2015. Millions of Catholics and others wanted get a glimpse of the Pope. But there was limited room along the parade route and in Central Park where the Pope would speak. So, how to accommodate the throngs who wanted to see the Pope? The church decided to distribute 40,000 pairs of tickets to the faithful, in a sort of lottery. The lucky winners got tickets for free. The losers? They were willing to *pay* for those tickets. So, a *market* in papal tickets arose instantaneously, with "free" tickets priced as high as $3,000. The "scalpers" who were reselling tickets were blessed with huge profits. Had the tickets been priced at the market equilibrium initially, there wouldn't have been such an opportunity for scalping.

NEWS WIRE MARKET SHORTAGE

©Giulio Napolitano/Shutterstock

SCALPERS PROFITING GREATLY FROM POPE'S VISIT

New York. Pope Francis' visit to New York City was a blessed event. It was also a blessed opportunity for ticket scalpers. 93,000 New Yorkers applied for tickets to watch the Pope's procession through Central Park. But church officials had only 40,000 tickets to distribute, which they did by lottery—for free. That left 53,000 New Yorkers without tickets. It was a scalper's heaven. Sinful resellers immediately started hawking tickets online. The free tickets were simply mailed in a PDF to lottery winners, with no ID required, making them easy to resell. Scalped tickets sold for as much as $3,000 a pair. Although Church officials urged scalpers to repent, the opportunity for profit was irresistible.

Source: News accounts of September 2015.

NOTE: A below-equilibrium price creates a market shortage. When that happens, another method of distributing tickets—like scalping or time in line—must be used to determine who gets the available tickets.
注：市价低于均衡价格会造成市场短缺。当这种情况发生时，市场必定会出现别的分配方式（如"倒卖黄牛票"或排队），来决定谁得到票。

---

accommodate 容纳。faithful 忠实的。

A similar but less dramatic situation occurred when the iPhone 7 and 7 Plus were released in September 2016. At the initial list price of $649 for the 32GB model of the iPhone 7 and $769 for the 7 Plus, the quantity demanded greatly exceeded the quantity supplied (see the News Wire "Market Shortage"). To get one of the first iPhone 7s, people either had to wait for weeks or pay a premium price in resale markets like eBay or Craigslist.

> **NEWS WIRE MARKET SHORTAGE**
>
> **APPLE iPHONE 7 SELLS OUT: SHIPPING DELAYS EXPECTED**
>
> The new iPhone 7 was supposed to hit store shelves on September 16, but the shelves were mostly empty. Apple reported that online orders—which began at 3:01 a.m. ET on September 9 in 28 nations—have already absorbed all available inventory of the iPhone 7 Plus and nearly all of the smaller iPhone 7s. The entry-level iPhone 7 is priced at $649, and the larger iPhone 7 Plus starts out at $769. Both phones offer better cameras than their predecessors, as well as water resistance, a faster processor, an improved home button, and new colors. The new jet-black version of the 7 Plus is especially popular and now has a seven- to eight-week shipping delay. The basic iPhone 7 has a two- to three-week delay as Apple ramps up production to meet the high demand.
>
> Source: News accounts of September 9–20, 2016.
>
> NOTE: If price is below equilibrium, the quantity demanded exceeds the quantity supplied. Consumers who were willing to pay the announced price of $649 for an iPhone 7 didn't necessarily get one.
> 注：如果市价低于均衡价格，需求量就会超过供给量。只愿意支付 649 美元购买 iPhone 7 的人，并不能保证一定会买到。

Market Surplus 市场过剩

A very different sequence of events occurs when a market surplus exists. Suppose for the moment that the web designers at Clearview College believed tutoring services could be sold for $25 per hour rather than the equilibrium price of $20. From the demand and supply schedules depicted in Figure 2.6, we can foresee the consequences. At $25 per hour, campus web designers would be offering more web tutoring services (point *y*) than Tom, George, and Lisa would be willing to buy at that price (point *x*). A **market surplus** of web services would exist, in that more tutoring was being offered for sale (supplied) than students cared to purchase (demanded) at the available price.

As Figure 2.6 indicates, at a price of $25 per hour, a market surplus of 32 hours per semester exists. Under these circumstances, campus web designers would be spending many idle hours at their computers, waiting for customers to appear. Their waiting will be in vain because the quantity of tutoring demanded will not increase until the price of tutoring falls. That is the clear message of the demand curve. The tendency of quantity demanded to increase as price falls is illustrated in Figure 2.6 by a movement along the demand curve from point *x* to lower prices and greater quantity demanded. As we move down the market demand curve, the desire for tutoring does not change, but the quantity of people who are able and willing to buy increases. Web designers at Clearview would have to reduce their price from $25 (point *y*) to $20 per hour in order to attract enough buyers.

U2 learned the difference between market shortage and surplus the hard way. Cheap tickets ($28.50) for its 1992 concerts not only filled up every concert venue but left thousands of fans clamoring for entry. The group began another tour in April 1997, with scheduled concerts in 80 cities over a period of 14 months. This time around, however, U2 was charging as much as $52.50 a ticket—nearly double the 1992 price. By the time it got to the second city, the group was playing in stadiums with lots of empty seats. The apparent market surplus led critics to label the 1997 PopMart tour a disaster. For its 2009, 360° Tour, U2 offered festival seating for only $30 and sold out every performance. By this process of trial and error, U2 ultimately located the equilibrium price for its concerts.

当市场过剩存在时，就会发生完全不同的情况。暂且假定，Clearview 学院的设计者相信自己的网页辅导服务能以每小时 25 美元的价格售出，而不是每小时 20 美元的均衡价格。从图 2.6 描述的需求和供给表中，我们能够预见到结果。在价格为每小时 25 美元时，校园里的网页设计者提供的网页辅导服务（*y* 点）多于汤姆、乔治和莉莎在这一价格下愿意购买的数量（*x* 点），就会存在网页辅导服务的**市场过剩**。在这种情况下，提供的用来销售（供给）的网页辅导服务多于学生在既定价格下愿意购买的数量。

---

premium 溢价。 in vain 徒然，无效。 clamor 大声地要求或抗议。 stadium 体育场，露天大型运动场。 process of trial and error 试错过程。

我们发现，无论何时，只要市场价格高于或低于均衡价格，就会出现市场过剩或市场短缺。为了克服过剩或短缺，买方和卖方将会改变他们的行为。只有在均衡价格下，才不需要进一步调整。

What we observe, then, is that ***whenever the market price is set above or below the equilibrium price, either a market surplus or a market shortage will emerge***. To overcome a surplus or shortage, buyers and sellers will change their behavior. Only at the *equilibrium* price will no further adjustments be required.

Business firms can discover equilibrium market prices by trial and error. If they find that consumer purchases are not keeping up with production, they may conclude that price is above the equilibrium. To get rid of their accumulated inventory, they will have to lower their prices (by a grand end-of-year sale, perhaps). In the happy situation where consumer purchases are outpacing production, a firm might conclude that its price was a trifle too low and give it a nudge upward. In either case, the equilibrium price can be established after a few trials in the marketplace.

Taylor Swift adopted this strategy for her 2018 "Reputation" tour. Earlier concerts had sold out within days of their announcement. Then thousands of tickets were resold on StubHub and other resale sites at much higher prices. Taylor concluded that she was pricing her tickets too low, permitting scalpers to take a big chunk of ticket revenue. For her Reputation tour, she chose "dynamic" pricing. That meant starting out with prices so high that scalpers couldn't make a resale profit. Then adjusting prices lower, moving down the demand curve and filling up the stadiums. In the early weeks of ticket sales, this strategy left thousands of tickets unsold. Critics began to assert that Taylor's popularity was waning and that her concerts would prove disastrous. But the strategy proved to be a success, with sales and attendance breaking all previous records. Trial and error worked in this case.

Changes in Equilibrium   均衡的变化

The collective actions of buyers and sellers will quickly establish an equilibrium price for any product. ***No equilibrium price is permanent,*** however. The equilibrium price established in the Clearview College web services market, for example, was the unique outcome of specific demand and supply schedules. Those schedules are valid for only a certain time and place. They will rule the market only so long as the assumption of *ceteris paribus* holds.

实际上，偏好、收入、其他商品的价格和可获得性或者预期在任何时候都会改变的。当这些改变发生时，其他条件不变的假设将被破坏，从而需求曲线必须重新绘制。需求曲线的移动将会导致一个新的均衡价格和数量。实际上，只要供给或需求曲线移动，均衡价格就一定发生变化。

In reality, tastes, incomes, the price and availability of other goods, or expectations could change at any time. When this happens, *ceteris paribus* will be violated, and the demand curve will have to be redrawn. Such a shift of the demand curve will lead to a new equilibrium price and quantity. Indeed, ***the equilibrium price will change whenever the supply or demand curve shifts.***

DEMAND SHIFTS   需求变化

We can illustrate how equilibrium prices change by taking one last look at the Clearview College web services market. Our original supply and demand curves, together with the resulting equilibrium point (point E_1), are depicted in Figure 2.7. Now suppose that the professors at Clearview begin requiring more technical expertise in their web design courses. These increased course requirements will affect market demand. Tom, George, and Lisa will suddenly be willing to buy more web tutoring at every price than they were before. That is to say, the *demand* for web services will increase. We represent this increased demand by a rightward *shift* of the market demand curve, as illustrated in Figure 2.7.

注意：这条新的需求曲线与（未改变的）市场供给曲线相交于一个新的价格点（E_2点）；现在的均衡价格是每小时30美元。这个新的均衡价格将会一直持续到需求曲线或供给曲线再一次移动。

Note that the new demand curve intersects the (unchanged) market supply curve at a new price (point E_2); the equilibrium price is now $30 per hour. This new equilibrium price will persist until either the demand curve or the supply curve shifts again.

---

get rid 处理。 outpace 超过，赶过。 trifle 少量。 nudge 微移，轻推。 dynamic 动态的。

SUPPLY AND DEMAND SHIFTS 供给曲线和需求曲线的移动

Even more dramatic price changes may occur when *both* demand and supply shift. Suppose the demand for tutoring increased at the same time supply decreased. With demand shifting right and supply shifting left, the price of tutoring would jump.

The kinds of price changes described here are quite common. A few moments in a stockbroker's office or a glance through the stock pages of the daily newspaper should be testimony enough to the fluid character of market prices. If thousands of stockholders decide to sell Facebook shares tomorrow, you can be sure that the market price of that stock will drop. Notice how often other prices—in the grocery store, in the music store, or at the gas station—change. Then determine whether it was supply, demand, or both curves that shifted.

当需求曲线和供给曲线都移动时，均衡价格可能会发生更剧烈的变化。假如对辅导服务的需求增加的同时，供给却减少了，那么随着需求曲线右移和供给曲线左移，辅导服务的价格将会大幅上涨。

DISEQUILIBRIUM PRICING 非均衡价格

The ability of the market to achieve an equilibrium price and quantity is evident. Nevertheless, people are often unhappy with those outcomes. At Clearview College, the students buying tutoring services feel that the price of such services is too high. On the other hand, campus web designers may feel that they are getting paid too little for their tutorial services.

Price Ceilings 价格上限

Sometimes consumers are able to convince the government to intervene on their behalf by setting a limit on prices. In many cities, for example, poor people and their advocates have convinced local governments that rents are too high. High rents, they argue, make housing prohibitively expensive for the poor, leaving them homeless or living in crowded,

有时，消费者能够说服政府通过限定价格来保护他们的利益。例如，在许多城市，穷人和他们的支持者就使当地政府

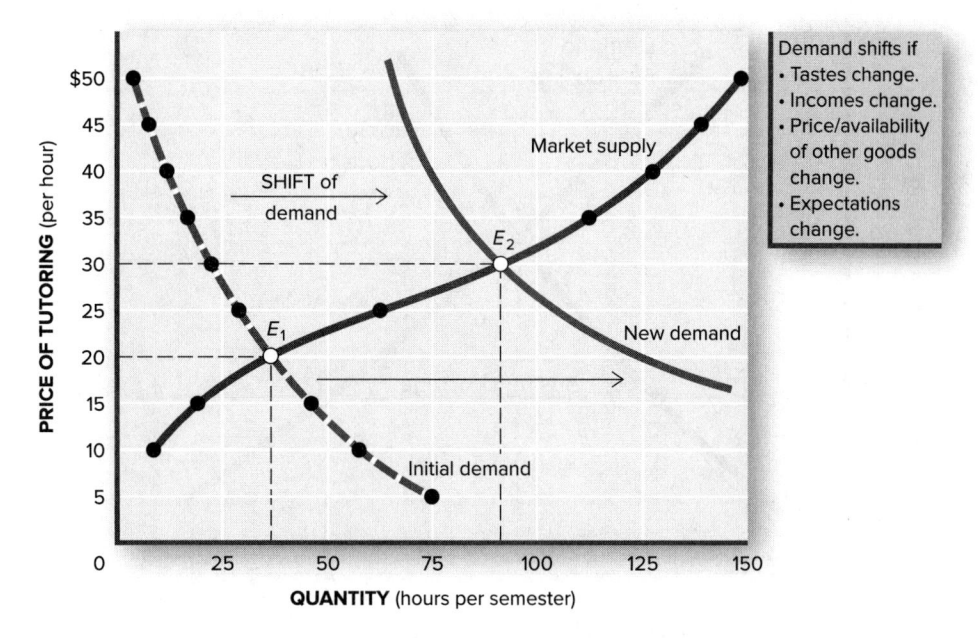

Figure 2.7 A New Equilibrium A rightward shift of the demand curve indicates that consumers are willing and able to buy a larger quantity at every price. As a consequence, a new equilibrium is established (point E_2), at a higher price and greater quantity. A shift of the demand curve occurs only when the assumption of *ceteris paribus* is violated—when one of the determinants of demand changes.

The equilibrium would also be altered if the determinants of supply changed, causing a shift of the market supply curve.

确信租金过高。他们认为，对穷人来说高额租金使有房住变得极其昂贵，使他们无家可归或住在拥挤的、不安全的地方。为了让每个人都能付得起住房费用，他们要求政府对租金加以限制。200个地方政府——包括纽约、波士顿、华盛顿和旧金山，已经对租金控制作出了反应。在所有情况下，租金控制都是一种**价格上限**——对商品和服务价格所设立的上限。

unsafe quarters. They ask government to impose a *limit* on rents in order to make housing affordable for everyone. Two hundred local governments—including New York City, Boston, Washington, DC, and San Francisco—have responded with rent controls. In all cases, rent controls are a **price ceiling**—an upper limit imposed on the price of a good or service.

Rent controls have a very visible effect in making housing more affordable. But such controls are *disequilibrium* prices and will change housing decisions in less visible and unintended ways. Figure 2.8 illustrates the problem. In the absence of government intervention, the quantity of housing consumed (q_e) and the prevailing rent (p_e) would be established by the intersection of market supply and demand curves (point E). Not everyone would be housed to his or her satisfaction in this equilibrium. Some of those people on the low end of the demand curve (below p_e) simply do not have enough income to pay the equilibrium rent p_e. They may be living with relatives or roommates they would rather not know. Or in extreme cases, they may even be homeless.

To remedy this situation, the city government imposes a rent ceiling of p_c. This lower price seemingly makes housing more affordable for everyone, including the poor. At the controlled rent p_c, people are willing and able to consume a lot more housing: The quantity *demanded* increases from q_e to q_d at point A.

But what about the quantity of housing *supplied*? Rent controls do not increase the number of housing units available. On the contrary, price controls tend to have the opposite effect. Notice in Figure 2.8 how the quantity *supplied* falls from q_e to q_s when the rent ceiling is enacted. When the quantity supplied slides down the supply curve from point E to point B, less housing is available than there was before.

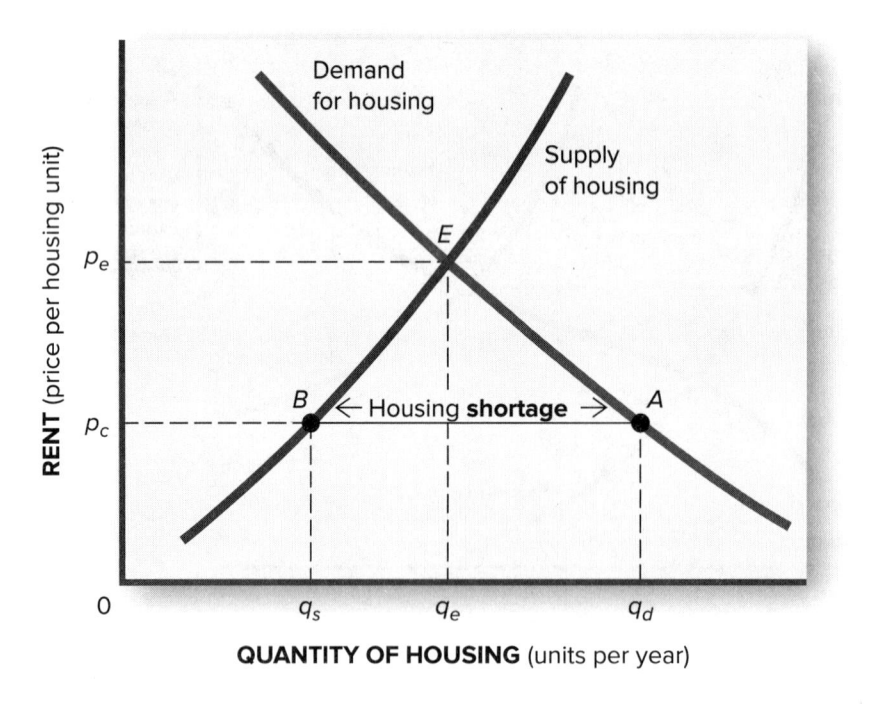

Figure 2.8 Price Ceilings Create Shortages Many cities impose rent controls to keep housing affordable. Consumers respond to the below-equilibrium price ceiling (p_c) by demanding more housing (q_d vs. q_e). But the quantity of housing supplied diminishes as landlords convert buildings to other uses (e.g., condos) or simply let rental units deteriorate. New construction also slows. The result is a housing shortage ($q_d - q_s$) and an actual reduction in available housing ($q_e - q_s$). ■

---

disequilibrium 非均衡，不均衡。enact 颁布、制定法律。

Thus *price ceilings have three predictable effects; they*

- *Increase the quantity demanded.*
- *Decrease the quantity supplied.*
- *Create a market shortage.*

因此，价格上限有三个可预见的效果，它们是：
- 增加需求数量
- 减少供给数量
- 引起市场短缺

You may well wonder where the "lost" housing went. The houses did not disappear. Some landlords simply decided that renting their units was no longer worth the effort. They chose, instead, to sell the units, convert them to condominiums, or even live in them themselves. Other landlords stopped maintaining their buildings, letting the units deteriorate. The rate of new construction slowed too, as builders decided that rent control made new construction less profitable. Slowly but surely the quantity of housing declines from q_e to q_s. Hence, *imposing rent controls to make housing more affordable for some means there will be less housing for all.*

你可能觉得奇怪：那些"消失的"住房哪去了？那些住房并没有消失。可是，一些房主认为不值得再出租他们的住房。于是他们选择出售这些住房，把它们改造成公寓，甚至干脆自己居住。其他一些房主不再维护他们的房屋，任其荒废下去。由于房屋建造者认为，租金控制使建造新房的利润降低，因此新房屋的建设速度也会放缓。房屋的供给量虽然下降缓慢但却是真实地从 q_e 降到了 q_s。因此，为了使一些人能够付得起房租而施加的租金控制，却使每个人的住房减少了。

Figure 2.8 illustrates another problem. The rent ceiling p_c has created a housing shortage—a gap between the quantity demanded (q_d) and the quantity supplied (q_s). Who will get the increasingly scarce housing? The market would have settled this FOR WHOM question by permitting rents to rise and allocating available units to those consumers willing and able to pay the rent p_e. Now, however, rents cannot rise, and we have lots of people clamoring for housing that is not available. A different method of distributing goods must be found. Vacant units will go to those who learn of them first, patiently wait on waiting lists, or offer a gratuity to the landlord or renting agent. In New York City, where rent control has been the law for 80 years, people "sell" their rent-controlled apartments when they move elsewhere.

Price Floors 价格下限

Artificially high (above-equilibrium) prices create similar problems in the marketplace. A **price floor** is a minimum price imposed by the government for a good or service. The objective is to raise the price of the good and create more income for the seller. Federal minimum wage laws, for example, forbid most employers from paying less than $7.25 an hour for labor.

市场上，人为的（均衡以上的）高价也会产生类似问题。价格下限是政府给某种商品或服务设定的最低价格。目的是抬高这种商品的价格，以便给卖方带来更多收入。例如，联邦最低工资法规定，雇主向劳工支付的工资不得低于每小时7.25美元。

Price floors are also common in the farm sector. To stabilize farmers' incomes, the government offers price guarantees for certain crops. The government sets a price guarantee of 18.75 cents per pound for domestically grown cane sugar. If the market price of sugar falls below 18.75 cents, the government promises to buy at the guaranteed price. Hence farmers know they can sell their sugar for 18.75 cents per pound, regardless of market demand.

Figure 2.9 illustrates the consequences of this price floor. The price guarantee (18.75¢) lies above the equilibrium price p_e (otherwise it would have no effect). At that higher price, farmers supply more sugar (q_s versus q_e). However, consumers are not willing to buy that much sugar: at that price they demand only the quantity q_d. Hence the *price floor has three predictable effects: It*

- *Increases the quantity supplied.*
- *Reduces the quantity demanded.*
- *Creates a market surplus.*

因此，价格下限有三个可预见的效果它们是：
- 增加供给数量
- 减少需求数量
- 引起市场过剩

In 2018 the government-guaranteed price (18.75¢) was 9 cents above the world price. That may not sound like a big difference, but it amounts to over $2 billion a year for U.S. consumers. At that higher price U.S. cane and beet sugar growers are willing to supply far more sugar than consumers demand. To prevent such a market surplus, the federal government sets limits on sugar production—and decides who gets to grow it. This is a classic case of **government failure**: Society ends up with the wrong mix of output (too much sugar), an increased tax burden (to pay for the surplus), an altered distribution of income (enriched sugar growers)—and a lot of political favoritism.

---

vacant 空缺的。gratuity 小费，赏金。government failure 政府失灵。

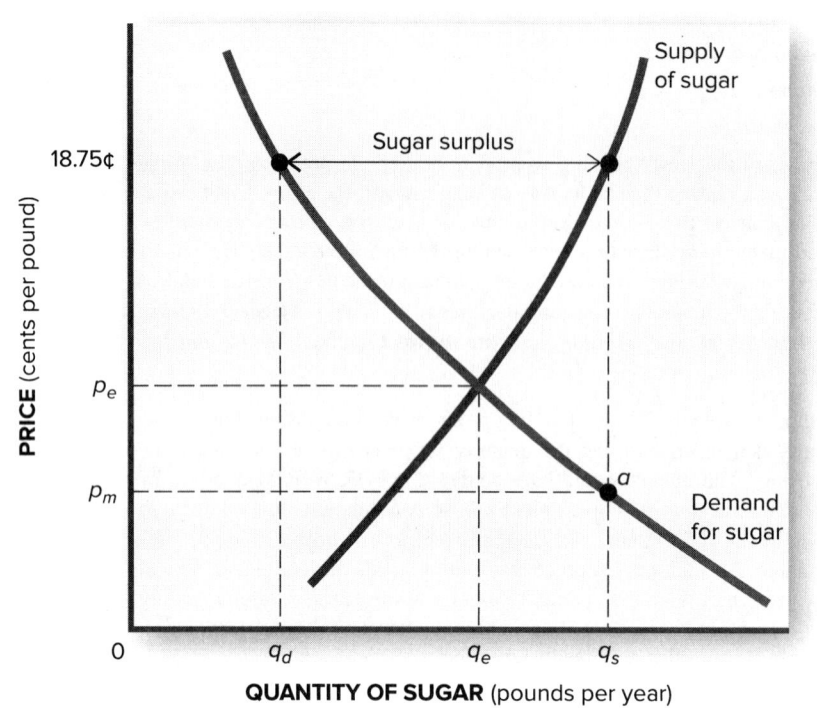

Figure 2.9 Price Floors Create Surplus The U.S. Department of Agriculture sets a minimum price for sugar at 18.75 cents. If the market price drops below 18.75 cents, the government will buy the resulting surplus.
Farmers respond by producing the quantity q_s. Consumers would purchase the quantity q_s, however, only if the market price dropped to p_m (point a on the demand curve). The government thus has to purchase and store the surplus ($q_s - q_d$). ■

Laissez Faire 自由放任

价格上限和价格下限明显的无效率暗示我们：最好不要干预市场。现代经济理论的创始人亚当·斯密在很久以前就得出了这个结论。在 1776 年，他提出了**自由放任**政策——字面意思是"别管它"。正如亚当·斯密所理解的那样，市场机制是一个配置资源和分配收入的有效手段。政府应该制定并执行市场规则，但是不应对其他方面进行干预。干预市场（通过价格上限、价格下限或其他调节方式）所引起的问题可能比它本身所希望解决的问题还多。

The apparent inefficiencies of price ceilings and floors imply that market outcomes are best left alone. This is a conclusion reached long ago by Adam Smith, the founder of modern economic theory. In 1776 he advocated a policy of **laissez faire**—literally, "leave it alone." As he saw it, the market mechanism was an efficient procedure for allocating resources and distributing incomes. The government should set and enforce the rules of the marketplace, but otherwise not interfere. Interference with the market—through price ceilings, floors, or other regulation—was likely to cause more problems than it could hope to solve.

The policy of laissez faire is motivated not only by the potential pitfalls of government intervention but also by the recognition of how well the market mechanism can work. Recall our visit to Clearview College, where the price and quantity of tutoring services had to be established. There was no central agency that set the price of tutoring service or determined how much tutoring service would be provided at Clearview College. Instead both the price of web services and its quantity were determined by the **market mechanism**—the interactions of many independent (decentralized) buyers and sellers.

WHAT, HOW, FOR WHOM 生产什么，如何生产，为谁生产

Notice how the market mechanism resolved the basic economic questions of WHAT, HOW, and FOR WHOM. The WHAT question refers to how much web tutoring to include in society's mix of output. The answer at Clearview College was 39 hours per semester. This

---

pitfall 陷阱。market mechanism 市场机制。

decision was not reached in a referendum but instead in the market equilibrium (see Figure 2.6). In the same way, but on a larger scale, millions of consumers and a handful of auto producers decide to include 17 million cars and trucks in each year's mix of output.

The market mechanism will also determine HOW these goods are produced. Profit-seeking producers will strive to produce web services and automobiles in the most efficient way. They will use market prices to decide not only WHAT to produce but also what resources to use in the production process.

Finally, the invisible hand of the market will determine who gets the goods produced. At Clearview College, who got tutorial help in web design? Only those students who were willing and able to pay $20 per hour for that service. FOR WHOM are all those automobiles produced each year? The answer is the same: Consumers who are willing and able to pay the market price for a new car.

OPTIMAL, NOT PERFECT 最优不等于完美

Not everyone is happy with these answers, of course. Tom would like to pay only $10 an hour for web tutoring. And some of the Clearview students do not have enough income to buy any assistance. They think it is unfair that they have to master web design on their own while richer students can have someone tutor them. Students who cannot afford cars are even less happy with the market's answer to the FOR WHOM question.

Although the outcomes of the marketplace are not perfect, they are often *optimal*. Optimal outcomes are the best possible given the level and distribution of incomes and scarce resources. In other words, we expect the choices made in the marketplace to be the best possible choices for each participant. Why do we draw such a conclusion? Because Tom and George and everyone else in our little Clearview College drama had (and continue to have) absolute freedom to make their own purchase and consumption decisions. And also because we assume that sooner or later they will make the choices they find most satisfying. The results are thus *optimal* in the sense that everyone has done as well as can be expected, given his or her income and talents.

The optimality of market outcomes provides a powerful argument for laissez faire. In essence, the laissez faire doctrine recognizes that decentralized markets not only work but also give individuals the opportunity to maximize their satisfaction. In this context, government interference is seen as a threat to the attainment of the "right" mix of output and other economic goals. Since its development by Adam Smith in 1776, the laissez faire doctrine has had a profound impact on the way the economy functions and what government does (or doesn't do).

尽管市场结果不是完美的,但它们往往是最优的。在一定的收入水平、收入分配以及资源稀缺的条件下,最优结果就是最可能实现的最好结果。换句话说,我们认为市场做出的选择对于每个参与者来说都是可能的最佳选择。我们为什么会得出这个结论呢?因为在Clearview学院,汤姆、乔治和其他人在做出自己的购买和消费决策时,都拥有(并且继续拥有)绝对的自由。而且,还因为我们假设他们迟早都会做出令自己感到最满意的选择。因此,在给定的收入和智力水平下,从每个人都达到自己最期待的结果这一角度来说,市场结果是最优的。

POLICY PERSPECTIVES

CAP WATER PRICES IN NATURAL DISASTERS?

Hurricane Harvey was the second most costly natural disaster in the United States since 1900. When it slammed into the Houston area in August 2017, it destroyed thousands of homes, forced the evacuation of nearly 40,000 people, and caused massive flooding. It also damaged 10 water systems, temporarily cutting off water to thousands of homes and businesses. Bottled water became the only option for thousands of people.

The market response to the water crisis was predictable: The price of bottled water skyrocketed overnight. A bottle of water that cost $1 before Harvey struck was selling for $7–$9 a day later.

©Adrin Snider/The Daily Press/AP Images

---

doctrine 学说。decentralized 分散,使分权。interference 干涉,干预。evacuation 疏散,撤离。skyrocket 猛涨。

> Consumers accused retailers of profiteering from the natural disaster and demanded that the government intervene to outlaw "price gouging." Church groups and nonprofit organizations said it was immoral to hit consumers with such outrageous price hikes on a truly essential commodity. The Consumer Protection Division of the Texas Attorney General's office received more than 500 complaints of price gouging in the first few days of Harvey's aftermath.
>
> Economists cautioned the attorney general about intervening. They said the high price of water would help solve the water crisis more quickly, for two reasons. First, the high price would induce consumers to use water as sparingly as possible. Second, that high price of water in the Houston area would induce sellers to truck in more water from Louisiana and other states. In other words, the high price would move consumers up the market demand curve and water companies up the market supply curve. Within days, more bottled water became available and prices eased.
>
> What would have happened if the government had capped the price of bottle water at $1? Who would have gotten the water? Would the quantity supplied have increased?

CHAPTER 2 REVIEW

SUMMARY

- Consumers, business firms, government agencies, and foreigners participate in the marketplace by offering to buy or sell goods and services, or factors of production. Participation is motivated by the desire to maximize utility (consumers), profits (business firms), or the general welfare (government agencies). **LO1**
- All interactions in the marketplace involve the exchange of either factors of production or finished products. Although the actual exchanges can take place anywhere, we say that they take place in product markets or factor markets, depending on what is being exchanged. **LO1**
- People who are willing and able to buy a particular good at some price are part of the market demand for that product. All those who are willing and able to sell that good at some price are part of the market supply. Total market demand or supply is the sum of individual demands or supplies. **LO2**
- Supply and demand curves illustrate how the quantity demanded or supplied changes in response to a change in the price of that good. Demand curves slope downward; supply curves slope upward. **LO2**
- The determinants of market demand include the number of potential buyers and their respective tastes (desires), incomes, other goods, and expectations. If any of these determinants change, the demand curve shifts. Movements along a demand curve are induced only by a change in the price of that good. **LO4**
- The determinants of market supply include technology, factor costs, other goods, taxes, expectations, and the number of sellers. Supply shifts when these underlying determinants change. **LO4**
- The quantity of goods or resources actually exchanged in each market depends on the behavior of all buyers and sellers, as summarized in market supply and demand curves. At the point where the two curves intersect, an equilibrium price—the price at which the quantity demanded equals the quantity supplied—will be established. **LO3**
- A distinctive feature of the market equilibrium is that it is the only price–quantity combination that is acceptable to buyers and sellers alike. At higher prices, sellers supply more than buyers are willing to purchase (a market surplus); at lower prices, the amount demanded exceeds the quantity supplied (a market shortage). Only the equilibrium price clears the market. **LO3**
- Price ceilings and floors are disequilibrium prices imposed on the marketplace. Such price controls create an imbalance between quantities demanded and supplied. **LO5**
- The market mechanism is a device for establishing prices and product and resource flows. As such, it may be used to answer the basic economic questions of WHAT to produce, HOW to produce it, and FOR WHOM. Its apparent efficiency prompts the call for laissez faire—a policy of government nonintervention in the marketplace. **LO3**

---

price gouging 哄抬物价。aftermath 后果，余波。

TERMS TO REMEMBER

Define the following terms:

market
factor market
product market
barter
supply
demand
opportunity cost
demand schedule
demand curve
law of demand
ceteris paribus
shift in demand

market demand
market supply
law of supply
equilibrium price
market shortage
market surplus
price ceiling
price floor
government failure
laissez faire
market mechanism

QUESTIONS FOR DISCUSSION

1. What does the supply and demand for human kidneys look like? If a market in kidneys were legal, who would get them? How does a law prohibiting kidney sales affect the quantity of kidney transplants or their distribution? **LO2**

2. In the web tutoring market, what forces might cause **LO4**
   a. a rightward shift of demand?
   b. a leftward shift of demand?
   c. a rightward shift of supply?
   d. a leftward shift of supply?
   e. an increase in the equilibrium price?

3. Did the price of tuition at your school change this year? What might have caused that? **LO3**

4. Illustrate the market shortage for tickets to the Pope's New York City procession (see the News Wire "Market Shortage"). **LO5**

5. How does a reduction in the price of concert tickets affect
   a. the quantity of tickets demanded?
   b. the desire of fans for tickets? **LO2**

6. When concert tickets are priced below equilibrium, who gets them? Is this distribution of tickets fairer than a pure market distribution? Is it more efficient? Who gains or loses if all the tickets are resold (scalped) at the market-clearing price? **LO5**

7. Is there a shortage of on-campus parking at your school? How might the shortage be resolved? **LO5**

8. If rent controls are so counterproductive, why do cities impose them? How else might the housing problems of poor people be solved? **LO5**

9. Why did Apple set the initial price of the iPhone 7 below equilibrium (see the News Wire "Market Shortage")? Should Apple have immediately raised the price? **LO5**

10. **POLICY PERSPECTIVES** In the wake of Hurricane Harvey, gasoline prices doubled at many locations, with prices reaching as high as $20 per gallon. Who got gas at those prices? Should the government have put a lid on prices? If it did, who would have gotten the available gasoline? **LO5**

PROBLEMS

1. Using the "new demand" in Figure 2.7 as a guide, determine the size of the market surplus or shortage that would exist at a price of (*a*) $40 (*b*) $20 **LO5**

2. Based on the News Wire "Supply Shift," **LO3, LO5**
   a. what is the initial (pre-hurricane) equilibrium rent per month?
   b. how large is the pre-hurricane shortage?

c. what is the post-hurricane equilibrium rent?
d. what is the pre-hurricane equilibrium quantity?
e. what is the post-hurricane equilibrium quantity?
f. how large is the post-hurricane shortage at the pre-hurricane equilibrium rent?

3. According to the News Wire "Market Shortage," **LO5**
   a. how large was the market shortage at the Church-set price of $0?
   b. if the Church had sold the tickets for $100, how would have quantity demanded changed? (increased, decreased, not changed)
   c. if the Church sold the tickets for $100, would the market shortage been larger or smaller?
   d. if the Church sold the tickets for the equilibrium price, would a market shortage exist?

4. In September 2014 Apple was selling a gold version of the 128GB iPhone 6 for $949. Two days later that phone was advertised on eBay for a starting bid of $1,625. **LO5**
   a. Was this evidence of a market shortage or a market surplus?
   b. Graph this situation.

5. Given the following data, **LO2**
   a. complete the following tables;
   b. construct market supply and demand curves;
   c. identify the equilibrium price; and
   d. identify the amount of shortage or surplus that would exist at a price of $4.

Participant	Quantity Demanded (per Week)				
Price	$5	$4	$3	$2	$1
Demand side					
Al	1	2	3	4	5
Betsy	1	2	2	2	3
Casey	2	2	3	3	4
Daisy	2	3	4	4	6
Eddie	2	2	2	3	5
Market total	___	___	___	___	___

Participant	Quantity Supplied (per Week)				
Price	$5	$4	$3	$2	$1
Supply side					
Firm A	3	3	3	3	3
Firm B	7	5	4	4	2
Firm C	6	4	3	3	1
Firm D	6	5	4	3	0
Firm E	4	3	3	3	2
Market total	___	___	___	___	___

6. If a product becomes more popular, **LO4**
   a. Which curve will shift?
   b. Along which curve will price and quantity move?
   At the new equilibrium price, will
   c. price
   d. quantity be higher or lower?
7. Which curve shifts, and in what direction, when the following events occur in the domestic car market? **LO4**
   a. The U.S. economy falls into a recession.
   b. U.S. autoworkers go on strike.
   c. Imported cars become more expensive.
   d. The price of gasoline increases.
8. Assume the following data describe the gasoline market: **LO3**

Price per gallon	$3.50	3.25	3.00	2.75	2.50	2.25	2.00
Quantity demanded	30	31	32	33	34	35	36
Quantity supplied	36	34	32	30	28	26	24

   a. Graph the demand and supply curves.
   b. What is the equilibrium price?
   c. If supply at every price is reduced by 6 gallons, what will the new equilibrium price be?
   d. If the government freezes the price of gasoline at its initial equilibrium price, how much of a surplus or shortage will exist when supply is reduced as described in part *c*?
9. Using the News Wire "Law of Demand," answer the following questions: **LO2**
   a. According to the News Wire, what would be the response of students to a tax on alcohol that raises the price of alcoholic drinks by $1?
   b. Graph the response of students to higher alcohol prices.
10. If the equilibrium price for tickets to a Taylor Swift concert is $100 each, and she sells them for $80, **LO5**
    a. does she create a market surplus or shortage?
    b. Suppose scalpers buy 10,000 tickets and resell them for $100 each. How much profit do the scalpers earn?
11. **POLICY PERSPECTIVES** Hurricane Harvey damaged water systems, cutting off water to thousands in Houston. **LO5**
    a. What was the immediate impact on demand for bottled water?
    b. If the government capped the price of bottled water at $1, what would have happened?

CHAPTER THREE

Consumer Demand 消费者需求

©Ira Berger/Alamy Stock Photo

LEARNING OBJECTIVES

After reading this chapter, you should be able to:

1. Explain why demand curves slope downward.
2. Describe what the price elasticity of demand measures.
3. Depict the relationship of price elasticity, price, and total revenue.
4. Recite the factors that influence the degree of price elasticity.
5. Discuss how advertising affects consumer demand.

"Shop until you drop" is apparently a way of life for many Americans. The *average* American (man, woman, or child) spends a whopping $40,000 per year on consumer goods and services. This adds up at the cash register to a consumption bill of roughly $15 *trillion* a year.

A major concern of microeconomics is to explain this shopping frenzy. What drives us to department stores, grocery stores, and every big sale in town? More specifically,

- How do we decide how much of any good to buy?
- How does a change in a product's price affect the quantity we purchase or the amount of money we spend on it?
- What factors other than price affect our consumption decisions?

The law of demand, first encountered in Chapter 2, gives us some clues for answering these questions. But we need to look beyond that law to fashion more complete answers. Knowing that demand curves are downward-sloping is important, but that knowledge won't get us far in the real world. In the real world, producers need to know the exact quantities demanded at various prices. Producers also need to know what forces will shift consumer demand.

The specifics of consumer demand are also important to public policy decisions. Suppose a city wants to relieve highway congestion and encourage more people to use public transit. Will public appeals be effective in changing commuter behavior? Probably not. But a change in relative prices might do the trick. Experience shows that raising the *price* of private auto use (e.g., higher parking fees, bridge tolls) and lowering transit fares *are* effective in changing commuters' behavior. Economists try to predict just how much prices should be altered to elicit the desired response.

Your school worries about the details of consumer demand as well. If tuition goes up again, some students will go elsewhere. Other students may take fewer courses. As enrollment begins to drop, school administrators may ask economics professors for some advice on tuition pricing. Their advice will be based on studies of consumer demand. ■

---

roughly 大约，粗略地。frenzy 疯狂。commuter 通勤者，经常往返者。toll 通行费。elicit 引出，得出。

PATTERNS OF CONSUMPTION 消费模式

开始研究消费者需求的一个好方法是观察消费者是怎样花掉他们的收入的。图 3.1 提供了一个简要概括。图中显示，消费者全部支出的一半用于食品和住房。在消费者花掉的每 1 美元中有 33 美分用于住房——包括租金、房屋修缮、水电和草籽等各项费用。另外有 13 美分用于食物，包括购买食品和去麦当劳这样的餐厅吃饭。我们还把许多钱花在了汽车上：交通支出（汽车的购买和保养、汽油、保险）占这 1 美元中的 16 美分。

A good way to start a study of consumer demand is to observe how consumers spend their incomes. Figure 3.1 provides a quick summary. Note that close to half of all consumer spending is for food and shelter. Out of the typical consumer dollar, 33 cents is devoted to housing—everything from rent and repairs to utility bills and grass seed. Another 13 cents is spent on food, including groceries and trips to McDonald's. We also spend a lot on cars; transportation expenditures (car payments, maintenance, gasoline, insurance) eat up 16 cents of the typical consumer dollar.

Taken together, housing, transportation, food, and health expenditures account for 70 percent of the typical household budget. Most people regard these items as the "basic essentials." However, there is no rule that says 13 cents of every consumer dollar must be spent on food or that 33 percent of one's budget is "needed" for shelter. What Figure 3.1 depicts is how the average consumer has *chosen* to spend his or her income. We could choose to spend our incomes in other ways.

A closer examination of consumer patterns reveals that we do in fact change our habits on occasion. In the last 10 years, our annual consumption of red meat has declined from 125 pounds per person to 65 pounds. In the same time, our consumption of chicken has increased from 47 pounds to 85 pounds. We now consume less coffee, whiskey, beer, and eggs but more wine, asparagus, and ice cream compared to 10 years ago. Smartphones and computer tablets are regarded as essentials today, even though no one had these products 20 years ago. What prompted these changes in consumption patterns?

Some changes in consumption are more sudden. In the recession of 2008–2009, Americans abruptly stopped buying new cars. Does that mean that cars were no longer essential? When oil prices rose sharply in 2018, people *drove* their cars less. Does that mean they *liked* driving less? Or did changes in income and prices alter consumer behavior?

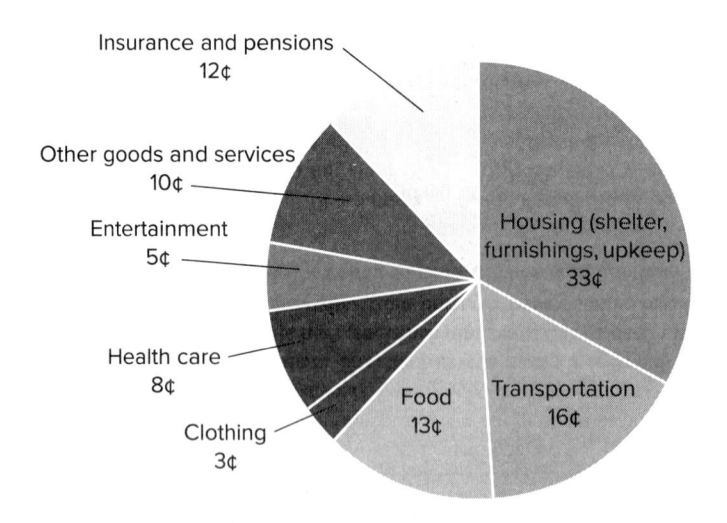

Figure 3.1 How the Consumer Dollar Is Spent Consumers spend their incomes on a vast array of goods and services. This figure summarizes those consumption decisions by showing how the average consumer dollar is spent. The goal of economic theory is to explain and predict these consumption choices. ■

Source: "Consumer Expenditure Survey, 2016," U.S. Department of Labor, April 2018.

---

asparagus 芦笋。prompt 促使，导致。upkeep 维修费。

DETERMINANTS OF DEMAND 需求的决定因素

In seeking explanations for consumer behavior, we have to recognize that economics doesn't have all the answers. But it does offer a unique perspective that sets it apart from other fields of study.

The Sociopsychiatric Explanation 社会精神病学的解释

Consider first the explanations of consumer behavior offered by other fields of study. Psychiatrists and psychologists have had a virtual field day formulating such explanations. The Austrian psychiatrist Sigmund Freud (1856–1939) was among the first to describe us as bundles of subconscious (and unconscious) fears, complexes, and anxieties. From a Freudian perspective, we strive for ever-higher levels of consumption to satisfy basic drives for security, sex, and ego gratification. Like the most primitive of people, we clothe and adorn ourselves in ways that assert our identity and worth. We eat and smoke too much because we need the oral gratification and security associated with the mother's breast. Self-indulgence, in general, creates in our minds the safety and satisfactions of childhood. Oversized homes and cars provide us with a source of warmth and security remembered from the womb. On the other hand, we often buy and consume some things we expressly don't desire just to assert our rebellious feelings against our parents (or parent substitutes). In Freud's view, it is the constant interplay of id, ego, and superego drives that motivates us to buy, buy, buy.

Sociologists offer additional explanations for our consumption behavior. They emphasize our yearning to stand above the crowd, to receive recognition from the masses. For people with exceptional talents, such recognition may come easily. But for the ordinary person, recognition may depend on conspicuous consumption. Owning a larger car, wearing the newest fashion, and taking an exotic vacation become expressions of identity that provoke recognition, even social envy. Thus we strive for higher levels of consumption—so as to *surpass* the Joneses, rather than just keep up with them.

Not *all* consumption is motivated by ego or status concerns, of course. Some food is consumed for the sake of self-preservation, some clothing is chosen because it provides warmth, and some housing simply offers shelter. The typical American consumer has more than enough income to satisfy these basic needs, however. In today's economy, consumers have a lot of *discretionary* income that can be used to satisfy psychological or sociological longings. As a result, single women are able to spend a lot of money on clothing and pets, while men spend freely on entertainment, food, and drink (see the accompanying News Wire "Consumption Patterns"). As for teenagers, who collectively spend over $300 million a year, they show off their affluence with purchases of electronic goods, cars, and clothes.

在寻求对消费者行为的解释时，我们要知道经济学并不能回答所有问题，但是它能为我们提供一种不同于其他研究领域的视角。

对于我们的消费行为，社会学家给出了另外的解释。他们强调，我们渴望出类拔萃和得到众人的赏识。对具有杰出才能的人来说，很容易就能得到别人的认可。但对于普通人来说，要获得这种认可可能要依靠炫耀性的消费。一辆更大的汽车、一件更时尚的衣服、一次更具有异国情调的度假都成了身份的象征，都能获得认可甚至引发嫉妒。因此，我们不断地追求更高的消费水平——就是为了超越别人，而不仅仅是与他们保持一致。

NEWS WIRE CONSUMPTION PATTERNS

MEN VERSUS WOMEN: HOW THEY SPEND

Are men really different from women? If spending habits are any clue, males do differ from females. That's the conclusion one would draw from the latest Bureau of Labor Statistics (BLS) survey of consumer expenditures. Here's what BLS found out about the spending habits of young (under age 25) men and women who are living on their own.

Distinctive Traits

- Young men have a lot more income to spend ($19,493) than do young women ($12,456).
- Young women pile on more credit card debt (average $10,000 per year) than do men ($2,000).
- Young men spend much more ($2,048) at fast-food outlets, restaurants, and carryouts than do young women ($1,673).
- Men spend twice as much on alcoholic beverages and smoking.

---

subconscious 潜意识的，下意识的。 ego gratification 自我满足。 adorn 装饰。 self-indulgence 自我放任。 womb 子宫。 rebellious 叛逆的，反抗的。 superego 超我。 discretionary 自由支配的。

- Men spend nearly twice as much as women do on television, cars, and stereo equipment.
- Young women spend a lot more money on education, clothing, pets, and personal care items.
- Neither sex spends much on charity, reading, or health care.

Source: "Consumer Expenditure Survey 2016," U.S. Bureau of Labor Statistics.

NOTE: Consumer patterns vary by gender, age, and other characteristics. Economists try to isolate the common influences on consumer behavior.
注：消费模式因性别、年龄及其他特征的不同而不同。经济学家试图分别研究这些因素对消费行为的影响。

The Economic Explanation 经济学的解释

Although psychiatrists and sociologists offer many reasons for these various consumption patterns, their explanations all fall a bit short. At best, sociopsychiatric theories tell us why teenagers, men, and women *desire* certain goods and services. They don't explain which goods will actually be *purchased*. Desire is only the first step in the consumption process. To acquire goods and services, one must be willing and able to *pay* for one's wants. Producers won't give you their goods just because you want to satisfy your Freudian desires. They want money in exchange for their goods. Hence *prices and income are just as relevant to consumption decisions as are more basic desires and preferences.*

In explaining consumer behavior, then, economists focus on the demand for goods and services. To say that someone **demands** a particular good means that he or she is able and willing to buy it at some price(s). In the marketplace, money talks: *The willingness and ability to pay* are critical. Many people with a strong desire for a Porsche (see photo) have neither the ability nor the willingness to actually buy it; they do not *demand* Porsches. Similarly, there are many rich people who are willing and able to buy goods they only remotely desire; they *demand* all kinds of goods and services.

You may desire this car, but are you able and willing to buy it?
©Roman Belogorodov/Alamy Stock Photo

What determines a person's willingness and ability to buy specific goods? As we saw in Chapter 2, economists have identified four different influences on consumer demand: tastes, income, expectations, and the prices of other goods. Note again that desire (tastes) is only one determinant of demand. Other determinants of demand (income, expectations, and other goods) also influence whether a person will be willing and able to buy a certain good at a specific price.

如第 2 章所述，一种商品的**市场需求**就等于所有单个消费者的需求总和。因此，某特定商品的市场需求由以下因素决定：

- 偏好（对这种商品和其他商品的欲望）
- 收入（消费者的）
- 预期（对收入、价格、偏好）
- 其他商品（它们的可获得性和价格）
- 市场中的消费者数量

As we observed in Chapter 2, the **market demand** for a good is simply the sum of all individual consumer demands. Hence *the market demand for a specific product is determined by*

- *Tastes* (desire for this and other goods).
- *Income* (of consumers).
- *Expectations* (for income, prices, tastes).
- *Other goods* (their availability and price).
- *The number of consumers in the market.*

In the remainder of this chapter we shall see how these determinants of demand give the demand curve its downward slope. Our objective is not only to explain consumer behavior but also to see (and predict) how consumption patterns *change* in response to *changes* in the price of a good or service or to *changes* in the underlying determinants of demand.

---

stereo equipment 立体声设备。 Porsches 保时捷。 remotely（程度）极微地。

THE DEMAND CURVE 需求曲线

Utility Theory 效用理论

The starting point for an economic analysis of demand is straightforward. Economists accept consumer tastes as the outcome of sociopsychiatric and cultural influences. They don't look beneath the surface to see how those tastes originated. Economists simply note the existence of certain tastes (desires) and then look to see how those tastes affect consumption decisions. We assume that the more pleasure a product gives us, the higher the price we would be willing to pay for it. If gobbling buttered popcorn at the movies really pleases you, you're likely to be willing to pay dearly for it. If you have no great taste or desire for popcorn, the theater might have to give it away before you'd eat it.

Total versus Marginal Utility 总效用和边际效用

Economists use the term **utility** to refer to the expected pleasure, or satisfaction, obtained from goods and services. **Total utility** refers to the amount of satisfaction obtained from your *entire* consumption of a product. By contrast, **marginal utility** refers to the amount of satisfaction you get from consuming the *last* (i.e., marginal) unit of a product.

经济学家用**效用**一词来指我们预期从商品和服务中所获得的快乐或满足感。**总效用**是指从一种产品的全部消费中所获得的满足感。相反，**边际效用**是指从一种产品最后（即边际）一单位的消费中所获得的满足感。

Diminishing Marginal Utility 边际效用递减

The concepts of total and marginal utility explain not only why we buy popcorn at the movies but also why we stop eating it at some point. Even people who love popcorn (i.e., derive great total utility from it), and can afford it, don't eat endless quantities of popcorn. Why not? Presumably because the thrill diminishes with each mouthful. The first box of popcorn may bring gratification, but the second or third box is likely to bring a stomachache. We express this change in perception by noting that the *marginal* utility of the first box of popcorn is higher than the additional or *marginal* utility derived from the second box.

The behavior of popcorn connoisseurs is not that unusual. Generally speaking, the amount of *additional* utility we obtain from a product declines as we continue to consume larger quantities of it. The third slice of pizza is not as desirable as the first, the sixth soda not so satisfying as the fifth, and so forth. Indeed, this phenomenon of diminishing marginal utility is so commonplace that economists have fashioned a law around it. This **law of diminishing marginal utility** states that each successive unit of a good consumed yields less *additional* utility.

爆米花偏爱者的行为并不奇怪。一般说来，随着我们持续消费更多数量的某一种产品，我们从中获得的新增效用是下降的。第二块比萨没有第一块那样诱人，第六瓶汽水也没有第五瓶那样好喝，等等。实际上，这种边际效用递减的现象非常普遍，经济学家因此提出了一个规律——**边际效用递减规律**：每多消费一个单位的某种商品，其产生的效用增量是递减的。

The law of diminishing marginal utility does *not* say that we won't like the third box of popcorn, the second pizza, or the sixth soda; it just says we won't like them as much as the ones we've already consumed. Note also that time is important here: If the first pizza was eaten last year, the second pizza, eaten now, may taste just as good. The law of diminishing marginal utility applies to short time periods.

The expectation of diminishing marginal utility is illustrated in Figure 3.2. The graph on the left depicts the *total* utility obtained from eating popcorn. Notice that total utility continues to rise as we consume the first five boxes of popcorn. But total utility increases by smaller and smaller increments. Each successive step of the total utility curve in Figure 3.2 is a little shorter.

The height of each step of the total utility curve in Figure 3.2 represents *marginal* utility—the increments to total utility. The graph on the right in Figure 3.2 illustrates these marginal increments—the height of each step of the total utility curve (left graph). This graph shows more clearly how *marginal* utility diminishes.

Do not confuse *diminishing* marginal utility with dislike. Figure 3.2 doesn't imply that the second box of popcorn isn't desirable. It only says that the second box isn't as satisfying as the

不要将边际效用递减理解为不喜欢。图 3.2 并不是说第二桶

---

straightforward 简单的，径直的。 gobble 狼吞虎咽地吃。 popcorn 爆米花。 derive from 获得，得自。

爆米花令人不满意。它只是说第二桶令人满意的程度没有第一桶高。但第二桶仍然很好吃。我们从何而知呢？因为它的边际效用是正的（右面的图），所以当吃完第二桶以后，总效用（左图）增加了。只要边际效用是正的，总效用就一定增加。

first. It still tastes good, however. How do we know? Because its *marginal* utility is positive (right graph), and therefore *total* utility (left graph) rises when the second box is consumed. ***So long as marginal utility is positive, total utility must be increasing.***

The situation changes abruptly with the sixth box of popcorn. According to Figure 3.2, the good sensations associated with popcorn consumption are completely forgotten by the time the sixth box arrives. Nausea and stomach cramps dominate. Indeed, the sixth box is absolutely *distasteful*, as reflected in the downturn of total utility and the *negative* value for marginal utility. We were happier—in possession of more total utility—with only five boxes of popcorn. The sixth box—yielding *negative* marginal utility—has reduced total satisfaction. This is the kind of sensation you'd also experience if you ate too much pizza (see the accompanying cartoon).

Marginal utility explains not only why we stop eating before we explode but also why we pay so little for drinking water. Water has a high *total* utility: We would die without it. But its *marginal* utility is low, so we're not willing to pay much for another glass of it.

并不是所有商品都会到达零边际效用（或更少的负边际效用）。但更普遍的边际效用递减规律却是我们每天都会经历的。也就是说，新增的某一商品的数量所产生的满足感的增量总是越来越小。总效用在继续增加，但随着消费数量的增加，总效用增加的速度越来越慢。边际效用递减规律也存在一些例外，但是并不多。（你能想到一些吗？）

Not all goods approach zero (much less negative) marginal utility. Yet the more general principle of diminishing marginal utility is experienced daily. That is to say, ***additional quantities of a good eventually yield increasingly smaller increments of satisfaction.*** Total utility continues to rise, but at an ever slower rate as more of a good is consumed. There are exceptions to the law of diminishing marginal utility, but not many. (Can you think of any?)

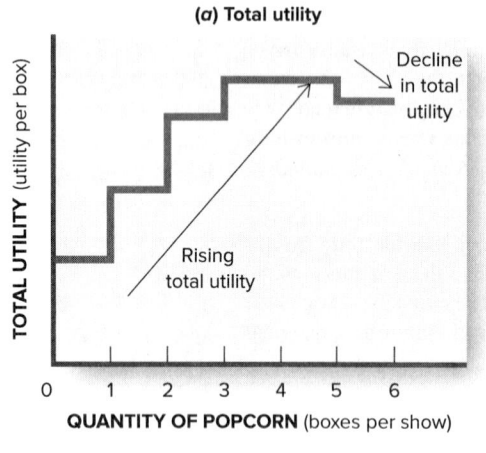

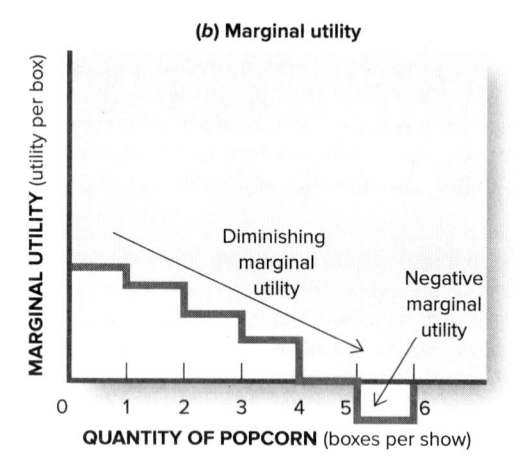

Figure 3.2 Total versus Marginal Utility The *total* utility (*a*) derived from consuming a product comes from the *marginal* utilities of each successive unit. The total utility curve shows how each of the first five boxes of popcorn contributes to total utility. Note that each successive step is smaller. This reflects the law of diminishing marginal utility.

The sixth box of popcorn causes the total utility steps to descend; the sixth box actually *reduces* total utility. This means that the sixth box has *negative* marginal utility.

The marginal utility curve (*b*) shows the change in total utility with each additional unit. It is derived from the total utility curve. Marginal utility here is positive but diminishing for the first five boxes. For the sixth box, marginal utility is negative.

---

sensation 感觉。nausea 恶心。cramps 痉挛，绞痛。distasteful 令人不快的，不合口味的。

Price and Quantity 价格与数量

Marginal utility is essentially a measure of how much we *desire* particular goods. But which ones will we *buy*? Clearly, we don't always buy the products we most desire. *Price* is often a problem. All too often we have to settle for goods that yield less marginal utility simply because they are less expensive. This explains why most people don't drive Porsches. Our desire ("taste") for a Porsche may be great, but its price is even greater. The challenge for most people is to somehow reconcile our tastes with our bank balances.

In deciding whether to buy something, our immediate focus is typically on a single variable—namely *price*. Assume that a person's tastes, income, and expectations are set in stone and that the prices of other goods are fixed as well. This is the ***ceteris paribus*** assumption we first encountered in Chapter 1. It doesn't mean that other influences on consumer behavior are unimportant. Rather, **the *ceteris paribus* simply allows us to focus on one variable at a time.** In this case, we are focusing on *price*. What we want to know is how high a price a consumer is willing to pay for another unit of a product.

You can have too much of a good thing. No matter how much we like a product, marginal utility is likely to diminish as we consume more of it.
©Lillian Dougherty

The concepts of marginal utility and *ceteris paribus* enable us to answer this question. The more marginal utility a good delivers, the more you're willing to pay for it. But marginal utility *diminishes* as increasing quantities of a product are consumed. Hence you won't be willing to pay so much for additional quantities of the same good. The moviegoer who is willing to pay 50 cents for that first mouthwatering ounce of buttered popcorn may not be willing to pay so much for a second or third ounce. The same is true for the second pizza, the sixth soda, and so forth. **With given income, taste, expectations, and prices of other goods and services, people are willing to buy additional quantities of a good only if its price falls.** In other words, as the marginal utility of a good diminishes, so does our willingness to pay.

This inverse relationship between the quantity demanded of a good and its price is referred to as the **law of demand**. Figure 3.3 illustrates this relationship again for the case of popcorn. Notice that the **demand curve** slopes downward: More popcorn is purchased at lower prices.

The law of demand and the law of diminishing marginal utility tell us nothing about why we crave popcorn or why our cravings subside. That's the job of psychiatrists, sociologists, and physiologists. The laws of economics simply describe our market behavior.

PRICE ELASTICITY 价格弹性

The theory of demand helps explain consumer behavior. Often, however, much more specific information is desired. Imagine you owned a theater and were actually worried about popcorn sales. Knowing that the demand curve is downward-sloping wouldn't tell you a whole lot about what price to charge. What you'd really want to know is *how much* popcorn sales would change if you raised or lowered the price.

Airlines want the same kind of hard data. Airlines know that around Christmas they can charge full fares and still fill all their planes. After the holidays, however, people have less desire to travel. To fill planes in February, the airlines must offer discount fares. But how far should they lower ticket prices? That depends on *how much* passenger traffic *changes* in response to reduced fares.

Apple Computer confronted a similar problem in June 2007. Apple was launching the very first iPhone at a price of $599. The product was an instant hit. But Apple wanted even greater sales. So it cut the price to $399 two months later, and unit sales skyrocketed from 9,000 iPhones a day to 27,000 a day. The *desire* for iPhones hadn't changed, but the *price* had. In 2018, Apple again used price cuts to accelerate the pace of sales, this time for the iPhone 8 (see the News Wire "Price Elasticity").

边际效用的概念和其他条件不变的假设使我们能够回答这一问题。一种商品带来的边际效用越多，你愿意支付的钱就越多。但是，随着一种产品消费数量的增加，边际效用会递减。因此，你不愿意为了购买更多数量的同种商品而花费那么多钱。一个愿意花50美分来购买一盎司令人垂涎的奶油爆米花的电影院常客，可能并不愿意花那么多钱来购买第二或第三盎司。对第二块比萨、第六瓶汽水等也是如此。假设消费者的收入、喜好和预期以及其他商品和服务的价格不变，那么只有当一种商品的价格下降时，消费者才愿意购买更多数量。也就是说，当一种商品的边际效用递减时，我们的购买意愿也是递减的。

---

reconcile 使一致，使和谐。set in stone 固定不变。sociologist 社会学家。physiologist 生理学家。

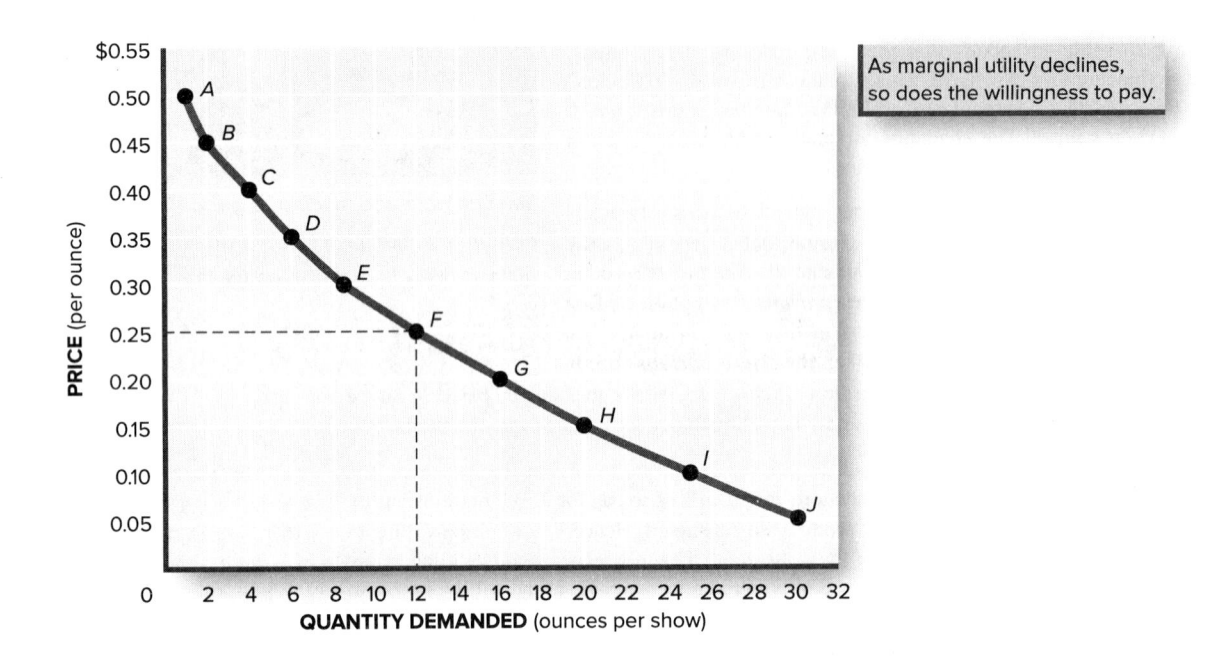

> As marginal utility declines, so does the willingness to pay.

	Price (per Ounce)	Quantity Demanded (Ounces per Show)
A	$0.50	1
B	0.45	2
C	0.40	4
D	0.35	6
E	0.30	9
F	0.25	12
G	0.20	16
H	0.15	20
I	0.10	25
J	0.05	30

Figure 3.3 A Demand Schedule and Curve Because marginal utility diminishes, consumers are willing to buy larger quantities of a good only at lower prices. This demand schedule and curve illustrate the specific quantities demanded at alternative prices.

Notice that points A through J on the curve correspond to the rows of the demand schedule. If popcorn sold for 25 cents per ounce, this consumer would buy 12 ounces per show (point F). More popcorn would be demanded only if the price were reduced (points G–J).

NEWS WIRE PRICE ELASTICITY

APPLE SLASHES THE PRICE OF IPHONE 8

Apple cut the price of the iPhone 8 by 15 percent, to $599. The price cut is intended to boost sales for last year's phone as a cheaper alternative to the new and more expensive iPhone XS and XS Max models that were launched this week. The cheapest XS is priced at $999. Apple expects unit sales of the cheaper iPhone 8 to increase by 20 percent this quarter, in response to the lower price.

Source: News accounts of September 12–15, 2018.

©INNA FINKOVA/Alamy Stock Photo

NOTE: According to the law of demand, quantity demanded increases when price falls. The price elasticity of demand measures how price sensitive consumers are.
注：根据需求法则，当价格下降时，需求量会增加。需求的价格弹性衡量的是消费者对价格变化的敏感程度。

The central question in all these decisions is the response of quantity demanded to a change in price. ***The response of consumers to a change in price is measured by the price elasticity of demand.*** Specifically, the **price elasticity of demand** refers to the *percentage* change in quantity demanded divided by the *percentage* change in price:

$$\text{Price elasticity } (E) = \frac{\text{percentage change in quantity demanded}}{\text{percentage change in price}}$$

Suppose we increased the price of popcorn by 20 percent. We know from the law of demand that the quantity of popcorn demanded will fall. But we need to observe market behavior to see *how far* sales drop. Suppose that unit sales (quantity demanded) fall by 10 percent. We could then compute the price elasticity of demand as

$$E = \frac{\text{percentage change in quantity demanded}}{\text{percentage change in price}} = \frac{-10\%}{+20\%} = -0.5$$

Because price and quantity demanded always move in opposite directions (the law of demand), E is a negative value (−0.5 in this case). For convenience, however, we use the absolute value of E (without the minus sign). What we learn here is that popcorn sales decline at half (0.5) the rate of price increases. Moviegoers cut back grudgingly on popcorn consumption when popcorn prices rise.

Elastic versus Inelastic Demand 需求富有弹性和缺乏弹性

We characterize the demand for various goods in one of three ways: *elastic*, *inelastic*, or *unitary elastic*. If E is larger than 1, we say demand is elastic: Consumer response is large relative to the change in price.

If E is less than 1, we say demand is inelastic. This is the case with popcorn, where E is only 0.5. ***If demand is inelastic, consumers aren't very responsive to price changes.***

If E is equal to 1, demand is unitary elastic. In this case, the percentage change in quantity demanded is exactly equal to the percentage change in price.

所有这些决策的核心问题都是需求量对价格变化的反应。消费者对价格变化的反应由需求的价格弹性来衡量。具体来说，**需求的价格弹性**指需求量变化的百分比除以价格变化的百分比：

$$需求的价格弹性（E）= \frac{需求量变化的百分比}{价格变化的百分比}$$

我们可以用富有弹性、缺乏弹性和单一弹性来描述对不同商品需求的特征。如果 E 大于 1，我们就说需求是富有弹性的——消费者对价格变化的反应很强烈。

如果 E 小于 1，我们就说需求缺乏弹性。爆米花就是这种情况，它的价格弹性只有 0.5。如果需求缺乏弹性，就说明消费者对价格的变化不是很敏感。

---

grudgingly 勉强地，不情愿地。

Degree of Elasticity	Estimate
Relatively elastic (E > 1)	
Airline travel, long run	2.4
Fresh fish	2.2
New cars, short run	1.2–1.5
Unitary elastic (E = 1)	
Private education	1.1
Radios and televisions	1.2
Shoes	0.9
Relatively inelastic (E < 1)	
Cigarettes	0.4
Coffee	0.3
Gasoline, short run	0.2
Long-distance telephone calls	0.1

Table 3.1 Elasticity Estimates Price elasticities vary greatly. When the price of gasoline increases, consumers reduce their consumption only slightly: Demand for gasoline is *in*elastic. When the price of fish increases, however, consumers cut back their consumption substantially: Demand for fish is elastic. These differences reflect the availability of immediate substitutes, the prices of the goods, and the amount of time available for changing behavior.

Sources: Hendrick S. Houthakker and Lester D. Taylor, *Consumer Demand in the United States, 1929–1970* (Cambridge, MA: Harvard University Press, 1966), p. 214; Frederick W. Bell, "The Pope and Price of Fish," *American Economic Review* 58, no. 5 (December 1968), pp. 1346–1350; and Michael R. Ward, Abstract, "Product Substitutability and Competition in Long-Distance Telecommunications," *Economic Inquiry* 37, no. 4 (October 1999), pp. 657–677.

Consider the case of smoking. Many smokers claim they would "pay anything" for a cigarette if they ran out. But would they? Would they continue to smoke just as many cigarettes if prices doubled or tripled? Research suggests not: Higher cigarette prices *do* curb smoking. There is at least *some* elasticity in the demand for cigarettes. But the elasticity of demand is low; Table 3.1 indicates that the elasticity of cigarette demand is only 0.4. As a result, the *tripling* of the federal tax on cigarettes in 2009 had only a modest effect on adult smoking, as the News Wire "Tax Hikes and Demand" explains.

NEWS WIRE TAX HIKES AND DEMAND

SMOKERS GASPING AT OBAMA'S TAX HIKE

Washington, D.C. President Obama signed a law that *tripled* the federal excise tax on cigarettes. The new law hiked the cigarette tax from 39 cents per pack to $1.01 per pack, effective April 1, 2009. That's the biggest cigarette tax hike ever. It increased the price of a 10-pack carton of Marlboros by $6.20. Cigar smokers were hit with an even heftier tax hike: The maximum tax on a cigar jumped from 4.9 cents to a whopping 40.26 cents.

These higher taxes hit smokers hard. A pack-a-day smoker is paying Uncle Sam an extra $226 a year in excise taxes. The National Bureau of Economic Research estimated that higher tax is costing smokers a total of $10 billion a year. Smokers say this isn't fair, especially in light of President Obama's campaign pledge not to raise taxes on any family making less than $250,000 a year. 96 percent of smokers fall into that category, and one in four smokers are officially classified as poor. So, the tax hikes hurt.

---

triple 三倍的；增至三倍。curb 控制，抑制。tax hike 增税。heftier 异常大的（hefty 的比较级）。

Mathew McKenna, of the Centers for Disease Control and Prevention, says the news isn't all bad. A 10 percent price increase reduced cigarette consumption by about 4 percent.

Source: News accounts of April 2009.

NOTE: Higher prices reduce quantity demanded. How much? It depends on the price elasticity of demand.
注：提价会使需求量降低。降低多少取决于需求的价格弹性。

Although the average adult smoker is not very responsive to changes in cigarette prices, teen smokers apparently are: Teen smoking drops by almost 7 percent when cigarette prices increase by 10 percent. Thus the price elasticity of *teen* demand for smoking is

$$E = \frac{\text{percent drop in quantity demanded}}{\text{percent increase in price}} = \frac{-7\%}{+10\%} = -0.7$$

Hence higher cigarette prices can be an effective policy tool for curbing teen smoking. The decline in teen smoking after the 2009 tax increase confirms this expectation.

According to Table 3.1, the demand for airline travel is even more price elastic. Whenever a fare cut is announced, the airlines get swamped with telephone inquiries. If fares are discounted by 25 percent, the number of passengers may increase by as much as 60 percent. As Table 3.1 shows, the elasticity of airline demand is 2.4, meaning that the percentage change in quantity demanded (60 percent) will be 2.4 times larger than the price cut (25 percent). The price elasticity of demand for the iPhone 8 wasn't that large in 2018, according to the News Wire "Price Elasticity," but iPhone 8 sales still increased a lot in response to Apple's price cut on that phone.

Price Elasticity and Total Revenue 价格弹性和总收益

The concept of price elasticity refutes the popular misconception that producers charge the highest price possible. Except in the rare case of completely inelastic demand ($E = 0$), this notion makes no sense. Indeed, higher prices may actually *reduce* total sales revenue.

The **total revenue** of a seller is the amount of money received from product sales. It is determined by the quantity of the product sold and the price at which it is sold. Specifically,

价格弹性的概念有力驳斥了这样一种普遍存在的误解，即生产商总是给商品制定尽可能高的价格。除非在商品完全没有价格弹性（$E = 0$）这样极其特殊的情况下，否则这样的定价策略一般是不明智的。事实上，更高的价格反而可能会降低总的销售收入。

卖者的**总收益**是指卖者出售商品得到的货币数量。总收益取决于售出商品的数量和价格。

Total revenue = price × quantity sold

If the price of popcorn is 25 cents per ounce and 12 ounces are sold (point *F* in Figure 3.4), total revenue equals $3.00 per show. This total revenue is illustrated by the shaded rectangle in Figure 3.4. (Recall that the area of a rectangle is equal to its height, *p*, times its width, *q*.)

Effect of a Price Cut 降价的影响

Now consider what happens to total revenue when the price of popcorn is reduced. Will total revenue decline along with the price? Maybe not. Remember the law of demand: As price falls, the quantity demanded *increases*. Hence total revenue *might* actually *increase* when the price of popcorn is reduced. Whether it does or not depends on *how much* quantity demanded goes up when price goes down. This brings us back to the concept of elasticity.

Suppose we reduce popcorn prices from 25 cents to only 20 cents per ounce. What happens to total revenue? We know from Figure 3.4 that total revenue at point *F* was $3.00. When the price drops to 20 cents, unit sales increase significantly (to 16 ounces). In fact, they increase so much that total revenue actually increases as well. Total revenue at point *G* ($3.20) is larger than at point *F* ($3.00). Because total revenue *rose* when price *fell*, demand must be *elastic* in this price range. (See the last column in Table 3.2.)

现在考虑爆米花降价后总收益如何变化。总收益会随之下降吗？也许不会。我们回忆一下需求法则：随着价格的下降，需求量上升。因此，总收益事实上可能随着爆米花价格的下降而增长。总收益是增长还是下降取决于价格下降时需求量变化多少。这就把我们带回到需求的价格弹性概念上。

---

swamp 使应接不暇。teen 青少年。

Total revenue can't continue rising as price falls. At the extreme, price would fall to zero, and there would be no revenue. So somewhere along the demand curve falling prices will begin to pinch total revenue. In Figure 3.4 this happens when the price of popcorn drops from 20 cents to 15 cents. Unit sales again increase (from 16 to 20 ounces) but not enough to compensate for the price decline. As a result, total revenue at point H ($3.00) is less than at point G ($3.20). Total revenue falls in this case because the consumer response to a price reduction is small compared to the size of the price cut. In other words, demand is price *inelastic*.

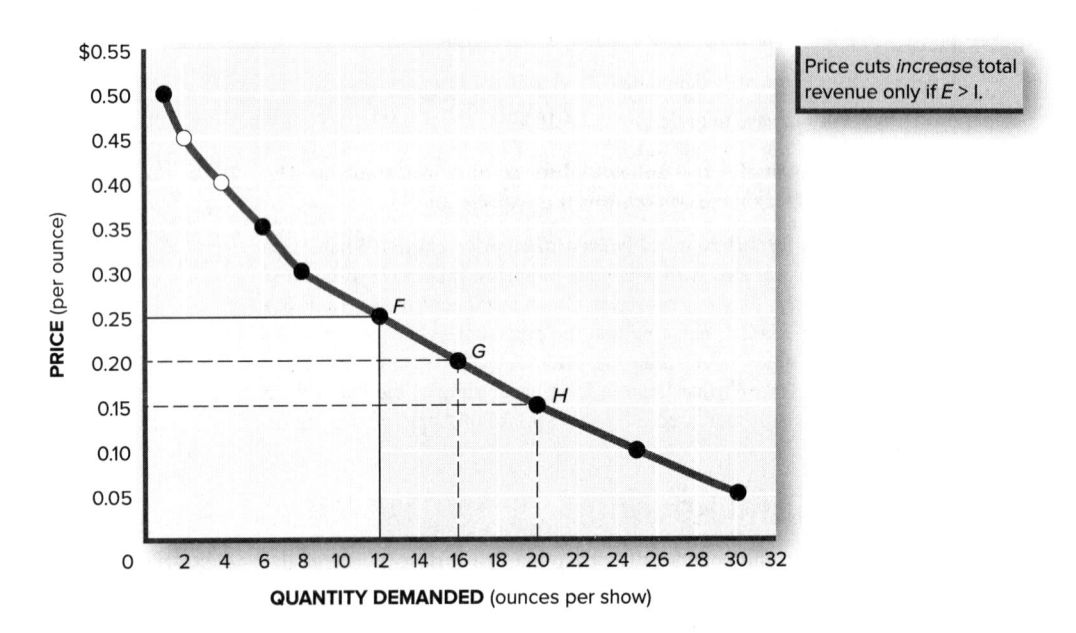

Price cuts *increase* total revenue only if $E > 1$.

	Price	×	Quantity Demanded	=	Total Revenue
A	$0.50		1		$0.50
B	0.45		2		0.90
C	0.40		4		1.60
D	0.35		6		2.10
E	0.30		8		2.40
F	0.25		12		3.00
G	0.20		16		3.20
H	0.15		20		3.00
I	0.10		25		2.50
J	0.05		30		1.50

Total revenue increasing as price drops.

Total revenue decreasing as price drops.

Figure 3.4 Elasticity and Total Revenue Total revenue is equal to the price of the product times the quantity sold. It is illustrated by the area of the rectangle formed by $p \times q$. The shaded rectangle illustrates total revenue ($3.00) at a price of 25 cents and a quantity demanded of 12 ounces.

When price is reduced to 20 cents, the rectangle and total revenue expand (see the dashed lines connected to point G) because demand is elastic ($E > 1$) in that price range.

Price cuts reduce total revenue only if demand is inelastic ($E < 1$), as it is here for prices below 20 cents (compare the total revenue at points G and H).

If Demand Is:	When Price Increases, Total Revenue Will:	When Price Decreases, Total Revenue Will:
Elastic (E > 1)	Decrease	Increase
Inelastic (E < 1)	Increase	Decrease
Unitary elastic (E = 1)	Not change	Not change

Table 3.2 Price Elasticity of Demand and Total Revenue The impact of higher prices on total revenue depends on the price elasticity of demand. Higher prices result in higher total revenue only if demand is inelastic. If demand is elastic, *higher* prices result in *lower* revenues. ■

Thus we can conclude that

- *A price cut reduces total revenue if demand is inelastic (E < 1).*
- *A price cut increases total revenue if demand is elastic (E > 1).*
- *A price cut does not change total revenue if demand is unitary elastic (E = 1).*

Table 3.2 summarizes these responses as well as responses to price increases.

- 如果需求缺乏价格弹性（E <1），降价会减少总收益。
- 如果需求富有价格弹性（E >1），降价会增加总收益。
- 如果需求具有单一价格弹性（E = 1），降价不会引起总收益的变化。

Once we know the price elasticity of demand, we can predict how consumers will respond to changing prices. We can also predict what will happen to total revenue when a seller raises or lowers the price. Presumably Starbucks performed these calculations before increasing coffee prices in 2018 (see the News Wire "Inelastic Demand").

NEWS WIRE INELASTIC DEMAND

A STARBUCKS JAVA JOLT JUST GOT MORE EXPENSIVE

Starbucks announced today that it is increasing the price of its brewed coffee by 10–20 cents a cup, or about 9 percent. A "tall" cup of java will now cost $1.95 to $2.15 in Starbucks' 8,000 U.S. locations. The company said the price increase was justified by rising costs, including rent and labor.

Analysts predicted that the price hike wouldn't deter most customers, as company loyalty is extremely high. Whatever sales might be lost for price-sensitive customers would be more than offset by higher revenues from loyal customers. The company's stock rose after the announcement.

Source: News accounts of June 7–9, 2018.

©Deposit Photos/Glow Images

NOTE: The impact of a price increase on unit sales and total revenue depends on the price elasticity of demand. Starbucks was counting on *in*elastic demand when it increased its prices in 2018.
注：涨价对单位销售额和总收益的影响取决于需求的价格弹性。星巴克在2018年涨价靠的就是需求缺乏弹性。

Determinants of Price Elasticity 价格弹性的决定因素

Table 3.1 indicates the actual price elasticity for a variety of familiar goods and services. These large differences in elasticity are explained by several factors.

Necessities versus Luxuries 必需品与奢侈品

Some goods are so critical to our everyday life that we regard them as necessities. A hairbrush, toothpaste, and perhaps textbooks might fall into this category. Our taste for such goods is so strong that we can't imagine getting along without them. As a result, we don't change our consumption of necessities much when the price increases; ***demand for necessities is relatively inelastic.***

必需品的需求相对缺乏价格弹性。

---

offset 抵消。 loyal 忠诚的。 category 种类，类别。

奢侈品的需求相对富有价格弹性。

A luxury good, by contrast, is something we'd *like* to have but aren't likely to buy unless our income jumps or the price declines sharply; vacation travel, new cars, and 4K television sets are examples. We want them, but we can get by without them. Thus ***demand for luxury goods is relatively elastic.***

Availability of Substitutes 替代品的可得性

Our notion of what goods are necessities is also influenced by the availability of substitute goods. The high elasticity of demand for fish recorded in Table 3.1 reflects the fact that consumers can always eat tofu, chicken, beef, or pork if fish prices rise. On the other hand, most coffee drinkers cannot imagine any substitute for a cup of coffee. As a consequence, when coffee prices rise, consumers do not reduce their purchases very much at all. Likewise, the low elasticity of demand for gasoline reflects the fact that most cars can't run on alternative fuels. In general, ***the greater the availability of substitutes, the higher the price elasticity of demand.*** This is a principle that San Francisco learned when it introduced a "butt tax" of 20 cents per pack of cigarettes in 2009 (see the accompanying News Wire "Substitute Goods"). In-city sales declined as smokers turned to adjoining states and cities, Indian reservations, and the Internet for their cigarette purchases. There were lots of substitutes for cigarettes sold (and taxed) in San Francisco.

一般说来，一种商品的替代品的可得性越大，这种商品的需求价格弹性就越大。

NEWS WIRE SUBSTITUTE GOODS

SAN FRANCISCO: THE BUTTS STOP HERE

San Francisco mayor Gavin Newsom says there are far too many butts in the City by the Bay. Not human butts, of course, but cigarette butts. Picking up the discarded butts costs the city $6 million a year. To make careless smokers pay these cleanup costs, he levied a tax of 20 cents on every pack of cigarettes sold in the city, effective October 2009. With 30 million packs being sold in the city annually, the 20 cent "fee" looked high enough to cover the costs of the butt cleanup ($6 million).

Mayor Gavin shouldn't count those chickens before they hatch. The only way the new 20-cent fee can generate $6 million a year is if San Franciscans continue to purchase 30 million packs per year. That just isn't going to happen. The law of demand is more powerful than the laws of San Francisco, and the law of demand clearly states that the quantity demanded goes down when price goes up. Finding substitute goods for San Francisco cigarettes is easy. Buy a carton of cigarettes in the neighboring communities of Daly City, Oakland, or Sausalito and you save $2.00. Buy cigarettes online from an Indian reservation (which does not pay federal or state taxes) and save even more. As a quick search on Google or Yahoo will confirm, over 2,000 websites offer to facilitate those untaxed shipments. So untaxed substitutes for San Francisco cigarettes are literally only a click away. Mayor Gavin should have consulted New York City Mayor Michael Bloomberg, who saw in-city cigarette sales plunge by 50 percent when he raised that city's tax in 2002.

—Bradley Schiller

Source: Bradley Schiller, "San Francisco: The Butts Stop Here," *The Economy Today News Flash*, August 2009.

NOTE: Demand for cigarettes in general is inelastic. However, demand for San Francisco's cigarettes is elastic because smokers can purchase cigarettes elsewhere.
注：香烟需求一般是缺乏价格弹性的。不过，旧金山的香烟之所以富有价格弹性，是因为烟民能够从其他地方买到香烟。

Price Relative to Income 相对于收入的价格

Another important determinant of elasticity is the price of the good itself. If the price of a product is very high in relation to the consumer's income, then price *changes* will be important. Airline travel and new cars, for example, are quite expensive, so even a small percentage change in their prices can have a big impact on a consumer's budget (and consumption decisions). The demand for such big-ticket items tends to be elastic. By contrast, coffee is so cheap for most people that even a large *percentage* change in price doesn't affect consumer behavior much. Starbucks loves that math.

---

butt tax 烟头税。facilitate 使便利。plunge 突然下降。

Other Changes in Consumer Behavior 消费者行为的其他变化

We stated at the outset of this discussion that we were going to focus on the *price* of a product and its quantity demanded. So we ignored everything else. It's time, however, to consider other influences on consumer behavior.

Substitute Goods 替代品

When Hurricane Harvey sent gasoline prices higher in August 2017, consumers cut back on their driving. So how did they get around? In part, they simply traveled less, but they also made more use of public transportation like buses, subways, and trains. Thus public transportation became a *substitute* for higher gas prices and private transportation. **The demand for substitute goods increases (shifts to the right) when the price of a product goes up.** When movie theater prices go up, the demand for streaming movies (e.g., Netflix) and DVDs increases. When airfares go down, the demand for bus and rail travel decreases. When Starbucks raised its prices in 2018, demand for Dunkin' Donuts coffee increased.

当某种商品的价格上升时，其替代商品的需求量增加（向右移）。当电影票价格上升时，对流媒体电影（如 Netflix）和 DVD 的需求量就会上升；当机票价格下降时，对汽车和火车旅行的需求随之下降。当星巴克在 2018 年提价时，对唐恩都乐咖啡的需求随之增加。

Complementary Goods 互补品

Plunging oil prices in 2015 had a very different effect. When gasoline prices dropped below $3 a gallon in early 2015, people drove more and bought more gas (the law of demand). But they also bought more trucks and gas-guzzling SUVs. The demand for pick-up trucks and SUVs *increased* when gasoline prices *decreased*. Light trucks and gasoline are *complementary goods*, not substitute goods. If the demand for another good moves in the opposite direction (up or down) of the price of a product, the two goods are *complements* (e.g., gas prices go *down*, truck demand goes *up*). Hybrid and electric cars didn't fare so well when gasoline prices fell in 2015. As the accompanying News Wire "Substitutes vs. Complementary Goods" affirms, the demand for hybrid cars *fell* when gasoline prices *fell*. When the demand for one product moves in the same direction as the price of another good, the goods are substitutes (e.g., gas prices go *down*, hybrid demand goes *down*).

The important thing to notice here is that *a change in the price of one product will affect not only the quantity of that product demanded (as measured by price elasticity) but also the demand for other goods* (substitute goods and complementary goods). This is why auto manufacturers worry a lot about gasoline prices and record companies worry about the price of music downloads.

这里要注意的重要一点是，一种商品价格的变化不仅会影响该商品的需求量（由价格弹性衡量），而且会影响其他商品的需求量（替代品和互补品）。这就是为什么汽车制造商担心汽油价格、唱片公司担心音乐下载价格的原因。

NEWS WIRE **SUBSTITUTE VS. COMPLEMENTARY GOODS**

FALLING GAS PRICES JUMP-START AUTO SALES

Detroit. U.S. auto sales jumped last year to a record 17.4 million vehicles. Falling prices at the pump were a major catalyst for the banner sales. The average price for regular gasoline fell from $3.44 per gallon in 2014 to $2.52 this year, a 27 percent decline. That price plunge benefited SUV and pick-up truck sales the most, with unit sales jumping 11.5 percent. But electric vehicles suffered, with EV sales declining 6 percent. The data again confirm that the price of gasoline is a critical factor in auto sales, especially what kind of vehicle to purchase.

©Philipus/Alamy Stock Photo

Source: Auto industry reports, January 2016.

NOTE: Changes in the price of one good will affect the demand for other goods. Lower gasoline prices increase the demand for pickup trucks and SUVs (complementary goods) and decrease the demand for hybrids (a substitute good).

注：一种商品价格的变化会影响人们对其他商品的需求。汽油价格下降增加了对皮卡和 SUV（互补品）的需求，降低了对混合动力车（替代品）的需求。

Changes in Income 收入变化

如果收入发生了变化，情况会有所不同。如果我们的收入增加了，在任何价格上我们都能购买更多商品。我们用需求曲线的移动来解释收入的变化，而不是沿着曲线移动（这是由价格变化引起的）。当经济进入衰退期时，人们失去工作和收入，对多数商品——尤其是昂贵商品，例如汽车、度假和新房子的需求将会下降（需求曲线向左移动）。在经济更繁荣的时期，收银机则忙个不停。

Auto manufacturers and record companies would worry less if consumers had more money to spend. As we observed earlier, income is a *determinant* of demand. Our analysis of the demand curve was based on the *ceteris paribus* assumption that only *one* thing was changing—namely, price. This assumption allowed us to observe how price changes propel consumers up and down the demand curve, altering both unit sales and total revenue.

The picture would look different if *incomes* were to change. If our incomes increased, we could buy *more* products at every price. **We illustrate income changes with shifts of the demand curve** rather than movements along it (due to changes in price). When the economy falls into a recession and people are losing jobs and income, demand for most products—especially big-ticket items like cars, vacations, and new homes—declines (shifts left). In more prosperous times, cash registers keep humming.

POLICY PERSPECTIVES

DOES ADVERTISING CHANGE OUR BEHAVIOR?

Marketing people have been quick to recognize the importance of demand curve *shifts*. Producers can't change consumer incomes, but what about the other determinants of demand? Wasn't *tastes* one of those determinants?

A whole new range of profit opportunities suddenly appears. If producers can change consumers' tastes, they can *shift* the demand curve and sell *more* output at *higher* prices. How will they do this? By advertising. As noted earlier, psychiatrists see us as complex bundles of basic drives, anxieties, and layers of consciousness. They presume that we enter the market with confused senses of guilt, insecurity, and ambition. Economists, on the other hand, regard the consumer as the rational *Homo economicus,* aware of his or her wants and knowledgeable about how to satisfy them. In reality, however, we do not always know what we want or which products will satisfy us. This uncertainty creates a vacuum into which the advertising industry has eagerly stepped.

The efforts of producers to persuade us to buy, buy, buy are as close as the nearest television, radio, magazine, web page, or billboard. American producers now spend over $200 *billion* per year to change our tastes. This spending works out to over $400 per consumer, the highest per capita advertising rates in the world. Much of this advertising (including product labeling) is intended to provide information about existing products or to bring new products to our attention. A great deal of advertising, however, is also designed to exploit our senses and lack of knowledge. Recognizing that we are guilt-ridden, insecure, and sex-hungry, advertisers offer us pictures and promises of exoneration, recognition, and love: All we have to do is buy the right product.

One of the favorite targets of advertisers is our sense of insecurity. Brand images are developed to give consumers a sense of identity. Smoke a Marlboro cigarette, and you're a virile cowboy. Drink the right beer or vodka, and you'll be a social success. Use the right perfume, and you'll be irresistibly sexy. Wear Brand X jeans, and you'll be way cool. Or at least that's what advertisers want you to believe.

ARE WANTS CREATED?

Advertising cannot be blamed for all of our "foolish" consumption. Even members of the most primitive tribes, uncontaminated by the seductions of advertising, adorn themselves with rings, bracelets, and pendants. Furthermore, advertising has grown to massive proportions only in the last 50 years, but consumption spending has been increasing throughout recorded history.

Although advertising cannot be charged with creating our needs, it does encourage specific outlets for satisfying those needs. The objective of all advertising is to alter the choices we make. Advertising seeks to increase our desire (taste) for particular products and therewith our willingness to pay. **A successful advertising campaign is one that shifts the demand curve for a product to the right,** inducing consumers to increase their purchases of a product at every price (see Figure 3.5). Advertising may also increase brand loyalty, making the demand curve less elastic, thereby reducing consumer responses to price increases.

---

propel 推动，促使。

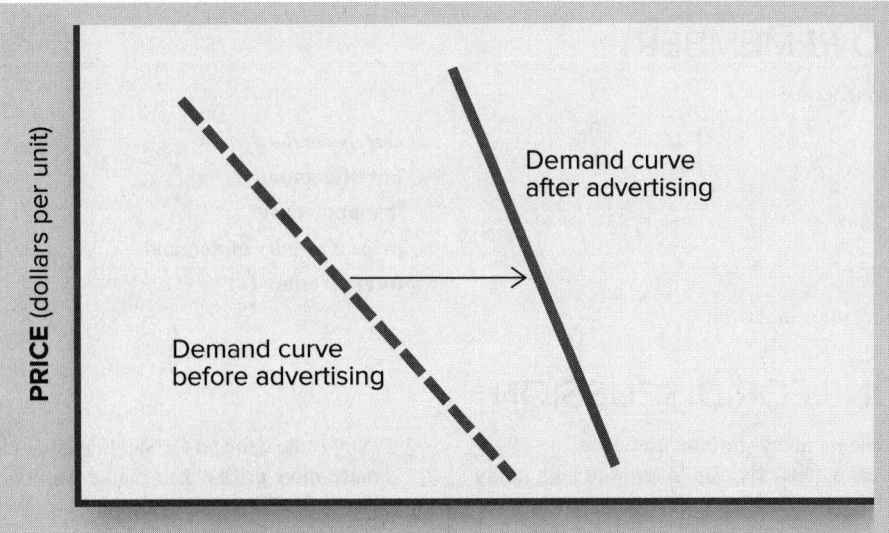

Figure 3.5 The Impact of Advertising on a Demand Curve Advertising seeks to increase our taste for a particular product. If our taste (the product's perceived marginal utility) increases, so will our willingness to buy. The resulting change in demand is reflected in a rightward shift of the demand curve, often accompanied by a diminished price elasticity of demand.

CHAPTER 3 REVIEW

SUMMARY

- Our desires for goods and services originate in the structure of personality and social dynamics and are not explained by economic theory. Economic theory focuses on *demand*—that is, our ability and willingness to buy specific quantities of a good or service at various prices. **LO1**
- *Utility* refers to the satisfaction we get from consumer goods and services. *Total utility* refers to the amount of satisfaction associated with all consumption of a product. *Marginal utility* refers to the satisfaction obtained from the last unit of a product. **LO1**
- The law of diminishing marginal utility says that the more of a product we consume, the smaller the increments of pleasure we get from each additional unit. This is the foundation for the law of demand. **LO1**
- The price elasticity of demand (E) is a numerical measure of consumer response to a change in price (*ceteris paribus*). It equals the percentage change in quantity demanded divided by the percentage change in price. **LO2**
- If demand is elastic ($E > 1$), a small change in price induces a large change in quantity demanded. "Elastic" demand indicates that consumers are very price sensitive. **LO2**
- If demand is *elastic*, a price increase will reduce total revenue. Price and total revenue move in the *same* direction only if demand is *inelastic*. **LO3**
- The shape and position of any particular demand curve depend on a consumer's income, tastes, expectations, and the price and availability of other goods. Should any of these things change, the assumption of *ceteris paribus* will no longer hold, and the demand curve will shift. **LO4**
- Advertising seeks to change consumer tastes and thus the willingness to buy. If tastes do change, the demand curve will shift. **LO5**

TERMS TO REMEMBER

Define the following terms:

demand
market demand
utility
total utility
marginal utility
law of diminishing marginal utility

ceteris paribus
law of demand
demand curve
price elasticity of demand
total revenue

QUESTIONS FOR DISCUSSION

1. Why do people routinely stuff themselves at all-you-can-eat buffets? Explain in terms of both utility and demand theories. **LO1**
2. What does the demand for education at your college look like? What is on each axis? Is the demand elastic or inelastic? How could you find out? **LO1**
3. What would happen to unit sales and total revenue for this textbook if the publisher reduced its price? **LO3**
4. Should Starbucks have increased its prices in 2018? Should it raise prices again? (See the News Wire "Inelastic Demand.") **LO4**
5. Identify three goods for which your demand is (*a*) elastic and (*b*) inelastic. What accounts for the differences in elasticity? **LO2**
6. Utility companies routinely ask state commissions for permission to raise utility rates. What does this suggest about the price elasticity of demand? Why is demand so (in)elastic? **LO3**
7. Why is the demand for San Francisco cigarettes so much more price elastic than the overall market demand for cigarettes (see the News Wire "Substitute Goods")? **LO4**
8. When gasoline prices go up, how is demand for the following products affected: (*a*) SUVs; (*b*) electric cars; (*c*) beach hotels; (*d*) Netflix? **LO4**
9. What goods do people buy a lot more of when their incomes go up? What goods are unaffected by income changes? **LO4**
10. If Apple cuts the price of the iWatch, what will happen to (*a*) unit sales and (*b*) total revenue? (*c*) Should Apple do it? **LO3**
11. **POLICY PERSPECTIVES** If *all* soda advertisements were banned, how would Pepsi sales be affected? How about total soda consumption? **LO5**

PROBLEMS

1. *a.* In Figure 3.2, which box of popcorn first shows diminished marginal utility?
   b. In the cartoon "You can have too much of a good thing," which pizza slice first yields negative marginal utility? **LO1**
2. Using the demand schedule below, plot the demand curve on the graph and answer four questions about demand and elasticity: **LO3**

Price (per pair)	$120	$100	$80	$60	$40
Quantity demanded (in pairs per year)	6	10	15	20	26

   a. Illustrate the demand curve on the following graph.
   b. How much will consumers spend on shoes at the price of (i) $120, (ii) $100, (iii) $80, (iv) $60, (v) $40?
   c. As the price drops from $120 to $100 a pair, is demand elastic, unitary elastic, or inelastic?
   d. As the price drops from $80 to $60 a pair, is demand elastic, unitary elastic, or inelastic?
   e. As the price drops from $60 to $40 a pair, is demand elastic, unitary elastic, or inelastic?

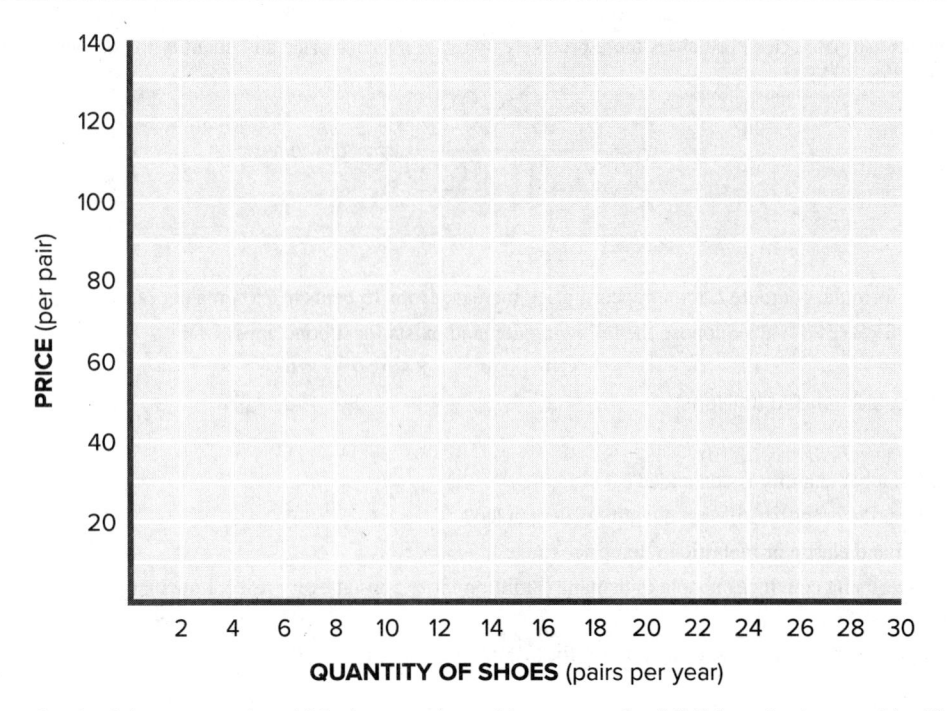

3. According to the elasticity computation, (a) by how much would popcorn sales fall if the price increased by 10 percent? (b) By 30 percent? **LO2**

4. According to Table 3.1, if price increases by 10 percent, how much will unit sales decline for (a) coffee, (b) shoes, and (c) airline travel? Will total revenue increase or decrease for (d) coffee, (e) shoes, (f) airline travel? **LO3**

5. (a) According to Table 3.1, by how much would coffee sales decline if the price of coffee increased 10 percent? (b) If your local coffee shop raised *its* coffee prices by the same amount (10 percent), would sales decline by more, less, or the same amount as calculated in part *a*? **LO4**

6. According to the News Wire "Tax Hikes and Demand," the average cigarette price rose by 12 percent on April 1, 2009. According to the story, by what percentage might smoking be expected to decline? **LO2**

7. Suppose the following table reflects the total satisfaction (utility) derived from eating pizza: **LO1**

Quantity consumed	1	2	3	4	5	6	7
Total utility	47	92	122	135	137	120	70

   a. What is the marginal utility of each pizza?
   b. When does marginal utility first diminish?
   c. When does marginal utility first turn negative?

8. According to the News Wire "Inelastic Demand," LO3
   a. by what percent did Starbucks raise brewed coffee prices?
   b. If unit sales didn't decline at all, what would the price elasticity of demand have been?
   Now, suppose unit sales fell by 2 percent.
   c. Calculate price elasticity.
   d. Would demand be elastic or inelastic?
   e. Would total revenue have increased decreased?

9. According to the News Wire "Price Elasticity," what was the price elasticity of demand for the iPhone 8? **LO2**

10. Economists estimate price elasticities more precisely by using *average* price and quantity to compute percentage changes. Thus, **LO3**

$$E = \frac{Q_2 - Q_1}{\frac{Q_1 + Q_2}{2}} \div \frac{P_2 - P_1}{\frac{P_1 + P_2}{2}}, \text{ in absolute value}$$

Using this formula, compute E for a popcorn price increase from 15 cents to 25 cents per ounce (Figure 3.4).

11. **POLICY PERSPECTIVES** Suppose the following demand exists for iPhone apps: **LO5**

Price	$10	9	8	7	6	5	4	3
Quantity demanded (millions)	2	3	4	5	6	7	8	9

   a. At $9, what quantity is demanded?
   b. If the price drops to $6, what quantity is demanded?
   c. Is demand elastic or inelastic in that price range?
   d. If advertising convinces people to demand 3 million more apps at every price, how many apps will be demanded at a price of $9?
   e. Graph the above answers, using point A for (a), point B for (b), and point C for (d).

CHAPTER FOUR

Supply Decisions 供给决策

©Heorshe/Alamy Stock Photo

LEARNING OBJECTIVES

After reading this chapter, you should be able to:

1. Explain what the production function reveals.
2. Explain why the law of diminishing returns applies.
3. Describe the nature of fixed, variable, and marginal costs.
4. Illustrate the difference between production and investment decisions.
5. Discuss how accounting costs and economic costs differ.

Most consumers think that producers reap huge profits from every market sale. Most producers wish that were true. The average producer earns a profit of only four to six cents on every sales dollar. And those profits don't come easily. Producers earn a profit only if they make the correct supply decisions. They have to keep a close eye on prices and costs and produce the right quantity at the right time. If they do all the right things, they *might* make a profit. Even when a producer does everything right, however, profits are not assured. Over 50,000 U.S. businesses fail every year despite their owners' best efforts to make a profit.

In this chapter we look at markets from the supply side, examining two distinct concerns. First, how much output *can* a firm produce? Second, how much output will it *want* to produce? As we'll see, the answers to these two questions are rarely the same.

The question of how much *can* be produced is largely an engineering and managerial problem. The question of how much *should* be produced is an *economic* issue. If costs escalate as capacity is approached, it might make sense to produce less than capacity output. In some situations, the costs of production might even be so high that it doesn't make sense to produce *any* output from available facilities. The end result will be a **supply** decision—that is, an expressed *ability* and *willingness* to produce a good at various prices.

supply
The ability and willingness to sell (produce) specific quantities of a good at alternative prices in a given time period, *ceteris paribus*.

A producer's supply decision is similar to your homework decision. The amount of homework you *could* do in the next two hours is determined by available resources (e.g., brain power, computer access, tutorial help, space). How much homework you *actually* do ("produce") will be determined by how you *choose* to use your time. You rarely produce at capacity, and neither do business firms: They *choose* how much of their capacity to utilize.

---

reap 收获，从……获得（利润）。escalate 逐步提高。

Chapter Four: Supply Decisions

This chapter focuses on those *supply* decisions. We look first at the capacity to produce and then at how choices are made about how much of that capacity to utilize. The discussion revolves around three questions:

- What limits a firm's ability to produce?
- What costs are incurred in producing a good?
- How do costs affect supply decisions?

Once we have answered these questions, we should be able to understand how supply-side forces affect the price and availability of the goods and services we demand in product markets.

产能约束：生产函数
CAPACITY CONSTRAINTS: THE PRODUCTION FUNCTION

无论规模大小，所有者是谁，企业全都面临同一个核心问题：生产商品需要资源。农民生产玉米需要土地、水、种子、设备和劳动力。牙医补牙需要一把椅子、一台钻孔机、一定的空间和劳动力。甚至教育服务（例如这节经济学课）的"生产"也需要利用劳动力（你的老师）、土地（学校用地）和一些资本（砖、灰浆或电子教室）。简而言之，除非你正在生产的是未经提炼、未经包装的空气，否则你都需要**生产要素**，也就是可以用来生产商品或服务的资源。

No matter how large a business is or who owns it, all businesses confront one central fact: You need resources to produce goods. To produce corn, a farmer needs land, water, seed, equipment, and labor. To produce fillings, a dentist needs a chair, a drill, some space, and labor. Even the "production" of educational services (e.g., this economics class) requires the use of labor (your teacher), land (on which the school is built), and some capital (bricks and mortar or electronic classrooms). In short, unless you are producing unrefined, unpackaged air, you need **factors of production**—that is, resources that can be used to produce a good or service.

The factors of production used to produce a good or service provide the basic measure of economic cost. If someone asked you what the cost of your econ class was, you'd probably quote the tuition you paid for it. But tuition is the *price of consuming* the course, not the *cost of producing* it. The cost of producing your economics class is measured by the amounts of land, labor, and capital it requires. These are *resource* costs of production.

The first question a producer must ask is: How many resources are actually needed to produce a given product? You could use a lot of resources to produce a product or perhaps just a few. What we really want to know is how *best* to produce the product. What is the *smallest* amount of resources needed? Or we could ask the same question from a different perspective: What is the *maximum* amount of output attainable from a given quantity of input resources?

These aren't easy questions to answer. But if we knew the technology of the production process, we could come up with an answer. The answer would tell us the *maximum* amount of output attainable from a given quantity of resources. These limits to the production of any good are reflected in the **production function**. The production function tells us the maximum amount of good X producible from various combinations of factor inputs. With one chair and one drill, a dentist can fill a maximum of 32 cavities per day. With two chairs, a drill, and an assistant, a dentist can fill up to 55 cavities per day.

如果企业全力生产，我们想知道利用可得资源究竟能生产多少条牛仔裤。为使问题简化，我们假定厂房已经建成，并且假定只有一台租赁的缝纫机可用。因此，土地和资本投入是固定的。在这种情况下，只有劳动力数量可变。我们能够生产的牛仔裤数量直接取决于雇用的劳动力数量。生产函数的目的正是告诉我们，利用不同数量的要素投入所能生产的最大产出。图4.1提供了牛仔裤生产的相关信息。

A production function is a technological summary of our ability to produce a particular good. It's not about economics, it's about technology. Figure 4.1 provides a partial glimpse of one such function. In this case, the desired output is designer jeans, as produced by Tight Jeans Corporation. The essential inputs in the production of jeans are land, labor (garment workers), and capital (a factory and sewing machines). With these inputs, Tight Jeans can produce and sell fancy jeans to status-conscious consumers.

As in all production endeavors, we want to know how many pairs of jeans we can produce with available resources. To make things easy, we will assume that the factory is already built. We will also assume that only one leased sewing machine is available. Thus both land and capital inputs are fixed. Under these circumstances, only the quantity of labor can be varied. In this case, the quantity of jeans we can produce depends directly on the amount of labor we employ. *The purpose of a production function is to tell us just how much output we can produce with varying amounts of factor inputs.* Figure 4.1 provides such information for jeans production.

---

price of consuming 消费价格。 perspective 视角，观点。 attainable 可达到的。 glimpse 概况。 garment 衣服，服装。 fancy 精美的，花哨的。

Column A of the table in Figure 4.1 confirms the obvious: You can't manufacture jeans without any workers. Even though land, capital (an empty factory and an idle machine), and denim are available, essential labor inputs are missing, and jeans production is impossible. Maybe advances in robotics will change that reality. For now, however, the factory depicted in Figure 4.1 isn't nearly that advanced. It still needs live bodies in the production process.

Column B in the table shows what happens to jeans output when just one worker is employed. With only one machine and one worker, the jeans start rolling out the front door. Maximum output under these circumstances (row 2, column B) is 15 pairs of jeans per day. Now we're in business!

The remaining columns of the table tell us how many additional jeans we can produce if we hire more workers, while still leasing only one sewing machine. With one machine and two workers, maximum output rises to 34 pairs per day (column C). If a third worker is hired, output could increase to 44 pairs.

Labor is a vital but variable input in production.
©Rob Crandall/SCPhotos/Alamy Stock Photo

Short-Run Production Function

	A	B	C	D	E	F	G	H	I
Labor input (workers per day)	0	1	2	3	4	5	6	7	8
Output (pairs of jeans per day)	0	15	34	44	48	50	51	51	47

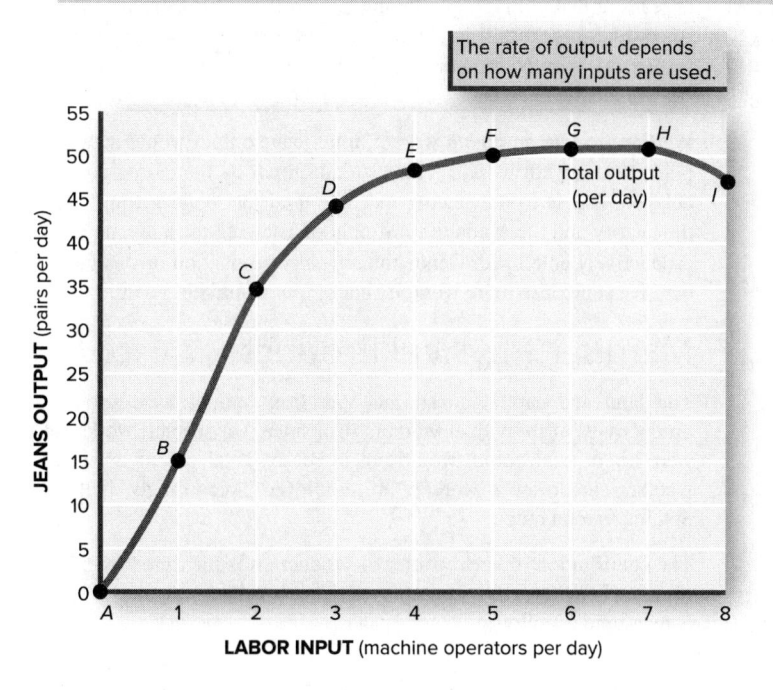

The rate of output depends on how many inputs are used.

Figure 4.1 A Production Function A production function tells us the *maximum* amount of output attainable from alternative combinations of factor inputs. This particular function tells us how many pairs of jeans we can produce in a factory that has only one sewing machine and varying quantities of labor.

With only one operator, we can produce a maximum of 15 pairs of jeans per day, as indicated in column B of the table and point *B* on the graph. To produce more jeans, we need more labor. The short-run production function shows how output changes when more labor is used.

denim 斜纹粗棉布，牛仔布。robotics 机器人学（技术）。

This information on our production capabilities is also illustrated graphically in Figure 4.1. Point A illustrates the fact that we can't produce any jeans without some labor. Points B through I show how production increases as additional labor is employed.

Efficiency 效率

Every point on the production function in Figure 4.1 represents the *most* output we could produce with a specific number of workers. Point D, for example, tells us we could produce as many as 44 pairs of jeans with three workers. We recognize, however, that we might also produce less. If the workers goof off or the sewing machine isn't maintained well, total output might be less than 44 pairs per day. In that case, we wouldn't be making the best possible use of scarce resources: We would be producing *inefficiently*. In Figure 4.1, this would imply a rate of output *below* point D. Only if we produce with maximum *efficiency* will we end up at point D or some other point on the production function. **All points on the production function represent efficient production.**

Capacity 生产能力

尽管生产函数强调了产出如何随着工人数量的增加而提高，但这种提高却不是无止境的。劳动力并不是生产牛仔裤所需的唯一要素，我们还需要资本。在本例中，我们只拥有一间小型厂房和一台缝纫机。如果我们持续雇用工人，将很快耗尽空间和可用设备。土地和资本的约束设定了潜在产出的上限。

Although the production function emphasizes how output increases with more workers, the progression can't go on forever. Labor isn't the only factor of production needed to produce jeans. We also need capital. In this case, we have only a small factory and one sewing machine. If we keep hiring workers, we will quickly run out of space and available equipment. ***Land and capital constraints place a ceiling on potential output.***

Notice in Figure 4.1 how total output peaks at point G. We can produce a total of 51 pairs of jeans at that point by employing six workers. What happens if we hire still more workers? According to Figure 4.1, if we employed a seventh worker, total output would not increase further. At point H, total output is still 51 pairs, just as it was at point G, when we hired only six workers.

Were we to hire an *eighth* worker, total jeans output would actually *decline*, as illustrated by point I. An eighth worker *reduces* total output by increasing congestion on the factory floor, delaying access to the sewing machine, and just plain getting in the way. Given the size of the factory and the availability of only one sewing machine, no more than six workers can be productively employed. Hence the *capacity* production of this factory is 51 pairs of jeans per day. We could hire more workers, but output would not go up.

Marginal Physical Product 边际物质产品

The land and capital constraints that limit output have some interesting effects on the productivity of individual workers. Consider that seventh worker at the jeans factory. If she were hired, total output would not increase: Total output is 51 pairs of jeans regardless of whether six or seven workers are employed. Accordingly, that seventh worker contributes nothing to total output.

每一名工人对生产的贡献，是用这名工人被雇用后带来的总产出的变化量来衡量的。这个概念被称为**边际物质产品**，可根据下述公式计算：

边际物质产品（MPP）= 总产出的变化量 / 投入量的变化量

The contribution of each worker to production is measured by the change in *total* output that occurs when the worker is employed. This is called **marginal physical product (MPP)** and it is measured as follows:

$$\text{Marginal physical product (MPP)} = \frac{\text{change in total output}}{\text{change in input quantity}}$$

In this case, total output doesn't change when the seventh worker is hired, so her MPP equals zero. She contributes nothing to production.

---

goof off 混日子，游手好闲。 inefficiently 缺乏效率的。 decline 下降。

Contrast that experience with that of the *first* worker hired. When the first worker is employed at the jeans factory, total output jumps from zero (point A in Figure 4.1) to 15 pairs of jeans per day (point B). This *increase* in output reflects the marginal physical product (MPP) of that first worker—that is, the *change* in total output that results from employment of one more unit of (labor) input.

If we employ a second operator, jeans output more than doubles to 34 pairs per day (point C). Whereas the marginal physical product of the first worker was only 15 pairs, a second worker increases total output by 19 pairs.

The higher MPP of the second worker raises a question about the first. Why was the first worker's MPP lower? Laziness? Is the second worker faster, less distracted, or harder working?

The higher MPP of the second worker is not explained by superior talents or effort. We assume in this exercise that all units of labor are equal—that is, one worker is just as good as another. Their different marginal products are explained by the structure of the production process, not by their respective abilities. The first garment worker had to not only sew jeans but also unfold bolts of denim, measure the jeans, sketch out the patterns, and cut them to approximate size. A lot of time was spent going from one task to another. Despite the worker's best efforts, this person simply could not do everything at once.

A second worker alleviates this situation. With two workers, less time is spent running from one task to another. Now there is an opportunity for each worker to specialize a bit. While one is measuring and cutting, the other can continue sewing. This improved *ratio* of labor to other factors of production results in the large jump in total output. The superior MPP of the second worker is not unique to this person: It would have occurred even if we had hired the workers in the reverse order. What matters is the amount of capital or land each unit of labor can work with. In other words, **a worker's productivity (MPP) depends in part on the amount of other resources in the production process.**

第2名工人缓解了这种情况。由于有了两名工人，工种转换过程中所浪费的时间减少。此时对于每一名工人而言，都有了专攻某项工作的机会。当一名工人测量和裁剪时，另一名工人可以继续缝纫。这样就提高了劳动力对其他生产要素的比率，从而使总产出大幅上升。第2名工人较高的MPP并非是她独有的：即使我们以相反的顺序雇用这两名工人，仍会发生同样的情况。关键在于每一单位劳动力所能使用的资本或土地的数量。换句话说，工人的生产力（MPP）部分取决于生产过程中其他资源的数量。

Law of Diminishing Returns 收益递减规律

Unfortunately, output cannot keep increasing at this rate. Look what happens when a third worker is hired. Total jeans production continues to increase. But the increase from point C to point D in Figure 4.1 is only 10 pairs per day. Hence the MPP of the third worker (10 pairs) is *less* than that of the second (19 pairs). Marginal physical product is *diminishing*.

Resource Constraints 资源约束

What accounts for this decline in MPP? The answer again lies in the ratio of labor to other factors of production. A third worker begins to crowd our facilities. We still have only one sewing machine. Two people cannot sew at the same time. As a result, some time is wasted as the operators wait for their turns at the machine. Even if they split up the various jobs, there will still be some downtime, since measuring and cutting are not as time-consuming as sewing. In this sense, we cannot make full use of a third worker. ***The relative scarcity of other inputs (capital and land) constrains the marginal physical product of labor.***

Resource constraints are even more evident when a fourth worker is hired. Total output increases again, but the increase this time is very small. With three workers, we got 44 pairs of jeans per day (point D); with four workers, we get a maximum of 48 pairs (point E). Thus the marginal physical product of the fourth worker is only four pairs of jeans. A fourth worker really begins to strain our productive capacity. There simply aren't enough machines to make productive use of so much labor.

是什么造成了MPP的下降呢？答案仍然与劳动力对其他生产要素的比率有关。从第3名工人开始，设备使用变得紧张，我们仍然只有一台缝纫机，两人不能同时使用。因此，由于工人们排队轮流使用机器而浪费了一些时间。即使他们分工进行不同的工作，仍然会有窝工现象，这是由于测量和裁剪的工作没有缝纫耗时。从这个角度讲，我们没有充分利用第3名工人。其他投入（资本和土地）的相对稀缺性限制了劳动力的边际物质产品。

Negative MPP 负的边际物质产品

If a seventh worker is hired, the operators get in each other's way, argue, and waste denim. As we observed earlier, total output does not increase at all when a seventh worker is hired. The MPP of the seventh worker is zero. The seventh worker is being wasted in the sense that she

---

distract 转移，分心。unfold 打开，铺开。diminish 递减，减少。

设备的紧张状况在大多数生产过程都会发生。短期内生产过程的特点是，可用土地和资本的数量固定。通常情况下，短期内唯一可变的要素是劳动力。然而，随着更多劳动力被雇用，分摊到每个劳动力的资本和土地减少了。这是个简单的除法：可用设备被越来越多的工人共享。到了某个点，这种矛盾变得尖锐起来。此时边际物质产品开始下降。这种情况非常普遍，从而构成经济规律的基础：**收益递减规律**。该规律指出，在既定的生产条件下，随着某种生产要素（如劳动力）的不断增加，其边际物质产品将在达到某点后开始下降。

contributes nothing to total output. At Tight Jeans, however, the company does not want to hire someone who doesn't contribute to output. And it certainly doesn't want to hire an *eighth* worker because total output actually *declines* from 51 pairs of jeans (point *H* in Figure 4.1) to 47 pairs (point *I*) when an eighth worker is hired. In other words, the eighth worker has a *negative* MPP.

The problem of crowded facilities applies to most production processes. In the short run, a production process is characterized by a fixed amount of available land and capital. Typically the only factor that can be varied in the short run is labor. Yet *as more labor is hired, each unit of labor has less capital and land to work with.* This is simple division: The available facilities are being shared by more and more workers. At some point, this constraint begins to pinch. When it does, marginal physical product starts to decline. This situation is so common that it is the basis for an economic principle: the **law of diminishing returns**. This law says that the marginal physical product of any factor of production (e.g., labor) will begin to diminish at some point as more of it is used in a given production setting.

You could put the law of diminishing returns to an easy test. Start a lawn-mowing service. Assuming you have only one electric mower and a few rakes, what will happen to total output (lawns mowed per day) as you hire more workers? How soon before marginal physical product reaches zero? Then visit a Starbucks outlet. How much would output (drinks per day) increase if it hired more baristas? What keeps output from increasing faster in the short run? Would marginal physical product decline as more baristas competed for access to the espresso machines?

有限的可用空间或设备是收益递减的原因。一旦我们购买或租赁了一间厂房，它就会对当前的牛仔裤生产构成约束。当作为投入的资本（如厂房和机器）固定时，我们所面临的就是**短期**生产问题。如果不存在土地或资本限制——我们可以建造或租赁任何规模的厂房，我们面临的就是长期决策问题。**长期**内我们还可以学习生产牛仔裤的更新、更先进的方法，从而提高生产能力。然而，我们暂时必须接受一个事实，即图4.1中的生产函数描述了牛仔裤生产的短期约束。我们的短期目标是尽可能充分利用已经获得的厂房。这是生产者每天面临的挑战。

Short Run versus Long Run 短期与长期

The limited availability of space or equipment is the cause of diminishing returns. Once we have purchased or leased a specific factory, it sets a limit to current jeans production. When such commitments to fixed inputs (e.g., the factory and machinery) exist, we are dealing with a **short-run** production problem. If no land or capital were in place—if we could build or lease any size factory—we would be dealing with a *long-run* decision. In the **long run** we might also learn new and better ways of making jeans and so increase our production capabilities. For the time being, however, we must accept the fact that the production function in Figure 4.1 defines the *short-run* limits to jeans production. Our short-run objective is to make the best possible use of the factory we have acquired. This is the challenge producers face every day.

---

mower 割草机。rake 耙子。

Cost of Producing Jeans (15 Pairs per Day)		
Resource Used ×	Unit Price =	Total Cost
1 factory	$100 per day	$100
1 sewing machine	20 per day	20
1 operator	80 per day	80
1.5 bolts of denim	30 per bolt	45
Total cost		$245

Table 4.1 The Total Costs of Production The total cost of producing a good equals the market value of all the resources used in its production. In this case, we have assumed that the production of 15 pairs of jeans per day requires resources worth $245.

COSTS OF PRODUCTION 生产成本

A production function tells us how much output a firm *could* produce with its existing plant and equipment. It doesn't tell us how much the firm will *want* to produce: that's an *economic* decision. The level of desired output depends on prices and costs. A firm *might* want to produce at capacity if the profit picture is bright enough. On the other hand, a firm might not produce *any* output if costs always exceed sales revenue. ***A firm's goal is to maximize profits, not production.*** The most desirable rate of output is the one that maximizes total **profit**—the difference between total revenue and total costs.

The production function, then, is just a starting point for supply decisions. To decide how much output to produce with that function, a firm must next examine the dollar costs of production.

Total Cost 总成本

The economic cost of producing a good is ultimately gauged by the amount of scarce resources used to produce it. In a market economy, however, we want a more convenient measure of cost. Instead of listing all the input quantities used, we want a single dollar figure. To get that dollar amount, we must identify all the resources used in production, compute their value, and then add everything up. The end result will be a dollar figure for the **total cost** of production.

In the production of jeans, the resources used include land, labor, and capital. Table 4.1 identifies these resources, their unit values, and the total costs associated with their use. This table is based on an assumed output of 15 pairs of jeans per day, with the use of one machine operator and one sewing machine (point *B* in Figure 4.1). The rent on the factory is $100 per day, a sewing machine costs $20 per day, and the wages of a garment worker are $80 per day. We will assume Tight Jeans Corporation can purchase bolts of denim for $30 apiece, each of which provides enough denim for 10 pairs of jeans. In other words, one-tenth of a bolt ($3 worth of material) is required for one pair of jeans. We will ignore any other potential expenses. With these assumptions, the total cost of producing 15 pairs of jeans per day amounts to $245, as shown in Table 4.1.

Fixed Costs 固定成本

Total costs will change, of course, as we alter the rate of production. But not all costs increase. In the short run, some costs don't increase at all when output is increased. These are **fixed costs** in the sense that they do not vary with the rate of output. The factory lease is an example. Once you lease a factory, you are obligated to pay for it whether you use it or not. The person who owns the factory wants $100 per day. Even if you produce no jeans, you still have to pay that rent. That is the essence of fixed costs.

---

lease 租赁。 obligate 使负义务，迫使。

生产函数告诉我们，企业借助现有厂房和设备能够生产多少产出，但是并没有为我们回答，企业愿意生产多少产出：这是一个经济决策。合意的产出水平取决于价格和成本。如果获利前景明朗，企业可能愿意尽其所能地去生产。另一方面，如果成本总是超过销售收入，企业也可能不进行任何生产。企业的目标是使利润而非生产最大化。最合意的产出水平是使总**利润**——总收益和总成本之差最大化的产出水平。

生产产品的经济成本，最终是由生产过程中所使用的稀缺资源的数量来衡量的。但是在市场经济中，我们需要更加便捷的方法来衡量成本。我们只想要一个美元数，而不是将所有投入的数量一一列举。为了得到这一数字，我们必须明确生产中所使用的全部资源，计算它们的价值并加总。最后计算出来的美元数即为生产的**总成本**。

The leased sewing machine is another fixed cost. When you rent a sewing machine, you must pay the rental charge. It doesn't matter whether you use it for a few minutes or all day long—the rental charge is fixed at $20 per day.

Variable Costs 可变成本

劳动力成本完全是另一回事。生产牛仔裤所雇用的劳动力数量可以轻易被改变。如果我们决定明天关闭厂房，只要通知唯一的那名工人不要来上班就可以了。我们仍然需要支付房租和缝纫机的租金，但是可以降低工资费用。另外，如果我们想增加日产出，也可以方便又快速地招到工人。在这个行当中，劳动力被看作**可变成本**，也就是随着产出水平的改变而变化的成本。

Labor costs are another story altogether. The amount of labor employed in jeans production can be varied easily. If we decide not to open the factory tomorrow, we can just tell our only worker to take the day off. We will still have to pay rent and the sewing machine lease, but we can cut back on wages. Alternatively, if we want to increase daily output, we can also hire workers easily and quickly. Labor is regarded as a **variable cost** in this line of work—that is, a cost that *varies* with the rate of output.

The denim itself is another variable cost. Denim not used today can be saved for tomorrow. Hence how much we "spend" on denim today is directly related to how many pairs of jeans we produce. In this sense, the cost of denim input varies with the rate of jeans output.

Figure 4.2 illustrates how these various costs are affected by the rate of production. On the vertical axis are the costs of production in dollars per day. Notice that the total cost of producing 15 pairs per day is still $245, as indicated by point B. This figure consists of $120

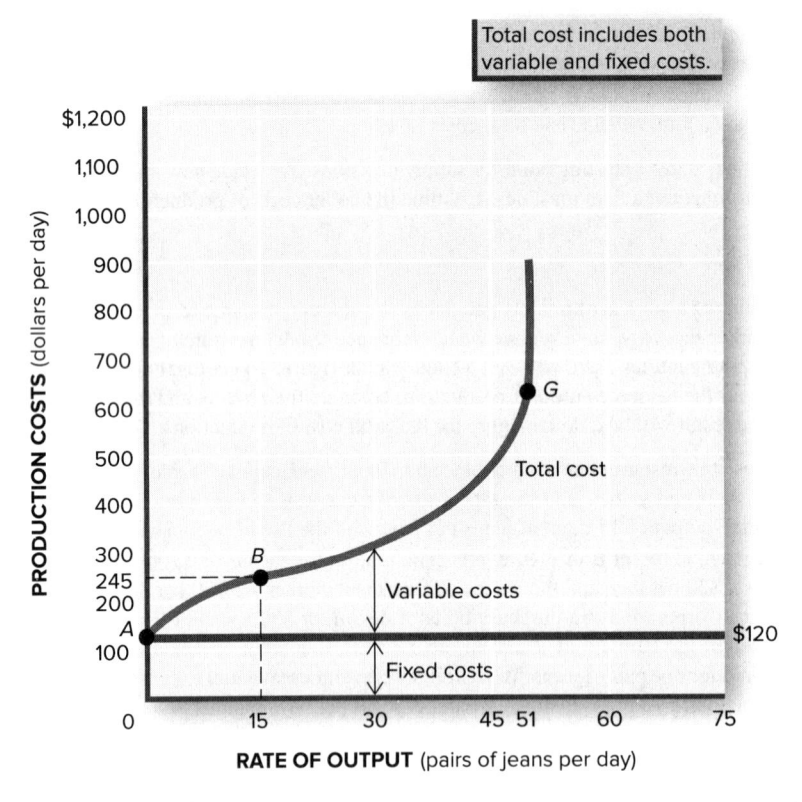

Figure 4.2 The Costs of Jeans Production Total cost includes both fixed and variable costs. Fixed costs must be paid even if no output is produced (point A). Variable costs start at zero and increase with the rate of output. The total cost of producing 15 pairs of jeans (point B) includes $120 in fixed costs (rent on the factory and sewing machines) and $125 in variable costs (denim and wages). Total cost rises as output increases.

In this example, the short-run capacity is equal to 51 pairs (point G). If still more inputs are employed, costs will rise but not total output. ■

---

vertical axis 纵轴。

of fixed costs (factory and sewing machine rents) and $125 of variable costs ($80 in wages and $45 for denim). If we increase the rate of output, total costs will rise. ***How fast total costs rise depends on variable costs only,*** however, since fixed costs remain at $120 per day. (Notice the horizontal fixed cost curve in Figure 4.2.)

With one sewing machine and one factory, there is an absolute limit to daily jeans production. As we observed in the production function (Figure 4.1), the capacity of a factory with one machine is 51 pairs of jeans per day. If we try to produce more jeans than this by hiring additional workers, total *costs* will rise, but total *output* will not. In fact, we could fill the factory with garment workers and drive total costs sky-high. But the limits of space and one sewing machine do not permit output in excess of 51 pairs per day. This limit to productive capacity is represented by point *G* on the total cost curve. Further expenditure on inputs will increase production costs but not output.

Although there is no upper limit to costs, there is a lower limit. If output is reduced to zero, total costs fall only to $120 per day, the level of fixed costs. This is illustrated by point *A* in Figure 4.2. As before, ***there is no way to avoid fixed costs in the short run.*** If you have leased a factory or machinery, you must pay the rent whether or not you produce any jeans.

Which Costs Matter? 哪个成本重要

The different nature of fixed and variable costs raises some intriguing questions about how to measure the cost of producing a pair of jeans. In figuring how much it costs to produce one pair, should we look only at the denim and labor time used to produce that pair? Or should we also take into account the factory rent and lease payments on the sewing machines?

A similar problem arises when you try to figure out whether a restaurant overcharges you for a steak dinner. What did it cost the restaurant to supply the dinner? Should only the meat and the chef's time be counted? Or should the cost include some portion of the rent, the electricity, and the insurance?

The restaurant owner, too, needs to figure out which measure of cost to use. She has to decide what price to charge for the steak. She wants to earn a profit. Can she do so by charging a price just above the cost of meat and wages? Or must she charge a price high enough to cover some portion of her fixed costs as well?

To answer these questions, we need to introduce two distinct measures of cost: *average* cost and *marginal* cost.

Average Cost 平均成本

Average total cost (ATC) is simply total cost divided by the rate of output:

$$\text{Average total cost (ATC)} = \frac{\text{total cost}}{\text{total output}}$$

If the total cost (including both fixed and variable costs) of supplying 10 steaks is $62, then the *average* cost of the steaks is $6.20.

As we observed in Figure 4.2, total costs change as the rate of output increases. Hence both the numerator and the denominator in the ATC formula change with the rate of output. This complicates the arithmetic a bit, as Figure 4.3 illustrates.

Figure 4.3 shows how average total cost *changes* as the rate of output varies. Row *J* of the cost schedule, for example, again indicates the fixed, variable, and total costs of producing 15 pairs of jeans per day. Fixed costs are still $120 (for factory and machine rentals); variable

---

sky-high 极高。expenditure 支出，花费。intriguing 有趣的。overcharge 对……要价（或收费）过高。numerator（分数的）分子。denominator（分数的）分母。

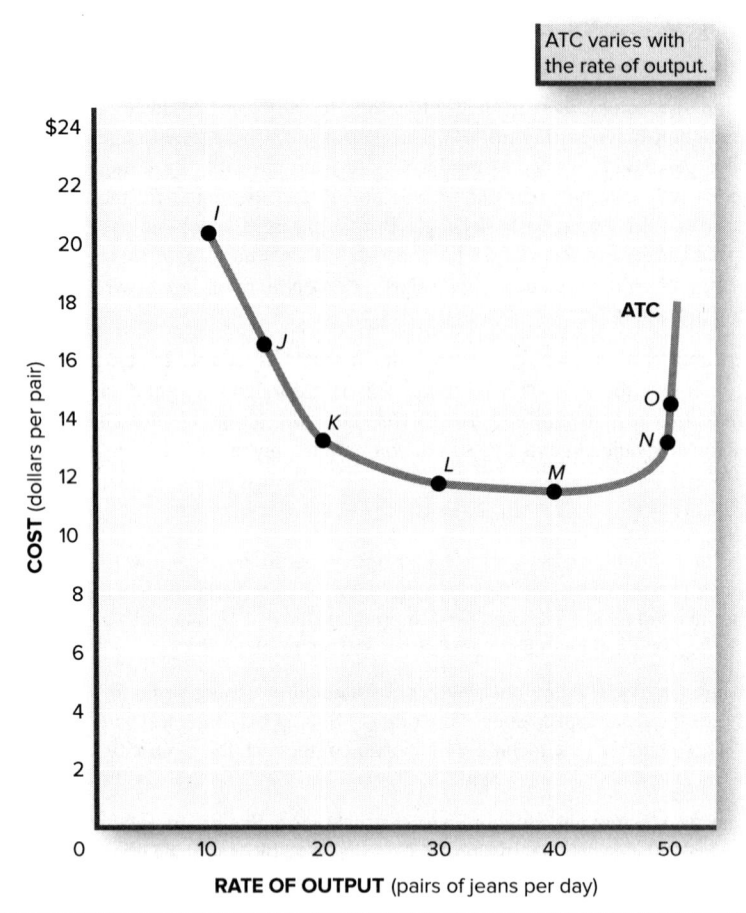

	(1) Rate of Output	(2) Fixed Costs	+	(3) Variable Costs	=	(4) Total Cost	(5) Average Total Cost
H	0	$120		$ 0		$120	—
I	10	120		85		205	$20.50
J	15	120		125		245	16.33
K	20	120		150		270	13.50
L	30	120		240		360	12.00
M	40	120		350		470	11.75
N	50	120		550		670	13.40
O	51	120		633		753	14.76

Figure 4.3 Average Total Cost Average total cost (ATC) is total cost divided by the number of units produced. In the accompanying table the ATC in column 5 is computed by dividing Total Cost (column 4) by the rate of output (column 1). Notice how ATC falls initially as output increases and then later rises. This gives the ATC curve a distinctive U shape, as illustrated in the graph.

costs (denim and labor) are $125. Thus the total cost of producing 15 pairs per day is $245. The *average* cost for this rate of output is simply total cost ($245) divided by quantity (15), or $16.33 per day. This ATC is indicated in column 5 of the table and by point *J* on the graph.

U-Shaped ATC Curve   U形平均总成本曲线

An important feature of the ATC curve is its shape. ***Average costs start high, fall, then rise once again, giving the ATC curve a distinctive U shape.***

ATC 曲线的一个重要特征是它的形状。平均成本曲线经历先递减再递增的过程，形成独特的 U 形。

The initial decline in ATC is largely due to fixed costs. At low rates of output, fixed costs are a high proportion of total costs. Quite simply, it's very expensive to lease (or buy) an entire factory to produce only a few pairs of jeans. The entire cost of the factory must be averaged out over a small quantity of output. This results in a high average cost of production. To reduce *average* costs, we must make fuller use of our leased plant and equipment.

The same problem of cost spreading would affect a restaurant that served only two dinners a day. The *total* cost of operating a restaurant might easily exceed $500 a day. If only two dinners were served, the *average* total cost of each meal would exceed $250. That's why restaurants need a high volume of business to keep average total costs—and meal prices—low.

As output increases, the fixed costs of production are distributed over an increasing quantity of output. Fixed costs no longer dominate total costs as production increases (compare columns 2 and 3 in Figure 4.3). As a result, average total costs tend to decline.

Average total costs don't fall forever, however. They bottom out at point *M* in Figure 4.3 and then start rising. What accounts for this turnaround?

Marginal Cost   边际成本

The upturn of the ATC curve is caused by rising *marginal* costs. **Marginal cost (MC)** *refers to the change in total costs when one more unit of output is produced.* In practice, marginal cost is easy to measure; just observe how much total costs increase when one more unit of output is produced. For larger increases in output, marginal cost can also be approximated by the formula

$$\text{Marginal cost} = \frac{\text{change in total cost}}{\text{change in total output}}$$

ATC 曲线的上升源于增加的边际成本。**边际成本**表示增加一单位产出时，总成本的变化量。在实践中，边际成本易于衡量，只需关注增加一单位产出时总成本的增加量。当产出增加很多时，可以通过如下公式近似计算边际成本：

$$边际成本 = \frac{总成本的变化量}{总产出的变化量}$$

Using this formula and Figure 4.3, we could confirm how marginal costs rise in jeans production. Take this slowly. Notice that as jeans production increases from 20 pairs (row *K*) to 30 pairs (row *L*) per day, total costs rise from $270 to $360. Hence the *change* in total cost ($90) divided by the *change* in total output (10) equals $9. This is the *marginal* cost of jeans in that range of output (20 to 30 pairs).

Figure 4.4 shows how marginal costs change as jeans output increases. As output continues to increase further from 30 to 40 pairs per day, marginal costs rise. *Total* cost rises from $360 (row *L*) to $470 (row *M*), a *change* of $110. Dividing this by the *change* in output (10) reveals that *marginal* cost is now $11. Marginal costs are rising as output increases.

Rising marginal cost implies that each additional unit of output becomes more expensive to produce. Why is this? Why would the third pair of jeans cost more to produce than the second pair? Why would it cost a restaurant more to serve the twelfth dinner than the eleventh dinner?

The explanation for this puzzle of rising marginal cost lies in the production function. As we observed earlier, output increases at an ever-slower pace as capacity is approached. The law of diminishing marginal product tells us that we need an increasing amount of labor to eke out

---

turnaround 转变，（经济、营业等的）突然好转。

each additional pair of jeans. The same law applies to restaurants. As more dinners are served, the waiters and cooks get pressed for space and equipment. It takes a little longer (and requires more wages) to prepare and serve each meal. So the *marginal* costs of each meal increase as the number of patrons rises.

SUPPLY HORIZONS 供给水平

All these cost calculations can give you a real headache. They can also give you second thoughts about jumping into Tight Jeans, restaurant management, or any other business. There are tough choices to be made. Any firm can produce many different rates of output, each of which entails a distinct level of costs. Someone has to choose which level of output to produce

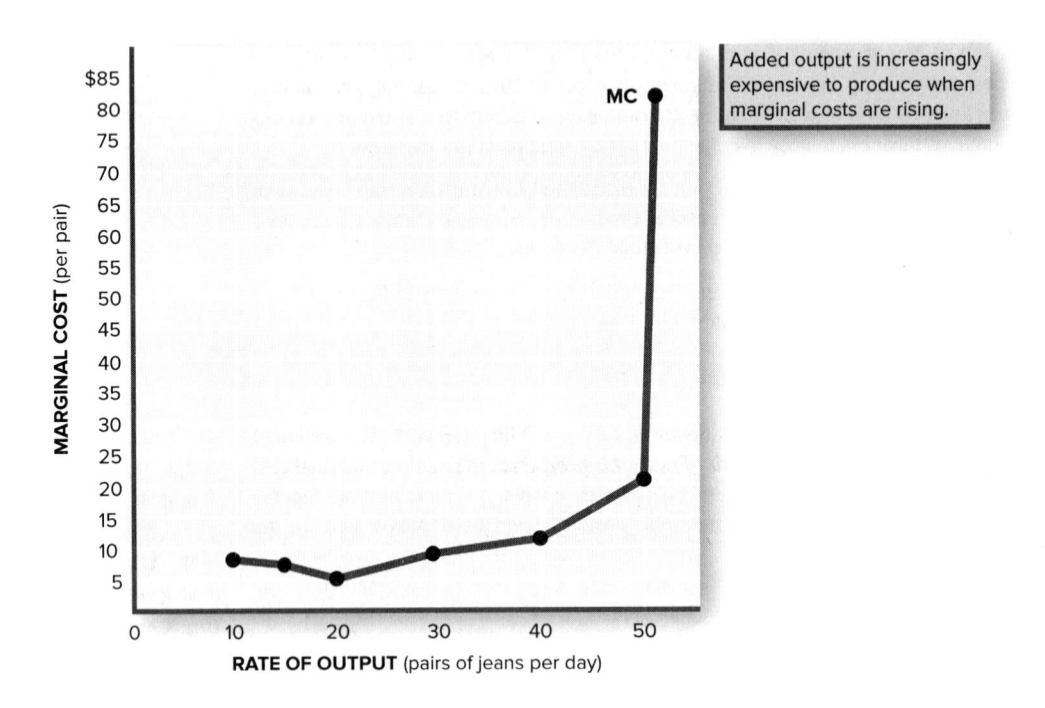

	Rate of Output	Total Cost	$\frac{\Delta TC}{\Delta q} = MC$	
H	0	$120		
I	10	205	$ 85/10 = $ 8.5	
J	15	245	$ 40/5 = $ 8.0	MC declining
K	20	270	$ 25/5 = $ 5.0	
L	30	360	$ 90/10 = $ 9.0	
M	40	470	$110/10 = $11.0	MC increasing
N	50	670	$200/10 = $20.0	
O	51	753	$ 83/1 = $83.0	

Figure 4.4 Marginal Cost Marginal cost is the *change* in total cost that occurs when more output is produced. *MC* equals $\Delta TC/\Delta q$.

Marginal costs rise as more workers have to share limited space and equipment (fixed costs) in the short run. This "crowding" reduces marginal physical product and increases marginal costs. ■

---

patron 顾客，常客。

and thus how many goods to supply to the market. That decision has to be based not only on the *capacity* to produce (the production function) but also on the *costs* of production (the cost functions). Only those who make the right decisions will succeed in business.

The Short-Run Production Decision 短期生产决策

The nature of supply decisions also varies with the relevant time frame. In this regard, we must distinguish *short*-run decisions from *long*-run decisions.

The Short Run 短期

The *short run* is characterized by the existence of fixed costs. A commitment has been made: a factory has been built, an office leased, or machinery purchased. The only decision to make is how much output to produce with these existing facilities. This is the **production decision**, the choice of how intensively to use available plant and equipment. This choice is typically made daily (e.g., jeans production), weekly (e.g., auto production), or seasonally (e.g., farming).

Focus on Marginal Cost 关注边际成本

The most important factor in the short-run production decision is marginal costs. Producers will be willing to supply output only if they can at least cover marginal costs. If the marginal cost of producing a product exceeds the price at which it is sold, it doesn't make sense to produce that last unit. Price must exceed marginal cost for the producer to reap any profit from the last unit produced. Accordingly, *marginal cost is a basic determinant of short-run supply (production) decisions*.

Look back at Figure 4.4. Suppose Tight Jeans is producing 40 pairs per day (row M in the table) and selling them for $18 each. In that case, total revenue is $720 ($18 × 40 pairs) and total cost is $470, yielding a profit of $250 per day.

Now suppose the plant manager is so excited by these profits that she increases total output to 50 pairs per day. Will profits increase? Not according to Figure 4.4. When output increases to 50 pairs (row N in the table), *marginal* cost rises to $20. At this rate of output, the cost of producing those extra 10 pairs ($20 each) is more than what the company can sell them for ($18 each). At this level of output, then, marginal costs dictate *not* producing the additional jeans. If they are produced, total profits will decline (from $250 to only $230). Marginal costs put a brake on production decisions.

Marginal costs may also dictate short-run *pricing* decisions. Suppose the average total cost of serving a steak dinner is $12, but the marginal cost is only $7. How low a price can the restaurant charge for the dinner? Ideally, it would like to charge at least $12 and cover all of its costs. It could at least cover *marginal* costs, however, if it charged only $7. At that price the restaurant would be neither better nor worse off for having served an extra dinner. The additional cost of serving that one meal would be covered.

It must be emphasized that covering marginal cost is a *minimal* condition for supplying additional output. A restaurant that covers only marginal costs but not average total cost will lose money. It may even go out of business. This is a lesson lots of now-defunct Internet companies learned the hard way. They spent millions of dollars building telecommunications networks to produce Internet services. The *marginal* costs of producing Internet service was low, so they sold their services at low prices. Those low prices didn't bring in enough revenue to cover *fixed* costs, however, so legions of dot.com companies went bankrupt. As they quickly learned, you can get by just covering marginal costs. To stay in the game, however, you've got to cover average *total* costs as well. In Chapter 5 we examine more closely just how marginal cost considerations affect short-run supply behavior.

短期的特点是存在固定成本。我们已进行如下投资：建造厂房、租赁办公室或购买设备。唯一要做的决策就是利用这些现有设施生产多少产出。这就是**生产决策**，即决定在何种程度上利用现有车间和设备。此决策通常每天（如牛仔裤生产）、每周（如汽车生产）或每季度（如农业生产）进行一次。

短期生产决策中最重要的因素是边际成本。只有生产所得至少能够弥补边际成本时，生产者才愿意生产。如果生产某产品的边际成本超过了它的市场价格，就没有必要生产这最后一单位产品了。对于想从最后一单位产品中获利的生产者而言，价格必须超过边际成本。因此，边际成本是短期供给（生产）决策的基本决定因素。

---

distinguish 区分，辨别。 dictate 决定。 minimal 最低的，最小限度的。 bankrupt 破产。

The Long-Run Investment Decision 长期投资决策

The long run opens up a whole new range of options. In the *long run,* we have no lease or purchase commitments. We are free to start all over again, with whatever scale of plant and equipment we desire. ***There are no fixed costs in the long run.*** Accordingly, long-run supply decisions are more complicated. If no commitments to production facilities have been made, a producer must decide how large a facility to build, buy, or lease. Hence the size (scale) of plant and equipment becomes an additional option for long-term supply decisions. In a long-run (no fixed costs) situation, a firm can make the **investment decision**.

No Fixed Costs 不存在固定成本

Note that the distinction between short- and long-run supply decisions is not based on time. The distinction instead depends on whether commitments have been made. If no leases have been signed, no construction contracts awarded, no acquisitions made, a producer still has a free hand. With no fixed costs, the producer can walk away from the potential business at a moment's notice.

Once fixed costs are incurred, the options narrow. Then the issue becomes one of making the best possible use of the assets (e.g., factory, office space, equipment) that have been acquired. Once fixed costs have been incurred, it's hard to walk away from the business. The goal then becomes to make as much profit as possible from the investments already made. The accompanying News Wire "Production and Investment Decisions" illustrates the distinction between these production and investment decisions. The decision by Tesla to produce more vehicles at its Fremont, California, plant is a short-run production decision. By contrast, Tesla's decision to build a "Gigafactory" in Shanghai is an investment decision.

NEWS WIRE PRODUCTION AND INVESTMENT DECISIONS

Tesla to Boost Production in 2019

Tesla produced 5,000 Model 3 cars last week at its Freemont, California, factory, finally reaching its long-promised production goal. CEO Elon Musk noted, however, that Tesla plans to ramp up production further, to at least 6,000 cars week by early 2019.

Tesla Plans "Gigafactory"

Tesla CEO Elon Musk confirmed that an agreement has been signed with the Shanghai government to build another "Gigafactory," this time in Shanghai, China. The super-sized plant will have the capacity to produce 500,000 cars per year plus enough lithium-ion batteries to power the electric cars.

Source: News accounts of July 2018.

NOTE: Production decisions focus on the (short-run) use of existing facilities. Investment decisions relate to the (long-run) acquisition of productive facilities.
注：生产决策注重（短期）现有设备的使用。投资决策与可获得的（长期）生产设施有关。

经济成本与会计成本
ECONOMIC VERSUS ACCOUNTING COSTS

The cost concepts we have discussed here are based on *real* production relationships. The dollar costs we compute reflect underlying resource costs—the land, labor, and capital used in the production process. Not everyone counts this way. On the contrary, accountants and businesspeople often count dollar costs only and ignore any resource use that doesn't result in an explicit dollar cost. This kind of tunnel vision can cause serious mistakes.

---

walk away from 退出，撤出。boost 增加，提高。

Return to Tight Jeans for a moment to see the difference. When we computed the dollar cost of producing 15 pairs of jeans per day, we noted the following resource inputs:

Inputs	Cost
1 factory rent	@ $100
1 machine rent	@ 20
1 machine operator	@ 80
1.5 bolts of denim	@ 45
Total cost	$245

The total value of the resources used in the production of 15 pairs of jeans was thus $245 per day. But this economic cost need not conform to *actual* dollar costs. Suppose the owners of Tight Jeans decided to sew the jeans themselves. Then they would not have to hire a worker or pay $80 per day in wages. *Dollar* costs would drop to $165 per day. The producers and their accountant would consider this to be a remarkable achievement. They would assert that the costs of producing jeans had fallen.

Economic Cost 经济成本

An economist would draw no such conclusions. *The essential economic question is how many resources are used in production.* This has not changed. One unit of labor is still being employed at the factory; now it's simply the owner, not a hired worker. In either case, one unit of labor is not available for the production of other goods and services. Hence society is still incurring an opportunity cost of $245 for jeans, whether the owners of Tight Jeans write checks in that amount or not. We really don't care who sews the jeans—the essential point is that someone (i.e., a unit of labor) does.

The same would be true if Tight Jeans owned its factory rather than rented it. If the factory was owned rather than rented, the owners probably would not write any rent checks. Accounting costs would drop by $100 per day. But society would not be saving any resources. The factory would still be in use for jeans production and therefore unavailable for the production of other goods and services. Hence the *opportunity cost* of the factory would still be $100 per day. As a result, the economic (resource) cost of producing 15 pairs of jeans would still be $245.

The distinction between an economic cost and an accounting cost is essentially one between resource and dollar costs. *Dollar cost* refers to the explicit dollar outlays made by a producer; it is the lifeblood of accountants. **Economic cost**, in contrast, refers to the dollar *value* of all resources used in the production process; it is the lifeblood of economists. The accountant's dollar costs are usually *explicit* in the sense that someone writes a check. The economist takes into consideration *implicit* costs as well—that is, even those costs for which no direct payment is made. In other words, economists count costs as

Economic cost = explicit costs + implicit costs

As this formula suggests, *economic and accounting costs will diverge whenever any factor of production is not paid an explicit wage (or rent, etc.).*

The Cost of Homework 作业成本

These distinctions between economic and accounting costs apply also to the "production" of homework. You can pay people to write term papers for you or even buy them off the Internet. At large schools you can often buy lecture notes as well. But most students end up doing their own homework so that they will learn something and not just turn in required assignments.

经济学家不会得出这样的结论。最根本的经济问题是生产中使用了多少资源。这一点没有改变。工厂仍然使用着一单位劳动力；只不过现在这个劳动力是所有者本人，而不是雇用的工人。无论哪一种情况，这一单位劳动力都不能进行其他商品和服务的生产。因此，无论 Tight Jeans 的所有者是否以这个数字记账，社会都要承担生产牛仔裤的 245 美元的机会成本。我们根本不关心是谁生产了牛仔裤——关键在于，有人（也就是一单位劳动力）在生产。

经济成本和会计成本之间的区别本质上是资源成本和美元成本的区别。美元成本指生产者显性的美元支出，是会计师的"命根子"。相反，**经济成本**指生产过程中所使用的全部资源的美元价值，是经济学家的"命根子"。由于通常是签发支票，所以会计师的美元成本是显性的；而经济学家还要考虑隐性成本，也就是那些并未直接支付的成本。换句话说，经济学家这样计算成本：

经济成本 = 显性成本 + 隐性成本

正如公式所表明的，当任何生产要素没有以显性工资（或租金）支付时，经济成本与会计成本就存在差异。

---

conform to 符合，遵照。remarkable 卓越的，非凡的。

Doing homework is expensive, however, even if you don't pay someone to do it. The time you spend reading this chapter is valuable. You could be doing something else if you weren't reading right now. What would you be doing? The forgone activity—the best alternative use of your time—represents the opportunity cost of doing homework. Even if you don't pay yourself for reading this chapter, you'll still incur that *economic* cost.

Economic Profit 经济利润

经济成本和会计成本的主要区别直接影响了利润的计算。提供商品和服务的生产者都想从付出中得到利润，但究竟什么是"利润"呢？经济学上，利润是总收入和总经济成本的差额，即

利润 = 总收入 – 总成本

The distinction between economic cost and accounting cost directly affects profit computations. People who supply goods and services want to make a profit from their efforts. But what exactly *is* "profit"? In economic terms, profit is the difference between total revenues and *total* economic costs:

$$\text{Profit} = \text{total revenue} - \text{total cost}$$

Economists don't rely on accountants to compute profits. Instead they factor in not just the explicit costs that accountants keep track of but also the implicit costs that arise when resources are used but not explicitly paid (e.g., an owner's time and capital investment). Suppose total revenue at Tight Jeans was $300 per day. With total costs of $245 per day (see the foregoing cost computation), profit would be $55 per day. If the owner did her own stitching, *accounting* costs would drop by $80 and *accounting* profits would increase by the same amount. *Economic* profits would *not* change, however. By keeping track of *all* costs (implicit and explicit), economists can keep a consistent eye on profits. In the next chapter we'll see how business firms use supply decisions to maximize those profits.

POLICY PERSPECTIVES

CAN WE OUTRUN DIMINISHING RETURNS?

For more than a century people have been predicting that living standards are destined to fall—that the growth of the world's population will exceed the growth of production. If that were to happen, the future would indeed be bleak. But is that outcome inevitable?

Fears about future living standards have their roots in the law of diminishing returns. As we add more and more people to the fixed resources of the planet, each person will have fewer resources to work with. As a result, marginal physical productivity will decline, along with our standard of living.

But declining marginal physical product (MPP) isn't inevitable. We can postpone that scenario—perhaps indefinitely. To beat the law of diminishing marginal productivity, we can *increase* the productivity of all workers. This means that we have to *shift* production functions upward, as shown graphically in Figure 4.5a.

How can we achieve such across-the-board productivity gains? There are several possibilities. One possibility is to invest in labor by increasing education and training. Better-educated workers are apt to squeeze more output from any production facility. In the world's poorest nations, one out of every two workers is illiterate. In those nations, even basic literacy training can boost labor productivity substantially. In the United States, most workers have at least some college education. That isn't the end of skill training, however. Skill training in classrooms and on the job continues to boost U.S. labor productivity. The government encourages such training with student loans, school subsidies, and training programs. In 2018, the federal government spent over $100 billion on education, and state and local governments spent 10 times that much.

---

keep track of 记录。 stitch 缝合。 squeeze 挤出，压榨。 illiterate 文盲的，不识字的，没受教育的。

Spending on *capital* investment also boosts productivity. American workers have the productivity advantage of not just more education but also far more capital resources in the workplace. Additional investment in capital not only adds to the stock (quantity) of resources in the world but increases its *quality* as well. New machines, factories, and networks almost always embody the latest technology. Hence **more capital investment typically results in improved technology as well, giving a double boost to production possibilities.** The government can encourage such investments with targeted tax incentives.

Investments in either human or nonhuman capital shift the production function upward, as in Figure 4.5a. In either case, the marginal physical product of labor rises and marginal costs fall (Figure 4.5b). This not only increases worker productivity, but also expands (shifts) society's production possibilities outward. Those outward shifts of the production function are what allow the Earth to accommodate more and more people without lowering living standards.

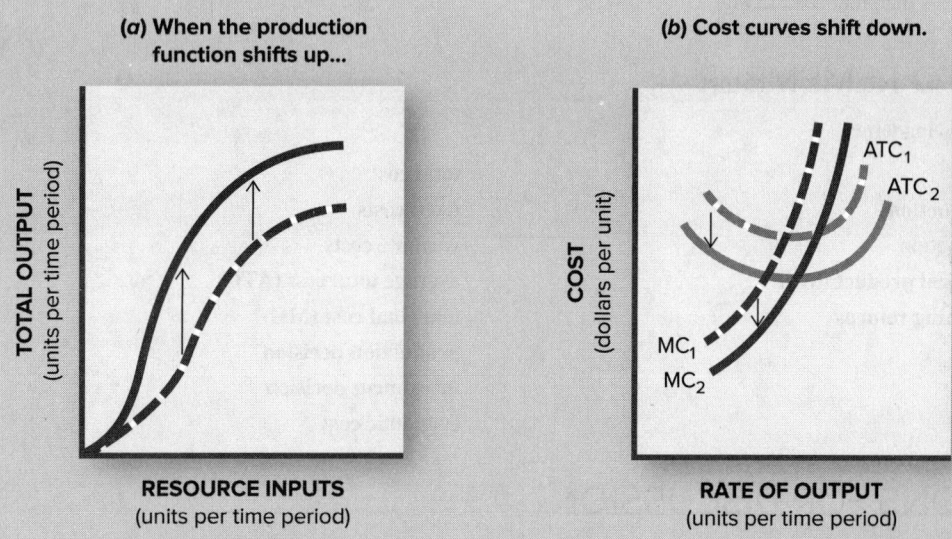

Figure 4.5 Improvements in Productivity Reduce Costs Advances in technological or managerial knowledge increase our productive capability. This is reflected in upward shifts of the production function (*a*) and downward shifts of production cost curves (*b*). Investments in either labor (education and training) or capital (new plant and equipment) propel such shifts. ■

CHAPTER 4 REVIEW

SUMMARY

- Supply decisions are constrained by the *capacity* to produce and the *costs* of using that capacity. **LO1**
- In the short run, some inputs (e.g., land and capital) are fixed in quantity. Increases in (short-run) output result from more use of variable inputs (e.g., labor). **LO1**
- A production function indicates how much output can be produced from available facilities using different amounts of variable inputs. Every point on the production function represents efficient production.

Capacity output refers to the maximum quantity that can be produced from a given facility. **LO1**

- Output tends to increase at a diminishing rate when more labor is employed in a given facility. Additional workers crowd existing facilities, leaving each worker with less space and machinery to work with. **LO2**
- The costs of production include both fixed and variable costs. Fixed costs (e.g., space and equipment leases) are incurred even if no output is produced. Variable costs

(e.g., labor and material) are incurred when plant and equipment are put to use. **LO3**
- Average cost is total cost divided by the quantity produced. The average total cost (ATC) curve is typically U-shaped. **LO3**
- Marginal cost is the increase in total cost that results when one more unit of output is produced. Marginal costs increase because of diminishing returns in production. **LO3**
- The production decision is the short-run choice of how much output to produce with existing facilities. A producer will be willing to supply output only if price at least covers marginal cost. **LO4**
- The long run is characterized by an absence of fixed costs. The investment decision entails the choice of whether to acquire fixed costs—that is, whether to build, buy, or lease plant and equipment. **LO4**
- The economic costs of production include the value of *all* resources used. Accounting costs typically include only those dollar costs actually paid (explicit costs). **LO5**
- Historically, advances in technology and the quality of our inputs have been the major source of productivity growth. These advances have shifted production functions up and pushed cost curves down. **LO1**

TERMS TO REMEMBER

Define the following terms:

supply
factors of production
production function
marginal physical product (MPP)
law of diminishing returns
short run
long run
profit

total cost
fixed costs
variable costs
average total cost (ATC)
marginal cost (MC)
production decision
investment decision
economic cost

QUESTIONS FOR DISCUSSION

1. Is your school currently producing at capacity (i.e., teaching as many students as possible)? What considerations might inhibit full capacity utilization? **LO1**
2. What are the production costs of your economics class? What are the fixed costs? The variable costs? What is the marginal cost of enrolling more students? **LO3**
3. Suppose you set up a lawn-mowing service and recruit friends to help you. Would the law of diminishing returns apply? Explain. **LO2**
4. What are the fixed and variable costs of (*a*) a pizza shop, (*b*) a corn farm, (*c*) a movie theater, (*d*) Netflix? Which needs the highest sales volume to earn a profit? **LO3**
5. How do marginal costs "put a brake on production decisions"? **LO3**
6. Is it possible for a company to show an accounting profit even while it is incurring an economic loss? How? What might happen with such a company? **LO5**
7. Why does marginal physical product decline at a fast-food outlet (e.g., McDonald's) when more employees are hired? What are the fixed input constraints that limit worker productivity? **LO2**
8. If Tesla is planning to increase production at its Fremont, California, factory (News Wire "Production and Investments Decisions"), what must be the relationship between marginal cost and price? **LO3**
9. What will be the capacity of Tesla's Shanghai Gigafactory (News Wire "Production and Investment Decisions"). How many cars will Tesla want to produce in that factory? **LO4**
10. **POLICY PERSPECTIVES** If capital investment ceased, what would happen over time to worker productivity and living standards? **LO1**

PROBLEMS

1. (*a*) What is the marginal physical product of each successive worker in Figure 4.1? For which worker is marginal physical product (*b*) first diminishing? (*c*) zero? **LO2**

2. (*a*) Compute *average* fixed costs and *average* variable costs in Figure 4.3 for all rates of output. At what rate of output is (are) **LO3**
    b. Average fixed costs the lowest?
    c. Average variable costs the lowest?
    d. Average total cost the lowest?

3. (*a*) Complete the following table; (*b*) then plot the marginal cost and average total cost curves on the same graph. (*c*) What output has the lowest per-unit cost? (*d*) What is the value of fixed costs? **LO3**

Rate of Output	Total Cost	Marginal Cost	Average Total Cost
0	$ 80	___	___
1	90	___	___
2	100	___	___
3	120	___	___
4	160	___	___
5	250	___	___

4. Suppose the mythical Tight Jeans Corporation leased a *second* sewing machine, giving it the following production function: **LO1**

Number of workers:	0	1	2	3	4	5	6	7	8
Quantity of output:	0	10	36	56	68	74	76	76	74

    a. Graph the production function.
    b. On a separate graph, illustrate marginal physical product.
    At what level of employment does
    c. The law of diminishing returns become apparent?
    d. MPP hit zero?
    e. MPP become negative?

5. Using the data in problem 4 and a price of $30 per pair of jeans, calculate the marginal physical product and the value of the marginal physical product. Note the value of the marginal physical product is the price of the product multiplied by the marginal physical product. **LO3**

6. Using Figure 4.3 as a guide, compute total profits at a price of $15 per pair of jeans and output of (*a*) 40 pairs, and (*b*) 50 pairs. **LO3**

7. Suppose a company incurs the following costs:
    Labor $800
    Equipment $400
    Materials $300

    It owns the building, so it doesn't have to pay the usual $900 in rent. **LO5**

    a. What is the total accounting cost?
    b. What is the total economic cost?
    c. How would accounting and economic costs change if the company sold the building and then leased it back?
8. **POLICY PERSPECTIVES** If investment in new machinery doubles the productivity of every worker, what will be the MPP of the fifth worker in Figure 4.1? **LO4**
9. **POLICY PERSPECTIVES** If the world's population is growing by 1 percent a year, (*a*) how fast does production have to increase to keep living standards from falling? (*b*) Will living standards rise, fall, or stay the same if the workforce and productivity (MPP) also increase by 1 percent each year? **LO1**

CHAPTER FIVE

Competition 竞 争

©Marek Zuk/Alamy Stock Photo

LEARNING OBJECTIVES

After reading this chapter, you should be able to:

1. Identify the unique characteristics of perfectly competitive firms and markets.
2. Illustrate how total profits change as output expands.
3. Describe how the profit-maximizing rate of output is found.
4. Recite the determinants of competitive market supply.
5. Explain how profits get eliminated in competitive markets.

Catfish farmers in the South are upset. During the last two decades they have invested millions of dollars in converting cotton farms into breeding ponds for catfish. They now have over 60,000 acres of ponds and supply over 90 percent of the nation's catfish. From January 2013 to January 2016, catfish prices rose dramatically, from 82 cents a pound to $1.14 a pound. That made catfish farming look pretty good. But then prices started slipping again, falling as low as 95 cents a pound by January 2018. This abrupt price decline killed any hopes the farmers had of making huge profits. Indeed, catfish prices got so low that many farmers started draining their ponds and planting crops again.

The dilemma the catfish farmers find themselves in is a familiar occurrence in competitive markets. When the profit prospects look good, everybody wants to get in on the act. As more and more firms start producing the good, however, prices and profits tumble. This helps explain why more than 200,000 new firms are formed each year as well as why 50,000 others fail.

In this chapter we examine how supply decisions are made in competitive markets—markets in which all producers are relatively small. Our focus on competition centers on the following questions:

- What are the unique characteristics of competitive markets?
- How do competitive firms make supply decisions?
- How are production levels, prices, and profits determined in competitive markets?

By answering these questions, we will develop more insight into supply decisions and thus the core issues of WHAT, HOW, and FOR WHOM goods and services are produced. ■

---

convert 改建。breed 养殖。dramatically 显著地，大幅地。dilemma 困境。tumble（价格或利润）暴跌，骤降。

MARKET STRUCTURE 市场结构

追逐利润是商业企业的共同目标，但是并非所有企业都有同样的获得利润的机会。与南部的鲶鱼养殖场一样，数以百万计的厂商规模都很小，它们完全受市场支配。其产品市场价格的轻微下降往往都会导致经济损失。即使获利，也必须时刻关注新竞争、新产品或技术方面的改进。

巨型企业和微型企业都是**市场结构**的极端情况，这两种极端情况确定了企业可能拥有的权力范围。从没有权力到权力强大，市场结构的分布如同光谱，而现实世界中的大多数企业都落在这个光谱上。光谱（图5.1）的一端是完全**竞争性厂商**——不能左右其产品价格的厂商。如同南部的鲶鱼养殖者，一个完全竞争性厂商必须接受其产品的市场价格，它是一个价格接受者。完全由竞争性厂商所构成的市场（并且没有任何厂商控制需求方）被称为（完全）**竞争性市场**。在完全竞争性市场中，任何生产者或消费者都不能控制产品的价格和数量。

The quest for profits is the common denominator of business enterprises. But not all businesses have the same opportunity to pursue profits. Millions of firms, like the southern catfish farms, are very small and entirely at the mercy of the marketplace. A small decline in the market price of their product often spells financial ruin. Even when such firms make a profit, they must always be on the lookout for new competition, new products, or changes in technology.

Larger firms don't have to work quite so hard to maintain their standing. Huge corporations often have the power to raise prices, change consumer tastes (through advertising), or even prevent competitors from taking a slice of the profit pie. Such powerful firms can protect and perpetuate their profits. They are more likely to dominate markets than to be at their mercy.

Business firms aren't always either giants or dwarfs, however. Those are extremes of **market structure** that illustrate the range of power a firm might possess. Most real-world firms fall along a spectrum that stretches from the powerless to the powerful. At one end of the spectrum (Figure 5.1) we place perfectly **competitive firms**—firms that have no power over the price of goods they produce. Like the catfish farmers in the South, a perfectly competitive firm must take whatever price for its wares the market offers; it is a *price taker*. A market composed entirely of competitive firms—and without anyone dominating the demand side either—is referred to as a (perfectly) **competitive market**. *In a perfectly competitive market, no single producer or consumer has any control over the price or quantity of the product.*

At the other end of the spectrum of market structures are monopolies. A **monopoly** is a single firm that produces the entire supply of a particular good. Despite repeated legal and technological attacks, Microsoft still supplies 9 out of 10 computer operating systems. That near-monopoly gives Microsoft the power to *set* market prices rather than simply respond to them. With nearly 75 percent of the soft drink market between them, The Coca-Cola Company and PepsiCo are a virtual duopoly (two-firm market). Together they have the power to set prices for their beverages. All firms with such power are price *setters*, not price *takers*.

Monopolies are the extreme case of market power. In Figure 5.1 they are at the far right end of the spectrum, easily distinguished from the small, competitive firms that reside at the low (left) end of the power spectrum.

Among the 30 million or so business enterprises in the United States, there are relatively few monopolies. Local phone companies, cable TV companies, and utility firms often have a monopoly in specific geographic areas. The National Football League has a monopoly on professional football. The NFL owners know that if they raise ticket prices, fans won't go elsewhere to watch a football game. These situations are the exception to the rule, however. Typically more than one firm supplies a particular product.

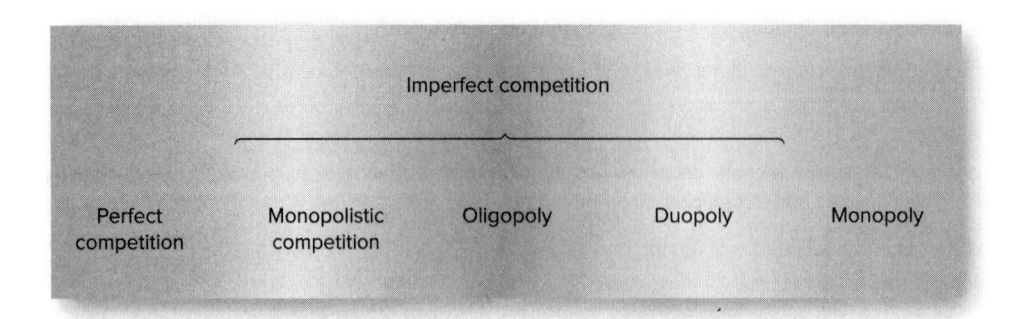

Figure 5.1 Market Structures The number and relative size of firms producing a good vary across industries. Market structures range from perfect competition (a great many firms producing the same goods) to monopoly (only one firm). Most real-world firms are along the continuum of *imperfect* competition. ■

---

at the mercy of 受……支配。price setters 价格制定者。price takers 价格接受者。

Consider the case of Apple Inc. Apple is a megacorporation with over $250 billion in annual sales revenue and more than 125,000 employees. It is not a monopoly, however. Other firms produce smartphones that are virtually identical to Apple products. These other smartphone companies (Samsung, LG, etc.) limit Apple's ability to set prices for its own output. In other words, other firms in the same market limit Apple's **market power**. Apple is not completely *powerless*, however; it is still large enough to have some direct influence on smartphone prices and output. Because it has some market power over smartphone prices, Apple is not a *perfectly* competitive firm.

Economists have created categories to distinguish the degrees of competition in product markets. These various market structures are illustrated in Figure 5.1. At one end of the spectrum is perfect competition, where lots of small firms vie for consumer purchases. At the other extreme is monopoly, where only one firm supplies a particular product.

In between the extremes of monopoly (no competition) and perfect competition lie various forms of imperfect competition:

- *Duopoly:* Only two firms supply a particular product.
- *Oligopoly:* A few large firms supply all or most of a particular product.
- *Monopolistic competition:* Many firms supply essentially the same product, but each enjoys significant brand loyalty.

在垄断（没有竞争）与完全竞争这两个极端情况之间，包括以下几种不同形式的不完全竞争：

- 双头垄断：仅由两家企业控制某一产业。
- 寡头垄断：少数几家大企业完全或几乎完全控制某一产业。
- 垄断竞争：许多家企业共同生产本质上相同的产品，但是每个品牌都享有显著的品牌忠诚度。

How a firm is classified across this spectrum depends not only on its size but also on how many other firms produce identical or similar products. A decade ago IBM, for example, would be classified in the oligopoly category for servers. IBM supplied nearly 70 percent of all servers and confronted only a few rival producers. In the personal computer market, however, IBM had a small market share (under 10 percent) and faced dozens of rivals. In that market IBM fit into the category of monopolistic competition. These days, more firms are producing servers, PCs and tablet computers leading to increased competition. Gasoline stations, fast-food outlets, and even colleges are other examples of monopolistic competition. In this category, many firms are trying to rise above the crowd and get the consumer's attention (and purchases).

Market structure has important effects on the supply of goods. How much you pay for a product depends partly on how many firms offer it for sale. This textbook would be even more expensive if other publishers weren't offering substitute goods. And long-distance telephone service didn't become inexpensive until competing firms broke AT&T's monopoly control of that market. The number of firms in the market has had a significant effect on price.

The *quality* of the product also depends on the degree of competition in the marketplace. Why do the look, the feel, and the features of an iPhone change so fast? Largely because dozens of firms are nipping at Apple's heels, trying to get a larger piece of the smartphone market that Apple created. Apple isn't a perfectly competitive firm, but it still feels the heat of competitive pressure. By contrast, the U.S. Department of Justice contended that the lack of effective competition allowed Microsoft to sell operating systems that were too complex and unwieldy for the typical computer user. With more firms in the market, consumers would have gotten a *better* product at a *lower* price.

With other firms also producing smartphones, Apple has to keep improving its product.
©BestPhotoPlus/Shutterstock

In this chapter we focus on only one market structure—namely, perfect competition. Our goal is to see how perfectly competitive firms make supply decisions. In the next chapter we contrast *monopoly* behavior with this model of perfect competition.

PERFECT COMPETITION 完全竞争

It's not easy to visualize a perfectly competitive firm. None of the corporations you could name are likely to fit the model of perfect competition. Perfectly competitive firms are pretty much faceless. They have no brand image and no real market recognition.

---

megacorporation 特大企业，巨型企业。　market power 市场权力。　powerless 无权利的。　vie 争夺，激烈竞争。　unwieldy 笨拙的，不易操作的。

No Market Power 没有市场权力

完全竞争最重要的特征就是行业里的每个企业都完全没有市场权力。在完全竞争性市场中，每个企业的产出相对于市场规模而言都是如此之小，以至于它们的产出决策对市场价格没有明显影响。竞争性厂商能够以现行市场价格将其产出全部销售出去。如果该企业想提高价格，那么它什么也卖不出去，因为消费者会去其他地方购买。在这点上，完全竞争性厂商没有市场权力——没有能力控制它所销售产品的市场价格。

The critical factor in perfect competition is the total absence of market power for individual firms. *A perfectly competitive firm is one whose output is so small in relation to market volume that its output decisions have no perceptible impact on price.* A competitive firm can sell all its output at the prevailing market price. If it tries to charge a higher price, it will not sell anything because consumers will shop elsewhere. In this sense, a perfectly competitive firm has no *market power*—no ability to control the market price for the good it sells.

At first glance, it might appear that all firms have market power. After all, who is to stop a producer from raising prices? The critical concept here, however, is *market* price—that is, the price at which goods are actually sold. You might want to resell this textbook for $90. But you will discover that the bookstore will not buy it at that price. Anyone can change the *asking* price of a good, but actual sales will occur only at the market price. With so many other students offering to sell their books, the bookstore knows it does not have to pay the $90 you are asking. Because you do not have any market power, you have to accept the "going price" for used texts if you want to sell this book.

The same kind of powerlessness is characteristic of the small catfish farmer. Like any producer, the lone catfish farmer can increase or reduce his rate of output. But this production decision will not affect the market price of catfish.

甚至年产量达10万磅的养殖大户，也不能影响鲶鱼的市场价格。为什么？因为每年都有超过5亿磅鲶鱼进入市场，10万磅的数目便显得微乎其微了。换句话说，相对于整个市场供给而言，单个养殖者的产出是如此之小，以至于对市场中的总数量或价格没有显著影响。

Even a larger farmer who can alter a harvest by as much as 100,000 pounds of fish per year will not influence the market price of catfish. Why not? Because over 500 *million* pounds of catfish are brought to market every year, and another 100,000 pounds simply won't be noticed. In other words, *the output of the lone farmer is so small relative to the market supply that it has no significant effect on the total quantity or price in the market.*

One can visualize the difference between competitive firms and firms with market power by considering what happened in 2008 to U.S. catfish supplies and prices when Farmer Seamans drained some of his catfish ponds (see the News Wire "Competitive Markets"). No one really noticed: Total U.S. catfish production and market prices were unaffected. Farmer Seamans was a tiny player in a very big market. The same kind of powerlessness was evident in 2018 when falling prices again forced catfish farmers to drain their ponds and plant soybeans instead.

NEWS WIRE COMPETITIVE MARKETS

CATFISH FARMERS ON THE HOOK

Foreign imports and rising feed prices are destroying the prospects for catfish farming. Jerry Seamans, whose catfish farm is just outside Lake Village, is converting 20 percent of his 1,200 acres of catfish ponds back to acreage for planting soybeans and rice. He says cheap imports and the rising price of grain feed have made catfish farming unprofitable. Returning his ponds to rice and soybean production looks like a much better bet. He noted that some catfish farmers are going out of business altogether, and nearly every farmer is adjusting his production.

Six years ago, the situation was much better. Back in 2002, there were 195 catfish farmers in Arkansas operating 38,000 acres of ponds. In the last few years the number of catfish farms has dwindled to 128 with only 29,900 acres of ponds. Annual production has dropped from 107,821 pounds two years ago to the only 90,400 this year. The catfish industry just can't stay ahead of foreign competition and rising production costs.

Source: Arkansas news accounts of May 2008.

NOTE: In competitive markets, new firms enter quickly when profitable opportunities exist. As a result of such entry, profits often don't last long, forcing some firms to quit the business.
注：在竞争性市场中，当有盈利机会时，新企业进入市场的速度非常快。由于进入如此迅速，利润通常都不会持续很久，这迫使一些企业退出行业。

Contrast that scenario with the likely consequences for U.S. auto supplies and prices if the Ford Motor Company were to close down suddenly. Farmer Seamans's cutbacks had no impact on market outcomes; the impact of a Ford shutdown, however, would be dramatic. Ford is a big player in the auto market and its production decisions can change the market price of cars.

The same contrast is evident when a firm's output is increased. Were Farmer Seamans to double his production capacity (build another 10 ponds), the added catfish output wouldn't even show up in commerce statistics. U.S. catfish production is calibrated in the hundreds of millions of pounds, and no one is going to notice another 100,000 pounds of fish. Were Ford, on the other hand, to double its production, the added output would depress automobile prices as Ford tried to unload its heavy inventories.

Price Takers 价格接受者

The critical distinction between Ford and Farmer Seamans is not in their motivation but in their ability to alter market outcomes. Both are out to make a profit. What makes Farmer Seamans's situation different is the fact that his output decisions do not influence catfish prices. All catfish look alike, so Farmer Seamans's catfish will fetch the same price as everyone else's catfish. Were he to attempt to enlarge his profits by raising his catfish prices above market levels, he would find himself without customers because consumers would go elsewhere to buy their catfish. To maximize his profits, Farmer Seamans can only strive to run an efficient operation and make the right supply decisions. He is a *price taker*, taking the market price of catfish as a fact of life and doing the best he can within that constraint.

Ford Motor Company, on the other hand, can behave like a *price setter*. Instead of waiting to find out what the market price is and making appropriate output adjustments, Ford has the discretion to announce prices at the beginning of every model year. Fords are not exactly like Chevrolets or Toyotas in the minds of consumers. Because Fords are *differentiated*, Ford knows that sales will not fall to zero if its car prices are set a little higher than those of other car manufacturers. Ford confronts a downward-sloping, rather than a perfectly horizontal, demand curve for its output.

福特与鲶鱼养殖者西门斯的显著区别并不在于它们的动机，而在于它们改变市场状况的能力。两者都想赚钱。农民西门斯的情况之所以不同，是因为他的产出决策不能影响鲶鱼价格。所有鲶鱼看起来都一样，因此西门斯的鲶鱼与其他人的鲶鱼价格一样。假如他试图通过使自己的鲶鱼价格高于市场水平来增加利润，他会发现顾客流失了，因为顾客将到其他地方购买鲶鱼。为了实现利润最大化，鲶鱼养殖者西门斯只能努力提高工作效率，并做出正确的供给决策。他是一个价格接受者，只能将鲶鱼的市场价格作为既定价格来接受，并在此约束下尽可能做到最好。

Market Demand versus Firm Demand 市场需求与企业需求

To appreciate the unique nature of perfect competition, ***you must distinguish between the market demand curve and the demand curve confronting a particular firm.*** Farmer Seamans's small operation does not contradict the law of demand. The quantity of catfish purchased in the supermarket still depends on catfish prices. That is to say, the *market* demand curve for catfish is downward-sloping, just as the market demand for cars is downward-sloping.

The Firm's Horizontal Demand Curve 厂商的水平需求曲线

Although the market demand curve for catfish is downward-sloping, the demand curve facing Farmer Seamans has a unique shape: It is *horizontal*. Remember, if he charges a price above the prevailing market price, he will lose *all* his customers. So a higher price results in quantity demanded falling to zero. On the other hand, he can double or triple his output and still sell every fish he produces at the prevailing market price. As a result, ***the demand curve facing a perfectly competitive firm is horizontal.*** Farmer Seamans himself faces a horizontal demand curve because his share of the market is so tiny that changes in his output do not disturb the market equilibrium.

为了了解完全竞争的独特性，必须区分市场需求曲线与单个企业所面对的需求曲线。鲶鱼养殖者西门斯的小规模经营与需求规律并不矛盾。超市中鲶鱼的购买量仍然取决于鲶鱼的价格。也就是说，鲶鱼的市场需求曲线仍然是向下倾斜的，正如汽车的市场需求曲线是向下倾斜的一样。

Collectively, though, individual farmers do count. If 10,000 small, competitive farmers expand their catfish production at the same time, the market equilibrium will be disturbed. That is to say, a competitive market composed of 10,000 individually powerless producers still sees a lot of action. The power here resides in the collective action of all the producers, however, not in the individual action of any one producer. Were catfish production to increase abruptly, the catfish could be sold only at lower prices, in accordance with the downward-sloping nature of the *market* demand curve.

---

calibrate 标定。 discretion 自行决定权。 differentiated 可区分的，有差异的。 disturb 干扰，妨碍。 in accordance with 与……一致。

The distinction between the actions of a single producer and those of the market are illustrated in Figure 5.2. Notice that

- 产品的市场需求曲线总是向下倾斜的；
- 完全竞争性厂商所面对的需求曲线是水平的。

- ***The market demand curve for a product is always downward-sloping.***
- ***The demand curve facing a perfectly competitive firm is horizontal.***

That horizontal demand curve is the distinguishing feature of *perfectly* competitive firms. If a firm can raise its price without losing *all* its customers, it is not a perfectly competitive firm. (Does McDonald's meet this condition? United Airlines? Apple? Your college?)

厂商的生产决策
THE FIRM'S PRODUCTION DECISION

因为竞争性厂商是价格接受者，所以不必进行价格决策，他们生产的所有产品都以市场价格出售。但他们仍然需要做一个重要决策——竞争性厂商需要决定在这种价格水平下该生产多少产品。

Because a competitive firm is a price taker, it doesn't have to make a *pricing decision*: Everything it produces will be sold at the prevailing *market* price. It still has an important decision to make, however. The competitive firm must decide *how much* output to sell at the going price.

产出水平的选择就是厂商的**生产决策**。厂商是应该尽其所能进行生产，还是应该使产出少于最大产出呢？

Choosing a rate of output is a firm's **production decision**. Should it produce all the output it can? Or should it produce less than its capacity output?

Output and Revenues   产出与收益

If a competitive firm produces more output, its sales revenue will definitely increase. **Total revenue** is the price of the good multiplied by the quantity sold:

$$\text{Total revenue} = \text{price} \times \text{quantity}$$

(a) Market demand

(b) Demand for individual farmer's catfish

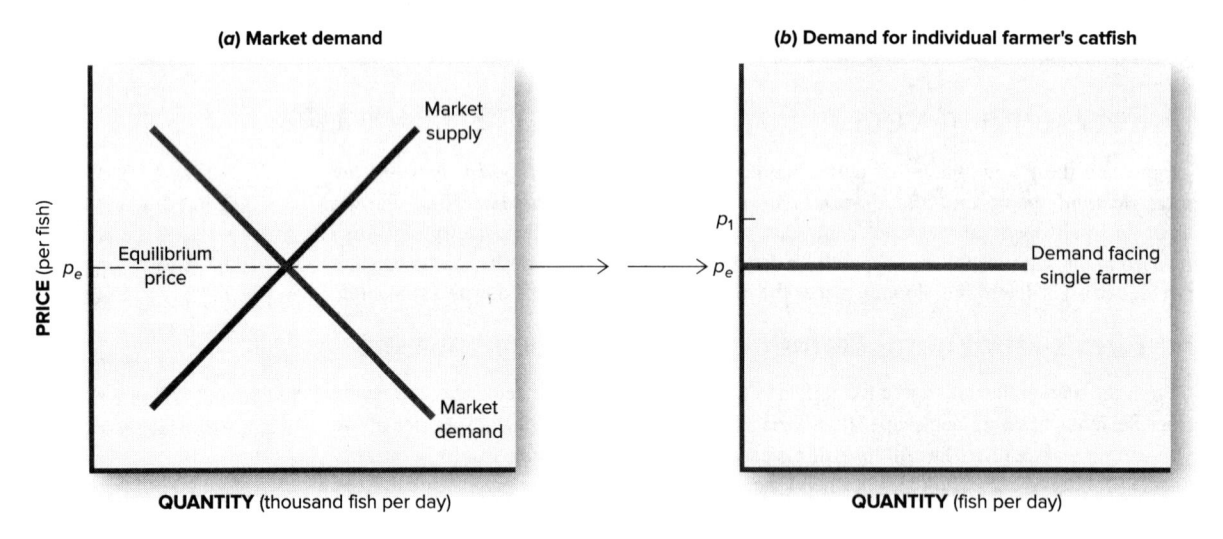

Figure 5.2 Market Demand versus Firm Demand The *market* demand for any product is downward-sloping. The equilibrium price (p_e) of catfish is established by the intersection of *market demand* and *market supply*, as shown in Figure 5.2a.

This market-established price is the only one at which an individual farmer can sell catfish. If the farmer asks a higher price (e.g., p_1), no one will buy his catfish since people can buy identical catfish from other farmers at p_e. But a farmer can sell all of his catfish at the equilibrium price. The lone farmer thus confronts a horizontal demand curve for his own output, as shown in Figure 5.2b. (Notice the difference in quantities on the horizontal axes of the two graphs.) ■

Since a competitive firm can sell all of its output at the market price, total revenue is a simple multiple of that price. That is why the total revenue line in Figure 5.3 keeps rising in a straight line: *More output means more revenue.*

Revenues versus Profits 收益与利润

If a competitive firm wanted to maximize total *revenue,* its strategy would be obvious: It would simply produce as much output as possible. But maximizing total revenue isn't the goal. Business firms try to maximize total *profits,* not total *revenue.*

As we saw in Chapter 4, total **profit** is the *difference* between total revenues and total costs. Hence a profit-maximizing firm must look not only at revenues but at costs as well. As output increases, total revenues go up, but total costs do as well. If costs rise too fast, profits may actually decline as output increases.

正如在第 4 章学到的，总**利润**是总收益与总成本之间的差额。因此一个追求利润最大化的企业不仅需要关注收益，还要关注成本。随着产出增加，总收益上升，但总成本也会上升。假如成本上升过快，利润很可能随着产出的增加而减少。

We may embark on the search for maximizing profits with two clues:

- *Maximizing output or revenue is not the way to maximize profits.*
- *Total profits depend on how both revenues and costs increase as output expands.*

我们可以从以下两条线索出发寻求利润最大化：

- 产出最大化或收益最大化并不是寻求利润最大化的途径；
- 总利润取决于随着产出的扩大，收益与成本增加的程度。

Notice in Figure 5.3 how total costs start out above total revenue. Do you remember why this is the case? Because of fixed costs—costs that are incurred even when no output is produced. At zero output, the firm must pay its fixed costs (rent, insurance, overhead, etc.) but has no sales and, therefore, no revenue. That means the firm is incurring a loss for sure is it doesn't produce anything from its fixed assets. At zero output, the firm must pay its fixed costs (rent, insurance, overhead, etc) but has no sales and, therefore, no revenue. That means that the firm is incurring a loss for sure if it doesn't produce anything from its fixed assets. As production increases, however, revenues increase faster than costs (beginning at q_1), making production profitable. But profits don't keep growing. At some point (q_2), escalating costs may overtake revenues, creating economic losses again.

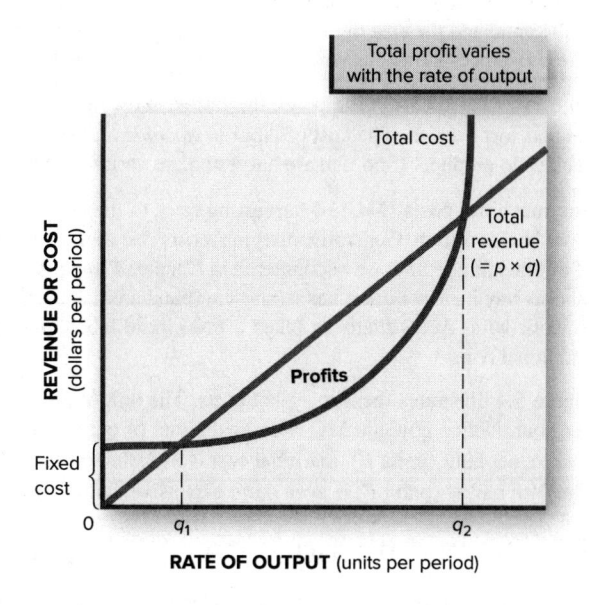

Figure 5.3 The Profitable Range of Output Total revenue rises as output expands. But profits depend on how fast revenues rise in comparison to total costs. Only in the range of output between q_1 and q_2 is this business profitable (i.e., total revenue exceeds total cost). The goal is to find the output level within this range that *maximizes* total profits. ■

---

multiple 倍数。 incur 招致，蒙受。 escalating 逐步上升的。

Notice in Figure 5.3 how the Total Cost line rises above the Total Revenue line again at point q_2. The firm starts losing money again if it produces more than the quantity q_2. Hence ***a business is profitable only within a certain range of output*** (q_1 to q_2 in Figure 5.3).

The goal of the firm is to find the single rate of output that *maximizes* total profit. That output rate must lie somewhere between q_1 and q_2 in Figure 5.3. But how can we locate it?

PROFIT MAXIMIZATION 利润最大化

We can advance still further toward the goal of maximum profits by employing a simple rule of thumb: Produce an additional unit of output only if that unit brings in more revenue than it costs. A producer who follows this rule will move steadily closer to maximum profits. We will explain this rule by looking first at the revenue side of production (what it brings in) and then at the cost side (what it costs).

Price 价格

For a perfectly competitive firm, it is easy to see how much revenue a unit of output brings in. All we have to look at is price. ***Since competitive firms are price takers, they must take whatever price the market has put on their products.*** Thus a catfish farmer can readily determine the value of his fish by looking at the market price of catfish.

Marginal Cost 边际成本

Once we know what one more unit brings in (its price), all we need to know for profit maximization is the cost of producing an additional unit.

The production process for catfish farming is fairly straightforward. The "factory" in this case is a pond; the rate of production is the number of fish harvested from the pond per hour. A farmer can alter the rate of production at will, up to the breeding capacity of the pond.

Assume that the *fixed* cost of the pond is $10 per hour. The fixed costs include the rental value of the pond and the cost of electricity for keeping the pond oxygenated so the fish can breathe. These fixed costs must be paid no matter how many fish the farmer harvests.

To harvest catfish from the pond, the farmer must incur additional costs. Labor is needed to net and sort the fish. The cost of labor is *variable,* depending on how much output the farmer decides to produce. If no fish are harvested, no variable costs are incurred.

The **marginal costs (MC)** of harvesting refer to the additional costs incurred to harvest *one* more basket of fish. Generally, marginal costs rise as the rate of production increases. The law of diminishing returns we encountered in Chapter 4 applies to catfish farming as well. As more labor is hired, each worker has less space (pond area) and capital (access to nets, sorting trays) to work with. Accordingly, it takes a little more labor time (marginal cost) to harvest each additional fish.

Figure 5.4 illustrates these marginal costs. The unit of production used here is baskets of fish per hour. Notice how the MC rises as the rate of output increases. At the output rate of four baskets per hour (point E), marginal cost is $13; the fourth basket increases total costs by $13. The fifth basket (point F) is even more expensive, with a marginal cost of $17.

Profit-Maximizing Rate of Output 利润最大化的产出率

We are now in a position to make a production decision. All we have to know is the price of the product and its marginal cost. We do not want to produce an additional unit of output if its MC exceeds its price. If MC exceeds price, we are spending more to produce that extra unit than we are getting back: Total profits will decline if we produce it.

---

rule of thumb 经验准则。steadily 稳定地，不断地。

The opposite is true when price exceeds MC. If an extra unit brings in more revenue than it costs to produce, it is adding to total profit. Total profits must increase in this case. Hence *a competitive firm wants to expand the rate of production whenever price exceeds MC.*

Since we want to expand output when price exceeds MC and contract output if price is less than MC, the profit-maximizing rate of output is easily found. *Short-run profits are maximized at the rate of output where price equals marginal cost.* The **competitive profit maximization rule** is summarized in Table 5.1.

Figure 5.5 illustrates the application of our profit maximization rule. The market price of catfish is $13 a basket. At this price we can sell as many fish as we like, up to our short-run capacity. The fish cannot be sold at a higher price because lots of farmers grow fish and sell them for $13. If we try to charge a higher price, consumers will buy their fish from these other producers. Hence the demand curve facing this one firm is horizontal at the price of $13 a basket.

当价格超过 MC 时，情况正好相反。如果额外一单位产出带来的收益大于其生产成本，就使总利润增加。总利润在这种情况下必然增加。因此，只要价格超过 MC，竞争性厂商就会扩大生产。

由于价格超过 MC 时我们会扩大产出，价格低于 MC 时会缩减产出，因此很容易找到利润最大化的产出水平。短期利润在价格等于边际成本的产出水平时达到最大化。表 5.1 总结了**竞争性利润最大化原则**。

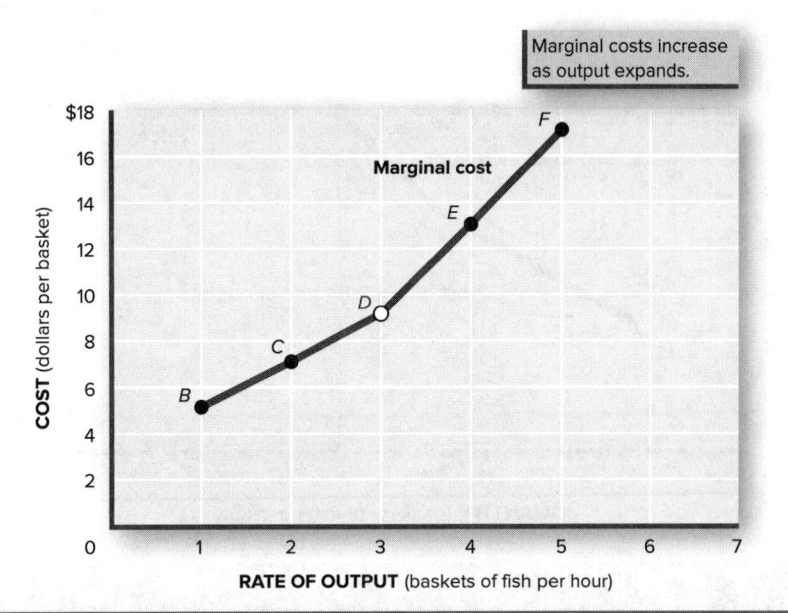

	Rate of Output (Baskets per Hour)	Total Cost (per Hour)	Marginal Cost (per Unit)	Average Total Cost (per Unit)
A	0	$10	—	—
B	1	15	$5	$15.00
C	2	22	7	11.00
D	3	31	9	10.33
E	4	44	13	11.00
F	5	61	17	12.20

Figure 5.4 Increasing Marginal Cost Marginal cost (MC) is the cost of producing one more unit. When production expands from two to three units per hour, total costs increase by $9 (from $22 to $31 per hour). The marginal cost of the third basket is therefore $9, as seen in row *D* of the table and point *D* in the graph. Marginal costs increase as output expands (remember why?). ∎

Price Level	Production Decision
Price > MC	Increase output rate.
Price = MC	Maintain output rate (profits maximized).
Price < MC	Decrease output rate.

Table 5.1 Short-Run Decision Rules for a Competitive Firm The relationship between price and marginal cost dictates short-run production decisions. For competitive firms, profits are maximized at that rate of output where price = MC.

The costs of harvesting catfish were already examined in Figure 5.4. The key concept illustrated here is marginal cost. The MC curve slopes upward.

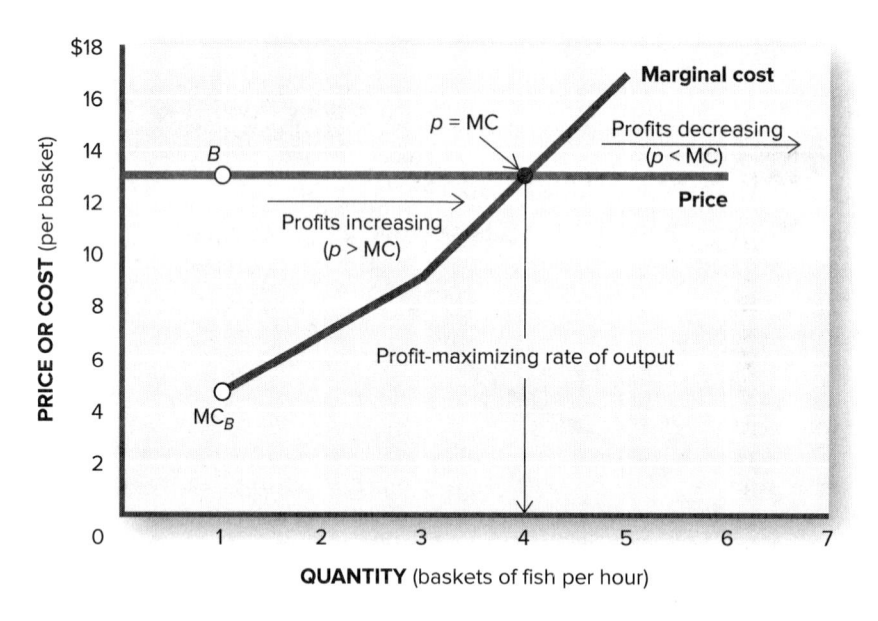

	(1) Number of Baskets (per Hour)	(2) Price	(3) Total Revenue	(4) Total Cost	(5) Total Profit	(6) Price	(7) Marginal Cost
A	0	—	0	$10.00	−$10.00	—	—
B	1	$13.00	$13.00	15.00	− 2.00	$13.00	$ 5.00
C	2	13.00	26.00	22.00	+ 4.00	13.00	7.00
D	3	13.00	39.00	31.00	+ 8.00	13.00	9.00
E	4	13.00	52.00	44.00	+ 8.00	13.00	13.00
F	5	13.00	65.00	61.00	+ 4.00	13.00	17.00

Figure 5.5 Maximizing Profits for a Competitive Firm A competitive firm maximizes total profits at the output rate where MC = p. If MC is less than price, the firm can increase profits by producing more. If MC exceeds price, the firm should reduce output. In this case, profit maximization occurs at an output of four baskets of fish per hour.

Also depicted in Figure 5.5 are the total revenues, costs, and profits of alternative production rates. Study the table in Figure 5.5 first. Notice that the firm loses $10 per hour if it produces no fish (row A). At zero output, total revenue is zero ($p \times q = 0$). However, the firm must still contend with fixed costs of $10 per hour. Total profit—total revenue minus total cost—is therefore *minus* $10; the firm incurs a loss.

Row *B* of the table shows how this loss is reduced when one basket of fish is produced per hour. The production and sale of just one basket per hour brings in $13 of total revenue (column 3). The total cost of producing that one basket is $15 (column 4). Hence the total loss associated with an output rate of one basket per hour is $2 (column 5). This $2 loss may not be what we hoped for, but it is certainly better than the $10 loss incurred at zero output.

If a firm had a complete table of revenues and costs, it could identify the profit-maximizing rate of output. But it would be nice to have a shortcut to that conclusion. Fortunately there is an easier way to make production decisions.

Decision When *p* > MC   *p* > MC 时的决策

The superior profitability of producing one basket of fish per hour rather than none is evident in columns 6 and 7 of row *B*. The first basket fetches a price of $13. But its *marginal cost* is only $5. Hence it brings in more added revenue ($13) than it costs to produce ($5). Under these circumstances—whenever price exceeds MC—output should definitely be expanded. That is one of the decision rules summarized in Table 5.1.

The excess of price over MC for the first unit of output is also illustrated by the graph in Figure 5.5. Point *B* ($13) lies above MC_B ($5); the *difference* between these two points measures the contribution that the first basket of fish makes to the total profits of the firm. In this case, that contribution equals $13 − $5 = $8, and production losses are reduced by that amount when the rate of output is increased from zero to one basket per hour.

So long as price exceeds MC, further increases in the rate of output are desirable. Notice what happens to profits when the rate of output is increased from one to two baskets per hour (row *C*). The price of the second basket is $13; its MC is $7. Therefore, it *adds* $6 to total profits. Instead of losing $2 per hour, the firm is now making a profit of $4 per hour.

The firm can make even more profits by expanding the rate of output further. Look what happens when the rate of output reaches three baskets per hour (row *D* of the table). The price of the third basket is $13; its marginal cost is $9. Therefore, the third basket makes a $4 contribution to profits. By increasing its rate of output to three baskets per hour, the firm doubles its total profits.

This firm will never make huge profits. The fourth unit of output has a price of $13 and an MC of $13 as well. It does not contribute to total profits, nor does it subtract from them. The fourth unit of output represents the highest rate of output the firm desires. ***At the rate of output where price = MC, total profits of the firm are maximized.***

Decision When *p* < MC   *p* < MC 时的决策

Notice what happens if we expand output beyond four baskets per hour. The price of the fifth basket is still $13, but its MC is $17. The fifth basket costs more than it brings in. If we produce that fifth basket, total profit will decline by $4. The fifth unit of output makes us worse off. This is evident in the graph in Figure 5.5: At the output rate of five baskets per hour, the MC curve lies above the price curve. The lesson here is clear: ***Output should not be increased if MC exceeds price.***

Maximum Profit at *p* = MC   *p* = MC 时利润最大化

The outcome of the production decision is illustrated in Figure 5.5 by the intersection of the price and MC curves. At this intersection, price equals MC and profits are maximized. If we produced less, we would be giving up potential profits. If we produced more, total profits would also fall. Hence the point where MC = *p* is the limit to profit maximization.

---

fetch 卖得（若干价钱）。expand 扩张，扩大。

Total Profit 总利润

所以我们在这里学到了什么呢？很简单：为了得到正确的生产决策，我们只需比较价格与边际成本。然而，当找到了合意的产出率之后，我们也许还想进一步考察正在累积的利润。当然，我们可以满足于图 5.5 表格中的统计数字。但如果能有一幅图——尤其是能反映我们在生产上的成功，那就更好了。图 5.6 便提供了这样一张图。

So what have we learned here? The message is simple: To reach the right production decision, we need only compare price and marginal costs. Having found the desired rate of output, however, we may want to take a closer look at the profits we are accumulating. We could, of course, content ourselves with the statistics shown in the table of Figure 5.5. But a picture would be nice, too, especially if it reflected our success in production. Figure 5.6 provides such a picture.

Figure 5.6 takes advantage of the fact that total profit can be computed in one of two ways:

$$\text{Total profit} = \text{total revenue} - \text{total cost}$$

or

$$\text{Total profit} = \text{average profit} \times \text{quantity sold}$$
$$(\text{profit per unit})$$

In Figure 5.6, the focus is on the second formula. To use it, we compute profit per unit as price *minus* average total cost—that is,

$$\text{profit per unit} = p - \text{ATC}$$

Figure 5.6 adds an *average* total cost curve to the graphs of Figure 5.4. This curve allows us to see how *profit per unit* changes as the rate of output increases. Like the ATC curve we first encountered in Chapter 4 (Figure 4.3), this ATC curve has the distinctive U shape.

We compute profit per unit as price minus ATC. As before, the market price of catfish is assumed to be $13 per basket, as illustrated by the horizontal price line at that level. Therefore, the *difference* between price and average cost—profit per unit—is illustrated by the vertical distance between the price and ATC curves. At four baskets of fish per hour, for example, profit per unit equals $13 − $11 = $2.

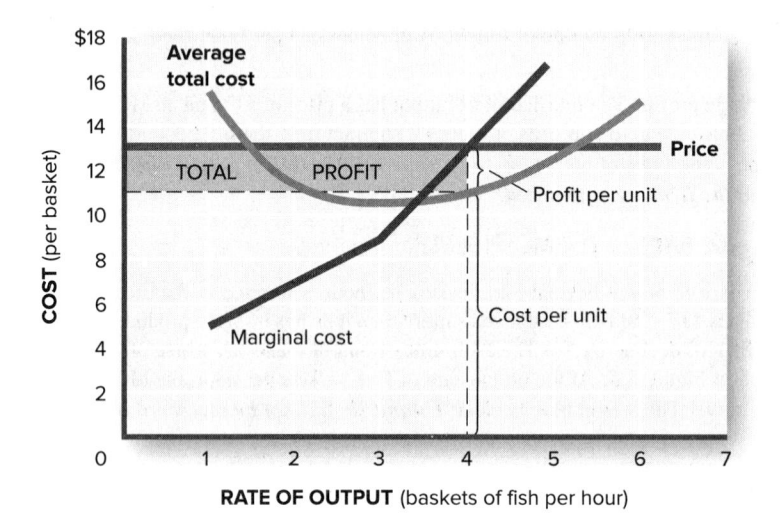

Figure 5.6 Illustrating Total Profit Total profits can be computed as profit *per unit* (*p* − ATC) multiplied by the quantity sold. This is illustrated by the shaded rectangle. To find the desired profit-maximizing rate of output, we could use this graph or just the MC and price curves of Figure 5.5. ∎

---

take advantage of 利用。

To compute *total* profits at the output rate of four baskets, we note that

$$\begin{aligned}\text{Total profit} &= \text{profit per unit} \times \text{quantity} \\ &= (p - ATC) \times q \\ &= (\$13 - \$11) \times 4\end{aligned}$$

In this case, the *total* profit would be $8 per hour. *Total* profits are illustrated in Figure 5.6 by the shaded rectangle. (Recall that the area of a rectangle is equal to its height [profit per unit] multiplied by its width [quantity sold].)

Profit per unit is used to compute total profits but it is often of interest in its own right as well. Businesspeople like to cite statistics on markups, which are a crude index to per-unit profits. However, ***the profit-maximizing producer never seeks to maximize per-unit profits.*** **What counts is *total* profits,** not the amount of profit per unit. This is the age-old problem of trying to sell ice cream for $8 a cone. You might be able to maximize profit per unit if you could sell one cone for $8, but you would make a lot more money if you sold 100 cones at a per-unit profit of only 50 cents each.

Similarly, ***the profit-maximizing producer has no particular desire to produce at that rate of output where ATC is at a minimum.*** Minimum ATC does represent least-cost production. But additional units of output, even though they raise average costs, will increase total profits. This is evident in Figure 5.6: Price exceeds MC for some output to the right of minimum ATC (the bottom of the U). Therefore, total profits are increasing as we increase the rate of output beyond the point of minimum average costs. ***Total profits are maximized only where p = MC.***

SUPPLY BEHAVIOR   供给行为

Right about now you may be wondering why we're memorizing formulas for profit maximization. Who cares about MC, ATC, and all these other cost concepts? Maybe we all do. If we don't know how firms make production decisions, we'll never figure out how the market establishes prices and quantities for the products we desire. Knowledge of supply decisions can also be valuable if you are purchasing a car, a vacation package, or even something in an electronic auction. What we're learning here is how much of a good sellers are *willing* to offer at any given price.

A Firm's Supply   单个厂商的供给

The most distinctive feature of perfectly competitive firms is the lack of pricing decisions. As price takers, the only decision competitive firms make is how much output to produce at the prevailing market price. Their **supply** behavior is determined by the rules for profit maximization (Table 5.1). Specifically, ***competitive firms adjust the quantity supplied until MC = price.***

Suppose the price of catfish was only $9 per basket instead of $13. Would it still make sense to harvest four baskets per hour? No. Four baskets is the profit-maximizing rate of output only when the price of catfish is $13. At a price of $9 a basket, it would not make sense to produce four baskets because the MC of the fourth basket ($13) would exceed its price. The decision rule (Table 5.1) in this case requires a cutback in output. At a market price of $9, the most profitable rate of output would be only three baskets of fish per hour (see Figure 5.5).

The marginal cost curve thus tells us how much output a firm will supply at different prices. Once we know the price of catfish, we can look at the MC curve to determine exactly how many fish Farmer Seamans should harvest. In other words, ***the marginal cost curve is the short-run supply curve for a competitive firm.***

---

auction 拍卖。make sense 有意义。cutback 削减，减少。

Supply Shifts　供给移动

Since marginal costs determine the supply decisions of a firm, *anything that alters marginal cost will change supply behavior.* The most important influences on marginal cost (and supply behavior) are

- *The price of factor inputs.*
- *Technology.*
- *Expectations.*

A catfish farmer will supply more fish at any given price if the price of feed declines. If fish can be bred faster because of advances in genetic engineering, productivity will increase and the farmer's MC curve will shift downward. With lower marginal costs, the firm will supply more output at any given price.

Conversely, if wages increased, the marginal cost of producing fish would rise as well. This upward shift of the MC curve would cause the firm to supply fewer fish at any prevailing price. Finally, if producers expect factor prices to rise or demand to diminish, they may be more willing to supply output now.

You can put the concept of marginal cost pricing to use the next time you buy a car. The car dealer wants to get a price that covers all costs, including a share of the rent, electricity, and insurance (fixed costs). The dealer might, however, be willing to sell the car for only its *marginal* cost—that is, the wholesale price paid for the car plus a little labor time (variable costs). So long as the price exceeds marginal cost, the dealer is better off selling the car than not selling it.

Market Supply　市场供给

Up until now we have focused on the supply behavior of a single competitive firm. But what about the **market supply** of catfish? We need a *market* supply curve to determine the *market* price the individual farmer will confront. In the previous discussion, we simply set the price arbitrarily at $13 per basket. Now our objective is to find out how the market actually sets market price.

Like the market supply curves we first encountered in Chapter 2, the market supply of catfish is obtained by simple addition. All we have to do is add up the quantities each farmer stands ready to supply at each and every price. Then we will know the total number of fish to be supplied to the market at that price. Figure 5.7 illustrates this summation. Notice that *the market supply curve is the sum of the marginal cost curves of all the firms.* Hence whatever determines the marginal cost of a typical firm will also determine industry supply. Specifically, the *market supply of a competitive industry is determined by*

- *The price of factor inputs.*
- *Technology.*
- *Expectations.*
- *The number of firms in the industry.*

INDUSTRY ENTRY AND EXIT　行业进入与退出

With a market supply curve and a market demand curve, we can identify the **equilibrium price**—the price that matches the quantity demanded to the quantity supplied. This equilibrium is shown as E_1 in Figure 5.8.

If truth be told, locating a market's equilibrium is neither difficult nor terribly interesting—certainly not in competitive markets. In *competitive markets, the real action is*

---

genetic engineering 基因工程，遗传工程。　dealer 经销商。　arbitrarily 武断地。

in changes to market equilibrium. In competitive markets, new firms are always beating down the door, trying to get a share of industry profits. Entrepreneurs are always looking for ways to improve products or the production process. Nothing stays in equilibrium very long. Hence, to understand how competitive markets really work, we have to focus on *changes* in equilibrium rather than on the identification of a static equilibrium. One of the forces driving those changes is the entry of new firms into an industry.

Entry 进入

竞争性市场中。竞争性市场的实际情况是时刻变化的，并不存在长久的市场均衡。在竞争性市场中，新厂商总是拼命地想挤入行业，分食一部分行业利润。企业家们也总是在寻找改进产品或生产流程的方法。均衡不会长久。因此，要理解竞争性市场的实际运行，与其关注某一确定的静态均衡，倒不如关注均衡的变化。驱使这些变化的力量之一是行业中新厂商的进入。

Suppose that the equilibrium price in the catfish industry is $13. This short-run equilibrium is illustrated in Figure 5.8 by the point E_1 at the intersection of market demand and the market supply curve S_1. At that price, the typical catfish farmer would harvest four baskets of fish per hour and earn a profit of $8 per hour (as seen earlier in Figure 5.6). All the farmers together would be producing the quantity q_1 in Figure 5.8.

The profitable equilibrium at E_1 is not likely to last, however. Farmers still growing cotton or other crops will see the profits being made by catfish farmers and lust after them. They, too, will want to dig up their crops and replace them with catfish ponds.

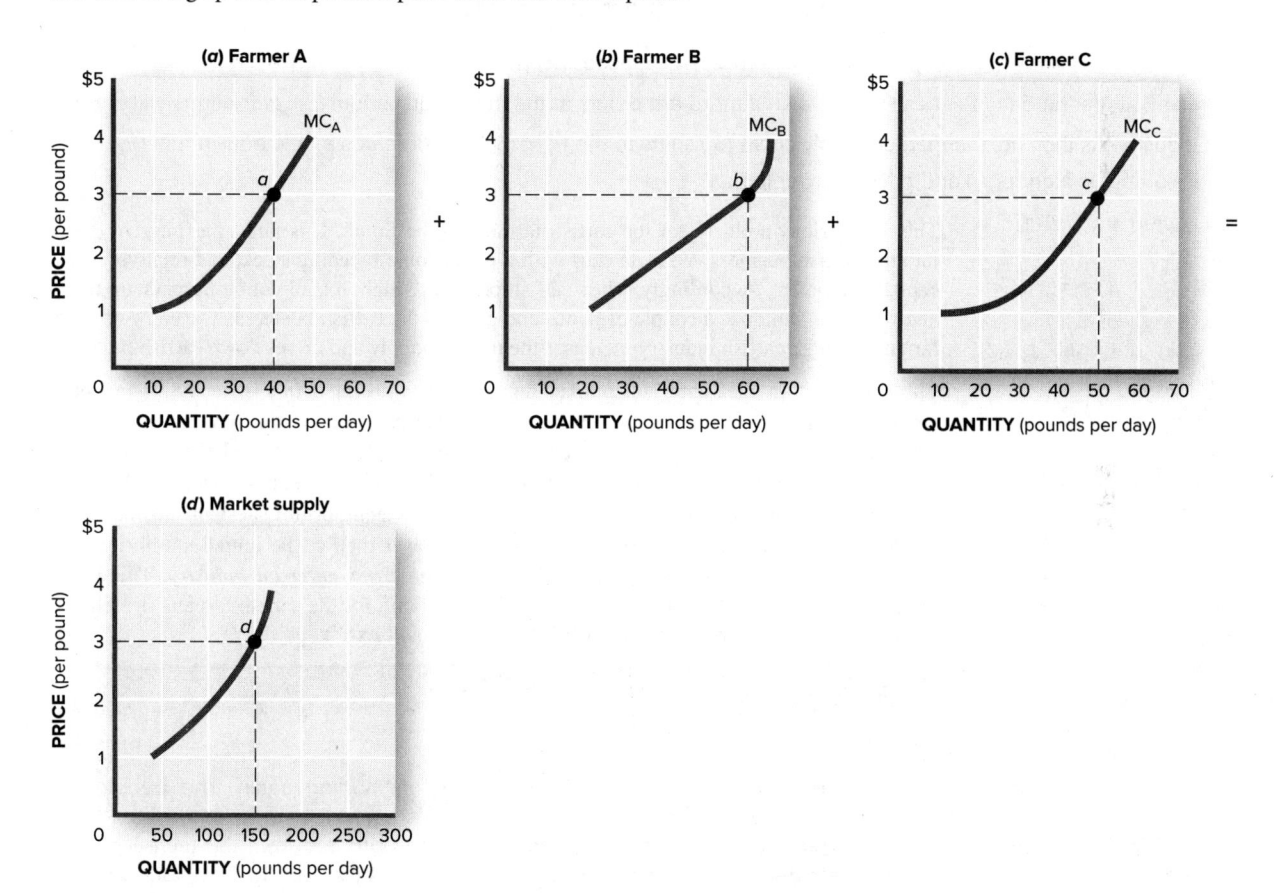

Figure 5.7 Competitive Market Supply The MC curve is a competitive firm's short-run supply curve. The curve MC_A tells us that Farmer A will produce 40 pounds of catfish per day if the market price is $3 per pound; Farmer B will produce 60 pounds per day (curve MC_B); and Farmer C will produce 50 pounds per day (curve MC_C).

To determine the *market supply,* we add up the quantities supplied by each farmer. The total quantity supplied to the market here is 150 pounds per day (= *a* + *b* + *c*). Market supply depends on the number of firms in an industry and their respective marginal costs. ∎

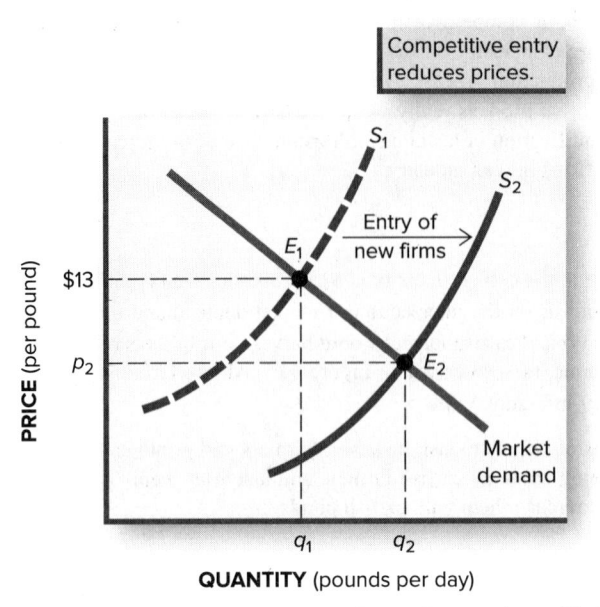

Figure 5.8 Market Entry Pushes Prices Down If there are profits at the initial equilibrium (E_1), more firms will enter the industry. As they do, the market supply curve (S_1) shifts to the right (S_2). This creates a new equilibrium (E_2), where output is higher (q_2) and price is lower (p_2).

进入市场对市场结果的影响如图 5.8 所示。最初的均衡 E_1 由现有生产者的供给行为决定。但是如果这些生产者能赚钱,其他厂商也将进入此行业。当他们进入后,行业供给曲线向右移动(S_2)。这一进入导致的市场供给曲线的移动改变了市场均衡。新的均衡在 E_2 建立起来。E_2 与起初的均衡 E_1 相比,供给数量更多,价格更低。因此当新厂商进入某行业时,行业产出增加而价格下降。

This is a serious problem for the catfish farmers in the South. It is fairly inexpensive to get into the catfish business. You can start with a pond, some breeding stock, and relatively little capital equipment. Accordingly, when catfish prices are high, lots of cotton farmers are ready and willing to bulldoze a couple of ponds and get into the catfish business. The entry of more farmers into the catfish industry increases the market supply and drives down catfish prices.

The impact of market entry on market outcomes is illustrated in Figure 5.8. The initial equilibrium at E_1 was determined by the supply behavior of existing producers. If those producers are earning a profit, however, other firms will want to enter the industry. When they do, the industry supply curve shifts to the right (S_2). This entry-induced shift of the market supply curve changes market equilibrium. A new equilibrium is established at E_2. At E_2, the quantity supplied is larger and the price is lower than at the initial equilibrium E_1. Hence ***industry output increases and price falls when firms enter an industry.*** This is the kind of competitive behavior that has made life so difficult for the catfish farmers in Belzoni, Mississippi (see the accompanying News Wire "Entry and Exit").

NEWS WIRE   ENTRY AND EXIT

CATFISH FARMERS QUITTING

Belzoni, Mississippi. This self-proclaimed "Catfish Capital of the World" is hurting again. The people of Belzoni rode the catfish boom for a couple of decades. As Americans developed a taste for this delicate, low-fat, high-protein fish in the 1970s, row-crop farmers dug fish ponds and profited from the increased demand for their product. When president Ronald Reagan proclaimed "National Catfish Day" on June 25, 1987, catfish farmers were spawning huge profits. As Reagan noted, catfish production increased by an astonishing 1,200 percent in only 10 years (1975–1985).

The situation in Belzoni isn't so heady today. The farmers are facing increasing feed and electricity costs, which have made production more expensive in Belzoni. Increased domestic production together with a flood of imports from Vietnam have pushed market prices down. Belzoni catfish farmers can't do much to stop this. As Jimmy Avery, an aquaculture professor at Mississippi State Extension, has noted, "The biggest

---

bulldoze 用推土机清除。   self-proclaimed 自称的,自我标榜的。

challenge financially is that you don't have control over the price of your inputs or the sales price of your product. As corn and soybean prices go up, catfish feed costs rise accordingly ... and catfish farmers have to take what someone is willing to pay on the day they harvest fish." With market prices down as low as 94 cents per pound and costs averaging about $1 a pound, local catfish farmers are throwing in the towel. Pond acreage in the county has declined by 50 percent in the last five years.

Source: Belzoni, Mississippi State University Extension and news accounts of 2018.

NOTE: When more firms enter an industry, the market supply increases (shifts right) and price declines.
注：随着更多的厂商进入一个行业，市场供给将增加（曲线右移），价格将下降。

Tendency toward Zero Economic Profits 零经济利润趋势

Whether more cotton farmers enter the catfish industry depends on their expectations for profit. If catfish farming looks more profitable than cotton, more farmers will flood their cotton fields. As they do, the market supply curve will continue shifting to the right, driving catfish prices down.

How far can catfish prices fall? *The force that drives catfish prices down is market entry.* **New firms continue to enter a competitive industry so long as profits exist.** Hence the price of catfish will continue to fall until all economic profits disappear.

鲶鱼价格能降低多少呢？驱使鲶鱼价格下降的力量是市场进入。只要存在利润，新厂商就会继续进入竞争性行业。因此鲶鱼价格将持续下降，直到所有经济利润消失。

Notice in Figure 5.9 where this occurs. When price drops from p_1 to p_2, the typical firm reduces its output from q_1 to q_2. At the price p_2, however, the firm is still making a profit because price exceeds average cost at the output q_2. This profit is illustrated by the shaded rectangle that appears in Figure 5.9b.

The persistence of profits lures still more firms into the industry. As they enter the industry, the market price of fish will be pushed ever lower (Figure 5.9a). When the price falls to p_3, the most profitable rate of output will be q_3 (where MC = p). But at that level, price no longer exceeds average cost. ***Once price falls to the level of minimum average cost, all economic profits disappear.*** This zero-profit outcome occurs at the bottom of the U-shaped ATC curve.

一旦价格下降到最低平均成本的水平，所有经济利润都将消失。这种零利润的情况发生在 U 形 ATC 曲线底部。

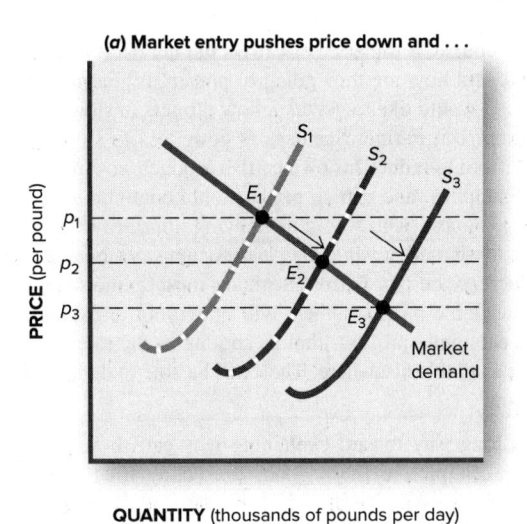

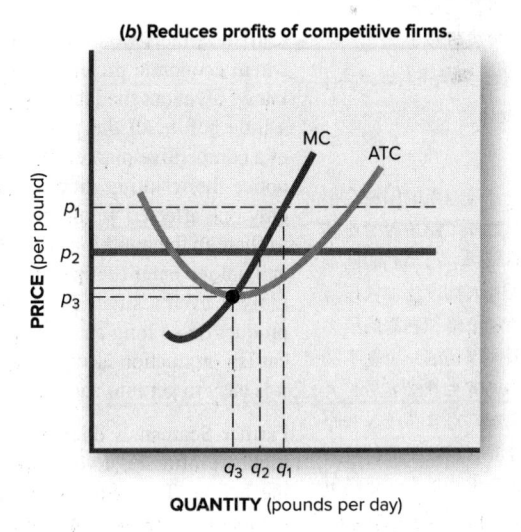

Figure 5.9 The Lure of Profits If economic profits exist in an industry, more firms will want to enter it. As they do, the market supply curve will shift to the right and cause a drop in the market price (Figure 5.9a). The lower market price, in turn, will reduce the output and profits of the typical firm (Figure 5.9b). Once the market price is driven down to p_3, all profits disappear and entry ceases.

When economic profits vanish, market entry ceases. No more cotton farmers will switch to catfish farming once the price of catfish falls to the level of minimum average total cost.

Exit 退出

In the short run, catfish prices might actually fall *below* average total cost. This is what happened in 2012 when Vietnamese and Chinese catfish farmers increased exports to the United States, hoping to take advantage of high prices. The resultant shift of market supply pushed prices so low (from $1.25 to 75 cents a pound) that many U.S. catfish farmers incurred an economic *loss* ($p < $ ATC).

Suddenly fields of rice looked a lot more enticing than ponds full of fish. Before long, some catfish farmers started filling in their ponds and planting rice. As they exited the catfish industry, the market supply curve shifted to the left and catfish prices rose in 2015–2016. Eventually, price rose to the level of average total costs, at which point further exits ceased. Once entry and exit cease, the market price stabilizes. At least for awhile. As the residents of Belzoni can attest, even seemingly "stable" prices don't last forever. When falling feed prices and higher "equilibrium" prices lured more farmers into catfish production in 2015–2017, the market price of catfish was pushed down again to a new equilibrium in 2018.

Equilibrium 均衡

The lesson to be learned from catfish farming is straightforward:

- *The existence of profits in a competitive industry induces entry.*
- *The existence of losses in a competitive industry induces exits.*

Accordingly, we can anticipate that prices in a competitive market will continue to adjust until all entry and exit cease. At that point, the market will be in equilibrium. ***In long-run competitive market equilibrium,***

- *Price equals minimum average total cost.*
- *Economic profit is eliminated.*

Catfish farmers would be happier, of course, if the price of catfish did not decline to the point where economic profits disappeared. But how are they going to prevent it? Farmer Seamans knows all about the law of demand and would like to get his fellow farmers to slow production a little before all the profits disappear. But Farmer Seamans is powerless to stop the forces of a competitive market. He cannot afford to reduce his own catfish production. Nobody would notice the resulting drop in market supplies, and catfish prices would continue to slide. The only one affected would be Farmer Seamans, who would be denying himself the opportunity to share in the good fortunes of the catfish market while they last. As long as others are willing and able to enter the industry and increase output, Farmer Seamans must do the same or deny himself even a small share of the available profits. Others will be willing to expand catfish production so long as catfish breed economic profits—that is, so long as the rate of return in catfish production is superior to that available elsewhere. They will be able to do so as long as it is easy to get into catfish production.

Farmer Seamans's dilemma goes a long way toward explaining why catfish farming is not highly profitable. Every time the profit picture looks good, everybody tries to get in on the action. This kind of pressure on prices and profits is a fundamental characteristic of competitive markets. ***As long as it is easy for existing producers to expand production or for new firms to enter an industry, economic profits will not last long.*** Industry output will expand, market prices will fall, and rates of profit will diminish. Thus the rate of profits in catfish farming is kept down by the fact that anyone with a pond and a couple of catfish can get into the business fairly easily.

---

cease 停止，终止。 enticing 有吸引力的。

Low Barriers to Entry 低进入壁垒

New producers will be able to enter a profitable industry and help drive down prices and profits as long as there are no significant **barriers to entry**. Such barriers may include patents, control of essential factors of production, brand loyalty, and various forms of price control. All such barriers make it expensive, risky, or impossible for new firms to enter into production. In the absence of such barriers, new firms can enter an industry more readily and at less risk.

Not surprisingly, firms already entrenched in a profitable industry do their best to keep newcomers out by erecting barriers to entry. As we saw, there are few barriers to entering the catfish business. When catfish imports from Vietnam first soared in 2002–2003, domestic farmers sought to stem the inflow with new entry barriers, including country-of-origin labeling, tougher health inspections, and outright import quotas. Such entry barriers would have impeded rightward shifts of the market supply curve and kept catfish prices higher. Without such protection, domestic farmers who couldn't keep up with falling prices and increased productivity exited the industry. Owners of T-shirt shops also fret over the low entry barriers that keep their prices and profits low (see the accompanying News Wire "Competitive Pressure").

只要没有很高的**进入壁垒**，新厂商就会进入有利可图的行业，并使价格和利润下降。这种壁垒包括专利权、对关键生产要素的控制、品牌忠诚度和各种形式的价格控制。所有这些壁垒都使新厂商进入该行业的代价变得昂贵、需要冒风险或根本无法进入。如果没有这些壁垒，新厂商进入行业就更加容易，风险也更小。

NEWS WIRE COMPETITIVE PRESSURE

THE T-SHIRT BUSINESS: TOO MUCH COMPETITION

At first blush, the T-shirt business looks like a sure thing. All you need is a bunch of blank T-shirts, a wall full of jazzy transfers, and a heat press. You can buy blank shirts for as little as $1.60 apiece and stock transfers for $1.50 a shot. That's a $3.10 investment. Sell the shirt for $15 and you've got a nice, fat profit margin. What could be easier?

The trouble is that everyone knows the formula. In fact there are dozens of websites that offer not only the necessary supplies, but also sage advice on how to set up your T-shirt shop, either online or in a real store. They all promise you can get rich selling T-shirts.

T-shirt shop owners aren't so sanguine about getting rich. Quite simply, there are far too many T-shirt shops and online outlets. The competition is fierce. So T-shirt shops have to battle for customers every day. As a shop owner in South Padre Island lamented, "Every day you have to compete with other shops. And if you invent something new, they will copy you."

©Ellen Isaacs/Alamy Stock Photo

Source: Industry websites and news, 2015.

NOTE: The ability of a single firm to increase the price of its product depends on how many other firms offer identical products. A perfectly competitive firm has no market power.
注：单个厂商提高其产品价格的能力，取决于提供相同产品的其他厂商的数量。完全竞争性厂商没有市场权力。

Market Characteristics 市场特征

This brief review of catfish economics illustrates a few general observations about the structure, behavior, and outcomes of a competitive market:

- ***Many firms.*** A competitive market will include a great many firms, none of which has a significant share of total output.
- ***Horizontal firm demand.*** Perfectly competitive firms confront horizontal demand curves; they don't have the power to raise their price above the prevailing market price.

- 众多厂商。竞争性市场包括很多厂商，每个厂商的产量只占总产出微不足道的一部分。
- 水平的厂商需求。完全竞争性厂商面对的是水平的需求曲线，他们没有权力将其产品的价格提高到市场价格之上。

---

entrench 确立，牢固。erect 竖立。lament 悲伤，哀悼。

- *Identical products.* Products are homogeneous. One firm's product is virtually indistinguishable from any other firm's product.
- *MC = p.* All competitive firms will seek to expand output until marginal cost equals price.
- *Low barriers to entry.* Barriers to enter the industry are low. If economic profits are available, more firms will enter the industry.
- *Zero economic profit.* The tendency of production and market supplies to expand when profit is high puts heavy pressure on prices and profits in competitive industries. Economic profit will approach zero in the long run as prices are driven down to the level of average production costs.
- *Perfect information.* All buyers and sellers are fully informed of market opportunities.

POLICY PERSPECTIVES

DOES COMPETITION HELP US OR HURT US?

This profile of competitive markets has important implications for public policy. As we noted in Chapter 2, a strong case can be made for the market mechanism. In particular, we observed that the market mechanism permits individual consumers and producers to express their views about WHAT to produce, HOW to produce, and FOR WHOM to produce by "voting" for particular goods and services with market purchases and sales. How well this market mechanism works depends in part on how competitive markets are.

THE RELENTLESS PROFIT SQUEEZE

The unrelenting squeeze on prices and profits that we have observed in this chapter is a fundamental characteristic of the competitive process. Indeed, the **market mechanism** works best under such circumstances. The existence of economic profits implies that consumers place a high value on a particular product and are willing to pay a comparatively high price to get it. The high price and profits signal this information to profit-hungry entrepreneurs, who eagerly come forward to satisfy consumer demands. Thus **high profits in a particular industry indicate that consumers want a different mix of output** (more of that industry's goods). They get that desired mix when more firms enter the industry, increasing its total output (and reducing output in the industries they left). Low entry barriers and the competitive quest for profits enable consumers to get more of the goods they desire, and at a lower price. We get a good answer to the WHAT question.

MAXIMUM EFFICIENCY

When the competitive pressure on prices is carried to the limit, the products in question are also produced at the least possible cost. This is HOW we want goods produced—at minimum cost. This was illustrated by the tendency of catfish prices to be driven down to the level of minimum average costs (Figure 5.9). Once the market equilibrium has been established, society is getting the most it can from its available (scarce) resources.

ZERO ECONOMIC PROFITS

At the limit of the process, all economic profit is eliminated. This doesn't mean that producers are left empty-handed, however. To begin with, the zero profit limit is rarely, if ever, reached. New products are continually being introduced, consumer demands change, and more efficient production processes are

---

relentless 不停的。

discovered. In fact, **the competitive process creates strong pressures to pursue product and technological innovation.** In a competitive market, the adage about the early bird getting the worm is particularly apt. As we observed in the catfish market, the first ones to take up catfish farming were the ones who made the greatest profits.

The sequence of events common to a competitive market situation includes the following:

- High prices and profits signal consumers' demand for more output.
- Economic profit attracts new suppliers.
- The market supply curve shifts to the right.
- Prices slide down the market demand curve.
- A new equilibrium is reached at which increased quantities of the desired product are produced and its price is lowered. Average costs of production are at or near a minimum, more of the product is supplied and consumed, and economic profit approaches zero.
- Throughout the process producers experience great pressure to keep ahead of the profit squeeze by reducing costs, a pressure that frequently results in product and technological innovation.

What is essential to note about the competitive process is that the potential threat of other firms to expand production or new firms to enter the industry keeps existing firms on their toes. Even the most successful firm cannot rest on its laurels for long. To stay in the game, competitive firms must continually improve technology, improve their products, and reduce costs.

THE SOCIAL VALUE OF LOSSES

Not all firms can maintain a competitive pace. Throughout the competitive process, many firms incur economic losses, shut down production, and exit the industry. These losses are a critical part of the market mechanism. **Economic losses are a signal to producers that they are not using society's scarce resources in the best way.** Consumers want those resources reallocated to other firms or industries that can better satisfy consumer demands. In a competitive market, money-losing firms are sent packing, making scarce resources available to more efficient firms.

The dog-eat-dog character of competitive markets troubles many observers. Critics say competitive markets are "all about money," with no redeeming social attributes. But such criticism is ill-founded. The economic goals of society are to produce the best possible mix of output, in the most efficient way, and then to distribute the output fairly. In other words, society seeks optimal answers to the basic WHAT, HOW, and FOR WHOM questions. What makes competitive markets so desirable is that they are most likely to deliver those outcomes.

CHAPTER 5 REVIEW
SUMMARY

- Market structures range from perfect competition (many small firms in an industry) to monopoly (one firm). **LO1**

- A perfectly competitive firm has no power to alter the market price of the goods it sells: It is a *price taker*. The firm confronts a horizontal demand curve for its

---

attribute 属性。

own output even though the relevant *market* demand curve is negatively sloped. **LO1**

- The competitive firm maximizes profit at that rate of output where marginal cost equals price. This represents the short-term equilibrium of the firm. **LO3**
- A competitive firm's supply curve is identical to its marginal cost curve. In the short run, the quantity supplied will rise or fall with price. **LO3**
- The determinants of supply include the price of inputs, technology, and expectations. If any of these determinants change, the *firm's* supply curve will shift. *Market* supply will shift if costs or the number of firms in the industry changes. **LO4**
- If short-term profits exist in a competitive industry, new firms will enter the market. The resulting shift of supply will drive market prices down the market demand curve. As prices fall, the profit of the industry and its constituent firms will be squeezed. **LO5**
- The limit to the competitive price and profit squeeze is reached when price is driven down to the level of minimum average total cost. Additional output and profit will be attained only if technology is improved (lowering costs) or if demand increases. **LO5**
- If the market price falls below ATC, firms will exit an industry. Price will stabilize only when entry and exit cease (and zero profit prevails). **LO5**
- The most distinctive thing about competitive markets is the persistent pressure they exert on prices and profits. The threat of competition is a tremendous incentive for producers to respond quickly to consumer demands and to seek more efficient means of production. In this sense, competitive markets do best what markets are supposed to do—efficiently allocate resources. **LO1**

TERMS TO REMEMBER

Define the following terms:

market structure
competitive firm
competitive market
monopoly
market power
production decision
total revenue
profit
marginal cost (MC)
competitive profit maximization rule
supply
market supply
equilibrium price
barriers to entry
market mechanism

QUESTIONS FOR DISCUSSION

1. What industries do you regard as being highly competitive? Can you identify any barriers to entry in those industries? **LO1**
2. If there were more bookstores around your campus, would textbook prices rise or fall? Why aren't there more bookstores? **LO5**
3. Why doesn't The Coca-Cola Company lose all its customers when it raises its price? Why would a catfish farmer lose all her customers if she raised her price? **LO1**
4. Why doesn't a corn farmer have to make pricing decision? **LO1**
5. If the price of a catfish is 95 cents a pound and the market price of the fish is $1 a pound, should an existing farmer stop producing? **LO3**
6. What is making life so difficult for the catfish farmers in Belzoni, Mississippi? (see the News Wire "Entry and Exit"). What can they do to make their lives better? **LO5**
7. Why would anyone want to enter a profitable industry knowing that profits would eventually be eliminated by competition? **LO5**
8. In the News Wire "Competitive Pressure," what types of costs are cited? Which are not mentioned? If the shop owner wanted to increase production and sales, what additional costs would he incur? Should he do so? **LO3**
9. **POLICY PERSPECTIVES** If Apple had no competitors, would it be improving iPhone features as fast? **LO5**
10. **POLICY PERSPECTIVES** Adam Smith in *The Wealth of Nations* asserted that the pursuit of self-interest by competitive firms promoted the interests of society. What did he mean by this? **LO1**

PROBLEMS

1. If feed prices were to rise **LO3**
   a. which curve in Figure 5.5 would be affected?
   b. how would it change?
   c. how would the profit-maximizing rate of output change?
2. Use Figure 5.5 to determine the following: **LO3**
   a. How many baskets of fish should be harvested at market prices of
      i. $9?
      ii. $13?
      iii. $17?
   b. How much total revenue is collected at each price?
   c. How much profit does the farmer make at each of these prices?
3. In Figure 5.5, what rate of output **LO2**
   a. maximizes total revenue?
   b. maximizes profit per unit?
   c. maximizes total profit? (Choose the higher level of output.)
4. Graph a situation where the typical catfish farmer is incurring a loss at the prevailing market price p_1. **LO3, LO4**
   a. What is MC equal to at the best possible rate of output?
   b. Is ATC above or below p_1?
   c. Which of the following would raise the market price?
      i. A reduction in the firm's output.
      ii. An increase in the firm's input costs.
      iii. Exits from the industry.
      iv. An improvement in technology.
   d. What price would prevail in long-term equilibrium?
5. Suppose a firm has the following costs: **LO3**

Output (units):	10	11	12	13	14	15	16	17	18	19
Total cost:	$50	$52	$56	$62	$70	$80	$92	$106	$122	$140

   a. If the prevailing market price is $14 per unit, how much should the firm produce?
   b. How much profit will it earn at that output rate?
   c. If it increases output by 2 units, will it make more profit or less?
6. What curve is shifting to alter the market equilibrium in the News Wire "Entry and Exit"? **LO5**
7. Graphically show the market outcome for a typical catfish farmer in Mississippi today as described by Jimmy Avery in the News Wire "Entry and Exit." **LO3**
8. Consider the case of a T-shirt shop for which the following data apply: Rent = $200/day; Labor cost = $4/shirt; and Output (sales) = 40 T-shirts/day. Using these data and the information contained in the News Wire "Competitive Pressure," compute: **LO3**
   a. total revenue per day.
   b. average total cost.
   c. per unit profit.
   d. total profit per day.
9. **POLICY PERSPECTIVES** *(a)* What are expected profits for a perfectly competitive firm in the long run? *(b)* Create a graph that shows a firm's long run outcome. **LO5**

10. **POLICY PERSPECTIVES** Suppose that the monthly market demand schedule for Frisbees is

Price	$8	$7	$6	$5	$4	$3	$2	$1
Quantity demanded	1,000	2,000	4,000	8,000	16,000	32,000	64,000	150,000

Suppose further that the marginal and average costs of Frisbee production for every competitive firm are

Rate of output	100	200	300	400	500	600
Marginal cost	$2.00	$3.00	$4.00	$5.00	$6.00	$7.00
Average total cost	$2.00	$2.50	$3.00	$3.50	$4.00	$4.50

Finally, assume that the equilibrium market price is $6 per Frisbee. **LO5**

a. Draw the cost curves of the typical firm.
b. Draw the market demand curve and identify market equilibrium.
c. How many Frisbees are being sold in equilibrium?
d. How many (identical) firms are initially producing Frisbees?
e. How much profit is the typical firm making?
f. In view of the profits being made, more firms will want to get into Frisbee production. In the long run, these new firms will shift the market supply curve to the right and push the price down to minimum average total cost, thereby eliminating profits. At what equilibrium price are all profits eliminated?
g. How many firms will be producing Frisbees at this price?

CHAPTER SIX

Monopoly 垄断

©Bettmann/Getty Images

LEARNING OBJECTIVES

After reading this chapter, you should be able to:

1. Define what a monopoly is.
2. Explain why price exceeds marginal revenue in monopoly.
3. Describe how a monopoly sets output and price.
4. Illustrate how monopoly and competitive outcomes differ.
5. Discuss the pros and cons of monopoly structures.

In 1908 Ford produced the Model T, the car "designed for the common man." It was cheap, reliable, and as easy to drive as the horse and buggy it was replacing. Ford sold 10,000 Model Ts in its first full year of production (1909). After that, sales more than doubled every year. In 1913 nearly 200,000 Model Ts were sold, and Ford was fast changing American patterns of consumption, travel, and living standards.

During this early development of the U.S. auto industry, Henry Ford dominated the field. There were other producers, but the Ford Motor Company was the only producer of an inexpensive "motorcar for the multitudes." In this situation, Henry Ford could dictate the price and the features of his cars. When he opened his new assembly line factory at Highland Park, he abruptly raised the Model T's price by $100—an increase of 12 percent—to help pay for the new plant. Then he decided to paint all Model Ts black. When told of consumer complaints about the lack of colors, Ford advised one of his executives in 1913, "Give them any color they want so long as it's black."[1]

Henry Ford had market power. He could dictate what color car Americans would buy. And he could raise the price of Model Ts without fear of losing all his customers. Such power is alien to competitive firms. Competitive firms are always under pressure to reduce costs, improve quality, and cater to consumer preferences.

In this chapter we will continue to examine how market structure influences market outcomes. Specifically, we examine how a market controlled by a single producer—a monopoly—behaves. We are particularly interested in the following questions:

- What price will a monopolist charge for its output?
- How does a monopolist keep potential competitors at bay?
- Are consumers better or worse off when only one firm controls an entire market?

---

[1] Charles E. Sorensen, *My Forty Years with Ford* (New York: W. W. Norton & Co., 1956), p. 127.

multitude 大众。cater 满足，迎合。at bay 陷入绝境。

MONOPOLY STRUCTURE 垄断结构

The essence of **market power** is the ability to alter the price of a product. The catfish farmers of Chapter 5 had no such power. Because many other farms were producing and selling the same good, each catfish producer had to act as a *price taker*. Each farm could sell all the fish it harvested at the prevailing market price. If a farmer tried to charge a higher price for his catfish, that individual farmer would lose all his customers. This inability to set the price of their output is the most distinguishing characteristic of perfectly competitive firms.

市场权力的本质就是改变产品价格的能力。第5章提及的鲶鱼养殖者就没有这种能力。因为还有许多其他养殖场也生产、销售同样的产品,所以每个鲶鱼养殖者不得不作为价格接受者行事。按照现行的市场价格,每个渔场都可以卖掉其捕捞到的全部鲶鱼。如果有人试图索取较高的价格,他将会失去所有顾客。不能为其产出的产品定价,是完全竞争性厂商最显著的特征。

Catfish don't, of course, violate the law of demand. As tasty as catfish are, people are not willing to buy unlimited quantities of them at $13 per pound. The marginal utility of extra fish, in fact, diminishes rapidly. To induce consumers to buy more fish, the price of fish must be reduced.

This seeming contradiction between the law of demand and the situation of the competitive firm was explained by the existence of two distinct demand curves. The demand for catfish refers to the **market demand** for that good. Like all other consumer demand curves, this market demand curve is downward-sloping. A second demand curve was constructed to represent the situation confronting a *single firm* in the competitive catfish market; that demand curve was horizontal.

Monopoly = Industry 垄断者=整个行业

We now confront an entirely different market structure. Suppose that the entire output of catfish could be produced by a single large producer. Assume that Universal Fish has a patent on the oxygenating equipment needed to maintain commercial-size fish ponds. A **patent** gives a firm the exclusive right to produce or license a product. With its patent, Universal Fish can deny other farmers access to oxygenating equipment and thus establish itself as the sole supplier of catfish. Such a firm is a **monopoly**—that is, a single firm that produces the entire market supply of a good.

In view of the fact that a monopoly has no direct competition, you'd hardly expect it to behave like a competitive firm. Competitive firms are always under pressure from other firms in the industry to hold down costs and improve product quality. Competitive firms also have to worry about new entrants into their industry and the resultant downward pressure on prices. A monopolist, however, owns the ballpark and can set the rules of the game. Is a monopoly going to charge the same price for fish as a competitive industry would? Not likely. As we'll see, a monopolist can use its market power to charge higher prices and retain larger profits.

垄断的出现消除了行业需求曲线与厂商面对的需求曲线之间的差别。垄断者就是整个行业,因此只需考虑一条需求曲线,即市场(行业)需求曲线。在垄断情况下,厂商所面对的需求曲线与该产品的市场需求曲线是一致的。

The emergence of a monopoly obliterates the distinction between industry demand and the demand curve facing the firm. A monopolistic firm *is* the industry. Hence there is only *one* demand curve to worry about, and that is the market (industry) demand curve. *In monopoly situations, the demand curve facing the firm is identical to the market demand curve for the product.*

Price versus Marginal Revenue 价格与边际收益

Although monopolies simplify the geometry of the firm, they complicate the arithmetic of supply decisions. Competitive firms maximize profits by producing at that rate of output where *price* equals marginal cost. Monopolies do not maximize profits in the same way. They still heed the advice about never producing anything that costs more than it brings in. But as strange as it may seem, what is brought in from an additional sale is not the price in this case.

增加额外一单位产出所增加的总收益称为**边际收益**。为计算边际收益,我们可比较在该产出水平下增加1单位产出前后的总收益,两者之差就是边际收益。

The contribution to total revenue of an additional unit of output is called **marginal revenue (MR)**. To calculate marginal revenue, we compare the total revenues received before and after a one-unit increase in the rate of production; the difference between the two totals equals *marginal* revenue.

---

violate 违反,违背。 oxygenate 供氧。 patent 专利。 ballpark 活动领域。 geometry 几何形状。

If every unit of output could be sold at the same price, marginal revenue would equal price. But what would the demand curve look like in such a case? It would have to be *horizontal*, indicating that consumers were prepared to buy everything produced at the existing price. As we have observed, however, a horizontal demand curve applies only to small competitive firms—firms that produce only a tiny fraction of total market output. ***Only for perfectly competitive firms does price equal marginal revenue.***

The situation in a monopoly is different. The firm is so big that its output decisions affect market prices. Keep in mind that a monopolist confronts the *market* demand curve, which is always downward-sloping. As a consequence, a monopolist can sell additional output only if it *reduces* prices.

Suppose Universal Fish could sell one ton of fish for $6,000. If it wants to sell two tons, however, it has to heed the law of demand and reduce the price per ton. Suppose it has to reduce the price to $5,000 in order to get the additional sales. In that case, we would observe

Total revenue　　　＝　1 ton × $ 6,000 ＝ $ 6,000
before price reduction　　　　　per ton

Total revenue　　　＝　2 tons × $ 5,000 ＝ $ 10,000
after price reduction　　　　　per ton

To compute marginal revenue, we observe that

Marginal revenue　＝　total revenue　－　total revenue
　　　　　　　　　　　　@ 2 tons　　　　　@ 1 ton
　　　　　　　　　＝　$ 10,000　　　－　$ 6,000　　　＝ $ 4,000

Notice how the quantity demanded in the marketplace increases from 1 ton to 2 tons as the unit price is reduced (the law of demand again). Notice, also, however, what happens to total revenue when unit sales increase: Total revenue here *increases* by $4,000. This *change* in total revenue represents the *marginal* revenue of the second ton.

Focus for a moment on the fact that marginal revenue ($4,000) is less than price ($5,000) in this example. This will always be the case when the demand curve facing the firm is downward-sloping. To get added sales, price must be reduced. The additional quantity sold is a plus for total revenue, but the reduced price per unit is a negative. The net result of these offsetting effects represents *marginal* revenue. Since the demand curve facing a monopolist is always downward-sloping, ***marginal revenue is always less than price for a monopolist***, as shown in Figure 6.1.

Figure 6.1 provides more detail on how marginal revenue is calculated. The demand curve and schedule represent the market demand for catfish and thus the sales opportunities for the Universal Fish monopoly. According to this information, Universal Fish can sell one pound of fish per hour at a price of $13. If the company wants to sell a larger quantity of fish, it has to reduce its price. According to the market demand curve shown here, the price must be lowered to $12 to sell two pounds per hour. This reduction in price is shown by a movement along the demand curve from point A to point B.

Our primary focus here is on marginal revenue. We want to show what happens to total revenue when unit sales increase by one pound per hour. To do this, we must compute the total revenue associated with each rate of output and then observe the changes that occur.

The calculations necessary for computing MR are summarized in Figure 6.1. Row A of the table indicates that the total revenue resulting from one sale per hour is $13. To increase unit sales, price must be reduced. Row B indicates that total revenues rise to $24 per hour when catfish sales double. The *increase* in total revenues resulting from the added sale is thus $11. The marginal revenue of the second pound is therefore $11. This is illustrated in the last column of the table and by point b on the marginal revenue curve.

---

heed 听从，留心。

Notice that the MR of the second pound of fish ($11) is *less* than its price ($12). This is because both pounds are being sold for $12 apiece. In effect, the firm is giving up the opportunity to sell only one pound per hour at $13 in order to sell a *larger* quantity at a *lower* price. In this sense, the firm is sacrificing $1 of potential revenue on the first pound of fish in order to increase *total* revenue. Marginal revenue measures the *change* in total revenue that results.

只要需求曲线是向下倾斜的，边际收益就总是低于价格。比较图 6.1 中表格的第 2 栏和第 4 栏，在每个超过 1 磅的产出率下，边际收益低于价格。这在曲线图中表现得也很明显：除了起始点，边际收益曲线的每一点都位于需求（价格）曲线的下方。

So long as the demand curve is downward-sloping, MR will always be less than price. Compare columns 2 and 4 of the table in Figure 6.1. At each rate of output in excess of one pound, marginal revenue is less than price. This is also evident in the graph: ***The MR curve lies below the demand (price) curve at every point but the first.***

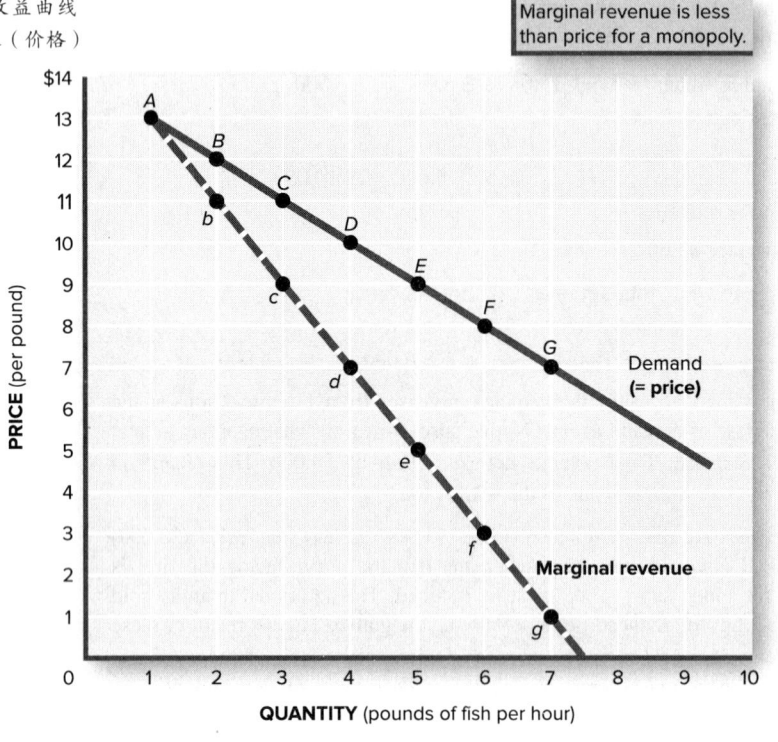

	(1) Quantity	×	(2) Price	=	(3) Total Revenue	(4) Marginal Revenue
A	1		$13		$13	
B	2		12		24	$11
C	3		11		33	9
D	4		10		40	7
E	5		9		45	5
F	6		8		48	3
G	7		7		49	1

Figure 6.1 Price Exceeds Marginal Revenue in Monopoly If a firm must lower its price to sell additional output, marginal revenue is less than price. If this monopoly firm wants to increase its sales from one to two pounds of fish per hour, for example, price must be reduced from $13 to $12. The marginal revenue of the second pound is therefore only $11 (= $24 of total revenue at *p* = $12 *minus* $13 of total revenue at *p* = $13). This is indicated in row *B* of the table and by point *b* on the graph. ∎

MONOPOLY BEHAVIOR 垄断行为

Like all producers, a monopolist wants to maximize total profits. A monopolist does this a bit differently than a competitive firm, however. Recall that a perfectly competitive firm is a *price taker*. It maximizes profits by adjusting its rate of output to a *given* market price. A monopolist, by contrast, *sets* the market price. Hence *a monopolist must make a pricing decision that perfectly competitive firms never make.*

Profit Maximization 利润最大化

In setting its price, the monopolist first identifies the profit-maximizing rate of output (the production decision) and then determines what price is compatible with that much output.

To find the best rate of output, a monopolist will follow the general **profit maximization rule** about equating marginal cost (what an additional unit costs to produce) and marginal revenue (how much more revenue an additional unit brings in). Hence *a monopolist maximizes profits at the rate of output where MR = MC.*

Note that competitive firms actually do the same thing. In their case, MR and price are identical. Hence a competitive firm maximizes profits where MC = MR = p. Thus the general profit maximization rule (MR = MC) applies to *all* firms; only those firms that are perfectly competitive use the special case of MC = p = MR.

The Production Decision 生产决策

Figure 6.2 shows how a monopolist applies the profit maximization rule to the **production decision**. The demand curve represents the market demand for catfish; the marginal revenue curve is derived from it, as shown in Figure 6.1. The marginal cost curve in Figure 6.2 represents the costs incurred by Universal Fish in supplying the market. As we've seen before, the MC curve slopes upward. Universal's goal is to use these curves to find the one rate of output that maximizes total profit.

Competitive firms make the production decision by locating the intersection of marginal cost and price. A monopolist, however, looks for the rate of output at which marginal cost equals marginal revenue. This is illustrated in Figure 6.2 by the intersection of the MR and MC curves (point d). Looking down from that intersection, we see that the associated rate of output is four pounds per hour. Thus four pounds is the profit-maximizing rate of output for this monopoly; this is the only rate of output where MC = MR.

The Monopoly Price 垄断价格

How much should Universal Fish charge for these four pounds of fish? Naturally, the monopolist would like to charge a very high price. But its ability to charge a high price is limited by the demand curve. The demand curve always tells us the *most* consumers are willing to pay for any given quantity. Once we have determined the quantity that is going to be supplied (four pounds per hour), we can look at the demand curve to determine the price ($10 at point D) that consumers will pay for these catfish. That is to say,

- *The intersection of the marginal revenue and marginal cost curves (point d) establishes the profit-maximizing rate of output.*
- *The demand curve tells us the highest price consumers are willing to pay for that specific quantity of output (point D).*

If Universal Fish ignored these principles and tried to charge $13 per pound, consumers would buy only one pound, leaving it with three unsold pounds of fish. As the monopolist will soon learn, *only one price is compatible with the profit-maximizing rate of output.* In this case the

---

compatible 相匹配的，相一致的。

price is $10. This price is found in Figure 6.2 by moving up from the intersection of MR = MC until reaching the demand curve at point D. Point D tells us that consumers are able and willing to buy exactly four pounds of fish per hour at the price of $10 each. A monopolist that tries to charge more than $10 will not be able to sell all four pounds of fish. That could turn out to be an unprofitable (and smelly) situation.

Could a monopolist charge *less* than $10? Of course he could. But why would he? At lower prices, consumers would purchase more fish. But the marginal cost of producing those extra fish would exceed the price he was charging. Notice how the marginal cost line lies *above* the marginal revenue line to the right of point d. That makes no sense. The monopolist is trying to maximize total profits not total unit sales, and added sales beyond four pounds reduce profits. Again, only *one* price and *one* output is consistent with profit maximization.

Monopoly Profits 垄断利润

Figure 6.2 illustrates the maximum profits of the Universal Fish monopoly. To compute total profits, we again take advantage of the average total cost (ATC) curve. The distance between the price (point D) and ATC at the output rate of 4 represents profit *per unit*. In this case, profit per unit is $2 (price of $10 minus ATC of $8). Multiplying profit per unit ($2) by the quantity sold (4) gives us total profits of $8 per hour, as illustrated by the shaded rectangle.

We could also compute total profit by comparing *total* revenue and *total* cost. Total revenue at q = 4 is price ($10) times quantity (4), or $40. Total cost is quantity (4) times average total cost ($8), or $32. Subtracting total cost ($32) from total revenue ($40) gives us the total profit of $8 per hour already illustrated in Figure 6.2.

我们也可以通过比较总收益和总成本来计算总利润。当 q = 4 时，总收益等于价格（10 美元）乘以销售量（4），即 40 美元。总成本等于销售量（4）乘以平均总成本（8 美元），即 32 美元。如图 6.2，用总收益（40 美元）减去总成本（32 美元），我们就得到了总利润为 8 美元。

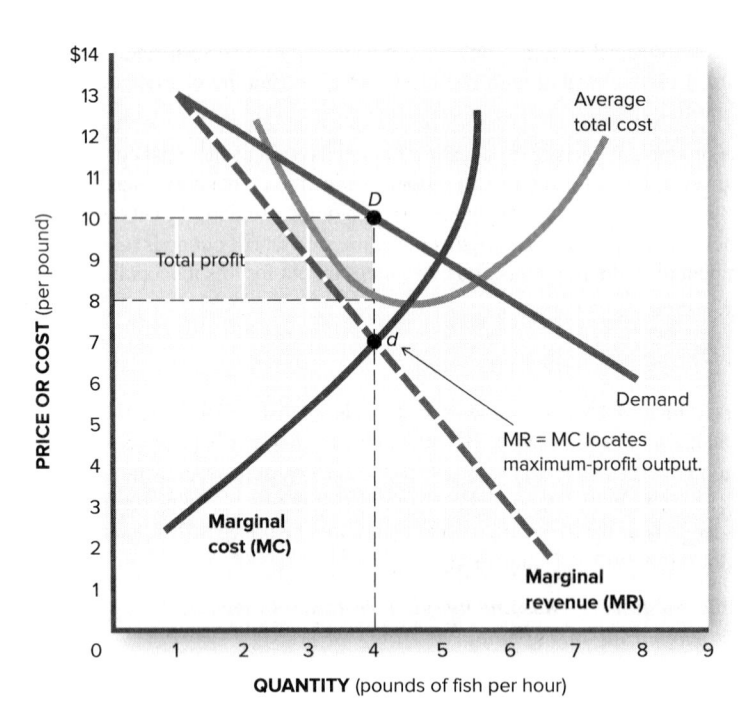

Figure 6.2 Profit Maximization The most profitable rate of output is indicated by the intersection of marginal revenue and marginal cost (point d). In this case, marginal revenue and marginal cost intersect at an output of four pounds per hour. Point D indicates that consumers will pay $10 per pound for this much output. Total profits equal price ($10) minus average total cost ($8), multiplied by the quantity sold (4 pounds).

smelly 有难闻气味的，发臭的。

BARRIERS TO ENTRY 进入壁垒

The profits attained by Universal Fish as a result of its monopoly position are not the end of the story. The existence of economic profit tends to bring profit-hungry entrepreneurs swarming. Indeed, in the competitive catfish industry of Chapter 5, the lure of high profits brought about an enormous expansion in domestic catfish farming, a flood of imported fish, and a steep decline in catfish prices. What, then, can we expect to happen in the catfish industry now that Universal has a monopoly position and is enjoying economic profits?

The consequences of monopoly on prices and output can be seen in Figure 6.3. In this case, we must compare monopoly behavior to that of a competitive *industry*. Remember that a monopoly is a single firm that constitutes the entire industry. What we want to depict, then, is how a different market structure (perfect competition) would alter industry prices and the quantity supplied.

If a *competitive* industry were producing at point D it too would be generating an economic profit with the costs shown in Figure 6.3. A competitive industry would not stay at that rate of output, however. All the firms in a competitive industry try to maximize profits by equating price and marginal cost. But at point D, price ($10) exceeds marginal cost ($7). Hence a competitive industry would quickly move from point D (the monopolist's equilibrium) to point E, where marginal cost and price are equal. At point E (the short-run competitive equilibrium), more fish are supplied, their price is lower, and industry profits are smaller.

Threat of Entry 进入威胁

At point E, catfish farming is still profitable, since price ($9) exceeds average cost ($8) at that rate of production. Although total profits at the competitive point E ($5 per hour) are less than at the monopolist's point D ($8 per hour), they are still attractive. These remaining profits will lure more entrepreneurs into a competitive industry. As more firms enter, the market supply curve will shift to the right, driving prices down further. As we observed in Chapter 5, output will increase and prices will decline until all economic profit is eliminated and entry ceases (long-run competitive equilibrium).

Universal Fish 因其垄断地位获取了利润，但是故事并没有结束。如前文所述，经济利润的存在将吸引那些追逐利润的企业家蜂拥而入。事实上，在第 5 章的竞争性鲶鱼行业中，高额利润的诱惑导致美国鲶鱼养殖业的迅速扩张、鱼的大量进口和鲶鱼价格的急剧下跌。既然 Universal Fish 现在处于垄断地位并享有经济利润，那么我们预期鲶鱼行业会发生什么呢？

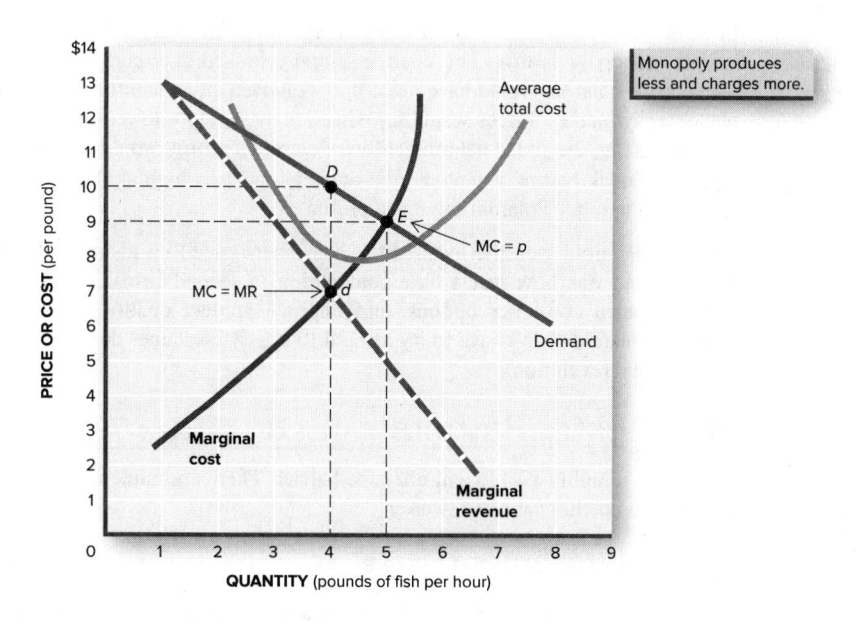

Figure 6.3 Monopoly versus Competitive Outcomes A monopoly will produce at the rate of output where MR = MC. A competitive industry will produce where MC = p. Hence a monopolist produces less (q = 4) than a competitive industry (q = 5). It also charges a higher price ($10 versus $9). ∎

---

eliminate 剔除，消除。

Will this sequence of events occur in a monopoly? Absolutely not. Remember that Universal Fish is now assumed to have an exclusive patent on oxygenating equipment and can use this patent as an impassable barrier to entry. Consequently, would-be competitors can swarm around Universal's profits until their wings drop off; Universal is not about to let them in on the spoils. Universal Fish has the power to maintain production and price at point D in Figure 6.3. In the absence of competition, monopoly outcomes won't budge. We conclude, therefore, that *a monopoly attains higher prices and profits by restricting output.*

The secret to a monopoly's success lies in its **barriers to entry**. So long as entry barriers exist, a monopoly can control (restrict) the quantity of goods supplied. The barrier to entry in this catfish saga is the patent on oxygenating equipment. Without access to that technology, would-be catfish farmers must continue to farm cotton or other crops.

专利保护：宝丽来与柯达之争
Patent Protection: Polaroid versus Kodak

A patent was also the source of monopoly power in the historic battle between Polaroid and Eastman Kodak. Edwin Land invented the instant development camera in 1947 and got a patent on his invention. Over the subsequent 29 years, the company he founded was the sole supplier of instant photography cameras and racked up billions of dollars in profits.

Polaroid's huge profits were too great a prize to ignore. In 1976 the Eastman Kodak Company decided to enter the market with an instant camera of its own. The availability of a second camera quickly depressed camera prices and squeezed Polaroid's profits.

Polaroid cried foul and went to court to challenge Kodak's entry into the instant photography market. Polaroid claimed that Kodak had infringed on Polaroid's patent rights and was producing cameras illegally. Kodak responded that it had developed its cameras independently and used no processes protected by Polaroid's patents.

The ensuing legal battle lasted 14 years. In the end, a federal judge concluded that Kodak had violated Polaroid's patent rights. Kodak not only stopped producing instant cameras but also offered to repurchase all of the 16 million cameras it had sold (for which film would no longer be available).

In addition to restoring Polaroid's monopoly, the court ordered Kodak to pay Polaroid for its lost monopoly profits. The court essentially looked at Figure 6.3 and figured out how much profit Polaroid would have made had it enjoyed an undisturbed monopoly in the instant photography market. Prices would have been higher, output lower, and profits greater. Using such reasoning, the judge determined that Polaroid's profits would have been $909.5 million higher if Kodak had never entered the market—*twice* as high as the profits actually earned. Kodak had to repay Polaroid these lost profits.

Although Polaroid won the legal battle, consumers ended up losing. What the Kodak entry demonstrated was how just a little competition (a second firm) can push consumer prices down, broaden consumer options, and improve product quality. Once its monopoly was restored, Polaroid didn't have to try as hard to satisfy consumer desires (it was later upended by the digital revolution).

Other Entry Barriers 其他进入壁垒

Patents are a highly visible and effective barrier. There are numerous other ways of keeping potential competitors at bay, however.

Legal Harassment 法律诉讼

An increasingly effective way of suppressing competition is to sue new entrants. Even if a new competitor hasn't infringed on a monopolist's patents or trademarks, it is still fair game for legal challenges. Recall that Kodak spent 14 years battling Polaroid in court. Small firms

---

rack up 积累。 cry foul 强烈抗议错误或不公平。 infringe 侵犯，侵害（权益）。 ensuing 因而发生的，随后的。 demonstrate 证明，示范。

can't afford all that legal skirmishing. When Napster, one of the first companies to offer free music downloads, got sued for copyright infringement in 2000, its fate was sealed. It simply didn't have the revenues needed to wage an extended legal battle. Even before the court ruled against it, Napster chose to compromise rather than fight. Because lengthy legal battles are so expensive, even the *threat* of legal action may dissuade entrepreneurs from entering a monopolized market. Even a company as large as Costco can be intimidated by legal action. When it started selling golf balls in 2016, it was promptly sued by Acushnet, the largest manufacturer of golf balls (Titleist). Although Costco countersued, claiming that Titleist's claim were unfounded, it chose to stop selling the competing golf balls. Other, smaller golf manufacturers had similarly chosen to quit rather than fight (see the News Wire "Legal Barriers").

> **NEWS WIRE LEGAL BARRIERS**
>
> **BIG LEGAL BILLS FOR LITTLE GOLF BALLS**
>
> To the average golfer, most golf balls look strikingly alike. But Acushnet Holdings Corp. says its Titleist ball is the "number one ball in golf," better than all others. To keep it that way, Acushnet has obtained 11 patents on the design of its Titleist balls. When retail giant Costco started selling its own Kirkland balls in 2016, Acushnet felt threatened. Costco was selling its golf balls for $1.25 apiece, while the Titleist ProV1 balls were $4 apiece, and reviewers found them to be comparable. Acushnet promptly sued Costco, claiming it had infringed on Titleist's design patents. Costco stopped selling the Kirkland balls. Previously, Acushnet had sued another 10 golf-ball manufactures, most of whom ceased production rather than fight in court. Dean Snell, a former Titleist ball designer, said the purpose of all the patents isn't merely to protect ball designs, but also to prevent competitors from innovating new designs.
>
> Source: News accounts of March 2017.
>
> **NOTE:** Legal action—or even the *threat* of legal action—may dissuade potential competitors from entering an industry.
>
> 注：法律诉讼，甚至是要采取法律诉讼的威胁，都会阻止潜在竞争者进入某个行业。

Exclusive Licensing 独家授权

Nintendo allegedly used another tactic to control the videogame market in the early 1990s. Nintendo forbade game creators from writing software for competing firms. Such exclusive licensing made it difficult for potential competitors to acquire the factors of production (game developers) they needed to compete against Nintendo. Only after the giant electronics company Sony entered the market in 1995 with new technology (PlayStation) did Nintendo have to share its monopoly profits.

据称，任天堂在20世纪90年代初期曾使用另一种策略来控制电子游戏市场。任天堂禁止游戏开发者为与其竞争的公司编写软件。这种独占许可使潜在竞争者很难获得所需要的生产要素（游戏开发者）来与任天堂竞争。直到1995年电子巨头索尼凭借新技术（PlayStation）进入这个市场，任天堂才不得不分享其垄断利润。

Bundled Products 捆绑产品

Another way to thwart competition is to force consumers to purchase complementary products. The U.S. Justice Department repeatedly accused Microsoft Corporation of "bundling" its applications software (e.g., Internet Explorer) with its Windows operating software. With a near monopoly on operating systems, Microsoft could charge a high price for Windows and then give "free" applications software with each system. Such bundling makes it almost impossible for potential competitors in the *applications* market to sell their products at a profitable price. The News Wire "Bundling Barriers" cites this practice as one of the many "oppressive" tactics that Microsoft used to protect and exploit its monopoly position. Bundling helped Microsoft gain 96 percent of the Internet browser market (displacing Netscape), 94 percent of the office suites markets (displacing Word Perfect), and an increased share of money management applications (gaining on Intuit). The federal courts concluded that consumers would have enjoyed better products and lower prices had the market for computer operating systems been more competitive.

---

skirmish 小争论，小冲突。 seal 确定，使成定局。 compromise 妥协，让步。 thwart 阻挠，阻止。 oppressive 压迫的，压制的。

> **NEWS WIRE** **BUNDLING BARRIERS**
>
> **JUDGE RULES MICROSOFT ABUSED MONOPOLY POWER**
>
> Washington, DC—U.S. District Judge Thomas Penfield Jackson ruled that Microsoft violated U.S. antitrust laws by unfairly hindering potential competitors from gaining access to the Internet. He concluded that the computer giant has kept "an oppressive thumb on the scale of competitive fortune, thereby effectively guaranteeing its continued dominance" in Internet access. Jackson's ruling affirms his earlier ruling in November that Microsoft is a monopoly that has used its power to stifle competition and ultimately hurt consumers. Judge Jackson was particularly upset by how Microsoft had "unlawfully tied its Web browser" to its Windows operating system, which powers over 90 percent of computers worldwide. Such "bundling" of products effectively locks competitors out of the browser market, thereby guaranteeing Microsoft's continued dominance of Internet access. Jackson concluded that Microsoft violated the Sherman Antitrust Act, just as had Standard Oil and AT&T did in earlier milestone cases.
>
> Source: News accounts of April 4–5, 2000.
>
> **NOTE:** Microsoft tried to keep competitors out of its operating system and applications software markets by erecting various barriers to entry. This behavior slowed innovation, restricted consumer choices, and kept prices too high.
>
> 注：微软试图通过设置各种进入壁垒来阻止竞争者进入操作系统和应用软件市场。这种行为延缓了技术创新，限制了消费者的选择权，并且抬高了价格。

Similar antitrust charges were made against Google. Google commands nearly 90 percent of all Internet searches. According to complaints filled by European Union anti-trust regulators, Google required smartphone manufactures to install its search engine and Chrome browser on all Android devices. Further, it uses its search dominance to steer consumers to its own services, effectively locking out would-be competitors. In July 2018, the European Union fined Google a record-setting $5 *billion* for its monopoly behavior.

Government Franchises 政府特权

在许多情况下，垄断得以维持的原因仅仅在于政府给某一个公司在某一特定市场上生产特定产品的特权。在这里，进入壁垒不是产品专利权，而是销售这种产品的专有权力。地方有线电视和电话公司常常是被赋予特权的垄断者。在邮递一类邮件上，美国邮政服务公司就是这样的垄断者。你们学校的书店也可能拥有在校园内销售教科书的特权。

In many cases, a monopoly persists just because the government gave a single firm the exclusive right to produce a particular good in a specific market. The entry barrier here is not a patent on a product but instead an exclusive franchise to sell that product. Local cable and telephone companies are often franchised monopolies. So is the U.S. Postal Service in the provision of first-class mail. Your campus bookstore might also have exclusive rights to sell textbooks on campus.

COMPARATIVE OUTCOMES 比较结果

These and other entry barriers are the ultimate sources of monopoly power. With that power, monopolies can change the way the market responds to consumer demands.

Competition versus Monopoly 竞争与垄断

By way of summary, we recount the different ways in which perfectly competitive and monopolized markets behave. The likely sequence of events that occurs in each type of market structure is as follows:

Competitive Industry	Monopoly Industry
• High prices and profits signal consumers' demand for more output.	• High prices and profits signal consumers' demand for more output.
• The high profits attract new suppliers.	• Barriers to entry are erected to exclude potential competition.
• Production and supplies expand.	• Production and supplies are constrained.

---

dominance 优势，支配地位。 unlawfully 不正当地，不合法地。

Competitive Industry	Monopoly Industry
• Prices slide down the market demand curve.	• Prices don't move down the market demand curve.
• A new equilibrium is established in which more of the desired product is produced, its price falls, average costs of production approach their minimum, and economic profits approach zero.	• No new equilibrium is established, average costs are not necessarily at or near a minimum, and economic profits are at a maximum.
• Price equals marginal cost throughout the process.	• Price exceeds marginal cost at all times.
• Throughout the process, there is great pressure to keep ahead of the profit squeeze by reducing costs or improving product quality.	• There is no squeeze on profits and thus no pressure to reduce costs or improve product quality.

Near Monopolies 近乎垄断

These comparative sequences aren't always followed exactly. Nor is the monopoly sequence available only to a single firm. In reality, two or more firms may rig the market to replicate monopoly outcomes and profits.

这些比较结果并不总是绝对的。同样，垄断也不单单局限于单一厂商的情况，实际上，两个或多个厂商同样可以操纵市场以取得垄断结果和利润。

Duopoly 双头垄断

In a duopoly there are two firms rather than only one. They may literally be the only two firms in the market, or two firms may so dominate the market that they can still control price and output even if other firms are present.

How would you expect duopolists to behave? Will they slug it out, driving prices and profits down to competitive levels? Or will they recognize that less intense competition will preserve industry profits? If they behave like true competitors, they risk losing economic profits. If they work together, they assure themselves a continuing share of monopoly-like profits.

The two giant auction houses, Sotheby's and Christie's, figured out which strategy made more sense. Together the two companies control 90 percent of the $4 billion auction market. Rather than compete for sales by offering lower prices to potential sellers, Sotheby's and Christie's agreed to fix commission prices at a high level. When they got caught in 2000, the two firms agreed to pay a $512 million fine to auction customers.

Oligopoly 寡头垄断

In an oligopoly, *several* firms (rather than one or two) control the market. Here, too, the strategic choice is whether to compete feverishly or live somewhat more comfortably. To the extent that the dominant firms recognize their mutual interest in higher prices and profits, they may avoid the kind of price competition common in perfectly competitive industries. Coca-Cola and Pepsi, for example, much prefer to use clever advertising rather than lower prices to lure customers away from each other. With 75 percent of industry sales between them, Coca-Cola and Pepsi realize that price competition is a no-win strategy.

In some instances, an oligopoly may have explicit limits on production and price. The 14 nations that constitute the Organization of Petroleum Exporting Countries (OPEC), for example, meet every six months or so to limit output (quantity supplied) and maintain a high price for oil (see the accompanying News Wire "Mimicking Monopoly"). OPEC operates outside U.S. borders and is therefore immune to U.S. laws against price fixing. The canned tuna industry doesn't enjoy such immunity, however. In 2017–2018 the three largest suppliers of canned tuna pled guilty to fixing the price of canned tuna. Together, the three companies controlled 80 percent of the canned tuna market, with sales of nearly $2 billion per year. To bolster profits, they agreed to reduce can size, curb promotional discounts, and take other steps to keep tuna prices and profits high (see the News Wire "Price Fixing"). Fines and jail sentences were imposed.

---

literally 确实地，真正地。 slug it out 决一雌雄，一决高下。 feverishly 激烈地，狂热地。 explicit 清楚明白的，明确的。 immune 不受影响的。

NEWS WIRE MIMICKING MONOPOLY

OPEC EASES OIL RESTRAINTS

Vienna. Two years ago, OPEC took decisive action to push up the price of oil. Meeting here in Vienna, the 14 nations belonging to the Organization of Petroleum Exporting Countries (OPEC) agreed to cut back production by 1.2 million barrels a day. The curtailed supply, they knew, would force prices higher. And it worked. The price of oil has risen from a low $27 a barrel in early 2016 to more than $80 a barrel last month.

OPEC's success in raising the price of oil has been a mixed blessing. American shale producers couldn't produce oil profitably at $27 a barrel. But they are ready and willing at prices above $50. So, the higher OPEC-managed price brought a gush of U.S. shale oil to the market. Russia, too, increased exports to take advantage of the higher prices. The flood of non-OPEC oil worried Saudi Arabia, the largest OPEC producer. To discourage further loss of market share, the Saudis convinced a reluctant Iran and other members to *increase* production limits now. At the June meeting, OPEC agreed to increase production quotas by 1 million barrels a day, raising their collective target to roughly 33 million barrels a day. If adhered to, the new limits should keep a lid on world oil prices for awhile.

Source: News accounts of June 22–25, 2018.

NOTE: The 14 member-nations of OPEC collectively set their combined rate of output. In doing so, they are trying to duplicate monopoly outcomes.
注：欧佩克的14个成员国共同设定其总的产出率。它们以这样的形式努力达到垄断结果。

NEWS WIRE PRICE FIXING

TUNA FIRMS GUILTY OF PRICE FIXING

Washington, DC—The Justice Department says that the three largest suppliers of canned tuna conspired to fix prices from at least November 2010 to December 2013. U.S. consumption of tuna has been declining since the 1990s, in part due to alerts about mercury poisoning. To make up for the declining sales, Bumble Bee, StarKist, and Chicken of the Sea executives met regularly and agreed to protect profits with higher prices. They reduced can size from 6 ounces to 5 ounces, raising the price per ounce. And they agreed to cut back on promotional discounts. Bumble Bee pled guilty to the conspiracy charges in May 2017 and agreed to pay a fine of at lease $25 million. Chicken of the Sea confessed and was given amnesty for cooperating with Justice Department Investigators. Four executives of the companies pled guilty earlier this year, and the CEO of Bumble Bee was indicted in May.

©McGraw-Hill Education

Source: News accounts of September 2018.

NOTE: When a handful of companies dominate an industry, they may conspire to fix prices at monopoly levels.
注：当少数公司主导一个行业时，它们或许会合谋，确定垄断价格。

Monopolistic Competition 垄断竞争

Starbucks, too, has the power to set prices for its products even though many other firms sell coffee. But it has much less power than Coca-Cola or OPEC because so many firms sell coffee. A market made up of many firms, each of which has some distinct brand image, is called *monopolistic competition*. Each company has a monopoly on its brand image but still must

---

keep a lid on 抑制。

contend with competing brands. This is still very different from *perfect* competition, in which no firm has a distinct brand image or price-setting power. As a result, any industry dominated by relatively few firms is likely to behave more like a monopoly than like perfect competition.

WHAT Gets Produced 生产什么

To the extent that dominating firms behave as we have discussed, they alter the output of goods and services in two specific ways. You remember that competitive industries tend, in the long run, to produce at minimum average total costs. Competitive industries also pursue cost reductions and product improvements relentlessly. These pressures tend to expand our production possibilities and enrich our consumption choices. No such forces are at work in the monopoly we have discussed here. Hence there is a basic tendency for monopolies to inhibit economic growth and limit consumption choices.

Another important feature of competitive markets is their tendency toward **marginal cost pricing**. Marginal cost pricing is important to consumers because it informs consumers of the true opportunity costs of various goods. This allows us to choose the mix of output that delivers the most utility with available resources. In our monopoly example, recall that consumers ended up getting fewer catfish than they wanted, while the economy continued to produce cotton and other goods that were less desired. The mix of output shifted away from catfish when Universal took over the industry. The presence of a monopoly therefore alters society's answer to the question of WHAT to produce.

在某种程度上，占主导地位的厂商会像我们已经讨论过的那样行事。它们通过两种特殊方式来改变商品和服务的产出量。请记住，从长期看，竞争性行业倾向于以最低的平均总成本进行生产。竞争性行业也在不懈地追求成本的降低和产品质量的提高，这些压力有助于扩大生产的可能性，丰富我们的消费选择。但在我们讨论过的垄断性行业中并不存在这种压力。因此就垄断本身而言，它有抑制经济增长和限制消费选择的倾向。

FOR WHOM 为谁生产

Monopoly also changes the answer to the FOR WHOM question. The reduced supply and higher price of catfish imply that some people will have to eat canned tuna instead of breaded catfish. The monopolist's restricted output will also reduce job opportunities in the South, leaving some families with less income. The monopolist will end up with fat profits and thus greater access to all goods and services.

HOW 如何生产

Finally, monopoly may also alter the HOW response. Competitive firms are likely to seek out new ways of breeding, harvesting, and distributing catfish. A monopoly, however, can continue to make profits from existing equipment and technology. Accordingly, monopolies tend to inhibit technology—how things are produced—by keeping potential competition out of the market.

ANY REDEEMING QUALITIES? 垄断亦有益

Despite the strong case to be made against monopoly, it is conceivable that monopolies could also benefit society. One of the arguments made for concentrations of market power is that monopolies have greater ability to pursue research and development. Another is that the lure of monopoly power creates a tremendous incentive for invention and innovation. A third argument in defense of monopoly is that large companies can produce goods more efficiently than smaller firms. Finally, it is argued that even monopolies have to worry about *potential competition* and will behave accordingly. We must pause to reflect, then, on whether and how market power might be of some benefit to society.

虽然有充分的理由反对垄断，但可以想象得出，垄断也可能对社会有利。关于市场权力集中的争论之一是，垄断者更有能力进行研发。另一方面，垄断权力的诱惑为发明和创新创造了巨大的动力。支持垄断的第三个理由是，大型厂商比小厂商的生产效率更高。最后，即使是垄断者也要担心潜在的竞争，并采取相应的行动。因此，我们必须停下来反思一下，市场权力是否有益于社会？市场权力又该如何造福社会？

Research and Development 研究和开发

In principle, monopolies are well positioned to undertake valuable research and development. First, such firms are sheltered from the constant pressure of competition. Second, they have the resources (monopoly profits) with which to carry out expensive R&D functions. The manager of a perfectly competitive firm, by contrast, has to worry about day-to-day production decisions and profit margins. As a result, she is unable to take the longer view necessary for significant research and development and could not afford to pursue such a view even if she could see it.

---

marginal cost pricing 边际成本定价。 tuna 金枪鱼。 fat profit 巨额利润，利润丰厚。 carry out 执行，实施。

The basic problem with the R&D argument is that it says nothing about *incentives*. Although monopolists have a clear financial advantage in pursuing research and development, they have no clear incentive to do so. They can continue to make substantial profits just by maintaining market power. Research and development are not necessarily required for profitable survival. In fact, research and development that make existing products or plant and equipment obsolete run counter to a monopolist's vested interest and so may actually be suppressed.

The Federal Drug Administration (FDA) in 2018 suggested that the biggest pharmaceutical companies were in fact suppressing R&D in the production of generic substitutes for expensive, branded drugs. By blocking access of generic drugs to supplies of branded drugs, the big companies could effectively halt the testing of generic substitutes (see the News Wire "R&D Barriers"). This barrier protected the prices and profits of the branded drugs.

NEWS WIRE **R&D BARRIERS**

STIFLING WOULD-BE COMPETITION

Washington, DC—The Federal Drug Administration (FDA) today "named and shamed" the biggest pharmaceutical companies for stifling the development of generic drugs. Companies wanting to develop generic substitutes for branded drugs must prove the bioequivalence of their products to their branded counterparts. To do that, they need large supplies—typically 1,500 to 5,000 units—of the branded drug for testing. The generic companies complain that the branded companies deny or delay access to the needed inventory. When that happens, the generic companies can lodge a complaint with the FDA. The FDA today released a list of those complaints. Celegne topped the list, with 31 "inquiries," the largest number concerning access to its Revlimid drug, which sells for $20,000 a month to treat blood cancer and raked in over $8 billion in sales last year. The branded producers claim that they limit the distribution of their pricey drugs for safety reasons. Dr. Scott Gottlieb, FDA's commissioner, says the branded companies are "gaming the system" to suppress the development of generic substitutes.

Source: FDA news release of August 13, 2018.

NOTE: A firm that dominates a market may not have sufficient incentive to improve its product or reduce costs. It may even try to suppress would-be competition and product improvements that weaken its monopoly hold.

注：一家占主导地位的企业也许没有足够的动机去改进产品或降低成本。它甚至还会大力压制削弱其垄断地位的潜在竞争和产品改进。

Entrepreneurial Incentives 对企业家的激励

The second defense of market power tries to use the incentive argument in a novel way. As we observed in Chapter 5, every business is out to make a profit, and it is the quest for profits that keeps industries running. Thus, it is argued, even greater profit prizes will stimulate more entrepreneurial activity. Little Horatio Algers will work harder and longer if they can dream of one day possessing a whole monopoly.

关于垄断的市场权力的第二个辩护试图以一种新方式使用激励理论。如同我们在第 5 章所看到的，每家企业都是为了盈利，正是对利润的追求让行业得以运转。因此有人认为，更大的利润回报将会刺激更多的企业家采取行动。如果小霍雷肖·阿尔杰们梦想有一天拥有对行业的完全垄断，他们就会更勤奋，并且工作时间会更长。

The incentive argument for market power is enticing but not entirely convincing. After all, an innovator can make substantial profits in a competitive market, as it typically takes a considerable amount of time for the competition to catch up. Recall that the early birds did get the worm in the catfish industry in Chapter 5 even though profit margins were later squeezed. Hence it is not evident that the profit incentives available in a competitive industry are inadequate.

Economies of Scale 规模经济

A third defense of market power is the most convincing. A large firm, it is argued, can produce goods at a lower unit (average) cost than a small firm. That is, there are **economies of scale** in production. Thus if we desire to produce goods in the most efficient way—with the least amount of resources per unit of output—we should encourage and maintain large firms.

---

substantial 大量的，价值巨大的。　pharmaceutical 制药的，药品的。　Horatio Alger 美国儿童小说家，其作品大多讲述孩子如何通过勤奋和诚实获得财富和成功。

Consider once again the comparison we made earlier between Universal Fish and the competitive catfish industry. We explicitly assumed that Universal confronted the same production costs as the competitive industry. Thus Universal was not able to produce catfish any more cheaply than the competitive counterpart. We concerned ourselves only with the different production decisions made by competitive and monopolistic firms.

It is conceivable, however, that Universal Fish might use its size to achieve greater efficiency. Perhaps the firm could build one enormous pond and centralize all breeding, harvesting, and distributing activities. If successful, this centralization might reduce production costs, making Universal more efficient than a competitive industry composed of thousands of small farms (ponds).

Even though large firms *may* be able to achieve greater efficiencies than smaller firms, there is no assurance that they actually will. Increasing the size (scale) of a plant may actually *reduce* operating efficiency. Workers may feel alienated in a massive firm and perform below their potential. Centralization might also increase managerial red tape and increase costs. In evaluating the economies-of-scale argument for market power, then, we must recognize that **efficiency and size do not necessarily go hand in hand.** In fact, monopolies may generate *dis*economies of scale, producing at higher cost than a competitive industry.

Even where economies of scale do exist, there is no guarantee that consumers will benefit. Consider the case of multiplex theaters that offer multiple movie screens. Multiplex theaters have significant economies of scale (e.g., consolidated box office, advertising, snack bar, restrooms, projection) compared to single-screen theaters. Once they drive smaller theaters out of business, however, they rarely lower ticket prices.

Natural Monopolies 自然垄断

There is a special case where the economies-of-scale argument is potentially more persuasive. In this case—called **natural monopoly**—a single firm can produce the entire market supply more efficiently than any larger number of (smaller) firms. As the size (scale) of the one firm increases, its average total costs continue to fall. These economies of scale give the one large producer a decided advantage over would-be rivals. Hence economies of scale act as a "natural" barrier to entry.

Local telephone, cable, and utility services are classic examples of natural monopoly. They have extraordinarily high fixed costs (e.g., transmission lines and switches) and exceptionally small marginal costs. Hence average total costs keep declining as output expands. As a result, it is much cheaper to install one system of cable or phone lines than a maze of competing ones. Accordingly, a single telephone or power company can supply the market more efficiently than a large number of competing firms.

Although natural monopolies are economically desirable, they may be abused. We must ask whether and to what extent consumers are reaping some benefit from the efficiency a natural monopoly makes possible. Do consumers end up with lower prices, expanded output, and better service? Or does the monopoly tend to keep the benefits for itself in the form of higher profits, better wages, and more comfortable offices? Typically, federal, state, and local governments are responsible for regulating natural monopolies to ensure that the benefits of increased efficiency are shared with consumers.

Contestable Markets 可竞争市场

Governmental regulators are not necessarily the only force keeping monopolists in line. Even though a firm may produce the entire supply of a particular product at present, it may face *potential* competition from other firms. Potential rivals may be sitting on the sidelines, watching how well the monopoly fares. If it does too well, these rivals may enter the industry, undermining the monopoly structure and profits. In such **contestable markets**, monopoly behavior may be restrained by potential competition.

---

counterpart 竞争对手。 extraordinarily 极其，极端地。 switch 交换机。 a maze of 错综的，像迷宫般的。

市场的可竞争程度与其说取决于市场结构，不如说取决于进入壁垒。如果壁垒难以逾越，潜在的竞争者就被市场排斥在外。但如果进入壁垒适中，而垄断利润的诱惑又难以抗拒，它们就会被攻破。如果国内的垄断利润和价格居高不下，国外生产同样产品的竞争者很可能就会进入国内市场。

How contestable a market is depends not so much on its structure as on entry barriers. If entry barriers are insurmountable, would-be competitors are locked out of the market. But if entry barriers are modest, they will be surmounted when the lure of monopoly profits becomes irresistible. Foreign rivals already producing the same goods are particularly likely to enter domestic markets when monopoly prices and profits are high.

Structure versus Behavior   市场结构与市场行为

From the perspective of contestable markets, the whole case against monopoly is misconceived. Market *structure* per se is not a problem; what counts is market *behavior*. If potential rivals force a monopolist to behave like a competitive firm, then monopoly imposes no cost on consumers or on society at large.

The experience with the Model T Ford illustrates the basic notion of contestable markets. At the time Henry Ford decided to increase the price of the Model T and paint all Model Ts black, the Ford Motor Company enjoyed a virtual monopoly on mass-produced cars. But potential rivals saw the profitability of offering additional colors and features (e.g., self-starter, left-hand drive). When they began producing cars in volume, Ford's market power was greatly reduced. In 1926 the Ford Motor Company tried to regain its dominant position by again supplying cars in colors other than black. By that time, however, consumers had more choices. Ford ceased production of the Model T in May 1927.

The experience with the Model T suggests that potential competition can force a monopoly to change its ways. Critics point out, however, that even contestable markets don't force a monopolist to act exactly like a competitive firm. There will always be a gap between competitive outcomes and those monopoly outcomes likely to entice new entry. That gap can cost consumers a lot. The absence of *existing* rivals is also likely to inhibit product and productivity improvements. From 1913 to 1926, all Model Ts were black, and consumers had few alternatives. Ford changed its behavior only after *potential* competition became *actual* competition. Even after 1927, when the Ford Motor Company could no longer act like a monopolist, it still didn't price its cars at marginal cost.

POLICY PERSPECTIVES

WHY IS FLYING MONOPOLY AIR ROUTES SO EXPENSIVE?

Ever wonder why it's so cheap to fly to one place yet so expensive to fly somewhere else of equal distance? The answer is likely to be market structure. As we've observed in this and the previous chapter, the greater the number of firms in a market, the lower prices are likely to be. More competition also increases the quantity supplied.

INDUSTRY STRUCTURE

From a national perspective, the airline industry looks pretty competitive. More than 90 domestic airline companies offer scheduled passenger service, and at least 150 foreign carriers serve U.S. cities. So there are a lot of firms competing for the $100 billion that Americans spend annually on airline travel.

All those airlines don't fly to the places you want to go, however. If you're looking for a nonstop flight from Los Angeles to Palm Springs, don't bother calling US Airways, Southwest, or Delta, much less Air France. None of those firms fly that route. In fact, only one airline (United) was flying that route in 2018. Hence travelers in the Los Angeles–Palm Springs market end up paying monopoly fares ($1 per mile, as compared to 10 cents per mile on the more competitive Los Angeles–New York route).

---

at large 一般来说，普遍。   notion 概念。   other than 不同于，除了。

How much it costs to fly depends on how many airlines compete.
©Greg Balfour Evans/Alamy Stock Photo

Travelers between Huntsville, Alabama, and Houston Intercontinental confront outright monopoly fares since only United Airlines flies that route. When other carriers entered US Airways' monopoly Pittsburgh–Philadelphia route in 2005, the round-trip fare fell from $680 to $186.

When assessing market structure, it is essential to specify the relevant market. In this case the relevant market is best defined by specific intercity routes. The number of airlines serving a particular route is a far better measure of market power than the number of airlines flying anywhere. By this yardstick, the airline industry is beset with market power.

INDUSTRY BEHAVIOR

If market structure really matters, airline fares should vary with the number of firms serving a particular route. And so they do. A study by the U.S. General Accounting Office (GAO) found that fares from airports dominated by one or two carriers were 45–85 percent higher than at more competitive airports.

ENTRY EFFECTS

Another way to assess the impact of market structure on prices is to observe how airline fares *change* when airlines enter or exit a specific market. According to an antitrust suit filed by the U.S. Justice Department, American Airlines slashed fares whenever a new carrier entered a market it dominated. As soon as the new carrier was forced out of the market, American raised fares to monopoly levels again. The accompanying News Wire "Predatory Pricing" offers some examples of this **predatory pricing**.

NEWS WIRE PREDATORY PRICING

FOLLOWING THE FARES

The Justice Department says American Airlines cut its fares when low-cost carriers arrived—then raised them when they left. Fares* shown are for 1995–1996 from the Dallas–Fort Worth airport to three cities.

---

entry effects 进入效应。 predatory pricing 掠夺性定价。

	Colorado Springs	Wichita	Kansas City
Before low-cost	$180	$110	$113
Low-cost in the market	$88	$57	$83
After low-cost exit	$133	$96	$125

*Average for all local carriers, nonstop.

Source: "United States of America vs. AMR Corporation, American Airlines, Inc., and AMR Eagle Holding Corporation," The United States Department of Justice, April 27, 2001.

NOTE: A monopoly carrier may use a sharp but temporary cut in fares to drive a new entrant out of the market—or to discourage others from entering.
注：一家垄断性的航空公司也许会采用大幅降低票价的临时性措施，把新的进入者赶出市场，或者阻止其他航空公司进入。

BARRIERS TO ENTRY

For the largest carriers to maintain high profits on specific routes, they must be able to keep new firms from entering those markets. One of the most formidable entry barriers is their ownership of slots (landing rights) and gates. At Washington, DC's Reagan Airport, for example, the six largest carriers owned 97 percent of available takeoff/landing slots in 2000. To offer service from that airport, a new entrant would have to buy or lease a slot from one of them. It would also have to secure a gate so passengers could access the plane. Would-be competitors complain that the dominant carriers unfairly withhold access to slots and gates, thereby thwarting competition.

The U.S. Department of Transportation has examined options for giving would-be entrants more access to airline markets. One proposal envisions a lottery system for redistributing some slots. In a prior lottery, however, almost all the new entrants that were awarded slots simply resold them to the largest carriers, choosing quick, sure cash over uncertain competition. That left travelers with the all-too-familiar choice of either staying home or flying Monopoly Air.

CHAPTER 6 REVIEW

SUMMARY

- Market power is the ability to influence the market price of a good or service. The extreme case of market power is monopoly, where only one firm produces the entire supply of a particular product. **LO1**
- The distinguishing feature of any firm with market power is that the demand curve it faces is downward-sloping. In a monopoly, the demand curve facing the firm and the market demand curve are identical. **LO1**
- The downward-sloping demand curve facing a monopolist creates a divergence between marginal revenue and price. To sell larger quantities of output, the monopolist must lower product prices. Marginal revenue is the *change* in total revenue divided by the *change* in output. **LO2**
- A monopolist maximizes total profit at the rate of output at which marginal revenue equals marginal cost (MC = MR). **LO3**
- A monopolist will produce less output than will a competitive industry confronting the same market demand and cost opportunities. That reduced rate of output will be sold at higher prices, in accordance with the (downward-sloping) market demand curve. **LO4**
- A monopoly will attain a higher level of profit than a competitive industry because of its ability to equate industry (i.e., its own) marginal revenues and costs. By

thwart 反对，阻挠。

contrast, a competitive industry ends up equating marginal costs and *price* because its individual firms have no control over the market supply curve. **LO4**

- Because the higher profits attained by a monopoly attract envious entrepreneurs, barriers to entry are needed to prohibit other firms from expanding market supplies. Patents are one such barrier to entry. Other barriers are legal harassment, exclusive licensing, product bundling, and government franchises. **LO4**
- The defense of market power rests on (1) the ability of large firms to pursue research and development, (2) the incentives implicit in the chance to attain market power, (3) the efficiency that larger firms may attain, and (4) the contestability of even monopolized markets. The first two arguments are weakened by the fact that competitive firms are under much greater pressure to innovate and can stay ahead of the profit game only if they do so. The contestability defense at best concedes some amount of monopoly exploitation. **LO5**
- A natural monopoly exists when one firm can produce the output of the entire industry more efficiently than can a number of smaller firms. This advantage is attained from economies of scale. Large firms are not necessarily more efficient, however. **LO5**

TERMS TO REMEMBER

Define the following terms:

market power
market demand
patent
monopoly
marginal revenue (MR)
profit maximization rule
production decision

barriers to entry
marginal cost pricing
economies of scale
natural monopoly
contestable market
predatory pricing

QUESTIONS FOR DISCUSSION

1. If you owned the only bookstore on or near campus, what would you charge for this textbook? How much would you pay students for their used books? **LO3**
2. Why don't competitive industries produce at the rate of output that maximizes industry profits, as a monopolist does? **LO4**
3. Is single ownership of a whole industry necessary to exercise monopoly power? How might an industry with several firms achieve the same result? Can you think of any examples? **LO1**
4. Despite its reaffirmed monopoly position, Polaroid went bankrupt in 2001 and stopped making instant development cameras in 2007. What happened? **LO4**
5. Why don't monopolists try to establish the highest price possible, as many people allege? What would happen to sales? To profits? **LO3**
6. What circumstances might cause a monopolist to charge less than the profit-maximizing price? **LO3**
7. How could free Internet-search software (on Android phones) possibly harm consumers? **LO4**
8. What entry barriers exist in (*a*) the coffee-bar business; (*b*) cable TV; (*c*) the taxi-cab industry; (*d*) the illegal drug trade? **LO1**
9. Why would any firm pay another firm to *not* produce? (See the News Wire "R&D Barriers.") **LO4**
10. **POLICY PERSPECTIVES** The U.S. airline industry generated over $38 billion in profits in 2018. Is that outcome representative of a competitive industry? Why don't more companies get into the airline business? **LO4**

PROBLEMS

1. In Figure 6.1, **LO2**
   a. what is the highest price the monopolist could charge and still sell fish?
   b. what is total revenue at that highest price?
   c. what happens to total revenue as price is reduced from *A* to *F*?
   d. what is the value of marginal revenue as price is reduced from *F* to *G*?

2. In Figure 6.1's graph, **LO3**
   a. at what output rate (from *A* to *G*) is total revenue maximized?
   b. what is MR at that output rate?
   c. if the firm is currently producing at that rate of output identified in part *a*, should the firm increase, decrease, or not change the rate of production?
3. Use Figure 6.2 to answer the following questions: **LO2**
   a. What rate of output maximizes total profit?
   b. What is the MR at that rate of output?
   c. What is the price?
   d. If output is increased by 1 pound beyond that point, is MC (i) larger or (ii) smaller than MR?
   e. What happens to total profits?
4. Compute marginal revenues from the following data on market demand: **LO2**

Price per unit	$38	36	34	32	30	28	26
Units demanded	10	11	12	13	14	15	16
Marginal revenue		—	—	—	—	—	—

   a. At what price does MR = 0?
   b. At what price is MR < 0?
   c. At what price is MR < price?
5. Suppose the following data represent the market demand for catfish: **LO2**

Price (per unit)	$20	19	18	17	16	15	14	13	12	11
Quantity demanded (units per day)	12	13	14	15	16	17	18	19	20	21
Total revenue		—	—	—	—	—	—	—	—	—
Marginal revenue		—	—	—	—	—	—	—	—	—

   a. Compute total and marginal revenue to complete the table above.
   b. At what rate of output is total revenue maximized?
   c. At what rate of output is MR less than price?
   d. At what rate of output does MR first become negative?
   e. Graph the demand and MR curves.
6. Assume that the following marginal costs exist in catfish production: **LO4**

Quantity produced (units per day)	10	11	12	13	14	15	16	17
Marginal cost (per unit)	$4	6	8	10	12	14	16	18

   a. Graph the MC curve.
   b. Use the data on market demand below and graph the demand and MR curves on the same graph.

Price (per unit)	$25	24	23	22	21	20	19	18
Quantity demanded (units per day)	10	11	12	13	14	15	16	17

   c. At what rate of output is MR = MC?
   d. What price will a monopolist charge for that much output?
   e. If the market were perfectly competitive, what price would prevail?
   f. How much output would be produced in perfect competition?

7. *a.* According to the News Wire "Mimicking Monopoly," by what percentage did oil prices rise between 2016–2018? **LO3**
   b. What is the minimum price per barrel required for U.S. shale producers to be profitable? **LO3**
8. If generic producers were able to produce a substitute for Revlimid that reduced Revlimid's sales by 50 percent, how much less revenue would Celegne take in per year (see the News Wire " R&D Barriers"). **LO4**
9. Assume the on-campus demand for soda is as follows: **LO4**

Price ($ per can)	2.00	1.75	1.50	1.25	1.00	0.75	0.50	0.25
Quantity demanded (per day)	30	40	50	60	70	80	90	100

   If the marginal cost of supplying a soda is 50 cents, what price will students end up paying in
   a. A perfectly competitive market?
   b. A monopolized market?
10. Titleist sells about 15 million golf balls a year. If it has to sell them at Costco's price rather than the ProV1 price, how much less revenue would Titleist take in? (See the News Wire "Legal Barriers.") **LO3**
11. **POLICY PERSPECTIVES**
    a. Classify the airline industry in general as a competitive or monopolistic industry. **LO 4**
    b. How about the specific route between Los Angeles and Palm Springs? **LO 4**
    c. What are two important barriers to entry for airlines to maintain high profits? **LO 4**

CHAPTER SEVEN

The Labor Market 劳动力市场

LEARNING OBJECTIVES

After reading this chapter, you should be able to:

1. Cite the forces that influence the supply of labor.
2. Explain why the labor demand curve slopes downward.
3. Describe how the equilibrium wage and employment levels are determined.
4. Depict how a legal minimum wage alters market outcomes.
5. Explain why wages are so unequal.

Dale Earnhardt Jr. raked in around $14 million a year from winning NASCAR races. But that's just the beginning for Dale Jr.: He got another $10–$15 million a year from product endorsements—everything from Nationwide Insurance (his primary sponsor) to Wrangler jeans, Chevrolet, eye glasses, and Dale Jr. "88" stogies. Even after he retired from full-time racing in 2017, "Junior" continued to receive millions of dollars a year from product endorsements, part-time racing, broadcasting, and various businesses. Yet the president of the United States gets paid only $400,000. And the assistant who typed the manuscript of this book is paid just $19,000. What accounts for these tremendous disparities in earnings?

And why is it that the average college graduate earns over $55,000 a year, while the average high school graduate earns just $32,000? Are such disparities simply a reward for enduring four years of college, or do they reflect real differences in talent? Are you really learning anything that makes you that much more valuable than a high school graduate? For that matter, what are you worth—not in metaphysical terms but in terms of the wages you would be paid in the marketplace?

The FOR WHOM question is one of society's three central economic concerns. How large a share of output individuals get is largely determined by their paychecks. The distribution of income in the United States and elsewhere is far from equal. How does this inequality arise? Why do some people earn a great deal of income while others earn very little? To answer this question, we have to consider both the *supply* and the *demand* for labor. In this regard, the following questions arise:

- How do people decide how much time to spend working?
- What determines the wage rate an employer is willing to pay?
- Why are some workers paid so much and others so little?

To answer these questions, we need to examine the behavior of labor *markets*. ■

---

product endorsement 产品代言。manuscript 手稿，原稿。disparity 不同，差距。metaphysical 形而上学的。

LABOR SUPPLY 劳动供给

The following two ads appeared in the campus newspaper of a well-known university:

> Will do ANYTHING for money: able-bodied liberal-minded male needs money, will work to get it. Have car. Call Tom 555-0244.

> Web Architect: Computer sciences graduate, strong programming skills and software knowledge (e.g., JavaScript, Python, C++). Please call Margaret 555-3247, 9–5.

在广告中，汤姆和玛格丽特所表达的工作意愿代表了**劳动供给**。对任何能付给他们适当工资的人，他们乐意提供自己的时间和才能。他们的明确意愿与其他任何寻找工作的人是一样的。求职者在学生就业办公室查询当前工作机会的信息，或者向潜在的雇主投递简历，都表达了接受雇用的意愿——也就是说，提供劳动。

Although placed by individuals with very different talents, the ads clearly expressed Tom's and Margaret's willingness to work. We don't know how much money they were asking for their respective talents or whether they ever found jobs, but we can be sure that they were prepared to take a job at some wage rate. Otherwise they would not have paid for the ads in the "Jobs Wanted" column of their campus newspaper.

The advertised willingness to work expressed by Tom and Margaret represents a **labor supply**. They are offering to sell their time and talents to anyone who is willing to pay the right price. Their explicit offers are similar to those of anyone who looks for a job. Job seekers who check the current job openings at the student employment office or send résumés to potential employers are demonstrating a willingness to accept employment—that is, to *supply* labor. The 4,500 people who showed up at the Amazon job fair in Baltimore (see the News Wire "Labor Supply") were also offering to supply labor.

NEWS WIRE LABOR SUPPLY

THOUSANDS OF JOB SEEKERS BRAVE HEAT TO GET AMAZON JOBS

Baltimore MD. The line started forming at 4 AM. By 8 AM, there were over 3,000 people in the line snaking around Amazon's fulfillment center. Despite 85-degree heat and equally high humidity, these people were willing to stand in line for hours just for a chance to land a job at Amazon's local fulfillment center. By the end of the day, over 4,500 job-seekers had applied for the 1,200 jobs Amazon had posted, which pay wages of around $14 an hour. Amazon held similar job fairs in 11 other cities around the nation, promising to hire as many as 50,000 new employees.

Source: News accounts of August 2–4, 2017.

©Julio Cortez/AP Images

NOTE: People supply labor by demonstrating a willingness to work. The quantity of labor supplied increases as the wage rate rises.
注：人们通过表达工作意愿来提供劳动。劳动的供给数量随着工资水平的升高而增加。

Our first concern in this chapter is to explain these labor supply decisions. As Figure 7.1 illustrates, we expect the quantity of labor supplied—the number of hours people are willing to work—to increase as wage rates rise.

But how do people decide how many hours to supply at any given wage rate? Do people try to maximize their income? If they did, we would all be holding three jobs and sleeping on the commuter bus. Few of us actually live this way. Hence we must have other goals than simply maximizing our incomes.

---

architect 建筑师，工程师。humidity 湿度。

Income versus Leisure 收入与闲暇

The most visible benefit obtained from working is a paycheck. In general, the fatter the paycheck—the greater the wage rate offered—the more willing a person is to go to work.

As important as paychecks are, however, people recognize that working entails real sacrifices. Every hour we spend working implies one less hour available for other pursuits. If we go to work, we have less time to watch TV, go to a soccer game, or simply enjoy a nice day. In other words, there is a real **opportunity cost** associated with working. Generally, we say that *the opportunity cost of working is the amount of leisure time that must be given up in the process.*

但是与工资同等重要的是，人们意识到工作也意味着某种意义上的牺牲。我们每花一小时去工作，就意味着我们少了一小时来从事其他活动。如果我们去上班，我们看电视、看球赛或者在家悠然自得的时间就变少了。换句话说，确实存在与工作相关的**机会成本**。一般说来，我们认为工作的机会成本就是工作过程中我们必须放弃的用于闲暇的时间。

Because both leisure and income are valued, **we confront a trade-off** when deciding whether to go to work. Going to work implies more income but less leisure. Staying home has the opposite consequences.

The inevitable trade-off between labor and leisure explains the shape of individual labor supply curves. As we work more hours, our leisure time becomes more scarce and thus more valuable. We become increasingly reluctant to give up any remaining leisure time as it gets scarcer. People who work all week long are reluctant to go to work on Saturday. It's not that they are physically exhausted. It's just that they want some time to enjoy the fruits of their labor. In other words, *as the opportunity cost of job time increases, we require correspondingly higher rates of pay.* We will supply additional labor—work more hours—only if higher wage rates are offered: This is the message conveyed by the upward-sloping labor supply curve.

换句话说，随着工作时间的机会成本增加，我们相应地会要求更高的工资。

The upward slope of the labor supply curve is reinforced with the changing value of income. Our primary motive for working is the income a job provides. Those first few dollars are really precious, especially if you have bills to pay. As you work and earn more, however, you discover that your most urgent needs have been satisfied. You may still want more things, but your consumption desires aren't so urgent. In other words, *the marginal utility of income declines as you earn more.* Accordingly, the wages offered for more work lose some of their allure. You may not be willing to work more hours unless offered a higher wage rate.

换句话说，随着你收入的增加，收入的边际效用是递减的。

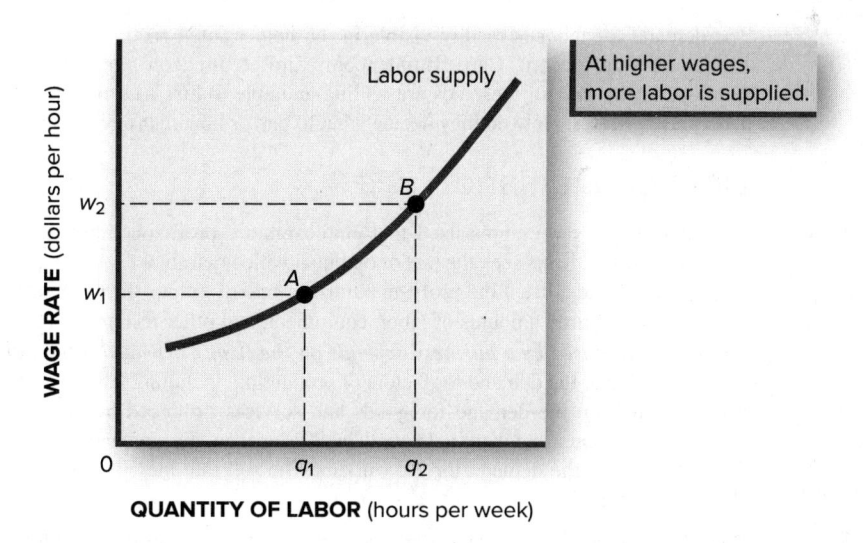

Figure 7.1 The Supply of Labor The quantity of any good or service offered for sale typically increases as its price rises. Labor supply responds in the same way. At the wage rate w_1, the quantity of labor supplied is q_1 (point A). At the higher wage w_2, workers are willing to work more hours per week—that is, to supply a larger quantity of labor (q_2).

因此，向上倾斜的个人劳动供给曲线反映了两个现象：
- 劳动的机会成本递增；
- 随着工作时间的增加，个人收入的边际效用递减。

The upward slope of an individual's labor supply curve is thus a reflection of two phenomena:
- The increasing opportunity cost of labor.
- The decreasing marginal utility of income as a person works more hours.

Nearly one of every two U.S. workers now says he or she would be willing to give up some pay for more leisure. As wages and living standards have risen, the urge for more money has abated. What people want is more leisure time to *spend* their incomes. As a result, ever-higher wages are needed to lure people into working longer hours.

Money isn't necessarily the only thing that motivates people to work, of course. People *do* turn down higher-paying jobs in favor of lower-wage jobs that they like. Many parents forgo high-wage "career" jobs in order to have more flexible hours and time at home. Volunteers offer their services just for the sense of contributing to their communities; no paycheck is required. Even MBA graduates say they are motivated more by the challenge of high-paying jobs than by the money. When push comes to shove, however, money almost always makes a difference: People *do* supply more labor when offered higher wages.

Market Supply　　市场供给

劳动的市场供给是指人们在各种工资水平下愿意提供劳动的总时数。它也是向上倾斜的。当工资水平上升时，不仅现有工人愿意提供更长时间的劳动，而且其他工人也被吸引到劳动力市场。如果工作机会充足并且工资够高，许多学生会离开学校而开始工作。同样，许多家庭主妇也很难抗拒高工资的诱惑而外出工作。工资水平高的时候，进入劳动力市场的移民人数也会增多。随着劳动力市场进入者的各种流动增加，劳动力市场上的劳动供给总量也随之增加。

The **market supply of labor** refers to all the hours people are willing to work at various wages. It, too, is upward-sloping. As wage rates rise, not only do existing workers offer to work longer hours but other workers are drawn into the labor market as well. If jobs are plentiful and wages high, many students leave school and start working. Likewise, many homemakers decide that work outside the home is too hard to resist. The flow of immigrants into the labor market also increases when wages are high. As these various flows of labor market entrants increase, the total quantity of labor supplied to the market goes up.

LABOR DEMAND　　劳动需求

Regardless of how many people are *willing* to work, it is up to employers to decide how many people will *actually* work. Employers must be willing and able to hire workers if people are going to find the jobs they seek. That is to say, there must be a **demand for labor**.

The demand for labor is readily visible in the help wanted section of the newspaper or the listings at Monster.com, CareerBuilder.com, ZipRecruiter.com, and other online job sites. Employers who pay for these ads are willing and able to hire a certain number of workers at specific wage rates. How do they decide what to pay or how many people to hire?

Derived Demand　　派生需求

在以前的章节中，我们强调了雇主是追求利润最大化的。在追求利润最大化的过程中，企业寻求边际收益等于边际成本时的产出率。企业一旦确定了利润最大化的产出率，就会进入要素市场购买所需要的劳动、设备和其他资源。因此，企业购入的资源量取决于它的预期产出量和销售量。在这个意义上讲，我们认为对包括劳动在内的生产要素的需求是一种**派生需求**，它源于对这些要素产生的商品和服务的需求。

In earlier chapters we emphasized that employers are profit maximizers. In their quest for maximum profits, firms seek the rate of output at which marginal revenue equals marginal cost. Once they have identified the profit-maximizing rate of output, firms enter factor markets to purchase the required amounts of labor, equipment, and other resources. Thus *the quantity of resources purchased by a business depends on the firm's expected sales and output.* In this sense, we say that the demand for factors of production, including labor, is a **derived demand**; it is derived from the demand for goods and services produced by these factors. As 5,500 employees of Sears and Kmart learned in 2018, when the demand for Sears merchandise declines, so does the demand for the workers who sell that merchandise (see the News Wire "Derived Demand").

Consider also the plight of strawberry pickers. Strawberry farming is a $2 billion industry. Yet the thousands of pickers who toil in the fields earn only $9 an hour. The United Farm Workers union blames greedy growers for the low wages. They say if the farmers would only raise the price of strawberries by a nickel a pint, they could raise wages by 50 percent.

---

abate 减弱，减少。　flexible 灵活的，有弹性的。　push comes to shove 紧要关头。　plight 困境。　toil 辛勤劳动。

NEWS WIRE DERIVED DEMAND

SEARS TO LAY OFF 5,500 WORKERS

The first wave of termination notices went out on April 12, informing Sears employees that their jobs were disappearing. The struggling retailer, which lost over $400 million in the first quarter of this year, announced that it is closing 39 Sears stores and 64 Kmart stores this year. The closures will result in at least 5,500 employee layoffs.

Source: News accounts of April–September 2018.

NOTE: A firm's demand for labor depends on the demand for the products the firm produces.
注：企业对劳动力的需求取决于人们对企业生产出的产品的需求。

Unfortunately, employer greed is not the only force at work here. Strawberry growers, like most producers, would love to sell more strawberries at higher prices. If they did, the growers might hire more pickers and even pay them a higher wage rate. But the growers must contend with the market demand for strawberries. If they increase the price of strawberries—even by only 5 cents a pint—the quantity of berries demanded will decline. They'd end up hiring fewer workers. Wage rates might suffer as well.

The link between the product market and the labor market also explains why graduates with engineering or computer science degrees are paid so much (see the News Wire "Unequal Wages"). Demand for related products is growing so fast that employers are desperate to hire individuals with the necessary skills. By contrast, the wages of philosophy majors suffer from the fact that the search for meaning is no longer a growth industry.

NEWS WIRE UNEQUAL WAGES

MOST LUCRATIVE COLLEGE DEGREES

College graduation does improve a person's income prospects. But all graduates aren't treated equally: What you majored in counts for a lot. Annual salary surveys by PayScale Inc. confirm that a student majoring in engineering can expect to earn nearly twice the salary of a journalism major.

What Does Your Major Pay?

Major	Median Starting Salary	Major	Median Starting Salary
Chemical engineering	$63,200	Business	$43,000
Computer engineering	61,400	Marketing	40,800
Electrical engineering	60,900	Political science	40,800
Nursing	54,200	Philosophy	39,900
Physics	50,300	History	39,200
Economics	**50,100**	Sociology	36,500
Finance	47,900	Journalism	35,600
Accounting	46,000		

Source: "College Salary Report," *PayScale*, 2018, www.payscale.com.

NOTE: The pay of college graduates depends in part on what major they studied. Graduates who can produce goods and services in great demand get the highest pay.
注：大学毕业生的工资部分取决于他们所学的专业。能够生产（或提供）社会需求量大的商品或服务的毕业生工资最高。

---

desperate 不顾一切的。 lucrative 获利丰厚的。

The principle of derived demand suggests that if consumers really want to improve the lot of strawberry pickers, they should eat more strawberries. An increase in consumer demand for strawberries will motivate growers to plant more berries and hire more labor to pick them. Until then, the plight of the pickers is not likely to improve.

The Wage Rate 工资率

The number of strawberry pickers hired by the growers is not completely determined by consumer demand for strawberries. A farmer with tons of strawberries to harvest might still be reluctant to hire many workers at $30 an hour. At $9 per hour, however, the same farmer would hire a lot of help. That is to say, ***the quantity of labor demanded depends on its price (the wage rate)***. In general, we expect that strawberry growers will be *willing to hire* more pickers at low wages than at high wages. Hence the demand for labor is not a fixed quantity; instead there is a varying relationship between quantity demanded and price (wage rate). Like virtually all other demand curves, the labor demand curve is downward-sloping (see Figure 7.2).

这就是说，劳动需求量取决于劳动的价格（工资率）。总的说来，我们预计草莓农场主愿意以低工资雇用更多的采摘工人，而不是高工资。所以对劳动力的需求不是一个固定的量，需求量与价格（工资率）之间存在一个变化关系。与几乎所有其他需求曲线一样，劳动的需求曲线是向下倾斜的（如图7.2）。

Marginal Physical Product 边际物质产品

The downward slope of the labor demand curve reflects the changing productivity of workers as more are hired. Each worker isn't as valuable as the last. On the contrary, each additional worker tends to be *less* valuable as more workers are hired. In the strawberry fields, a worker's value is measured by the number of boxes he or she can pick in an hour. More generally, we measure a worker's value to the firm by his or her **marginal physical product (MPP)**—that is, the *change* in total output that occurs when an additional worker is hired. In most situations, ***marginal physical product declines as more workers are hired.***

一般地说，我们用他的**边际物质产品**来衡量一个工人对雇主的价值，即多雇用一个工人时总产出的变化量。在大多数情况下，边际物质产品随着所雇用人数的增多而减少。

Suppose for the moment that Marvin, a college dropout with three summers of experience as a canoe instructor, can pick five boxes of strawberries per hour. These five boxes represent Marvin's marginal physical product (MPP)—in other words, the *addition* to total output that occurs when the grower hires Marvin:

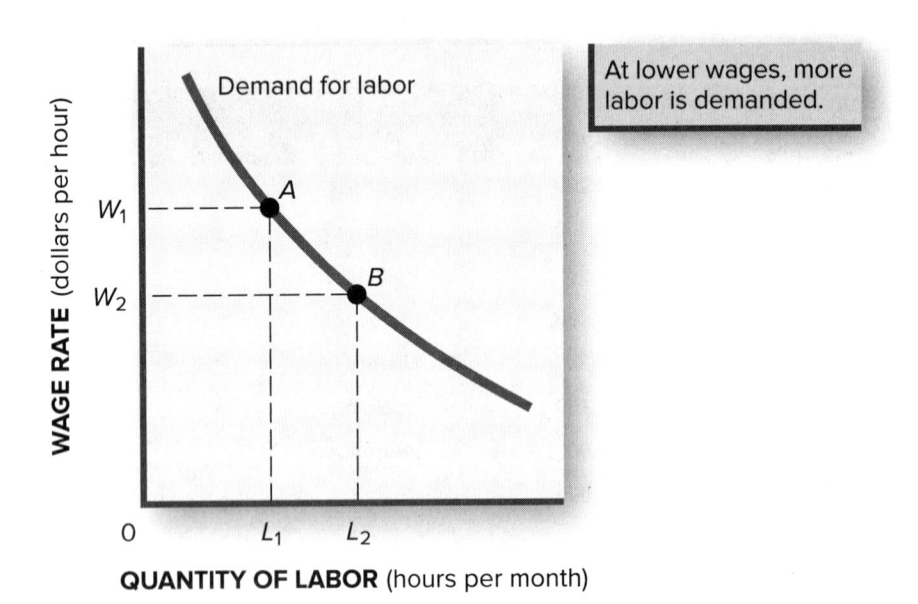

Figure 7.2 The Demand for Labor The higher the wage rate, the smaller the quantity of labor demanded (*ceteris paribus*). At the wage rate W_1, only L_1 of labor is demanded (point A). If the wage rate falls to W_2, a larger quantity of labor (L_2) will be demanded. The labor demand curve obeys the law of demand. ■

---

dropout 辍学者。canoe 独木舟。

$$\text{Marginal physical product} = \frac{\text{change in total output}}{\text{change in quantity of labor}}$$

边际物质产品 = $\frac{\text{总产出的变化量}}{\text{劳动的变化量}}$

Marginal physical product establishes an *upper limit* to the grower's willingness to pay. Clearly the grower can't afford to pay Marvin more than five boxes of strawberries for an hour's work; the grower will not pay Marvin more than he produces.

Marginal Revenue Product 边际收益产品

Most strawberry pickers don't want to be paid in strawberries, of course. At the end of a day in the fields, the last thing a picker wants to see is another strawberry. Marvin, like the rest of the pickers, wants to be paid in cash. To find out how much cash he might be paid, all we need to know is what a box of strawberries is worth. This is easy to determine. The market value of a box of strawberries is simply the price at which the grower can sell it. Thus Marvin's contribution to output can be measured in either marginal *physical* product (five boxes per hour) or the dollar *value* of that product.

The dollar value of a worker's contribution to output is called **marginal revenue product (MRP)**. Marginal revenue product is the change in total revenue that occurs when more labor is hired:

$$\text{Marginal revenue product} = \frac{\text{change in total revenue}}{\text{change in quantity of labor}}$$

边际收益产品 = $\frac{\text{总收益的变化量}}{\text{劳动的变化量}}$

If the grower can sell strawberries for $2 a box, Marvin's marginal revenue product is five boxes per hour × $2 per box, or $10 per hour. This is Marvin's value to the grower. Accordingly, the grower can afford to pay Marvin up to $10 per hour. Thus *marginal revenue product sets an upper limit to the wage rate an employer will pay.*

But what about a lower limit? Suppose that the pickers aren't organized and that Marvin is desperate for money. Under such circumstances, he might be willing to work—to supply labor—for only $6 an hour.

Should the grower hire Marvin for such a low wage? The profit-maximizing answer is obvious. If Marvin's marginal revenue product is $10 an hour and his wages are only $6 an hour, the grower will be eager to hire him. The difference between Marvin's marginal revenue product ($10) and his wage ($6) implies additional profits of $4 an hour. In fact, the grower will be so elated by the economics of this situation that he will want to hire everybody he can find who is willing to work for $6 an hour. After all, if the grower can make $4 an hour by hiring Marvin, why not hire 1,000 pickers and accumulate profits at an even faster rate?

The 25,000 pickers who harvest America's $2 billion strawberry crop are paid only $9 an hour. Why is their pay so low?
©David Butow/Corbis/Getty Images

The Law of Diminishing Returns 收益递减规律

The exploitive possibilities suggested by Marvin's picking are too good to be true. For starters, how could the grower squeeze 1,000 workers onto one acre of land and still have any room left over for strawberry plants? You don't need two years of business school to recognize a potential problem here. Sooner or later the farmer will run out of space. Even before that limit is reached, the rate of strawberry picking may slow. Indeed, the grower's eagerness to hire additional pickers will begin to fade long before 1,000 workers are hired. The critical concept here is *marginal productivity*.

---

upper limit 上限。 eager 热切的，渴望的。 elate 使……欢欣，使……兴高采烈。 exploitive 剥削的。 fade 逐渐消失，消退。 marginal productivity 边际生产率。

Diminishing MPP 边际物质产品递减

做出雇用马文的决定源于他的边际物质产品——就是每小时马文能采摘 5 盒草莓。要评估雇用更多工人是否明智，我们就要考虑随着更多工人被雇用后总产出的变化。要做到这一点，我们需要了解当更多工人被雇用时边际物质产品的变化。

The decision to hire Marvin was based on his marginal physical product—that is, the five boxes of strawberries he can pick in an hour's time. To assess the wisdom of hiring additional pickers, we have to consider what happens to total output as more workers are employed. To do so, we need to keep track of how marginal physical product *changes* when more workers are hired.

Figure 7.3 shows how strawberry output changes as additional pickers are hired. We start with Marvin, who picks five boxes of strawberries per hour. Total output and Marvin's marginal physical product are identical because he is initially the only picker employed.

When the grower hires George, Marvin's old college roommate, we observe that the total output increases to 10 boxes per hour (point *B* in Figure 7.3). This figure represents another increase of five boxes per hour. Accordingly, we may conclude that George's *marginal physical product* is five boxes per hour, the same as Marvin's. Naturally, the grower will want to hire George and continue looking for more pickers.

As more workers are hired, total strawberry output continues to increase, but not nearly as fast. Although the later hires work just as hard, the limited availability of land and capital constrains their marginal physical product. One problem is the number of boxes. There are only a dozen boxes, and the additional pickers often have to wait for an empty box. The time spent waiting depresses marginal physical product. The worst problem is space: As additional workers are crowded onto the one-acre patch, they begin to get in one another's way. The picking process is slowed, and marginal physical product is further depressed. Note that the MPP of the fifth picker (row E of the table) is two boxes per hour, while the MPP of the sixth picker is only one box per hour. By the time we get to the seventh picker (row G), marginal physical product actually falls to zero—no further increases in total strawberry output take place.

So, what is that seventh worker doing? Why doesn't total output increase when that seventh worker is hired? The marginal physical product of zero isn't that worker's fault. The problem is the lack of land and tools to accommodate so many workers. The seventh worker is as busy as the other six. But lack of space and tools is limiting strawberry production.

Things get even worse if the grower hires still more pickers. If eight pickers are employed, total output actually *declines*. The pickers can no longer work efficiently under such crowded conditions. Hence the MPP of the eighth worker is *negative*, no matter how ambitious or hardworking this person may be. Points *H* and *h* in Figure 7.3 illustrate this negative marginal physical product.

我们对草莓生产的这种观察适用于大多数行业。事实上，收益递减甚至在最简单的生产过程中也十分明显。设想你叫一个朋友来帮你做作业。一点点的帮助也许会对你提高成绩大有帮助。那是否意味着你请两个朋友来帮忙，你的进步就会加倍呢？你叫 5 个朋友来又会怎样呢？他们会一时兴起在你家里聊天，你的家庭作业就别想再做了。总之，边际物质产品随着所雇劳动力数量的增加而最终下降。

Our observations on strawberry production apply to most industries. Indeed, diminishing returns are evident in even the simplest production processes. Suppose you ask a friend to help you with your homework. A little help may go a long way toward improving your grade. Does that mean that your grade improvement will *double* if you get *two* friends to help? What if you get five friends to help? Suddenly everyone's chatting, and your homework performance deteriorates. In general, **the marginal physical product of labor eventually declines as the quantity of labor employed increases.**

你可能已经意识到**收益递减规律**在这里起作用。当更多的人要共享有限的设施时，边际生产率会降低。通常收益递减的原因是工人数量的增加使每个工人可利用的土地和资本减少了。

You may recognize the **law of diminishing returns** at work here. **Marginal productivity declines as more people must share limited facilities.** Typically, diminishing returns result from the fact that an increasing number of workers leaves each worker with less land and capital to work with.

Diminishing MRP 边际收益产品递减

As marginal *physical* product diminishes, so does marginal *revenue* product (MRP). As noted earlier, marginal revenue product is the increase in the *value* of total output associated with an added unit of labor (or other input). In our example, it refers to the increase in strawberry revenues associated with one additional picker.

---

identical 完全相同的。 ambitious 野心勃勃的，有雄心的。

The decline in marginal revenue product (MRP) mirrors the drop in marginal physical product (MPP). Recall that a box of strawberries sells for $2. With this price and the output statistics of Figure 7.3, we can readily calculate marginal revenue product, as summarized in Table 7.1. As the growth of output diminishes, so does marginal revenue product. Marvin's marginal revenue product of $10 an hour has fallen to $6 an hour by the time four pickers are employed and reaches zero when seven pickers are employed.

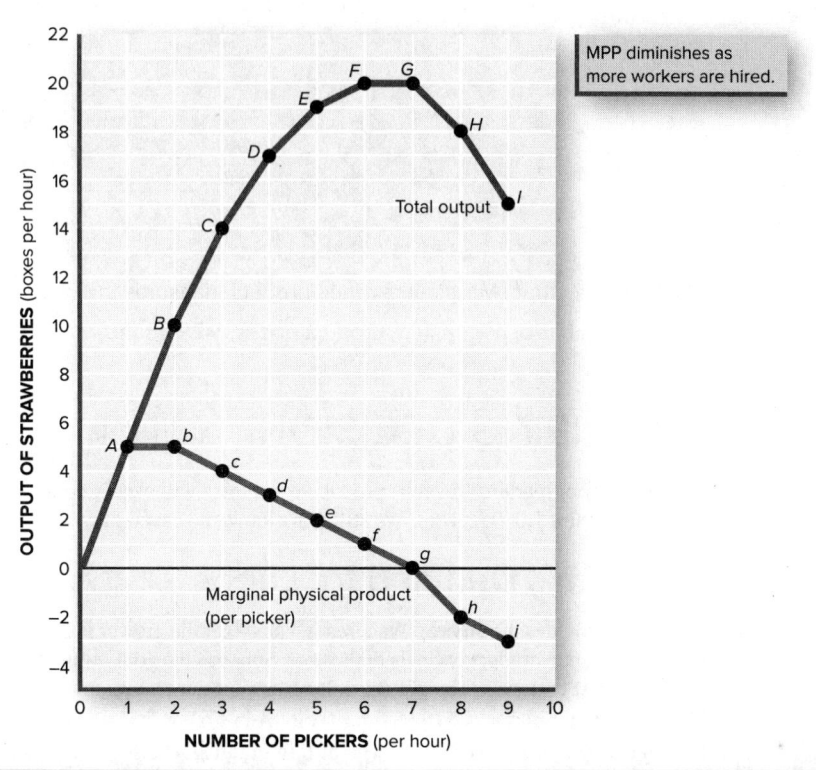

	Number of Pickers (per Hour)	Total Strawberry Output (Boxes per Hour)	Marginal Physical Product (Boxes per Hour)
A	1 (Marvin)	5	5
B	2 (George)	10	5
C	3	14	4
D	4	17	3
E	5	19	2
F	6	20	1
G	7	20	0
H	8	18	−2
I	9	15	−3

Figure 7.3 Diminishing Marginal Physical Product The marginal physical product of labor is the increase in total production that results when one additional worker is hired. Marginal physical product tends to fall as additional workers are hired. This decline occurs because each worker has increasingly less of other factors (e.g., land) with which to work.

When the second worker (George) is hired, total output increases from 5 to 10 boxes per hour. Hence the second worker's MPP equals five boxes per hour. Thereafter, capital and land constraints diminish marginal physical product.

Number of Pickers (per Hour)	Total Strawberry Output (Boxes per Hour)	× Price of Strawberries (per Box)	= Total Strawberry Revenue (per Hour)	Marginal Revenue Product
0	0	$2	0	
1 (Marvin)	5	$2	$10	$10
2 (George)	10	$2	$20	$10
3	14	$2	$28	$8
4	17	$2	$34	$6
5	19	$2	$38	$4
6	20	$2	$40	$2
7	20	$2	$40	$0
8	18	$2	$36	$-4
9	15	$2	$30	$-6

Table 7.1 Diminishing Marginal Revenue Product Marginal revenue product measures the change in total revenue that occurs when one additional worker is hired. At constant product prices, MRP equals MPP × price. Hence MRP declines along with MPP.

THE HIRING DECISION 雇用决策

边际收益产品递减的趋势肯定会给农场主雇用 1 000 个工人的愿望泼一盆冷水。但是我们仍然不知道到底有多少工人会被雇用。

The tendency of marginal revenue product to diminish will clearly cool the strawberry grower's eagerness to hire 1,000 pickers. We still don't know, however, how many pickers will be hired.

The Firm's Demand for Labor 厂商对劳动的需求

Figure 7.4 provides the answer. We already know that the grower is eager to hire pickers whose marginal revenue product exceeds their wage. Suppose the going wage for strawberry pickers is $6 an hour. At that wage, the grower will certainly want to hire at least one picker because the MRP of the first picker is $10 an hour (point *A* in Figure 7.4). A second worker will be hired as well because that picker's MRP (point *B* in Figure 7.4) also exceeds the going wage rate. In fact, ***the grower will continue hiring pickers until the MRP has declined to the level of the market wage rate.*** Figure 7.4 indicates that this intersection of MRP and the market wage rate (point *C*) occurs after four pickers are employed. Hence we can conclude that the grower will be willing to hire—will *demand*—four pickers if wages are $6 an hour.

事实上，农场主将继续雇用新的采摘工人，直到工人的边际收益产品降到市场工资水平。

The folly of hiring more than four pickers is also apparent in Figure 7.4. The marginal revenue product of the fifth worker is only $4 an hour (point *D*). Hiring a fifth picker will cost more in wages than the picker brings in as revenue. The *maximum* number of pickers the grower will employ at prevailing wages is four (point *C*).

The law of diminishing returns also implies that all of the four pickers will be paid the same wage. Once four pickers are employed, we cannot say that any single picker is responsible for the observed decline in marginal revenue product. Marginal revenue product diminishes because each worker has less capital and land to work with, not because the last worker hired is less able than the others. Accordingly, the fourth picker cannot be identified as any particular individual. Once four pickers are hired, Marvin's MRP is no higher than any other picker's. ***Each (identical) worker is worth no more than the marginal revenue product of the last worker hired, and all workers are paid the same wage rate.***

每一个（相同的）工人的价值都不会比最后一个被雇用工人的边际收益产品更高，而且他们的工资率相同。

The principles of marginal revenue product apply to football coaches as well as strawberry pickers. Nick Saban, Alabama's football coach, earns $7 million a year (see the accompanying News Wire "Marginal Revenue Product"). Why does he get paid 10 times more than the

---

folly 愚蠢的事。apparent 显然的，明显的。

university's president? Because a winning football team brings in tens of thousands of paying fans per game, lots of media exposure, and grateful alumni. The university thinks his MRP easily justifies the high salary.

NEWS WIRE MARGINAL REVENUE PRODUCT

ALABAMA'S NICK SABAN GETS $74 MILLION CONTRACT

Nick Saban, the 65-year-old coach of the Crimson Tide football team, will be staying in Tuscaloosa for many more years. He just signed a contract that extends his coaching job until 2025. Saban was paid $11.125 million this year for garnering another national championship (his fifth in nine years). The new contract will pay him at least $74 million over the next eight seasons, continuing his reign as the nation's highest paid college coach.

Source: News accounts of July 2018.

©Don Juan Moore/Getty Images

NOTE: Colleges are willing to pay more for football coaches than professors. Successful coaches bring in much more revenue.
注：各大学均愿意向橄榄球教练支付比教授更高的工资。成功的教练将会带来更多收益。

If we accept the notion that marginal revenue product sets the wages of both football coaches and strawberry pickers, must we give up all hope for low-paid workers? Can anything be done to create more jobs or higher wages for pickers? To answer this, we need to see how market demand and supply interact to establish employment and wage levels.

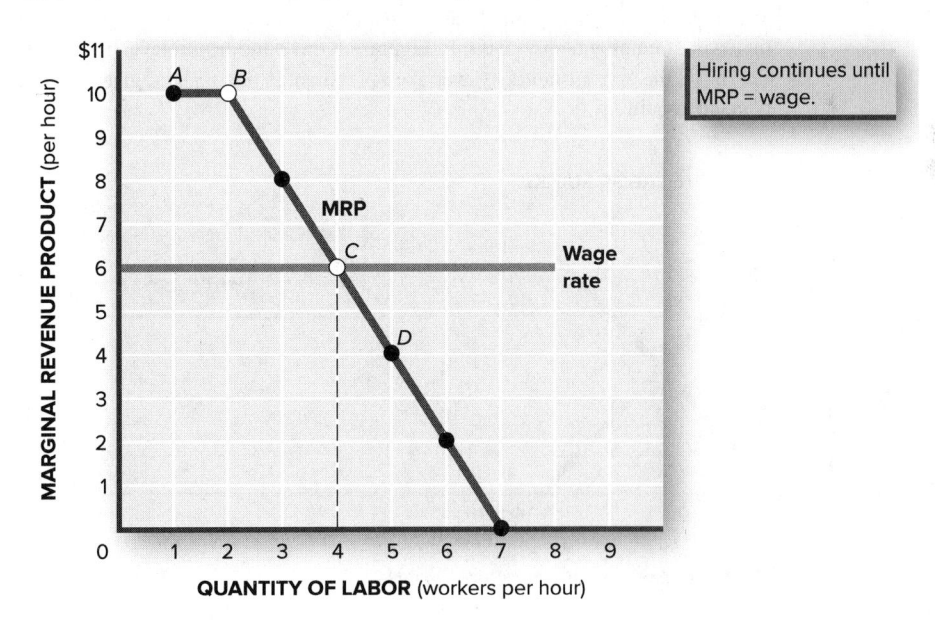

Hiring continues until MRP = wage.

Figure 7.4 The Marginal Revenue Product Curve Is the Firm's Labor Demand Curve An employer is willing to pay a worker no more than his or her marginal revenue product. In this case, a grower would gladly hire a second worker because that worker's MRP (point *B*) exceeds the wage rate ($6). The fifth worker will not be hired at that wage rate, however, since that worker's MRP (at point *D*) is less than $6. The MRP curve is the firm's labor demand curve. ■

alumni 校友。championship 冠军。

MARKET EQUILIBRIUM 市场均衡

指导单个草莓种植者雇用决策的原则可以延伸到整个劳动力市场。这表明劳动力的市场需求取决于：

- 雇主的数量；
- 每家企业、每个行业中劳动力的边际收益产品。

在劳动力的市场供给方面，我们已经观察到劳动力的供给取决于：

- 可获得的工人数量；
- 在可选择的工资水平上，每个工人的工作意愿。

图 7.5 综合了这些市场影响因素。市场供给与需求曲线的交点决定了**均衡工资**。在前面的例子中，我们假设现行的工资水平是每小时 6 美元。在现实中，市场价格是 w_e，如图 7.5 所示。均衡工资就是使劳动力的供给等于其需求时的工资水平。在这一工资水平，每一个愿意并且能够工作的人将会找到工作。

The principles that guide the hiring decisions of a single strawberry grower can be extended to the entire labor market. This suggests that the *market* demand for labor depends on

- The number of employers.
- The marginal revenue product of labor in each firm and industry.

On the supply side of the labor market we have already observed that the market supply of labor depends on

- The number of available workers.
- Each worker's willingness to work at alternative wage rates.

The supply decisions of each worker are in turn a reflection of tastes, income, wealth, expectations, other prices, and taxes.

Equilibrium Wage 均衡工资

Figure 7.5 brings these market forces together. ***The intersection of the market supply and demand curves establishes the*** **equilibrium wage**. In our previous example we assumed that the prevailing wage was $6 an hour. In reality, the market wage will be w_e, as illustrated in Figure 7.5. ***The equilibrium wage is the only wage at which the quantity of labor supplied equals the quantity of labor demanded.*** Everyone who is willing and able to work for this wage will find a job.

Many people will be unhappy with the equilibrium wage. Employers may grumble that wages are too high. Workers may complain that wages are too low. Nevertheless, the equilibrium wage is the only one that clears the market.

Equilibrium Employment 均衡就业

The intersection of labor supply and demand determines not just the prevailing wage rate but the level of employment as well. In Figure 7.5 this equilibrium level of employment occurs at q_e. That is the only sustainable level of employment in that market, given prevailing supply and demand conditions.

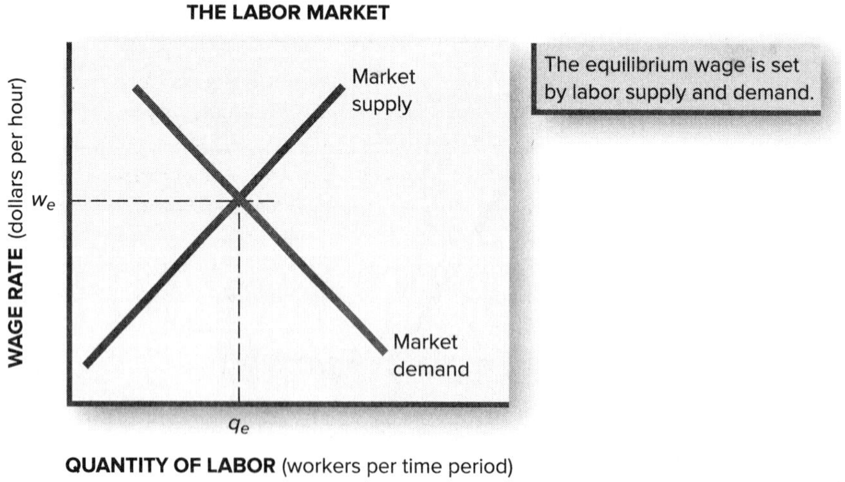

THE LABOR MARKET

Figure 7.5 Equilibrium Wage The intersection of *market supply* and *demand* determines the equilibrium wage in a competitive labor market. All of the firms in the industry can then hire as much labor as they want at that equilibrium wage. Likewise, anyone who is willing and able to work for the wage w_e will be able to find a job.

---

grumble 抱怨。

CHANGING MARKET OUTCOMES 改变市场结果

The equilibrium established in any market is subject to change. If Alabama's football team started losing too many games, ticket and ad revenues would fall. Then the coach's salary might shrink. Likewise, if someone discovered that strawberries cure cancer, those strawberry pickers might be in great demand. In this section we examine how changing market conditions alter wages and employment levels.

Changes in Productivity 生产率的变化

The law of diminishing returns is responsible for the trade-off between wage and employment levels. The downward slope of the labor demand curve does not mean wages *and* employment can never rise together, however. ***If labor productivity (MPP) rises, wages can increase without sacrificing jobs.***

Suppose that Marvin and his friends enroll in a local agricultural extension course and learn new methods of strawberry picking. With these new methods, the marginal physical product of each picker increases by one box per hour. With the price of strawberries still at $2 a box, this productivity improvement implies an increase in marginal *revenue* product of $2 per worker. Now farmers will be more eager to hire pickers. This increased demand for pickers is illustrated by the upward *shift* of the labor demand curve in Figure 7.6.

Notice how the improvement in productivity has altered the value of strawberry pickers. The MRP of the fourth picker is now $7 an hour (point *S*) rather than $6 (point *C*). Hence the grower can now afford to pay higher wages. Or the grower could employ more pickers than before, moving from point *C* to point *E*. ***Increased productivity implies that workers can get either higher wages without sacrificing jobs or more employment without lowering wages.*** Historically, increased productivity has been the most important source of rising wages and living standards.

收益递减规律导致工资水平和就业水平之间需要权衡，但是向下倾斜的劳动力需求曲线并不意味着工资和就业不能同时增长。如果劳动生产率提高了，工资的增长就不会以牺牲就业量为前提。

劳动生产率的提高意味着工人们不用牺牲就业量就可以获得更高的工资，或者说不用降低工资就可以提高就业量。从历史上看，生产率的提高是工资和生活水平提高最重要的源泉。

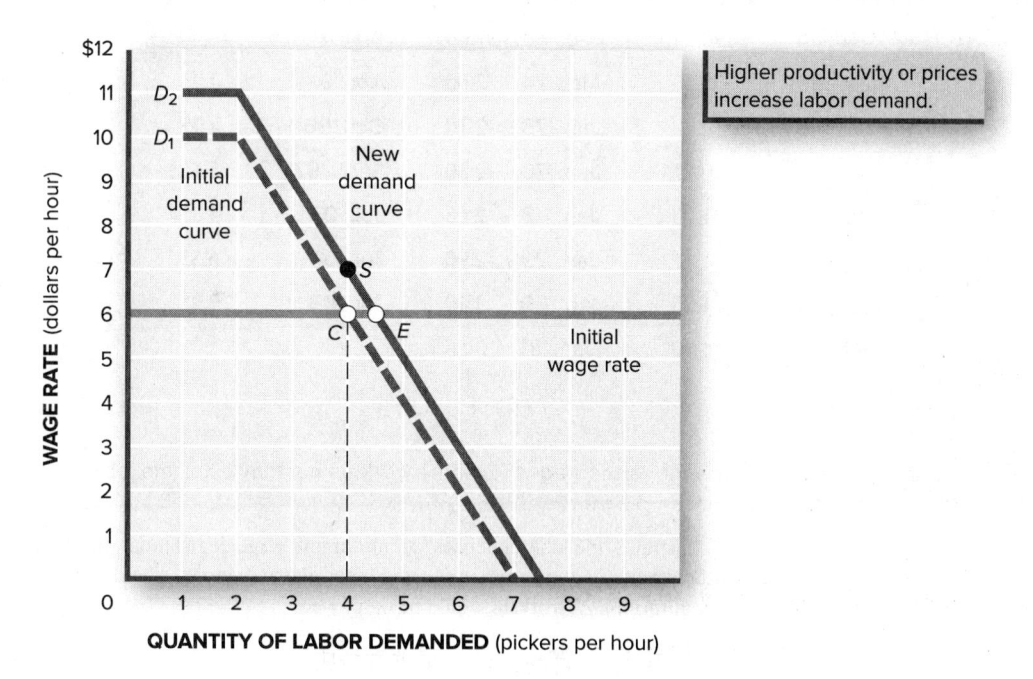

Figure 7.6 Increased Productivity Wage and employment decisions depend on marginal revenue product. If productivity improves, the labor demand curve shifts upward (e.g., from D_1 to D_2), raising the MRP of all workers. The grower can now afford to pay higher wages (point *S*) or hire more workers (point *E*). ■

---

be subject to 易受到，常遭到。cure 治疗，治愈。

Changes in Price 价格的变化

草莓价格的提高也会帮助草莓采摘者。边际收益产品反映了生产率和产品价格的相互影响。如果草莓的价格加倍，草莓采摘工人甚至在不用增加其物质生产率的情况下就使其产出价值翻倍，但是产品价格的这种变化取决于市场上草莓的供求变化。

An increase in the price of strawberries would also help the pickers. Marginal revenue product reflects the interaction of productivity and product prices. If strawberry prices were to double, strawberry pickers would become twice as valuable, even without an increase in *physical* productivity. Such a change in product prices depends, however, on changes in the market supply and demand for strawberries.

Legal Minimum Wages 法定最低工资

Rather than waiting for *market* forces to raise their wages, the strawberry pickers might seek *government* intervention. The U.S. government decreed in 1938 that no worker could be paid less than 25 cents per hour. Since then the U.S. Congress has repeatedly raised the legal minimum wage, bringing it to $7.25 in 2009. In 2017 Congressional Democrats proposed another increase—to $15 an hour by 2024 (see the News Wire "Minimum Wage Hikes"), but their bill was never voted on.

NEWS WIRE MINIMUM WAGE HIKES

DEMS PROPOSE $15 MINIMUM WAGE

Washington, DC. Democrat leaders submitted the "Raise the Wage Act of 2017" in the House of Representatives today. Bernie Sanders, one of the chief sponsors of the bill, declared that a $7.25 minimum wage is a "starvation minimum wage" and called for Congress to approve an immediate increase to $9.25, followed by gradual increase to $15 an hour by 2024. With Republicans in charge of the House, most observers said the bill was unlikely to come up for a vote.

Source: News accounts of May 25, 2017.

Minimum Wage History

Oct. '38	$0.25	Feb. '68	$1.60	Apr. '90	$3.80
Oct. '39	0.30	May '74	2.00	Apr. '91	4.25
Oct. '45	0.40	Jan. '75	2.10	Oct. '96	4.75
Jan. '50	0.75	Jan. '76	2.30	Sept. '97	5.15
Mar. '56	1.00	Jan. '78	2.65	Jul. '07	5.85
Sept. '61	1.15	Jan. '79	2.90	Jul. '08	6.55
Sept. '63	1.25	Jan. '80	3.10	Jul. '09	7.25
Feb. '67	1.40	Jan. '81	3.35		

NOTE: An increase in the minimum wage raises wages for some workers but may eliminate jobs for others.
注：最低工资的提高使一些工人的工资提高了，但也有一些人失业了。

Figure 7.7 illustrates the consequences of minimum wage legislation. In the absence of government intervention, the labor supply and labor demand curves would establish the wage w_e. At that equilibrium q_e, workers would be employed.

Demand-Side Effects 需求方效应

When a legislated minimum wage of w_m is set, things change. Suddenly the quantity of labor *demanded* declines. In the prior equilibrium employers kept hiring workers until their marginal

---

decree 颁布法令。legislation 立法。prior 先前的。

revenue product fell to w_e. If a minimum wage of w_m must be paid, it no longer makes sense to hire that many workers. So employers back up on the labor demand curve from point E to point D. At D, marginal revenue product is high enough to justify paying the legal minimum wage. At D, only q_d workers are demanded, not the previous q_e. As a result of this retrenchment, some workers ($q_e - q_d$) lose their jobs.

Supply-Side Effects 供给方效应

Note in Figure 7.7 what happens on the *supply* side as well. The higher minimum wage attracts more people into the labor market. The number of workers willing to work jumps from q_e (point E) to q_s (point S). Everybody wants one of those better-paying jobs.

但是没有那么多的工作机会眷顾你，法定最低工资水平下的工作岗位数量只有 q_d，但是有 q_s 的求职者在找工作，求职者比工作职位多，失业就产生了。现在出现了**市场过剩**（$q_s - q_d$），这些工人将会失业。

There aren't enough jobs to go around, however. The number of jobs available at the minimum wage is only q_d; the number of job seekers at that wage is q_s. With more job seekers than jobs, unemployment results. We now have a **market surplus** (equal to q_s minus q_d). Those workers are unemployed.

Government-imposed wage floors thus have two distinct effects. *A minimum wage*

- ***Reduces the quantity of labor demanded.***
- ***Increases the quantity of labor supplied.***

Thus it

- ***Creates a market surplus.***

因此，政府设定的工资下限有两个明显影响。最低工资：

- 减少了劳动力的需求量；
- 增加了劳动力的供给量。

最低工资进而

- 造成了市场过剩。

The market surplus creates inefficiency and frustration, especially for workers who are ready and willing to work but can't find a job. Not everyone suffers, however. Those workers who keep their jobs (at q_d in Figure 7.7) end up with higher wages than they had before. Accordingly, ***a legal minimum wage entails a trade-off: Some workers end up better off, while others end up worse off.*** Those most likely to end up worse off are teenagers and other inexperienced workers whose marginal revenue product is below the legal minimum wage. They will have the hardest time finding jobs when the legal wage floor is raised.

市场过剩带来了低效率和挫败感，特别是对那些愿意工作但是找不到工作的人。并不是所有人都会遭受这些。那些保住工作的人（图7.7中的 q_d）就会拿到比以前更高的工资。因此，法定最低工资的限制造成了一种此消彼长的情况：一些人的境况比以前更好了，一些人比以前更差了。

How many potential jobs are lost to minimum wage hikes depends on how far the legal minimum is raised. The elasticity of labor demand is also important. Democrats argue that labor demand is inelastic, so few jobs will be lost. Republicans argue that labor demand is

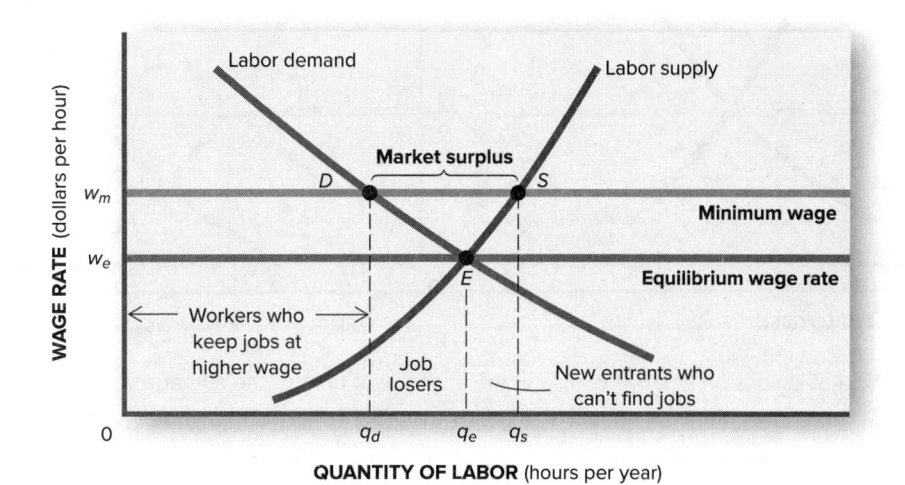

Figure 7.7 Minimum Wage Effects A minimum wage increases the quantity of labor supplied but reduces the quantity demanded. Some workers (q_d) end up with higher wages, but others ($q_s - q_d$) remain or become jobless. ■

---

make sense 有意义，讲得通。 retrenchment 削减，紧缩。 wage floor 最低工资。

elastic, so more jobs will be lost. The state of the economy is also critical. If the economy is growing rapidly, increases (shifts) in labor demand will help offset job losses resulting from a minimum wage hike.

Inflation may also effect the impact of a minimum wage hike. 2009 was the year the minimum wage was last increased. By 2019, consumer prices had risen by an average of 19 percent and general wages by 23 percent. So, the *real* (inflation-adjusted) minimum wage had fallen substantially, perhaps even below the equilibrium wage. Proponents of another wage hike noted that this would dull the negative employment effects of a further minimum-wage hike.

Labor Unions   工会

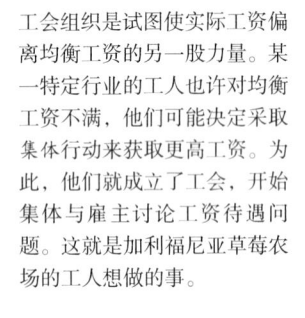

工会组织是试图使实际工资偏离均衡工资的另一股力量。某一特定行业的工人也许对均衡工资不满，他们可能决定采取集体行动来获取更高工资。为此，他们就成立了工会，开始集体与雇主讨论工资待遇问题。这就是加利福尼亚草莓农场的工人想做的事。

因此，工会如果想获得并保持高于市场均衡的工资，它就必须将一部分工人排除在市场之外。

Labor unions are another force that attempts to set aside equilibrium wages. The workers in a particular industry may not be satisfied with the equilibrium wage. They may decide to take *collective* action to get a higher wage. To do so, they form a labor union and bargain collectively with employers. This is what the United Farm Workers has tried to do in California's strawberry fields.

The formation of a labor union does not set aside the principles of supply and demand. The equilibrium wage remains at w_e, the intersection of the labor supply and demand curves (see Figure 7.8a). If the union were successful in negotiating a higher wage (w_u in the figure), a labor market surplus would appear ($l_3 - l_2$ in Figure 7.8a). These jobless workers would compete for the union jobs, putting downward pressure on the union-negotiated wage. Hence ***to get and maintain an above-equilibrium wage, a union must exclude some workers from the market.*** Effective forms of exclusion include union membership, required apprenticeship programs, and employment agreements negotiated with employers.

What happens to the excluded workers? In the case of a national minimum wage (Figure 7.7), the surplus workers remain unemployed. A union, however, sets above-equilibrium wages in only one industry or craft. Accordingly, there are lots of other potential jobs for the excluded nonunion workers. Their wages will suffer, however. As workers excluded from the unionized market (Figure 7.8a) stream into the nonunionized market (Figure 7.8b), they shift the nonunionized labor supply curve to the right. This influx of workers depresses nonunion wages, dropping them from w_e to w_n.

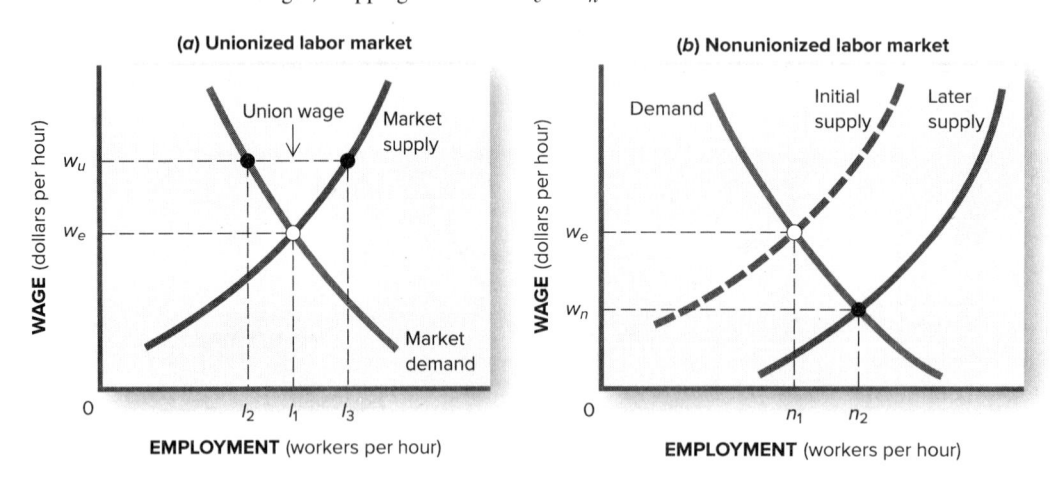

Figure 7.8 The Effect of Unions on Relative Wages In the absence of unions, the average wage rate would be equal to w_e. As unions take control of the market, however, they seek to raise wage rates to w_u. The higher wage reduces the amount of employment in the unionized market from l_1 to l_2. The workers displaced from the unionized market will seek work in the nonunionized market, thereby shifting the nonunion supply curve to the right. The result will be a reduction of wage rates (to w_n) in the nonunionized market. Thus union wages (w_u) end up higher than nonunion wages (w_n). ■

---

offset 抵消，补偿。 apprenticeship 学徒制。 influx 大量涌入。

Although the theoretical impact of union exclusionism on relative wages is clear, empirical estimates of that impact are fairly rare. We do know that union wages in general are significantly higher than nonunion wages ($1,041 versus $829 per week in 2017). But part of this differential is due to the fact that unions are more common in industries that have always been more capital-intensive and have paid relatively high wages. When comparisons are made within particular industries or sectors, the differential narrows considerably. Nevertheless, there is a consensus that unions have managed to increase their relative wages from 15 to 20 percent above the competitive equilibrium wage.

POLICY PERSPECTIVES

SHOULD CEO PAY BE CAPPED?

The chairman of the Walt Disney Company signed a four-year contract in 2018 that will pay him as much as $423 million over four years. If Disney could pay that much to its chairman, surely it could afford to pay more than the legal minimum wage to its least skilled workers. But Disney says such a comparison is irrelevant. When challenged to defend his pay, Disney's board of directors insisted that Bob Iger had earned every penny of it by enhancing the value of the company's stock.

Critics of CEO pay don't accept this explanation. They make three points. First, the rise in the price of Disney's *stock* is not a measure of marginal revenue product. Stock prices rise in response to both company performance and general changes in financial markets. Hence only part of the stock increase could be credited to the CEO. Second, the revenues of the Walt Disney Company probably wouldn't be $400 million less in the absence of CEO Bob Iger. Hence his marginal revenue product is less than $400 million. Finally, Iger probably would have worked just as hard for, say, just $100 million or so. Therefore, his actual pay was more than required to elicit the desired supply response.

Critics conclude that many CEO paychecks are out of line with the realities of supply and demand. Bernie Sanders was particularly outraged by the multimillion-dollar salaries and bonuses paid to Disney's CEO (see the News Wire "Cap CEO Pay?") He wants corporations to reduce CEO pay and revise the process used for setting CEO pay levels.

NEWS WIRE   CAP CEO PAY?

SANDERS BLASTS DISNEY CEO'S PAY

Anaheim, CA. Senator Sanders took aim at the pay package for Disney CEO Bob Iger. In a tweet this morning, Sanders asked why CEO Iger is paid hundreds of millions of dollars while workers at Disney theme parks struggle to make ends meet. Sanders went on to ask, "Does Disney CEO Bob Iger have a good explanation for why he is being compensated more than $400 million while workers at Disneyland are homeless and relying on food stamps to feed their families?"

Source: News accounts of July 13, 2018.

NOTE: The enormous gap between CEO pay and average wages prompts calls for limits on executive compensation.
注：CEO 薪酬与平均工资之间的巨大差距促使人们呼吁限制高管薪酬。

---

theoretical 理论上的。empirical 实证的。considerably 相当地，非常地。consensus 一致看法，共识。be credited to 归功于。

UNMEASURED MRP

One of the difficulties in determining the appropriate level of CEO pay is the elusiveness of marginal revenue product. It is easy to measure the MRP of a strawberry picker or even a sales clerk who sells Disney toys. But a corporate CEO's contributions are less well defined. A CEO is supposed to provide strategic leadership and a sense of mission. These are critical to a corporation's success but hard to quantify.

Congress confronts the same problem in setting the president's pay. We noted earlier that the President of the United States is paid $400,000 a year. Can we argue that this salary represents his marginal revenue product? The wage we actually pay the President of the United States is less a reflection of his contribution to total output than a matter of custom. His salary also reflects the price voters believe is required to induce competent individuals to forsake private-sector jobs and assume the responsibilities of the presidency. In this sense, the wage paid to the president and other public officials is set by their **opportunity wage**—that is, the wage they could earn in private industry.

The same kinds of considerations influence the wages of college professors. The marginal revenue product of a college professor is not easy to measure. Is it the number of students he or she teaches, the amount of knowledge conveyed, or something else? Confronted with such problems, most universities tend to pay college professors according to their *opportunity wage*—that is, the amount the professors could earn elsewhere.

Opportunity wages also help explain the difference between the wage of the chairman of Disney and that of the workers who peddle its products. The lower wage of sales clerks reflects not only their marginal revenue product at Disney stores, but also the fact that they are not trained for many other jobs. That is to say, their opportunity wages are low. By contrast, Disney's CEO has impressive managerial skills that are in demand by many corporations; his opportunity wages are high.

Opportunity wages help explain CEO pay but don't fully justify such high pay levels. If Disney's CEO pay is justified by opportunity wages, that means that another company would be willing to pay him that much. But what would justify such high pay at another company? Would his MRP be any easier to measure? Maybe *all* CEO paychecks have been inflated.

Critics of CEO pay conclude that the process of setting CEO pay levels should be changed. All too often, executive pay scales are set by self-serving committees composed of executives of the same or similar corporations. Critics want a more independent assessment of pay scales, with nonaffiliated experts and stockholder representatives. Some critics want to go a step further and set mandatory caps on CEO pay.

If markets work efficiently, such government intervention should not be necessary. Corporations that pay their CEOs excessively will end up with smaller profits than companies that pay market-based wages. Over time, lean companies will be more competitive than fat companies, and excessive pay scales will be eliminated. Legislated CEO pay caps imply that CEO labor markets aren't efficient or that the adjustment process is too slow.

---

appropriate 恰当的；合适的。elusiveness 难以衡量。opportunity wage 机会工资。nonaffiliated 没有附属关系的，无关联的。

CHAPTER 7 REVIEW

SUMMARY

- The economic motivation to work arises from the fact that people need income to buy the goods and services they desire. As a consequence, people are willing to work (i.e., to supply labor). **LO1**
- There is an opportunity cost involved in working—namely, the amount of leisure time one sacrifices. People willingly give up additional leisure only if offered higher wages. Hence the labor supply curve is upward-sloping. **LO1**
- A firm's demand for labor reflects labor's marginal revenue product. A profit-maximizing employer will not pay a worker more than the value of what the worker produces. **LO2**
- The marginal revenue product of labor diminishes as additional workers are employed in a particular job (the law of diminishing returns). This decline occurs because additional workers have to share existing land and capital, leaving each worker with less land and capital to work with. The decline in MRP gives labor demand curves their downward slope. **LO2**
- The equilibrium wage is determined by the intersection of labor supply and labor demand curves. Attempts to set above-equilibrium wages cause labor surpluses by reducing the jobs available and increasing the number of job seekers. **LO3**
- Labor unions attain above-equilibrium wages by excluding some workers from a particular industry or craft. The excluded workers increase the labor supply in the nonunion market, depressing wages there. **LO4**
- Differences in marginal revenue product are an important explanation of wage inequalities. But the difficulty of measuring MRP in many instances leaves many wage rates to be determined by custom, power, discrimination, or opportunity wages. **LO5**

TERMS TO REMEMBER

Define the following terms:

labor supply
opportunity cost
market supply of labor
demand for labor
derived demand
marginal physical product (MPP)

marginal revenue product (MRP)
law of diminishing returns
equilibrium wage
market surplus
opportunity wage

QUESTIONS FOR DISCUSSION

1. Why are you doing this homework? What are you giving up? What do you expect to gain? If homework performance determined course grades, would you spend more time doing it? **LO1**
2. Why does the opportunity cost of doing homework increase as you spend more time doing it? **LO1**
3. How do "supply and demand" explain the wage gap between chemical engineering and sociology majors (News Wire "Unequal Wages")? **LO3**
4. Explain why marginal physical product would diminish as **LO2**
    a. more administrative assistants are hired in an office.
    b. more professors are hired in the economics department.
    c. more construction workers are hired to build a school.
5. Under what conditions might an increase in the minimum wage *not* reduce the number of low-wage jobs? How much of a job loss is acceptable? **LO4**
6. The United Farm Workers want strawberry pickers to join its union. It hopes then to convince consumers to buy only union-picked strawberries. Will such activities raise picker wages? Increase employment? **LO3**
7. Why did Sears eliminate so many jobs (News Wire "Derived Demand")? **LO1**

8. How might you measure the marginal revenue product of (*a*) a quarterback, (*b*) the team's coach, and (*c*) the team's owner? **LO5**
9. **POLICY PERSPECTIVES** In response to Bernie Sanders' critique of his pay (News Wire "Cap CEO Pay?"), Disney's CEO pointed out that he had created 11,000 new jobs at Disneyland in the prior 10 years. Had Sanders succeeded in raising the minimum wage to $15 an hour, would that many jobs have been created? **LO4**
10. **POLICY PERSPECTIVES** Why do people want to cap Bob Iger's salary but not Beyonce's? **LO5**

PROBLEMS

1. According to the News Wire, "Labor Supply," **LO3**
    a. what was the apparent market surplus at the Amazon job fair in Baltimore?
    b. if Amazon increased wages to $16 per hour, what do you predict will happen to that market surplus?
2. According to Figure 7.4, how many workers would be hired if the prevailing wage were **LO3**
    a. $10 an hour?
    b. $2 an hour?
3. The following table depicts the number of grapes that can be picked in an hour with varying amounts of labor: **LO2**

Number of pickers (per hour)	1	2	3	4	5	6	7	8
Output of grapes (in flats)	10	28	43	54	61	64	65	61

    Calculate marginal physical product (MPP) and then graph the total product (output) and MPP curves.
4. a. Assuming that the price of grapes is $3 per flat, use the data in problem 3 to calculate total revenue and marginal revenue product (MRP) and graph the MRP curve.
    b. How many pickers will be hired if the going wage rate is $9 per hour? **LO2**
5. Using the production information contained in Table 7.1 and assuming that the price of strawberries is $3 per box, how many workers would be hired at a wage of (*a*) $12 per hour and (*b*) $6 per hour? **LO3**
6. The University of Alabama increased the capacity of its Bryant-Denny stadium by 10,000 seats when it hired Nick Saban as its football coach. (*a*) If the average price of a season ticket is $1,000, how much additional revenue is the university getting from those added seats per year? (*b*) Does that exceed coach Saban's annual pay for his new contract (see the News Wire "Marginal Revenue Product")? **LO3**
7. In Figure 7.7, **LO4**
    a. how many workers lose their jobs when the minimum wage is enacted?
    b. how many workers are unemployed at the minimum wage?
8. If the price elasticity of demand for labor is 0.1 and the wage increased from $10 to $15 an hour, what is the predicted decrease in the level of employment in percentage terms? **LO4**
9. In November 2014, the Miami Marlins agreed to pay Giancarlo Stanton $325 million over 10 years. If this salary were to be covered by ticket sales only, how many more tickets per game would the Marlins have to sell to cover Stanton's salary in the 81 home games per year if the average ticket price is $60? **LO4, LO5**
10. Assuming that a college graduate on average earns his or her MRP, what is the MRP for a newly hired Economics major? (See the News Wire "Unequal Wages.") **LO4**
11. **POLICY PERSPECTIVES** If Nick Saban (News Wire "Marginal Revenue Product") were offered a CEO position at a sporting goods company, what would his opportunity cost be? **LO5**

CHAPTER EIGHT

Government Intervention 政府干预

©Zack Frank/Shutterstock

LEARNING OBJECTIVES

After reading this chapter, you should be able to:

1. Define what market failure means.
2. Explain why the market underproduces public goods.
3. Tell how externalities distort market outcomes.
4. Describe how market power prevents optimal outcomes.
5. Define what government failure is.

The market has a keen ear for private wants, but a deaf ear for public needs.

–Robert Heilbroner

Adam Smith was the eighteenth-century economist who coined the phrase **laissez faire**. He wanted the government to "leave it [the market] alone" so as not to impede the efficiency of the marketplace. But even Adam Smith felt the government had to intervene on occasion. He warned in *The Wealth of Nations* (1776), for example, that firms with market power might meet together and conspire to fix prices or restrain competition. He also recognized that the government might have to give aid and comfort to the poor. So he didn't really believe that the government should leave the market *entirely* alone. He just wanted to establish a *presumption* of market efficiency.

Economists, government officials, and political scientists have been debating the role of government ever since. So has the general public. Although people are quick to assert that government is too big, they are just as quick to demand more schools, more police, and more income transfers.

The purpose of this chapter is to help define the appropriate scope of government intervention in the marketplace. To this end, we try to answer the following questions:

- Under what circumstances do markets fail?
- How can government intervention help?
- How much government intervention is desirable?

---

laissez faire 自由放任。impede 阻止，妨碍。conspire 共谋。presumption 假设。

As we'll see, there is substantial agreement about how and when markets fail to give us the best WHAT, HOW, and FOR WHOM answers. There is much less agreement about whether government intervention improves the situation. Indeed, Americans are strikingly ambivalent about government intervention. They want the government to fix the mix of output, protect the environment, and ensure an adequate level of income for everyone. But voters are equally quick to blame government meddling for many of our economic woes.

MARKET FAILURE 市场失灵

我们能通过聚焦生产什么的问题，来设想政府干预的可能性。在这里，我们的目标是用现有资源生产出最优产出组合。在前面我们已用生产可能性曲线说明了这一目标。图 8.1 列出了我们能生产的所有可能的产出组合，在 X 点处的唯一组合代表了最想要的产出组合，即**最优产出组合**。X 点在图中的位置是随意的，我们只是用这个点来说明，某个特定的产出组合肯定优于其他所有组合。X 点被假设为考虑到所有其他选择、机会成本和社会偏好之后，社会选择的最优产出组合。

We can visualize the potential for government intervention by focusing on the WHAT question. Our goal is to produce the best possible mix of output with existing resources. We illustrated this goal earlier with the production possibilities curve. Figure 8.1 assumes that of all the possible combinations of output we could produce, the unique combination at point X represents the most desirable—that is, the **optimal mix of output**. The exact location of X in the graph is arbitrary—we're just using that point to remind us that some specific mix of output must be better than all other combinations. Thus point X is *assumed* to be *optimal*—the mix of output society would choose after examining all other options, their opportunity costs, and social preferences.

The Nature of Market Failure 市场失灵的本质

We have seen how the market mechanism can help us find this desired mix of output. The **market mechanism** moves resources from one industry to another in response to consumer demands. If we demand more computers—offer to buy more at a given price—more resources (labor) will be allocated to computer manufacturing. Similarly, a fall in demand will encourage producers to stop making computers and offer their services in another industry. Changes in market prices direct resources from one industry to another, moving us along the perimeter of the production possibilities curve.

The big question is whether the mix of output the market mechanism selects is the one society most desires. If so, we don't need government intervention to change the mix of output. If not, we may need government intervention to guide the invisible hand of the market.

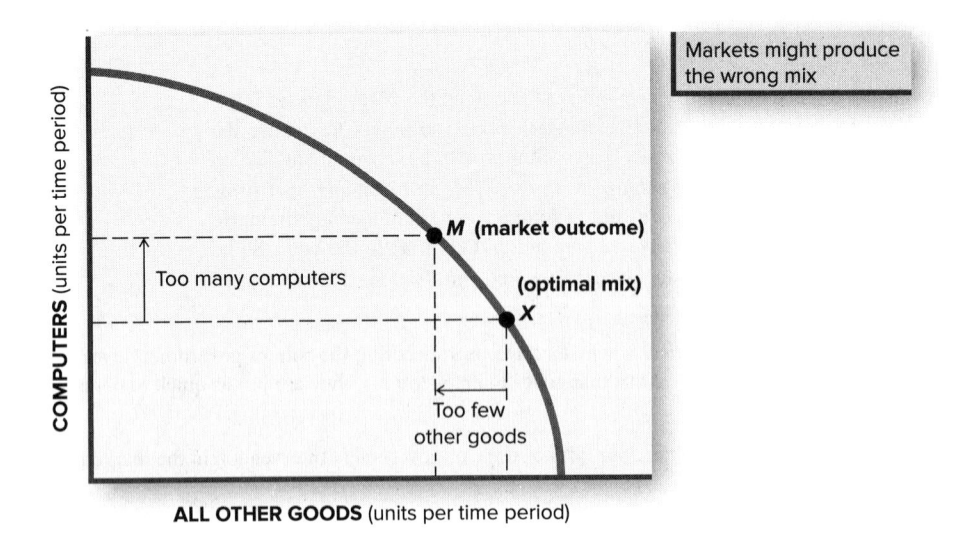

Figure 8.1 Market Failure We can produce any mix of output on the production possibilities curve. Our goal is to produce the optimal (best possible) mix of output, as represented by point *X*. Market forces, however, may produce another combination, such as point *M*. In that case, the market fails—it produces a *sub*optimal mix of output.

· ambivalent 矛盾的。meddle 干涉，干预。woe 困境。

We use the term **market failure** to refer to less than perfect (suboptimal) outcomes. If the invisible hand of the marketplace produces a mix of output that is different from the one society most desires, then it has failed. *Market failure implies that the forces of supply and demand have not led us to the best point on the production possibilities curve.* Such a failure is illustrated by point *M* in Figure 8.1.

Point *M* is assumed to be the mix of output generated by market forces. Notice that the market mix (point *M*) is not identical to the optimal mix (point *X*). The market in this case *fails*; we get the wrong answer to the WHAT question. Specifically, at point *M*, too many computers and too few other goods are produced. It's not that we have no use for more computers—additional computers are still desired. But we'd *rather* have more of the other goods. In other words, we'd be better off with a slightly different mix of output, such as that at point *X*.

Market failure opens the door for government intervention. If the market can't do the job, we need some form of *nonmarket* force to get the right answers. In terms of Figure 8.1, we need something to change the mix of output—to move us from point *M* (the market mix of output) to point *X* (the optimal mix of output). Accordingly, *market failure establishes a basis for government intervention.*

Sources of Market Failure   市场失灵的来源

Because market failure is the justification for government intervention, we need to know how and when market failure occurs. *There are four specific sources of microeconomic market failure:*

- *Public goods.*
- *Externalities.*
- *Market power.*
- *Inequity.*

We examine the nature of these micro problems in this chapter. We also take note of failures due to *macro* instability. Along the way we'll see why government intervention is called for in each case.

PUBLIC GOODS   公共物品

The market mechanism has the unique capability to signal consumer demands for various goods and services. By offering to pay higher or lower prices for specific products, we express our collective answer to the question of WHAT to produce. However, the market mechanism works efficiently only if the benefits of consuming a particular good or service are available only to the individuals who purchase that product.

Consider doughnuts, for example. When you eat a doughnut, you alone enjoy its greasy, sweet taste—that is, you derive a *private* benefit. No one else reaps any significant benefit from your consumption of a doughnut: The doughnut you purchase in the market is yours alone to consume. Accordingly, your decision to purchase the doughnut will be determined only by your anticipated satisfaction, your income, and your opportunity costs.

Joint Consumption   共同消费

Many goods and services produced in the public sector are different from doughnuts—and not just because doughnuts look, taste, and smell different from nuclear submarines. When you buy a doughnut, you *exclude* others from consumption of that product. If Dunkin' Donuts sells a particular pastry to you, it cannot supply the same pastry to someone else. If you devour it, no one else can. In this sense, the transaction and product are completely private.

---

signal 用信号通知，引导。 pastry 油酥糕点。 devour 吞食。

从这个意义上说，你和你的邻居要么共同消费核潜艇防卫的好处，要么都不消费核潜艇防卫的好处。这里没有排他性的消费。不管谁为核防卫埋单，对它们的消费都是公共行为。正是由于这个原因，国防被认为是**公共物品**。从这个意义上来说，一个人对公共物品的消费不能排除其他人对同一物品的消费。相反，甜甜圈是**私人物品**，因为如果我吃了它，其他人就不能吃了。

The same exclusiveness is not characteristic of public goods such as national defense. If you buy a nuclear submarine to patrol the Pacific Ocean, there is no way you can exclude your neighbors from the protection your submarine provides. Either the submarine deters would-be attackers or it doesn't. In the former case, both you and your neighbors survive happily ever after; in the latter case, we are all blown away together. In that sense, you and your neighbors either consume or don't consume the benefits of nuclear submarine defenses *jointly*. There is no such thing as exclusive consumption here. The consumption of nuclear defenses is a communal feat, no matter who pays for them. For this reason, national defense is regarded as a **public good** in the sense that *consumption of a public good by one person does not preclude consumption of the same good by another person.* By contrast, a doughnut is a **private good** because if I eat it, nobody else can consume it.

The Free-Rider Dilemma   搭便车困境

The communal nature of public goods leads to a real dilemma. If you and I will *both* benefit from nuclear defenses, which one of us should buy the nuclear submarine? I would prefer, of course, that *you* buy it, thereby providing me with protection at no direct cost. Hence I may profess no desire for nuclear subs, secretly hoping to take a **free ride** on your market purchase. Unfortunately, you, too, have an incentive to conceal your desire for national defense. As a consequence, neither one of us may step forward to demand nuclear subs in the marketplace. We will both end up defenseless.

Flood control is also a public good. No one in the valley wants to be flooded out. But each landowner knows that a flood control dam will protect *all* the landowners, regardless of who pays. Either the entire valley is protected or no one is. Accordingly, individual farmers and landowners may say they don't *want* a dam and aren't willing to *pay* for it. Everyone is waiting and hoping that someone else will pay for flood control. In other words, everyone wants a *free ride*. Thus, if we leave it to market forces, no one will *demand* flood control and everyone in the valley will be washed away.

Flood protection is a public good: Downriver nonpayers can't be excluded from flood protection.
©Andrew Zarivny/Shutterstock

Exclusion   排他性

The difference between public goods and private goods rests on *technical* considerations, not political philosophy. **The central question is whether we have the technical capability to exclude nonpayers.** In the case of national defense or flood control, we simply don't have that capability. Even city streets have the characteristics of public goods. Although we could theoretically restrict the use of streets to those who pay to use them, a toll gate on every corner would be exceedingly expensive and impractical. Here, again, joint or public consumption appears to be the only feasible alternative. As the News Wire "Public Goods" about Israel's "Iron Dome" emphasizes, the technical capability to exclude nonpayers is the key factor in identifying public goods.

NEWS WIRE PUBLIC GOODS

ISRAEL'S "IRON DOME" WORKS!

Israel's Iron Dome is an air defense system designed to intercept and destroy incoming missiles and mortars fired across the border by Hamas and other Palestinian factions. It works. Israel's Defense Minister claims the Iron Dome has been 90 percent effective in shielding population centers in the latest barrage of artillery fired into Israel by Hamas.

Source: News accounts of July 20–28, 2014.

NOTE: An air-defense system is a public good because nonpayers cannot be excluded from its protection. Consumption by one person does not preclude consumption by others.

注：防空系统是一种公共物品，因为未付费者不能被排除在它的保护之外。一个人对它的消费不能排除其他人对它的消费。

---

exclusiveness 排他性。patrol 巡逻，巡查。valley 流域，山谷。dam 大坝。rest on 基于。

To the list of public goods we could add the administration of justice, the regulation of commerce, and the conduct of foreign relations. These services—which cost tens of *billions* of dollars and employ thousands of workers—provide benefits to everyone, no matter who pays for them. More important, there is no evident way to exclude *nonpayers* from the benefits of these services.

The free rides associated with public goods upset the customary practice of paying for what you get. If I can get all the streets, defenses, and laws I desire without paying for them, I am not about to complain. I am perfectly happy to let you pay for the services while all of us consume them. Of course, you may feel the same way. Why should you pay for these services if you can consume just as much of them when your neighbors foot the whole bill? It might seem selfish not to pay your share of the cost of providing public goods. But you would be better off in a material sense if you spent your income on doughnuts, letting others pick up the tab for public services.

Underproduction 生产不足

Because the familiar link between paying and consuming is broken, public goods cannot be peddled in the supermarket. People are reluctant to buy what they can get free. This is a perfectly rational response for a consumer who has only a limited amount of income to spend. Hence ***if public goods were marketed like private goods, everyone would wait for someone else to pay.*** The end result might be a total lack of public services. This is the kind of dilemma Robert Heilbroner had in mind when he spoke of the market's "deaf ear for public needs" (see the quote at the beginning of this chapter).

由于常见的付费和消费之间的联系被打破，所以我们不能在超市销售公共物品。人们不愿意为那些可免费得到的东西付费。对于收入有限的消费者来说，这是很理性的反应。因此，如果公共物品像私人物品那样在市场上交易，那么每个人都会等待其他人去购买。最后的结果可能是完全没有公共服务。这正是罗伯特·海尔布罗纳在谈及市场"对公共需求充耳不闻"（见本章开头的引用）时提出的困境。

The production possibilities curve in Figure 8.2 illustrates the dilemma created by public goods. Suppose that point X again represents the optimal mix of private and public goods. It is the mix of goods and services we would select if everyone's preferences were known and reflected in production decisions. The market mechanism will not lead us to point X, however, because the demand for public goods will be hidden. If we rely on the market, nearly everyone will withhold demand for public goods, waiting for a *free ride* to point X. As a result,

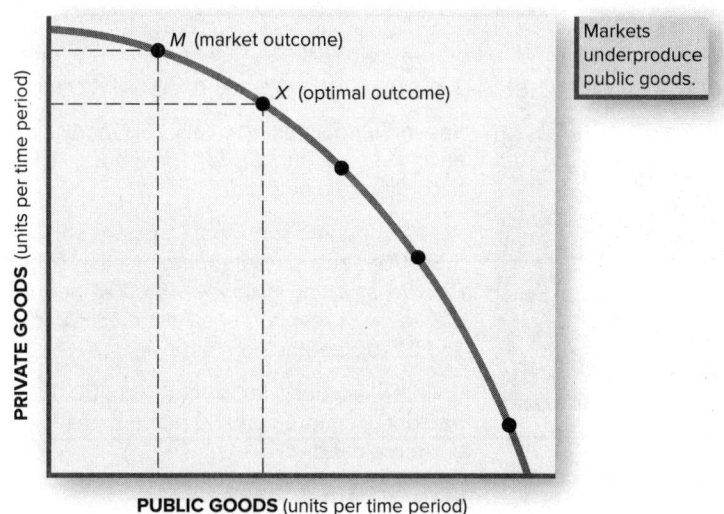

Figure 8.2 Underproduction of Public Goods Suppose point X represents the optimal mix of output—the mix of private and public goods that maximizes society's welfare. Because consumers will not demand purely public goods in the marketplace, the price mechanism will not allocate enough resources to the production of public goods. Instead the market will tend to produce a mix of output like point M, which includes fewer public goods and more private goods than is *optimal*. ■

---

justice 司法。 nonpayer 未付款者。 customary 照惯例的。 optimal 最优的。

the market tends to underproduce public goods and overproduce private goods. The market mechanism will leave us at a mix of output like that at point *M*, with few, if any, public goods. Since point *X* is assumed to be optimal, point *M* must be *suboptimal* (inferior to point *X*).

Figure 8.2 illustrates how the market fails: We cannot rely on the market mechanism to allocate resources to the production of public goods, no matter how much they might be desired. If we want more public goods, we need a *nonmarket* force—government intervention—to get them. The government will have to force people to pay taxes and then use the tax revenues to pay for the production of defense, flood control, and other public goods.

注意，我们这里所使用的术语公共物品不同于大多数人使用它时的含义。对大多数人来说，术语公共物品指政府生产的任何商品或服务。然而，在经济学中，该术语的含义受到更加严格的限制。公共物品和私人物品的区别在于商品的性质，而不在于是由谁生产的。术语"公共物品"仅指那些被支付者和未支付者共同消费的商品和服务。无论是公共物品还是私人物品，政府部门和私营部门都可以生产。

Note that we are using *public good* in a different way than most people use it. To most people, the term *public good* refers to any good or service the government produces. In economics, however, the meaning is much more restrictive. ***The distinction between public goods and private goods is based on the nature of the goods, not who produces them.*** The term "public good" refers only to those goods and services that are consumed jointly, both by those who pay for them and by those who don't. Public goods can be produced by either the government or the private sector. Private goods can be produced in either sector as well.

EXTERNALITIES 外部性

The free-rider problem associated with public goods provides an important justification for government intervention into the market's decision about WHAT to produce. It is not the only justification, however. Further grounds for intervention arise from the tendency of the costs or benefits of some market activities to "spill over" onto third parties.

Your demand for a good reflects the amount of satisfaction you expect from its consumption. Often, however, your consumption may affect others. The purchase of cigarettes, for example, expresses a smoker's demand for that good. But others may suffer from that consumption. In this case, smoke literally spills over onto other consumers, causing them discomfort, ill health, and even death (see the accompanying News Wire "Externalities"). Yet their loss is not reflected in the market—the harm caused to nonsmokers is *external* to the market price of cigarettes.

NEWS WIRE EXTERNALITIES

SECONDHAND SMOKE KILLS MORE THAN 600,000 PEOPLE A YEAR: STUDY

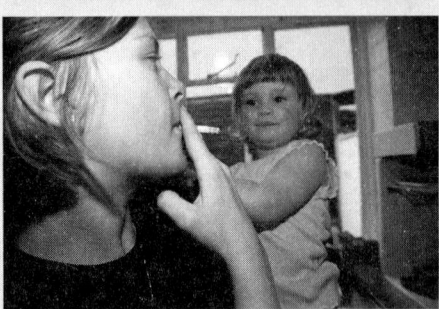

Secondhand smoke globally kills more than 600,000 people each year, accounting for 1 percent of all deaths worldwide, according to a new study.

Researchers estimate that ("passive smoking") causes about 379,000 deaths from heart disease, per year, worldwide. Passive smoking also kills 165,000 people each each year due to lower respiratory disease, 36,900 deaths from asthma, and 21,400 deaths from lung cancer.

Children account for about 165,000 of the deaths. Forty percent of children and 30 percent of adults regularly breathe in secondhand smoke.

Source: World Health Organization.

Secondhand smoke has deadly effects for nonsmokers too, according to a recent study.
©Image Source/Getty Images

NOTE: People who smoke feel the pleasures of smoking justify the cost (price). But nonsmokers end up bearing an external cost—secondhand smoke—that they don't voluntarily assume.
注：吸烟的人觉得吸烟带来的乐趣相对于其付出的成本（价格）是值得的。但不吸烟的人最终会承担二手烟带来的外部成本，而这并不是他们自愿承担的。

---

suboptimal 次优的。 inferior to 不好，次于。 spill over 溢出，外溢。

The term **externalities** refers to all costs or benefits of a market activity borne by a third party—that is, by someone other than the immediate producer or consumer. Whenever externalities are present, the preferences expressed in the marketplace will not be a complete measure of a good's value to society. As a consequence, the market will fail to produce the right mix of output. Specifically, *the market will underproduce goods that yield external benefits and overproduce those that generate external costs.* Government intervention may be needed to move the mix of output closer to society's optimal point.

术语**外部性**是指市场活动产生的所有成本或收益由第三方承担，也就是由直接生产者或消费者以外的方承担。当存在外部性时，市场对一种商品的偏好将不能完全衡量这种商品对社会的价值。因此，市场将不能生产正确的产出组合。具体而言，市场对产生外部收益的商品生产不足，而对产生外部成本的商品生产过剩。这可能就需要政府干预，将产出组合移动到靠近社会最优点的位置。

Consumption Decisions 消费决策

Externalities often originate on the demand side of markets. Consumers are always trying to maximize their personal well-being by buying products that deliver the most satisfaction (marginal utility) per dollar spent. In the process, they aren't likely to consider how the well-being of others is affected by their consumption behavior.

External Costs 外部成本

Automobile driving illustrates the problem. The amount of driving one does is influenced by the price of a car and the marginal costs of driving it. But automobile use involves not only *private costs* but *external costs* as well. When you cruise down the highway, you are adding to the congestion that slows other drivers down. You're also fouling the air with the emissions (carbon monoxide, hydrocarbons, etc.) your car spits out. The quality of the air other people breathe gets worse. You may even be accelerating climate change. Hence other people are made *worse* off at the same time as your auto consumption is making you *better* off.

Do you take account of such *external* costs when you buy a car? Not likely. Your willingness to buy a car is more likely to reflect only *your* expected satisfaction. Hence the *market* demand for cars doesn't fully represent the interests of society. Instead market demand reflects only *private* benefits.

To account more fully for our *collective* well-being, we must distinguish the *social* demand for a product from the *market* demand whenever externalities exist. This isn't that difficult. We simply recognize that

> Social demand = market demand + externalities

In the case of autos, the externality is *negative*—that is, an external *cost*. Hence the social demand for cars is less than the (private) market demand. Put simply, this means we'd own and drive fewer cars if we took into account the external costs (pollution, congestion) that our cars caused. We don't, of course, since we're always trying to maximize our personal well-being. Market failure results.

Figure 8.3 illustrates the divergence of the *social* demand for automobiles and the *market* demand. The market demand expresses the anticipated *private* benefits of driving. Because of the *external* costs (congestion, pollution) associated with driving, the market demand *overstates* the social benefits of auto consumption. **To represent the social demand for cars, we must subtract external costs from the private benefits.** This leaves us with the *social demand* curve in Figure 8.3. Notice that the social demand curve lies below the market demand curve. The vertical distance between the market demand curve and the social demand curve represents the amount of external cost.

The divergence between the social and market demand curves leads to market failure. At the price p_1 the socially desired number of cars is q_S, as determined by the intersection at point B. The market, however will produce q_M number of cars at the price p_1, as indicated by the intersection at point A. Hence, the market ends up producing *more* cars than is socially desirable (optimal). That is what we call market failure.

图 8.3 说明了汽车的社会需求和市场需求之间的差异。市场需求表达的是驾驶的预期私人收益。因为驾驶会带来外部成本（拥堵、污染），所以市场需求夸大了汽车消费的社会收益。为了体现汽车的社会需求，我们必须从私人收益中减去外部成本。这样我们就得到了图 8.3 中的社会需求曲线。

---

foul 弄脏，污染。carbon monoxide 一氧化碳。hydrocarbon 碳氢化合物。

A divergence between social and private costs can be observed even in the simplest consumer activities, such as throwing an empty soda can out the window of your car. To hang on to the soda can and later dispose of it in a trash barrel involves personal effort and thus private marginal costs. Throwing it out the window transfers the burden of disposal costs to someone else. Thus private costs can be distinguished from social costs. The resulting externality ends up as roadside litter.

The same kind of divergence between private and social costs helps explain why people abandon old cars in the street rather than haul them to scrap yards. It also explains why people use vacant lots as open dumps. In all these cases, *the polluter benefits by substituting external costs for private costs*. In other words, market incentives encourage environmental damage.

External Benefits 外部收益

Not all consumption externalities are negative. Completing this course will benefit you personally, but it may benefit society as well. If more knowledge of economics makes you a better-informed voter, your community will reap some benefit from your education. If you share the lessons of supply and demand with friends, they will benefit without ever attending class. If you complete a research project that helps markets function more efficiently, others will sing your praises. In all these cases, an *external* benefit augments the private benefit of education. *Whenever external benefits exist, the social demand exceeds the market demand.* In Figure 8.3, the social demand would lie *above* the market demand if external *benefits* were present. Society wants more of those goods and services generating external benefits than the market itself will demand. This is why governments subsidize education and flu shots.

Production Decisions 生产决策

Externalities also exist in production. A power plant that burns high-sulfur coal damages the surrounding environment. Yet the damage inflicted on neighboring people, vegetation, and buildings is *external* to the cost calculations of the firm. Because the cost of such pollution is not reflected in the price of electricity, the firm will tend to produce more electricity (and pollution) than is socially desirable. To reduce this imbalance, the government has to step in and change market outcomes.

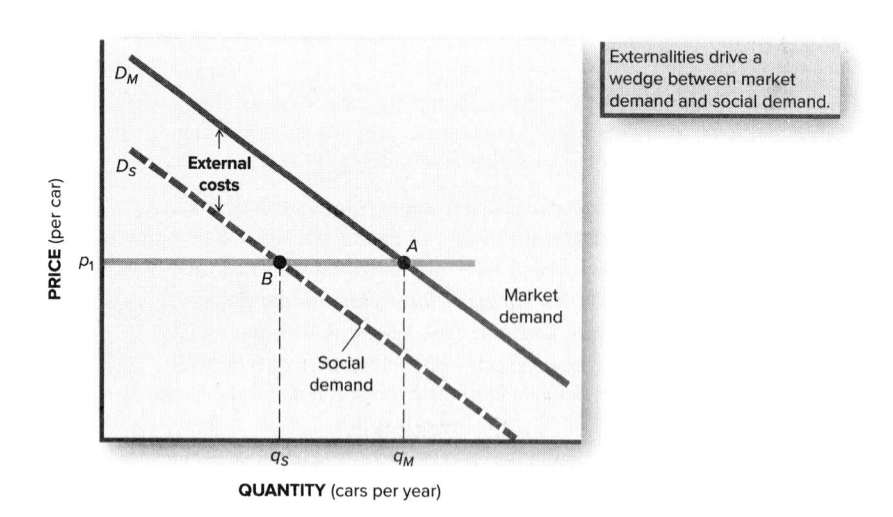

Figure 8.3 Social versus Market Demand Whenever external costs exist, market demand overstates (lies above) social demand. At p_1 the market would demand q_M cars. Because of external costs, however, society wants only q_S cars at that price. Hence the market *over*produces goods with external costs.

hang on to 保留。trash barrel 垃圾桶。inflict 使遭受，使承受。

Suppose you're the manager of an electric power plant. Power plants are major sources of air pollution and are responsible for nearly all thermal water pollution. Hence your job automatically puts you on the most-wanted list of environmental enemies. But suppose you bear society no grudges and would truly like to help eliminate pollution. Let's consider the alternatives.

Profit Maximization 利润最大化

Figure 8.4a depicts the marginal and average total costs (MC and ATC) associated with the production of electricity. By equating marginal cost (MC) to price (= marginal revenue, MR), we observe (point A) that profit maximization occurs at an output of 1,000 kilowatt-hours per day. Total profits are illustrated by the shaded rectangle between the price line and the average total cost (ATC) curve.

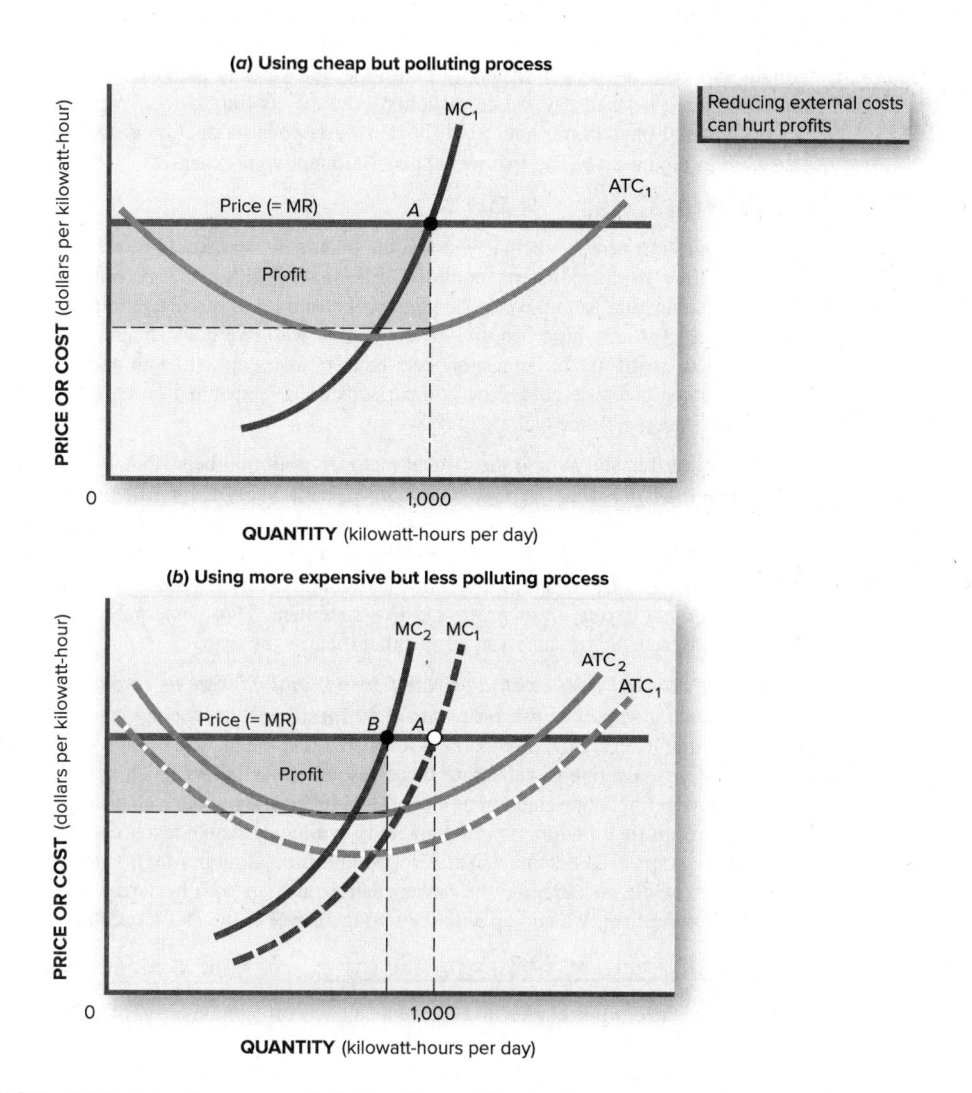

Figure 8.4 Profit Maximization versus Pollution Control Production processes that control pollution may be more expensive than those that do not. If they are, the MC and ATC curves will shift upward (to MC_2 and ATC_2). These higher *internal* costs will reduce output and profits. In this case, environmental protection moves the profit-maximizing output to point *B* from point *A* and total profit shrinks. Hence a producer has an incentive to continue polluting, using cheaper technology and *external* costs. ■

---

thermal 热的。

The profits illustrated in Figure 8.4*a* are achieved in part by use of the cheapest available fuel under the boilers (which create the steam that rotates the generators). Unfortunately, the cheapest fuel is high-sulfur coal, a major source of air pollution. Other fuels (e.g., low-sulfur coal, fuel oil, natural gas) pollute less but cost more. Were you to switch to one of them, the ATC and MC curves would both shift upward, as shown in Figure 8.4*b*. Under these conditions, the most profitable rate of output (point *B*) would be less than before (point *A*), and total profits would decline (note the smaller profit rectangle in Figure 8.4*b*). Thus pollution abatement can be achieved, but only by sacrificing some profit. If you were the manager of this power plant, would you sacrifice profits for the sake of cleaner air? Would the owners of the power plant agree? Would your competitors make such a sacrifice?

The same kinds of cost considerations lead the plant to engage in thermal pollution. Cool water must be run through an electric utility plant to keep the turbines from overheating. And once the water runs through the plant, it is too hot to recirculate. Hence it must be either dumped back into the adjacent river or cooled off by being circulated through cooling towers. As you might expect, it is cheaper simply to dump the hot water in the river. The fish don't like it, but they don't have to pay the construction costs of cooling towers. Were you to get on the environmental bandwagon and build those towers, your production costs would rise, just as they did in Figure 8.4*b*. The fish would benefit, but at your expense.

External Cost   外部成本

The big question here is whether you and the plant's owners would be willing to incur higher costs in order to cut down on pollution. Eliminating either the air pollution or the water pollution emanating from the electric plant will cost a lot of money; eliminating both will cost much more. And to whose benefit? To the people who live downstream and downwind? We don't expect profit-maximizing producers to take such concerns into account. The behavior of profit maximizers is guided by comparisons of revenues and costs, not by philanthropy, aesthetic concerns, or the welfare of fish.

The moral of this story—and the critical factor in pollution behavior—is that ***people tend to maximize their personal welfare, balancing*** *private **benefits against** private **costs.*** For the electric power plant, this means making production decisions on the basis of revenues received and costs incurred. The fact that the power plant imposes costs on others, in the form of air and water pollution, is irrelevant to its profit-maximizing decision. Those costs are *external* to the firm and do not appear on its profit-and-loss statement. Those external costs are no less real, but they are incurred by society at large rather than by the firm.

Whenever external costs exist, a private firm will not allocate its resources and operate its plant in such a way as to maximize social welfare. In effect, society is permitting the power plant the free use of valued resources—clean air and clean water. Thus the power plant has a tremendous incentive to substitute those resources for others (such as high-priced fuel or cooling towers) in the production process. The inefficiency of such an arrangement is obvious when we recall that the function of markets is to allocate scarce resources in accordance with consumers' expressed demands. Yet here we are, proclaiming a high value for clean air and clean water while encouraging the power plant to use up both resources by offering them at zero cost to the firm. We end up with the wrong answer to the HOW question.

Social versus Private Costs   社会成本与私人成本

The inefficiency of this market arrangement can be expressed in terms of a distinction between social costs and private costs. **Social costs** are the total costs of all the resources that are used in a particular production activity. On the other hand, **private costs** are the resource costs that are incurred by the specific producer.

Ideally, a producer's private costs will encompass all the attendant social costs, and production decisions will be consistent with our social welfare. Unfortunately, this happy identity does not always exist, as our experience with the power plant illustrates. ***When social costs differ from private costs, external costs exist. In fact, external costs are equal to the difference between the social and private costs***:

---

rotate 使旋转。 emanate 产生。 philanthropy 慈善。 aesthetic 美学的，审美的。 encompass 包括，涵盖。

> External costs = social costs − private costs

外部成本 = 社会成本 − 私人成本

When external costs are present, the market mechanism will not allocate resources efficiently. The price signal confronting producers is flawed. By not conveying the full (social) cost of scarce resources, the market encourages excessive pollution. We end up with a suboptimal mix of output, the wrong production processes, and a polluted environment. This is another case of market failure.

Policy Options 政策选择

What should the government do to remedy market failures caused by externalities?

Our goal is to discourage production and consumption activities that impose external costs on society. We can do this in one of two ways:

- *Alter market incentives.*
- *Bypass market incentives.*

Emission Fees 排污费

Consider our pollution problem. The key to market-based environmental protection is to eliminate the gap between private costs and social costs. The opportunity to shift some costs onto others lies at the heart of the pollution problem. If we could somehow compel producers to *internalize* all costs—pay for both private and previously external costs—the gap would disappear, along with the incentive to pollute.

One possibility is to establish a system of **emission charges**, direct costs attached to the act of polluting. Suppose that we let you keep your power plant job and even permit you to operate it according to profit-maximizing principles. The only difference is that we no longer supply you with clean air and cool water at zero cost. Instead we will charge you for these scarce resources. We might, say, charge you 2 cents for every gram of noxious emission you discharge into the air. We might also charge you 3 cents for every gallon of water you use, heat, and discharge back into the river.

Confronted with such emission charges, a plant manager would have to rethink the production decision. ***An emission charge increases private marginal cost and thus encourages lower output.*** Figure 8.5 illustrates this effect.

面对这样的排污收费，工厂管理者不得不重新考虑其生产决策。排污收费增加了私人的边际成本，并因此导致了较低的产出。图 8.5 就描述了这种结果。

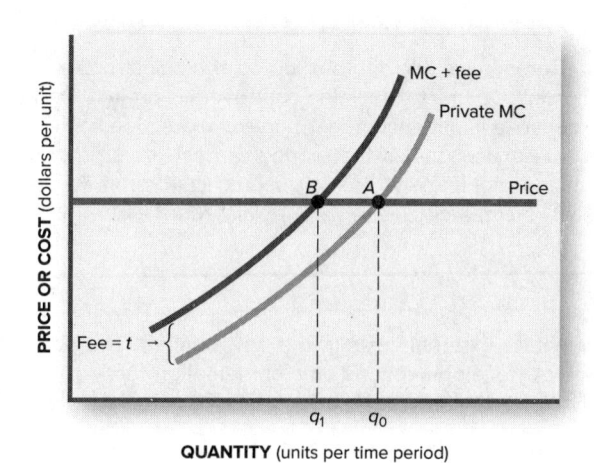

Figure 8.5 Emission Fees Emission charges can be used to close the gap between social costs and private costs. Faced with an emission charge of t, a private producer will reduce output from q_0 to q_1. ∎

---

flawed 有缺陷的。 remedy 解决，纠正。 internalize 内部化。 compel 强迫。 emission charge 排污收费。

Consider again the choice of fuels to be used in our fictional power plant. Earlier, we chose high-sulfur coal because it was the cheapest fuel available. Now, however, there is an added cost to burning such fuel, in the form of an emission charge on noxious pollutants. This higher marginal cost might prompt a switch to less polluting fuels. The actual response of producers will depend on the relative costs involved. If emission charges are too low, it may be more profitable to continue burning and polluting with high-sulfur coal and pay a nominal fee. This is a simple pricing problem. The government can set the emission price higher, prompting the desired behavioral responses.

What works on producers will also sway consumers. Surely you've heard of deposits on returnable bottles. At one time the deposits were imposed by beverage producers to encourage you to bring the bottle back for reuse. Thirty years ago, virtually all soft drinks and most beer came in returnable bottles. But producers discovered that such deposits discouraged sales and yielded little cost savings. The economics of returnable bottles were further undermined by the advent of metal cans and, later, plastic bottles. Today returnable bottles are rarely used. One result is the inclusion of over 30 billion bottles and 65 billion cans in our solid waste disposal problem.

We could reduce this solid waste problem by imposing a deposit on all beverage containers. This would internalize pollution costs for the consumer and render the throwing of a soda can out the window equivalent to throwing away money. Some people would still find the thrill worthwhile, but they would be followed around by others who attached more value to money. When Oregon imposed a 5-cent deposit on beverage containers, related litter in that state declined by 81 percent! Ten states now have "bottle bills," with required deposits of 5–10 cents per container. Recycling rates in those states are roughly double the rate in states without bottle bills.

Regulation   管制

Although emission fees can be used to alter market incentives, the government can also choose to bypass market signals altogether. This was the approach President Obama took in vetoing the Keystone XL pipeline. As he saw it, any project that added to environmental damage was undesirable, regardless of what economic benefits it might generate. In his mind, there was no need to weigh benefits versus costs and no reason to alter production decisions at the margin. President Trump disagreed, arguing that the benefits of cheaper and more abundant energy outweighed environmental (external) costs (see the News Wire "External Costs")

NEWS WIRE EXTERNAL COSTS

TRUMP OKS KEYSTONE PIPELINE

Washington, DC—President Trump gave the thumbs up to the construction of the Keystone Pipeline, reversing the decision of President Obama to block the controversial project. Environmental groups oppose the 1,180-mile-long pipeline because it will encourage more oil extraction, increase carbon emissions, and potentially pollute the Ogalla Acquifer, one of the world's largest underground deposits of fresh water. Native Americans also claim the pipeline will destroy sacred cultural sites. President Trump was more impressed that the pipeline will increase U.S. energy supplies, reduce energy costs, spur oil exports, and create thousands of jobs.

Source: News accounts of March 2017.

NOTE: Energy development entails external costs to the environment. The policy challenge is to find the optimal balance between energy development and environmental protection.
注：能源开发必定对环境造成外部成本。政策挑战是在能源开发和环境保护间找到最佳平衡点。

Aside from outright prohibitions, the government can also choose to regulate market behavior. The federal government began regulating auto emissions in 1968 and got tough under the provisions of the Clean Air Act of 1970. The act required auto manufacturers to reduce hydrocarbon, carbon monoxide, and nitrogen oxide emissions by 90 percent within six years of the act's passage. Although the timetable for reducing pollutants was later extended, the act forced auto manufacturers to reduce auto emissions dramatically: By 1990, new cars were emitting only 4 percent as much pollution as 1970 models. This dramatic reduction in per-vehicle emissions enabled auto production to increase even while pollution declined (see the accompanying News Wire "Changing Market Behavior").

NEWS WIRE CHANGING MARKET BEHAVIOR

BREATHING EASIER

America's air has become a great deal cleaner over the last generation. Since measurement began in 1970, U.S. emissions have fallen dramatically, even while GDP and travel have more than doubled. America, in other words, is producing much more while polluting less.

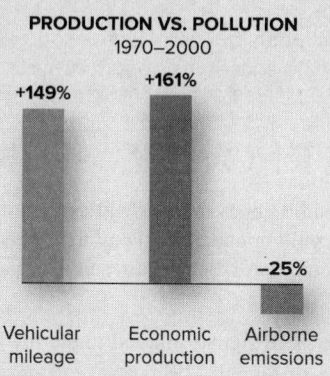

PRODUCTION VS. POLLUTION
1970–2000

- Vehicular mileage: +149%
- Economic production: +161%
- Airborne emissions: −25%

Source: *The American Enterprise*, July/August 2003, p. 17.

NOTE: A combination of market incentives and government mandates has enabled output to increase even while the volume of pollution has diminished. The market alone would not have done as well.
注：市场激励和政府管制相结合使产出增加，而污染物却减少了。单凭市场是做不到这一点的。

Regulatory standards may specify not only the required reduction in emissions, but also the *process* by which those reductions are to be achieved. Clean air legislation mandated not only fewer auto emissions but also specific processes (e.g., catalytic converters, lead-free gasoline) for attaining them. Specific processes and technologies are also required for toxic waste disposal and water treatment. Laws requiring the sorting and recycling of trash are also examples of process regulation.

Although such hands-on regulation can be effective, this policy option also entails risks. By requiring market participants to follow specific rules, the regulations may impose excessive costs on some activities and too low a constraint on others. Some communities may not need the level of sewage treatment the federal government prescribes. Individual households may not generate enough trash to make sorting and separate pickups economically sound. Some producers may have better or cheaper ways of attaining environmental standards. ***Excessive process regulation may raise the costs of environmental protection*** and discourage cost-saving innovation. There is also the risk of regulated processes becoming entrenched long after they are obsolete.

尽管这种管制在实际中可能是有效的，但是这种政策选择也存在风险。通过要求所有的市场参与者遵守特定的规则，这种管制可能对某些活动造成过高的成本，而对其他活动约束过低。一些社区可能不需要联邦政府规定的污水处理程度。单个家庭产生的垃圾可能不足以让垃圾分类和分拣变得经济。有些生产者可能有更好或更便宜的方法来达到环保标准。过度的流程管制可能会增加环境保护的成本，并有可能阻碍成本节约创新。在管制流程过时以后，它们也有变成制约因素的风险。

There are cost considerations, too. Recycling, for example, is popular but not costless. The plants that process recycled materials are expensive to build and operate. So, too, are the fleets of vehicles that are used to collect recyclables from homes and businesses. Furthermore, both the collection and processing functions generate their own pollution. Hence, recycling programs create both internal and external costs. Former New York City mayor Michael Bloomberg concluded that recycling was not worth the cost and ended the city's recycling programs (see the News Wire "Opportunity Costs"). He decided the city would be better off spending that money on schools, transit, and public safety.

---

toxic 有毒的。

NEWS WIRE OPPORTUNITY COSTS

BLOOMBERG: FORCED RECYCLING A WASTE

Looking for ways to cut the city's budget, Mayor Michael Bloomberg has zeroed in on the city's recycling program. Local law 19 mandates that the city recycle 25 percent of its waste. But that's a very expensive mandate. It costs about $240 per ton to recycle plastic, glass, and metal, while the cost of simply sending that trash to landfills is only $130 per ton. If the city suspended its recycling program, it could save New Yorkers $57 million per year. Mayor Bloomberg wants to do exactly that. Otherwise, he warns, the city will have to make painful cuts to its police and fire department budgets. "You could do a lot better things in the world with $57 million," the mayor says.

Source: News accounts of March 9, 2002.

NOTE: Recycling programs reduce pollution but also use resources that could be employed for other purposes. The benefits of recycling should exceed its opportunity costs.
注：回收项目减少了污染，但也占用了可用于其他目的的资源。回收的收益应该大于其机会成本。

MARKET POWER 市场权力

当公共物品或外部性存在时，市场的价格信号是有缺陷的。消费者愿意并能够为某一特定商品支付的价格，并不能反映出生产那种商品的所有收益或成本。因此市场无法生产社会所需要的产出组合。

When either public goods or externalities exist, the market's price signal is flawed. The price consumers are willing and able to pay for a specific good does not reflect all the benefits or costs of producing that good. As a result, the market fails to produce the socially desired mix of output.

Even when the price signals emitted in the market are accurate, however, we may still get a suboptimal mix of output. The *response* to price signals, rather than the signals themselves, may be flawed.

Restricted Supply 有限的供给

Market power is often the cause of a flawed response. Suppose there were only one airline company in the world. As a monopolist, the airline could charge extremely high prices without worrying that travelers would flock to a competing airline. Ideally, such high prices would act as a signal to producers to build and fly more planes—to change the mix of output. But a monopolist does not have to cater to every consumer whim. It can limit airline travel and thus obstruct our efforts to achieve an optimal mix of output.

Monopoly is the most severe form of **market power**. More generally, market power refers to any situation where a single producer or consumer has the ability to alter the market price of a specific product. If the publisher (McGraw-Hill) charges a high price for this book, you will have to pay the tab. McGraw-Hill has market power because there are relatively few economics textbooks and your professor has required you to use this one. You don't have power in the textbook market because your purchase decision will not alter the market price of this text. You are only one of the million students taking an introductory economics course this year.

不管市场权力的来源是什么，市场权力的直接后果是，一个或多个生产者获得了市场对价格信号反应的自由决策权。它们可能利用这种决策权力使自己变得富有，而不是将经济推向最优产出组合。在这种情况下，市场在生产社会最需要的商品和服务方面将会又一次失灵。正如我们在第6章所观察到的，政府认为微软利用它在计算机操作系统上的实质性垄断限制了消费者选择，并因此让自己获利。

The market power McGraw-Hill possesses is derived from the copyright on this text. No matter how profitable textbook sales might be, no one else is permitted to produce or sell this particular text. Patents are another source of market power because they also preclude others from making or selling a specific product. Market power may also result from control of resources, restrictive production agreements, or efficiencies of large-scale production.

Whatever the source of market power, *the direct consequence of market power is that one or more producers attain discretionary power over the market's response to price signals.* They may use that discretion to enrich themselves rather than to move the economy toward the optimal mix of output. In this case, the market will again fail to deliver the most desired goods and services. As we observed in Chapter 6, the government concluded that Microsoft used its virtual monopoly in computer operating systems to limit consumer choice and enrich itself.

---

mandate 指令，要求。 flock to 蜂拥而至。 cater to 迎合，为……服务。 whim 奇想，一时的兴致。 tab 账单。 preclude 排除。

Antitrust Policy 反垄断政策

A primary goal of government intervention in such cases is to prevent or dismantle concentrations of market power. That is the essential purpose of **antitrust** policy. The legal foundations of federal antitrust activity are contained in three laws:

- **The Sherman Act (1890).** The Sherman Act prohibits "conspiracies in restraint of trade," including mergers, contracts, or acquisitions that threaten to monopolize an industry. Firms that violate the Sherman Act are subject to fines of up to $1 million, and their executives may be subject to imprisonment. In addition, consumers who are damaged—for example, via high prices—by a conspiracy in restraint of trade may recover treble damages. The U.S. Department of Justice has used this trust-busting authority to block attempted mergers and acquisitions, force changes in price or output behavior, require companies to sell some of their assets, and even send corporate executives to jail for conspiracies in restraint of trade.

- **The Clayton Act (1914).** The Clayton Act of 1914 was passed to outlaw specific antitrust behavior not covered by the Sherman Act. The principal aim of the act was to prevent the development of monopolies. To this end the Clayton Act prohibits price discrimination, exclusive dealing agreements, certain types of mergers, and interlocking boards of directors among competing firms.

- **The Federal Trade Commission Act (1914).** The increased antitrust responsibilities of the federal government created the need for an agency that could study industry structures and behavior so as to identify anticompetitive practices. The Federal Trade Commission was created for this purpose in 1914.

In the early 1900s this antitrust legislation was used to break up the monopolies that dominated the steel and tobacco industries. In the 1980s the same legislation was used to dismantle AT&T's near monopoly of telephone service. The court forced AT&T to sell off its local telephone service companies (the Baby Bells) and allow competitors more access to long-distance service. The resulting competition pushed prices down and spawned a new wave of telephone technology and services.

Although antitrust policy has produced some impressive results, its potential is limited. There are over 30 million businesses in the United States, and the trustbusters can watch only so many. Even when they decide to take action, antitrust policy entails difficult decisions. What, for example, constitutes a monopoly in the real world? Must a company produce 100 percent of a particular good to be a threat to consumer welfare? How about 99 percent? Or even 75 percent?

And what specific monopolistic practices should be prohibited? Should we be looking for specific evidence of price gouging? Or should we focus on barriers to entry and unfair market practices? In the antitrust case against Microsoft (see the News Wire "Barriers to Entry" in Chapter 6), the Justice Department asserted that bundling its Internet Explorer with Windows was an anticompetitive practice. Microsoft Chairman Bill Gates responded that the attorney general didn't understand how the fiercely competitive software market worked. Who was right?

These kinds of questions determine how and when antitrust laws will be enforced. Just the threat of enforcement, however, may help push market outcomes in the desired direction. In the Microsoft case, for example, the company changed some of its exclusionary licensing practices soon after the government filed its antitrust case. Google, too, reassessed some of its self-serving search-engine routines when confronted with antitrust complaints from the European Union.

INEQUITY 不公平

Public goods, externalities, and market power all cause resource misallocations. Where these phenomena exist, the market mechanism will fail to produce the optimal mix of output.

在这些情况下，政府干预的一个主要目标是防止或消除市场权力的集中。这也是**反垄断政策**的根本目的。以下三项法案包含了联邦反垄断行为的法律基础：

- **谢尔曼法案** 谢尔曼法案禁止"会限制贸易的共谋"，包括可能导致垄断一个行业的兼并、契约或收购。

- **克莱顿法案** 克莱顿法案于1914年通过，用来禁止谢尔曼法案没有包括的一些特定的反垄断行为。

- **联邦贸易委员会法案** 随着联邦政府反垄断责任的增加，有必要建立一个机构来研究产业结构和产业行为，从而确定反竞争行为。基于这一目的，1914年成立了联邦贸易委员会。

---

prohibit 禁止。 conspiracy 共谋，合谋。 discrimination 歧视。 spawn 引发，造成。 price gouging 价格欺诈。 fiercely 激烈地。

Beyond the question of WHAT to produce, we are also concerned about FOR WHOM output is to be produced. Is the distribution of goods and services generated by the marketplace fair? If not, government intervention may be needed to redistribute income.

In general, the market mechanism tends to answer the basic question of FOR WHOM to produce by distributing a larger share of total output to those with the most income. Although this result may be efficient, it is not necessarily equitable. Individuals who are aged or disabled, for example, may be unable to earn much income yet may still be regarded as worthy recipients of goods and services. In such cases, we may want to change the market's answer to the basic question of FOR WHOM goods are produced.

The government alters the distribution of income with taxes and transfers. The federal income tax takes as much as 37 percent of income from rich individuals. A big chunk of this tax revenue is then used to provide **income transfers** for poor people.

政府利用税收和转移支付来改变收入的分配。联邦税收向富人征收高达 37% 的所得税。这种税收收入的很大一部分用来给穷人提供**收入转移**。

As Figure 8.6 illustrates, poor people would get only a tiny sliver of the economic pie—about 1 percent—without government intervention. The tax and transfer system more than sextuples the amount of income they end up with. Although poor people still don't have enough income, government intervention clearly remedies some of the inequities the market alone creates.

Table 8.1 indicates some of the larger income transfer programs. The largest transfer program is Social Security. Although Social Security benefits are paid to virtually all retirees, they are particularly important to the aged poor. In the absence of those monthly Social Security checks, almost half of this country's aged population would be poor. For younger families, food stamps, welfare checks, and Medicaid are all important income transfers for reducing poverty.

MACRO INSTABILITY 宏观不稳定性

The micro failures of the marketplace imply that we are at the wrong point on the production possibilities curve or inequitably distributing the output produced. There is another basic question we have swept under the rug, however. How do we get to the production possibilities curve in the first place? To reach the curve, we must utilize all available resources and technology. Can we be confident that the invisible hand of the marketplace will use all of our resources? Or will some people remain unemployed—that is, willing to work but unable to find a job?

市场的微观失灵意味着我们正处于生产可能性曲线上一个错误的点，或者对产出的分配是不公平的。

And what about prices? Price signals are a critical feature of the market mechanism. But the validity of those signals depends on some stable measure of value. What good is a doubling of salary when the price of everything you buy doubles as well? Generally, rising prices enrich people who own property and impoverish people who rent. That is why we strive to avoid inflation—a situation where the *average* price level is increasing.

LOW-INCOME HOUSEHOLDS SHARE OF TOTAL INCOME

Before government intervention: 1.1%

After taxes and transfers: 6.9%

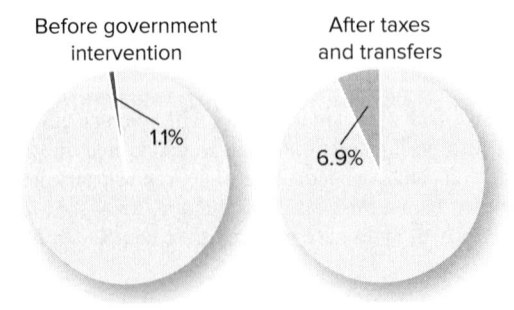

Figure 8.6 Moderating Inequity The market alone would distribute only 1.1 percent of total income to the poor. Government taxes and transfers raise that share to 6.9 percent.

Source: "The Distribution of Household Income, 2014," Congressional Budget Office, 2018.

---

validity 有效性。 impoverish 使贫穷。

Program	Recipient Group	Number of Recipients	Value of Transfers
Social Security	Retired and disabled workers	67 million	$1,002 billion
Medicare	Individuals over age 65	59 million	$ 620 billion
Medicaid	Medically needy individuals	75 million	$ 400 billion
Unemployment compensation	Unemployed workers	6 million	$ 30 billion
Food stamps	Low-income households	42 million	$ 63 billion
Earned Income Tax Credit	Low-wage workers	30 million	$ 70 billion
Temporary Aid to Needy Families	Poor families	3 million	$ 17 billion

Table 8.1 Income Transfers The market mechanism might leave some people with too little income and others with too much. The government uses taxes and transfers to redistribute income more fairly.

Source: Congressional Budget Office, 2018.

Historically, the marketplace has been wracked with bouts of both unemployment and inflation. These experiences have prompted calls for government intervention at the macro level. *The goal of macro intervention is to foster economic growth—to get us on the production possibilities curve (full employment), maintain a stable price level (price stability), and increase our capacity to produce (growth).* The means for achieving this goal are examined in the macro section of this course.

从历史上看，市场一直被失业和通货膨胀所困扰。这些经历促使人们呼吁政府在宏观层面进行干预。宏观干预的目标是促进经济增长——使我们到达生产可能性曲线（充分就业），保持一个稳定的价格水平（价格稳定），并提高我们的生产能力（增长）。实现这个目标的方法会在本书的宏观部分进行探讨。

POLICY PERSPECTIVES

WILL THE GOVERNMENT GET IT RIGHT?

The potential micro and macro failures of the marketplace provide specific justifications for government intervention. The question then turns to how well the government responds to these implied mandates. Can we trust the government to fix the shortcomings of the market?

INFORMATION

If the government is going to fix things, it must not only confirm market failure but identify the social optimum. This is no easy task. Back in Figure 8.1 we arbitrarily designated point X as the social optimum. In the real world, however, only the *market* outcome is visible. The social optimum isn't visible; it must be inferred. To locate it, we need to know the preferences of the community as well as the dimensions of any externalities. Likewise, if we want the government to change the market distribution of income, we need to know what society regards as fair. No one really has all the required information. Consequently, government intervention typically entails a lot of groping in the dark for *better*, if not *optimal*, outcomes.

VESTED INTERESTS

Vested interests often try to steer the search away from the social optimum. Cigarette manufacturers don't want people to stop smoking. Car companies don't want consumers to reject the fuel technology they have developed. So they try to keep the government from altering market outcomes. To do so, they may generate studies that minimize the size of external costs. They may try to sway public opinion with public interest advertising. And they may use their wealth to finance the campaigns of sympathetic politicians. Government officials, too, may have personal agendas that don't reflect society's interests. In these circumstances it becomes more difficult to figure out where the social optimum is, much less how to get there.

---

shortcomings 缺陷，短处。 designate 指定。

GOVERNMENT FAILURE

These are just a couple of reasons why government intervention won't always improve market outcomes. Yes, an unregulated market might produce the wrong mix of output, generate too much pollution, or leave too many people in poverty. However, **government intervention might *worsen*, rather than improve, market outcomes.** In such cases, we would have to conclude that government intervention has *failed*.

The possibility of government failure is illustrated in Figure 8.7. The WHAT choice depicted here is between consumers goods and military goods. We now know that national defense is a *public good*, so don't expect consumers to *demand* military goods directly. As a consequence, fewer military goods will be produced at point M than society really wants (point X). This is the market failure we want the government to fix.

Government intervention doesn't always improve economic outcomes.

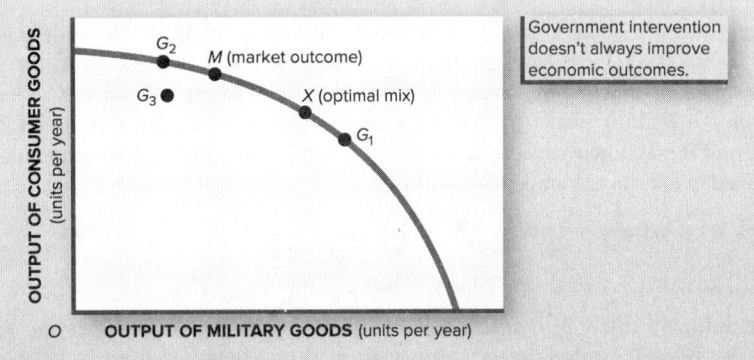

Figure 8.7 Government Failure The goal of government intervention is to correct market failure (e.g., by changing the mix of output from M to X). It is possible, however, that government policy might move the economy beyond the optimal mix (to point G_1), in the wrong direction (to point G_2), or even inside the production possibilities curve (to point G_3).

Will the government move us to point X? Maybe. But it might also move us to point G_1, where *too many* resources are being allocated to the military. Or pacifists might move us to point G_2, where *too little* military output is produced. Maybe government procurement will be so inefficient that we end up at G_3, producing *less* output than possible. Any of these outcomes (G_1, G_2, G_3) fall short of our goal; they may even be worse than the initial market outcome (point M).

Government failure refers to any intervention that fails to improve market outcomes. Perhaps the mix of output or the income distribution got worse when the government intervened. Or the regulatory/administrative cost of intervention outweighed its benefits. Clearly, **there is no guarantee that the visible hand of government will be any better than the invisible hand of the marketplace.**

The average citizen clearly understands that government intervention does not always succeed as hoped. Opinion polls reveal considerable doubt about the government's ability to improve market outcomes. As Figure 8.8 illustrates, only one out of seven Americans believes the federal government will do the right thing all or most of the time when it intervenes. One out of five believes this never happens. Confidence levels are higher for state and local governments but still far short of comfort levels.

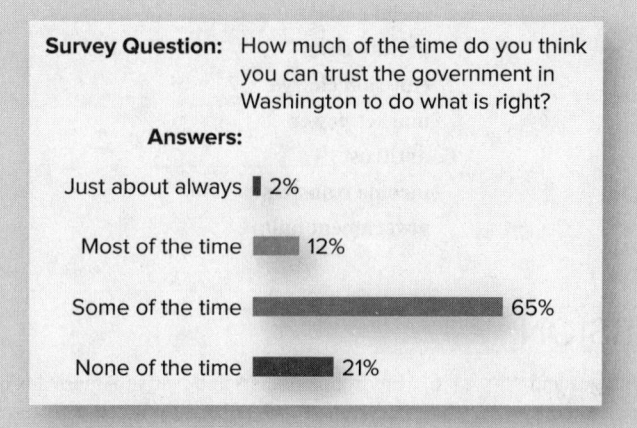

> **Survey Question:** How much of the time do you think you can trust the government in Washington to do what is right?
>
> **Answers:**
> - Just about always — 2%
> - Most of the time — 12%
> - Some of the time — 65%
> - None of the time — 21%

Figure 8.8 Low Expectations The public has substantial doubts about the ability of government to fix market failures.
Source: "Trump's Job Approval Remains Low While Most Americans Don't See the Effects of the Tax Cuts," Hart Research Associates, March 27, 2018.

Neither market failure nor government failure is inevitable. The challenge for public policy is to decide when *any* government intervention is justified and, when deemed necessary, to intervene in a way that improves outcomes in the least costly way.

CHAPTER 8 REVIEW

SUMMARY

- Government intervention in the marketplace is justified by market failure—that is, suboptimal market outcomes. **LO1**
- The micro failures of the market originate in public goods, externalities, market power, and inequity. These flaws deter the market from achieving the optimal mix of output or distribution of income. **LO1**
- Public goods are those that cannot be consumed exclusively; they are jointly consumed regardless of who pays. Because everyone seeks a free ride, no one demands public goods in the marketplace. Hence the market underproduces public goods. **LO2**
- Externalities are costs (or benefits) of a market transaction borne by a third party. Externalities create a divergence of social and private costs (or benefits), causing suboptimal market outcomes. The market overproduces goods with external costs and underproduces goods with external benefits. **LO3**
- Market power enables a producer to thwart market signals and maintain a suboptimal mix of output. Antitrust policy seeks to prevent or restrict market power. **LO4**
- The market-generated distribution of income may be regarded as unfair. This equity concern may prompt the government to intervene with taxes and transfer payments that redistribute incomes. **LO5**
- The macro failures of the marketplace are reflected in unemployment and inflation. Government intervention at the macro level is intended to achieve full employment and price stability. **LO5**
- Government failure occurs when intervention fails to improve, or even worsens, economic outcomes. **LO5**

TERMS TO REMEMBER

Define the following terms:

laissez faire
optimal mix of output
market mechanism
market failure
public good
private good
free rider
externalities

social costs
private costs
emission charge
market power
antitrust
income transfers
government failure

QUESTIONS FOR DISCUSSION

1. Why should taxpayers subsidize public colleges and universities? What external benefits are generated by higher education? **LO3**
2. If everyone seeks a free ride, what mix of output will be produced in Figure 8.2? Why would anyone voluntarily contribute to the purchase of public goods like flood control or snow removal? **LO2**
3. Could local fire departments be privately operated, with services sold directly to customers? What problems would be involved in such a system? **LO3**
4. Identify a specific government activity that is justified by each source of market failure. **LO1**
5. Given the effectiveness of Israel's Iron Dome (News Wire "Public Goods"), why wouldn't individuals want to pay for its protective services? Could this be a profitable venture in the private market? **LO2**
6. Environmentalists and Native Americans oppose the Keystone Pipeline because it causes external costs (News Wire "External Costs"). Should any activity that generates external costs be prohibited? **LO5**
7. Does anyone have an incentive to maintain auto exhaust control devices in good working order? How can we ensure that they will be maintained? **LO5**
8. What are the costs of New York City's recycling program (see the News Wire "Opportunity Costs")? Are these costs justified? **LO5**
9. Most cities are served by only one cable company. How might this monopoly power affect prices and service? What should the government do, if anything? **LO4, LO5**
10. **POLICY PERSPECTIVES** Why might the market underproduce and the government overproduce flood-control dams? **LO1**

PROBLEMS

1. In Figure 8.3, by how much is the market overproducing cars? **LO3**
2. How much global output is lost annually as a result of adult deaths from secondhand smoke if the average adult produces (*a*) $15,000 output per year, (*b*) $20,000 output per year? (see the News Wire "Externalities")? **LO3**
3. *a.* Draw a production possibilities curve (PPC) with cars on the horizontal axis and other goods on the vertical axis.
   b. Illustrate on your PPC the market failure that occurs in Figure 8.3. **LO3**
4. Draw market demand and social demand curves for flu shots. What is the source of market failure? **LO3**
5. In Figure 8.2, identify the market and optimal outcomes. Does the market under or overproduce (*a*) public goods? (*b*) private goods? **LO2**
6. Suppose the annual cost of the Iron Dome is $500 million. What is the opportunity cost of this defense spending in terms of private housing assuming a new home can be constructed for $100,000? (see the News Wire "Public Goods"). **LO2**
7. The market demand for cigarettes are given in the following table. **LO3**

Price ($ per pack)	6.50	6.00	5.50	5.00	4.50	4.00	3.50
Quantity (packs per day)	40	50	60	70	80	90	100

Suppose further that smoking creates external costs valued at 50 cents per pack.

a. Draw the social and market demand curves.

Given a market price of $5.00,

b. What quantity is demanded in the market?

c. What is the socially optimal quantity?

8. Graph the following data on social and market demand: **LO3**

Price ($)	Market Quantity Demanded (units per month)	Social Quantity Demanded (units per month)
20	10	20
18	20	30
16	30	40
14	40	50
12	50	60
10	60	70

a. Does this product have external benefits or external costs?

b. How large ($) is that externality?

9. **POLICY PERSPECTIVES** According to Table 8.1 (Income Transfers), calculate the average benefit a Medicare recipient receives. **LO1**

10. **POLICY PERSPECTIVES** The production possibilities curve shows the trade-off between housing and all other goods. **LO5**

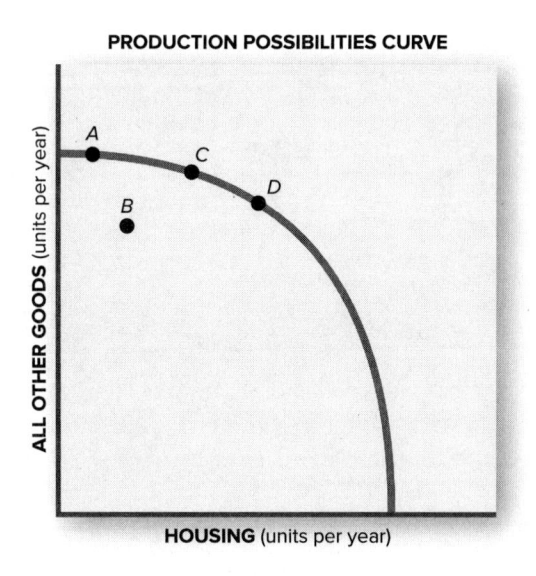

a. If the market mix of output is at point A and the optimal mix of output is at point C, does a market failure exist?

b. If the government has a laissez-faire approach, will it intervene?

c. If the government intervenes and the economy moves to point D, is this a government failure?

CHAPTER NINE

The Business Cycle 商业周期

©Everett Historical/Shutterstock

LEARNING OBJECTIVES

After reading this chapter, you should be able to:

1. Explain how growth of the economy is measured.
2. Tell how unemployment is measured and affects us.
3. Discuss why inflation is a problem and how it is measured.
4. Define full employment and price stability.
5. Recite the U.S. track record on growth, unemployment, and inflation.

In 1929 it looked as though the sun would never set on the American economy. For eight years in a row, the U.S. economy had been expanding rapidly. During the Roaring Twenties, the typical American family drove its first car, bought its first radio, and went to the movies for the first time. With factories running at capacity, virtually anyone who wanted to work readily found a job.

Under these circumstances everyone was optimistic. In his acceptance address in November 1928, President-elect Herbert Hoover echoed this optimism by declaring, "We in America today are nearer to the final triumph over poverty than ever before in the history of any land. . . . We shall soon with the help of God be in sight of the day when poverty will be banished from this nation."

The booming stock market seemed to confirm this optimistic outlook. Between 1921 and 1927, the stock market's value more than doubled, adding billions of dollars to the wealth of American households and businesses. The stock market boom accelerated in 1927, causing stock prices to double again in less than two years. The roaring stock market made it look easy to get rich in America.

---

at capacity 以最大程度，以最大生产能力。banish 消除。

The party ended abruptly on October 24, 1929. On what came to be known as Black Thursday, the stock market crashed. In a few hours, the market value of U.S. corporations fell abruptly in the most frenzied selling ever seen (see the accompanying News Wire "The Crash of 1929"). The next day President Hoover tried to assure America's stockholders that the economy was "on a sound and prosperous basis." But despite his assurances and the efforts of leading bankers to stem the decline, the stock market continued to plummet. The following Tuesday (October 29) the pace of selling quickened. By the end of the year, over $40 billion of wealth had vanished in the Great Crash. Rich men became paupers overnight; ordinary families lost their savings, their homes, and even their lives.

NEWS WIRE THE CRASH OF 1929

MARKET IN PANIC AS STOCKS ARE DUMPED IN 12,894,600-SHARE DAY; BANKERS HALT IT

Effect Is Felt on the Curb and throughout Nation—Financial District Goes Wild

The stock markets of the country tottered on the brink of panic yesterday as a prosperous people, gone suddenly hysterical with fear, attempted simultaneously to sell a record-breaking volume of securities for whatever they would bring.

The result was a financial nightmare, comparable to nothing ever before experienced in Wall Street. It rocked the financial district to its foundations, hopelessly overwhelmed its mechanical facilities, chilled its blood with terror.

In a society built largely on confidence, with real wealth expressed more or less inaccurately by pieces of paper, the entire fabric of economic stability threatened to come toppling down.

Into the frantic hands of a thousand brokers on the floor of the New York Stock Exchange poured the selling orders of the world. It was sell, sell, sell—hour after desperate hour until 1:30 p.m.

—Laurence Stern

Source: "Stock Market Crash of 1929," *The World*, October 25, 1929.

NOTE: The stock market is often a barometer of business cycles. The 1929 crash both anticipated and worsened the Great Depression.
注：股票市场通常是商业周期的晴雨表。1929 年的经济崩溃不仅预示了大萧条的到来，还加剧了大萧条。

The devastation was not confined to Wall Street. The financial flames engulfed farms, banks, and industries. Between 1930 and 1935, millions of rural families lost their farms. Automobile production fell from 4.5 million cars in 1929 to only 1.1 million in 1932. So many banks were forced to close that newly elected President Roosevelt had to declare a "bank holiday" in March 1933, closing all the nation's banks for four days. It was a desperate move to stem the outflow of cash to anxious depositors.

Throughout those years, the ranks of the unemployed continued to swell. In October 1929 only 3 percent of the workforce was unemployed. A year later over 9 percent of the workforce was unemployed. Still, things got worse. By 1933 over one-fourth of the labor force was unable to find work. People slept in the streets, scavenged for food, and sold apples on Wall Street.

The Great Depression seemed to last forever. In 1933 President Roosevelt lamented that one-third of the nation was ill clothed, ill housed, and ill fed. Thousands of unemployed workers marched to the Capitol to demand jobs and aid. In 1938, nine years after the Great Crash, nearly 20 percent of the workforce was still unemployed.

The Great Depression shook not only the foundations of the world economy but also the self-confidence of the economics profession. No one had predicted the depression, and few could explain it. How could the economy perform so poorly for so long? What could the government do to prevent such a catastrophe? Suddenly there were more questions than answers.

The scramble for answers became the springboard for modern **macroeconomics**, the study of aggregate economic behavior. A basic purpose of macroeconomic theory is to *explain* the **business cycle**—to identify the forces that cause the overall economy to expand or contract. Macro *policy* tries to *control* the business cycle, using the insights of macro theory.

---

abruptly 突然地。stem 阻止，遏制。plummet 暴跌。pauper 乞丐，穷人。totter 摇摇欲坠。hysterical 歇斯底里的。fabric 结构，架构。devastation 毁灭，破坏。engulf 吞没，吞噬。scavenge for food (在垃圾或废物中) 捡拾食物。lament 悲叹。springboard 基础。

In this chapter we focus on the nature of the business cycle and the related problems of unemployment and inflation. Our goal is to acquire a sense of why the business cycle is so feared. To address these concerns, we need to know

- What are business cycles?
- What damage does unemployment cause?
- Who is hurt by inflation?

As we answer these questions, we will get a sense of why people worry so much about the macro economy and why they demand that Washington do something about it. We'll also see why Washington policymakers were determined not to let the 2008–2009 recession turn into another Great Depression.

ASSESSING MACRO PERFORMANCE 评估宏观表现

Doctors gauge a person's health with a few simple measurements such as body temperature, blood pressure, and blood content. These tests don't tell doctors everything they need to know about a patient, but they convey some important clues about a patient's general health. In macroeconomics, economic "doctors" need comparable measures of the economy's health. The macro economy is a complex construction, encompassing all kinds of economic activity. To get a quick reading of how well it is doing, economists rely on three gauges. ***The three basic measures of macro performance are***

- *Output (GDP) growth*
- *Unemployment*
- *Inflation*

The macro economy is in trouble when output growth slows down—or worse, turns negative, as it did during the Great Depression. Economic doctors also worry about the macro economy when they see either unemployment or inflation rising. Any one of these symptoms is painful and may be the precursor to a more serious ailment. Someone has to decide whether to intervene or instead wait to see if the economy can overcome such symptoms by itself.

GDP GROWTH   GDP 增长

The first test of the economy's macro health is the rate of output growth. As we first saw in Chapter 1, an economy's *potential* output is reflected in its **production possibilities** curve. That curve tells us how much output the economy *could* produce with available resources and technology. The relevant performance test is whether we are living up to that potential. Are we fully using available resources—or producing at less than capacity? If we are producing *inside* the production possibilities curve, some resources (e.g., workers) are unnecessarily idle. If we are inside the production possibilities curve, the macro economy isn't doing well.

In reality, output has to *keep* increasing if an economy is to stay healthy. The population increases, and technology advances every year. So the production possibilities curve keeps shifting outward. This means *output* has to keep expanding at a healthy clip just to keep from falling further behind that expanding capacity.

Business Cycles   商业周期

The central concern in macroeconomics is that the rate of output won't always keep up with ever-expanding production possibilities. Indeed, when macro doctors study the patient's charts, they often discern a pattern of fits, starts, and stops in the growth of output. Sometimes the volume of output grows at a healthy clip. At other times, the growth rate slips. And in some cases total output actually contracts, as it did in 2008–2009 (see the News Wire "Declining Output").

- 什么是商业周期?
- 失业会引起哪些损失?
- 通货膨胀会对谁产生危害?

医生通过一些简单的测量（例如体温、血压和血液指标）来判断一个人的健康状况。这些测量并不能为医生提供了解病人所需要的全部信息，但是却可为其提供了解病人大体健康状况的重要线索。在宏观经济学中，"经济医生"们也需要对"病人"的健康进行同样的测量。宏观经济是一个包含了所有经济行为的复杂架构。为了迅速摸清它的运行情况，经济学家依赖于三个指标。衡量宏观经济表现的三个基本指标是:

- 产出（GDP）增长
- 失业
- 通货膨胀

对宏观经济健康的第一个测试即产出增长率。正如我们在第1章首次提到的，一个经济体的潜在产出是由**生产可能性**曲线来反映的。这条曲线告诉我们，利用可用资源和技术，经济能够生产多少产出。相关的对宏观经济表现的测试，是看我们是否达到生产潜能。我们是否充分利用了可用资源，还是生产低于产能？如果我们在生产可能性曲线内部进行生产，一些资源（例如工人）就被不必要地闲置。如果我们处于生产可能性曲线内部，宏观经济的表现就不尽人意。

---

symptom 症状。precursor 先兆。ailment 疾病，不适。discern 区分，识别。

188 Chapter Nine: The Business Cycle

> **NEWS WIRE DECLINING OUTPUT**
>
> **Economy: Sharpest Decline in 26 Years**
> Economic Activity Shrank by 6.3 Percent in Last Three Months of 2008
>
> Washington, DC—The U.S. economy suffered its biggest slowdown in 26 years in the final months of last year. According to the U.S. Bureau of Labor Statistics, gross domestic product—the broadest measure of the economy's performance—fell by 6.3 percent. Leading the decline was a 22.8 percent drop in housing construction, accompanied by a 28.1 percent decline in equipment production.
>
> The 6.3 percent drop in GDP was just a sliver less than the 6.4 percent decline registered in the first quarter of 1982, when the U.S. economy was in another deep recession.
>
> Source: U.S. Bureau of Economic Analysis, March 26, 2009.
>
> **NOTE:** A contraction in output indicates that the economy has moved to a point inside its production possibilities curve. Such contractions lower living standards and create more joblessness.
> 注：产出的收缩表明经济已经移到了生产可能性曲线之内的某一点。这样的收缩降低了生活水平，造成了更多失业。

Figure 9.1 illustrates this typical business cycle chart. During an economic expansion total output grows rapidly. Then a peak is reached, and output starts dropping. Once a trough is reached, the economy prospers again. This roller-coaster pattern begins to look like a recurring cycle.

Real GDP 实际 GDP

When we talk about output expanding or contracting, we envision changes in the physical quantity of goods and services produced. But the physical volume of output is virtually impossible to measure. Millions of different goods and services are produced every year, and no one has figured out how to add up their physical quantities (e.g., 30 million grapefruits + 128 million music downloads = ?). So *we measure the volume of output by its market value*, not by its physical volume (e.g., the dollar *value* of grapefruits + the dollar *value* of electronic commerce = a dollar value total). We refer to the dollar value of all the output produced in a year as **gross domestic product (GDP)**.

因此，我们用市场价值来衡量产出量，而不是用它们的实物数量（例如，葡萄柚的美元价值 + 电子商务的美元价值 = 1 美元的总值）。我们将一年中生产的所有产出的美元价值称为国内生产总值。

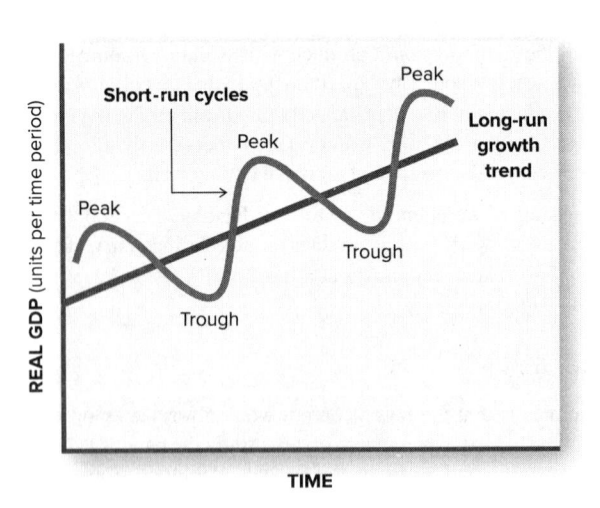

Figure 9.1 The Business Cycle The model business cycle resembles a roller coaster. Output first climbs to a peak and then decreases. After hitting a trough, the economy recovers, with real GDP again increasing.
A central concern of macroeconomic theory is to determine whether a recurring business cycle exists and, if so, what forces cause it. ■

---
roller-coaster pattern 过山车模式。 recurring 循环的。 envision 想象，设想。

Because prices vary from one year to the next, GDP yardsticks must be adjusted for inflation. Suppose that from one year to the next all prices doubled. Such a general price increase would double the *value* of output even if the *quantity* of output were totally unchanged. So an unadjusted measure of **nominal GDP** would give us a false reading: We might think output was racing ahead when in fact it was standing still.

To avoid such false readings, we adjust our measure of output for changing price levels. The yardstick of **real GDP** does this by valuing output at constant prices. Thus changes in real GDP are a proxy for changes in the number of grapefruits, houses, cars, items of clothing, movies, and everything else we produce in a year.

为了避免这样的错误理解，我们对产出的衡量做出适应价格水平变化的调整。**实际 GDP** 通过以不变价格衡量产出价值而实现了这种调整。因此，实际 GDP 的变动就代表了我们一年中所生产的葡萄柚、房屋、汽车、服装、电影以及所有其他产品数量的变化。

Economic activity in 2008 illustrates the distinction between real and nominal GDP. Nominal GDP increased from $14.498 trillion in the second quarter of 2008 to $14.547 trillion in the third quarter, a rise of $49 billion. But that increase in *nominal* GDP growth was due solely to rising prices. *Real* GDP *fell* by more than $90 billion: the *quantity* of output was falling. This decline in *real* GDP was what made people anxious about their livelihoods (see the previous News Wire "Declining Output").

Erratic Growth 不稳定增长

Fortunately, declines in real GDP are more the exception than the rule. As Figure 9.2 illustrates, the annual rate of real GDP growth between 1992 and 2000 was never less than 2.7 percent and got as high as 4.7 percent. Those may not sound like big numbers. In a $20 *trillion* economy, however, even small growth rates imply a *lot* of added output. Moreover, the GDP growth of those years exceeded the rate of expansion in production possibilities. Hence the economy kept moving closer to the limits of its (expanding) production possibilities. In the process, living standards rose, and nearly every job seeker could find work.

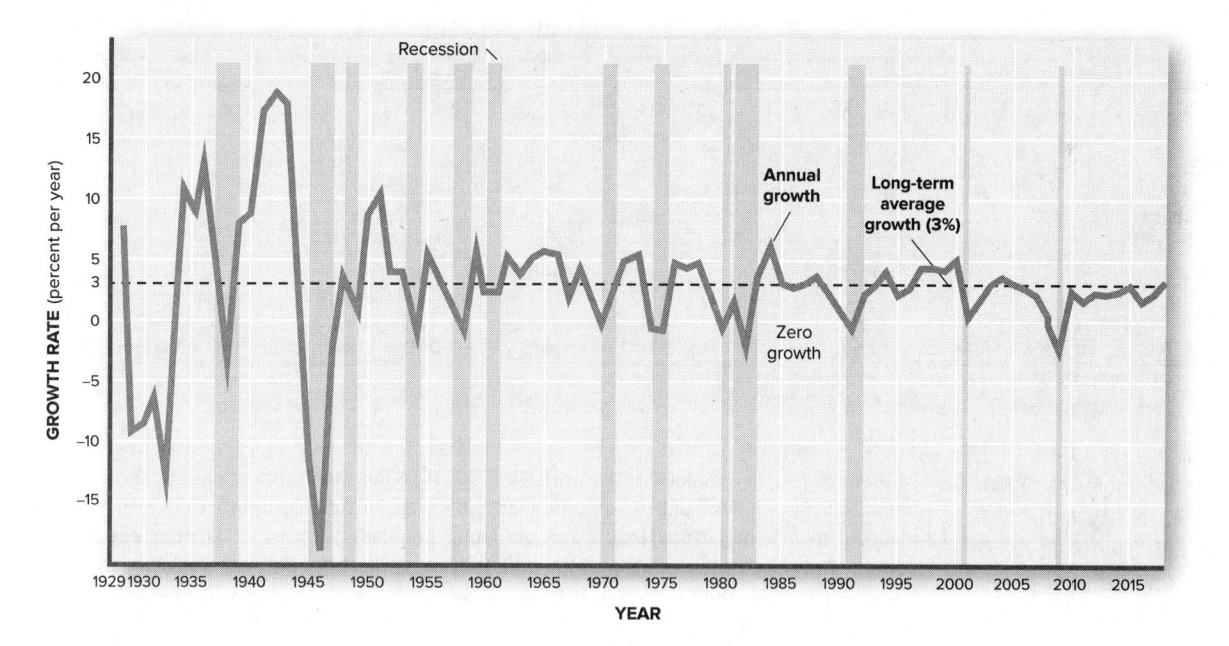

Figure 9.2 The Business Cycle in U.S. History From 1929 to 2018, real GDP increased at an average rate of 3 percent a year. But annual growth rates have departed widely from that average. Years of above-average growth seem to alternate with years of sluggish growth and years in which total output actually *declines*. Such *recessions* occurred in 1980, 1981–1982, 1990–1991, 2001, and again in 2008–2009. ■

Source: U.S. Bureau of Economic Analysis.

---

depart widely 相去甚远。 alternate 交替。 sluggish 缓慢的。

经济并不总是运行得这么好。仔细观察图 9.2。横穿图表中部的水平虚线代表实际 GDP 增长率的长期平均值，即每年 3.0%。注意经济增长经常低于此平均值，并且当增长率低于 0、总产出从某一年到下一年实际上出现下降时，会发生周期性的经济衰退，如 2009 年。这些经历证实了，实际 GDP 并不会保持持续平稳的增长，而是以阶段性的、时断时续的形式增长，甚至有时会倒退。

The economy doesn't always perform so well. Take a closer look at Figure 9.2. The dashed horizontal line across the middle of the chart illustrates the long-term *average* real GDP growth rate, at 3.0 percent a year. Then notice how often the economy grew more slowly than that. Notice also the periodic economic busts when the growth rate fell below zero and total output actually *decreased* from one year to the next, as in 2009. This experience confirms that **real GDP increases not in consistent, smooth increments but in a pattern of steps, stumbles, and setbacks.**

The Great Depression　大萧条

The most prolonged setback occurred during the Great Depression. Between 1929 and 1933, total U.S. output steadily declined. Real GDP fell by nearly 30 percent in those four years. Industrial output declined even further, as investments in new plants and equipment virtually ceased. Economies around the world came to a grinding halt (see the News Wire "Worldwide Losses").

NEWS WIRE　WORLDWIDE LOSSES

DEPRESSION SLAMS WORLD ECONOMIES

The Great Depression was not confined to the U.S. economy. Most other countries suffered substantial losses of output and employment over a period of many years. Between 1929 and 1932, industrial production around the world fell 37 percent. The United States and Germany suffered the largest losses, while Spain and the Scandinavian countries lost only modest amounts of output. For specific countries, the decline in output is shown in the accompanying table.

Country	Percentage Decline in Industrial Output
Chile	−22%
France	−31
Germany	−47
Great Britain	−17
Japan	−2
Norway	−7
Spain	−12
United States	−46

NOTE: Trade and financial links make countries interdependent. When one economy falls into a recession, other economies may suffer as well.
注：贸易和金融往来使国家之间相互依存。当一个经济体陷入衰退状态时，其他经济体也可能受到影响。

美国经济于 1934 年再次开始增长，但是增长率却非常有限，数百万人仍然没有工作。1937—1938 年，形势再次恶化，总产出再次下降。因此，1939 年的总产出率几乎与 1929 年持平。由于人口持续增长，1939 年的人均 GDP 实际上低于 1929 年。1939 年美国家庭的生活水平低于他们 10 年前的水平。这在以前从未发生过。

The U.S. economy started to grow again in 1934, but the rate of expansion was modest. Millions of people remained out of work. In 1937–1938 the situation worsened again, and total output once more declined. As a consequence, the rate of total output in 1939 was virtually identical to that in 1929. Because of continuing population growth, **GDP per capita was actually *lower* in 1939 than it had been in 1929**. American families had a *lower* standard of living in 1939 than they had enjoyed 10 years earlier. That had never happened before.

World War II　第二次世界大战

World War II greatly increased the demand for goods and services and ended the Great Depression. During the war years, output grew at unprecedented rates—almost 19 percent in a single year (1942). Virtually everyone was employed, either in the armed forces or in the factories. Throughout the war, our productive capacity was strained to the limit.

---

setback 倒退。　a grinding halt 突然停下。　substantial 重大的，巨大的。　unprecedented 史无前例的。　be strained to the limit 达到了极限，竭尽全力。

Dates	Duration (Months)	Percentage Decline in Output	Peak Unemployment Rate
Aug. 1929–Mar. 1933	43	−26.7%	24.9%
May 1937–June 1938	13	−18.2	19.0
Feb. 1945–Oct. 1945	8	−12.7	5.2
Nov. 1948–Oct. 1949	11	−1.7	7.9
July 1953–May 1954	10	−2.6	6.1
Aug. 1957–Apr. 1958	8	−3.7	7.5
Apr. 1960–Feb. 1961	10	−1.6	7.1
Dec. 1969–Nov. 1970	11	−0.6	6.1
Nov. 1973–Mar. 1975	16	−3.2	9.0
Jan. 1980–July 1980	6	−2.2	7.8
July 1981–Nov. 1982	16	−2.7	10.8
July 1990–Feb. 1991	8	−1.4	7.8
Mar. 2001–Nov. 2001	8	−0.3	6.3
Dec. 2007–June 2009	18	−5.1	10.0

Table 9.1 Business Slumps, 1929–2009 The U.S. economy has experienced 14 business slumps since 1929. None of the post–World War II recessions came close to the severity of the Great Depression of the 1930s. Recent slumps have averaged 10 months in length (versus 10 *years* for the 1930s depression). ∎

Recent Recessions 近代的衰退

After World War II the U.S. economy resumed a pattern of alternating growth and contraction. The contracting periods are called recessions. Specifically, the term **recession** refers to a decline in real GDP that continues for at least two successive calendar quarters. As Table 9.1 indicates, there have been 12 recessions since 1944. The most severe recession occurred immediately after World War II ended, when sudden cutbacks in defense production caused sharp declines in output. That first postwar recession lasted only eight months, however, and raised the rate of unemployment to just 5.2 percent. By contrast, the recession of 1981–1982 was much longer (16 months) and pushed the national unemployment rate to 10.8 percent. That was the highest unemployment rate since the Great Depression of the 1930s. The recession of 2008–2009 again pushed the unemployment rate up to 10 percent.

UNEMPLOYMENT 失业

Although the primary measure of the economy's health is the real GDP growth rate, that measure is a bit impersonal. *People*, not just output, suffer in recessions. When output declines, *jobs* are eliminated. In the 2008–2009 recession, more than 8 million American workers lost their jobs. Other would-be workers—including graduating students—had great difficulty finding jobs. These are the human dimensions of a recession.

The Labor Force 劳动力

Our concern about the human side of recession doesn't mean that we believe *everyone* should have a job. We do, however, strive to ensure that jobs are available for all individuals who *want* to work. This requires us to distinguish the general population from the smaller number of individuals who are ready and willing to work—that is, those who are in the **labor force**. The ***labor force consists of everyone over the age of 16 who is actually working plus all those who***

在经济衰退中我们对人的关注并不意味着我们认为人人都应该有份工作。事实上，我们所做的是确保所有想要工作的人都得到工作。这就要求我们将

---

slump 低迷期。 severity 严重性。 resume 恢复。 calendar quarter 季度。

are not working but are actively seeking employment. As Figure 9.3 shows, only about half of the population participates in the labor market. The rest of the population (nonparticipants) are too young, in school, retired, sick or disabled, institutionalized, or taking care of household needs.

Note that our definition of labor force participation excludes most household and volunteer activities. A woman who chooses to devote her energies to household responsibilities or to unpaid charity work is not counted as part of the labor force, no matter how hard she works. Because she is neither in paid employment nor seeking such employment in the marketplace, she is regarded as outside the labor market (a nonparticipant). But if she decides to seek a paid job outside the home and engages in an active job search, we would say that she is "entering the labor force." Students, too, are typically out of the labor force until they leave school and actively look for work, either during summer vacations or after graduation.

The Unemployment Rate 失业率

To assess how well labor force participants are faring in the macro economy, we compute the **unemployment rate** as follows:

$$\text{Unemployment rate} = \frac{\text{number of unemployed people}}{\text{size of the labor force}}$$

To be counted as *unemployed*, a person must be both jobless *and* actively looking for work. A full-time student, for example, may be jobless but would not be counted as unemployed. Likewise, a full-time homemaker who is not looking for paid employment outside the home would not be included in our measure of **unemployment**.

Figure 9.3 indicates that 7 million Americans were counted as unemployed in 2017. The civilian labor force (excluding the armed forces) at that time included 156 million individuals. Accordingly, the civilian unemployment *rate* was

$$\text{Civilian unemployment rate in 2017} = \frac{7 \text{ million unemployed}}{160 \text{ million in labor force}} = 4.4\%$$

Total population (326 million)

Out of the labor force (166 million)   In the **labor force** (160 million)

Under age 16 (66 million)
Homemakers (13 million)
In school (15 million)
Retired (45 million)
In institutions (4 million)
Other (23 million)

Employed (153 million)
Unemployed (7 million)

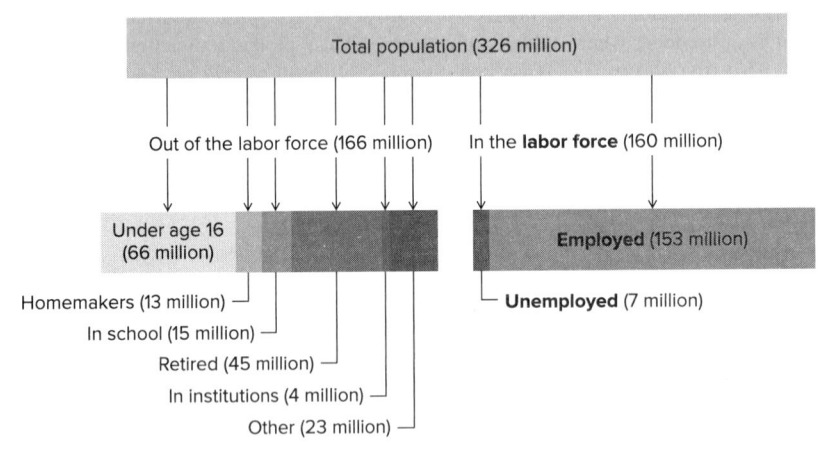

Figure 9.3 The U.S. Labor Force Only half of the total U.S. population participates in the civilian labor force. The rest of the population is too young, in school, at home, retired, or otherwise unavailable. Unemployment statistics count only those participants who are not currently working *and* who are actively seeking paid employment. Nonparticipants are neither employed nor actively seeking employment. ■

Source: "Labor Force Statistics from the Current Population Survey," U.S. Department of Labor, 2017; and "The U.S. Labor Force," U.S. Bureau of Census, 2017.

As Figure 9.4 illustrates, the unemployment rate in 2017 was well below the peaks reached in the Great Recession of 2008–2009. The unemployment rate continued to fall in 2018, as the economy expanded.

As noted earlier, the unemployment rate is our second measure of the economy's health. It is often regarded as an index of human misery. The people who lose their jobs in a recession experience not only a sudden loss of income, but also losses of security and self-confidence. Extended periods of unemployment may undermine families as well as finances. One study showed that every percentage increase in the unemployment rate causes an additional 10,000 divorces. An unemployed person's health may suffer too. Thomas Cottle, a lecturer at Harvard Medical School, stated the case more bluntly: "I'm now convinced that unemployment is *the* killer disease in this country—responsible for wife beating, infertility, and even tooth decay." The News Wire "Social Costs of Job Loss" documents some of the symptoms on which such diagnoses are based.

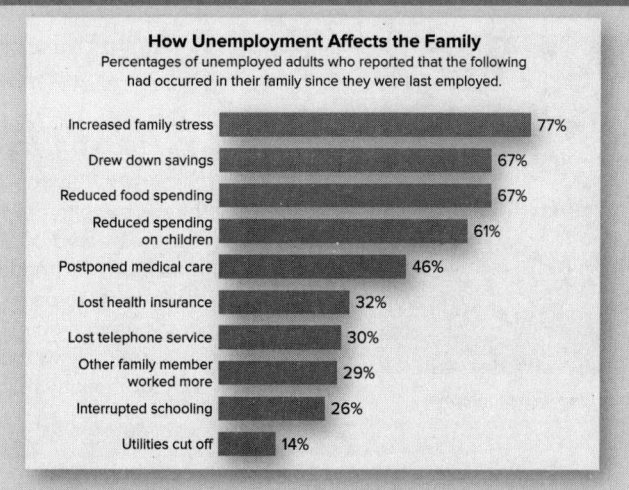

NEWS WIRE SOCIAL COSTS OF JOB LOSS

How Unemployment Affects the Family
Percentages of unemployed adults who reported that the following had occurred in their family since they were last employed.

Increased family stress	77%
Drew down savings	67%
Reduced food spending	67%
Reduced spending on children	61%
Postponed medical care	46%
Lost health insurance	32%
Lost telephone service	30%
Other family member worked more	29%
Interrupted schooling	26%
Utilities cut off	14%

Source: Peter D. Hart, "Unemployed in America: The Job Market, the Realities of Unemployment, and the Impact of Unemployment Benefits," National Employment Law Project, April 2003.

NOTE: The cost of unemployment goes beyond the implied loss of output. Unemployment may breed despair, crime, ill health, and other social problems.
注：失业的代价超出了潜在产出的损失。失业可能滋生绝望、犯罪、疾病和其他社会问题。

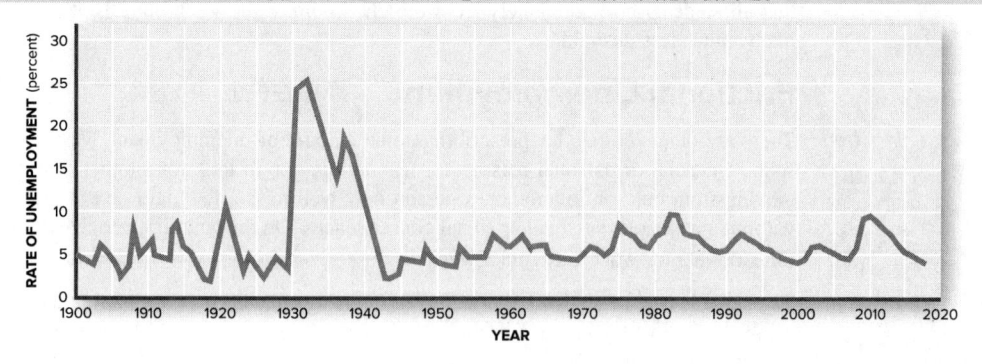

Figure 9.4 The Unemployment Record Unemployment rates reached record heights during the Great Depression. The postwar record is much better than the prewar record, even though full employment has been infrequent.

Source: "Unemployment Record," U.S. Department of Labor, 2019.

---

undermine 破坏。bluntly 坦率地。infertility 不孕症。diagnose 诊断。

The Full Employment Goal 充分就业目标

考虑到高失业率给人们带来的痛苦，保证所有劳动力参与者都能得到工作似乎是应该的。然而事情永远不会如此简单。"宏观经济医生"从不提议消除失业。相反，他们会开出一个低水平失业率但不是零失业率的"处方"。他们得出这一结论有以下几个理由。

In view of the human misery caused by high unemployment rates, it might seem desirable to guarantee every labor force participant a job. But things are never that simple. The macroeconomic doctors never propose to *eliminate* unemployment. They instead prescribe a *low*, but not a *zero*, unemployment rate. They come to this conclusion for several reasons.

Seasonal Unemployment 季节性失业

Seasonal variations in employment conditions are a persistent source of unemployment. Some joblessness is inevitable as long as we continue to grow crops, build houses, go skiing, or send holiday gifts (see the News Wire "Seasonal Unemployment") during certain seasons of the year. At the end of each of these seasons, thousands of workers must search for new jobs, experiencing some seasonal unemployment in the process.

NEWS WIRE SEASONAL UNEMPLOYMENT

©McGraw-Hill Education/Andrew Resek, photographer

SHIPPERS, RETAILERS HIRING THOUSANDS FOR THE HOLIDAY SEASON

The holiday season not only brings gifts and decorations, but also thousands of temporary jobs. United Parcel Service (UPS), the world's largest courier company, will hire an additional 100,000 employees to help deliver the expected avalanche of Christmas packages. Amazon, the nation's second largest employer after Walmart, expects to hire an additional 125,000 temporary employees. Retailers like Walmart, Macy's, and Kohl's are looking to hire more than 50,000 each to cope with the holiday rush.

Source: News accounts of October 2018.

NOTE: Some jobs are inherently seasonal. What happens to these UPS workers after the Christmas rush?
注：有些工作岗位本来就是季节性的。在圣诞节高峰过后，联邦快递的这些工人将何去何从？

Seasonal fluctuations also arise on the supply side of the labor market. Teenage unemployment rates, for example, rise sharply in the summer as students look for temporary jobs. To avoid such unemployment completely, we would either have to keep everyone in school or ensure that all students go immediately from the classroom to the workroom. Neither alternative is likely, much less desirable.

Frictional Unemployment 摩擦性失业

存在一定数量的失业人口还有其他原因。许多人有充分的经济或个人原因离开一份工作而去找另一份工作。在此过程中，这些人可能几天甚至几周没有工作，但是对于个人和社会都不会产生严重影响。相反，那些花很长时间去寻找工作的人，往往能找到更好的工作。

There are other reasons for prescribing some amount of unemployment. Many workers have sound financial or personal reasons for leaving one job to look for another. In the process of moving from one job to another, a person may well miss a few days or even weeks of work without any serious personal or social consequences. On the contrary, people who spend more time looking for work may find *better* jobs.

The same is true of students first entering the labor market. It is not likely that you will find a job the moment you leave school. Nor should you necessarily take the first job offered. If you spend some time looking for work, you are more likely to find a job you like. The job search period gives you an opportunity to find out what kinds of jobs are available, what skills they require, and what they pay. Accordingly, a brief period of job search for persons entering the labor market may benefit both the individual involved and the larger economy. The unemployment associated with this kind of job search is referred to as *frictional* unemployment.

---

fluctuation 波动。temporary 临时的。

Structural Unemployment 结构性失业

For many job seekers, the period between jobs may drag on for months or even years because they do not have the skills that employers require. In the early 1980s, the steel and auto industries downsized, eliminating over half a million jobs. The displaced workers had years of work experience. But their specific skills were no longer in demand. They were *structurally unemployed*. The same fate befell programmers and software engineers when the "dot.com" boom burst in 2000–2001, and then skilled craft workers in the 2006–2008 housing contraction.

High school dropouts suffer similar structural problems. They simply don't have the skills that today's jobs require. When such structural unemployment exists, more job creation alone won't necessarily reduce unemployment. On the contrary, more job demand might simply push wages higher for skilled workers, leaving unskilled workers unemployed.

Cyclical Unemployment 周期性失业

There is a fourth kind of unemployment that is more worrisome to the macroeconomic doctors. *Cyclical* unemployment refers to the joblessness that occurs when there are simply not enough jobs to go around. Cyclical unemployment exists when the number of workers demanded falls short of the number of persons in the labor force. This is not a case of mobility between jobs (frictional unemployment) or even of job seekers' skills (structural unemployment). Rather, it is simply an inadequate level of demand for goods and services and thus for labor.

The Great Depression is the most striking example of cyclical unemployment. The dramatic increase in unemployment rates that began in 1930 (see Figure 9.4) was not due to any increase in friction or sudden decline in workers' skills. Instead the high rates of unemployment that persisted for a *decade* were due to a sudden decline in the market demand for goods and services. How do we know? Just notice what happened to our unemployment rate when the demand for military goods and services increased in 1941!

The Policy Goal 政策目标

In later chapters, we examine the causes of cyclical unemployment and explore some potential policy responses. At this point, all we want to do is to set some goals for macro policy. We have seen that there are four types of unemployment, namely:

- Seasonal unemployment
- Frictional unemployment
- Structural unemployment
- Cyclical unemployment

Because some seasonal, frictional, and structural unemployment is both inevitable and desirable, zero unemployment is not an appropriate policy goal. But what, then, is a desirable level of *low* unemployment? If we want to assess macro policy, we need to know what specific rate of unemployment to shoot for.

There is some disagreement about the level of unemployment that constitutes **full employment**. Most macroeconomists agree, however, that the optimal unemployment rate lies somewhere between 4 and 6 percent.

INFLATION 通货膨胀

When the unemployment rate falls to its full employment level, you might expect everyone to cheer. This rarely happens, though. Indeed, when the jobless rate declines, a lot of macroeconomists start to fret. Too much of a good thing, they worry, might cause some harm. The harm they fear is *inflation*.

---

worrisome 令人担忧的。 striking 显著的，突出的。 fret 担心，焦虑。

The fear of inflation is based on the price pressures that accompany capacity production. When the economy presses against its production possibilities, idle resources are hard to find. An imbalance between the demand and supply of goods may cause prices to start rising. The resulting inflation may cause a whole new type of pain. Even a low level of inflation pinches family pocketbooks, upsets financial markets, and ignites a storm of political protest. Runaway inflations do even more harm; they crush whole economies and topple governments. In Germany prices rose more than twenty-five-fold in only one month during the *hyperinflation* of 1922–1923. As the News Wire "Hyperinflation" describes, those runaway prices forced people to change their market behavior radically. In 2018, the rate of inflation reached 200,000 percent in Venezuela. Such uncontrolled inflation sent consumers scrambling for goods that became increasingly hard to find at "reasonable" prices. In 2009 prices rose an incomprehensible 231 *million* percent in Zimbabwe. At the height of Zimbabwe's inflation, prices were rising by a factor of 10 per day. That means that a Starbucks latte that cost $4 today would cost $40 tomorrow. Such runaway inflation caused an economic and political crisis that shrank Zimbabwe's output by 30 percent. To avoid that kind of economic disruption, every American president since Franklin Roosevelt has expressed a determination to keep prices from rising.

NEWS WIRE HYPERINFLATION

HYPERINFLATION BRINGS WEIMAR REPUBLIC TO STANDSTILL

The world had never experienced the kind of hyperinflation that crippled the Weimar Republic in the 1920s. In 1920, wholesale prices rose fortyfold and retail prices rose even more. That kind of inflation wiped out consumer saving and made business planning near impossible.

But that was only the beginning: Prices skyrocketed at an unbelievable pace in 1923. In just one month (May 1923), consumer prices quadrupled. Between July and August, prices rose more than 15 times their July level. That was still not the end. In September, prices rose 25 times their base and another 10 times in October. The rate of inflation in October 1923 was nearly 30,000 percent. A dozen eggs that cost 3 Reichmarks in 1921 cost 500 Reichmarks in January 1923, 30 million Reichmarks in September 1923, and an astonishing 4 billion Reichmarks in October 1923. In early 1922, a U.S. dollar was worth 320 million Reichmarks; in November 1923, a dollar was worth 4.2 trillion Reichmarks.

How did Germans cope with such runaway prices? Consumers tried to buy anything and everything they could before prices rose further. Companies started paying their workers two or three times a day, before their paychecks lost more value. People needed barrels of currency to purchase goods—if they could find them. Production ground to a halt and unemployment mushroomed.

Source: Historical archives.

NOTE: When prices are rising quickly, people are forced to change their market behavior. Runaway inflation can derail an economy.
注：当价格迅速上涨时，人们被迫改变他们的市场行为。失控的通货膨胀会使一国经济脱轨。

Relative versus Average Prices 相对价格与平均价格

尽管大多数人都担心通货膨胀，却很少有人理解它。大多数人会将特定商品和服务的价格上涨与**通货膨胀**联系起来。然而，并不是每杯咖啡价格的每次上涨都必然意味着经济正在经历着通货膨胀。我们必须仔细地将通货膨胀现象与特定商品的价格上涨区分开来。通货膨胀是平均价格水平的上涨，而不是任何特定商品价格的改变。

Although most people worry about inflation, few understand it. Most people associate **inflation** with price increases on specific goods and services. The economy is not necessarily experiencing inflation, however, every time the price of a cup of coffee goes up. We must be careful to distinguish the phenomenon of inflation from price increases for specific goods. *Inflation is an increase in the average level of prices, not a change in any specific price.*

Suppose you wanted to know the average price of fruit in the supermarket. Surely you would not have much success in seeking out an average fruit—nobody would be quite sure what you had in mind. You might have some success, however, if you sought the prices of apples, oranges, cherries, and peaches. Knowing the price of each kind of fruit, you could then

---

press against 挤压，压在……上。 pinch 使收缩，缩小。 hyperinflation 恶性通货膨胀。 radically 彻底地，根本上。 quadruple 四倍，翻两番。 mushroom 快速增长。

compute the average price of fruit. The resultant figure would not refer to any particular product but would convey a sense of how much a typical basket of fruit might cost. By repeating these calculations every day, you could then determine whether fruit prices, *on average*, were changing. On occasion, you might even notice that apple prices rose while orange prices fell, leaving the *average* price of fruit unchanged.

The same kinds of calculations are made to measure inflation in the entire economy. We first determine the average price of all output—the average price level—then look for changes in that average. A rise in the average price level is referred to as *inflation*.

The average price level may fall as well as rise. A decline in average prices—**deflation**—occurs when price decreases on some goods and services outweigh price increases on all others. Although we have not experienced any general deflation since 1940, general price declines were common in earlier periods.

Because inflation and deflation are measured in terms of average price levels, it is possible for individual prices to rise or fall continuously without changing the average price level. We already noted, for example, that the price of apples can rise without increasing the average price of fruit, so long as the price of some other fruit (e.g., oranges) falls. In such circumstances, **relative prices** are changing, but not average prices. An increase in the relative price of apples, for example, simply means that apples have become more expensive in comparison with other fruits (or any other goods or services).

Changes in relative prices may occur in a period of stable average prices or in periods of inflation or deflation. In fact, in an economy as vast as ours—where literally millions of goods and services are exchanged in the factor and product markets—relative prices are always changing. Indeed, relative price changes are an essential ingredient of the market mechanism. If the relative price of apples increases, that is a signal to farmers that they should grow more apples and fewer other fruits.

General inflation—an increase in the *average* price level—does not perform this same market function. If all prices rise at the same rate, price increases for specific goods are of little value as market signals. In less extreme cases, when most but not all prices are rising, changes in relative prices do occur but are not so immediately apparent.

Redistributions 再分配

The distinction between relative and average prices helps us determine who is hurt by inflation—and who is helped. Popular opinion notwithstanding, it is simply not true that everyone is worse off when prices rise. *Although inflation makes some people worse off, it makes other people better off.* Some people even get rich when prices rise! These redistributions of income and wealth occur because people buy different combinations of goods and services, own different assets, and sell distinct goods or services (including labor). The impact of inflation on individuals, therefore, depends on how the prices of the goods and services each person buys or sells actually change. In this sense, *inflation acts just like a tax, taking income or wealth from some people and giving it to others.* This "tax" is levied through changes in prices, changes in incomes, and changes in wealth.

Price Effects 价格效应

Price changes are the most familiar of inflation's pains. If you have been paying tuition, you know how the pain feels. In 1975 the average tuition at public colleges and universities was $400 per year. In 2018, in-state tuition was $10,230 and still rising (see the News Wire "Price Effects"). At private universities, tuition has increased eightfold in the last 10 years, to roughly $36,000. You don't need a whole course in economics to figure out the implications of these tuition hikes. To stay in college, you (or your parents) must forgo increasing amounts of other goods and services. You end up being worse off because you cannot buy as many goods and services as you were able to buy before tuition went up.

---

deflation 通货紧缩。outweigh 超过。literally 确实地，真正地。forgo 放弃。

由于通货膨胀与通货紧缩都是根据平均价格水平来衡量的，因此在不改变平均价格水平的情况下，个别价格可以不断上涨或下降。例如我们已经注意到的，只要其他某种水果（如橘子）的价格下降，苹果价格上涨就不会改变水果的平均价格。在这种情况下，**相对价格**在发生变化，而不是平均价格。例如，苹果相对价格的上涨只是意味着苹果与其他水果（或任何其他商品或服务）相比变得更加昂贵。

相对价格和平均价格的区别有助于我们确定谁受到了通货膨胀的损害，谁在通货膨胀中受益。尽管大众的观点认为在价格上涨时所有人的状况都会变差，但事实并非如此。虽然通货膨胀使一些人处境更糟，但也使其他人从中受益。当价格上涨时，一些人甚至变得更加富有。这种收入和财富的重新分配之所以出现，是由于人们购买不同组合的商品和服务，拥有不同资产，并出售不同的商品或服务（包括劳动力）。因此，通货膨胀对个人的影响取决于人们购买或出售的商品和服务的价格变化情况。从这个意义上说，通货膨胀扮演了与税收同样的角色，它剥夺了一些人的收入或财富，再转交到其他人手中。而这种"税"是在价格、收入和财富的变化中征收的。

NEWS WIRE PRICE EFFECTS

COLLEGE COSTS KEEP RISING

The price of attending college has gone up again. According to the nonprofit College Board, in-state tuition at four-year public colleges rose to $10,230 this year, up another $400 from last year. Tuition at private colleges is up to nearly $36,000 a year. Over the last 10 years, college tuition has increased by 4.5 percent a year, while average consumer prices have risen by only 1.3 percent a year. These tuition hikes are making college attendance increasingly expensive and difficult for many families.

Source: "Trends in College Pricing," *The College Board*, 2018.

NOTE: An increase in tuition reduces the real income of college students, forcing them to reduce spending on other goods and services.
注：提高学费降低了大学生的实际收入，迫使他们减少了在其他商品和服务上的支出。

学费上涨对你的经济福利的影响反映在名义收入与实际收入的区别上。**名义收入**指你在特定时期内得到的货币额，以现时的美元衡量。相比之下，**实际收入**指这些货币的购买力，以你的美元所能购买的商品和服务的数量来衡量。如果你每年所得到的美元数都相同，那么你的名义收入不变；但是如果价格上涨，那么你的实际收入就会下降。

The effect of tuition increases on your economic welfare is reflected in the distinction between nominal income and real income. **Nominal income** is the amount of money you receive in a particular time period; it is measured in current dollars. **Real income**, by contrast, is the purchasing power of that money, as measured by the quantity of goods and services your dollars will buy. If the number of dollars you receive every year is always the same, your *nominal income* doesn't change, but your *real income* will fall if prices increase.

Suppose you have an income of $6,000 a year while you're in school. Out of that $6,000 you must pay for your tuition, room and board, books, and everything else. The budget for your first year at school might look like this:

First Year's Budget	
Nominal income	$6,000
Consumption	
Tuition	$3,000
Room and board	2,000
Books	300
Everything else	700
Total	$6,000

After paying for all your essential expenses, you have $700 to spend on "everything else"—the clothes, entertainment, or whatever else you want.

Now suppose tuition increases to $3,500 in your second year, while all other prices remain the same. What will happen to your nominal income? Nothing. You're still getting $6,000 a year. Your *real* income, however, will suffer. This is evident in the second year's budget:

Second Year's Budget	
Nominal income	$6,000
Consumption	
Tuition	$3,500
Room and board	2,000
Books	300
Everything else	200
Total	$6,000

---

tuition 学费。suffer 受损。

Item	Price Change in 2017 (percent)
Eggs	+11.6
Gasoline	+10.7
Oranges	+8.9
Cigarettes	+6.6
Cable TV service	+4.8
Average price level	+2.1
Apples	−2.6
Peanut butter	−3.5
Airfares	−4.0
Televisions	−6.3
Cell phone service	−10.2

Table 9.2 Not All Prices Rise at the Same Rate The average rate of inflation conceals substantial differences in the price changes of specific goods and services. The impact of inflation on individuals depends in part on which goods and services are consumed. People who buy goods whose prices are rising fastest lose more real income.
Source: "Average Price Data (in U.S. dollars)," *Graphics for Economic News Releases,* August 20, 2018.

You now have to use more of your income to pay tuition. This means you have less income to spend on other things. After paying for room and board, books, and the increased tuition, only $200 is left for everything else. That means fewer pizzas, movies, dates, or anything else you'd like to buy. The pain of higher tuition will soon be evident; your *nominal income* hasn't changed, but your *real income* has.

There are two basic lessons about inflation to be learned from this sad story:

- *Not all prices rise at the same rate during inflation.* In our example, tuition increased substantially while other prices remained steady. Hence the "average" rate of price increase was not representative of any particular good or service. Typically some prices rise rapidly, others rise only modestly, and some may actually fall. Table 9.2 illustrates some recent variations in price changes. In 2017 average prices rose by 2.1 percent. But the average rate of inflation disguised very steep price hikes for eggs, oranges, cable service, gasoline, and cigarettes.
- *Not everyone suffers equally from inflation.* This follows from our first observation. Those people who consume the goods and services that are rising faster in price bear a greater burden of inflation; their real incomes fall more. In 2017 people who ate oranges and eggs for breakfast were hurt badly by changing food prices. People who preferred a diet of apples and peanut butter scored real gains from falling prices. By contrast, students got ripped by rising tuition and textbook prices.

We conclude, then, that *the price increases associated with inflation redistribute real income.* In the example we have discussed, college students end up with fewer goods and services than they had before. Other consumers can continue to purchase at least as many goods as before, perhaps even more. Thus output is effectively *redistributed* from college students to others. Naturally, most college students aren't happy with this outcome. Fortunately for you, inflation doesn't always work out this way.

Income Effects 收入效应

The redistributive effects of inflation are not limited to changes in prices. Changes in prices automatically influence nominal incomes also.

- 在通货膨胀期间并不是所有价格都以相同的比率上涨。在我们的例子中，学费显著上涨，而其他价格保持稳定。因此"平均"价格涨幅并不代表任何特定商品或服务的上涨幅度。
- 并非所有人都在通货膨胀中遭受同样的损失。这是在我们的第一个观察中得出的结论。那些消费了价格上涨较快的商品和服务的人承受着更大的通胀负担；他们的实际收入下降更多。

于是我们得出结论，价格上涨总是伴随着通货膨胀对实际收入的重新分配。在我们讨论的例子中，大学生最后所得到的商品和服务比以前少。其他消费者可以继续购买至少和以前一样多的商品，甚至会更多。因此产出被有效地从大学生手中重新分配给了其他消费者。当然，大多数大学生都会对这个结果感到不满。幸运的是，通货膨胀并不总是以这样的方式进行。

---

conceal 隐藏，遮住。disguise 掩饰，掩盖。

If the price of tuition does in fact rise faster than all other prices, we can safely make three predictions:

- The *real income* of college students will fall relative to that of nonstudents (assuming constant nominal incomes).
- The *real income* of nonstudents will rise relative to that of students (assuming constant nominal incomes).
- The *nominal income* of colleges and universities will rise.

最后一个预测只是为了提醒我们，总有人因较高的价格而获益。对买方而言是价格，对卖方而言是收入。如果所有学生都缴纳更高的学费，学校将得到更多收入。当价格上涨以后，学校最终将有能力购买比以前更多的商品和服务（包括教员、建筑和图书馆藏书）。大学的名义收入和实际收入都增加了。

This last prediction simply reminds us that someone always pockets higher prices. ***What looks like a price to a buyer looks like income to a seller.*** If students all pay higher tuition, the university will take in more income. It will end up being able to buy *more* goods and services (including faculty, buildings, and library books) after the price increase than it could before. Both its nominal income and its real income have risen.

Not everyone gets more nominal income when prices rise. But you may be surprised to learn that *on average* people's incomes *do* keep pace with inflation. Again, this is a direct consequence of the circular flow: What one person pays out, someone else takes in. ***If prices are rising, incomes must be rising, too.*** Notice in Figure 9.5 that nominal wages have risen along with prices. In fact, nominal wages have risen *faster* than prices over time. As a result, *real* wages have risen. From this perspective, it makes no sense to say that "inflation hurts everybody." On *average*, at least, we are no worse off when prices rise, because our (average) incomes increase at the same time.

No one is exactly "average," of course. In reality, some people's incomes rise faster than inflation while others' increase more slowly. Hence the redistributive effects of inflation also originate in varying rates of growth in nominal income.

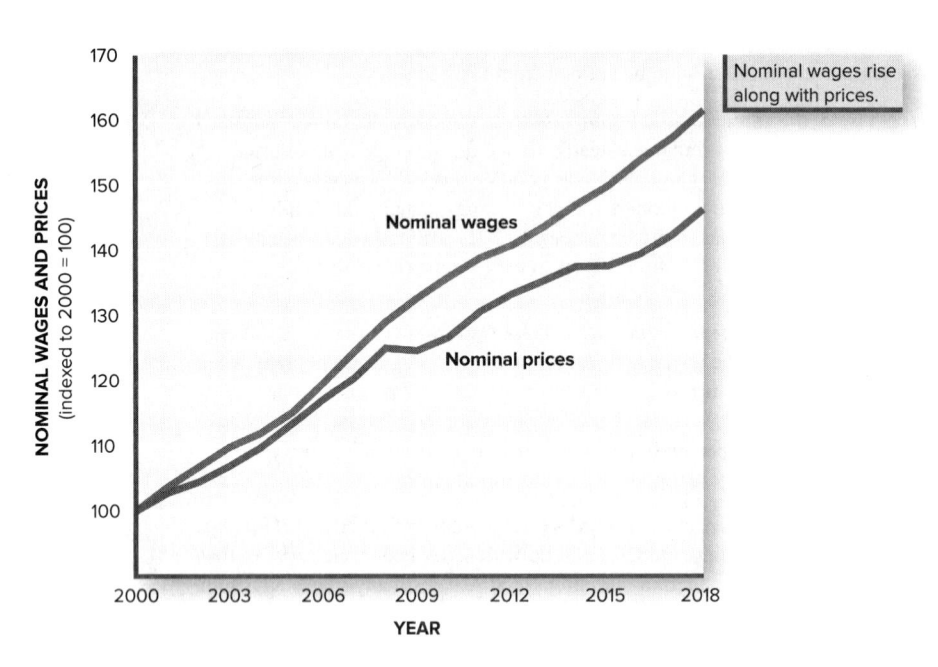

Figure 9.5 Nominal Wages and Prices Inflation implies not only higher prices but higher wages as well. What is a price to one person is income to someone else. Hence inflation cannot make *everyone* worse off. This graph confirms that average hourly wages have risen along with average prices. When nominal wages rise faster than prices, *real* wages are increasing.

Source: "Employment Cost Index Summary," News Release, Bureau of Labor Statistics, U.S. Department of Labor.

Year	Annual Inflation Rate				
	2 Percent	4 Percent	6 Percent	8 Percent	10 Percent
2019	$1,000	$1,000	$1,000	$1,000	$1,000
2020	980	962	943	926	909
2021	961	925	890	857	826
2022	942	889	840	794	751
2023	924	855	792	735	683
2024	906	822	747	681	621
2025	888	790	705	630	564
2026	871	760	665	584	513
2027	853	731	627	540	467
2028	837	703	592	500	424
2029	820	676	558	463	386

Table 9.3 Inflation's Impact, 2019–2029 In the 1990s, the U.S. rate of inflation ranged from a low of 1.6 percent to a high of 6.1 percent. Does a range of 4–5 percentage points really make much difference? One way to find out is to see how a specific sum of money will shrink in real value.

Here's what would happen to the *real* value of $1,000 from January 1, 2019, to January 1, 2029, at different inflation rates. At 2 percent inflation, $1,000 held for 10 years would be worth $820. At 10 percent inflation that same $1,000 would buy only $386 worth of goods in the year 2029. ■

Wealth Effects   财富效应

The same kind of redistribution occurs between those who hold some form of wealth and those who do not. Suppose that on January 1 you deposit $100 in a savings account, where it earns 5 percent interest until you withdraw it on December 31. At the end of the year you will have more nominal wealth ($105) than you started with ($100). But what if all prices have doubled in the meantime? At the end of the year, your accumulated savings ($105) buy less than they would have at the start of the year. In other words, inflation in this case reduces the *real* value of your savings. You end up with fewer goods and services than those individuals who spent all their income earlier in the year! Table 9.3 shows how even modest rates of inflation alter the real value of money hidden under the mattress for 10 years. German households saw the value of their savings approach zero when *hyper*inflation set in (see the News Wire "Hyperinflation").

Table 9.4 shows how the value of various assets actually changed in the 1990s. Between 1991 and 2001, the average price level rose by 32 percent. The price of stocks increased much faster, however, while the price of gold fell. Hence people who held their wealth in the form of stocks rather than gold came out far ahead. The *nominal* values of bonds and silver rose as well, but their *real* value fell.

Robin Hood?   罗宾汉

By altering relative prices, incomes, and the real value of wealth, then, inflation turns out to be a mechanism for redistributing incomes. ***The redistributive mechanics of inflation include***

- ***Price effects.*** People who prefer goods and services that are increasing in price are the slowest to end up with a larger share of real income.

● 价格效应　那些青睐价格上涨最慢的商品和服务的人，最后将得到更多的实际收入份额。

---

withdraw 提款，取钱。approach 接近，临近。

Asset	Change in Value, 1991–2001
Stocks	+250%
Diamonds	+71
Oil	+66
Housing	+56
U.S. farmland	+49
Average price of goods	**+32**
Silver	+22
Bonds	+20
Stamps	−9
Gold	−29

Table 9.4 The Real Story of Wealth As the value of various assets changes, so does a person's wealth. Between 1991 and 2001, prices rose an average of 32 percent. But the prices of stocks, diamonds, and oil rose even faster. People who held these assets gained in *real* (inflation-adjusted) wealth. Home prices also rose more than average prices. Hence the *real* value of homes also increased in the 1990s. Investors in silver, bonds, and gold did not fare as well.

- 收入效应 名义收入增速快于通货膨胀率的人，最后将得到更多的实际收入份额。
- 财富效应 拥有实际价值上涨的资产的人，最后将比其他人更加富有。

另一方面，名义收入跟不上通货膨胀步伐的人，最后只得到较少的总产出份额。喜欢价格上涨最快的商品或持有实际价值正在下降的资产的人，会有同样的遭遇。在此意义上，通货膨胀扮演了与税收同样的角色，剥夺一部分人的收入或财富，又转交到其他人手中。但是我们不能确保这种特殊的"税收"会像罗宾汉那样能够劫富济贫。也许结果刚好相反。难以获悉的是，谁能够获得通货膨胀的好处，谁又将在通货膨胀过程中遭受损失，这使每个人都对价格水平的上涨充满畏惧。

- *Income effects.* People whose nominal incomes rise faster than the rate of inflation end up with a larger share of total income.
- *Wealth effects.* People who own assets that are increasing in real value end up better off than others.

On the other hand, people whose nominal incomes do not keep pace with inflation end up with smaller shares of total output. The same thing is true of those who enjoy goods that are rising fastest in price or who hold assets that are declining in real value. In this sense, **inflation acts like a tax, taking income or wealth from one group and giving it to another.** But we have no assurance that this particular tax will behave like Robin Hood, taking from the rich and giving to the poor. It may do just the opposite. Not knowing who will win or lose the inflation sweepstakes may make everyone fear rising price levels.

Uncertainty 不确定性

The uncertainties of inflation may also cause people to change their consumption, saving, or investment behavior. When average prices are changing rapidly, economic decisions become increasingly difficult. Should you commit yourself to four years of college, for example, if you are not certain that you or your parents will be able to afford the full costs? In a period of stable prices you can at least be fairly certain of what a college education will cost over a period of years. But if prices are rising, you can no longer be sure how large the bill will be. Under such circumstances, many individuals may decide not to enter college rather than risk the possibility of being driven out later by rising costs. In extreme cases, fear of rapidly increasing prices may even deter diners from ordering a meal.

The uncertainties created by changing price levels affect production decisions as well. Imagine a firm that is considering building a new factory. Typically the construction of a factory takes two years or more, including planning, site selection, and actual construction. If construction costs change rapidly, the firm may find that it is unable to complete the factory or to operate it profitably. Confronted with this added uncertainty, the firm may decide to do without a new plant or at least to postpone its construction until a period of stable prices returns.

---

commit 承担，承诺。fairly 相当地。完全地。deter 阻止，使打消念头。

Measuring Inflation 衡量通货膨胀

Given the pain associated with inflation, it's no wonder that inflation rates are a basic barometer of macroeconomic health. To gauge that dimension of well-being, the government computes several price indexes. Of these indexes, the **consumer price index (CPI)** is the most familiar. As its name suggests, the CPI is a mechanism for measuring changes in the average price of consumer goods and services. It is analogous to the fruit price index we discussed earlier. The CPI refers not to the price of any particular good but, rather, to the average price of all consumer goods.

By itself, the "average price" of consumer goods is not a useful number. Once we know the average price of consumer goods, however, we can observe whether that average rises—that is, whether inflation is occurring. By observing how prices change, we can calculate the **inflation rate**—that is, the annual percentage increase in the average price level.

To compute the CPI, the Bureau of Labor Statistics periodically surveys families to determine what goods and services consumers actually buy. The Bureau of Labor Statistics then goes shopping in various cities across the country, recording the prices of 184 items that make up the typical market basket. This shopping survey is undertaken every month, in 85 areas and at a variety of stores in each area.

As a result of its surveys, the Bureau of Labor Statistics can tell us what's happening to consumer prices. Suppose, for example, that the market basket cost $100 last year and that the *same* basket of goods and services cost $110 this year. On the basis of those two shopping trips, we could conclude that consumer prices had risen by 10 percent in one year—that is, that the rate of inflation was 10 percent.

In practice, the CPI is usually expressed in terms of what the market basket cost in 1982–1984. For example, the CPI stood at 254 in January 2019. In other words, it cost $254 in 2019 to buy the same market basket that cost only $100 in the base period (1982–1984). Thus prices had more than doubled, on average, over that period. Each month the Bureau of Labor Statistics updates the CPI, telling us the current cost of that same market basket.

The Price Stability Goal 价格稳定目标

In view of the inequities, anxieties, and real losses caused by inflation, it is not surprising that price stability is a major goal of economic policy. As we observed at the beginning of this chapter, every American president since Franklin Roosevelt has decreed price stability to be a foremost policy goal. Unfortunately, few presidents (or their advisers) have stated exactly what they mean by *price stability*. Do they mean *no* change in the average price level? Or is some upward creep in the CPI consistent with the notion of price stability?

The Policy Goal 政策目标

An explicit numerical goal of **price stability** was established for the first time in the Full Employment and Balanced Growth Act of 1978. According to that act, the goal of economic policy is to hold the rate of inflation at under 3 percent.

Why did Congress choose 3 percent inflation rather than zero inflation as the benchmark for price stability? Two considerations were important. First, Congress recognized that efforts to maintain absolutely stable prices (zero inflation) might threaten full employment. Recall that our goal of full employment is defined as the lowest rate of unemployment *consistent with stable prices*. The same kind of thinking is apparent here. The amount of inflation regarded as tolerable depends in part on how anti-inflation strategies affect unemployment. If policies that promise zero inflation raise unemployment rates too high, people may prefer to accept a little inflation. After reviewing our experiences with both unemployment and inflation, Congress concluded that 3 percent inflation was a safe target.

---

price stability 价格稳定。benchmark 基准，标准。tolerable 可容忍的。

Quality Improvements 质量改进

将价格稳定目标定在零通货膨胀以上的第二个理由与衡量能力相关。尽管消费价格指数非常全面，却不是衡量通货膨胀的完美手段。本质上，CPI 只是监控了特定商品随时间发生的价格变化。然而，随着时间的推移，商品本身也发生了改变。原有产品由于质量改进而变得更好。今天的电视机比 1955 年价格更高，但同时也能传送更大、更清晰的图像——采用数字图像和立体声音响，甚至 3D 技术。因此电视机价格的上涨夸大了实际通货膨胀率：部分高价位代表了质量更高的产品。

The second argument for setting our price stability goal above zero inflation relates to our measurement capabilities. Although the consumer price index is very thorough, it is not a perfect measure of inflation. In essence, the CPI simply monitors the price of specific goods over time. Over time, however, the goods themselves change, too. Old products become better as a result of *quality improvements*. A television set costs more today than it did in 1955, but today's TV also delivers a bigger, clearer picture—in digital images, stereo sound, and even 3D. Hence increases in the price of television sets tend to exaggerate the true rate of inflation: Part of the higher price represents more product.

The same kind of quality changes distort our view of how car prices have changed. Since 1958 the average price of a new car has risen from $2,867 to roughly $36,000. But today's cars aren't really comparable to those of 1958. Since that time, the quality of cars has been improved with electronic ignitions, emergency flashers, rear window defrosters, crash-resistant bodies, air bags, antilock brakes, remote-control mirrors, seat belts, variable-speed windshield wipers, radial tires, GPS systems, a doubling of fuel mileage, and a hundredfold decrease in exhaust pollutants. Accordingly, the twelvefold increase in average car prices since 1958 greatly overstates the true rate of inflation.

New Products 新产品

The problem of measuring quality improvements is even more apparent in the case of new products. The smartphones most people have today did not exist when the Census Bureau conducted its 1982–1984 survey of consumer expenditures. The 2018 survey did include smartphones, but it couldn't fully capture the effects of their changing features. The iPhone XS (2018) has way more features than the original iPhone (2007), but the Census Bureau can't quantify those changes. All the Census Bureau can do is record the change in price. As new products and quality improvements continue to emerge, we end up getting more for our money. Hence, the recorded changes in prices will tend to overstate the burden of inflation. The goal of 3 percent inflation accommodates this measurement problem.

POLICY PERSPECTIVES

IS ANOTHER RECESSION COMING?

The simple answer to the above question is yes. There have been at least 47 recessions in the United States since 1790, 12 of them since 1944. So if history is any guide, we should expect to experience another recession.

But recessions don't occur on a regular schedule. Nor are they all equally severe. Recessions are like earthquakes: We know they will happen again but don't know exactly when, much less how severe the next one will be. Scientists (seismologists) who study the causes, magnitude, and timing of earthquakes have given us great insights into that natural phenomenon. But seismologists still aren't able to predict exactly when or where the next quake will erupt.

So it is with the economics profession. Economists have studied the origins, the magnitude, and the timing of past recessions. They have isolated a variety of factors (e.g., financial crises, natural disasters) that cause production to decline. And we know a lot about how production cutbacks spread from one industry to another, just like the flu. We even have a pretty good idea about how to contain and ultimately end recessions, as we'll see in later chapters. But we still don't know how to avoid them completely. The next one will probably surprise us.

Although recessions may be inevitable, the challenge for economic policy is to postpone, mitigate, and bring a quick end to future recessions. When we talk about business cycles, we are simply recognizing the inevitability of future downturns. We are not suggesting that they will occur on a set schedule or with

---

defrosters 除冰（或霜）装置。 crash-resistant 防撞击的。 exhaust pollutant 尾气污染物。

consistent force. On the contrary, we continue to develop policy tools for taming the business cycle, even if we can't eliminate it. Our experience since the Great Depression of the 1930s suggests we are making progress in that regard.

In the following chapters, we'll take a closer look at the policy tools we will use to cope with the next recession.

CHAPTER 9 REVIEW
SUMMARY

- The health of the macro economy is gauged by three measures: real GDP growth, the unemployment rate, and the inflation rate. **LO1**
- The long-term growth rate of the U.S. economy is 3 percent a year. But output doesn't increase by 3 percent every year. In some years real GDP grows faster; in other years growth is slower. Sometimes total output actually declines (recession). **LO5**
- These short-run variations in GDP growth are the focus of macroeconomics. Macro theory tries to explain the alternating periods of growth and contraction that characterize the business cycle; macro policy attempts to control the cycle. **LO1**
- To understand unemployment, we need to distinguish the labor force from the larger population. Only people who are working (employed) or spend some time looking for a job (unemployed) are participants in the labor force. People who are neither working nor looking for work are outside the labor force. **LO2**
- The most visible loss imposed by unemployment is reduced output of goods and services. Those individuals actually out of work suffer lost income, heightened insecurity, and even reduced longevity. **LO2**
- There are four types of unemployment: seasonal, frictional, structural, and cyclical. Because some seasonal and frictional unemployment is inevitable, and even desirable, full employment is not defined as zero unemployment. These considerations, plus fear of inflation, result in full employment being defined as an unemployment rate of 4–6 percent. **LO4**
- Inflation is an increase in the average price level. Typically it is measured by changes in a price index such as the consumer price index (CPI). **LO3**
- Inflation redistributes income by altering relative prices, incomes, and wealth. Because not all prices rise at the same rate and because not all people buy (and sell) the same goods or hold the same assets, inflation does not affect everyone equally. Some individuals actually gain from inflation, whereas others suffer a drop in real income. **LO3**
- Inflation threatens to reduce total output because it increases uncertainties about the future and thereby inhibits consumption and production decisions. **LO3**
- The U.S. goal of price stability is defined as an inflation rate of less than 3 percent per year. This goal recognizes potential conflicts between zero inflation and full employment, as well as the difficulties of measuring quality improvements and new products. **LO4**

TERMS TO REMEMBER

Define the following terms:

macroeconomics
business cycle
production possibilities
gross domestic product (GDP)
nominal GDP
real GDP
recession
labor force
unemployment rate
unemployment

full employment
inflation
deflation
relative price
nominal income
real income
consumer price index (CPI)
inflation rate
price stability

QUESTIONS FOR DISCUSSION

1. If auto sales are increasing but home construction is falling, is the economy growing or shrinking? **LO1**
2. If the price level is rising faster than nominal GDP, what is happening to real GDP? **LO1**
3. Why isn't a full-time college student who is not working not counted as "unemployed"? **LO2**
4. Why might inflation accelerate as the unemployment rate declines? **LO4**
5. During the time period shown in Table 9.4, what happened to the wealth of people holding hordes of silver? **LO3**
6. According to Table 9.2, what happened to the average price of fruit in 2017? **LO3**
7. How might the inflation numbers in Table 9.2 affected people's transportation choices? **LO3**
8. Which of the following people would we expect to be hurt by an increase in the rate of inflation from 3 percent to 6 percent? **LO3**
    a. A homeowner
    b. A retired person
    c. An automobile worker
    d. A bond investor
9. According to Table 9.4, what happened to *(a)* the nominal value of silver? *(b)* the real value of silver? **LO3**
10. **POLICY PERSPECTIVES** Why did the Great Depression last so long? What happened to all the jobs? **LO5**

PROBLEMS

1. How much *more* output will the average American have next year if the $20 trillion U.S. economy grows by **LO1**
    a. 2 percent?
    b. 5 percent?
    c. −1 percent?

    Assume a population of 340 million.

2. Suppose the following data describe a nation's population: **LO2**

	Year 1	Year 2
Population	320 million	330 million
Labor force	150 million	160 million
Unemployed	6.5 million	6.9 million

    a. What is the unemployment rate in each year?
    b. Has the economy experienced an increase or a decrease in
       i. the number of unemployed persons?
       ii. the unemployment rate?

3. If the average worker produces $100,000 of GDP, by how much will GDP increase if there are 150 million labor force participants and the unemployment rate drops from 5.0 to 4.5 percent? **LO1, LO2**

4. During the past 10 years by what percentage did *(a)* the nominal price and *(b)* the real price of college tuition increase per year (see the News Wire "Price Effects")? **LO3**

5. Nominal GDP increased from roughly $10 trillion in 2000 to $20 trillion in 2018. In the same period prices rose on average by roughly 50 percent. By how much did *real* GDP increase? **LO3**

6. What will the *real* value of $100 be in 10 years if you hide the money under your mattress and the inflation rate is: **LO3**
    a. 0%
    b. 2%
    c. 8%

    (*Hint:* Table 9.3 provides clues.)

7. According to the following data, **LO3**
   a. by what percentage did nominal wages increase between 2000 and 2019?
   b. by what percentage did consumer prices increase?
   c. did real wages increase?

	2000	2019
Average hourly wage	$ 14	$ 23
CPI	170	254

8. In Zimbabwe the rate of inflation hit 90 sextillion percent in 2009, with prices increasing tenfold every day. At that rate, how much would a $100 textbook cost one week later? **LO3**

9. The following table lists the prices of a small market basket purchased in both 2008 and 2018. Assuming that this basket of goods is representative of all goods and services, **LO3**
   a. compute the cost of the market basket in 2008.
   b. compute the cost of the market basket in 2018.
   c. by how much has the average price level risen between 2008 and 2018?
   d. the average household's nominal income increased from $40,000 to $60,000 between 2008 and 2018. What happened to its real income?

Item	Quantity	Price in 2008	Price in 2018
Coffee	20 pounds	$ 4	$ 5
Tuition	1 year	$4,000	$7,000
Pizza	100 pizzas	$ 8	$ 10
Movie download	90 movies	$ 10	$ 5
Gasoline	1,000 gallons	$ 2	$ 3

10. According to the information in Table 9.2, which product had (*a*) the largest price increase in 2017? (*b*) the biggest price decline? **LO3**

11. **POLICY PERSPECTIVES** Since 1940, **LO5**
    a. when did the longest recession begin?
    b. when did the shortest recession begin?
    c. when did the recession with the highest unemployment rate begin?
    d. when did the recession with the biggest decline in output begin?
    e. when did the recession with the smallest decline in output begin?
    (See Table 9.1.)

CHAPTER TEN

Aggregate Supply and Demand 总供给和总需求

©B&M Noskowski/iStock/Getty Images

LEARNING OBJECTIVES

After reading this chapter, you should be able to:

1. Cite the major macro outcomes and their determinants.
2. Explain how classical and Keynesian macro views differ.
3. Interpret the shapes of the aggregate demand and supply curves.
4. Tell how macro failure occurs.
5. Outline the major policy options for macro government intervention.

Recurrent recessions, unemployment, and inflation indicate that the economy isn't always in perfect health. Now it's time to start thinking about causes and cures. Why does the economy slip into recession? What causes unemployment or inflation rates to flare up? And what, if anything, can the government do to cure these ailments?

The central focus of **macroeconomics** is on these questions—that is, what causes business cycles and what, if anything, the government can do about them. Can government intervention prevent or correct market excesses? Or is government intervention likely to make things worse?

这些问题正是**宏观经济学**的核心，即什么引起了商业周期？政府能为此做些什么？政府干预能防止或纠正市场的过度行为吗？还是说，政府干预只能让情况变得更糟？

To answer these questions, we need a model of how the economy works. The model must show how the various pieces of the economy interact. The model must not only show how the macro economy works but also pinpoint potential causes of macro failure.

To develop such a macro model, some basic questions must be answered:

- What are the major determinants of macro outcomes?
- How do the forces of supply and demand fit into the macro picture?
- Why are there disagreements about causes and cures of macro ailments?

Answers to these questions will go a long way toward explaining the continuing debates about the causes of business cycles. A macro model can also be used to identify policy options for government intervention. ■

---

flare up 突然上升。pinpoint 精确地找到。

A MACRO VIEW 宏观视角
Macro Outcomes 宏观经济的结果

图 10.1 提供了一个关于宏观经济的鸟瞰图。宏观经济的主要结果列在图的右侧。这些基本的宏观经济结果包括：

Figure 10.1 provides a bird's-eye view of the macro economy. The primary outcomes of the macro economy are arrayed on the right side of the figure. These basic *macro outcomes include*

- *Output:* Total volume of goods and services produced (real GDP).
- *Jobs:* Levels of employment and unemployment.
- *Prices:* Average prices of goods and services.
- *Growth:* Year-to-year expansion in production capacity.
- *International balances:* International value of the dollar; trade and payments balances with other countries.

- 产出：生产的商品和服务的总量（实际 GDP）。
- 就业：就业和失业的水平。
- 价格：商品和服务的平均价格。
- 增长：生产能力逐年提高。
- 国际收支平衡：美元的国际价值，与其他国家的贸易和收支平衡。

These macro outcomes define our nation's economic welfare. As observed in Chapter 9, we gauge the health of the macro economy by its real GDP (output) growth, unemployment (jobs), and inflation (prices). To this list we now add an international measure—the balances in our trade and financial relations with the rest of the world.

Macro Determinants 宏观决定因素

图 10.1 还概括了影响宏观经济结果的各种力量，其中有三种主要力量。这些影响宏观经济表现的决定因素具体包括：

Figure 10.1 also provides an overview of the separate forces that affect macro outcomes. Three broad forces are depicted. These *determinants of macro performance include*

- *Internal market forces:* Population growth, spending behavior, invention and innovation, and the like.
- *External shocks:* Wars, natural disasters, terrorist attacks, trade disruptions, and so on.
- *Policy levers:* Tax policy, government spending, changes in interest rates, credit availability and money, trade policy, immigration policy, and regulation.

- 内部市场力量：人口增长、消费行为、发明和创新，以及其他类似因素。
- 外部冲击：战争、自然灾害、恐怖袭击、贸易中断，等等。
- 政策杠杆：税收政策、政府支出、利率变动、信贷投放和货币、贸易政策、移民政策、管制等。

In the absence of external shocks or government policy, an economy would still function—it would still produce output, create jobs, establish prices, and maybe even grow. The U.S. economy operated this way for much of its history. Even today, many less developed countries and areas operate in relative isolation from government and international events. In these situations, macro outcomes depend exclusively on internal market forces.

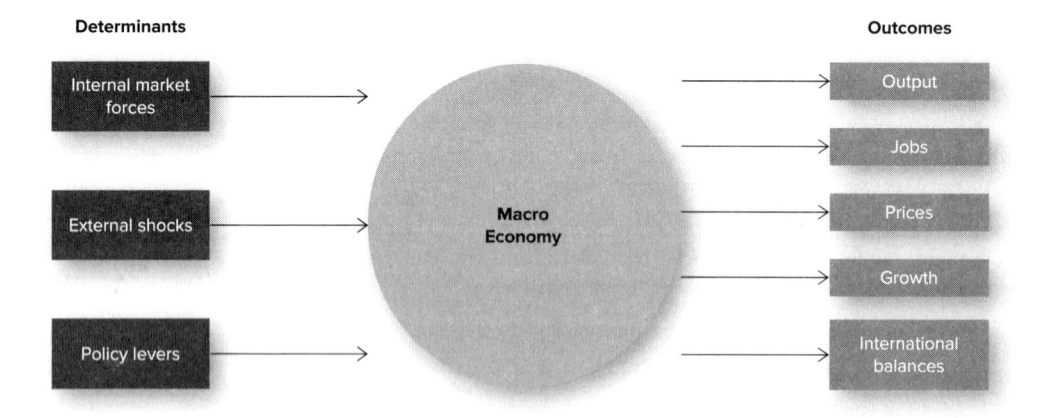

Figure 10.1 The Macro Economy The primary outcomes of the macro economy are output of goods and services, jobs, prices, economic growth, and international balances (trade, currency). These outcomes result from the interplay of internal market forces (e.g., population growth, innovation, spending patterns), external shocks (e.g., wars, weather, trade disruptions), and policy levers (e.g., tax and budget decisions).

STABLE OR UNSTABLE? 稳定还是不稳定

The central concern of macroeconomic theory is whether the internal forces of the marketplace will generate desired outcomes. Will the market mechanism assure us full employment? Will the market itself maintain price stability? Or will the market *fail*, subjecting us to recurring bouts of unemployment, inflation, and declining output?

Classical Theory 古典理论

Prior to the 1930s, macro economists thought there could never be a Great Depression. The economic thinkers of the time asserted that the economy was inherently stable. During the nineteenth century and the first 30 years of the twentieth century, the U.S. economy had experienced some bad years—years in which the nation's output declined and unemployment increased. But most of these episodes were relatively short-lived. The dominant feature of the industrial era was growth—an expanding economy, with more output, more jobs, and higher incomes nearly every year.

Self-Adjustment 自我调整

In this environment, classical economists, as they later became known, propounded an optimistic view of the macro economy. *According to the classical view, the economy self-adjusts to deviations from its long-term growth trend.* Producers might occasionally reduce their output and throw people out of work. But these dislocations would cause little damage. If output declined and people lost their jobs, the internal forces of the marketplace would quickly restore prosperity. **Economic downturns were viewed as temporary setbacks, not permanent problems.**

面对这种情形，后来被人们熟知的古典经济学家提出了一个关于宏观经济的乐观观点。按照古典学派的看法，任何对长期增长趋势的偏离，经济都能通过自我调整来校正。生产者可能会偶尔减产和解雇工人，不过这些小的紊乱造成的损害很小。如果产出下降并出现失业，市场的内部力量很快就可以使经济恢复到繁荣状态。经济低迷被视为短暂的倒退，而非永久性问题。

Flexible Prices 富有弹性的价格

The cornerstones of classical optimism were flexible prices and flexible wages. If producers were unable to sell all their output at current prices, they had two choices. They could reduce the rate of output and throw some people out of work. Or they could reduce the price of their output, thereby stimulating an increase in the quantity demanded. According to the law of demand, price reductions cause an increase in unit sales. If prices fall far enough, all the output produced can be sold. Thus flexible prices—prices that would drop when consumer demand slowed—virtually guaranteed that all output could be sold. No one would have to lose a job because of weak consumer demand.

Flexible Wages 富有弹性的工资

Flexible prices had their counterpart in factor markets. If some workers were temporarily out of work, they would compete for jobs by offering their services at lower wages. As wage rates declined, producers would find it profitable to hire more workers. Ultimately, flexible wages would ensure that everyone who wanted a job would have a job.

Say's Law 萨伊定律

These optimistic views of the macro economy were summarized in Say's law. **Say's law**—named after the nineteenth-century economist Jean-Baptiste Say—decreed that "supply creates its own demand." In Say's view, if you produce something, *somebody* will buy it. All you have to do is find the right price. In this classical view of the world, unsold goods could appear in the market. But they would ultimately be sold when buyers and sellers found an acceptable price.

The same self-adjustment was expected in the labor market. Sure, some people could lose jobs, especially when output growth slowed. But they could find new jobs if they were willing to accept lower wages. With enough wage flexibility, no one would remain unemployed.

这些对宏观经济乐观的观点可以用萨伊定律概括。**萨伊定律**以19世纪经济学家让·巴蒂斯特·萨伊的名字命名，认为"供给能够创造它自己的需求"。在萨伊看来，如果你生产了某种东西，就一定有某人买它，你需要做的就是确定正确的价格而已。在古典学派的世界里，尚未卖出的商品在市场上终将被卖掉，此时买卖双方将以他们找到的合适价格成交。

---

episode 一段时期。

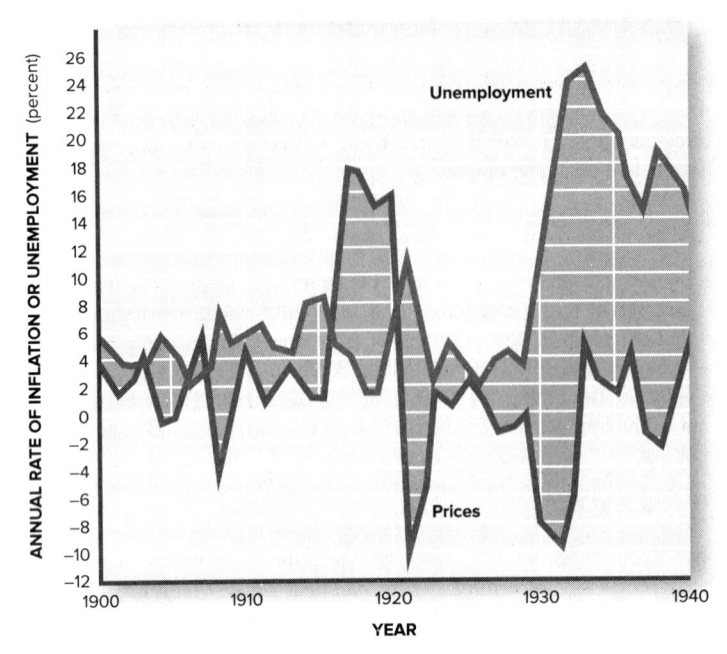

Figure 10.2 Inflation and Unemployment 1900–1940 In the early twentieth century, prices responded to both upward and downward changes in aggregate demand. Periods of high unemployment also tended to be brief. In the 1930s, however, unemployment rates rose to unprecedented heights and stayed high for a decade. Falling wages and prices did not restore full employment. This macro failure prompted calls for new theories and policies to control the business cycle.

Source: Mueller, Frederick H., *Historical Statistics of the United States.* U.S., Bureau of the Census, 1957, 73.

在古典学派的世界里，没有持久的宏观失灵——不会出现大萧条。确实，内部市场力量（比如，弹性价格和工资）能对威胁宏观经济稳定的外部冲击（如战争、干旱、贸易中断）进行自动调整。在古典经济学家看来，图 10.1 中的"政策杠杆"是没用的，政府对（可以自我调整的）宏观经济的干预是不必要的。

There could be no Great Depression—no protracted macro failure—in this classical view of the world. Indeed, internal market forces (e.g., flexible prices and wages) could even provide an automatic adjustment to external shocks (e.g., wars, droughts, trade disruptions) that threatened to destabilize the economy. *The classical economists saw no need for the box labeled "policy levers" in Figure 10.1; government intervention in the (self-adjusting) macro economy was unnecessary.*

The Great Depression was a stunning blow to classical economists. At the onset of the depression, classical economists assured everyone that the setbacks in production and employment were temporary and would soon vanish. Andrew Mellon, secretary of the U.S. Treasury, expressed this optimistic view in January 1930, just a few months after the stock market crash. Assessing the prospects for the year ahead, he said, "I see nothing . . . in the present situation that is either menacing or warrants pessimism . . . I have every confidence that there will be a revival of activity in the spring and that during the coming year the country will make steady progress."[1] Merrill Lynch, one of the nation's largest brokerage houses, was urging people to buy stocks. But the depression deepened. Indeed, unemployment grew and persisted *despite* falling prices and wages (see Figure 10.2). The classical self-adjustment mechanism simply did not work.

The Keynesian Revolution   凯恩斯革命

The Great Depression destroyed the credibility of classical economic theory. As John Maynard Keynes wrote in 1935, classical economists

---

[1] Shannon, David A., *The Great Depression.* Englewood Cliffs, NJ: Prentice Hall, 1960, 5.

stunning 令人震惊的。 at the onset of 在……开始的时候。 menacing 威胁的，险恶的。

were apparently unmoved by the lack of correspondence between the results of their theory and the facts of observation:—a discrepancy which the ordinary man has not failed to observe. . . .

The celebrated optimism of [classical] economic theory . . . is . . . to be traced, I think, to their having neglected to take account of the drag on prosperity which can be exercised by an insufficiency of effective demand. For there would obviously be a natural tendency towards the optimum employment of resources in a Society which was functioning after the manner of the classical postulates. It may well be that the classical theory represents the way in which we should like our Economy to behave. But to assume that it actually does so is to assume our difficulties away.[2]

No Self-Adjustment 自我调整的缺失

Keynes went on to develop an alternative view of the macro economy. Whereas the classical economists viewed the economy as inherently stable, **Keynes asserted that the private economy was inherently unstable.** Small disturbances in output, prices, or unemployment were likely to be magnified, not muted, by the invisible hand of the marketplace. The Great Depression was not a unique event, Keynes argued, but a calamity that would recur if we relied on the market mechanism to self-adjust. Macro failure was the rule, not the exception, for a purely private economy.

In Keynes's view, the inherent instability of the marketplace required government intervention. When the economy falters, we cannot afford to wait for some assumed self-adjustment mechanism. We must instead intervene to protect jobs and income. Keynes concluded that policy levers (see Figure 10.1) were both effective and necessary. Without such intervention, he believed, the economy was doomed to bouts of repeated macro failure.

Modern economists hesitate to give policy intervention that great a role. Nearly all economists recognize that policy intervention affects macro outcomes. But there are great arguments about just how effective any policy lever is. A vocal minority of economists even echoes the classical notion that policy intervention may be either ineffective or, worse still, inherently destabilizing.

凯恩斯接着对宏观经济提出了另外一种见解。尽管古典经济学家认为宏观经济具有内在稳定性，但凯恩斯断言私有经济是内在不稳定的。经由市场这只"看不见的手"，产出、价格和失业方面的较小扰动很可能会被放大，而不是减弱。凯恩斯认为，大萧条并非独特事件，而是一场灾难，如果我们依靠市场机制来自我调整，这场灾难就会重演。对于纯粹的私有经济来说，宏观上的失灵是常态，而非例外。

在凯恩斯看来，市场内在的不稳定性要求政府干预。

THE AGGREGATE SUPPLY–DEMAND MODEL 总供求模型

These persistent debates can best be understood in the familiar framework of supply and demand—the most commonly used tools in an economist's toolbox. All of the macro outcomes depicted in Figure 10.1 are the result of market transactions—an interaction between supply and demand. Hence ***any influence on macro outcomes must be transmitted through supply or demand.*** In other words, if the forces depicted on the left side of Figure 10.1 affect neither supply nor demand, they will have no impact on macro outcomes. This makes our job easier. We can resolve the question about macro stability by focusing on the forces that shape supply and demand in the macro economy.

Aggregate Demand 总需求

Economists use the term "aggregate demand" to refer to the collective behavior of all buyers in the marketplace. Specifically, **aggregate demand** refers to the various quantities of output that all market participants are willing and able to buy at alternative price levels in a given period. Our view here encompasses the collective demand for *all* goods and services rather than the demand for any single good.

To understand the concept of aggregate demand better, imagine that everyone is paid on the same day. With their income in hand, people then enter the product market. The question is, How much will people buy?

To answer this question, we have to know something about prices. If goods and services are cheap, people will be able to buy more with their given income. On the other hand, high prices will limit both the ability and willingness of people to purchase goods and services. Note that we are talking here about the average price level, not the price of any single good.

经济学家们用"总需求"这个词表示市场上所有买者的集体行为。具体而言，**总需求**表示某一给定时期，在各种价格水平下，所有市场参与者愿意并有能力购买的各种产出的数量之和。我们这里着眼的是对所有商品和服务的集体需求，而非对单个商品的需求。

---

[2] Keynes, John Maynard, *The General Theory of Employment, Interest and Money.* London, UK: Macmillan, 1936, 33–34.

celebrated 著名的，有名望的。 postulate 假定。 falter 衰退。 doomed 注定的，命定的。 vocal 直言不讳的。

Real GDP (Output) 实际 GDP

This simple relationship between average prices and real spending is illustrated in Figure 10.3. On the horizontal axis we depict the various quantities of output that might be purchased. We are referring here to **real GDP**, an inflation-adjusted measure of physical output.

Price Level 价格水平

On the vertical axis we measure prices. Specifically, Figure 10.3 depicts alternative levels of *average* prices. As we move up the vertical axis, the average price level rises (inflation); and as we move down, the average price level falls (deflation).

The aggregate demand curve in Figure 10.3 has a familiar shape. The message of this downward-sloping macro curve is a bit different, however. ***The aggregate demand curve illustrates how the volume of purchases varies with average prices.*** The downward slope of the aggregate demand curve suggests that with a given (constant) level of income, people will buy more goods and services at lower prices. The curve doesn't tell us *which* goods and services people will buy; it simply indicates the total volume (quantity) of their intended purchases.

At first blush, a downward-sloping demand curve hardly seems remarkable. But because *aggregate* demand refers to the total volume of spending, Figure 10.3 requires a distinctly macro explanation. That explanation includes three separate phenomena:

- ***Real balances effect:*** The primary explanation for the downward slope of the aggregate demand curve is that cheaper prices make the dollars you hold more valuable. That is to say, ***the real value of money is measured by how many goods and services each dollar will buy.*** In this respect, lower prices make you richer: The cash balances you hold in your pocket, in your bank account, or under your pillow are worth more when the price level falls. Lower prices also increase the value of other dollar-denominated assets (e.g., bonds), thus increasing the wealth of consumers.

When their real incomes and wealth increase because of a decline in the price level, consumers respond by buying more goods and services. They end up saving less of their incomes and spending more. This causes the aggregate demand curve to slope downward to the right.

图 10.3 中的总需求曲线看起来很眼熟，不过这个向下倾斜的宏观曲线所传递的信息有些不同。总需求曲线表明购买总量如何随平均价格水平的变化而变化。总需求曲线向下倾斜表示在给定的（不变的）收入水平下，面对较低的价格，人们将会购买更多的商品和服务。该曲线并没有告诉我们人们会购买哪些商品和服务，它只是表示人们愿意购买的总量（数量）。

● 实际余额效应：总需求向下倾斜的主要原因是较低的价格水平使你持有的美元更有价值。这就是说，货币的真实价值是由每一美元可以买到多少商品和服务来衡量的。

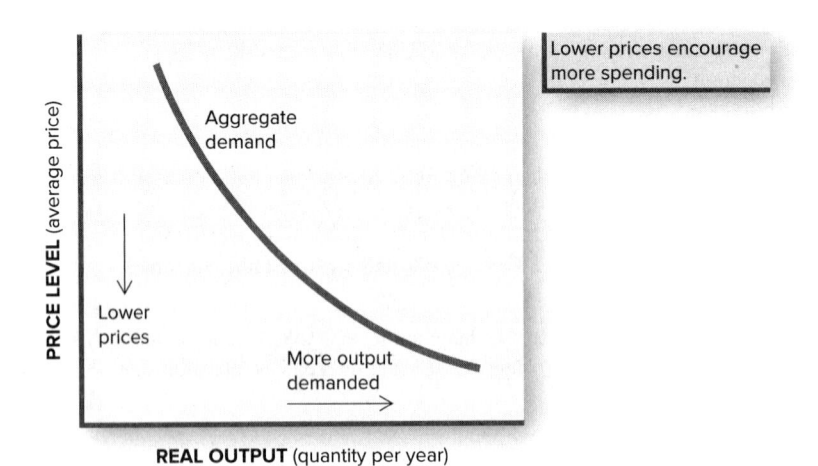

Figure 10.3 Aggregate Demand Aggregate demand refers to the total output demanded at alternative price levels (*ceteris paribus*). The vertical axis here measures the average level of all prices rather than the price of any single good. Likewise, the horizontal axis refers to the real value of all goods, not the quantity of any one product.

---

physical output 实物产出。 remarkable 引人注目的。 pillow 枕头。

- *Foreign trade effect:* The downward slope of the aggregate demand curve is reinforced by changes in imports and exports. When American-made products become cheaper, U.S. consumers will buy fewer imports and more domestic output. Foreigners will also step up their purchases of American-made goods when American prices are falling.

  The opposite is true as well. When the domestic price level rises, U.S. consumers are likely to buy more imports. At the same time, foreign consumers may cut back on their purchases of American-made products when American prices increase.

- *Interest rate effect:* Changes in the price level also affect the amount of money people need to borrow and so tend to affect interest rates. At lower price levels, consumer borrowing needs are smaller. As the demand for loans diminishes, interest rates tend to decline as well. This cheaper money stimulates more borrowing and loan-financed purchases.

The combined forces of these real balances, foreign trade, and interest rate effects give the aggregate demand curve its downward slope. **People buy a larger volume of output when the price level falls** (*ceteris paribus*). This makes perfect sense.

Aggregate Supply   总供给

While lower price levels tend to increase the volume of output *demanded*, they have the opposite effect on the aggregate quantity *supplied*.

Profit Margins   利润率

If the price level falls, producers are being squeezed. In the short run, producers are saddled with some relatively constant costs, such as rent, interest payments, negotiated wages, and inputs already contracted for. If output prices fall, producers will be hard-pressed to pay these costs, much less earn a profit. Their response will be to reduce the rate of output.

Rising output prices have the opposite effect. Because many costs are fixed in the short run, higher prices for goods and services tend to widen profit margins. As profit margins widen, producers will want to produce and sell more goods. Thus *we expect the rate of output to increase when the price level rises.* This expectation is reflected in the upward slope of the aggregate supply curve in Figure 10.4. **Aggregate supply** reflects the various quantities of real output that firms are willing and able to produce at alternative price levels in a given time period. The higher the price level, the greater the willingness to produce (supply).

Costs   成本

The upward slope of the aggregate supply curve is also explained by rising costs. To increase the rate of output, producers must acquire more resources (e.g., labor) and use existing plants and equipment more intensively. These greater strains on our productive capacity tend to raise production costs. Producers must therefore charge higher prices to recover the higher costs that accompany increased capacity utilization.

Cost pressures tend to intensify as capacity is approached. If there is a lot of excess capacity, output can be increased with little cost pressure. Hence the lower end of the aggregate supply (AS) curve is fairly flat. As capacity is approached, however, business isn't so easy. Producers may have to pay overtime wages, raise base wages, and pay premium prices to get needed inputs. This is reflected in the steepening slope of the AS curve at higher output levels, as shown in Figure 10.4.

Macro Equilibrium   宏观均衡

What we end up with here are two rather conventional-looking supply and demand curves. But these particular curves have special significance. Instead of describing the behavior of buyers

---

utilization 利用。premium 溢价，额外费用。

这些特定的曲线有特殊的意义。总供给和总需求曲线概括的是整个（宏观）经济的市场行为，而不是描述单一市场上买者和卖者的行为。这些曲线告诉我们，在各个价格水平下，商品和服务的供给和需求总量。

and sellers in a single market, ***aggregate supply and demand curves summarize the market activity of the whole (macro) economy.*** These curves tell us what *total* amount of goods and services will be supplied or demanded at various price levels.

These graphic summaries of buyer and seller behavior provide some initial clues to how macro outcomes are determined. The most important clue is point E in Figure 10.5, where the aggregate demand and supply curves intersect. This is the only point at which the behavior of buyers and sellers is compatible. We know from the aggregate demand curve that people are willing and able to *buy* the quantity Q_E when the price level is at P_E. From the aggregate supply curve we know that businesses are prepared to *sell* the quantity Q_E at the price level P_E. Hence buyers and sellers are willing to trade exactly the same quantity (Q_E) at that price level. We call this situation **macro equilibrium**—the unique combination of price level and output that is compatible with both buyers' and sellers' intentions. **At macro equilibrium, the rate of desired spending is exactly equal to the rate of production: Everything produced is sold.**

在宏观均衡状态，合意的支出水平恰好等于产出水平：生产的所有东西都卖出去了。

Disequilibrium 非均衡

To appreciate the significance of macro equilibrium, suppose that another price or output level existed. Imagine, for example, that prices were higher, at the level P_1 in Figure 10.5. How much output would people want to buy at that price level? How much would businesses want to produce and sell?

The aggregate demand curve tells us that people would want to buy only the quantity D_1 at the higher price level P_1. But business firms would want to sell the larger quantity, S_1. This is a *disequilibrium* situation in which the intentions of buyers and sellers are incompatible. The aggregate quantity supplied (S_1) exceeds the aggregate quantity demanded (D_1). Accordingly, a lot of the goods being produced will remain unsold at price level P_1.

Market Adjustments 市场调整

To unload these unsold goods, producers have to reduce their prices. As prices drop, producers will decrease the volume of goods sent to market. At the same time, the quantities consumers

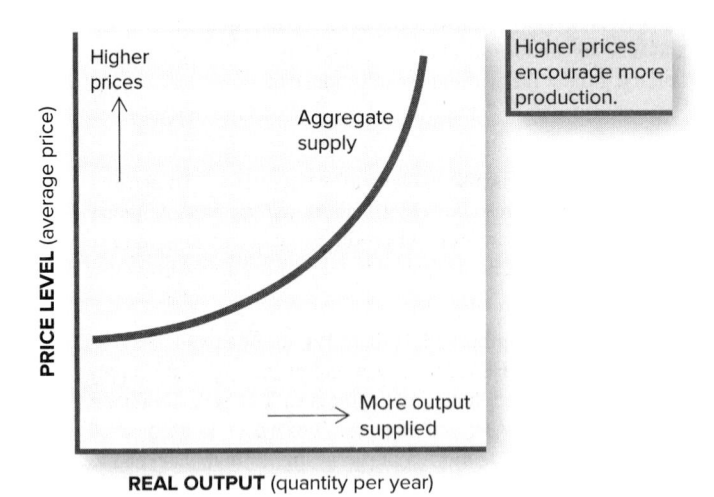

Figure 10.4 Aggregate Supply Aggregate supply refers to the total volume of output producers are willing and able to bring to the market at alternative price levels (*ceteris paribus*). The upward slope of the aggregate supply curve reflects the fact that profit margins widen when output prices rise (especially when short-run costs are constant). Producers respond to wider profit margins by supplying more output.

want to buy will increase. This adjustment process will continue until point E is reached and the quantities demanded and supplied are equal. At that macro equilibrium, the lower price level P_E will prevail.

The same kind of adjustment process would occur if a lower price level first existed. At lower prices, the aggregate quantity demanded would exceed the aggregate quantity supplied. As sales outpaced production, inventories would dwindle and shortages would emerge. The resulting shortages would permit sellers to raise their prices. As they did so, the aggregate quantity demanded would decrease, and the aggregate quantity supplied would increase. Eventually we would return to point E, where the aggregate quantities demanded and supplied are equal.

Equilibrium is unique; it is the only price–output combination that is mutually compatible with aggregate supply and demand. In terms of graphs, it is the only place where the aggregate supply and demand curves intersect. At point E there is no reason for the level of output or prices to change. The behavior of buyers and sellers is compatible: Desired spending equals current production. By contrast, any other level of output or prices creates a *dis*equilibrium that requires market adjustments. All other price and output combinations, therefore, are unstable. They will not last. Eventually the economy will return to point E.

均衡是唯一的；它是唯一使总需求和总供给相一致的价格—产出组合。如果用图形表示，它就是总供给曲线和总需求曲线的唯一交点。在 E 点，产出和价格水平都没有改变的动因，买卖双方的行为是一致的，合意的支出等于当前的产出。相比之下，任何其他的产出和价格水平会造成非均衡，并需要市场进行调整。因此，所有其他的价格和产出组合都是不稳定的，它们不会持续。最终经济将重新回到 E 点。

MACRO FAILURE 宏观失灵

There are ***two potential problems with the macro equilibrium*** depicted in Figure 10.5:

- ***Undesirability:*** The price–output relationship at equilibrium may not satisfy our macroeconomic goals.
- ***Instability:*** Even if the designated macro equilibrium is optimal, it may be displaced by macro disturbances.

宏观经济均衡伴有两个潜在问题，可以用图 10.5 来说明。

- 非合意性：均衡点的价格—产出关系可能无法满足我们的宏观经济目标。
- 不稳定性：即使给定的宏观均衡是最优的，它也可能被宏观扰动所取代。

Undesirable Outcomes 非合意的结果

The macro equilibrium depicted in Figure 10.5 is simply the intersection of two curves. All we know for sure is that people want to buy the same quantity of goods and services that businesses want to sell at the price level P_E. This quantity (Q_E) may be more or less than our full employment capacity. This contingency is illustrated in Figure 10.6.

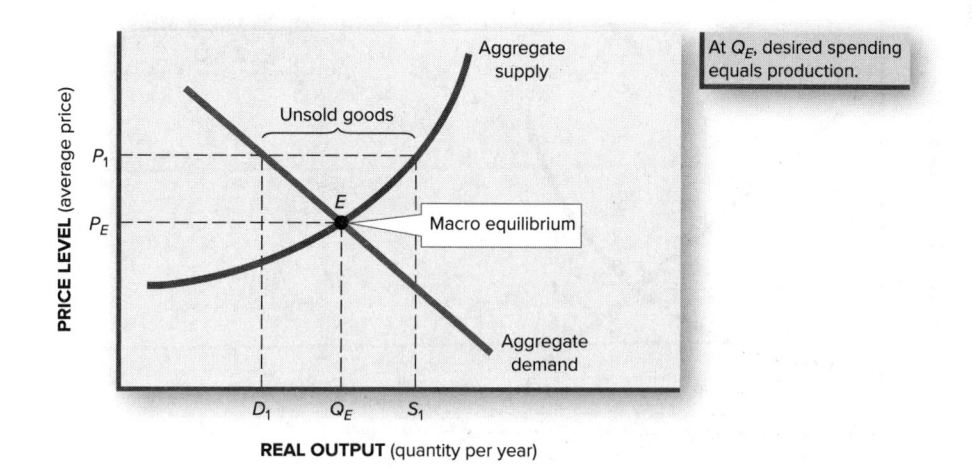

Figure 10.5 Macro Equilibrium The aggregate demand and supply curves intersect at only one point (E). At that point, the price level (P_E) and output (Q_E) combination is compatible with both buyers' and sellers' intentions. The economy will gravitate to those equilibrium price (P_E) and output (Q_E) levels. At any other price level the behavior of buyers and sellers is incompatible. At P_1, firms supply more output (S_1) than market participants demand (D_1). ■

---

contingency 可能发生的事。

图 10.6 的新内容是设计了一个**充分就业**的 GDP，也就是产出能力。图中的产出水平 Q_F 代表社会的充分就业目标，它指的是劳动力充分就业时能生产的产出总量。

What's new in Figure 10.6 is the designation of **full employment GDP**—that is, capacity output. The output level Q_F in the figure represents society's full employment goal. ***Q_F refers to the quantity of output that could be produced if the labor force were fully employed.*** If we produce less output than that, some workers will remain unemployed. This is exactly what happens at the macro equilibrium depicted here: Only the quantity Q_E is being produced. Since Q_E is less than Q_F, the economy is not fully utilizing its production possibilities. This is the dilemma that the U.S. economy confronted in 2008–2009 (see the News Wire "Undesirable Outcomes").

Unemployment 失业

The shortfall in equilibrium output illustrated in Figure 10.6 implies that the economy will be burdened with cyclical **unemployment**. Full employment is attained only if we produce at Q_F. Market forces, however, lead us to the lower rate of output at Q_E. Some workers can't find jobs.

Inflation 通货膨胀

Similar problems may arise with the equilibrium price level. Suppose that P^* represents the most desired price level. In Figure 10.6 we see that the equilibrium price level P_E exceeds P^*. If market behavior determines prices, the price level will rise above that desired level. The resulting increase in average prices is what we call **inflation**.

Macro Failure 宏观失灵

It could be argued, of course, that our apparent macro failures are simply an artifact. We could have drawn our aggregate supply and demand curves to intersect at point F in Figure 10.6. At that intersection we would enjoy both price stability and full employment. Why didn't we draw them there, rather than intersecting at point E?

On the graph we can draw curves anywhere we want. In the real world, however, only one set of curves will correctly express buyers' and sellers' behavior. We must emphasize here that those real-world curves may *not* intersect at point F, thus denying us price stability, full employment, or both. That is the kind of economic outcome illustrated in Figure 10.6. When that happens, we are saddled with macro failure.

均衡价格水平也会带来类似问题。假设 P^* 代表最合意的价格水平。在图 10.6 中，我们看到均衡价格水平 P_E 高于 P^*。如果由市场行为决定价格，价格水平将高于合意的水平。由此导致的平均价格水平上升就是我们所说的**通货膨胀**。

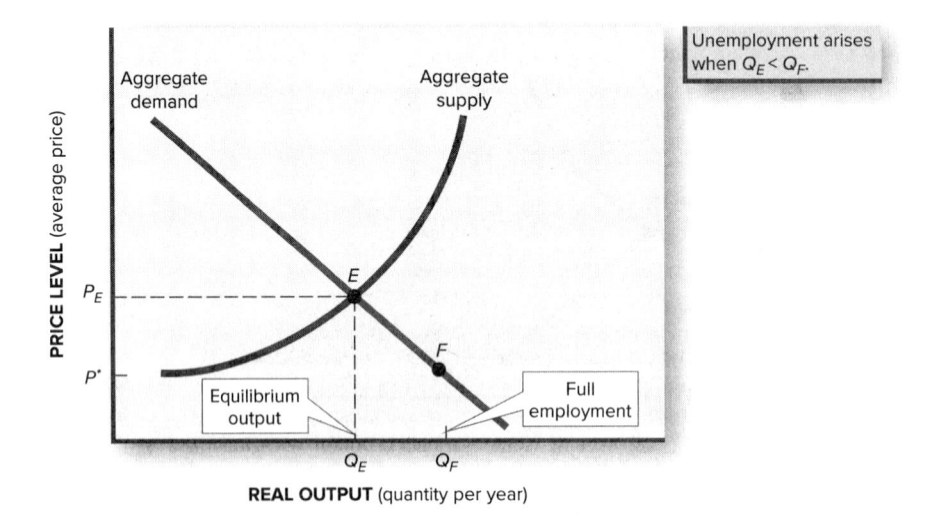

Figure 10.6 An Undesired Equilibrium Equilibrium establishes the only levels of prices and output that are compatible with both buyers' and sellers' intentions. These outcomes may not satisfy our policy goals. In the case shown here, the equilibrium output rate (Q_E) falls short of full employment GDP (Q_F). Unemployment results. ∎

shortfall 不足。artifact 人为因素，人为的结果。

NEWS WIRE UNDESIRABLE OUTCOMES

JOB LOSSES SURGE AS U.S. DOWNTURN ACCELERATES
Layoffs Spread beyond Construction to Rest of Economy

The U.S. Bureau of Labor Statistics (BLS) reported Friday that the economy shed another 533,000 jobs in November, bringing the total of jobs lost so far in the current recession to nearly 3 million. The downward job spiral that began in construction has spilled over into a broad range of industries. Since its employment peak in September 2006 the construction industry has hemorrhaged 780,000 jobs. Now unemployment is surging in other industries: Last month 91,000 jobs were lost in retailing, 85,000 in manufacturing, 76,000 in the leisure and hospitality industry, and 136,000 in business services.

"It's remarkable how fast the unemployment rate is increasing" in several states, said Luke Tilley, a senior economist at IHS Global Insight. "We are now seeing the full ripple effects." . . .

Source: U.S. Bureau of Labor Statistics, December 8, 2008.

NOTE: A contraction in one industry (such as housing) can have "ripple effects" that reduce aggregate demand across the entire economy, destroying jobs.
注：一个行业（如房地产业）的收缩可能会产生"连锁效应"，降低整个经济的总需求，从而导致失业。

Unstable Outcomes 不稳定的结果

Figure 10.6 is only the beginning of our macro worries. Suppose that the aggregate supply and demand curves actually intersected in the perfect spot. That is, imagine that macro equilibrium yielded the optimal levels of both employment and prices. This is pretty much the happy situation we enjoyed in 2007: We had full employment (4.6 percent unemployment), price stability (2.8 percent inflation), and decent real GDP growth (2.1 percent). With such good macro outcomes, couldn't we just settle back and enjoy our good fortune?

Unhappily, even a perfect macro equilibrium doesn't ensure a happy ending. The aggregate supply and demand curves that momentarily bring us macro bliss are not necessarily permanent. They can *shift*—and they will whenever the behavior of buyers and sellers changes.

Shift of Aggregate Demand 总需求曲线的移动

The behavior of U.S. producers and consumers *did* change in 2007, pushing the economy out of its full employment equilibrium. The problem began in the construction industry. From 2001 to 2006 home prices rose every year. That made home-owning consumers wealthier and kept construction companies busy building new homes. The party started to peter out in July 2006, however, when home prices stopped rising. Things got worse a few months later when home prices actually started falling. By 2007 the demand for new homes began falling rapidly. As it did, the aggregate demand (AD) curve *shifted* to the left. Suddenly more output (including new homes) was being produced at Q_F than people were willing to buy. Builders responded by cutting back construction and laying off workers. As the economy moved to a new and lower equilibrium (point H in Figure 10.7a), more and more workers lost their jobs and joined the ranks of the unemployed. The economy moved from the full employment equilibrium (point F) of 2007 to the recessionary equilibrium (point H) of 2008–2009. (See the News Wire "Shifting Aggregate Demand".)

Shift of Aggregate Supply 总供给曲线的移动

A shift of the aggregate supply (AS) curve can also push the economy out of full employment equilibrium. When Hurricane Harvey struck the Gulf Coast in August 2017, it destroyed roads, bridges, and ports, making transportation of goods more expensive. Refinery shutdowns also caused the price of oil to shoot up. This oil price hike directly increased the cost of production

图 10.6 仅仅是我们对宏观经济担忧的开始。假设总供给和总需求曲线正好相交于完美的一点。这就是说，宏观均衡所产生的结果，无论是价格水平还是就业，都是最优水平。这正是我们在 2007 年所遇到的令人欣慰的局面：我们实现了充分就业（失业率为 4.6%）、价格稳定（通胀水平为 2.8%）和可观的实际 GDP 增长（2.1%）。面对如此美好的宏观结果，难道我们就不能安安稳稳地享受我们的好运吗？

---

momentarily 暂时地。bliss 福祉。

in a wide range of U.S. industries, making producers less willing and able to supply goods at prevailing prices. Thus the aggregate supply curve *shifted to the left*, as shown in Figure 10.7b. The impact of a leftward supply shift on the economy is evident. Whereas macro equilibrium was originally located at the optimal point *F*, the new equilibrium was located at point *G*. At point *G*, less output was produced, and prices were higher. Full employment and price stability vanished before our eyes. This is the kind of "external shock" that can destabilize any economy.

Recurrent Shifts 周期性移动

当总供给曲线和总需求曲线沿不同方向反复移动时，情况就变得更令人不知所措了。总需求曲线左移会引起衰退，因为产出率下降。随后的右移会引致经济复苏，此时实际GDP（和就业）再次上升。总供给曲线的移动会引起类似的上升和下降。因此，**商业周期**源于总供给和总需求曲线的周期性移动。

The situation gets even crazier when the aggregate supply and demand curves shift repeatedly in different directions. A leftward shift of the aggregate demand curve can cause a recession as the rate of output falls. A later rightward shift of the aggregate demand curve can cause a recovery, with real GDP (and employment) again increasing. Shifts of the aggregate supply curve can cause similar upswings and downswings. Thus **business cycles *result from recurrent shifts of the aggregate supply and demand curves.***

Shift Factors 移动因素

There is no reason to believe that the aggregate supply and demand curves will always shift in such undesired ways. However, there are lots of reasons to expect them to shift on occasion.

Demand Shifts 需求移动

The aggregate demand curve might shift, for example, if consumer sentiment were to change. As noted, a plunge in home prices not only reduces consumers' wealth but also saps their confidence in their future. This combination of reduced wealth and shattered confidence might cause consumers to pare their spending plans—even if their current incomes remain

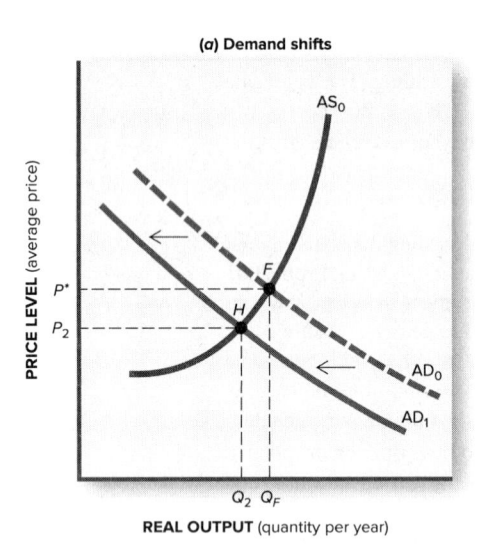

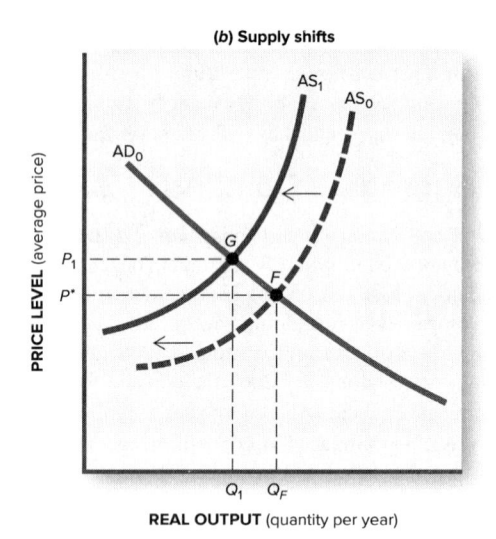

Figure 10.7 Macro Disturbances Point *F* represents the "perfect" macro equilibrium of full employment (Q_F) and price stability (P^*). But that outcome may be upset by

(a) Aggregate demand shifts: A decrease (leftward shift) in aggregate demand (AD) tends to reduce output and price levels. A fall in demand may be due to a plunge in housing prices or the stock market, an increased taste for imports, changes in expectations, higher taxes, or other events.

(b) Aggregate supply shifts: A decrease (leftward shift) of the aggregate supply (AS) curve tends to reduce real GDP and raise average prices. When supply shifts from AS_0 to AS_1, the equilibrium moves from *F* to *G*. Such a supply shift may result from natural disasters, higher import prices, changes in tax policy, or other events. ■

---

sentiment 观点，情绪。shatter 粉碎（梦想、希望、信仰等）。pare 削减。

unchanged. (See the News Wire "Shifting Aggregate Demand.") This would shift the AD curve to the left. A tax hike might have a similar effect. Higher taxes reduce disposable (after-tax) incomes, forcing consumers to cut back spending. Higher interest rates make credit-financed spending more expensive and so might also reduce aggregate demand (especially on big-ticket items like cars and houses).

NEWS WIRE SHIFTING AGGREGATE DEMAND

CONSUMER CONFIDENCE PLUMMETS

New York. American consumers are trimming their shopping lists. That's the latest finding from the monthly surveys of consumer sentiment conducted by the Conference Board. The shrinking economy, together with rising unemployment, have sapped consumer confidence. Declining confidence typically leads to reduced spending, a bad omen for the larger economy.

The Conference Board's index of consumer confidence fell to 25 in February, down from 37.4 in January. The index has been setting historic lows since September of last year. Consumers not only feel that the economy has stalled, but also that there is little hope of economic recovery in the next six months.

Source: News accounts of March 2009.

NOTE: Declining home and stock prices sap not only consumer wealth but consumer confidence as well. This prompts consumers to spend less, shifting the aggregate demand curve leftward.
注：房价和股价下挫不仅会摧毁消费者的财富，也会摧毁消费者的信心。这迫使消费者减少支出，从而引起总需求曲线左移。

Demand shifts aren't always bad. When the stock market is rising or home prices increasing, consumers will have more money to spend. They are also likely to be more confident about their financial future. This combination of greater wealth and confidence can prompt consumers to demand *more* output at any given price level. This kind of *rightward* shift of aggregate demand occurred in 2017–2018.

Supply Shifts 供给移动

Many factors may shift aggregate supply as well. As noted earlier, rising oil prices are another brake on GDP growth. Higher oil prices raise the cost of producing goods and services (e.g., airline travel, heating, delivery services), making producers less willing to supply output at a given price level. A similar shift occurred in the wake of the September 2001 terrorist attacks. Higher costs for stepped-up security made it more expensive to produce and ship goods. As a result, a smaller quantity of goods was available at any given price level. The same kind of leftward AS shift occurred when Hurricane Harvey destroyed transportation systems in August 2017 (see the News Wire "Shifting Aggregate Supply").

Higher business taxes could also discourage production, thereby shifting the aggregate supply curve to the left. Tougher environmental or workplace regulations could raise the cost of doing business, inducing less supply at a given price level. On the other hand, more liberal immigration rules might increase the supply of labor and increase the supply of goods and services (a rightward shift).

较高的营业税也可能抑制生产，从而使总供给曲线左移。过于严格的环境和工作场所法规也增加了商业成本，削弱了给定价格水平上的供给意愿。另一方面，更宽松的移民规定可能使劳动力供给增加，进而增加商品和服务的供给（右移）。

NEWS WIRE SHIFTING AGGREGATE SUPPLY

HARVEY SLAMS INTO HOUSTON AREA

Hurricane Harvey is turning into one of the costliest natural disasters in U.S. history. The Houston area was the hardest hit. Winds of up to 132 miles per hour and unrelenting rainfall have inflicted $125 billion of damage. Over 300,000 structures and 500,000 vehicles were damaged, displacing 32,000 people. Houston's two airports were shut down, and flooding closed most roadways. Houston-area oil refineries were also shut down, eliminating about 20 percent of the state's gasoline supply.

---

disposable income 可支配收入。credit-financed 信贷融资。stepped-up 增加的。

©Robert Coy/Alamy Stock Photo
Source: News accounts of August–September 2017.

NOTE: An external shock can disrupt both the demand and supply sides of the economy. The damage caused by Hurricane Harvey to transportation and production systems made supplying output more difficult, more time-consuming, and more expensive.
注：外部冲击会扰乱经济中的需求和供给。飓风"哈维"对运输和生产系统造成的破坏会使产出的供给变得更加困难、耗时且成本更高。

COMPETING THEORIES OF SHORT-RUN INSTABILITY 短期不稳定理论的比较

Although it is evident that either aggregate supply or aggregate demand *might* shift, economists disagree about how often such shifts might occur or what consequences they might have. What we have seen in Figures 10.6 and 10.7 is how things might go poorly in the macro economy.

Figure 10.6 suggests that the odds of the market generating an equilibrium at full employment and price stability are about the same as finding a needle in a haystack. Figure 10.7 suggests that if we are lucky enough to find the needle, we will probably drop it again when AS or AD shifts. From this perspective, it appears that our worries about the business cycle are well founded.

The classical economists had no such worries. As we saw earlier, they believed that the economy would gravitate toward full employment. Keynes, on the other hand, worried that the macro equilibrium might start out badly and get worse in the absence of government intervention.

总供给和总需求曲线为比较上述理论以及其他关于宏观经济如何运行的理论提供了一个很方便的框架。从本质上说，宏观问题的争论焦点是总供给和总需求曲线的形状以及促使它们移动的潜在力量。有了正确的形状（或者正确的移动），任何合意的均衡都能实现。正如我们将会看到的，关于令人满意的结果能否产生以及如何产生，存在许多不同观点。这些不同观点可以分为需求方面的解释、供给方面的解释以及二者的某种结合。

Aggregate supply and demand curves provide a convenient framework for comparing these and other theories on how the economy works. Essentially, ***macro controversies focus on the shape of aggregate supply and demand curves and the potential to shift them.*** With the right shape—or the correct shift—any desired equilibrium could be attained. As we will see, there are differing views as to whether and how this happy outcome might come about. These differing views can be classified as demand-side explanations, supply-side explanations, or some combination of the two.

Demand-Side Theories 需求方面的理论

Keynesian Theory 凯恩斯理论

凯恩斯的理论是需求方面理论中影响最为深远的。尽管古典学派经济学家们断言供给能够创造自己的需求，凯恩斯却背道而驰：需求创造供给。

Keynesian theory is the most prominent of the demand-side theories. ***Whereas the classical economists asserted that supply creates its own demand, Keynes argued the reverse: Demand it, and it will be supplied.***

---

odds 可能性。needle 缝衣针。needle in a haystack 海底针。

The downside of this demand-driven view is that a lack of spending will cause the economy to contract. If aggregate spending isn't sufficient, some goods will remain unsold and some production capacity will be idled. This contingency is illustrated in Figure 10.8a. The aggregate demand curve AD_0 generates full employment at Q_F. But when the AD curve shifts to AD_1, things fall apart. When the new AD curve intersects with the unchanged AS curve at E_1, we end up with output of Q_1. Since Q_1 is less than full-employment GDP, some workers become unemployed.

Keynes developed his theory during the Great Depression, when the economy seemed to be stuck at a very low level of equilibrium output, far short of full employment GDP. The only way to end the depression, he argued, was for someone to start demanding more goods. He advocated a big increase in government spending to start the economy moving toward full employment. At the time, his advice was largely ignored. When the United States mobilized for World War II, however, the sudden surge in government spending shifted the AD curve to the right, restoring full employment.

Although Keynes emphasized the potential of government spending to shift the AD curve rightward, he didn't really care where the added spending came from. An increase in spending by consumers, businesses, or foreigners could also shift the AD curve rightward. *What Keynes emphasized is that someone had to shift the AD curve rightward in order to restore full employment.*

尽管凯恩斯强调政府支出有可能使 AD 曲线向右移动，但他并不真正关心增加的支出从何而来。消费者、企业或外国人支出的增加也可能使支出曲线向右移动。凯恩斯强调的是，要恢复充分就业，必须有人将 AD 曲线向右移动。

The Keynesian strategy can also be used to dampen inflation. If *too much* aggregate demand were pushing the price level up, Keynes advocated moving these in the opposite direction—that is, shifting the AD curve to the left.

Monetary Theories 货币理论

Another demand-side theory emphasizes the role of money in financing aggregate demand. Money and credit affect the ability and willingness of people to buy goods and services. If credit isn't available or is too expensive, consumers won't be able to buy as many cars, homes, or other expensive products. Tight money might also curtail business investment. In these circumstances, aggregate demand might prove to be inadequate. In this case, an increase in the money supply may be required to shift the aggregate demand curve into the desired position. Monetary theories thus focus on the control of money and interest rates as mechanisms for shifting the aggregate demand curve.

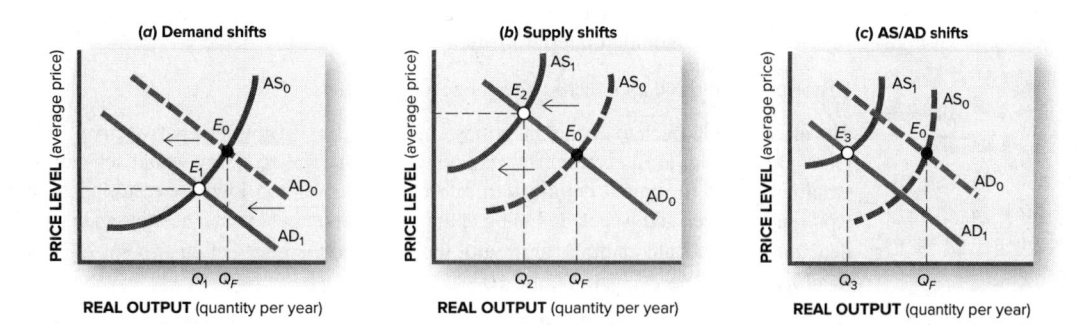

Figure 10.8 Origins of a Recession Unemployment can result from several kinds of market phenomena, including

(a) **Demand shifts:** Total output will fall if aggregate demand (AD) declines. The shift from AD_0 to AD_1 changes equilibrium from point E_0 to E_1 (reducing output from Q_F to Q_1).

(b) **Supply shifts:** Unemployment can also emerge if aggregate supply (AS) declines, as the shift from AS_0 to AS_1 shows.

(c) **AS/AD shifts:** If aggregate demand and aggregate supply both decline, output and employment also fall (from E_0 to E_3).

---

surge 剧增。tight money 收紧银根。curtail 减缩，限制。

Supply-Side Theories 供给方面的理论

Figure 10.8b illustrates an entirely different explanation of the business cycle. Notice that the aggregate *supply* curve is on the move in Figure 10.8b. The initial equilibrium is again at point E_0. This time, however, aggregate demand remains stationary while aggregate supply shifts. The resulting decline of aggregate supply causes output and employment to decline (to Q_2 from Q_F).

Figure 10.8b tells us that aggregate supply may be responsible for downturns as well. Our failure to achieve full employment may result from the unwillingness of producers to provide more goods at existing prices. That unwillingness may originate in rising costs, resource shortages, natural or terrorist disasters, or changes in government taxes and regulations. Whatever the cause, if the aggregate supply curve is AS_1 rather than AS_0, full employment will not be achieved with the demand AD_0. To get more output, the supply curve must shift back to AS_0. The mechanisms for shifting the aggregate supply curve in the desired direction are the focus of supply-side theories.

Eclectic Explanations 折衷解释

Not everyone blames either the demand side or the supply side exclusively. The various macro theories tell us that both supply and demand can help us achieve our policy goals—or cause us to miss them. These theories also demonstrate how various shifts of the aggregate supply and demand curves can achieve any specific output or price level. Figure 10.8c illustrates how undesirable macro outcomes can be caused by simultaneous shifts of both aggregate curves. Eclectic explanations of the business cycle draw from both sides of the market.

POLICY OPTIONS 政策选择

Aggregate supply and demand curves not only help illustrate the causes of the business cycle; they also imply a fairly straightforward set of policy options. Essentially, ***the government has three policy options:***

- ***Shift the aggregate demand curve.*** Find and use policy tools that stimulate or restrain total spending.
- ***Shift the aggregate supply curve.*** Find and implement policy levers that reduce the costs of production or otherwise stimulate more output at every price level.
- ***Do nothing.*** If we can't identify or control the determinants of aggregate supply or demand, we shouldn't interfere with the market.

Historically, all three approaches have been adopted.

The classical approach to economic policy embraced the "do nothing" perspective. Prior to the Great Depression, most economists were convinced that the economy would self-adjust to full employment. If the initial equilibrium rate of output was too low, the resulting imbalances would alter prices and wages, inducing changes in market behavior. The aggregate supply and demand curves would naturally shift until they reached the intersection at point E_0, where full employment (Q_F) prevails in Figure 10.8.

Recent versions of the classical theory—dubbed the new classical economics—stress not only the market's natural ability to self-adjust to *long-run* equilibrium but also the inability of the government to improve *short-run* market outcomes.

Fiscal Policy 财政政策

The Great Depression cast serious doubt on the classical self-adjustment concept. According to Keynes's view, the economy would *not* self-adjust. Rather, it might stagnate at point E_1 in Figure 10.8a until aggregate demand was forcibly shifted. An increase in government spending

---

simultaneous 同时发生的，同步的。dub 把……称为。

on goods and services might provide the necessary shift. Or a cut in taxes might be used to stimulate greater consumer and investor spending. These budgetary tools are the hallmark of fiscal policy. Specifically, **fiscal policy** is the use of government tax and spending powers to alter economic outcomes.

Fiscal policy is an integral feature of modern economic policy. Every year the president and the Congress debate the budget. They argue about whether the economy needs to be stimulated or restrained. They then argue about the level of spending or taxes required to ensure the desired outcome. This is the heart of fiscal policy. President Obama pursued this fiscal strategy as soon as he took office in 2009, convincing Congress to pass a massive increase in government spending. That spending surge helped shift the AD curve to the right, in the direction of fuller employment.

调整的能力。相反，它可能会在图 10.8a 中的 E_1 点停滞不前，直到总需求曲线被强制移动。政府增加对商品和服务的购买支出可能会带来必要的移动。另外，也可以采取减税的办法来刺激消费和投资支出。这些就是财政政策的工具。准确地说，**财政政策**就是政府运用税收和政府支出的力量来改变经济结果。

Monetary Policy 货币政策

The government budget doesn't get all the action. As suggested earlier, the amount of money in circulation may also affect macro equilibrium. If so, the policy arsenal must include some levers to control the money supply. These are the province of monetary policy. **Monetary policy** refers to the use of money and interest rates to alter economic outcomes.

The Federal Reserve (the Fed) has direct control over monetary policy. The Fed is an independent regulatory body charged with maintaining an "appropriate" supply of money. In practice, the Fed adjusts interest rates and the money supply in accordance with its views of macro equilibrium.

To help the economy escape from the Great Recession, the Fed cut interest rates repeatedly, beginning in September 2007. Interest rates hit an historic low in 2012, giving businesses and consumers an added incentive to borrow money for investment and big-ticket consumption like cars and houses. Once the economy got back to full employment in 2017, the Fed reversed course and began nudging interest rates up once again.

政府预算不是问题的全部。之前我们提到，流通中的货币量也可能影响宏观经济的均衡。如果这样的话，政策工具箱中就应该备上几种控制货币供给的杠杆。这就是货币政策的职责了。**货币政策**就是运用货币和利率来改变经济结果。

Supply-Side Policy 供给学派政策

Fiscal and monetary policies focus on the demand side of the market. Both policies are motivated by the conviction that appropriate shifts of the aggregate demand curve can bring about desired changes in output or price levels. **Supply-side policies** offer an alternative; they seek to shift the aggregate supply curve.

There are scores of supply-side levers. The most famous are the tax cuts implemented by the Reagan administration in 1981. Those tax cuts were designed to increase *supply*, not just demand (as traditional fiscal policy does). By reducing tax *rates* on wages and profits, the Reagan tax cuts sought to increase the willingness to supply goods at any given price level. The promise of greater after-tax income was the key incentive for the supply shift.

President Trump pursued a similar policy. His 2017 tax cuts focused on the supply side of the market, by cutting *corporate* taxes and giving special tax incentives for new investment. The idea was to increase investment in factories, equipment, office buildings, and other production facilities, thus shifting the AS curve to the right. As we noted earlier, a rightward shift of the AS curve could both increase output and reduce inflationary pressures.

Other supply-side levers are less well recognized but nevertheless important. Your economics class is an example. The concepts and skills you learn here should increase your productive capabilities. This expands the economy's capacity. With a more educated workforce, a greater supply of goods and services can be produced at any given price level. Hence government subsidies to higher education might be viewed as part of supply-side policy. Government employment and training programs also shift the aggregate supply curve to the right. Immigration policies that increase the inflow of workers get even quicker supply-side effects.

财政和货币政策着眼于市场中的需求方。它们的做法就是让总需求曲线适当移动，以达到合意的产出或价格水平。**供给学派政策**提供了另外一种选择，它们试图使总供给曲线移动。

---

integral 构成整体所必需的，不可或缺的。

Government regulation is another staple of supply-side policy. Regulations that slow innovation or raise the cost of doing business reduce aggregate supply. Removing unnecessary red tape can facilitate more output and reduce inflationary pressures.

POLICY PERSPECTIVES
WHICH POLICY LEVER TO USE?

The various policy levers in our basic macro model have all been used at one time or another. The "do nothing" approach prevailed until the Great Depression. Since that devastating experience, more active policy roles have predominated.

1960s: FISCAL POLICY EMPHASIS

Fiscal policy dominated economic debate in the 1960s. When the economy responded vigorously to tax cuts and increased government spending, it appeared that fiscal policy might be the answer to our macro problems. Many economists even began to assert that they could fine-tune the economy—generate very specific changes in macro equilibrium with appropriate tax and spending policies.

The promise of fiscal policy was tarnished by our failure to control inflation in the late 1960s. It was further compromised by the simultaneous outbreak of both inflation and unemployment in the 1970s. This new macro failure appeared to be chronic, immune to the cures proposed by fiscal policy. Solutions to our macro problems were sought elsewhere.

1970s: MONETARY POLICY EMPHASIS

Monetary policy was next in the limelight. The flaw in fiscal policy, it was argued, originated in its neglect of monetary constraints. More government spending, for example, might require so much of the available money supply that private spending would be crowded out. To ensure a net boost in aggregate demand, more money would be needed—a response only the Fed could make.

In the late 1970s the Fed dominated macro policy. It was hoped that appropriate changes in the money supply would foster greater macro stability. Reduced inflation and lower interest rates were the immediate objectives. Both were to be accomplished by placing greater restraints on the supply of money.

The heavy reliance on monetary policy lasted only a short time. When the economy skidded into yet another recession, the search for more effective policy tools resumed.

1980s: SUPPLY-SIDE EMPHASIS

Supply-side policies became important in 1980. In his 1980 presidential campaign, Ronald Reagan asserted that supply-side tax cuts, deregulation of markets, and other supply-focused policies would reduce both inflation and unemployment. According to Figure 10.8c, such an outcome appeared at least plausible. A rightward shift of the aggregate supply curve does reduce both prices and unemployment. Although the Reagan administration later embraced an eclectic mix of fiscal, monetary, and supply-side policies, its initial supply-side emphasis was distinctive.

1990s: POLICY RESTRAINT

The George H. W. Bush administration pursued a less activist approach. Bush Senior initially resisted tax increases but later accepted them as part of a budget compromise that also reduced government spending. When the economy slid into recession in 1990, President Bush maintained a hands-off policy. Like classical economists, Bush kept assuring the public that the economy would come around on its own. Not until the 1992 elections approached did he propose more active intervention. By then it was too late for him, however. Voters were swayed by Bill Clinton's promises to use tax cuts and increased government spending (fiscal policy) to create "jobs, jobs, jobs."

---

staple 重要部分。predominate 占主导地位。tarnish 使变暗淡。immune 有免疫力的，不受影响的。plausible 看似合理的。be swayed by 被……动摇。

After he was elected, President Clinton reversed policy direction. Rather than delivering the promised tax cuts, Clinton pushed a tax *increase* through Congress. He also pared the size of his planned spending increases.

2000s: ECLECTIC POLICY

The fiscal restraint of the late 1990s helped the federal budget move from deficits to surpluses. These budget surpluses grew so large and so fast that they prompted another turn in fiscal policy. One of the most heated issues in the 2000 presidential campaign was whether to use the federal budget surplus to cut taxes, increase government spending, or pay down the debt. By the time George W. Bush took office in January 2001, the economy had slowed so much that people feared another recession was imminent. This helped convince Congress to pull the fiscal policy lever in the direction of stimulus, with two more rounds of tax cuts in 2002 and 2003.

The fiscal stimulus and low interest rates of 2001–2004 gave the AD curve a big rightward boost. In fact, the economy started growing so fast again that people worried that inflation might accelerate. Since neither the White House nor Congress wanted to raise taxes or cut government spending, the Federal Reserve had to take the lead role again in managing the macro economy.

2008–2016: OBAMANOMICS

By the time Barack Obama took office in January 2009, the economy was deep into another recession. Moreover, the Fed had already exhausted its arsenal of interest rate cuts. So it appeared that only a renewed emphasis on fiscal policy could save the day. President Obama preferred the option of increased government spending rather than tax cuts. He vastly underestimated, however, how much time it would take for increased government spending on roads, bridges, and other infrastructure to actually take place. As a consequence, unemployment stayed high much longer than anticipated. President Obama also paid little heed to how increased regulation and taxes were dampening supply-side incentives. It was left to the Fed to keep interest rates at rock-bottom levels, using monetary policy to restore full employment.

2017–2020: TRUMPONOMICS

President Donald Trump heralded tax cuts as the cornerstone of his economic policy. As noted earlier, he favored tax cuts that would not only increase spending (AD), but also increase production capacity (AS). His 2017 tax cuts heavily favored incentives for business investment rather than consumer spending. To further shift AS to the right, President Trump pursued a vigorous program of deregulation, reducing obstacles to new investments. At the same, however, he pursued immigration restrictions that reduced the flow of labor and erected trade barriers that made production more expensive.

As is evident from this brief review, presidents and other policymakers have made extensive use of our macro-policy tools. Sometimes they have been successful; sometimes not. The continuing policy challenge is to assess the health of the economy, then select the right tools to remedy any macro failures that may exist. While perfection may be beyond our capabilities, the next couple of chapters offer some ideas about which policy levers to pull at any given time.

CHAPTER 10 REVIEW
SUMMARY

- The primary outcomes of the macro economy are output, prices, jobs, and international balances. These outcomes result from the interplay of internal market forces, external shocks, and policy levers. **LO1**

- All the influences on macro outcomes are transmitted through aggregate supply or aggregate demand. Aggregate supply and demand determine the equilibrium rate of output and prices. The economy

---

imminent 即将发生的。

will gravitate to that unique combination of output and price levels. **LO3**
- The market's macro equilibrium may not be consistent with our nation's employment or price goals. Macro failure occurs when the economy's equilibrium is not optimal—when unemployment or inflation is too high. **LO4**
- Macro equilibrium may be disturbed by changes in aggregate supply (AS) or aggregate demand (AD). Such changes are illustrated by shifts of the AS and AD curves, and they lead to a new equilibrium. Recurring AS and AD shifts cause business cycles. **LO4**
- Competing economic theories try to explain the shape and shifts of the aggregate supply and demand curves, thereby explaining the business cycle. Specific theories tend to emphasize demand or supply influences. **LO2**
- Macro policy options range from doing nothing (the classical approach) to various strategies for shifting either the aggregate demand curve or the aggregate supply curve. **LO5**
- Fiscal policy uses government tax and spending powers to alter aggregate demand. Monetary policy uses money and credit availability for the same purpose. **LO5**
- Supply-side policies include all interventions that shift the aggregate supply curve. Examples include tax incentives, (de)regulation, immigration, and resource development. **LO5**

TERMS TO REMEMBER

Define the following terms:

macroeconomics
Say's law
aggregate demand
real GDP
aggregate supply
equilibrium (macro)
full employment GDP

unemployment
inflation
business cycle
fiscal policy
monetary policy
supply-side policy

QUESTIONS FOR DISCUSSION

1. If the price level were below P_E in Figure 10.5, what macro problems would we observe? Why is P_E considered an equilibrium? **LO4**
2. What factors might cause a rightward shift of the aggregate demand curve? What might induce a rightward shift of aggregate supply? **LO3**
3. What kind of external shock would benefit an economy? **LO1**
4. What would a *horizontal* aggregate supply curve imply about producer behavior? How about a vertical AS curve? **LO3**
5. If equilibrium is compatible with both buyers' and sellers' intentions, how can it be undesirable? **LO4**
6. Th U.S. stock market increased in value by 25 percent in 2017. How might this have affected aggregate demand? What happens to aggregate demand when the stock market plunges? **LO3**
7. Why would job losses in the construction industry cause a loss of retail jobs, as the News Wire "Undesirable Outcomes" suggests? **LO4**
8. **POLICY PERSPECTIVES** Why did President Obama believe that government intervention was needed to get the economy out of the 2008–2009 recession? Could the economy have recovered on its own? **LO4, LO5**
9. **POLICY PERSPECTIVES** President Trump directed his 2017 tax cuts more to businesses than to consumers. Does it matter? How different would have been the impact of consumer tax cuts? **LO5**
10. **POLICY PERSPECTIVES** What is the condition of the U.S. economy now? Should the government intervene more? What policy levers should be pulled, if any? **LO5**

PROBLEMS

1. In Figure 10.8, (*a*) what is the level of full employment? How much is the rate of output reduced when (*b*) AD shifts leftward ? (*c*) AS shifts leftward? (*d*) both AD and AS shift leftward? **LO4**

2. In Figure 10.6, when AD shifts rightward, does *(a)* the price level increase or decrease and *(b)* output increase or decrease? **LO3**
3. Illustrate these events with AS or AD shifts: **LO3**
    a. government cuts defense spending.
    b. interest rates rise.
    c. imported oil gets cheaper.
    d. taxes on the rich are increased.

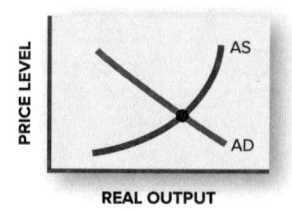

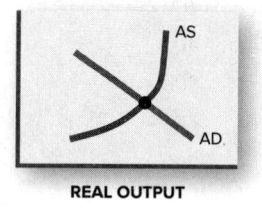

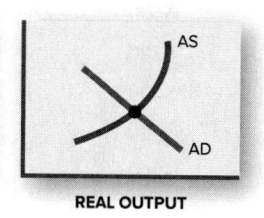

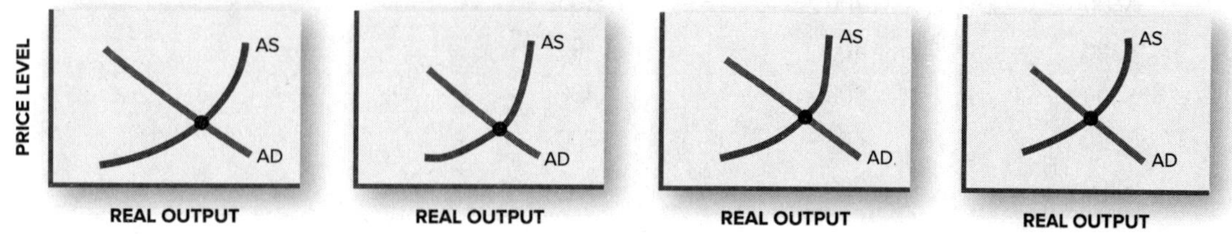

a. Government cuts defense spending.

b. Interest rates rise.

c. Imported oil gets cheaper.

d. Taxes on the rich are increased.

4. Based on the News Wire "Shifting Aggregate Supply," **LO4**
    a. illustrate the AS shift that occurs.
    b. identify the old (E_0) and new (E_1) macro equilibrium.
    c. what are the macro results?
    d. how can the economy stay healthy in this case?
5. Graph the following aggregate supply and demand curves (be sure to draw to scale). **LO3**

Price Level	Real GDP (in $ Trillions)	
	Supplied	Demanded
100	4	16
110	10	15
140	14	12
200	15	6

    a. What is the equilibrium price level?
    b. What is the equilibrium output?
    c. If the quantity of output demanded at every price level increases by $2 trillion, what happens to equilibrium output and prices? Graph your answer.
6. Draw a conventional aggregate demand curve on a graph. Then add three different aggregate supply curves, labeled **LO1, LO3**

    S_1: horizontal curve

    S_2: upward-sloping curve

    S_3: vertical curve

    all intersecting the AD curve at the same point. If AD were to increase (shift to the right), which AS curve would lead to
    a. the biggest increase in output?
    b. the largest jump in prices?
    c. the least inflation?

7. The following schedule provides information with which to draw both an aggregate demand curve and an aggregate supply curve. Both curves are assumed to be straight lines. **LO4**

Average Price (Dollars per Unit)	Quantity Demanded (Units per Year)	Quantity Supplied (Units per Year)
$800	100	700
$700	200	600
$600	300	500
$500	400	400
$400	500	300
$300	600	200
$200	700	100

   a. At what price level does equilibrium occur?
   b. What curve would have shifted if a new equilibrium were to occur at an output level of 700 and a price level of $800?
   c. What curve would have shifted if a new equilibrium were to occur at an output level of 700 and a price level of $500?
   d. What curve would have shifted if a new equilibrium were to occur at an output level of 700 and a price level of $200?
   e. Compared to the initial equilibrium (*a*), how have the outcomes in (*b*), (*c*), and (*d*) changed price levels or output?

8. Suppose AD shifts by $60 for every $1,000 change in consumer wealth. By how much will AD increase when the stock market rises in value by $300 billion? **LO3**

9. Suppose AS increases by $50 billion for every 1 percentage point decrease in business tax rates. By how much will AS shift to the right when the tax rate is reduced from 35 percent to 21 percent? **LO3**

10. **POLICY PERSPECTIVES** Suppose a nation's *maximum* GDP (with 0 percent unemployment) is $25 trillion. **LO5**

    a. Assuming that *full employment* occurs when there is 4 percent unemployment, how much is full employment GDP?
    b. If *equilibrium* GDP is $20 trillion, how far from full employment GDP is this economy?
    c. Which of the following shifts will move this economy closer to full employment?
        i. AD shifts to the right.
        ii. AD shifts to the left.
        iii. AS shifts to the right.
        iv. AS shifts to the left.

CHAPTER ELEVEN

Fiscal Policy 财政政策

©Susan Walsh/AP Images

LEARNING OBJECTIVES

After reading this chapter, you should be able to:

1. Define what fiscal policy is.
2. Explain why fiscal policy might be needed.
3. Illustrate what the multiplier is and how it works.
4. Tell how fiscal stimulus or restraint is achieved.
5. Specify how fiscal policy affects the federal budget.

During the Great Depression of the 1930s, as many as 13 million Americans were out of work. They were capable people and eager to work. But no one would hire them. As sympathetic as employers might have been, they simply could not use any more workers. Consumers were not buying the goods and services already being produced. Employers were more likely to cut back production and lay off still more workers than to hire any new ones. As a consequence, an "army of the unemployed" was created in 1929 and continued to grow for nearly a decade. It was not until the outbreak of World War II that enough jobs could be found for the unemployed, and most of those "jobs" were in the armed forces.

The Great Depression was the springboard for the Keynesian approach to economic policy. John Maynard Keynes concluded that the ranks of unemployed persons were growing because of problems on the *demand* side of product markets. People simply were not able and willing to buy all the goods and services the economy was capable of producing. As a consequence, producers had no incentive to increase output or to hire more labor. So long as the demand for goods and services was inadequate, unemployment was inevitable.

Keynes sought to explain how a deficiency of demand could arise in a market economy and then to show how and why the government had to intervene. Keynes was convinced that government intervention was necessary to achieve our macroeconomic goals, particularly full employment. To that end, Keynes advocated aggressive use of fiscal policy—that is, deployment of the government's tax and spending powers to alter macro outcomes. He urged policymakers to use these powers to minimize the swings of the business cycle.

---

sympathetic 有同情心的。lay off 解雇。swing 波动,震荡。

Chapter Eleven: Fiscal Policy

In this chapter we take a closer look at what Keynes intended. We focus on the following questions:

- Why did Keynes think the market was inherently unstable?
- How can fiscal policy help stabilize the economy?
- How will the use of fiscal policy affect the government's budget deficit?

We'll also examine how the Keynesian strategy of fiscal stimulus was used to help end the Great Recession of 2008–2009.

总需求的构成
COMPONENTS OF AGGREGATE DEMAND

财政政策的前提是：对商品和服务的总需求不总是与经济稳定性相一致。正如第10章（以图10.7为例）所观察到的，衰退出现在总需求下降时；只要总需求持续低于经济的生产能力，衰退就会继续存在。通货膨胀也是由类似的不均衡产生的。如果总需求比产出增长得快，价格就趋向于上涨，而且价格水平会持续上升，直到总需求与生产水平相一致。

The premise of **fiscal policy** is that the **aggregate demand** for goods and services will not always be compatible with economic stability. As we observed in Chapter 10 (e.g., Figure 10.7), *recessions occur when aggregate demand declines; recessions persist when aggregate demand remains below the economy's capacity to produce.* Inflation results from similar imbalances. If aggregate demand increases faster than output, prices tend to rise. The price level will keep rising until aggregate demand is compatible with the rate of production.

But why do such macro failures occur? Why wouldn't aggregate demand always reflect the economy's full employment potential?

To determine whether we are likely to have the right amount of aggregate demand, we need to take a closer look at spending behavior. Who buys the goods and services on which output decisions and jobs depend?

The four major components of aggregate demand are:

总需求的四个主要构成是：

C：消费支出

I：投资支出

G：政府支出

X−IM：净出口（出口减去进口）

C:	*Consumption*
I:	*Investment*
G:	*Government spending*
X − IM:	*Net exports (exports minus imports)*

Consumption 消费

消费是指所有家庭在商品和服务上的支出——从食品杂货到大学学费的所有商品和服务。环顾四周，你将发现以消费为导向的经济比比皆是。总的说来，消费支出占美国经济总支出的2/3以上（图11.1）。

Consumption refers to all household expenditures on goods and services—everything from groceries to college tuition. Just look around and you can see the trappings of our consumer-oriented economy. In the aggregate, consumption spending accounts for over two-thirds of total spending in the U.S. economy (Figure 11.1).

Because consumer spending looms so large in aggregate demand, any change in consumer behavior can have a profound impact on employment and prices. Life would be simple for policymakers if consumers kept spending their incomes at the same rate. Then there wouldn't be any consumer-induced shifts of aggregate demand (AD). But life isn't that simple: Consumers *do* change their behavior. From 2002 to 2005, for example, consumers went on a buying spree, purchasing new homes, new cars, big-screen TVs, and iPods. The consumption component of AD kept the AD curve shifting rightward, increasing equilibrium GDP.

By late 2007, however, the rush to consume appeared to be slowing. Declining home sales and prices, high gasoline prices, and continuing concerns about terrorism and the war in Iraq were giving consumers pause. As the News Wire "Shifts in Aggregate Demand" confirms, economists feared that a slowdown in consumer spending might reverse the path of the AD curve (they were right, as the 2008–2009 recession confirmed).

NEWS WIRE SHIFTS IN AGGREGATE DEMAND

RECESSION LOOMING

You don't have to be an economist to foresee a recession coming. There are ample warning signs everywhere. Housing prices have been falling sharply, depleting both the purchasing power and the confidence of American consumers. The 1,000-point drop in the Dow Jones Industrial Average since early

---

loom 逼近，临近。profound 意义深远的。deplete 大量减少，耗尽。

October has added to the consumer malaise. As if those trends in wealth were not depressing enough, job growth has slowed and wages gains have all but disappeared. More and more households are feeling a budget squeeze. This has got to put a dent in consumer spending soon.

Another bleak sign of looming recession is apparent at the gas station. Gasoline prices are rising, making the cost of driving, heating, and air-conditioning more expensive. Forced to pay more for energy, consumers will have to cut back their spending on other goods. Walmart and Target have already reported a slowdown in retail sales.

These early warning signs are more than just troubling. As David Rosenberg, the chief economist at Merrill Lynch, sees it, wealth and income trends make a recession next year inevitable. "Right now, the question is how bad it's going to get. The question is one of magnitude."

Source: News accounts of November 2007.

NOTE: Consumer spending accounts for two-thirds of aggregate demand. If consumer spending slows, the AD curve shifts left, increasing the risk of recession.
注：消费者支出占总需求的2/3。如果消费者支出放缓，总需求曲线将向左移动，这将增加经济衰退的风险。

To anticipate such changes in consumer behavior, the economic doctors regularly take consumers' pulse. Every month the University of Michigan and the Conference Board survey a cross-section of U.S. households to see how they are feeling. They ask how confident consumers are about their jobs and incomes and how optimistic they are about their economic future. The responses to such questions are combined into an index of consumer confidence, which is reported monthly. If confidence is rising, consumers are likely to keep spending. When consumer confidence declines, as in January 2009 (see the News Wire "Shifting Aggregate Demand" in Chapter 10), the economic doctors worry that the AD curve may shift backward.

Total spending: $20 trillion

Government spending: 18%

Investment spending: 17%

Consumption spending: 68%

Net exports: –3%

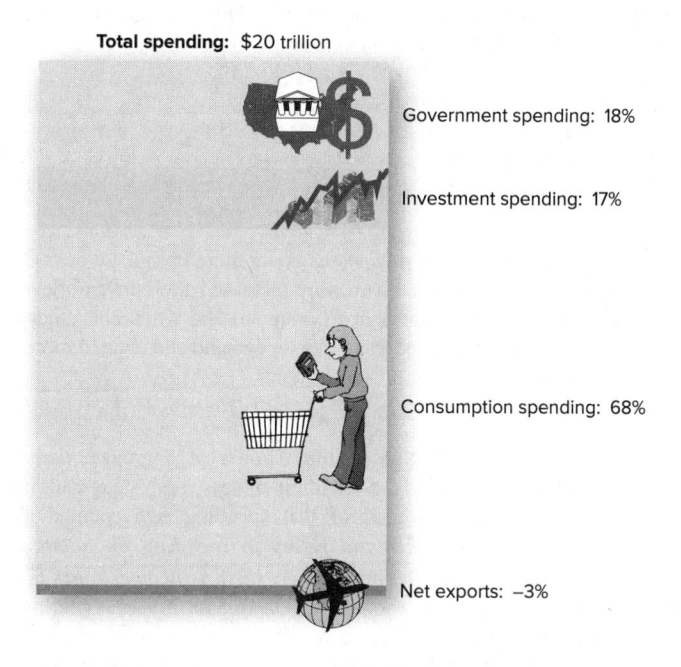

Figure 11.1 Components of Aggregate Demand In 2018, the output of the U.S. economy was $20 trillion. Over two-thirds of that output consisted of consumer goods and services. The government sectors (federal, state, and local) demanded 18 percent of total output. Investment spending took another 17 percent. Finally, because imports exceeded exports, the impact of net exports on aggregate demand was negative. ■
Source: U.S. Department of Commerce.

anticipate 预测，预期。

Investment 投资

总需求的第二个构成——投资，同样是容易改变的行为。**投资**是指企业在新厂房和设备上的支出。当企业决定建造新厂房或改造旧厂房时，所引发的支出将增加总需求。当农民更换旧拖拉机时，他们的购买行为也增加了商品和服务的总支出。新建住宅也视为（住宅）投资的一部分。

The second component of AD—investment—is also prone to behavioral shifts. **Investment** refers to business spending on new plant and equipment. When a corporation decides to build a new factory or modernize an old one, the resulting expenditure adds to aggregate demand. When farmers replace their old tractors, their purchases also increase total spending on goods and services. Construction of new homes is also counted as part of (residential) investment.

Changes in business inventory are counted as investment too. Retail stores stock their shelves with goods bought from other firms. Amazon stocks even more inventory in its 130 "fulfillment centers" scattered around the country (see News Wire "Inventory Investment"). The companies that stockpile inventory hope to sell these products later to consumers. But the inventory purchases are themselves part of aggregate demand, as they are acquisitions of newly produced products. When companies allow their inventories to shrink, then inventory investment is negative. During the Great Depression not only was inventory investment negative, but spending on plant and equipment also plummeted. As a result, total business investment plunged by 70 percent between 1929 and 1933. This plunge in investment spending wracked aggregate demand and eliminated millions of jobs.

NEWS WIRE INVENTORY INVESTMENT

Amazon Prime Day Approaches $3 Billion in Sales

For 36 hours Amazon's Prime members got some amazing deals on thousands of products. And they responded by buying nearly $3 billion of merchandise from the e-commerce giant. Amazon now has 130 "fulfillment centers" in the United States, with a total warehouse space of over 100 million square feet (equivalent to 60 times the size of America's largest stadium, the U.S. Bank stadium in Minneapolis). The nation's largest online retailer stores thousands of products in its warehouses, for itself and third-party vendors, then picks, packs, and ships them to customers in as little as one day. Sales this year are projected to exceed $200 billion, about 4 percent of all retail sales.

Source: News accounts of July 16–20, 2018.

NOTE: Inventory purchases are part of business investment and therefore aggregate demand. Businesses purchase inventory when they expect consumers to buy those products later.
注：库存采购是商业投资的一部分，因此也是总需求的一部分。当企业预期消费者以后会购买这些产品时，他们会进行库存采购。

Near the end of 2009, businesses had a more optimistic outlook. Sensing that the 2008–2009 recession was ending, businesses increased their inventories by roughly 40 percent. They wanted to be sure their shelves were stocked when consumers started shopping again. That inventory buildup added to aggregate demand and created more jobs.

Government Spending 政府支出

政府支出是总需求的第三个来源。美国联邦政府现在每年大约支出 4 万亿美元，州政府和地方政府的总支出则更多。然而，并不是所有这些支出都计入总需求的。总需求指花费在商品和服务上的支出。但是政府支出的很大一部分是用于收入转移——付给那些没有提供服务的人的款项。

Government spending is a third source of aggregate demand. The federal government currently spends nearly $4 trillion a year, and state and local governments collectively spend even more. Not all of that spending gets counted as part of aggregate demand, however. *Aggregate demand refers to spending on goods and services.* Much of what the government spends, however, is merely *income transfers*—payments to individuals for which no services are exchanged. Uncle Sam, for example, mails out over $1 trillion a year in Social Security checks—a fourth of all federal spending. These Social Security checks don't represent a demand for goods and services. That money will become part of aggregate demand only when the Social Security recipients spend their transfer income on goods and services.

Only that portion of government budgets that gets spent on goods and services represents part of aggregate demand. Aggregate demand includes federal, state, and local spending on highways, schools, police, national defense, and all other goods and services the public sector provides. Such spending now accounts for nearly one-fifth of aggregate demand.

---

recipient 接受者，受众。

Net Exports　净出口

The fourth component of aggregate demand, **net exports**, is the difference between export and import spending. The demand of foreigners for American-made products shows up as U.S. exports. At the same time, Americans spend some of their income on goods imported from other countries. The difference between exports and imports represents the *net* demand for domestic output.

U.S. net exports are negative. This means that Americans are buying more goods from abroad than foreigners are buying from us. The net effect of trade is thus to reduce domestic aggregate demand. That is why net exports is a negative amount in Figure 11.1.

Net export flows are also subject to abrupt changes. Strong growth in foreign nations may spur demands for U.S. exports. Increasing American incomes will have a similar effect on U.S. imports. Conversely, tariffs (import taxes) on imported good will reduce the volume of U.S. imports. Such changes in the flow of net exports will shift the AD curve.

总需求的第四个构成是**净出口**，它是出口与进口的差额。外国人对美国制造产品的需求表现为美国的出口。同时，美国人也将收入的一部分用于购买从其他国家进口的商品。出口与进口的差额代表国内产出的净需求。

Equilibrium　均衡

The four components of aggregate demand combine to determine the shape, position, and potential shifts of the aggregate demand curve. Notice that **aggregate demand is not a single number but instead a schedule of planned purchases**. The quantity of output market participants desire to purchase depends in part on the price level.

Suppose the existing price level is P_1, as seen in Figure 11.2, and the curve AS represents aggregate supply. Full employment is represented by the output level Q_F. We want to know whether aggregate demand will be just enough to ensure both price stability and full employment. This happy **equilibrium** occurs only if the aggregate demand curve intersects the aggregate supply curve at point *a*. The curve AD* achieves this goal.

总需求的四个构成共同决定了总需求曲线的形状、位置及潜在移动。注意，总需求不是一个单纯的数字，而是计划购买的一览表。市场参与者期望购买的产出数量部分取决于价格水平。

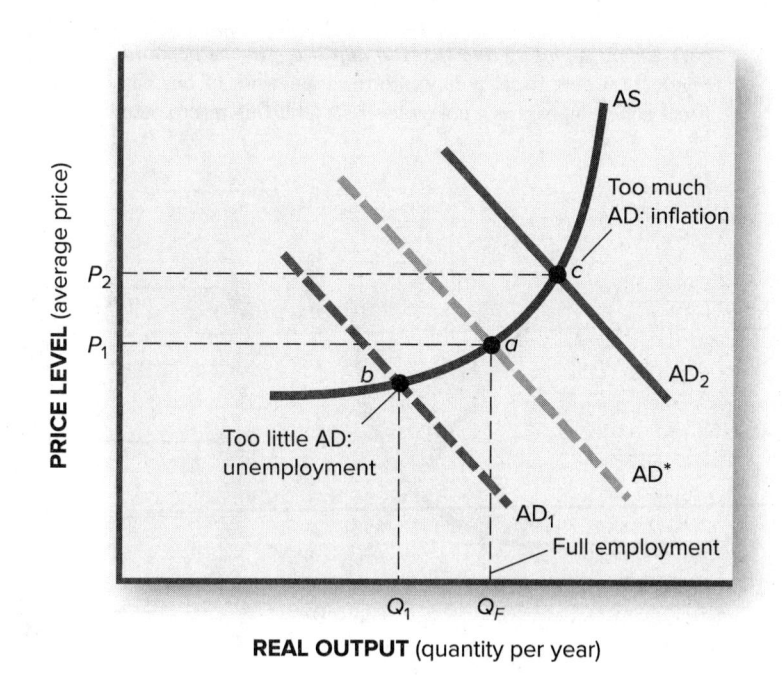

Figure 11.2 The Desired Equilibrium The goal of fiscal policy is to achieve price stability and full employment, the desired equilibrium represented by point *a*. This equilibrium will occur only if aggregate demand is equal to AD*. Less demand (e.g., AD$_1$) will cause unemployment; more demand (e.g., AD$_2$) will cause inflation. ■

spur 刺激，激励。

Inadequate Demand 需求不足

Aggregate demand may turn out to be less than perfect, however. Keep in mind that aggregate demand includes four different types of spending:

$$AD = C + I + G + (X - IM)$$

There is no evident reason these four distinct components of aggregate demand would generate exactly the output Q_F at the price level P_1 in Figure 11.2. They could in fact generate *less* spending, as illustrated by the curve AD_1. In this case, aggregate demand falls short, leaving some potential output unsold at the equilibrium point b.

Excessive Demand 需求过剩

In contrast, the curve AD_2 illustrates a situation of excessive aggregate demand. In this case, the combined expenditure plans of market participants *exceed* the economy's full employment output. The resulting scramble for available goods and services pushes prices up to the level P_2. This inflationary equilibrium is illustrated by the AS/AD_2 intersection at point c.

THE NATURE OF FISCAL POLICY 财政政策的本质

Clearly, we will fulfill our macroeconomic goals only if we get the right amount of aggregate demand (the curve AD* in Figure 11.2). But what are the chances of such a fortunate event? Keynes asserted that the odds are stacked against such an outcome. Indeed, Keynes concluded that ***it would be a minor miracle if $C + I + G + (X - IM)$ added up to exactly the right amount of aggregate demand.*** Consumers, investors, and foreigners all make independent decisions on how much to spend. Why should those separate decisions result in just enough demand to ensure either full employment or price stability? It is far more likely that the level of aggregate demand will turn out to be wrong. In these circumstances, government spending must be the safety valve that expands or contracts aggregate demand as needed. ***The use of government spending and taxes to adjust aggregate demand is the essence of fiscal policy.*** Figure 11.3 puts fiscal policy into the framework of our basic macro model. In this figure, fiscal policy appears as a policy lever for adjusting macro outcomes.

显然，只有达到合适的总需求数量（图 11.2 中的曲线 AD*），我们才能实现宏观经济目标。但是这样幸运的概率有多大呢？凯恩斯认为微乎其微。事实上，凯恩斯指出，使 $C + I + G + (X - IM)$ 刚好等于令人满意的总需求量可谓是奇迹。消费者、投资者和外国人各自做出支出决策。为什么这些独立的决策恰好能产生确保充分就业或价格稳定的充足需求呢？总需求水平不符合上述要求的可能性很大。在这些情况下，政府支出就必须充当安全阀：根据需要来扩大或缩小总需求。运用政府支出和税收来调整总需求是财政政策的本质。图 11.3 中我们将财政政策纳入了宏观模型的基本框架。在此图中，我们将财政政策视为调节宏观经济运行的政策杠杆。

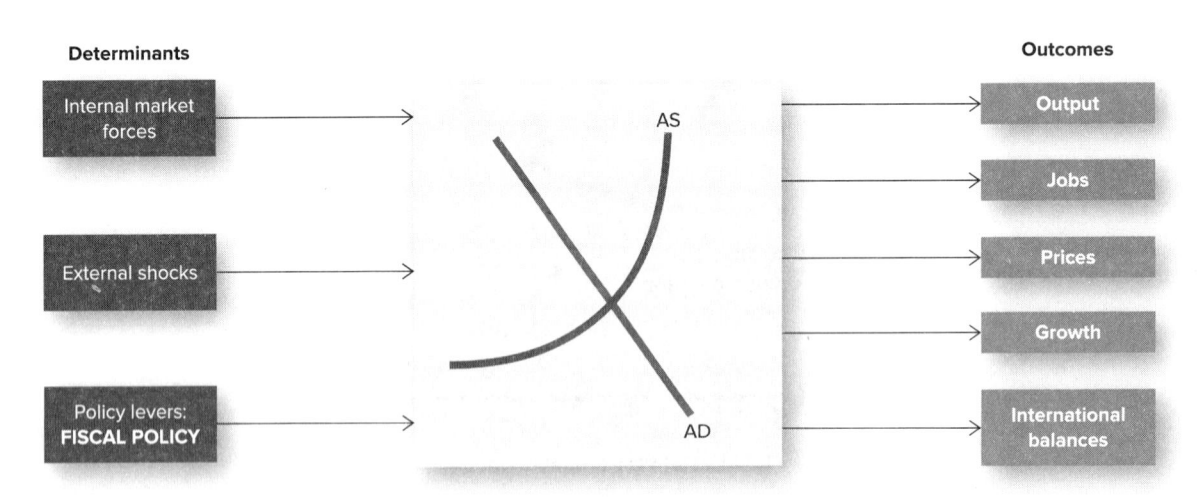

Figure 11.3 Fiscal Policy Fiscal policy refers to the use of the government tax and spending powers to alter macro outcomes. Fiscal policy works principally through shifts of the aggregate demand curve.

FISCAL STIMULUS 财政刺激

Suppose that aggregate demand has fallen short of our goals and unemployment rates are high. This scenario is illustrated in Figure 11.4. Full employment is reached when $6 trillion of output is demanded at current price levels, as indicated by Q_F. The quantity of output actually demanded at current price levels, however, is only $5.6 trillion ($Q_1$), as determined by the intersection at point *b*. Hence there is a gap between the economy's ability to produce (Q_F) and the amount of output people are willing to buy (Q_1) at the current price level (P_1). *The difference between equilibrium output and full employment output is called the GDP gap.* In Figure 11.4, this **GDP gap** amounts to $400 billion. If nothing is done, $400 billion of productive facilities will be idled and millions of workers will be unemployed.

The goal here is to eliminate the GDP gap by *shifting* the aggregate demand curve to the right. In this case, spending has to increase by $400 billion per year to close the GDP gap. How can fiscal policy make this happen?

President Obama relied on this policy lever when he convinced Congress to pass the American Recovery and Reinvestment Act in February 2009 (see the accompanying News Wire "Fiscal Stimulus: Government Spending"). The largest chunk of that act was a $308.3 billion increase in government spending on goods and services (e.g., highways, bridges, railroads, energy). Obama expected that increased spending to push the AD curve so far to the right that 3 million to 4 million jobs would be restored. He envisioned the GDP gap eventually closing.

假设总需求不能满足我们的目标，并且失业率也很高。图11.4 展示了上述假设情况。在目前的价格水平下，当需求为 6 万亿美元的产出（如图中 Q_F 所示）时，就实现了充分就业的目标。但是目前需求仅仅为 5.6 万亿美元的产出（Q_1）。这是由交点 *b* 确定的，因此在目前的价格水平（P_1）下，经济的生产能力（Q_F）和人们愿意购买的产出数量（Q_1）间产生了缺口。均衡产出和充分就业产出之间的差额称为 GDP 缺口。

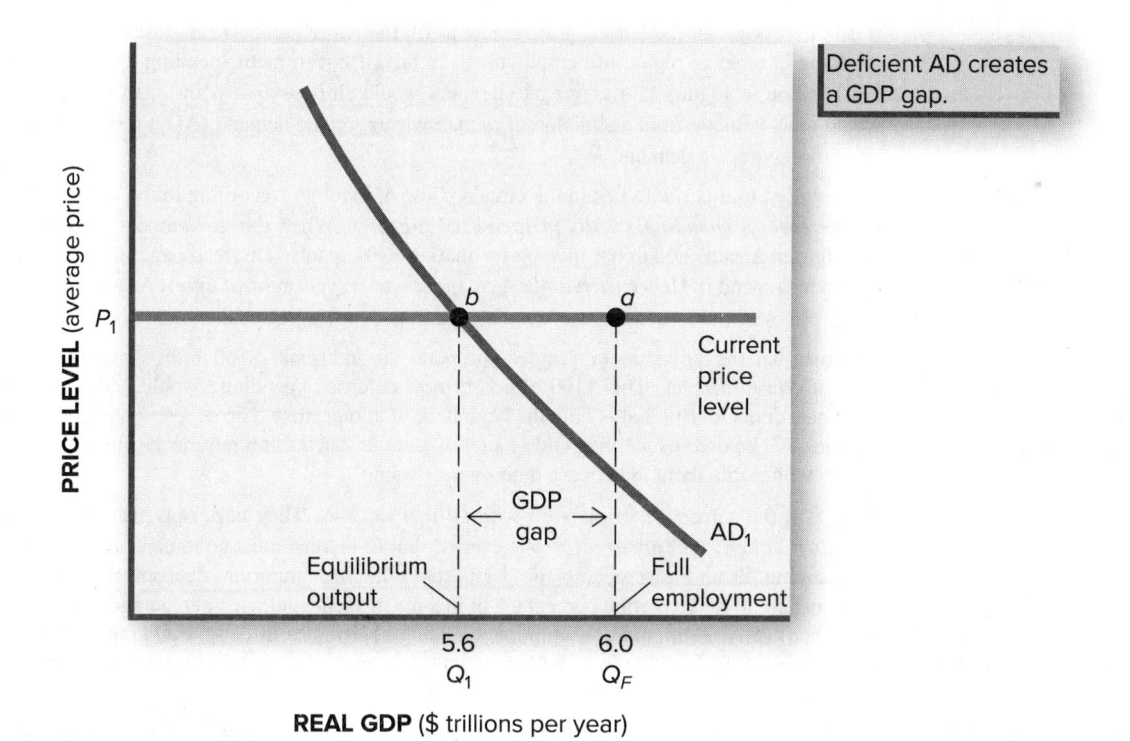

Figure 11.4 Deficient Demand The aggregate demand curve AD_1 results in only $5.6 trillion of final sales at current price levels (P_1). This is well short of full employment (Q_F), which occurs at $6.0 trillion of output. The fiscal policy goal is to close the GDP gap by shifting the AD curve rightward until it passes through point *a*. ■

productive facility 生产设施。chunk 一大块。

> **NEWS WIRE** FISCAL STIMULUS: GOVERNMENT SPENDING
>
> **SENATE OKS OBAMA STIMULUS PACKAGE**
>
> Washington, DC—The U.S. Congress gave final approval to President Obama's $787 billion stimulus package yesterday. The $787 billion package is intended to give a boost to the economy, lifting it out of the current recession. At the heart of the package is a half-trillion increase in spending for infrastructure construction, high-speed rail projects, increased unemployment benefits, and scores of other government programs. The package will pump $185 billion into the economy this year and $399 billion next year. Democrats say the plan will save or create 3.5 million jobs. The Senate passed the measure by a vote of 60–38 with the support of three Republicans. Earlier, the House passed the bill by a vote of 246–183 with no Republican support.
>
> Source: News accounts of February 13–15, 2009.
>
> **NOTE:** President Obama counted on increased government spending to shift the AD curve to the right, increasing GDP and employment.
> 注：奥巴马总统依靠增加政府支出，使 AD 曲线向右移动，增加 GDP 和就业。

More Government Spending 更多的政府支出

The simplest solution to the demand shortfall does appear to be increased government spending. If the government were to step up its purchases of tanks, highways, schools, and other goods, the increased spending would add directly to aggregate demand. This would shift the aggregate demand curve rightward, moving us closer to full employment. Hence *increased government spending is a form of* **fiscal stimulus.**

Multiplier Effects 乘数效应

It isn't necessary for the federal government to fill the entire gap between desired and current spending in order to regain full employment. In fact, if government spending did increase by $400 billion in Figure 11.4, aggregate demand would shift *beyond* point *a*. In that case we would quickly move from a situation of *inadequate* aggregate demand (AD_1) to a situation of *excessive* aggregate demand.

The solution to this riddle lies in the circular flow of income. According to the circular flow, *an increase in spending results in increased incomes.* When the government increases its spending, it creates additional income for market participants. The recipients of this income will in turn spend it. Hence *each dollar gets spent and respent several times.* As a result, every dollar of government spending has a *multiplied* impact on aggregate demand.

Suppose that the government decided to spend an additional $100 billion per year on a fleet of cruise missiles. This $100 billion of new defense expenditure would add directly to aggregate demand. But that is only the beginning of a long story. The people who build cruise missiles will be on the receiving end of a lot of income. Their fatter paychecks, dividends, and profits will enable them to increase their own spending.

What will the aerospace workers do with all that income? They have only two choices: *all income is either spent or saved.* Hence every dollar of income must go to consumer spending or to **saving**. From a macroeconomic perspective, the only important decision the aerospace workers have to make is what percentage of income to spend and what percentage to save (i.e., not spend). Any additional consumption spending contributes directly to aggregate demand. The portion of income that is saved (not spent) goes under the mattress or into banks or other financial institutions.

Suppose the aerospace workers decide to spend 75 percent of any extra income they get and to save the rest (25 percent). We call these percentages the marginal propensity to consume and the marginal propensity to save, respectively. The **marginal propensity to consume (MPC)** is the fraction of *additional* income people spend. The **marginal propensity to save (MPS)** is the fraction of new income that is saved.

---

cruise missile 巡航导弹。 fatter 更丰厚的。 aerospace 航空航天。 mattress 床垫。

Figure 11.5 illustrates how the spending and saving decisions are connected. In this case we have assumed that the MPC equals 0.75. Hence 75 cents out of any extra dollar get spent. By definition, the remaining 25 cents get saved. The MPC and MPS tell us how the aerospace workers will behave when their incomes rise.

According to these behavioral patterns, the aerospace workers will use their additional $100 billion of income as follows:

$$\text{Increased consumption} = \text{MPC} \times \text{additional income}$$
$$= 0.75 \times \$100 \text{ billion}$$
$$= \$75 \text{ billion}$$

$$\text{Increased saving} = \text{MPS} \times \text{additional income}$$
$$= 0.25 \times \$100 \text{ billion}$$
$$= \$25 \text{ billion}$$

Thus all of the new income is either spent ($75 billion) or saved ($25 billion).

According to our MPC calculations, the aerospace workers increase their consumer spending by $75 billion. This $75 billion of new consumption adds directly to aggregate demand. Hence aggregate demand has now been increased *twice*: first by the government expenditure on missiles ($100 billion) and then by the additional consumption of the aerospace workers ($75 billion). Thus aggregate demand has increased by $175 billion as a consequence of the stepped-up defense expenditure. ***The fiscal stimulus to aggregate demand includes both the initial increase in government spending and all subsequent increases in consumer spending triggered by the government outlays.*** That combined stimulus is already up to $175 billion.

The stimulus of new government spending doesn't stop with the aerospace workers. The circular flow of income is a *continuing* process. The money spent by the aerospace workers becomes income to *other* workers. As their incomes rise, we expect their spending to increase as well. In other words, ***income gets spent and respent in the circular flow.*** This multiplier process is illustrated in Figure 11.6.

我们通过 MPC 计算得出，航空航天工作者的消费支出增加了 750 亿美元。新增加的这 750 亿美元直接增加了总需求。因此总需求增加了两次：第一次是政府在导弹上的支出（1 000 亿美元），第二次是航空航天工作者新增的消费支出（750 亿美元）。因此，由于国防支出的增加，总需求增加了 1 750 亿美元。对总需求的财政刺激不仅包括最初的政府支出增加，而且包括所有由政府支出引发的消费支出。这些刺激合起来已达到 1 750 亿美元。

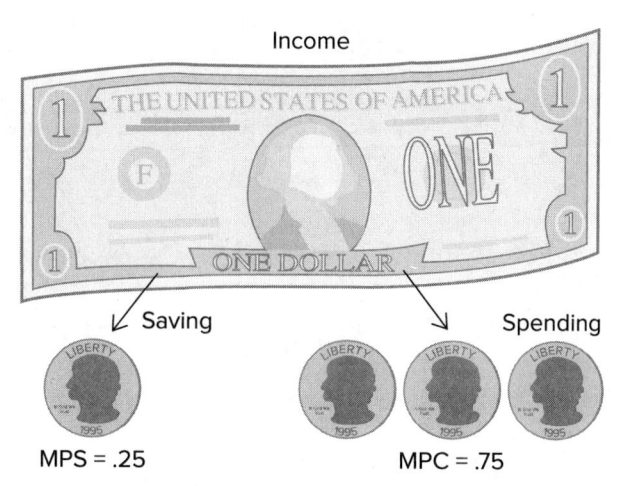

Figure 11.5 MPC and MPS The marginal propensity to consume (MPC) tells us what portion of an extra dollar of income will be spent. The remaining portion will be saved. The MPC and MPS help us predict consumer responses to changes in income.

Spending Cycles 支出循环

表 11.1 描述了乘数过程的细节。假设航空航天工作者花 750 亿美元用于购买新船。这样就增加了船舶制造者的收入，从而也增加了他们的支出。

Table 11.1 fills in the details of the multiplier process. Suppose the aerospace workers spend their $75 billion on new boats. This increases the income of boat builders. They, too, are then in a position to increase *their* spending.

Suppose the boat builders also have a marginal propensity to consume of 0.75. They will then spend 75 percent of *their* new income ($75 billion). This will add *another* $56.25 billion to consumption demand.

Notice in Table 11.1 what is happening to cumulative spending as the multiplier process continues. When the boat builders go on a spending spree, the cumulative increase in spending becomes:

Cycle 1: Government expenditure on cruise missiles	$100.00 billion
Cycle 2: Aerospace workers, purchase of boats	75.00 billion
Cycle 3: Boat builders' expenditure on beer	56.25 billion
Cumulative increase in spending after three cycles	$231.25 billion

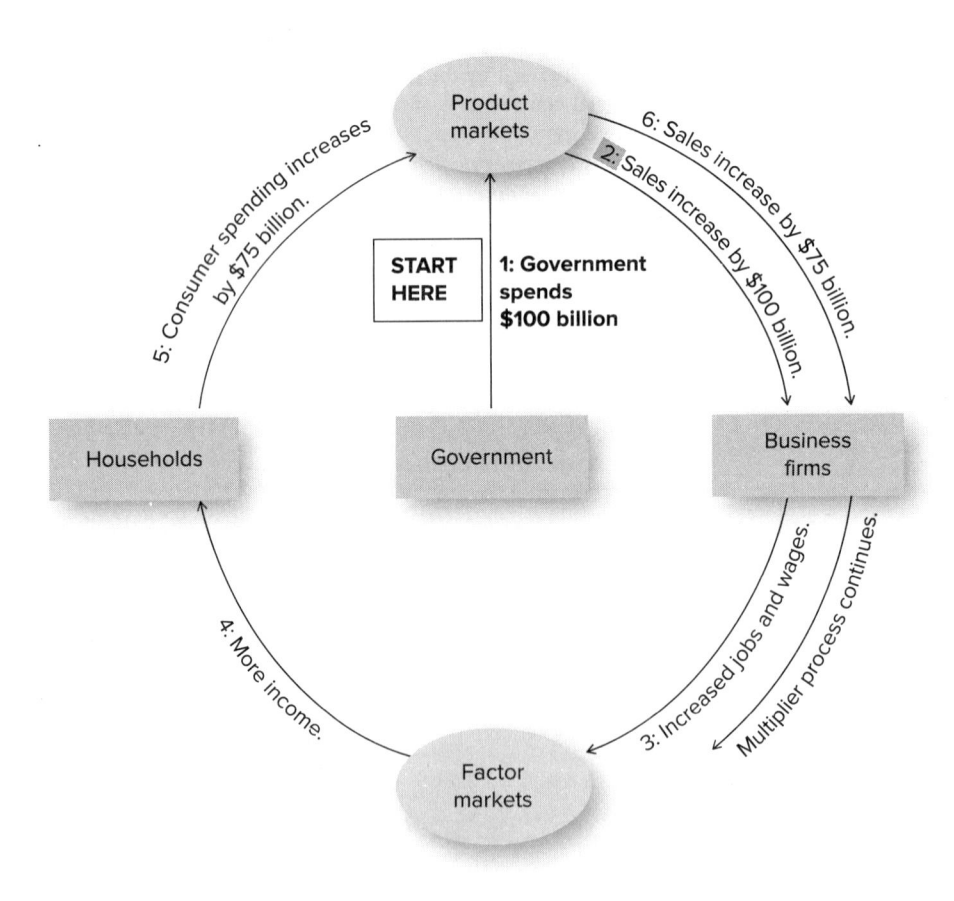

Figure 11.6 The Circular Flow In the circular flow of income, money gets spent and respent multiple times. As a result of this multiplier process, aggregate demand increases by much more than the initial increase in government spending. An MPC of 0.75 is assumed here.

---

spree 狂欢。

Spending Cycles	Change in Spending during Cycle (Billions per Year)	Cumulative Increase in Spending (Billions per Year)
First cycle: Government buys $100 billion worth of missiles.	$100.00	$100.00
Second cycle: Missile workers have more income ($100 billion), buy new boats (0.75 × $100).	75.00	175.00
Third cycle: Boat builders have more income ($75 billion), spend it on beer (0.75 × $75).	56.25	231.25
Fourth cycle: Bartenders and brewery workers have more income ($56.25 billion), spend it on new cars (0.75 × $56.25).	42.19	273.44
Fifth cycle: Autoworkers have more income, spend it on clothes (0.75 × $42.19).	31.64	305.08
Sixth cycle: apparel workers have more income ($42.19), spend it on movies and entertainment (0.75 × $31.64).	23.73	328.81
Nth cycle and beyond		400.00

Table 11.1 *The Multiplier Process at Work* Purchasing power is passed from hand to hand in the circular flow. The *cumulative* change in total expenditure that results from a new injection of spending into the circular flow depends on the MPC and the number of spending cycles that occur.

The limit to multiplier effects is established by the ratio 1/(1 − MPC). In this case MPC = 0.75, so the multiplier equals 4. That is, total spending will ultimately rise by $400 billion per year as a result of an increase in *G* of $100 billion per year. ■

As a result of the circular flow of spending and income, the impact of the initial government expenditure has already more than doubled.

Table 11.1 follows the multiplier process to its logical end. Each successive cycle entails less new income and smaller increments to spending. Ultimately the changes get so small that they are not even noticeable. By that time, however, the *cumulative* change in spending is huge. The cumulative change in spending is $400 billion: $100 billion of initial government expenditure and an additional $300 billion of consumption induced by multiplier effects. Thus ***the demand stimulus initiated by increased government spending is a multiple of the initial expenditure.***

表 11.1 遵循乘数过程得出了符合逻辑的结果。每一个连续循环，意味着更少的新收入和更小的支出增量。最后，变化小到难以察觉的程度。但是，到那时支出的累积变化将非常巨大。支出的累积变化是 4 000 亿美元：最初政府支出的 1 000 亿美元和由乘数效应引起的 3 000 亿美元的消费。因此，由政府支出的增加引发的需求扩张是最初政府支出的若干倍。

Multiplier Formula 乘数公式

To compute the cumulative change in spending, we need not examine each cycle of the multiplier process. There is a shortcut. The entire sequence of multiplier cycles is summarized in a single number, aptly named the *multiplier*. The **multiplier** tells us how much *total* spending will change in response to an initial spending stimulus. The multiplier is computed as

$$\text{Multiplier} = \frac{1}{1 - \text{MPC}}$$

---

shortcut 捷径。 aptly 适宜地，适当地。

In our case, where MPC = 0.75, the multiplier is

$$\text{Multiplier} = \frac{1}{1-\text{MPC}}$$

$$= \frac{1}{1-0.75} = \frac{1}{0.25} = 4$$

Using this multiplier, we can confirm the conclusion of Table 11.1 by observing that

Total change in spending = multiplier × initial change in government spending

$$= \frac{1}{1-\text{MPC}} \times \$100 \text{ billion per year}$$

$$= \frac{1}{1-0.75} \times \$100 \text{ billion per year}$$

$$= 4 \times \$100 \text{ billion per year}$$

$$= \$400 \text{ billion per year}$$

The impact of the multiplier on aggregate demand is illustrated in Figure 11.7. The AD_1 curve represents the inadequate aggregate demand that caused the initial unemployment problem (Figure 11.4). When the government increases its defense spending, the aggregate demand curve shifts rightward by $100 billion to AD_2. This increase in defense expenditure sparks a consumption spree, shifting aggregate demand further to AD_3. This combination of increased government spending ($100 billion) and induced consumption ($300 billion) is sufficient to restore full employment.

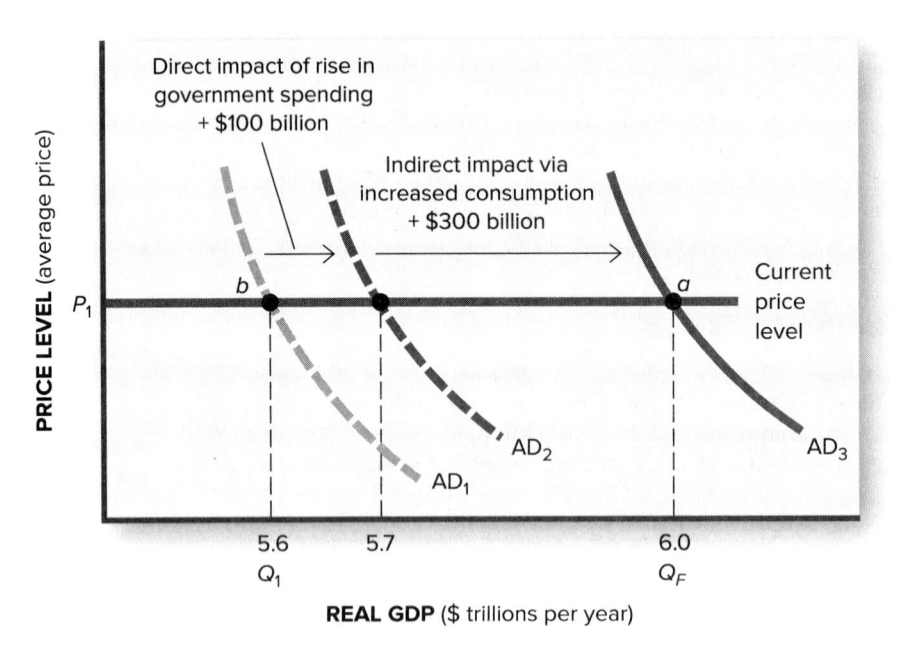

Figure 11.7 Multiplier Effects A $100 billion increase in government spending shifts the aggregate demand curve to the right by a like amount (i.e., AD_1 to AD_2). Aggregate demand gets another boost from the additional consumption induced by multiplier effects. In this case, an MPC of 0.75 results in $300 billion of additional consumption.

spark 引发，触发。restore 恢复。

The multiplier packs a lot of punch. ***Every dollar of fiscal stimulus has a multiplied impact on aggregate demand.*** This makes fiscal policy easier. The multiplier also makes fiscal policy riskier, however, by exaggerating any intervention mistakes.

Tax Cuts 减税

Although government spending (G) is capable of moving the economy to its full employment potential, increased G is not the only way to get there. The stimulus required to raise output and employment levels from Q_1 to Q_F could originate in consumption (C) or investment (I) as well as from G. It could also come from abroad, in the form of increased demand for our exports. In other words, any Big Spender would help. Of course, the reason we are initially at Q_1 instead of Q_F in Figure 11.7 is that consumers and investors have chosen not to spend as much as is required for full employment.

The government might be able to stimulate more consumer and business spending with a tax cut. A tax cut directly increases the **disposable income** of the private sector. As soon as people get more income in their hands, they're likely to spend it. When they do, aggregate demand gets a lift. This is what happened in 2018. In December 2017 President Trump signed the Tax Cuts and Jobs Act, a law that reduced taxes for both consumers and businesses. The law increased disposable incomes by about 2 percent, or roughly $40 per week for the average household. What did consumers do with that added income? Spend much of it, of course, as the News Wire "Fiscal Stimulus: Tax Cuts" reveals. That tax-cut-induced spending shifted the AD curve to the right, increasing both GDP and employment in 2018.

NEWS WIRE FISCAL STIMULUS: TAX CUTS

TRUMP TAX CUTS BOOST SPENDING

The Tax Cuts and Jobs Act of 2017 seems to be working. Although the lion's share of President Trump's tax cuts went to business, consumers got a tax break as well. For the average U.S. household, the tax cut amounts to roughly $40 a week in take-home pay. That may not sound like much, but with 130 million households, that extra income can pack some punch. According to the National Retail Federation, consumer spending was up 4.8 percent in the first six months of this year. And the government reports that GDP grew by 4.2 percent in the second quarter, the best performance since 2014. There may be other factors at work here, but tax-cut-fueled consumer spending is certainly a big contributor.

Source: News accounts of September–October 2018.

NOTE: Tax cuts increase disposable income and boost consumer spending. This shifts the AD curve rightward.
注：减税增加了可支配收入，从而促进了消费支出。这使 AD 曲线向右移动。

Taxes and Consumption 税收和消费

How much of an AD shift we get from a personal tax cut depends on the marginal propensity to consume (MPC). If consumers squirreled away their entire tax cut, AD wouldn't budge. But an MPC of zero is an alien concept. People *do* increase their spending when their disposable income increases. So long as the MPC is greater than zero, a tax cut *will* stimulate more consumer spending.

Suppose again the MPC is 0.75. If taxes are cut by $100 billion, the resulting consumption spree amounts to

$$\text{Initial increase in consumption} = \text{MPC} \times \text{tax cut}$$

$$= 0.75 \times \$100 \text{ billion}$$

$$= \$75 \text{ billion}$$

Hence ***a tax cut that increases disposable incomes stimulates consumer spending.***

---

squirrel away 储存。

The initial consumption spree induced by a tax cut starts the multiplier process in motion. Once in motion, the multiplier picks up steam. The new consumer spending creates additional income for producers and workers, who will then use the additional income to increase their own consumption. This will propel us along the multiplier path already depicted in Table 11.1. The cumulative change in total spending will be

$$\text{Cumulative change in spending} = \text{multiplier} \times \text{initial change in consumption}$$

In this case, the cumulative change is

$$\text{Cumulative change in spending} = \frac{1}{1 - \text{MPC}} \times \$75 \text{ billion}$$
$$= 4 \times \$75 \text{ billion}$$
$$= \$300 \text{ billion}$$

Here again we see that the multiplier increases the impact of a tax cut on aggregate demand. ***The cumulative increase in aggregate demand is a multiple of the initial tax cut.*** Thus the multiplier makes both increased government spending and tax cuts powerful policy levers.

Taxes and Investment   税收和投资

A tax cut may also be an effective mechanism for increasing investment spending. Investment decisions are guided by expectations of future profit, particularly after-tax profits. If a cut in corporate taxes raises after-tax profits, it should encourage additional investment. Once increased investment spending enters the circular flow, it has a multiplier effect on total spending like that which follows an initial change in consumer spending. Thus tax cuts for consumers or investors provide an alternative to increased government spending as a mechanism for stimulating aggregate spending.

Tax cuts designed to stimulate consumption (*C*) and investment (*I*) have been used frequently. In 1963 President John F. Kennedy announced his intention to reduce taxes in order to stimulate the economy, citing the fact that the marginal propensity to consume for the average American family at that time appeared to be exceptionally high. His successor, Lyndon Johnson, concurred with Kennedy's reasoning. Johnson agreed to "shift emphasis sharply from expanding federal expenditure to boosting private consumer demand and business investment." He proceeded to cut personal and corporate taxes by $11 billion.

One of the largest tax cuts in history was initiated by President Ronald Reagan in 1981. The Reagan administration persuaded Congress to cut personal taxes by $250 billion over a three-year period and to cut business taxes by another $70 billion. The resulting increase in disposable income stimulated consumer spending and helped push the economy out of the 1981–1982 recession.

President Trump's 2017 tax-cut package also included both personal tax cuts and business tax cuts. In fact, businesses got most of the tax breaks. The most notable break was a reduction in the corporate profits tax rate from 35 percent to 21 percent. The rate cut gave businesses a major incentive to invest and produce more. The Tax Cut and Jobs Act of 2017 further sweetened the pot for investors by increasing expense and depreciation allowances that effectively reduced tax burdens still further. The expectation was that businesses would respond to these tax incentives by increasing the volume of investment spending. And they did. Business spending on nonresidential structures and equipment increased by $78 billion in the first quarter of 2018, when the tax cuts first became effective. In the first half of 2018, business investment jumped by 7 percent, far ahead of earlier trends. This rightward shift of AD accelerated GDP growth throughout 2018.

---

successor 继任者。concur 同意，意见一致。

Inflation Worries 对通货膨胀的担忧

President Clinton had also promised fiscal stimulus when he ran for president in 1992. With the economy still far short of its productive capacity (Q_F), he called for more government spending and some tax cuts. After he was elected, however, President Clinton changed his mind about the need for fiscal stimulus. Rather than delivering the middle-class tax cut he had promised, Clinton instead decided to *raise* taxes. This abrupt policy U-turn was motivated in part by the recognition of how powerful the multiplier is. The economy was already expanding when Clinton was elected, and the multiplier was at work. As each successive spending cycle developed, the economy would move closer to full employment. Any *new* fiscal stimulus would accelerate that movement. As a result, the economy might end up expanding so fast that it would overshoot the full employment goal.

The pressure from any more fiscal stimulus could easily force prices higher. This risk was illustrated in Figure 11.2. ***Whenever the aggregate supply curve is upward sloping, an increase in aggregate demand increases prices as well as output.*** Notice in Figure 11.2 how the price level starts creeping up as aggregate demand increases from AD_1 to AD^*. If aggregate demand expands further to AD_2, the price level really jumps. This suggests that the degree of inflation caused by increased aggregate demand depends on the slope of the aggregate supply curve. Only if the AS curve were horizontal would there be no risk of inflation when AD increases. Keynes thought this might have been the case during the Great Depression. With so much excess capacity available, businesses were willing and able—indeed, eager—to supply more output at the existing price level.

来自财政刺激的任何压力将很容易导致价格的上涨。图 11.2 说明了这种风险。只要总供给曲线是向上倾斜的，任何总需求的增加都将导致价格和产出的增加。注意图 11.2 中价格水平是如何随着总需求由 AD_1 到 AD^* 的增加而增加的。如果总需求进一步扩大到 AD_2，价格水平就会猛增。这就说明由总需求增加引起的通货膨胀的程度，取决于总供给曲线的倾斜程度。

Businesses are not always so accommodating to an increase in aggregate demand. The economic situation was far rosier in January 2018 when the Trump tax cuts first became effective. The national unemployment rate in January (4.1%) was well within our notion of **full employment**. Accordingly, any rightward shifts of the AD curve threatened to stir up inflation, as depicted in Figure 11.2. The inflationary pressures would come from labor and resource shortages that emerged when the economy pushed up against its production possibilities.

FISCAL RESTRAINT 财政紧缩

The threat of inflation suggests that **fiscal restraint** may be an appropriate policy strategy at times. *If excessive aggregate demand is causing prices to rise, the goal of fiscal policy will be to* **reduce** *aggregate demand, not stimulate it* (see Figure 11.8).

通货膨胀的威胁说明**财政紧缩**有时或许可以成为适当的政策策略。如果过度的总需求导致价格上升，财政政策的目标就将转变为降低总需求，而不是刺激总需求（参看图 11.8）。

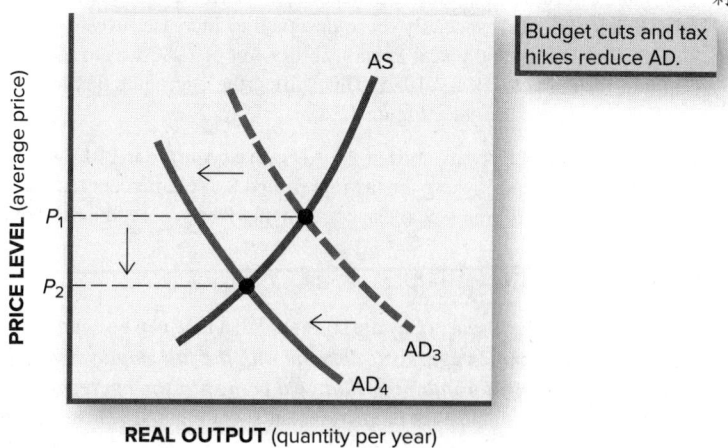

Figure 11.8 Fiscal Restraint Fiscal restraint is used to reduce inflationary pressures. The strategy is to shift the aggregate demand curve to the left with budget cuts or tax hikes. ∎

stir up 引起。

The means available to the federal government for restraining aggregate demand emerge again from both sides of the budget. The difference here is that we use the budget tools in reverse. We now want to *reduce* government spending or *increase* taxes.

Budget Cuts 缩减预算

Cutbacks in government spending on goods and services directly reduce aggregate demand. As with spending increases, the impact of spending cuts is magnified by the multiplier.

Multiplier Cycles 乘数循环

Suppose the government cut military spending by $100 billion. This would throw a lot of aerospace employees out of work. Thousands of workers would get smaller paychecks, or perhaps none at all. These workers would be forced to cut back on their own spending. Hence aggregate demand would take two hits: first a cut in government spending and then induced cutbacks in consumer spending. ***The multiplier process works in both directions.***

从这一点来讲，这些听起来应该非常熟悉。正如我们在表 11.1 中所详述的，政府支出减少 1 000 亿美元最终将导致消费支出减少 3 000 亿美元。因此支出一共减少了 4 000 亿美元。如同镜像一般，政府支出的减少对总需求产生了乘数效应。对总需求的总影响等于：

支出的累积减少 = 乘数 × 最初的预算削减

The marginal propensity to consume again reveals the power of the multiplier process. If the MPC is 0.75, the consumption of aerospace workers will drop by $75 billion when the government cutbacks reduce their income by $100 billion. (The rest of the income loss will be covered by a reduction in savings balances.)

From this point on the story should sound familiar. As detailed in Table 11.1, the $100 billion government cutback will ultimately reduce consumer spending by $300 billion. The *total* drop in spending is thus $400 billion. Like their mirror image, ***government cutbacks have a multiplied effect on aggregate demand.*** The total impact is equal to

$$\text{Cumulative reduction in spending} = \text{multiplier} \times \text{initial budget cut}$$

Tax Hikes 增税

Tax increases can also be used to shift the aggregate demand curve to the left. The direct effect of a tax increase is a reduction in disposable income. People will pay the higher taxes by reducing their consumption and depleting their savings. The reduced consumption results in less aggregate demand. As consumers tighten their belts, they set off the multiplier process, leading to a much larger cumulative shift of aggregate demand.

增税也可以使总需求曲线向左移动。增税产生的直接影响是可支配收入的减少。人们将通过降低消费和减少储蓄来支付更高的税收。消费的减少又导致了总需求的减少。消费者在勒紧裤腰带的同时，又引发了乘数过程，从而导致总需求曲线更大幅度地移动。

In 1982 there was great concern that the 1981 tax cuts had been excessive and that inflationary pressures were building up. To reduce that inflationary pressure, Congress withdrew some of its earlier tax cuts, especially those designed to increase investment spending. The net effect of the Tax Equity and Fiscal Responsibility Act of 1982 was to increase taxes by roughly $90 billion for the years 1983–1985. This shifted the aggregate demand curve leftward, reducing inflationary pressures (see Figure 11.8).

The same kind of leftward shift of the AD curve occurred in 2013 when Congress increased the payroll (FICA) tax. Raising the tax rate from 4.2 to 6.2 percent reduced consumers' disposable income by $110 billion (see the accompanying News Wire "Fiscal Restraint").

Fiscal Guidelines 财政方针

The basic rules for fiscal policy are so simple that they can be summarized in a small table. ***The policy goal is to match aggregate demand with the full employment potential of the economy. The fiscal strategy for attaining that goal is to shift the aggregate demand curve.*** The tools for doing so are (1) changes in government spending and (2) changes in tax rates. Table 11.2 summarizes the guidelines developed by John Maynard Keynes for using those tools.

政策目标是使总需求与经济的充分就业潜能相匹配。实现这一目标的财政策略是改变总需求曲线。实现这一目标的工具是：(1) 政府支出的变化；(2) 税率的变化。表 11.2 概括了约翰·梅纳德·凯恩斯为使用这些工具而制定的指导方针。

---

magnify 放大，扩大。

Problem	Solution	Policy Tools
Unemployment (recession)	Increase aggregate demand.	Increase government spending. Cut taxes.
Inflation	Reduce aggregate demand.	Cut government spending. Raise taxes.

Table 11.2 Fiscal Policy Guidelines The Keynesian emphasis on aggregate demand results in simple guidelines for fiscal policy: Reduce aggregate demand to fight inflation; increase aggregate demand to fight unemployment. Changes in government spending and taxes are the tools used to shift AD. ■

NEWS WIRE FISCAL RESTRAINT

RETAILERS BRACING FOR SPENDING SLOWDOWN

Retailers across the country are bracing for an anticipated slowdown in consumer spending. As of January 1, the Social Security payroll tax rate moved back up from 4.2 percent to 6.2 percent. That will reduce take-home pay by 2 percent. That means that the 153 million workers in this country will have an average of $1,500 less to spend this year. For retailers, that implies less spending on groceries, household goods, and dining out. According to an estimate by Citigroup, the jump in the payroll tax will leave $110 billion less in consumers' pockets. That has retailers worried.

Source: News accounts of January 2013.

Will people buy less when their paychecks shrink?
©McGraw-Hill Education/John Flournoy, photographer

NOTE: Tax increases leave consumers with less income to spend, reducing aggregate demand.
注：增税使消费者用于支出的消费减少了，从而减少了总需求。

POLICY PERSPECTIVES

MUST THE BUDGET BE BALANCED?

The primary lever of fiscal policy is the federal government's budget. As we have observed, changes in either federal taxes or outlays are the mechanism for shifting the aggregate demand curve. If used carefully, these fiscal tools can help us achieve our goals of full employment, price stability, and economic growth.

The use of the budget as a fiscal tool has other as well, which troubles many people. ***The use of the budget to manage aggregate demand implies that the budget will often be unbalanced.*** In the face of a recession, for example, the government has sound reasons both to cut taxes and to increase its own spending. By reducing tax revenues and increasing expenditures simultaneously, however, the federal government will throw its budget out of balance.

BUDGET DEFICIT

Whenever government expenditures exceed tax revenues, a **budget deficit** exists. The deficit is measured by the difference between expenditures and receipts

> Budget deficit = government spending > tax revenues

where spending exceeds revenues. In the years 2010–2012 the federal budget deficit was more than $1 *trillion* every year. To pay for such enormous deficit spending, the government had to borrow money, either directly from the private sector or from the banking sector. As Figure 11.9 reveals, the deficits of 2010–2012 were far larger than any earlier deficits. The series of deficits from 1970 to 1997 were tiny by comparison. Yet even those deficits caused recurrent political crises. Several times the federal government had to shut down for days at a time while Republicans and Democrats in Congress battled over how to cut the deficit. A majority of citizens even supported adding an amendment to the U.S. Constitution that would *force* Congress to balance the budget every year.

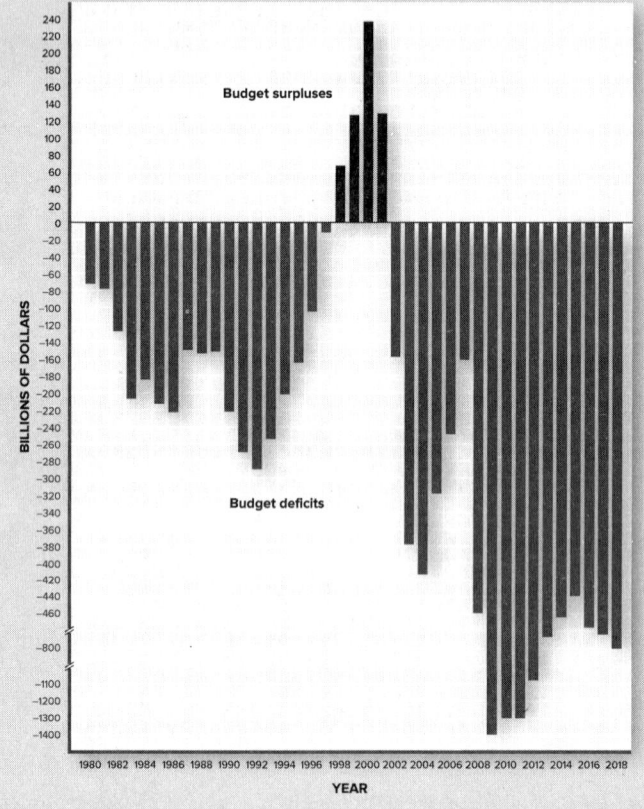

Figure 11.9 Unbalanced Budgets From 1970 until 1997 the federal budget was in deficit every year. From 1998 to 2001 the budget was briefly in surplus due to strong GDP growth and slowed federal spending.
An economic slowdown, tax cuts, and a surge in defense spending returned the budget to deficit in 2002. The recession of 2008–2009 and subsequent fiscal stimulus sent the deficit soaring to over $1 trillion for four years running (2009–2012). Economic growth and tax increases shrunk the deficit from 2012 to 2015. The Trump tax cuts widened the deficit again.
Source: Congressional Budget Office.

---

amendment 修正案。 soar 激增。

BUDGET SURPLUS

Ironically, while the U.S. Congress was debating such an amendment, the deficit started shrinking. The record-breaking expansion of the U.S. economy and the stock market boom of the late 1990s swelled tax collections. The Balanced Budget Act of 1997 also slowed the growth of government spending. This combination of growing tax revenues and slower government spending shrunk the deficit dramatically.

By 1998 the deficit had completely vanished, and a **budget surplus** appeared. For the first time in 30 years, tax revenues exceeded government spending.

> Budget surplus = government spending < tax revenues

The surpluses started out small but grew rapidly as the economy kept expanding.

The budget surpluses of 1998–2001 created a unique problem: what to do with the "extra" revenue. Should the government give it back to taxpayers? Expand government programs? Pay down accumulated debt? The government had not confronted that problem since 1969.

DEFICITS RESURFACE

The problem of managing a budget surplus vanished with the surplus itself in 2002. The September 11, 2001, terrorist attacks on New York City and Washington, DC, contributed to an economic contraction that reduced tax revenues. A subsequent surge in defense spending and new tax cuts widened the deficit further.

2008–2009 RECESSION

The Great Recession of 2008–2009 threw the federal budget completely out of whack. GDP growth turned negative in the last quarter of 2008 and stayed negative throughout 2009. As employment, payrolls, and profits shrank, so did tax revenues. The 2008 tax rebates took another $100 billion out of the revenue stream. Then the gigantic 2009 fiscal stimulus program (see the News Wire "Fiscal Stimulus: Government Spending") ratcheted up federal spending. All these policies helped widen the annual deficit to more than $1 trillion for several years' running (2010–2012).

COUNTERCYCLICAL POLICY

For John Maynard Keynes, the 2010–2012 deficit explosion would seem perfectly normal. From a Keynesian perspective, the desirability of a budget deficit or surplus depends on the health of the economy. If the economy is ailing, an injection of government spending or a tax cut is appropriate. On the other hand, if the economy is booming, some fiscal restraint (spending cuts, tax hikes) would be called for. Hence Keynes would first examine the economy and then prescribe fiscal restraint or stimulus. He might even prescribe neither, sensing that the economy was in optimal health. *In Keynes's view, an unbalanced budget is perfectly appropriate if macro conditions call for a deficit or surplus.* A balanced budget is appropriate only if the resulting aggregate demand is consistent with full employment equilibrium.

DEFICIT WORRIES

Not everyone is as comfortable as Keynes with soaring deficits. Most people understand that recessions can throw government budgets deep into the red.

---

ailing 处境困难的，每况愈下的。

> But those cyclical displacements should be *temporary*. What worried people so much in 2010–2012 was the perception that those trillion-dollar deficits would continue. The American Recovery and Reinvestment Act of 2009 authorized infrastructure and energy projects that would continue for years, long after the recession was over. Without cutbacks in other government programs or tax increases—both politically unpopular—huge deficits were bound to persist.
>
> In early 2013 public anxiety over massive deficits triggered a heated political battle. Republicans in Congress insisted that the growth of government spending had to be reined in. President Obama, on the other hand, refused to consider cuts in spending, especially for entitlements like Social Security. He preferred additional tax increases, especially for the rich. In February 2013 the issue came to a head when Congress had to authorize additional government borrowing (the debt ceiling). Both sides dug their heels in, threatening a temporary shutdown of the federal government. In the end, both parties took the easy way out, *promising* future deficit reduction but delivering little immediate fiscal restraint.
>
> The Congressional Budget Office (CBO) foresees greater problems down the road. CBO projects that the federal budget deficit will increase from $800 billion in 2018 to more than $1 trillion in 2020 and remain in excess of $1 trillion a year for the next decade. Much of the projected increase in the federal deficit comes from the Trump tax cuts, which reduce government revenues. By CBO's computations, those tax cuts add $1.7 trillion to budget deficits over the period 2018–2028. To avoid that kind of deficit expansion, Congress would have to raise taxes again or cut popular government programs. These are not welcome options.

CHAPTER 11 REVIEW

SUMMARY

- Fiscal policy is the use of government taxes and spending to alter macroeconomic outcomes. **LO1**
- The Keynesian explanation of macro instability requires government intervention to shift the aggregate demand curve to the desired rate of output. **LO2**
- To boost aggregate demand, the government may either increase its own spending or cut taxes. To restrain aggregate demand, the government may reduce its own spending or raise taxes. **LO4**
- Any change in government spending or taxes will have a multiplied impact on aggregate demand. The additional impact comes from changes in consumption caused by changes in disposable income. **LO3**
- The marginal propensity to consume (MPC) indicates how changes in disposable income affect consumer spending. The MPC is the fraction of each additional dollar spent (i.e., not saved). **LO3**
- The size of the multiplier depends on the marginal propensity to consume. The higher the MPC, the larger the multiplier, where the multiplier $= 1/(1 - \text{MPC})$. **LO3**
- Fiscal stimulus carries the risk of inflation. The steeper the upward slope of the aggregate supply (AS) curve, the greater the risk of inflation. **LO4**
- A balanced budget is appropriate only if the resulting aggregate demand is compatible with full employment and price stability. Otherwise *unbalanced* budgets (deficits or surpluses) are appropriate. **LO5**

TERMS TO REMEMBER

Define the following terms:

fiscal policy
aggregate demand
consumption
investment
net exports
equilibrium (macro)
GDP gap
fiscal stimulus
saving

marginal propensity to consume (MPC)
marginal propensity to save (MPS)
multiplier
disposable income
full employment
fiscal restraint
budget deficit
budget surplus

QUESTIONS FOR DISCUSSION

1. Why was the Merrill Lynch economist (see the News Wire "Shifts in Aggregate Demand") so confident that a recession was coming in 2007? **LO2**
2. How long does it take you to spend any income you receive? Where do the dollars you spend end up? **LO3**
3. What is your MPC? Would a welfare recipient and a millionaire have the same MPC? What determines a person's MPC? **LO3**
4. Why was Walmart worried about the 2013 payroll tax hike (News Wire "Fiscal Restraint")? **LO4**
5. If the guidelines for fiscal policy (Table 11.2) are so simple, why does the economy ever suffer from unemployment or inflation? **LO2**
6. In early 2018 businesses bought more inventory, increasing GDP. What would happen if consumers didn't buy those goods? **LO2**
7. When consumers use tax cuts to increase their own spending, what kind of "extra" purchases are they likely to make? **LO4**
8. Which is likely to give the economy a greater boost, household tax cuts or business tax cuts? **LO3**
9. **POLICY PERSPECTIVES** Would a constitutional amendment that would require the federal government to balance its budget (incur no deficits) be desirable? Explain. **LO5**
10. **POLICY PERSPECTIVES** What government programs would you cut in the pursuit of fiscal restraint? **LO4**

PROBLEMS

1. In Figure 11.2, (a) identify the GDP gap when the demand curve is at AD1. (b) is the economy in a recession or expansion? **LO2**
2. If the marginal propensity to save is 0.25, (a) what is the MPC? (b) how large is the multiplier? **LO3**
3. In 2017 consumers' disposable income increased by $626 billion and their spending increased by $555 billion. What was the MPC? **LO3**
4. According to the News Wire "Fiscal Stimulus: Tax Cuts," **LO3**
   a. how much did the weekly disposable income of the average household increase as a result of the Trump tax cut?
   b. how much did the weekly disposable income of *all* households increase?
   c. if the MPC was 0.6, by how much did total consumer spending increase (i) after a one-week boost to incomes and (ii) after all the spending cycles were completed after a one-week boost to incomes?
5. If the MPC were 0.8, (a) how much spending would occur in the third cycle of Figure 11.6? (b) how many spending cycles would occur before consumer spending increased by $200 billion? **LO3**
6. The multiplier process depicted in Table 11.1 is based on an MPC of 0.75. (a) Recompute the first four cycles using an MPC of 0.80. (b) How much more consumption occurs in the first four cycles? (c) What is the value of the multiplier in this case? **LO3**

7. Suppose the government increases education spending by $30 billion. If the marginal propensity to consume is 0.75, how much will total spending increase? **LO4**

8. If taxes were cut by $1 trillion and the MPC was 0.75, by how much would total spending **LO3**
   a. increase in the first year with two spending cycles per year?
   b. increase over three years, with two spending cycles per year?
   c. increase over an infinite time period per year?

9. If consumers had an MPC of 0.90, by how much would aggregate demand have eventually increased with Obama's spending stimulus assuming the stimulus was entirely government spending (see the News Wire "Fiscal Stimulus: Government Spending")? **LO3**

10. If the MPC was 0.90, and using the Citigroup estimate, (*a*) how much did consumer spending decline initially in response to the 2013 payroll tax hike? (News Wire "Fiscal Restraint")? (*b*) what was the ultimate decline in aggregate demand after all multiplier effects? **LO3**

11. **POLICY PERSPECTIVES** Assume MPC = 0.75. If an initial fiscal restraint of $100 billion is desired, by how much must **LO4**
    a. government spending be reduced?
    b. taxes be raised?

CHAPTER TWELVE

Money and Banks 货币与银行

©Zephyr_p/Shutterstock

LEARNING OBJECTIVES

After reading this chapter, you should be able to:

1. Detail what the features of money are.
2. Specify what is included in the money supply.
3. Describe how a bank creates money.
4. Explain how the money multiplier works.
5. Discuss why the money supply is important.

Sophocles, the ancient Greek playwright, had strong opinions about the role of money. As he saw it, "Of evils upon earth, the worst is money. It is money that sacks cities, and drives men forth from hearth and home; warps and seduces native intelligence, and breeds a habit of dishonesty."[1]

In modern times, people may still be seduced by the lure of money and fashion their lives around its pursuit. Nevertheless, it is hard to imagine an economy functioning without money. Money affects not only morals and ideals but also the way an economy works.

The purpose of this chapter and the following chapter is to examine the role of money in the economy today. We begin with a very simple question:

- What is money?

As we shall discover, money isn't exactly what you think it is. Once we have established the characteristics of money, we go on to ask,

- Where does money come from?
- What role do banks play in the macro economy?

In the next chapter we look at how the Federal Reserve System controls the supply of money and thereby affects macroeconomic outcomes. We will then have a second policy lever in our basic macro model.

---

[1] Sophocles, *The Oedipus Trilogy: Oedipus the King, Oedipus at Colonus, Antigone*. California, Irvine: Xist Publishing, 2015.

Sophocles 索福克勒斯,古希腊悲剧诗人。sack 洗劫。seduce 诱惑,引诱。

THE USES OF MONEY 货币的用途

To appreciate the significance of money in a modern economy, imagine for a moment that there were no such thing as money. How would you get something for breakfast? If you wanted eggs for breakfast, you would have to tend your own chickens or go see Farmer Brown. But how would you pay Farmer Brown for her eggs? Without money, you would have to offer her goods or services that she could use. In other words, you would have to engage in primitive **barter**—the direct exchange of one good for another. You would get those eggs only if Farmer Brown happened to want the particular goods or services you had to offer and if the two of you could agree on the terms of the exchange.

The use of money greatly simplifies market transactions. It's a lot easier to exchange money for eggs at the supermarket than to go into the country and barter with farmers. Our ability to use money in market transactions, however, depends on the grocer's willingness to accept money as a *medium of exchange*. The grocer sells eggs for money only because he can use the same money to pay his help and buy the goods he himself desires. He, too, can exchange money for goods and services. Accordingly, **money plays an essential role in facilitating the continuous series of exchanges that characterizes a market economy.**

Money has other desirable features. The grocer who accepts your money in exchange for a carton of eggs doesn't have to spend his income immediately. He can hold on to the money for a few days or months without worrying about it spoiling. Hence money is also a useful *store of value*—that is, a mechanism for transforming current income into future purchases. Finally, common use of money serves as a *standard of value* for comparing the market worth of different goods. A dozen eggs are more valuable than a dozen onions if they cost more at the supermarket.

We may identify, then, several essential characteristics of what we call money. Specifically, **anything that serves all the following purposes can be thought of as money:**

- *Medium of exchange:* It is accepted as payment for goods and services.
- *Store of value:* It can be held for future purchases.
- *Standard of value:* It serves as a yardstick for measuring the prices of goods and services.

The great virtue of money is that it facilitates the market exchanges that permit specialization in production. In fact, efficient division of labor requires a system whereby people can exchange the things they produce for the things they desire. Money makes this system of exchange possible.

Many Types of Money 货币的许多种类

Although markets cannot function without money, they can get along without *dollars*. U.S. dollars are just one example of money. In the early days of colonial America, there were no U.S. dollars. A lot of business was conducted with Spanish and Portuguese gold coins. Later people used Indian wampum, then tobacco, grain, fish, and furs, as media of exchange. Throughout the colonies, gunpowder and bullets were frequently used for small change. These forms of money weren't as convenient as U.S. dollars, but they did the job. So long as they served as a medium of exchange, a store of value, and a standard of value, they were properly regarded as money.

The first paper money issued by the U.S. federal government consisted of $10 million worth of "greenbacks," printed in 1861 to finance the Civil War. The Confederate states also issued paper money to finance their side of the Civil War. Confederate dollars became worthless, however, when the South lost and people no longer accepted Confederate currency in exchange for goods and services.

---

desirable 可取的，合意的。 spoil 破坏，毁坏。 facilitate 促进，使更容易。 greenback 美钞。

Similar problems arose in Eastern Europe. In Poland, the zloty was shunned as a form of money in the early 1980s. Poles preferred to use cigarettes and vodka as media of exchange and stores of value. So much Polish currency (zlotys) was available that its value was suspect. The same problem undermined the value of the Russian ruble in the 1990s. Russian consumers preferred to hold and use American dollars rather than the rubles that few people would accept in payment for goods and services. Cigarettes, vodka, and even potatoes were a better form of money than Russian rubles. Venezuelans had to resort to the same kind of barter in 2017–2019. Rather than accept worthless bolivars for their work or output, they insisted on payment in flour, rice cooking oil and other products. (see the News Wire "Barter").

NEWS WIRE BARTER

FISH FOR FLOUR: VENEZUELA'S BARTER ECONOMY

Rio Chico—Fishermen in this tiny village on the coast of Venezuela hope to sell their catch each day. But not for cash. The Venezuelan bolivar is just about worthless. It would take a shoebox full of bolivars to purchase just one fish. And with inflation running at an astronomical 25,000 percent a year, that box would be worthless in a couple of days. So, the fishermen want to sell their catch for real goods. They commonly sell their mullets and snappers for packages of flour, rice, and cooking oil. In urban areas, barter has also replaced money. In Caracas, a haircut costs five bananas and two eggs. Plumbers and electricians expect to be pain in groceries, not bolivars. Facebook pages are full of swap offers, covering everything from toothpaste to baby formula. Oil, pasta, corn flour, and cooking oil are especially desired commodities because they are needed to prepare arepas, Venezuela's famed grilled pancakes.

Source: News accounts of July–October 2018.

NOTE: When people lose faith in a nation's currency, they must use something else as a medium of exchange. This greatly limits market activity.
注：当人们对一个国家的货币丧失信心时，他们必定使用别的东西作为交换媒介。这极大地限制了市场活动。

THE MONEY SUPPLY 货币供给

Cash versus Money 现金与货币

In the U.S. economy today, such unusual forms of money are rarely used. Nevertheless, the concept of money includes more than the dollar bills and coins in your pocket or purse. Most people realize this when they offer to pay for goods with a check or debit card rather than cash. The money you have in a checking account can be used to buy goods and services, or it can be retained for future use. In these respects, your checking account balance is as much a part of your money as are the coins and dollars in your pocket or purse. In fact, you could get along without *any* cash if everyone accepted your checks and debit cards (and if they worked in vending machines and parking meters).

There is nothing unique about cash, then, insofar as the market is concerned. **Checking accounts can and do perform the same market functions as cash.** Accordingly, we must include checking account balances in our concept of **money**. The essence of money is not its taste, color, or feel but, rather, its ability to purchase goods and services.

那么就市场而言，现金并不是独一无二的。活期存款能够并且确实发挥了与现金相同的市场功能。因此，在**货币**的概念中我们必须包括活期存款账户余额。货币的本质并不在于它的味道、颜色或感觉，而在于它购买商品和服务的能力。

Transactions Accounts 交易账户

In their competition for customers, banks have created all kinds of different checking accounts. Credit unions and other financial institutions have also created checking account services. Although they have a variety of distinctive names, all checking accounts have a common feature: They permit depositors to spend their deposit balances easily without making a special trip to the bank to withdraw funds. All you need is a checkbook, a debit card, an ATM card, or a payment app on your smartphone.

---

zloty 兹罗提（波兰货币单位）。shun 避开，回避。ruble 卢布（俄罗斯货币单位）。balance 余额。depositor 存款人。

因为所有这些活期存款账户余额都可以在市场交易中直接使用（无需去银行），所以它们统称为交易账户。所有**交易账户**与众不同的特点是，它们允许直接向第三方付款，无需去银行提取存款。支付可以采取支票、借记卡划账或自动转账的形式。在所有这些情况下，交易账户余额都可以替代现金而成为货币的一种形式。

Because all such checking account balances can be used directly in market transactions (without a trip to the bank), they are collectively referred to as *transactions accounts*. The distinguishing feature of all **transactions accounts** is that they permit direct payment to a third party without requiring a trip to the bank to make a withdrawal. The payment itself may be in the form of a check, a debit card transfer, or an automatic payment transfer. In all such cases, ***the balance in your transactions account substitutes for cash, and is therefore a form of money.***

Basic Money Supply 基础货币供给

Because all transactions accounts can be spent as readily as cash, they are counted as part of our money supply. Adding transactions account balances to the quantity of coins and currency held by the public gives us one measure of the amount of "money" available—that is, the basic **money supply**. The basic money supply is typically referred to by the abbreviation **M1**.

图 12.1 说明了目前货币供给的实际构成。M1 的第一个构成部分是人们所持有的现金（商业银行以外流通的货币）。很显然，现金只是货币供给的一部分；大部分货币由交易账户余额构成。这一点不应该让人感到太惊讶。大多数市场交易仍然使用现金，但是这种现金交易通常金额很小（例如，购买咖啡、午餐、小商品）。每年 800 亿美元的非现金交易已经远远超过了这种现金交易。

Figure 12.1 illustrates the actual composition of our money supply. The first component of M1 is the cash people hold (currency in circulation outside of commercial banks). Clearly, ***cash is only part of the money supply; a lot of "money" consists of balances in transactions accounts.*** This really should not come as too much of a surprise. Most market transactions are still conducted in cash. But those cash transactions are typically small (e.g., for coffee, lunch, small items). They are vastly outspent by the 80 billion *non*cash retail payments made each year. People prefer to use checks rather than cash for most large market transactions and use debit cards just about everywhere (see the News Wire "Media of Exchange"). Checks and debit cards are more convenient than cash because they eliminate trips to the bank. Checks and debit cards are also safer: Lost or stolen cash is gone forever; checkbooks and debit cards are easily replaced at little or no cost.

Total money supply ($3,302 billion)

$1,600 — Currency in circulation

BILLIONS OF DOLLARS

$1,700 — Transactions account balances

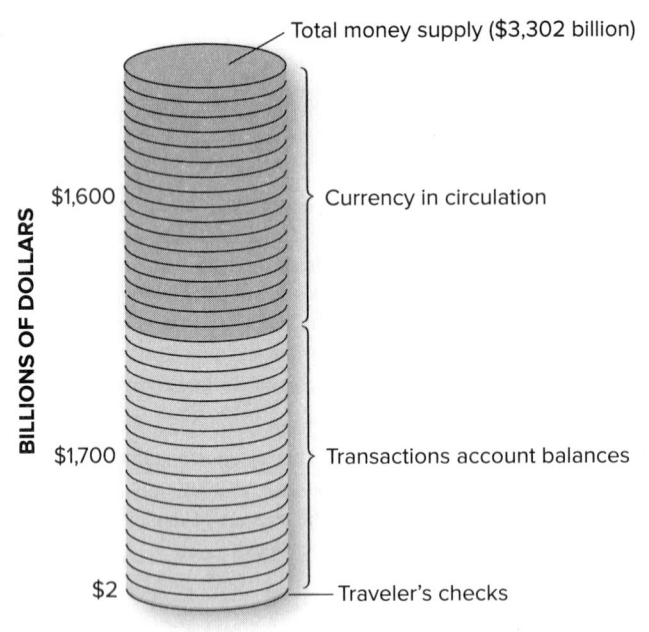

$2 — Traveler's checks

Figure 12.1 Composition of the Basic Money Supply (M1) The money supply (M1) includes all cash held by the public plus balances people hold in transactions accounts (e.g., checking, credit union share draft accounts). Cash is only part of our money supply. ■

Source: "Money Stock Measures—H.6," Federal Reserve Board of Governors, 2018.

NEWS WIRE MEDIA OF EXCHANGE

HOW WOULD YOU LIKE TO PAY FOR THAT?

As new payment technologies have developed, consumers have changed the way they pay for the goods and services they buy. But cash is still the most popular form of payment, accounting for a third of all consumer purchases. Those cash payments are typically small, however. Cash payments account for only 8 percent of the *value* of consumer purchases. More expensive purchases are made electronically or by check, debit card, or credit card.

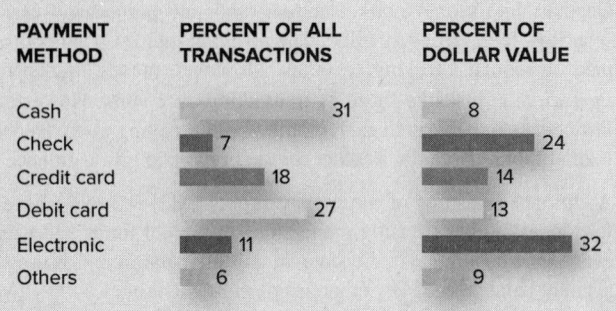

PAYMENT METHOD	PERCENT OF ALL TRANSACTIONS	PERCENT OF DOLLAR VALUE
Cash	31	8
Check	7	24
Credit card	18	14
Debit card	27	13
Electronic	11	32
Others	6	9

Source: O'Brien, Shaun, "Understanding Consumer Cash Use: Preliminary Findings from the 2016 Diary of Consumer Payment Choice," Federal Reserve Bank of San Francisco, April 2017.

NOTE: People pay for goods and services in many ways. Cash is still the most common form of payment but other payment methods account for most of the dollar value of purchases.
注：人们以多种方式为商品和服务进行支付。现金仍是最常见的支付方式，而其他支付方式占购买金额的大部分。

Credit cards are another popular medium of exchange. People use credit cards for about one-third of all purchases. This use is not sufficient, however, to qualify credit cards as a form of money. Credit card balances must be paid by check or cash. Hence credit cards are simply a payment *service,* not a final form of payment (credit card companies charge fees and interest for this service). The cards themselves are not a store of value, in contrast to cash or bank account balances.

Mobile payment services like ApplePay don't qualify as "money" either. Before you can pay for a skinny Frappuccino at Starbucks (see photo), you must first register a credit or debit card with ApplePay. All ApplePay does is allow you to access your credit or debit card through your iWatch, iPhone, or iPad. You just click and the payment is transmitted to Starbucks. You don't have to pull out your credit or debit card. ApplePay makes paying for coffee easier, but it isn't money—it's a payment service that gives you access to money (with the debit card) or credit (that must later be paid with money). The same is true of PayPal: It is a payment *service,* not a form of money.

The last component of our basic money supply consists of traveler's checks issued by nonbank firms (e.g., American Express). These, too, can be used directly in market transactions, just like cash.

Near Money 准货币

Transactions accounts are not the only substitute for cash. Even a conventional savings account can be used to finance market purchases. This use of a savings account may require a trip to the bank for a special withdrawal. But that is not too great a barrier to consumer spending. Many savings banks make that trip unnecessary by offering computerized withdrawals and transfers from their savings accounts—some even at supermarket service desks or cash machines. Others offer to pay your bills if you phone in instructions.

ApplePay is a payment service, *not a form of* money.
©Marcio Jose Sanchez/AP Images

---

barrier 障碍，壁垒。

Not all savings accounts are so easily spendable. Certificates of deposit, for example, require a minimum balance to be kept in the bank for a specified number of months or years; early withdrawal results in a loss of interest. Funds held in certificates of deposit cannot be transferred automatically to a checking account (like passbook savings balances) or to a third party. As a result, certificates of deposit are seldom used for everyday market purchases. Nevertheless, such accounts still function like "near money" in the sense that savers can go to the bank and withdraw cash if they really want to buy something.

Another popular way of holding money is to buy shares of money market mutual funds. Deposits into money market mutual funds are pooled and used to purchase interest-bearing securities (e.g., Treasury bills). The resultant interest payments are typically higher than those paid on regular checking accounts. Moreover, money market funds can often be withdrawn *immediately*, just like those in transactions accounts. However, such accounts allow only a few checks to be written each month without paying a fee. Hence consumers don't use money market funds as readily as other transactions accounts to finance everyday spending.

Additional measures of the money supply (M2, M3, etc.) have been constructed to account for the possibility of using money market mutual funds and various other deposits to finance everyday spending. At the core of all such measures, however, are cash and transactions account balances, the key elements of the basic money supply (M1). Accordingly, we limit our discussion to just M1.

Aggregate Demand　总需求

Why do we care so much about the specifics of money? Who cares what forms money comes in or how much of it is out there?

Our concern about the specific nature of money stems from our broader interest in macro outcomes. As we have observed, total output, employment, and prices are all affected by changes in **aggregate demand**. How much money people have (in whatever form) directly affects their spending behavior. That's why it's important to know what "money" is and where it comes from.

CREATION OF MONEY　货币创造

When people ponder where money comes from, they often have a simple answer: The government prints it. They may even have toured the Bureau of Engraving and Printing in Washington, DC, and seen dollar bills running off the printing presses. Or maybe they visited the U.S. Mint in Denver or Philadelphia and saw coins being stamped.

There is something wrong with this explanation of the origin of money, however. As Figure 12.1 illustrates, *most of what we call money is not cash but bank balances.* Hence the Bureau of Engraving and the four surviving U.S. mints play only a minor role in creating money. The real power over the money supply lies elsewhere.

Deposit Creation　派生存款

To understand the origins of money, think about your own bank balance. How did you acquire a balance in your checking account? Did you deposit cash? Did you deposit a check? Or did you receive an automatic payroll transfer?

If you typically make *non*cash deposits, your behavior is quite typical. Most deposits into transactions accounts are checks or computer transfers; hard cash is seldom used. When people get paid, for example, they typically deposit their paychecks at the bank. Some employers even arrange automatic payroll deposits, thereby eliminating the need for employees to go to the bank at all. The employee never sees or deposits cash in these cases.

---

certificates of deposit 定期存款单。checking account 活期存款账户。passbook 银行存折。ponder 仔细思考。

If checks are used to make deposits, then the supply of checks provides an initial clue about where money comes from. Anyone can buy blank checks and sign them, of course. But banks won't cash checks unless there are funds on deposit to make the check good. Banks, in fact, hold checks for a few days to confirm the existence of sufficient account balances to cover the checks. Likewise, retailers won't accept checks unless they get some deposit confirmation or personal identification. The constraint on check writing, then, is not the supply of paper but the availability of transactions account balances. The same is true of debit cards: If you don't have enough funds in your bank account, the purchase will be rejected.

Like a good detective novel, the search for the origins of money seems to be going in a circle. It appears that transactions account deposits come from transactions account balances. This seeming riddle suggests that money creates money. But it offers no clue regarding how the money got there in the first place. Who created the first transactions account balance? What was used as a deposit?

The solution to this mystery is totally unexpected: Banks themselves create money. They don't print dollar bills. But they do make loans. The loans, in turn, become transactions account balances and therefore part of the money supply. This is the answer to the riddle. Quite simply, *in making a loan, a bank effectively creates money because the resulting transactions account balance is counted as part of the money supply.* And you are free to spend that money, just as if you had earned it yourself.

这个谜题的答案完全是出人意料的：银行自己创造了货币。它们不印钞票，但它们却提供贷款。贷款转而又变成了交易账户余额，从而成为货币供给的一部分。这就是谜题的答案。非常简单，由于交易账户余额是货币供给的一部分，因此银行通过发放贷款有效地创造了货币。并且你可以自由花这笔钱，就像这笔钱是你自己赚的一样。

To understand where money comes from, then, we must recognize two basic principles:

- Transactions account balances are the largest part of the money supply.
- Banks create transactions account balances by making loans.

为了理解货币的来源，我们必须明确两个基本原则：

- 交易账户余额是货币供给的最大组成部分；
- 银行通过发放贷款创造了交易账户余额。

In the following two sections we examine this process of creating money—**deposit creation**—more closely.

A Monopoly Bank 垄断银行

Suppose, to keep things simple, that there is only one bank in town, University Bank, and no one regulates bank behavior. Imagine also that you have been saving some of your income by putting loose change into a piggy bank. Now, after months of saving, you break the bank and discover that your thrift has yielded $100. You immediately deposit this money in a new checking account at University Bank.

Your initial deposit will have no immediate effect on the money supply (M1). The coins in your piggy bank were already counted as part of the money supply because they represented cash held by the public (see Figure 12.1 again). **When you deposit cash or coins in a bank, you are changing the composition of the money supply, not its size.** The public (you) now holds $100 less of coins but $100 more of transactions deposits. Accordingly, no money is lost or created by the demise of your piggy bank (the initial deposit).

你最初的存款对货币供给（M1）并没有直接影响。这是因为储蓄罐里的硬币代表公众所持有的现金，已经被算作货币供给的一部分了（如图12.1所示）。当你将现金或硬币存到银行时，只是改变了货币供给的构成，而不是它的规模。公众（你）现在少持有100美元硬币，但是交易存款多了100美元。因此，货币并没有因储蓄罐（最初的储蓄）的破碎而变少或变多。

What will University Bank do with your deposit? Will it just store the coins in its safe until you withdraw them (in person or by check)? That doesn't seem likely. After all, banks are in business to earn a profit. And University Bank won't make much profit just storing your coins. To earn a profit on your deposit, University Bank will have to put your money to work. This means using your deposit as the basis for making a loan to someone else—someone who wants to buy something but is short on cash *and* willing to pay the bank interest for the use of money.

Typically a bank does not have much difficulty finding someone who wants to borrow money. Many firms and individuals have spending plans that exceed their current money balances. These market participants are eager to borrow whatever funds banks are willing to lend. The question is, How much money can a bank lend? Can it lend your entire deposit? Or must University Bank keep some of your coins in reserve, in case you want to withdraw them? The answer may surprise you.

---

detective novel 侦探小说。loose change 零钱。thrift 节俭，节省。

An Initial Loan 初始贷款

Suppose that University Bank decided to lend the entire $100 to Campus Radio. Campus Radio wants to buy a new antenna but doesn't have any money in its own checking account. To acquire the antenna, Campus Radio must take out a loan from University Bank.

How does University Bank lend $100 to Campus Radio? The bank doesn't hand over $100 in cash. Instead it credits the account of Campus Radio. University Bank simply adds $100 to Campus Radio's checking account balance. That is to say, the loan is made electronically with a simple bookkeeping entry.

This simple bookkeeping entry is the key to creating money. At the moment University Bank lends $100 to the Campus Radio account, it creates money. Keep in mind that transactions deposits are counted as part of the money supply. Once the $100 loan is credited to its account, Campus Radio can use this new money to purchase its desired antenna without worrying that its check will bounce.

Or can it? Once University Bank grants a loan to Campus Radio, both you and Campus Radio have $100 in your checking accounts to spend. But the bank is holding only $100 of **reserves** (your coins). Yet the increased checking account balance obtained by Campus Radio does not limit *your* ability to write checks. There has been a net *increase* in the value of transactions deposits, but no increase in bank reserves. How is that possible?

Using the Loan 使用贷款

What happens if Campus Radio actually spends the $100 on a new antenna? Won't this use up all the reserves held by the bank and endanger your check-writing privileges? Happily, the answer is no.

Consider what happens when Atlas Antenna receives the check from Campus Radio. What will Atlas do with the check? Atlas could go to University Bank and exchange the check for $100 of cash (your coins). But Atlas probably doesn't have any immediate need for cash. Atlas may prefer to deposit the check in its own checking account at University Bank (still the only bank in town). In this way, Atlas not only avoids the necessity of going to the bank (it can deposit the check by mail, ATM, or smartphone) but also keeps its money in a safe place. Should Atlas later want to spend the money, it can simply write a check or use a debit card. In the meantime, the bank continues to hold its entire reserves (your coins), and both you and Atlas have $100 to spend.

Fractional Reserves 部分准备金

Notice what has happened here. The money supply has increased by $100 as a result of deposit creation (the loan to Campus Radio). Moreover, the bank has been able to support $200 of transaction deposits (your account and either the Campus Radio or Atlas account) with only $100 of reserves (your coins). In other words, ***bank reserves are only a fraction of total transactions deposits.*** In this case, University Bank's reserves (your $100 in coins) are only 50 percent of total deposits. Thus the bank's **reserve ratio** is 50 percent—that is,

$$\text{Reserve ratio} = \frac{\text{bank reserves}}{\text{total deposits}}$$

The ability of University Bank to hold reserves that are only a fraction of total deposits results from two facts: (1) People use checks for most transactions, and (2) there is no other bank. Accordingly, reserves are rarely withdrawn from this monopoly bank. In fact, if people *never* withdrew their deposits in cash and *all* transactions accounts were held at University Bank, University Bank would not really need any reserves. Indeed, it could melt your coins and make a nice metal sculpture. So long as no one ever came to see or withdraw the coins, everybody would be blissfully ignorant. Merchants and consumers would just continue using

---

antenna 天线。 bounce 退回（支票等）。 sculpture 雕塑。 blissfully 幸福地，充满喜悦地。

checks, presuming that the bank could cover them when necessary. In this most unusual case, University Bank could continue to make as many loans as it wanted. Every loan made would increase the supply of money.

Reserve Requirements 法定准备金

If a bank could create money at will, if would have a lot of control over aggregate demand. In reality, no private bank has that much power. First, there are many banks available, not just a single monopoly bank. Hence **the power to create money resides in the banking system, not in any single bank.** Each of the thousands of banks in the system plays a relatively small role.

The second constraint on bank power is government regulation. The Federal Reserve System (the Fed) regulates bank lending. The Fed decides how many loans banks can make with their available reserves. Hence even an assumed monopoly bank could not make unlimited loans with your piggy bank's coins. **The Federal Reserve System requires banks to maintain some minimum reserve ratio.** The reserve requirement directly limits the ability of banks to grant new loans.

To see how Fed regulations limit bank lending (money creation), we have to do a little accounting. Suppose the Federal Reserve had imposed a minimum reserve requirement of 75 percent on University Bank. That means the bank must hold reserves equal to at least 75 percent of total deposits.

A 75 percent reserve requirement would have prohibited University Bank from lending $100 to Campus Radio. That loan would have brought *total* deposits up to $200 (your $100 plus the $100 Campus Radio balance). But reserves (your coins) would still be only $100. Hence the ratio of reserves to deposits would have been 50 percent ($100 of reserves ÷ $200 of deposits). That would have violated the Fed's assumed 75 percent reserve requirement. A 75 percent reserve requirement means that University Bank must hold at all times **required reserves** equal to 75 percent of *total* deposits, including those created through loans.

The bank's dilemma is evident in the following equation:

$$\text{Required reserves} = \text{required reserve ratio} \times \text{total deposits}$$

To support $200 of total deposits, University Bank would need to satisfy this equation:

$$\text{Required reserves} = 0.75 \times \$200 = \$150$$

But the bank has only $100 of reserves (your coins) and so would violate the reserve requirement if it increased total deposits to $200 by lending $100 to Campus Radio.

University Bank can still issue a loan to Campus Radio. But the loan must be less than $100 to keep the bank within the limits of the required reserve formula. Thus *a minimum reserve requirement directly limits deposit creation possibilities*.

Excess Reserves 超额准备金

Banks will sometimes hold reserves in excess of the minimum required by the Fed. Such reserves are called **excess reserves** and are calculated as

$$\text{Excess reserves} = \text{total reserves} - \text{required reserves}$$

Suppose again that University Bank's only asset is the $100 in coins you deposited. Assume also a Fed reserve requirement of 75 percent. In this case, the initial ledger of the bank would look like this:

---

ledger 分类账。

University Bank Balance Sheet ("T-account")			
Assets		**Liabilities**	
Required reserves	$75	Your account balance	$100
Excess reserves	$25		
Total assets (your coins)	$100		

Notice two things in this "T-account" ledger. First, total assets equal total liabilities: There are $100 in total assets on the left side of the T-account and $100 on the right. This equality must always exist because someone must own every asset. Second, the bank has $25 of excess reserves. It is *required* to hold only $75 (0.75 × $100); the remainder of its reserves ($25) are thus excess.

This bank is not fully using its lending capacity. *So long as a bank has excess reserves, it can make additional loans.* If it does, the nation's money supply will increase.

A Multibank World   多家银行并存的世界

In reality, there is more than one bank in town. Hence any loan University Bank makes may end up as a deposit in another bank rather than at its own. This complicates the arithmetic of deposit creation but doesn't change its basic character. Indeed, the existence of a multibank system makes the money creation process even more powerful.

In a multibank world, *the key issue is not how much excess reserves any specific bank holds but how much excess reserves exist in the entire banking system.* If excess reserves exist anywhere in the system, then some banks still have unused lending authority.

THE MONEY MULTIPLIER   货币乘数

Excess reserves are the source of bank lending authority. If there are no excess reserves in the banking system, banks can't make any more loans.

Although an *absence* of excess reserves precludes further lending activity, the *amount* of excess reserves doesn't define the limit to further loans. This surprising conclusion emerges from the way a multibank system works. Consider again what happens when someone borrows all of a bank's excess reserves. Suppose University Bank uses its $25 excess reserves to support a loan. If someone borrows that much money from University Bank, those excess reserves will be depleted. The money won't disappear, however. Once the borrower *spends* the money, someone else will *receive* $25. If that person deposits the $25 elsewhere, then another bank will acquire a new deposit.

If another bank gets a new deposit, the process of deposit creation will continue. The new deposit of $25 increases the second bank's *required* reserves as well as its *excess* reserves. We're talking about a $25 deposit. If the Federal Reserve minimum is 75 percent, then *required* reserves increase by $18.75. The remaining $6.25, therefore, represents *excess* reserves. This second bank can now make additional loans in the amount of $6.25.

Perhaps you are beginning to get a sense that the process of deposit creation will not come to an end quickly. On the contrary, it can continue indefinitely as loans get made and the loans are spent—over and over again. *Each loan made creates new excess reserves, which help fund the next loan.* This recurring sequence of loans and spending is much like the income multiplier, which creates additional income every time income is spent. People often refer to deposit creation as the money multiplier process, with the **money multiplier** expressed as the reciprocal of the required reserve ratio:

remainder 剩余部分。

$$\text{Money multiplier} = \frac{1}{\text{required reserve ratio}}$$

货币乘数 = $\dfrac{1}{\text{法定准备金率}}$

We've been assuming a 75 percent reserve requirement in this example. In that case, the money multiplier would be:

$$1/0.75 = 1.333$$

If the reserve requirement were only 20 percent, the money multiplier would be 5.

The money multiplier process is illustrated in Figure 12.2. When a new deposit enters the banking system at University Bank, it creates both excess and required reserves. The required reserves cannot be used to create new loans. Excess reserves, on the other hand, can be used for new loans. Once University Bank makes those loans, they become transactions deposits elsewhere in the banking system (Bank #2 in Figure 12.2).

What happens when the new deposit lands in Bank #2? Part of the new deposit goes into required reserves ($18.75) and the remainder goes into excess reserves ($6.25). Now Bank #2 is in a position to make a new loan. When it does, the money flow moves on to Banks #3 and #4, which make loans themselves. The process continues until all excess reserves have leaked into required reserves. Once excess reserves have all disappeared, the total value of new loans will equal initial excess reserves multiplied by the money multiplier.

Limits to Deposit Creation   派生存款的极限

The potential of the money multiplier to create loans is summarized by the equation

$$\text{Excess reserves of banking system} \times \text{money multiplier} = \text{potential deposit creation}$$

货币乘数创造贷款的潜力可概括为下述公式:

银行体系中的超额准备金 × 货币乘数 = 潜在派生存款

Notice how the money multiplier worked in our previous example. The value of the money multiplier was equal to 1.33, which is 1.0 divided by the required reserve ratio of 0.75. The banking system started out with the $25 of excess reserves created by your initial $100 deposit (the remaining $75 was required reserves). These excess reserves became the basis for bank lending. How much lending? According to the money multiplier, then, the deposit creation potential of the banking system was

$$\text{Excess reserves} (\$25) \times \text{money multiplier} (1.33) = \text{potential deposit creation} (\$33.25)$$

If all the banks fully utilize their excess reserves at each step of the money multiplier process, the banking system could make loans in the amount of $33.25. Not very impressive, but in the real world all these numbers would be in the billions—and that *would* be impressive.

Initial deposit ($100) → University Bank — Loan $25 / Deposit → Bank #2 — Loan $6.25 / Deposit → Bank #3 — Loan $1.56 / Deposit → Bank #4 → etc.

Excess reserves: $25
Required reserves: $75

Excess reserves: $6.25
Required reserves: $18.75

Excess reserves: $1.56
Required reserves: $4.69

Excess reserves: $0.39
Required reserves: $1.17

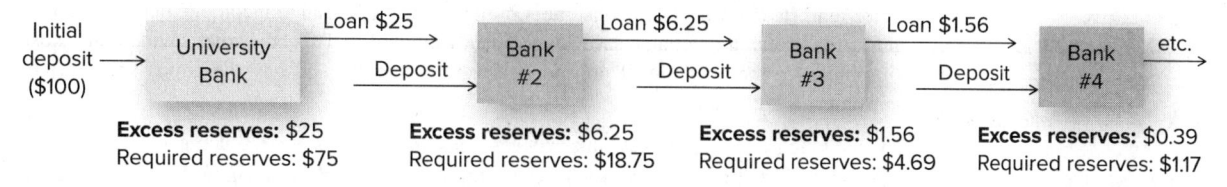

Figure 12.2 The Money Multiplier Process Each bank can use its excess reserves to make a loan. The loans will end up as deposits at other banks. These banks will then have some excess reserves and lending capacity of their own. If the required reserve ratio is 0.75, Bank #2 can lend 25 percent of the $25 deposit it receives. In this case, it lends $6.25, continuing the deposit creation process. ■

leak 漏出。

Excess Reserves as Lending Power

While you are struggling with the arithmetic of deposit creation, notice the critical role that excess reserves play in the process. A bank can make loans only if it has excess reserves. Without excess reserves, all of a bank's reserves are required, and no further liabilities (transactions deposits) can be created with new loans. On the other hand, a bank with excess reserves can make additional loans. In fact,

- *Each bank may lend an amount equal to its excess reserves and no more.*

As such loans enter the circular flow and become deposits elsewhere, they create new excess reserves and further lending capacity. As a consequence,

- *The entire banking system can increase the volume of loans by the amount of excess reserves multiplied by the money multiplier.*

By keeping track of excess reserves, then, we can gauge the lending capacity of any bank or, with the aid of the money multiplier, the entire banking system.

THE MACRO ROLE OF BANKS 银行的宏观角色

The bookkeeping details of bank deposits and loans are complex, frustrating, and downright boring. But they demonstrate convincingly that *banks can create money.* Since virtually all market transactions involve the use of money, banks must have some influence on macro outcomes.

Financing Aggregate Demand 融资总需求

What we have demonstrated in this chapter is that banks perform two essential functions:

- Banks transfer money from savers to spenders by lending funds (reserves) held on deposit.
- The banking system creates additional money by making loans in excess of total reserves.

In performing these two functions, banks change not only the size of the money supply but aggregate demand as well. The loans banks offer to their customers will be used to purchase new cars, homes, business equipment, and other output. All of these purchases will add to aggregate demand. Hence *increases in the money supply tend to increase aggregate demand.*

When banks curtail their lending activity, the opposite occurs. People can't get the loans or credit they need to finance desired consumption or investment. As a result, *aggregate demand declines when the money supply shrinks.*

The central role of the banking system in the economy is emphasized in Figure 12.3. In this depiction of the circular flow, income flows from product markets through business firms to factor markets and returns to consumers in the form of disposable income. Consumers spend most of their income but also save (don't spend) some of it. This consumer saving could pose a problem for the economy if no one else were to step up and buy the goods and services consumers leave unsold.

The banking system is the key link between consumer savings and the demand originating in other sectors of the economy. To see how important that link is, imagine that *all* consumer saving was deposited in piggy banks rather than depository institutions (banks) and that no one used checks. Under these circumstances, banks could not transfer money from savers to spenders by holding deposits and making loans. The banks could not create the money needed to boost aggregate demand.

---

gauge 衡量，判定。

In reality, a substantial portion of consumer saving *is* deposited in banks. These and other bank deposits can be used as the basis of loans, thereby returning purchasing power to the circular flow. Moreover, because the banking system can make *multiple* loans from available reserves, banks don't have to receive all consumer saving in order to carry out their function. On the contrary, **the banking system can create any desired level of money supply if allowed to expand or reduce loan activity at will.**

事实上，相当一部分消费者的储蓄是存放在银行的。这些存款和其他银行存款可用来作为贷款的资金基础，从而使购买力回归到循环流动过程。此外，由于银行体系能够利用可用的准备金发放成倍的贷款，因此银行无需收到所有消费者的储蓄也能履行其职能。相反，如果允许银行体系随意提高或降低放贷能力，它就能产生任意水平的货币供给。

Constraints on Money Creation 货币创造的局限

If banks had unlimited power to create money (make loans), they could control aggregate demand. Their power isn't quite so vast, however. There are four major constraints on their lending activity.

Bank Deposits 银行存款

The first constraint on the lending activity of banks is the willingness of people to keep deposits in the bank. If people preferred to hold cash rather than debit cards and checkbooks, banks would not be able to acquire or maintain the reserves that are the foundation of bank lending activity.

Willing Borrowers 自愿借款者

The second constraint on deposit creation is the willingness of consumers, businesses, and governments to borrow the money that banks make available. If no one wanted to borrow any money, deposit creation would never begin.

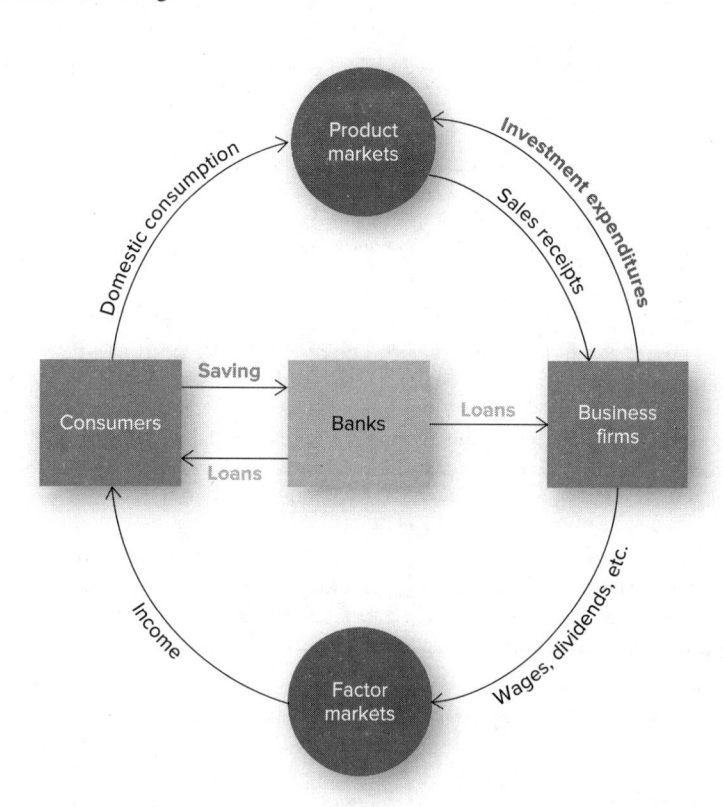

Figure 12.3 Banks in the Circular Flow Banks help transfer income from savers to spenders. They do this by using their deposits to make loans to business firms and consumers who desire to spend more money than they have. By lending money, banks help maintain any desired rate of aggregate spending. ■

Willing Lenders 自愿贷款者

The banks themselves may not be willing to satisfy all credit demands. This was the case in the 1930s when the banks declined to use their excess reserves for loans they perceived to be too risky. In the recession of 2008–2009 many banks again closed their loan windows. Consumers couldn't get mortgages to buy new homes; businesses couldn't get loans to purchase equipment or inventory.

Government Regulation 政府监管

The last and most important constraint on deposit creation is the Federal Reserve System. In the absence of government regulation, individual banks would have tremendous power over the money supply and therewith all macroeconomic outcomes. The government limits this power by regulating bank lending practices. The levers of Federal Reserve policy are examined in the next chapter.

POLICY PERSPECTIVES

ARE BITCOINS THE NEW MONEY?

Not everyone likes the idea that the government (mostly the Federal Reserve System) controls the supply of money. And many people worry about the privacy of their market purchases, especially those made with checks, credit cards, and debit cards: There is always a record of those transactions somewhere in the financial system. And consumers and merchants alike complain about the fees they have to pay to the financial institutions that process their payments. Is there a better way to buy goods and services? A way that would offer lower fees, more secure transactions, and anonymity?

Satoshi Nakamoto believes he invented such an alternative. In 2009 he unveiled a peer-to-peer online payment system, using a digital currency called "bitcoins." In this open-source software system, people can acquire, hold, and spend bitcoins. The bitcoins are identified digital entries in an electronic database maintained by computer programmers around the world. Individuals have "private keys," like passcodes, that allow them to access their bitcoins and transfer them to others. Such transfers can finance market purchases, much like debit or credit card payments. But there is no middleman in bitcoin transfers, nor is there any public disclosure of the buyer and seller.

At first blush, bitcoins sound like money. But they don't quite make the grade. Remember that to qualify as money, an item must possess three characteristics: (1) be accepted as a medium of exchange, (2) serve as a store of value, and (3) function as a standard of value. Bitcoins can pretty much pass the first test; they are accepted as a medium of exchange by many merchants and individuals. But even on that score, their acceptability is limited to just a tiny fraction of the marketplace. As for being a store of value, bitcoins don't come close to qualifying. In just a two-year period (2011–2013), the value of a bitcoin varied from a low of 30 cents to a high of $1,242! And that wasn't because the value kept going up; the value of a bitcoin has plummeted repeatedly. By early 2015, its value had fallen 80 percent from its November 29, 2013, peak. It spiked again to an all-time high of $19,783 in December 2017, then fell continuously to under $6,000 in 2018. Given its incredible volatility, it would be hard to think of bitcoins as a standard of value. So, bitcoins aren't about to become the new "money."

What has kept bitcoins in the news is their potential for anonymity. Bitcoin transactions can be used to move assets around without anyone knowing. This makes it an ideal vehicle for illicit activities, including money laundering, drug sales, tax evasion, and terrorism. The U.S. Department of Homeland Security, the FBI, and other international agencies have disrupted numerous bitcoin exchanges, seizing bitcoin assets. Ironically, the anonymity of bitcoin transactions has also made it a favorite target of hackers; stolen bitcoins are very hard to trace. There have been numerous instances of bitcoin thefts, amounting to tens of millions of dollars.

---

anonymity 匿名。bitcoin 比特币。volatility 波动。money laundering 洗钱。

CHAPTER 12 REVIEW

SUMMARY

- In a market economy, money serves a critical function in facilitating exchanges and specialization, thus permitting increased output. "Money" refers to anything that serves as a medium of exchange, store of value, and standard of value. **LO1**
- The most common measure of the money supply (M1) includes both cash and balances people hold in transactions accounts (e.g., checking accounts). **LO2**
- Banks have the power to create money simply by making loans. In making loans, banks create new transactions deposits (bank balances), which instantly become part of the money supply. **LO3**
- The ability of banks to make loans—create money—depends on their reserves. Only if a bank has excess reserves—reserves greater than those required by federal regulation—can it make new loans. **LO3**
- As loans are spent, they create deposits elsewhere, making it possible for other banks to make additional loans. The money multiplier (1 ÷ required reserve ratio) indicates the total value of deposits that can be created by the banking system from excess reserves. **LO4**
- The role of banks in creating money includes the transfer of money from savers to spenders as well as deposit creation in excess of deposit balances. Taken together, these two functions give banks direct control over the amount of purchasing power available in the marketplace. **LO5**
- The deposit creation potential of the banking system is limited by government regulation. It is also limited by the willingness of market participants to hold deposits or borrow money. At times, banks themselves may be unwilling to use all their lending ability. **LO4**

TERMS TO REMEMBER

Define the following terms:

barter
money
transactions account
money supply (M1)
aggregate demand
deposit creation
bank reserves
reserve ratio
required reserves
excess reserves
money multiplier

QUESTIONS FOR DISCUSSION

1. Do bananas satisfy the three conditions for money? Did barter make it easier or more difficult to get a haircut in Venezuela? (See the News Wire "Barter.") **LO1**
2. Why aren't mobile payments counted as money? **LO2**
3. What percentage of your monthly spending do you pay with (*a*) cash, (*b*) check, (*c*) credit card, (*d*) debit card, or (*e*) automatic transfers? How does your behavior compare to others? (See the News Wire "Media of Exchange.") **LO2**
4. If a friend asked you how much money you had to spend, what items would you include in your response? **LO2**
5. Does money have any intrinsic value? If not, why are people willing to accept money in exchange for goods and services? **LO1**
6. Have you ever borrowed money to buy a car, pay tuition, or for any other purpose? In what form did you receive the money? How did your loan affect the money supply? Aggregate demand? **LO3**
7. Does the fact that your bank keeps only a fraction of your account balance in reserve worry you? Why don't people rush to the bank and retrieve their money? What would happen if they did? **LO3**
8. If all banks heeded Shakespeare's admonition "Neither a borrower nor a lender be," what would happen to the supply of money? **LO3**
9. Why would a bank ever hold excess reserves rather than make new loans? **LO3**
10. If banks stopped making new loans, how would aggregate demand be affected? **LO5**
11. **POLICY PERSPECTIVES** If people want more anonymity in their market transactions, why don't they simply use cash instead of bitcoins? **LO1**

PROBLEMS

1. What percent of the money supply depicted in Figure 12.1 is cash? **LO2**
2. If a bank has $100 million in deposits and $17 million in reserves with a reserve requirement of 0.15, **LO3**
    a. how much are its required reserves?
    b. what is the required reserve ratio?
    c. how much can it lend?
3. If a bank has $10 million in deposits and excess reserves of $200,000 and required reserves of $1 million, **LO3**
    a. what are its total reserves?
    b. what is the required reserve ratio?
4. How large is the money multiplier when the required reserve ratio is 0.25? If the required reserve ratio decreases to 0.20, what happens to the money multiplier? **LO4**
5. If a bank has total reserves of $200,000 and $1 million in deposits, how much money can it lend if the required reserve ratio is **LO3**
    a. 4 percent?
    b. 6 percent?
6. How large a loan can Bank #2 in Figure 12.2 make? **LO3**
7. What volume of loans can the banking system in Figure 12.2 support? If the reserve requirement were 50 percent rather than 75 percent, what would the system's lending capacity be? **LO3, LO4**
8. Suppose that a lottery winner deposits $5 million in cash into her transactions account at the Bank of America. Assume a reserve requirement of 20 percent and no excess reserves in the banking system prior to this deposit. Show the changes on the Bank of America balance sheet when the $5 million is initially deposited. **LO3**
9. In December 1994, a man in Ohio decided to deposit all of the *8 million* pennies he had been saving for nearly 65 years. (His deposit weighed over 48,000 pounds!) With a reserve requirement of 10 percent, how did his deposit change the lending capacity of **LO3, LO4**
    a. his bank?
    b. the banking system?
10. **POLICY PERSPECTIVES** If the value of bitcoins increases from $5,000 to $6,000 this year, by how much will M1 increase? **LO2**

CHAPTER THIRTEEN

Monetary Policy 货币政策

The Washington, DC, headquarters of the Federal Reserve
©Jonathan Larsen/Getty Images

LEARNING OBJECTIVES

After reading this chapter, you should be able to:

1. Describe how the Federal Reserve is organized.
2. Identify the Fed's three primary policy tools.
3. Explain how open market operations work.
4. Tell how monetary stimulus or restraint is achieved.
5. Discuss how monetary policy affects macro outcomes.

Rarely do all the members of a congressional committee attend a committee hearing. But when the chair of the Fed is the witness, all 21 members of the U.S. Senate Committee on Banking, Housing, and Urban Affairs typically show up. So do staffers, lobbyists, and a throng of reporters and camera crews from around the world. They don't want to miss a word that Jerome ("Jay") Powell utters.

Tourists visiting the U.S. Capitol are often caught up in the excitement. Seeing all the press and the crowds, they assume some movie star is testifying. Maybe George Clooney is pleading for humanitarian aid for Sudan. Or Lars Ulrich, the drummer for Metallica, is asking for more copyright protection for music. Maybe Angelina Jolie is urging Congress to increase funding for AIDS research and global poverty. Or Ben Affleck is asking Congress to increase aid to Congo. Curious to see who's getting all the attention, the tourists often stand in line to get a brief look into the hearing room. Imagine their bewilderment when they finally get in: The star witness is a banker droning on about economic statistics. Who *is* this person? they wonder, as they head for the exit.

Why do so many people listen intently to Jay Powell, the Fed chair?
Source: Federalreserve.gov

---

hearing 听证会。Senate 参议院。show up 露面,到场。lobbyist 说客,游说者。bewilderment 困惑。drone on 喋喋不休地说下去。

"This person" is often described as the most powerful person in the U.S. economy. Even the president seeks his advice and approval. Why? Because this is the chair of the Federal Reserve—the government agency that controls the nation's money supply. As we saw in the previous chapter, changes in the money supply can alter aggregate demand. So whoever has a hand on the money supply lever has a lot of power over macroeconomic outcomes—which explains why so many people want to know what the Fed chair thinks about the health of the economy.

图 13.1 简单描绘了**货币政策**是怎样融入宏观经济模型的。很明显，很多人认为货币政策杠杆是十分重要的，否则就不会有人去参加美联储主席出席的枯燥的听证会了。要想理解货币政策为何如此重要，我们必须回答两个基本问题：

- 在经济运行中政府如何控制货币数量？
- 货币供给是怎样影响宏观经济结果的？

Figure 13.1 offers a bird's-eye view of how **monetary policy** fits into our macro model. Clearly a lot of people think the monetary policy lever is important. Otherwise no one would be attending those boring congressional hearings at which the Fed chair testifies. To understand why monetary policy is so important, we must answer two basic questions:

- How does the government control the amount of money in the economy?
- How does the money supply affect macroeconomic outcomes?

THE FEDERAL RESERVE SYSTEM 联邦储备系统

Control of the money supply in the United States starts with the Fed. The Federal Reserve System is actually a system of regional banks and central controls, headed by a chair of the board.

Federal Reserve Banks 联邦储备银行

The core of the Federal Reserve System consists of 12 Federal Reserve banks, located in the various regions of the country. Each of these banks acts as a central banker for the private banks in its region. In this role, the regional Fed banks perform many critical services, including the following:

- 私营银行间的支票结算。

- ***Clearing checks between private banks.*** Suppose the Bank of America in San Francisco receives a deposit from one of its customers in the form of a check written on a Wells Fargo bank branch in New York. The Bank of America doesn't have to go to New York to collect the cash or other reserves that support that check. Instead the Bank of America can deposit the check at its account with the Federal Reserve Bank of San Francisco. The Fed then collects from Wells Fargo. This vital clearinghouse service saves the Bank of America and other private banks a great deal of time and expense. In view of the fact that over 20 *billion* checks are written every year, this clearinghouse service is an important feature of the Federal Reserve System.

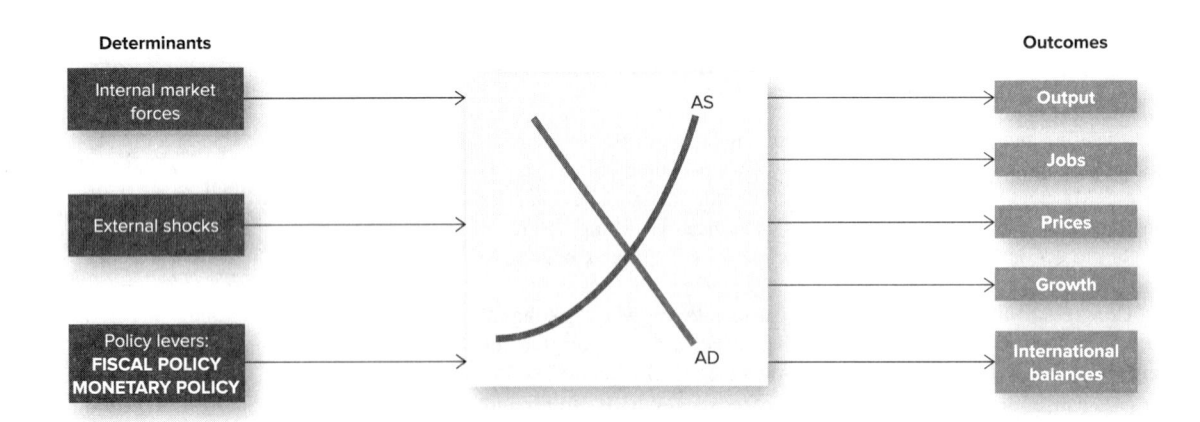

Figure 13.1 Monetary Policy Monetary policy tries to alter macro outcomes by managing the amount of money available in the economy. By changing the money supply and/or interest rates, monetary policy seeks to shift aggregate demand.

---

clearinghouse service 票据交换服务。

- ***Holding bank reserves.*** What makes the Fed's clearinghouse service work is the fact that the Bank of America and Wells Fargo both have their own accounts at the Fed. Recall from Chapter 12 that banks are *required* to hold some minimum fraction of their transactions deposits in reserve. Nearly all these reserves are held in accounts at the regional Federal Reserve banks. Only a small amount of reserves are held as cash in a bank's vaults. The accounts at the regional Fed banks provide greater security and convenience for bank reserves. They also enable the Fed to monitor the actual level of bank reserves.   • 持有银行准备金。
- ***Providing currency.*** Because banks hold little cash in their vaults, they turn to the Fed to meet sporadic cash demands. A private bank can simply call the regional Federal Reserve bank and order a supply of cash to be delivered (by armored truck) before a weekend or holiday. The cash will be deducted from the bank's own account at the Fed. When all the cash comes back in after the holiday, the bank can reverse the process, sending the unneeded cash back to the Fed.   • 提供现金。
- ***Providing loans.*** The Federal Reserve banks may also lend reserves to private banks. This practice, called *discounting*, will be examined more closely in a moment.   • 提供贷款。

The Board of Governors　　理事会

At the top of the Federal Reserve System's organization chart (Figure 13.2) is the Board of Governors. The Board of Governors is the key decision maker for monetary policy. The Fed Board, located in Washington, DC, consists of seven members appointed by the president of the United States and confirmed by the U.S. Senate. Board members are appointed for 14-year terms and cannot be reappointed. Their exceptionally long tenure is intended to give the Fed governors a measure of political independence. They are not beholden to any elected official and will hold office longer than any president.

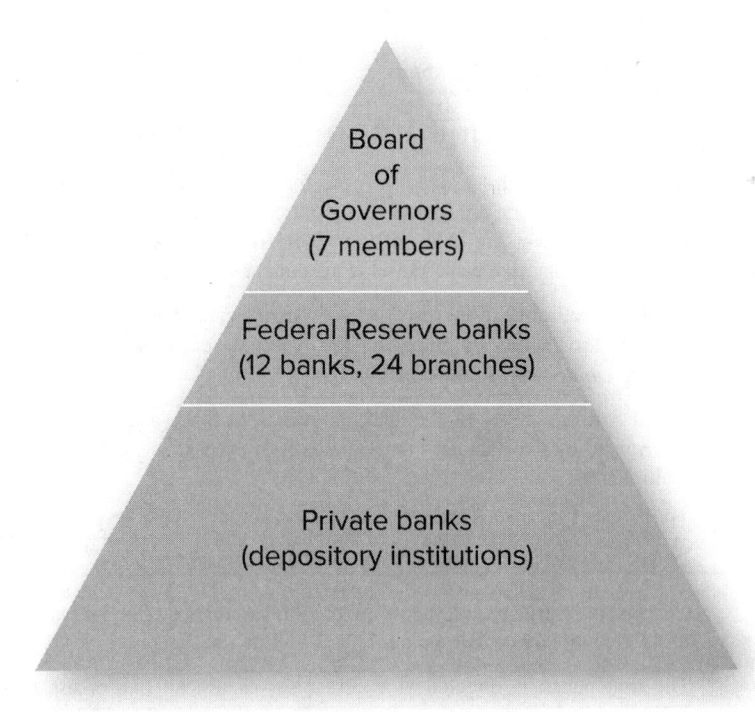

Figure 13.2 Structure of the Federal Reserve System The broad policies of the Fed are determined by the seven-member Board of Governors. Jerome Powell is the chair of the Fed Board.
The 12 Federal Reserve banks provide central banking services to individual banks in their respective regions. The private banks must follow Fed rules on reserves and loan activity.

---

sporadic 零星的，不定时发生的。 armored truck 运钞车。 tenure 任期。 be beholden to 受……的控制。

The intent of the Fed's independence is to keep control of the nation's money supply beyond the immediate reach of politicians (especially members of the House of Representatives, elected for two-year terms). The designers of the Fed system feared that political control of monetary policy would cause wild swings in the money supply and macro instability. Critics argue, however, that the Fed's independence makes it unresponsive to the majority will.

The Fed Chair   美联储主席

The most visible member of the Fed system is the Board's chair. The chair is selected by the president of the United States, subject to congressional approval. The chair is appointed for four years but may be reappointed for successive terms. Alan Greenspan was first appointed chairman by President Reagan and then reappointed by Presidents George H. W. Bush, Bill Clinton, and George W. Bush. When his term as a governor expired on January 31, 2006, he was replaced by Ben Bernanke, a former economics professor from Princeton University. President Obama reappointed Bernanke for another four-year term in January 2010. In January 2014 the president appointed a new chair, Janet Yellen—another economist. She served until 2018, at which time President Trump chose to replace her with Jerome ("Jay") Powell. Powell himself was appointed as a governor by President Obama in 2012 and had been serving on the Board until sworn in as the new chair in February 2018. He will serve as chair until at least 2022.

MONETARY TOOLS   货币工具

Our immediate interest is not in the structure of the Federal Reserve System but in the way the Fed can use its powers to alter the **money supply (M1)**. *The basic tools of monetary policy are*

- *Reserve requirements.*
- *Discount rates.*
- *Open market operations.*

Reserve Requirements   法定准备金

In Chapter 12 we emphasized the need for banks to maintain some minimal level of reserves. The Fed requires private banks to keep a certain fraction of their deposits in reserve. These **required reserves** are held either in the form of actual vault cash or, more commonly, as credits (deposits) in a bank's reserve account at a regional Federal Reserve bank.

The Fed's authority to set reserve requirements gives it great power over the lending behavior of individual banks. *By changing the reserve requirement, the Fed can directly alter the lending capacity of the banking system.*

Recall that the ability of the banking system to make additional loans—create deposits—is determined by two factors: (1) the amount of excess reserves banks hold and (2) the money multiplier:

$$\text{Available lending capacity of banking system} = \text{excess reserves} \times \text{money multiplier}$$

Changes in reserve requirements affect both variables on the right side of this equation, giving this policy tool a one–two punch.

The first punch is directed at excess reserves. Recall that **excess reserves** are simply the difference between total reserves and the amount required by Fed rules:

$$\text{Excess reserves} = \text{total reserves} - \text{required reserves}$$

---

reappoint 再任命。vault 保险库，金库。

	Required Reserve Ratio	
	25 Percent	20 Percent
1. Total deposits	$100 billion	$100 billion
2. Total reserves	30 billion	30 billion
3. Required reserves	25 billion	20 billion
4. Excess reserves	5 billion	10 billion
5. Money multiplier	4	5
6. Unused lending capacity	$20 billion	$50 billion

Table 13.1 *The Impact of a Decreased Reserve Requirement* A decrease in the required reserve ratio raises both excess reserves (row 4) and the money multiplier (row 5). As a consequence, changes in the reserve requirement have a huge impact on the lending capacity of the banking system (row 6). ■

Accordingly, with a given amount of total reserves, *a decrease in required reserves directly increases excess reserves.* The opposite is equally apparent: An increase in the reserve requirement reduces excess reserves. That's what the first punch is supposed to accomplish.

Then comes the second punch. A change in the reserve requirement also increases the *money multiplier*. Recall that the **money multiplier** is the reciprocal of the reserve requirement (i.e., 1 ÷ reserve requirement). Hence *a lower reserve requirement automatically increases the value of the money multiplier.* Both determinants of bank lending capacity thus are affected by reserve requirements.

法定准备金的变化也会增加货币乘数。回忆一下：**货币乘数**是法定准备金率的倒数（也就是1÷法定准备金率），所以较低的法定准备金率会增加货币乘数的值。银行放贷能力的两个决定因素都受到法定准备金的影响。

A Decrease in Required Reserves 法定准备金减少

The impact of a decrease in the required reserve ratio is summarized in Table 13.1. In this case, the required reserve ratio is decreased from 25 to 20 percent. Notice that this change in the reserve requirement has no effect on the amount of initial deposits in the banking system (row 1 of Table 13.1) or the amount of *total* reserves (row 2). They remain at $100 billion and $30 billion, respectively.

What the decreased reserve requirement *does* affect is the way those reserves can be used. Before the decrease, $25 billion in reserves was *required* (row 3), leaving $5 billion of *excess* reserves (row 4). Now, however, banks are required to hold only $20 billion (0.20 × $100 billion) in reserves, leaving them with $10 billion in excess reserves. Thus a decrease in the reserve requirement immediately increases excess reserves, as illustrated in row 4 of Table 13.1.

There is a second effect also. Notice in row 5 of Table 13.1 what happens to the money multiplier (1 ÷ reserve ratio). Previously it was 4 (= 1 ÷ 0.25); now it is 5 (= 1 ÷ 0.20). Consequently, a lower reserve requirement not only increases excess reserves but boosts their lending power as well.

A change in the reserve requirement, therefore, hits banks with a double whammy. *A change in the reserve requirement causes*

- *A change in excess reserves.*
- *A change in the money multiplier.*

These changes lead to a sharp rise in bank lending power. Whereas the banking system initially had the power to increase the volume of loans by only $20 billion (= $5 billion of excess reserves × 4), it now has $50 billion (= $10 billion × 5) of unused lending capacity, as noted in row 6 of Table 13.1. Were all this extra lending capacity put to use, the aggregate demand (AD) curve would shift noticeably to the right.

所以，法定准备金的变化对银行有双重效力。法定准备金的变化导致：

- 超额准备金的变化；
- 货币乘数的变化。

Changes in reserve requirements are a powerful weapon for altering the lending capacity of the banking system. The Fed uses this power sparingly so as not to cause abrupt changes in the money supply and severe disruptions of banking activity. From 1970 to 1980, for example, reserve requirements were changed only twice, and then by only half a percentage point each time (e.g., from 12.0 to 12.5 percent). In December 1990 the Fed lowered reserve requirements, hoping to create enough extra lending power to push the stalled U.S. economy out of recession.

The central bank of China pushed this policy lever in July 2018. Fearful that its economy wasn't growing fast enough, China *lowered* the reserve requirement (see the accompanying News Wire "Reserve Requirements"). In so doing, it *increased* the lending capacity of Chinese banks and helped stimulate AD.

NEWS WIRE RESERVE REQUIREMENTS

CHINA CUTS RESERVE REQUIREMENTS

BEIJING—For the third time this year China's central bank reduced the amount of reserves commercial banks are required to hold, freeing up money for lending in the latest easing measure to shore up the world's second-largest economy.

The People's Bank of China's half percentage point cut in the reserve requirement lowers the reserve-requirement ratio, or RRR, to 15.5 percent for large banks. The move frees up about US $108 billion in additional funds that banks can now lend.

Source: News accounts of July 5–10, 2018.

NOTE: A change in reserve requirements is such a powerful monetary lever that it is rarely used. A change in the reserve requirements immediately changes both the amount of excess reserves and the money multiplier.
注：改变法定准备金是一个非常有力的货币杠杆，因此很少被使用。法定准备金的变化会立即引起超额准备金数额和货币乘数的变化。

The Discount Rate 贴现率

美联储货币政策工具箱里的第二个工具是**贴现率**。贴现率是美联储向私营银行借出准备金时收取的利率。

要理解这个政策工具是如何使用的，你必须认识到银行是追求利润的。它们不想留存闲置的准备金，它们想利用所有可用的准备金来发放有息贷款。在追求利润的过程中，银行总是试图将准备金水平保持在或接近美联储规定的最低额度上。事实也是如此，银行总是有神奇的能力将准备金保持在或接近美联储规定的最低水平。

The second tool in the Fed's monetary policy toolbox is the **discount rate**. This is the interest rate the Fed charges for *lending* reserves to private banks.

To understand how this policy tool is used, you have to recognize that banks are profit seekers. They don't want to keep idle reserves; they want to use all available reserves to make interest-bearing loans. In their pursuit of profits, banks try to keep reserves at or close to the bare minimum established by the Fed. In fact, banks have demonstrated an uncanny ability to keep their reserves close to the minimum federal requirement. As Figure 13.3 illustrates, the only two times banks held huge excess reserves were during the Great Depression of the 1930s and again in 2008–2015. Banks didn't want to make any more loans during the depression and were fearful of panicky customers withdrawing their deposits. Excess reserves spiked up briefly again after the terrorist attacks of September 2001, when the future looked unusually uncertain. In 2008–2015 excess reserves flew off the charts (see Figure 13.3) as banks were waiting for clarity about the economic outlook and government regulation of lending practices.

Because banks typically seek to keep excess reserves at a minimum, they run the risk of occasionally falling below reserve requirements. A large borrower may be a little slow in repaying a loan, or deposit withdrawals may exceed expectations. At such times a bank may find that it doesn't have enough reserves to satisfy Fed requirements.

Banks could ensure continual compliance with reserve requirements by maintaining large amounts of excess reserves. But that is an unprofitable practice. On the other hand, a strategy of maintaining minimum reserves runs the risk of violating Fed rules. Banks can pursue this strategy only if they have some last-minute source of extra reserves.

---

sparingly 保守地，谨慎地。panicky 恐慌的。

Federal Funds Market 联邦基金市场

There are three possible sources of last-minute reserves. A bank that finds itself short of reserves can turn to other banks for help. If a reserve-poor bank can borrow some reserves from a reserve-rich bank, it may be able to bridge its temporary deficit and satisfy the Fed. Interbank borrowing is referred to as the *federal funds market*. The interest rate banks charge each other for lending reserves is called the **federal funds rate**.

紧急准备金有三个可能来源。发现自己准备金不足的银行可以向其他银行寻求帮助。如果准备金不足的银行能从准备金充足的银行借到准备金，就可以弥补暂时的赤字并且满足美联储的要求。银行间拆借指的是联邦基金市场。银行间拆借准备金的利率称为**联邦基金利率**。

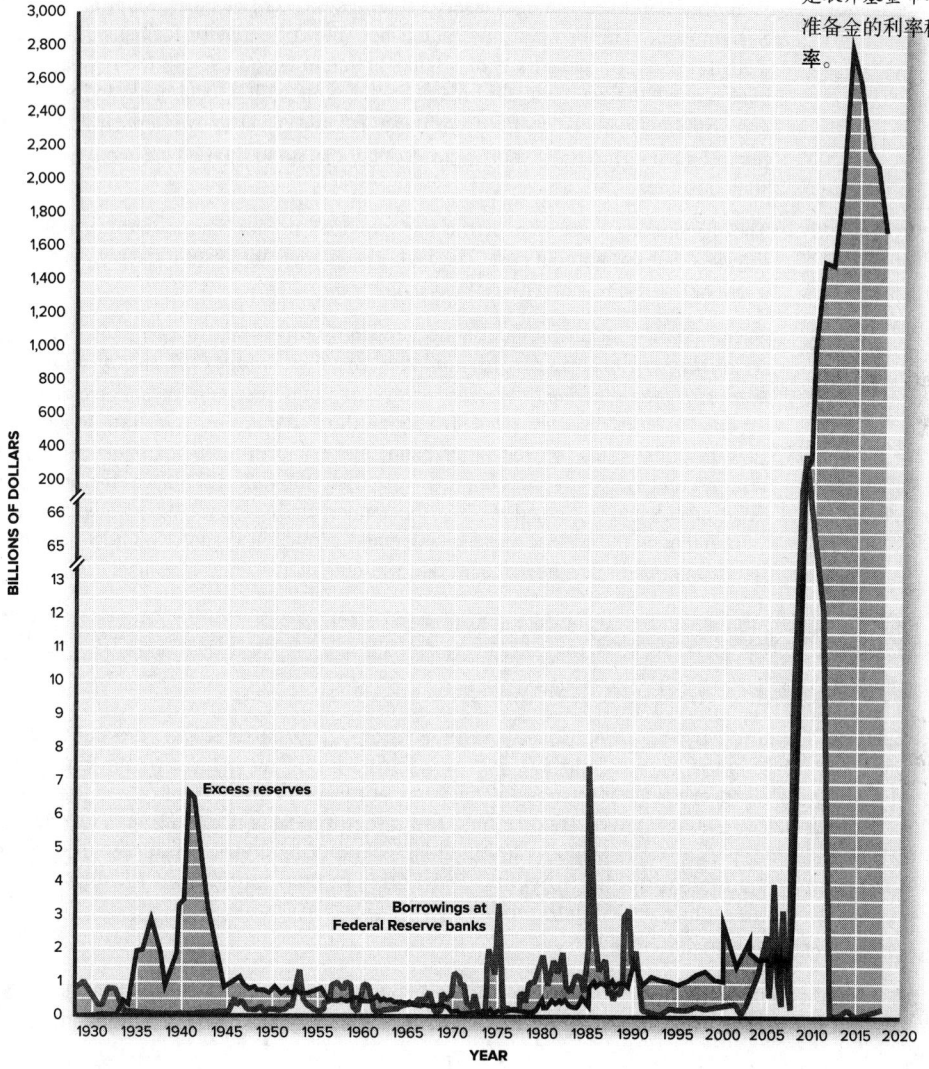

Figure 13.3 Excess Reserves and Borrowings Excess reserves represent unused lending capacity. Hence banks strive to keep excess reserves at a minimum. The only exception to this practice occurred during the Great Depression, when banks were hesitant to make any loans, and again in 2008–2014, when both the economic and regulatory outlooks were uncertain.

In trying to minimize excess reserves, banks occasionally fall short of required reserves. At such times they may borrow from other banks (the federal funds market), or they may borrow reserves from the Fed. Borrowing from the Fed is called *discounting*.

Source: Federal Reserve System.

Securities Sales 证券买卖

Another option available to reserve-poor banks is the sale of securities. Banks use some of their excess reserves to buy government bonds, which pay interest. If a bank needs more reserves to satisfy federal regulations, it may sell these securities and deposit the proceeds at the regional Federal Reserve bank. Its reserve position is thereby increased.

Discounting 贴现

A third option for avoiding a reserve shortage is to *borrow* reserves from the Federal Reserve System itself. The Fed not only establishes rules of behavior for banks, but also functions as a central bank, or banker's bank. Banks maintain accounts with the regional Federal Reserve banks, much the way you and I maintain accounts with a local bank. Individual banks deposit and withdraw *reserve credits* from these accounts, just as we deposit and withdraw dollars. Should a bank find itself short of reserves, it can go to the Fed's *discount window* and *borrow* some reserves.

贴现窗口提供了一种直接影响银行准备金规模的机制。通过提高或者降低贴现率，美联储改变了银行的资金成本和银行借取准备金的积极性。在高贴现率的情况下，从美联储借款成本高昂。高贴现率也表明美联储想要限制货币供给增长。另一方面，较低的贴现率使银行能够借入更多的准备金，并最大限度地利用自己的放贷能力。

The discounting operation of the Fed provides private banks with an important source of reserves, but not without cost. The Fed, too, charges interest on the reserves it lends to banks, a rate of interest referred to as the *discount rate*.

The discount window provides a mechanism for directly influencing the size of bank reserves. ***By raising or lowering the discount rate, the Fed changes the cost of money for banks and therewith the incentive to borrow reserves.*** At high discount rates, borrowing from the Fed is expensive. High discount rates also signal the Fed's desire to restrain money supply growth. Low discount rates, on the other hand, make it profitable for banks to borrow additional reserves and to exploit one's lending capacity to the fullest. This was the objective of the Fed's 2008 discount rate reductions (see the accompanying News Wire "Discount Rates"), which were intended to increase aggregate demand. Notice in Figure 13.3 how bank borrowing from the Fed jumped after the discount rate was cut.

NEWS WIRE DISCOUNT RATES

FED CUTS KEY INTEREST RATE EIGHTH TIME IN A YEAR

WASHINGTON, DC—Alarmed by the rapidly weakening economy, the Federal Reserve cut a key interest rate again yesterday. This is the eighth time this year the Fed had cut the discount rate, dropping it from 4.75 percent at the beginning of the year to a mere 0.50 percent now. The discount rate is the rate the Fed charges for loans it make to private banks. By dropping the rate, the Fed is hoping banks will borrow more money, then use that money to make new loans to businesses and consumers. What has spooked the Fed is that GDP is falling at the fastest rate in 50 years. The Fed is hoping that record low interest rates will prompt more spending, preventing a protracted recession.

Source: News accounts of December 16–18, 2008.

NOTE: A cut in the discount rate lowers the cost of bank borrowing. By cutting both the discount and federal funds rates, the Fed sought to reduce interest rates to consumers and business, thereby stimulating more spending.

注：贴现率的下调会降低银行借款成本。通过降低贴现率和联邦基金利率，美联储希望降低消费者和企业的利率，从而刺激更多的支出。

Open Market Operations 公开市场操作

法定准备金和贴现率是货币政策的重要工具，但是在对货币供给的日常影响方面它们比不上公开市场操作。公开市场操作是直接改变银行系统准备金的主要机制。

Reserve requirements and discount rates are important tools of monetary policy. But they do not come close to open market operations in terms of day-to-day impact on the money supply. ***Open market operations are the principal mechanism for directly altering the reserves of the banking system.*** Because reserves are the lifeblood of the banking system, open market operations have an immediate and direct impact on lending capacity. They are more flexible than changes in reserve requirements, thus permitting minor adjustments to lending capacity (and ultimately aggregate demand).

---

discount window 贴现窗口。protracted recession 长期衰退。

Portfolio Decisions　资产组合决策

To appreciate the impact of open market operations, you have to think about the alternative uses for idle funds. Just about everybody has some idle funds, even if they amount to a few dollars in your pocket or a minimal balance in your checking account. Other consumers and corporations have great amounts of idle funds, even millions of dollars at any time. What we're concerned with here is what people decide to do with such funds.

People, and corporations, do not hold all of their idle funds in transactions accounts or cash. Idle funds are also used to purchase stocks, build up savings account balances, and purchase bonds. These alternative uses of idle funds are attractive because they promise some additional income in the form of interest, dividends, or capital appreciation (e.g., higher stock prices).

Hold Money or Bonds?　持有现金还是债券

The open market operations of the Federal Reserve focus on one of the portfolio choices people make—whether to deposit idle funds in transactions accounts (banks) or use them to purchase government bonds (see Figure 13.4). In essence, the Fed attempts to influence this choice by making bonds more or less attractive as circumstances warrant. It thereby induces people to move funds from banks to bond markets, or vice versa. In the process, reserves either enter or leave the banking system. Hence the lending capacity of banks depends on how much of their wealth people hold in the form of *money* (bank balances) and how much they hold in the form of bonds.

美联储的公开市场操作关注人们所做的资产组合选择——是将闲置资金存进交易账户（银行）还是用来购买政府债券（见图13.4）。

Open Market Activity　公开市场活动

The Fed's interest in these portfolio choices originates in its concern over bank reserves. The more money people hold in the form of bank deposits, the greater the reserves and lending capacity of the banking system. If people hold more bonds and smaller bank balances, banks will have fewer reserves and less lending power. Recognizing this, *the Fed buys or sells bonds to alter the level of bank reserves.* This is the purpose of the Fed's bond market activity. In other words, **open market operations** entail the purchase and sale of government securities (bonds) for the purpose of altering the flow of reserves into and out of the banking system.

美联储对这些资产组合选择的兴趣源于其对银行准备金的关注。人们以银行存款的形式持有的货币越多，银行系统的准备金就会越多，其放贷能力也会越强。如果人们更多地持有债券并保留较少的银行账户余额，银行准备金就会减少，其放贷能力也会降低。因此，美联储通过买卖债券使银行准备金水平发生变化，这就是美联储在债券市场活动的目的。换句话说，**公开市场操作**包括购买和出售政府证券（债券），目的是改变准备金在银行系统的流入和流出。

Buying Bonds　购买债券

Suppose the Fed wants to increase the money supply. To do so, it must persuade people to deposit a larger share of their financial assets in banks and hold less in other forms, particularly government bonds. How can the Fed do this?

The solution lies in bond prices. If the Fed offers to pay a high price for bonds, people will sell some of their bonds to the Fed. They will then deposit the proceeds of the sale in their bank accounts. This influx of money into bank accounts will directly increase bank reserves.

Figure 13.4 Portfolio Choice People holding extra funds have to place them somewhere. If the funds are deposited in the bank, lending capacity increases. ■

---

idle fund 闲置资金。influx 流入。

图 13.5 展示了这个过程的运作。注意，在第 1 步中，当美联储从公众手中买入债券时，它支付的是自己开的支票。债券的卖家如果想要使用这些收入或者只是把钱保管好，就必须将美联储的支票存进银行账户（第 2 步）。接着，银行将这些支票存入地区联邦储备银行，作为自己的准备金（第 3 步）。银行准备金直接按支票面值增加。所以，通过购买债券，美联储增加了银行的准备金。当银行将新获得的准备金用于发放贷款时，这些准备金可以用来扩大货币供给。

Figure 13.5 shows how this process works. Notice in step 1 that when the Fed buys a bond from the public, it pays with a check written on itself. The bond seller must deposit the Fed's check in a bank account (step 2) if she wants to use the proceeds or simply desires to hold the money for safekeeping. The bank, in turn, deposits the check at a regional Federal Reserve bank, in exchange for a reserve credit (step 3). The bank's reserves are directly increased by the amount of the check. Thus **by buying bonds, the Fed increases bank reserves.** These reserves can be used to expand the money supply as banks put their newly acquired reserves to work making loans.

Selling Bonds   卖出债券

Should the Fed desire to slow the growth in the money supply, it can reverse the whole process. Instead of offering to *buy* bonds, the Fed in this case will try to *sell* bonds. If it sets the price sufficiently low, individuals, corporations, and government agencies will want to buy them. When they do so, they write a check, paying the Fed for the bonds. The Fed then returns the check to the depositor's bank, taking payment through a reduction in the bank's reserve account. The reserves of the banking system are thereby diminished. So is the capacity to make loans. Thus **by selling bonds, the Fed reduces bank reserves.**

To appreciate the significance of open market operations, one must have a sense of the magnitudes involved. The volume of trading in U.S. government securities exceeds $1 *trillion* per day. The Fed alone owned over $2 *trillion* worth of government securities at the beginning of 2019 and bought or sold enormous sums daily. Thus open market operations involve tremendous amounts of money and, by implication, potential bank reserves.

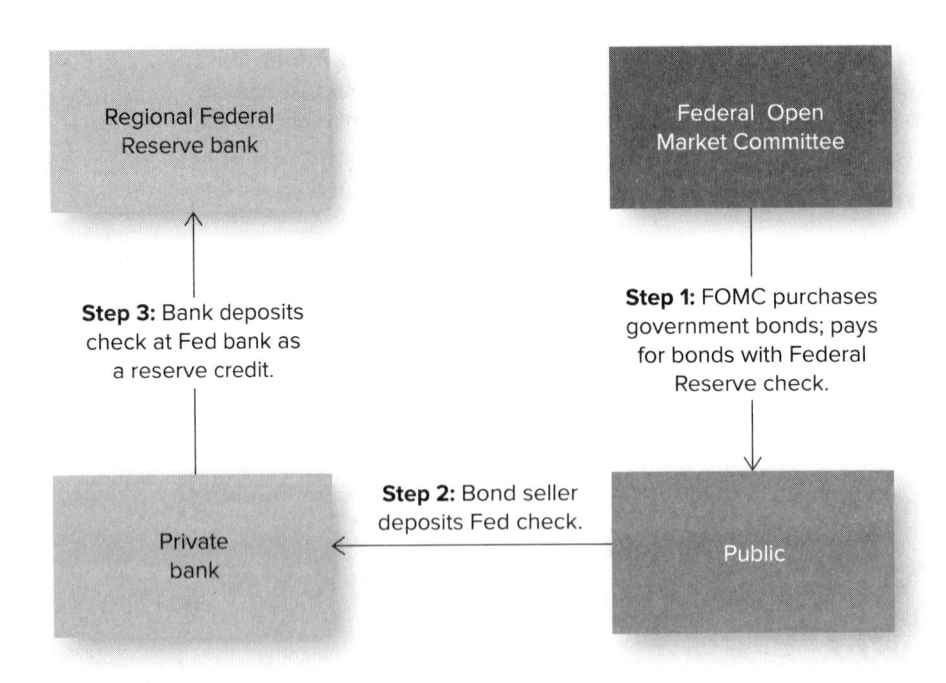

Figure 13.5 An Open Market Purchase The Fed can increase bank reserves by buying government securities from the public. The Fed check used to buy securities (step 1) gets deposited in a private bank (step 2). The bank returns the check to the Fed (step 3), thereby obtaining additional reserves (and lending capacity). To decrease bank reserves, the Fed would sell securities, thus reversing the flow of reserves.

---

trillion 万亿。

Problem	Solution	Policy Tools
Unemployment (slow GDP growth)	Increase aggregate demand.	Buy bonds. Lower discount rate. Reduce reserve requirement.
Inflation (excessive GDP growth)	Decrease aggregate demand.	Sell bonds. Raise discount rate. Increase reserve requirement.

Table 13.2 Monetary Policy Guidelines Monetary policy works by increasing or decreasing aggregate demand, as macro conditions warrant. The tools for shifting AD include open market operations, the discount rate, and bank reserve requirements. ■

Powerful Levers 强有力的杠杆

What we have seen in these last few pages is how the Fed can regulate the lending behavior of the banking system. By way of summary, we observe that the three levers of monetary policy are

- Reserve requirements.
- Discount rates.
- Open market operations.

By using these levers, the Fed can change the level of bank reserves and banks' lending capacity. Since bank loans are the primary source of new money, ***the Fed has effective control of the nation's money supply.*** The question then becomes, What should the Fed do with this policy lever?

通过使用这些杠杆，美联储可以改变银行准备金和它们的放贷能力。由于银行贷款是新增货币的主要来源，所以我们说美联储有效控制了国家的货币供给。下一步问题就变成，美联储应该如何使用这些政策杠杆？

SHIFTING AGGREGATE DEMAND 移动总需求

The ultimate goal of all macro policy is to stabilize the economy at its full employment potential. Monetary policy contributes to the goal by increasing or decreasing the money supply as economic conditions require. Table 13.2 summarizes the tools the Fed uses to pursue this goal.

Expansionary Policy 扩张性政策

Suppose the economy is in recession, producing less than its full employment potential. Such a situation is illustrated again by the equilibrium point E_1 in Figure 13.6. The objective in this situation is to stimulate the economy, increasing the rate of output from Q_1 to Q_F.

We earlier saw how fiscal policy can help bring about the desired expansion. Were the government to increase its own spending, **aggregate demand** would shift to the right. A tax cut would also stimulate aggregate demand by giving consumers and business more disposable income to spend.

前面我们看到了财政政策是如何帮助我们实现想要的经济扩张的。如果政府增加其自身的支出，**总需求**将会向右移动。通过增加消费者和企业的可支配收入，减税也可以刺激总需求。

Monetary policy may be used to shift aggregate demand as well. If the Fed lowers reserve requirements, drops the discount rate, or buys more bonds, it will increase bank lending capacity. The banks in turn will try to use that expanded capacity by making more loans. By offering lower interest rates or easier approvals, the banks can encourage people to borrow and spend more money. In this way, an increase in the money supply will result in a rightward shift of the aggregate demand curve. In Figure 13.6 the resulting shift propels the economy out of recession (Q_1) to its full employment potential (Q_F).

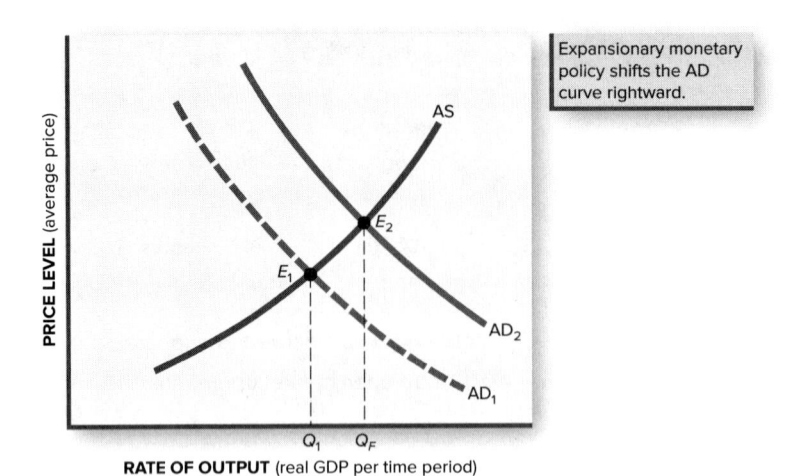

Figure 13.6 Demand-Side Focus Monetary policy tools change the size of the money supply. Changes in the money supply, in turn, shift the aggregate demand curve. In this case, an increase in M1 shifts demand from AD_1 to AD_2 restoring full employment (Q_F). ■

Restictive Policy   紧缩性政策

货币政策也可以用于给过热的经济降温。总需求过高会对我们的生产能力造成沉重的压力。随着市场参与者对紧缺商品竞相抬价,价格水平就会开始上涨。

Monetary policy may also be used to cool an overheating economy. Excessive aggregate demand may put too much pressure on our production capacity. As market participants bid against each other for increasingly scarce goods, prices will start rising.

The goal of monetary policy in this situation is to reduce aggregate demand—that is, to shift the AD curve leftward. To do this, the Fed can reduce the money supply by (1) raising reserve requirements, (2) increasing the discount rate, or (3) selling bonds in the open market. All of these actions will reduce bank lending capacity. The competition for this reduced pool of funds will drive up interest rates. The combination of higher interest rates and lessened loan availability will curtail investment, consumption, and even government spending.

Interest Rate Targets   利率目标

The federal funds rate typically plays a pivotal role in Fed policy. When the Fed wants to restrain aggregate demand, it sells more bonds. As it does so, it pushes interest rates up. Higher interest rates are intended to discourage consumer and investor borrowing, thereby slowing AD growth.

如果美联储想刺激总需求,它会通过购买债券增加货币供应量,当货币供应量增加时,利率下降。因此,利率是货币供给变化和总需求曲线移动之间的一个关键环节。

If the Fed wants to stimulate aggregate demand, it increases the money supply by buying bonds. As the supply of money increases, interest rates decline. Hence *interest rates are a key link between changes in the money supply and shifts of AD.*

In 2017–2018 the Fed raised the federal funds rate seven times, lifting it from 0.5 percent to 2.5 percent. It also announced that it would be raising the rate further in 2019–2020. What was the purpose of these rate increases and announcements? The intent was to signal to market participants that some slowing of aggregate demand was needed because the economy was fully employed and prices were starting to inch up. The market got the message: Interest rates on bonds increased and the stock market fell.

价格与产出效应
PRICE VERSUS OUTPUT EFFECTS

The successful execution of monetary policy depends on two conditions. The first condition is that aggregate *demand* must respond (shift) to changes in the money supply. The second prerequisite for success is that the aggregate *supply* curve must have the right shape.

---

pivotal 关键的。prerequisite 先决条件。

Aggregate Demand   总需求

The first prerequisite—responsive aggregate demand—usually isn't a problem. An increase in the money supply is typically gobbled up by consumers and investors eager to increase their spending. Only in rare times of economic despair (e.g., the Great Depression of the 1930s, the credit crisis of 2008–2009) do banks or their customers display a reluctance to use available lending capacity. In such situations, anxieties about the economy may overwhelm low interest rates and the ready availability of loans. If this happens, monetary policy will be no more effective than pushing on a string. In more normal times, however, increases in the money supply can shift aggregate demand rightward.

Aggregate Supply   总供给

The second condition for successful monetary policy is not so assured. As we first observed in Chapter 11, an increase in aggregate demand affects not only output but prices as well. How fast prices rise depends on **aggregate supply**. *Specifically, the effects of an aggregate demand shift on prices and output depend on the shape of the aggregate supply curve.*

货币政策成功的第二个条件就不那么确定了。就像我们在第11章中首先看到的那样，总需求的增加不仅会影响产出，而且还会波及价格水平。价格上涨的速度取决于**总供给**。确切地说，总需求曲线的移动对价格和产出的影响依赖于总供给曲线的形状。

Notice in Figure 13.6 what happened to output and prices when aggregate demand shifted rightward. This expansionary monetary policy *did* succeed in increasing output to its full employment level. In the process, however, prices also rose. The price level of the new macro equilibrium (E_2) is higher than it was before the monetary stimulus (E_1). Hence the economy suffers from inflation as it moves toward full employment. The monetary policy intervention is not an unqualified success.

Figure 13.7 illustrates how different slopes of the aggregate supply curve could change the impact of monetary policy. Figure 13.7*a* depicts the shape often associated with Keynesian theory. In Keynes's view, producers would not need the incentive of rising prices during a recession. They would willingly supply more output at prevailing prices, just to get back to full production. Only when capacity was reached would producers start raising prices. In this view, the aggregate supply curve is horizontal until full employment is reached, at which time it shoots up.

The horizontal aggregate supply curve in Figure 13.7*a* creates an ideal setting for monetary policy. If the economy is in recession (e.g., Q_1), expansionary policy (e.g., AD_1 to AD_2) increases output but not prices. If the economy is overheated, restrictive policy (e.g., AD_3 to AD_2) lowers prices but not output. In each case, the objectives of monetary policy are painlessly achieved.

Although a horizontal AS curve is ideal, there is no guarantee that producers and workers will behave in that way. The relevant AS curve is the one that mirrors producer behavior. Economists disagree, however, about the true shape of the AS curve.

Figure 13.7*b* illustrates a different theory about the shape of the AS curve, a theory that gives the Fed nightmares. The AS curve is completely vertical in this case. The argument here is that the quantity of goods produced is primarily dependent on production capacity, labor market efficiency, and other structural forces. These structural forces establish a "natural rate" of unemployment that is fairly immune to short-run policy intervention. From this perspective, there is no reason for producers to depart from this natural rate of output when the money supply increases. Producers are smart enough to know that both prices and costs will rise when spending increases. Hence rising prices will not create any new profit incentives for increasing output. Firms will just continue producing at the natural rate, with higher (nominal) prices and costs. As a result, increases in aggregate demand (e.g., AD_4 to AD_5) are not likely to increase output levels. Expansionary monetary policy causes only inflation in this case; the rate of output is unaffected.

---

nightmare 噩梦。

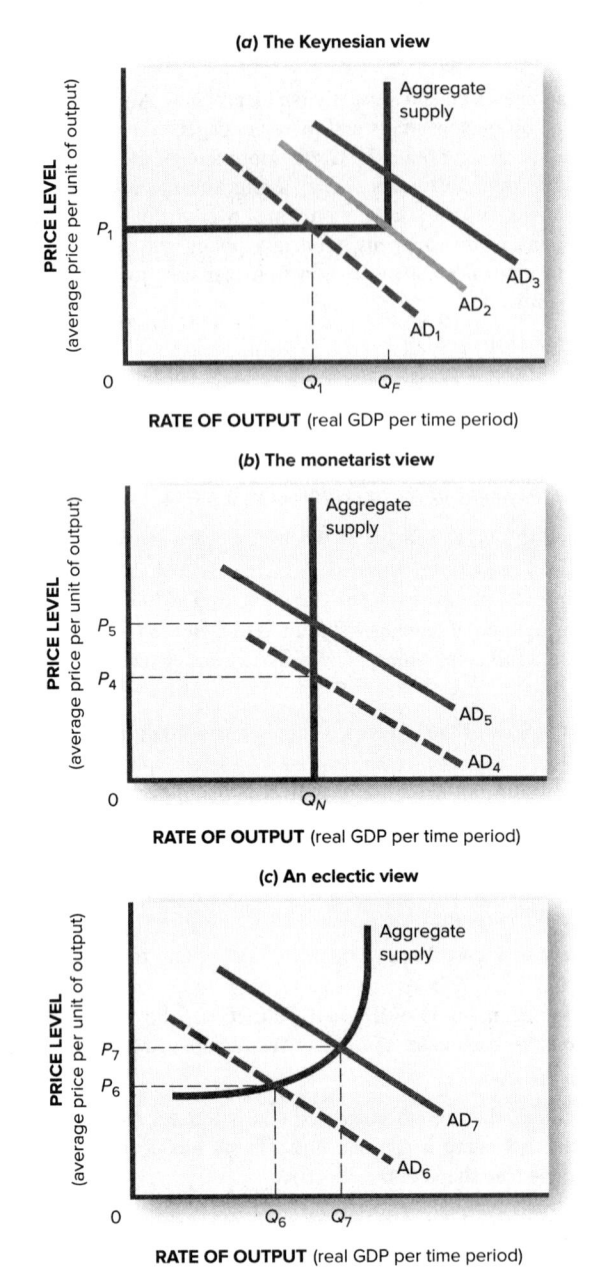

Figure 13.7 Contrasting Views of Aggregate Supply The impact of increased demand on output and prices depends on the shape of the aggregate supply curve.

(a) **Horizontal AS:** In the simple Keynesian model, the rate of output responds fully and automatically to increases in demand until full employment (Q_F) is reached. If demand increases from AD_1 to AD_2, output will expand from Q_1 to Q_F without any inflation. Inflation becomes a problem only if aggregate demand increases beyond capacity—to AD_3, for example.

(b) **Vertical AS:** Some critics assert that changes in the money supply affect prices but not output. They regard aggregate supply as a fixed rate of output, positioned at the long-run, "natural" rate of unemployment (here noted as Q_N). Accordingly, a shift of demand (from AD_4 to AD_5) can affect only the price level (from P_4 to P_5).

(c) **Sloped AS:** The eclectic view concedes that the AS curve may be horizontal at low levels of output and vertical at capacity. In the middle, however, the AS curve is upward-sloping. In this case, both prices and output are affected by monetary policy.

The third picture in Figure 13.7 is much brighter. The AS curve in Figure 13.7c illustrates a middle ground between the other two extremes. This upward-sloping AS curve renders monetary policy effective but not perfectly so. **With an upward-sloping AS curve, expansionary policy causes some inflation, and restrictive policy causes some unemployment.** There are no clear-cut winners or losers here. Rather, monetary (and fiscal) policy confronts a trade-off between the goals of full employment and price stability.

在向上倾斜的总供给曲线下，扩张性的货币政策会导致一定的通货膨胀，紧缩性货币政策会导致一定的失业。这里没有明确的赢家和输家。相反，货币（和财政）政策都会面临充分就业与价格稳定这两个目标的权衡取舍。

Many economists believe Figure 13.7c best represents market behavior. The Keynesian view (horizontal AS) assumes more restraint in raising prices and wages than seems plausible. The monetarist vision (vertical AS) assumes instantaneous wage and price responses. The eclectic view (upward-sloping AS), on the other hand, recognizes that market behavior responds gradually and imperfectly to policy interventions.

POLICY PERSPECTIVES

HOW MUCH DISCRETION SHOULD THE FED HAVE?

The debate over the shape of the aggregate supply curve spotlights a central policy debate. Should the Fed try to fine-tune the economy with constant adjustments of the money supply? Or should the Fed instead simply keep the money supply growing at a steady pace?

DISCRETIONARY POLICY

The argument for active monetary intervention rests on the observation that the economy itself is constantly beset by positive and negative shocks. In the absence of active discretionary policy, it is feared, the economy would tip first one way and then the other. To reduce such instability, the Fed can lean against the wind, restraining the economy when the wind accelerates, stimulating the economy when it stalls. This view of market instability and the attendant need for active government intervention reflects the Keynesian perspective. Applied to monetary policy, it implies the need for continual adjustments to the money supply.

FIXED RULES

Critics of discretionary monetary policy raise two objections. Their first argument relies on the vertical AS curve (Figure 13.7b). They contend that expansionary monetary policy inevitably leads to inflation. Producers and workers can't be fooled into believing that more money will create more goods. With a little experience, they'll soon realize that when more money chases available goods, prices rise. To protect themselves against inflation, they will demand higher prices and wages whenever they see the money supply expanding. Such defensive behavior will push the AS curve into a vertical position.

Even if one concedes that the AS curve isn't necessarily *vertical*, one still has to determine how much slope it has. This inevitably entails some guesswork and the potential for policy mistakes. If the Fed thinks the AS curve is less vertical than it really is, its expansionary policy might cause too much inflation. Hence discretionary policy is as likely to cause macro problems as to cure them. Critics conclude that fixed rules for money supply management are less prone to error. These critics, led by Milton Friedman, urge the Fed to increase M1 by a constant (fixed) rate each year.

THE FED'S ECLECTICISM

The Fed tries to walk a fine line between complete discretion and fixed rules by setting targets for the *outcomes* of its policy. It does this by setting specific targets for unemployment and inflation, two of the most important macroeconomic outcomes.

UNEMPLOYMENT TARGETING

The Fed embarked on a very aggressive stimulus program in 2008 in response to the emerging Great Recession of 2008–2009. It greatly expanded the money supply and pushed interest rates down to rock-bottom levels (see the News Wire "Discount Rates"). As we saw in Figure 13.3, these actions caused excess reserves in the banking system to soar to unprecedented heights. Critics worried that all of this monetary stimulus would ultimately ignite inflation. They wanted to know when the Fed was going to turn

---

instantaneous 即刻的。 spotlight 凸显。 fine-tune 微调。 concede（通常指不情愿地）承认。 be prone to 易于……。

off the money spigot. In 2012 the Fed responded. It said it would keep pursuing monetary stimulus until the national unemployment rate fell to 6.5 percent. The intent of this unemployment targeting was to give market participants a clearer signal about Fed intentions and policy. When the unemployment rate fell to 6.5 percent in 2014, the Fed started scaling back its stimulus program.

INFLATION TARGETING

Earlier the Fed had provided similar guidance with respect to the nation's inflation rate. It said that an inflation rate below 2 percent was tolerable and would not require any Fed intervention. Only when the inflation rate exceeded that target should market participants expect the Fed to introduce monetary restraint.

The unemployment and inflation targets set by the Fed reduce the uncertainty about the Fed's discretionary policy. But they are a far cry from fixed rules of conduct. Both the unemployment rate and the inflation rate change every month. Someone has to make a judgment call about whether an uptick in reported inflation or a downtick in unemployment is a temporary fluke or a meaningful change. In other words, the Fed still has to engage in some guesswork (i.e., use its discretionary powers).

CHAPTER 13 REVIEW

SUMMARY

- The Federal Reserve System controls the nation's money supply by regulating the loan activity (deposit creation) of private banks. **LO2**
- The core of the Federal Reserve System is the 12 regional Federal Reserve banks, which provide check clearance, reserve deposit, and loan (discounting) services to individual banks. **LO1**
- Private banks are required to maintain minimum reserves on deposit at one of the regional Federal Reserve banks. **LO1**
- The general policies of the Fed are set by its Board of Governors. The Board's chair is selected by the U.S. president and confirmed by Congress. The chair serves as the chief spokesperson for monetary policy. **LO1**
- The Fed has three basic tools for changing the money supply: reserve requirements, discount rates, and open market operations (buying and selling of Treasury bonds). With these tools, the Fed can change bank reserves and their lending capacity. **LO2**
- By buying or selling bonds in the open market, the Fed alters bank reserves and interest rates. **LO3**
- To boost aggregate demand, the Fed may either decrease the reserve requirement, lower the discount rate, or buy bonds. To restrain aggregate demand, the Fed may either increase the reserve requirement, raise the discount rate, or sell bonds. **LO4**
- Changes in the money supply directly affect aggregate demand. Increases in M1 shift the aggregate demand curve rightward; decreases shift it to the left. **LO5**
- The impact of monetary policy on macro outcomes depends on the slope of the aggregate supply curve. If the AS curve has an upward slope, a trade-off exists between the goals of full employment and price stability. **LO5**
- Advocates of discretionary monetary policy say the Fed must counter market instabilities. Advocates of fixed policy rules warn that discretionary policy may do more harm than good. The Fed tries to steer a middle course by setting unemployment and inflation targets that signal Fed policies. **LO5**

TERMS TO REMEMBER

Define the following terms:

monetary policy
money supply (M1)
required reserves
excess reserves
money multiplier

discount rate
federal funds rate
open market operations
aggregate demand
aggregate supply

QUESTIONS FOR DISCUSSION

1. Why do banks want to maintain as little excess reserves as possible? Under what circumstances might banks desire to hold excess reserves? (*Hint:* See Figure 13.3.) **LO4**
2. Why do people hold bonds rather than larger savings account or checking account balances? Under what circumstances might they change their portfolios, moving their funds out of bonds and into bank accounts? **LO3**
3. If the Federal Reserve banks mailed everyone a brand-new $100 bill, what would happen to prices, output, and income? Illustrate with aggregate demand and supply curves. **LO5**
4. Why would anyone sell a bond they owned to the Fed? **LO3**
5. How does an increase in the money supply get into the hands of consumers? What do they do with it? **LO4**
6. Is a reduction in interest rates likely to affect spending on pizza? What kinds of spending are sensitive to interest rate fluctuations? **LO5**
7. Which aggregate supply curve in Figure 13.6 does the Fed chair fear the most? Why? **LO5**
8. If the Fed successfully shifted the AD curve to the right and the price level didn't go up, which AS curve in Figure 13.7 was prevailing? **LO5**
9. **POLICY PERSPECTIVES** Like all human institutions, the Fed makes occasional errors in altering the money supply. Would a constant (fixed) rate of money supply growth eliminate errors? **LO5**
10. **POLICY PERSPECTIVES** The Fed cut the discount rate eight times in 2008 (see the News Wire "Discount Rates"), but the economy still fell into a recession. Why didn't the reduced interest rates end the recession? **LO5**

PROBLEMS

1. Suppose the following data apply: **LO2**

Total reserves:	$55 billion
Transactions deposits:	$500 billion
Cash held by public:	$400 billion
Bonds held by public:	$400 billion
Stocks held by public:	$140 billion
Gross domestic product:	$8 trillion
Interest rate:	6 percent
Required reserve ratio:	0.10

    a. How large is the money supply (M1)?
    b. How much excess reserves are there?
    c. What is the money multiplier?
    d. What is the available lending capacity?

2. Assume that the following data describe the condition of the commercial banking system: **LO2**

Total reserves:	$180 billion
Transactions deposits:	$800 billion
Cash held by public:	$300 billion
Required reserve ratio:	0.20

    a. How large is the money supply (M1)?
    b. Are the banks fully utilizing their lending capacity?

    Now assume that the public transfers $20 billion in cash into transactions accounts.

    c. What would happen to the money supply initially (before any lending takes place)?

d. How much would the total lending capacity of the banking system be after this portfolio switch?
   e. How large would the money supply be if the banks fully utilized their lending capacity?
   f. What three steps could the Fed take to offset this potential growth in M1?
3. Suppose the Federal Reserve decided to purchase $40 billion worth of government securities in the open market. **LO3**
   a. By how much will M1 change initially if the entire $40 billion is deposited into transaction accounts?
   b. How will the lending capacity of the banking system be affected if the reserve requirement is 10 percent?
   c. How will banks induce investors to utilize this expanded lending capacity?
4. Suppose the economy is initially in equilibrium at an output level of 100 and a price level of 100. The Fed then manages to shift aggregate demand rightward by 20. **LO4**
   a. Illustrate the initial equilibrium (E_1) and the shift of AD.
   b. Show what happens to output and prices if the aggregate supply curve is (i) horizontal, (ii) vertical, and (iii) upward-sloping.
5. What was the money multiplier in China **LO2**
   a. before the change in reserve requirements?
   b. after the change in reserve requirements? (See the News Wire "Reserve Requirements.")
6. According to the News Wire "Reserve Requirements," **LO2**
   a. by how much did excess reserves in China increase?
   b. by how much did the lending capacity of Chinese banks increase as a result?
7. If every one-point change in the federal funds rate alters aggregate demand by $200 billion, how far did AD shift in response to the News Wire "Discount Rates?" **LO5**
8. **POLICY PERSPECTIVES** From June 2008 to June 2009, M1 increased from $1,400 billion to $1,656 billion. **LO5**
   a. By what percentage did M1 increase?
   b. If the Fed had used a fixed rule of 3 percent growth of M1, how large would M1 have been in 2009?
9. **POLICY PERSPECTIVES** If the price level increases by 0.2 percent for every $100 billion increase in the money supply, by how much might prices rise if the Fed increases excess reserves by $80 billion and the reserve requirement is 0.05? **LO5**

CHAPTER FOURTEEN

Economic Growth 经济增长

Cuba, 2015: Waiting for economic growth.
©Douglas Scott/Alamy Stock Photo

LEARNING OBJECTIVES

After reading this chapter, you should be able to:

1. Specify how economic growth is measured.
2. Describe what GDP per capita and GDP per worker measure.
3. Discuss how productivity increases growth.
4. Explain how government policy affects growth.
5. Discuss why economic growth is desirable.

Fifty years ago there were no fax machines, no cell phones, no satellite TVs, and no iPods. Personal computers were still on the drawing board, and laptops weren't even envisioned. Home video didn't exist, and no one had yet produced microwave popcorn. Biotechnology had yet to produce any blockbuster drugs, and people used the same pair of athletic shoes for most sports.

New products are symptoms of our economic progress. Over time, we produce not only *more* goods and services but also *new* and *better* goods and services. In the process, we get richer: Our material living standards rise.

Rising living standards are not inevitable, however. According to World Bank estimates, nearly 3 *billion* people—close to half the world's population—continue to live in abject poverty (incomes of less than $2.50 per day). A quarter of the world's population has no electricity. And 80 percent of the world's population has an income of less than $10 per day. So not everyone enjoys the fruits of economic growth that are so common in the United States. Worse still, living standards in many of the poorest countries have *fallen* in the last decade.

The purpose of this chapter is to take a longer-term view of economic performance. Most macro policy focuses on the *short-run* variations in output and prices we refer to as business cycles. There are *long-run* concerns as well. As we ponder the future of the economy beyond the next business cycle, we have to confront the prospects for economic growth. In that longer-run context three questions stand out:

---

laptop 笔记本电脑。 biotechnology 生物技术。 symptom 征兆。

- How important is economic growth?
- How does an economy grow?
- What policies promote economic growth?

We develop answers to these questions by first examining the nature of economic growth and then examining its sources and potential.

THE NATURE OF GROWTH 增长的性质

Economic growth refers to increases in the output of goods and services. But there are two distinct ways in which output increases, and they have different implications for our economic welfare.

生产能力利用的短期变化
Short-Run Changes in Capacity Use

最简单的一种增长来自我们对生产能力的更多利用。在任何给定的年份都有一个经济潜在产出的极限,这个极限是由可以获得的资源数量和我们的技术知识决定的。在图 14.1a 中我们用**生产可能性**曲线来表示这些短期产出的极限。通过使用所有我们可以获得的资源和最好的技术,我们可以生产出生产可能性曲线上的任意产出组合。

The easiest kind of growth comes from increased use of our productive capabilities. In any given year there is a limit to an economy's potential output. This limit is determined by the quantity of resources available and our technological know-how. We have illustrated these short-run limits to output with a **production possibilities** curve, as shown in Figure 14.1a. By using all of our available resources and our best expertise, we can produce any combination of goods on the production possibilities curve.

We do not always take full advantage of our productive capacity. The economy often produces a mix of output that lies *inside* our production possibilities, like point A in Figure 14.1a. When this happens, the short-run goal of macro policy is to achieve full employment—to move us from point A to some point on the production possibilities curve (e.g., point B). This was the focus of macro policy during the 2008–2009 recession. The fiscal and monetary policy levers for attaining full employment were the focus of Chapters 11, 12, and 13.

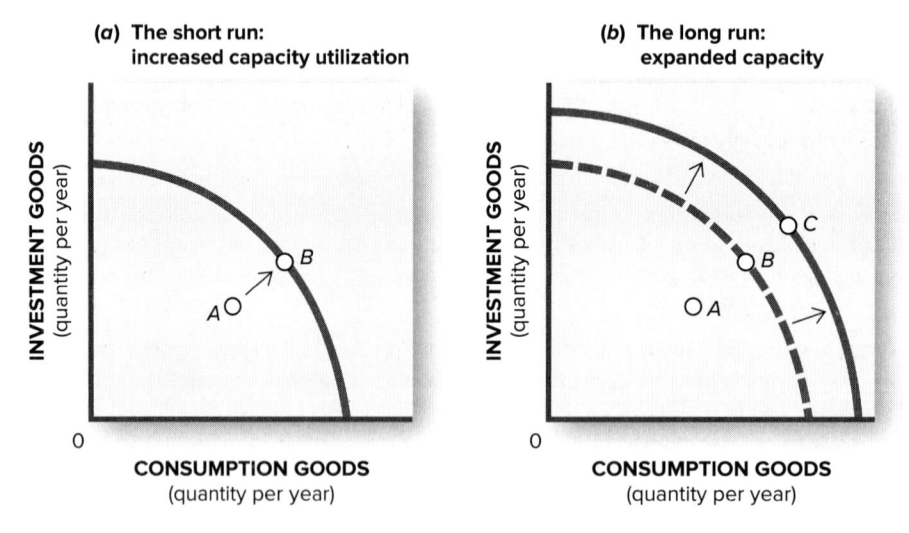

Figure 14.1 Two Types of Growth Increases in output may result from increased use of existing capacity or from increases in that capacity itself. In graph (a) the mix of output at point A does not make full use of production possibilities. Hence we can grow—get more output—by employing more of our available resources or using them more efficiently. This is illustrated by point B (or any other point on the curve).

Once we are on the production possibilities curve, we can increase output further only by *increasing* our productive capacity. This is illustrated by the outward *shift* of the production possibilities curve in graph (b).

Long-Run Changes in Capacity 生产能力的长期变化

As desirable as full employment is, there is an obvious limit to how much additional output we can obtain in this way. Once we are fully utilizing our productive capacity, further increases in output are attainable only if we *expand* that capacity. To do so, we have to *shift* the production possibilities curve outward, as shown in Figure 14.1b. Such shifts imply an increase in *potential* GDP—that is, our productive capacity.

Over time, increases in capacity are critical. Short-run increases in the utilization of existing capacity can generate only modest increases in output. Even high unemployment rates (e.g., 7 percent) leave little room for increased output. ***To achieve large and lasting increases in output we must push our production possibilities outward.*** For this reason, economists often define **economic growth** in terms of changes in *potential* GDP.

Aggregate Supply Focus 关注总供给

The unique character of economic growth can also be illustrated with aggregate supply and demand curves. Short-run macro policies focus on aggregate demand. Fiscal and monetary policy levers are used to shift the AD curve, trying to achieve the best possible combination of full employment and price stability. As we have observed, however, the aggregate supply (AS) curve sets a limit to demand-side policy. In the short run, the slope of the aggregate supply curve determines how much inflation we have to experience to get more output. In the long run, the position of the AS curve limits total output. To get a long-run increase in output, we must move the AS curve.

Figure 14.2 illustrates the supply-side focus of economic growth. Notice that ***economic growth—sustained increases in total output—is possible only if the AS curve shifts rightward.***

随着时间的推移，提高生产能力是至关重要的。利用现有生产能力的短期增长只能产生温和的产出增长。即使是很高的失业率（比如 7%）也没有给增加产出留下多少空间。为了达到大规模和持久的产出增长，我们必须推动我们的生产可能性（曲线）向外移动。所以，经济学家倾向于用潜在 GDP 的变化来定义**经济增长**。

图 14.2 表明了供给学派经济学家对经济增长的关注焦点。注意，经济增长（总产出的可持续增长）只有在总供给曲线向右移动时才成为可能。

Nominal versus Real GDP 名义 GDP 与实际 GDP

We refer to *real* GDP, not *nominal* GDP, in our concept of economic growth. **Nominal GDP** is the current dollar value of output—that is, the average price level (P) multiplied by the quantity of goods and services produced (Q). Accordingly, increases in nominal GDP can result from either increases in the price level or increases in the quantity of output. In fact, nominal GDP can rise even when the quantity of goods and services falls. This was the case in 1991, for example. The total quantity of goods and services produced in 1991 was less than the quantity produced in 1990. Nevertheless, prices rose enough during 1991 to keep nominal GDP growing.

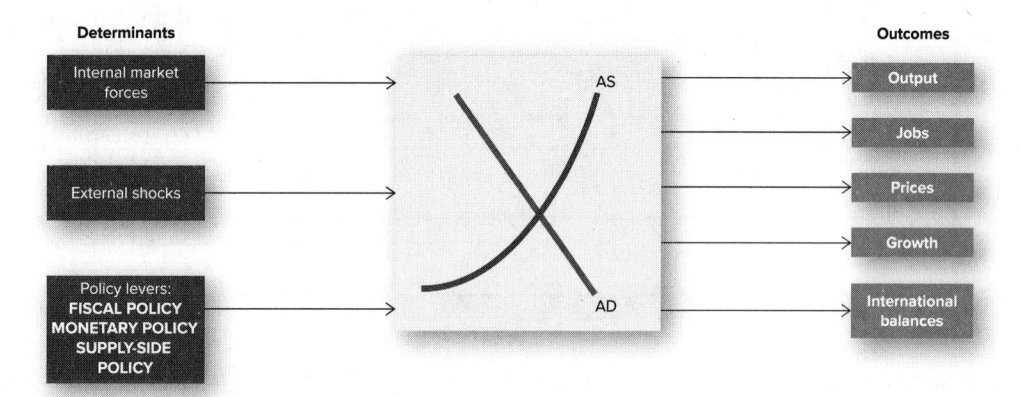

Figure 14.2 Supply-Side Focus Short-run macro policy uses shifts of the aggregate demand curve to achieve economic stability. To achieve long-run *growth,* however, the aggregate supply curve must be shifted as well.

实际 GDP 指的是商品和服务的实际产出量。实际 GDP 以不变价格衡量产出，避免了通货膨胀造成的扭曲。

Real GDP refers to the actual quantity of goods and services produced. Real GDP avoids the distortions of inflation by valuing output in *constant* prices.

GROWTH INDEXES 增长指数
The GDP Growth Rate GDP 增长率

一般说来，实际 GDP 的变化用百分比即增长率来表示。增长率就是用两个时期实际产出的变化量除以基期的总产出量。

Typically changes in real GDP are expressed in percentage terms as a growth *rate*. The **growth rate** is simply the change in real output between two periods divided by total output in the base period. In 2008, for example, real GDP was $15.605 trillion when valued in constant (2012) prices. Real GDP fell to $15.209 trillion in 2009, again measured in constant prices. Hence the growth rate between 2008 and 2009 was

$$\text{Growth rate} = \frac{\text{change in real GDP}}{\text{base period GDP}}$$

$$= \frac{-.396 \text{ trillion}}{15.605 \text{ trillion}} = -2.5\%$$

The negative growth rate in 2009 was an exception, not the rule. As Figure 14.3 illustrates, U.S. growth rates are usually positive, averaging about 3 percent a year. Although there is a lot of year-to-year variation around that average, years of actual decline in real GDP (e.g., 1980, 1982, 1991, 2008, 2009) are relatively rare.

The challenge for the future is to maintain higher rates of economic growth. After the recession of 1990–1991, the U.S. economy got back on its long-term growth track. The growth rate even moved a bit above the long-term average for several years (1997–1999). A brief recession and the 9/11 terrorist attacks put the brakes on economic growth in 2001. Then the economy really stalled in 2008–2009. Once again, policymakers were challenged to restore the GDP growth rate to 3 percent or better.

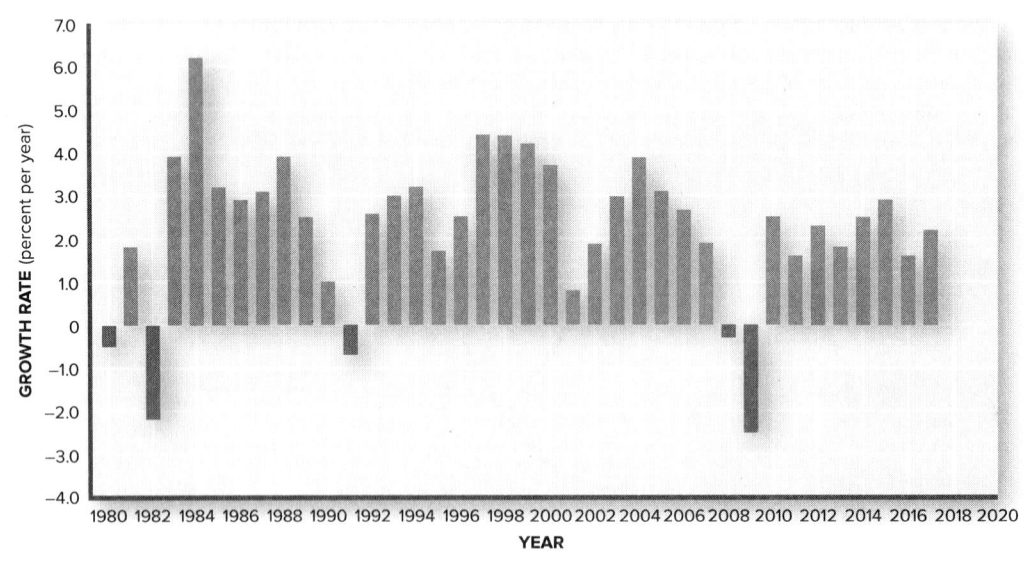

Figure 14.3 Recent U.S. Growth Rates Total output typically increases from one year to another. The focus of policy is on the growth rate—that is, how fast real GDP increases from one year to the next. Historically, growth rates have varied significantly from year to year and even turned negative on occasion. The policy challenge is to foster faster, steadier GDP growth. Is this possible?

The Exponential Process 指数过程

At first blush, the challenge of raising the growth rate from −2.5 percent to 3 percent may appear neither difficult nor important. Indeed, the whole subject of economic growth looks rather dull when you discover that big gains in economic growth are measured in fractions of a percent. However, this initial impression is not fair. First, even one year's low growth implies lost output. Consider the recession of 2009 (see Figure 14.3). If we had just *maintained* the rate of total output in 2009—that is, achieved a *zero* growth rate rather than a 2.5 percent decline—we would have had $396 billion more worth of goods and services. That works out to more than $1,300 worth of goods and services per person for 300 million Americans. Lots of people would have liked that extra output.

Second, economic growth is a *continuing* process. Gains made in one year accumulate in future years. It's like interest you earn at the bank. The interest you earn in a single year doesn't amount to much. But if you leave your money in the bank for several years, you begin to earn interest on your interest. Eventually you accumulate a nice little bankroll.

The process of economic growth works the same way. Each little shift of the production possibilities curve broadens the base for future GDP. As shifts accumulate over many years, the economy's productive capacity is greatly expanded. Ultimately we discover that those little differences in annual growth rates generate tremendous gains in GDP.

经济增长的过程也是如此。生产可能性曲线的每一次微小移动都会拓宽未来 GDP 的基础。随着多年曲线移动的积累，经济的生产能力将会得到极大的扩展。最终，我们将会发现，每年很少的增长率将会带来 GDP 的大幅增加。

This cumulative process, whereby interest or growth is compounded from one year to the next, is called an *exponential process*. To get a feel for its impact, consider the longer-run difference between annual growth rates of 3 percent and 5 percent. In 30 years, a 3 percent growth rate will raise our GDP to $51 trillion (in 2019 dollars). But a 5 percent growth rate would give us $91 trillion of goods and services in the same amount of time. Thus, in a single generation, 5 percent growth translates into a standard of living that is 78 percent higher than 3 percent growth. From this longer-term perspective, little differences in annual growth rates look big indeed.

人均 GDP：生活水平的衡量标准
GDP per Capita: A Measure of Living Standards

The exponential process looks even more meaningful when translated into *per capita* terms. **GDP per capita** is simply total output divided by total population. In 2018 the total output of the U.S. economy was about $20 trillion. Since there were 330 million of us to share that output, GDP per capita was

$$2018 \text{ GDP per capita} = \frac{\$20 \text{ trillion of output}}{330 \text{ million people}} = \$60,606$$

从人均 GDP 的角度来看指数过程将会更有意义。人均 GDP 就是用 GDP 总量除以人口总数。2018 年美国经济的总产出约为 20 万亿美元。

This does not mean that every man, woman, and child in the United States received $60,000 worth of goods and services in 2018. Rather, it simply indicates how much output was potentially available to the average person.

Growth in GDP per capita is attained only when the growth of output exceeds population growth. In the United States, this condition is usually achieved. Our population grows by an average of only 1 percent a year. Hence our average economic growth rate of 3 percent is more than sufficient to ensure steadily rising living standards.

只有当产出的增长超过人口增长时才能实现人均 GDP 的增长。美国通常能够实现这种情况。我们的年度平均人口增长率仅为 1%，所以我们 3% 的平均经济增长率足以确保生活水平的稳步提高。

The accompanying News Wire "Improved Living Standards" illustrates some of the ways rising per capita GDP has changed our lives. In the 20-year period between 1970 and 1990, the size of the average U.S. house increased by a third. Air conditioning went from the exception to the rule. And the percentage of college graduates nearly doubled. Had the economy grown more slowly, we wouldn't have gotten all these additional goods and services. The trend toward increasing creature comforts and less work continued from 1990 to 2010.

---

bankroll 资金。cumulative 积累的。

NEWS WIRE IMPROVED LIVING STANDARDS

WHAT ECONOMIC GROWTH HAS DONE FOR U.S. FAMILIES

As the economy grows, living standards rise. The changes are so gradual, however, that few people notice. After 20 years of growth, though, some changes are remarkable. We now live longer, work less, and consume a lot more. Some examples:

	1970	1990	2010
Average size of a new home (square feet)	1,500	2,080	2,600
New homes with central air conditioning	34%	76%	78%
People using computers	<100,000	76 million	200 million
Households with color TV	33.9%	96.1%	97.8%
Households with cable TV	4 million	55 million	92 million
Households with VCRs	0	67 million	64 million
Households with two or more vehicles	29.3%	54%	57%
Median household net worth (real)	$24,217	$48,887	$51,892
Households owning a microwave oven	<1%	79%	90%
Heart transplant procedures	<10	2,125	2,332
Average workweek	37.1 hours	34.5 hours	34.2 hours
Average daily time working in the home	3.9 hours	3.5 hours	2.4 hours
Annual paid vacation and holidays	15.5 days	22.5 days	25.0 days
Women in the workforce	31.5%	56.6%	58.9%
Recreational boats owned	8.8 million	16 million	17 million
Manufacturers' shipments of RVs	30,300	173,100	242,300
Adult softball teams	29,000	188,000	190,000
Recreational golfers	11.2 million	27.8 million	29.0 million
Attendance at symphonies and orchestras	12.7 million	43.6 million	—
Americans finishing high school	51.9%	77.7%	88.3%
Americans finishing four years of college	13.5%	24.4%	31.9%
Employee benefits as a share of payroll	29.3%	40.2%	49.0%
Life expectancy at birth (years)	70.8	75.4	79.0

Sources: Federal Reserve Bank of Dallas, 1993 Annual Report; and various government industry sources.

NOTE: Economic growth not only generated more and better output but also improved health and provided more leisure.
注：经济增长不仅带来了更多更好的商品和服务，它还会改善人们的健康状况，让人们拥有更多的休闲时间。

It's tempting to take the benefits of growth for granted. But that would be a serious mistake. As Figure 14.4 shows, rising GDP per capita is a relatively new phenomenon in the long course of history. World GDP per capita hardly grew at all for 1,500 years or so. It is only since 1820 that world output has grown significantly faster than the population.

Figure 14.4 also reveals that most of the non-Western world did not enjoy the robust GDP growth we experienced in the nineteenth and twentieth centuries. Even today, many poor countries continue to suffer from a combination of slow GDP growth and fast population

---

be tempting to 很容易……。　robust 强劲的。

growth. Zimbabwe, for example, is one of the poorest countries in the world, with GDP per capita of $900. Yet its population continues to grow more rapidly (1.8 percent per year) than GDP (0.7 percent growth), further depressing living standards. The population of Haiti grew by 1.5 percent per year from 2000 to 2017 while GDP grew at a slower rate of only 1.4 percent. As a consequence, GDP per capita *declined* by more than 0.1 percent per year. Even that dismal record was outstripped by the Central African Republic, where GDP itself *declined* by 0.4 percent a year from 2000 to 2017 while the population continued to grow at 1.3 percent a year.

By comparison with these countries, the United States has been most fortunate. Our GDP per capita has more than doubled since Ronald Reagan was president. This means that the average person today has twice as many goods and services as the average person had only a generation ago.

What about the future? Will we continue to enjoy substantial gains in living standards? It all depends on how fast output continues to grow in relation to population. Table 14.1 indicates some of the possibilities. If GDP per capita continues to grow at 2.0 percent per year, our average income will double again in 36 years.

单个工人的 GDP：生产率的衡量标准
GDP per Worker: A Measure of Productivity

As the people in Zimbabwe, Haiti, and the Central African Republic know, these projected increases in total output may never occur. Someone has to *produce* more output if we want GDP per capita to rise. One reason our living standard rose so nicely in the 1990s is that the **labor force** grew faster than the population. The baby boomers born after World War II had completed college, raised families, and were fully committed to the workforce. The labor force also continued to expand with a steady stream of immigrants and women taking jobs outside the home. The **employment rate**—the percentage of the adult population actually working—rose from under 60 percent in 1980 to over 63 percent in 2007.

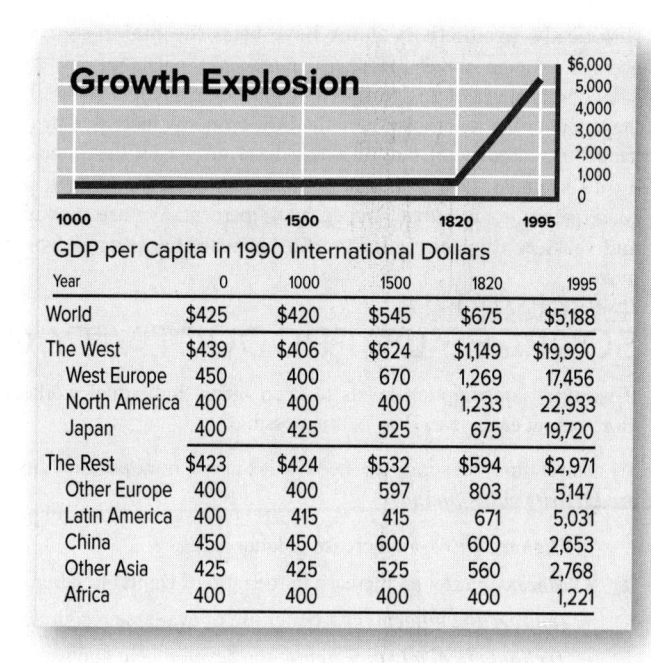

就像在津巴布韦、海地和中非共和国的人们所知道的那样，那些预计的总产出增长可能永远不会发生。如果我们想要提高人均 GDP，就得有人生产出更多的产品。我们的生活水平在 20 世纪 90 年代上升如此之快的一个原因就是**劳动力**的增长超过了人口的增长。第二次世界大战后出生的婴儿潮一代完成了大学学业，已经成家立业，他们都成为了劳动力大军中的一员。随着移民的涌入和妇女外出工作，劳动力的数量在持续增加。**就业率**（实际工作的成年人所占的百分比）从 1980 年的低于 60% 增至 2007 年的 63% 以上。

Growth Explosion

GDP per Capita in 1990 International Dollars

Year	0	1000	1500	1820	1995
World	$425	$420	$545	$675	$5,188
The West	$439	$406	$624	$1,149	$19,990
West Europe	450	400	670	1,269	17,456
North America	400	400	400	1,233	22,933
Japan	400	425	525	675	19,720
The Rest	$423	$424	$532	$594	$2,971
Other Europe	400	400	597	803	5,147
Latin America	400	415	415	671	5,031
China	450	450	600	600	2,653
Other Asia	425	425	525	560	2,768
Africa	400	400	400	400	1,221

Figure 14.4 The History of World Growth GDP per capita was stagnant for centuries. Living standards started rising significantly around 1820. Even then, most growth in per capita GDP occurred in the West. ■

Source: Maddison, Angus, "Poor until 1820," *The Wall Street Journal*, January 11, 1999.

---

stagnant 停滞不前的。

Growth Rate (Percent)	Doubling Time (Years)
0.0	Never
0.5	144
1.0	72
1.5	48
2.0	36
2.5	29
3.0	24
3.5	21
4.0	18
4.5	16
5.0	14

Table 14.1 The Rule of 72 Small differences in annual growth rates cumulate into large differences in GDP. Shown here are the number of years it would take to double GDP at various growth rates.
Doubling times can be approximated by the rule of 72. Seventy-two divided by the growth rate equals the number of years it takes to double.

就业率也不可能永远增长下去。在达到极限时，每一个人都进入了劳动力市场，再也找不到更多的工人了。在这种情况下，人均 GDP 的持续增长更有可能来源于人均产出的增加。产出的总量不仅取决于有多少工人被雇用，还取决于每个工人的生产率。如果生产率提高了，人均 GDP 很可能也会上升。

The employment rate cannot increase forever. At the limit, everyone would be in the labor market, and no further workers could be found. Sustained increases in GDP per capita are more likely to come from increases in output *per worker*. The total quantity of output produced depends not only on how many workers are employed but also on how productive each worker is. If **productivity** is increasing, then GDP per capita is likely to rise as well.

Historically, **productivity gains have been the major source of economic growth.** The average worker today produces *twice* as much output as his or her parents did. The consequences of this productivity gain are evident in Figure 14.5. Between 2000 and 2018, the amount of labor employed in the U.S. economy increased by only 5 percent. If productivity hadn't increased, total output would have grown by the same percentage. But productivity *wasn't* stagnant; output per labor-hour increased by 38 percent during that period. As a consequence, total output jumped by 43 percent. **We are now able to *consume* more goods and services than our parents did because the average worker *produces* more—much more.**

由于工人平均能生产更多的商品和服务，因此我们现在能消费比父辈更多的商品和服务。

生产率提高的源泉
SOURCES OF PRODUCTIVITY GROWTH

If we want consumption levels to keep rising, individual workers will have to produce still more output each year. How is this possible?

To answer this question, we need to examine how productivity increases. ***The sources of productivity gains include***

生产率提高的源泉包括：

- 更高的技能——劳动力技能的提高。
- 更多的资本——更高的资本对劳动力的比例。
- 改进的管理——在生产过程中更好地利用可用资源。
- 技术的进步——开发和使用更好的资本设备。

- *Higher skills*—an increase in labor skills.
- *More capital*—an increase in the ratio of capital to labor.
- *Improved management*—better use of available resources in the production process.
- *Technological advancement*—the development and use of *better* capital equipment.

Labor Quality　劳动力的素质

As recently as 1950, less than 8 percent of all U.S. workers had completed college. Today more than 30 percent of the workforce has completed four years of college. As a result, today's workers enter the labor market with much more knowledge. Moreover, they keep acquiring new skills through company-paid training programs, adult education classes, and distance learning options on the Internet. As education and training levels rise, so does productivity.

Capital Investment 资本投资

No matter how educated workers are, they need tools, computers, and other equipment to produce most goods and services. Thus *capital* **investment** *is a prime determinant of both productivity and growth.* More investment gives the average worker more and better tools to work with.

无论工人的受教育程度如何，他们还是需要工具、电脑和其他设备去生产大多数商品和服务。所以资本**投资**是生产率和经济增长的首要决定因素。更多的投资将为每一个工人提供更多和更好的劳动工具。

While labor force growth accelerated in the 1970s, the growth of capital slowed. The capital stock increased by 4.1 percent per year in the late 1960s but by only 2.5 percent per year in the 1970s and early 1980s. The stock of capital was still growing faster than the labor force, but the difference was getting smaller. This means that although the average worker was continuing to get more and better machines, the rate at which he or she was getting them was slower. As a consequence, productivity growth declined.

These trends reversed in the 1990s. Capital investment accelerated, with investments in computer networks and telecommunications surging by 10–12 percent a year. As a result, productivity gains accelerated into the 2.5–2.7 percent range. Those productivity gains shifted the production possibilities curve outward, permitting output to expand with less inflationary pressure.

Management 管理

The quantity and quality of factor inputs do not completely determine the rate of economic growth. Resources, however good and abundant, must be organized into a production process and managed. Hence entrepreneurship and the quality of continuing management are major determinants of economic growth.

要素投入的数量和质量并不完全决定经济增长率。无论资源多么优质和充足，都必须被组织到生产过程中，并且要得到很好的管理。所以企业家精神和持续管理的质量是经济增长的主要决定因素。

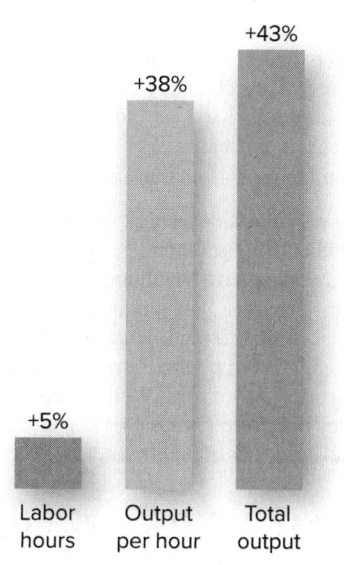

Figure 14.5 Rising Productivity and Living Standards From 2000 to 2018, work hours increased by only 5 percent but output increased by 43 percent. Rising output per worker (productivity) is the key to increased living standards (GDP per capita).

Source: U.S. Bureau of Labor Statistics.

It is difficult to characterize differences in management techniques or to measure their effectiveness. However, much attention has been focused in recent years on the potential conflict between short-term profits and long-term productivity gains. By cutting investment spending (a cost to the firm), a firm can increase short-run profits. In doing so, however, a firm may also reduce its growth potential and ultimately its long-term profitability. When corporate managers become fixated on short-run fluctuations in the price of corporate stock, the risk of such a trade-off increases.

Managers must also learn to motivate employees to their maximum potential. Workers who are disgruntled or alienated aren't likely to put out much effort. To maximize productivity, managers must develop personnel structures and incentives that make employees want to contribute to production.

Research and Development 研发

提高生产率的第四个重要源泉是研发（R&D）。研发是一个包括科学研究、产品开发、生产技术创新和管理改进在内的宽泛概念。研发活动可以是一个具体的、目标明确的活动（比如在实验室中），也可以是"干中学"过程中的一部分。无论哪种情况，从研发中获得的洞察力最终会促成新产品和更廉价的制造方式的诞生。随着时间的推移，人们认为研发对经济增长做出的贡献最大。爱德华·丹尼森在对1929—1982年美国经济增长的研究中得出结论：总的经济增长有26%归因于"知识的进步"。研发对生产率（单个工人产出）的相对贡献可能是这个数字的两倍还要多。

A fourth and vital source of productivity advance is research and development (R&D). R&D is a broad concept that includes scientific research, product development, innovations in production technique, and the development of management improvements. R&D activity may be a specific, identifiable activity (e.g., in a research lab), or it may be part of the process of learning by doing. In either case, the insights developed from R&D generally lead to new products and cheaper ways of producing them. Over time, R&D is credited with the greatest contributions to economic growth. In his study of U.S. growth during the period 1929–1982, Edward Denison concluded that 26 percent of *total* growth was due to "advances in knowledge." The relative contribution of R&D to productivity (output per worker) was probably twice that much.

There is an important link between R&D and capital investment. A lot of investment is needed to replace worn and aging equipment. However, new machines are rarely identical to the ones they replace. When you get a new computer, you're not just *replacing* an old one; you're *upgrading* your computing capabilities with more memory, greater speed, and a lot of new features. Indeed, the availability of *better* technology is often the motivation for such capital investment. The same kind of motivation spurs businesses to upgrade machines and structures. Hence, **advances in technology and capital investment typically go hand in hand.**

The fruits of research and development don't all reside in new machinery. New ideas may nurture products and processes that expand production possibilities even without additional capital equipment. Biotechnology has developed strains of wheat and rice that have multiplied the size of harvests, with no additional farm machinery. Likewise, the development of nonhierarchical databases revolutionized information technology, making it far less time-consuming to access and transmit data, with *less* hardware.

Corn farming provides an excellent illustration of how all these determinants of productivity can come together to boost output. From 1860 until 1930, corn productivity was stagnant at 30 bushels per acre. But then agricultural researchers discovered hybrid seeds that could increase yields. At the same time, the production of tractors greatly increased, giving corn farmers more and better capital to work with. New fertilizers were developed, increasing the amount of nitrogen going to corn plants. Farm extension programs were teaching improved tillage and herbicide practices. All of these factors have combined to increase corn productivity sixfold over the last century (see Figure 14.6). The same kind of productivity advances occur every year in a broad spectrum of industries.

POLICY LEVERS 政策杠杆

在很大程度上，经济增长的速度是由市场力量——市场参与者的教育、培训和投资决策决定的。政府的政策也起到了十分重要的作用。事实上，政府的政策对总供给曲线是否移动和移动多少有着重要影响。

To a large extent, the pace of economic growth is set by market forces—by the education, training, and investment decisions of market participants. Government policy plays an important role as well. Indeed, **government policies can have a major impact on whether and how far the aggregate supply curve shifts.**

---

disgruntle 使不满。alienate 使疏远。nurture 孕育，促进。nonhierarchical 非层次化的。

Education and Training 教育和培训

As noted earlier, the quality of labor largely depends on education and training. Accordingly, government policies that support education and training contribute directly to growth and productivity. From a fiscal policy perspective, money spent on schools and training has a dual payoff: It stimulates the economy in the *short* run (like all other spending) and increases the *long*-run capacity to produce. Hence we get positive aggregate demand (AD) and aggregate supply (AS) shifts. Tax incentives for training have the same effects.

Immigration Policy 移民政策

Both the quality and the quantity of labor are affected by immigration policy. Close to a million people immigrate to the United States each year. This influx of immigrants has been a major source of growth in the U.S. labor force—and thus a direct contributor to an outward shift of our production possibilities.

The impact of immigration on our productive capacity is a question not just of numbers, but also of the quality of these new workers. Recent immigrants have much lower educational attainment than native-born Americans and are less able to fill job vacancies in growing industries. This is largely due to immigration policy, which sets only country-specific quotas and gives preference to relatives of U.S. residents. Some observers have suggested that the United States should pay more attention to the educational and skill levels of immigrants and set preferences on the basis of potential productivity, as Canada and many other nations do. In December 2012, the U.S. House of Representatives set aside 55,000 visas for foreign students graduating with degrees in science, technology, engineering, and math, the so-called STEM fields.

Thousands of foreign workers seek access to American jobs, creating difficult policy decisions.
©Sandy Huffaker/Getty Images

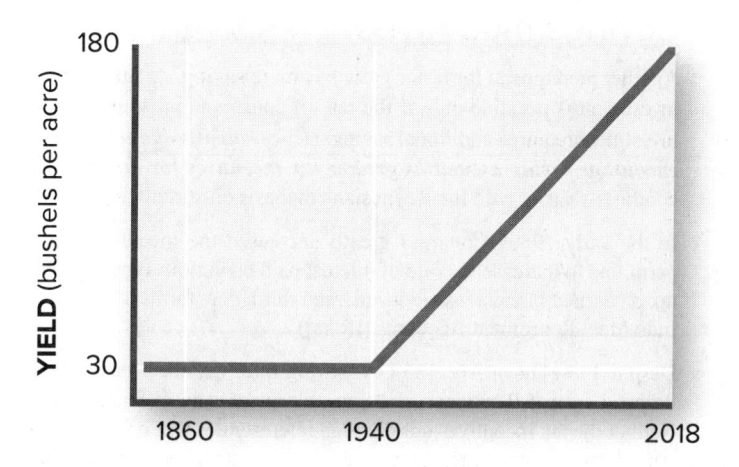

FIGURE 14.6 Skyrocketing Productivity on the Farm Corn output per acre was stagnant from 1860 until the late 1930s. After that, corn productivity increased nearly every year, bringing output per acre to more than 180 bushels in 2018, six times the level of 1930.

Source: "Estimating U.S. Crop Yields," National Agriculture Statistics Service, 2018.

---

attainment 学识，成就。

By 2016, the number of such visas had risen to 85,000. Another 600,000 foreign students applied for F-1 visas, which allow students graduating with STEM degrees to remain in the United States and work for up to three years. President Trump put more restrictions on F-1 visas, arguing that foreign students were taking jobs from Americans and engaging in industrial espionage. The number of visa applications dropped sharply in 2017, raising concerns among both American universities and employers about skill shortages. As the immigration debate continues, we have to recognize that the sheer number of people entering the country makes immigration policy an important growth policy lever.

Investment Incentives   投资激励政策

Government policy also affects the supply of capital. As a rule, lower tax rates encourage people to invest more—to build factories, purchase new equipment, and construct new offices. Hence, ***tax policy is not only a staple of short-term stabilization policy but a determinant of long-run growth as well.***

The tax treatment of capital gains is one of the most debated supply-side policy levers. Capital gains are increases in the value of assets. When stocks, land, or other assets are sold, any resulting gain is counted as taxable income. Many countries—including Japan, Italy, South Korea, and the Netherlands—do not levy any taxes on capital gains. The rest of the European Union and Canada impose lower capital gains taxes than does the United States. Lowering the tax rate on capital gains might stimulate more investment and encourage people to reallocate their assets to more productive uses. When the capital gains tax rate was cut from 28 to 20 percent in 1997, U.S. investment accelerated. That experience prompted President George W. Bush to push for further tax cuts in 2003. After the capital gains tax rate was cut to 15 percent (May 2003), nonresidential investment increased significantly. That pickup in investment may have accelerated GDP growth by as much as 2 percent in 2004.

Critics argue that a capital gains tax cut overwhelmingly favors the rich, who own most stocks, property, and other wealth. This inequity, they assert, outweighs any efficiency gains. That's why President Obama pushed Congress to increase the capital gains tax from 15 to 20 percent in 2013. Critics worried that the higher tax rates might slow capital investment and economic growth. President Trump convinced Congress to offer new tax incentives for investment (the Tax Cuts and Jobs Act of 2017) and in 2018 suggested reducing the effective tax rate on capital gains once again.

Savings Incentives   储蓄激励政策

Another prerequisite for faster growth is more **saving**. At full employment, a greater volume of investment is possible only if the rate of consumption is cut back. In other words, additional investment requires additional saving. Hence, ***supply-side economists favor tax incentives that encourage saving as well as greater tax incentives for investment.*** This kind of perspective contrasts sharply with the Keynesian emphasis on stimulating consumption.

In the early 1980s Congress greatly increased the incentives for saving. First, banks were permitted to increase the rate of interest paid on various types of savings accounts. Second, the tax on earned interest was reduced. And third, new forms of tax-free saving were created (e.g., Individual Retirement Accounts [IRAs]).

Despite these incentives, the U.S. saving rates declined during the 1980s. Household saving dropped from 6.2 percent of disposable income in 1981 to a low of 2.5 percent in 1987. Neither the tax incentives nor the high interest rates that prevailed in the early 1980s convinced Americans to save more. As a result, the U.S. saving rate fell considerably below that of other nations. By 2006 the U.S. saving rate was actually *negative*: Consumers were spending more than they were earning (see the accompanying News Wire "Saving Rates"). As a consequence, the United States is heavily dependent on foreign saving (deposited in U.S. banks and bonds) to finance investment and growth.

---

levy 征收，征税。outweigh（在重要性或意义上）超过。

NEWS WIRE SAVING RATES

AMERICANS SAVE LITTLE

American households save very little. In 2006 the average American actually spent *more* income than he or she earned—the saving rate was *negative*. As shown here, the United States continued to rank near the bottom of the savers' list in 2017.

Supply-siders are especially concerned about low saving rates. They argue that Americans must save more to finance increased investment and economic growth. Otherwise, they fear, the United States will fall behind other countries in the progression toward higher productivity levels and living standards.

Country	Saving Rate (2017)
Switzerland	18.5
Sweden	16.6
Luxembourg	13.6
South Korea	8.9
United States	**3.7**
Japan	2.7
Italy	1.7

Note: Saving rate equals household saving divided by disposable income.

Source: "Saving Rate," Organisation for Economic Co-operation and Development, 2017.

NOTE: Savings are a primary source of investment financing. Higher saving rates imply proportionately less consumption and more investment and growth.
注：储蓄是投资融资的主要来源。较高的储蓄率意味着较低比例的消费，以及较高比例的投资和增长。

Government Finances 政府财政

The dependence of economic growth on investment and savings adds an important dimension to the debate over budget deficits. When the government borrows money to finance its spending, it dips into the nation's savings pool. Hence the government ends up borrowing funds that could have been used to finance investment. If this happens, the government deficit effectively crowds out private investment. This process of **crowding out**—of diverting available savings from investment to government spending—directly limits private investment. From this perspective, government budget deficits act as a constraint on economic growth.

As we saw in earlier chapters, budget deficits aren't always bad. Short-run cyclical instability may require fiscal policies that unbalance the federal budget. The concern for long-run growth simply adds another wrinkle to fiscal policy decisions: *Fiscal and monetary policies must be evaluated in terms of their impact not only on short-run aggregate demand but also on long-run aggregate supply.* This was a major concern in 2009–2012 when massive federal government fiscal stimulus packages pushed the government's budget deficit into the trillion-dollar stratosphere. Similar concerns surfaced in the wake of President Trump's 2017 trillion-dollar tax cuts when interest rates started climbing.

经济增长对投资和储蓄的依赖，给有关政府预算赤字的争论增添了一个重要维度。当政府借款来为其支出融资时，它会动用整个国家的储蓄，这样会减少那些本可以用于投资的资金。如果这种情况发生，政府赤字实际上会挤出私人投资。这个**挤出**过程——将可用的储蓄由投资转为政府支出，直接限制了私人投资。从这个角度来说，政府预算赤字是经济增长的制约因素。

Deregulation 放松政府监管

There are still other mechanisms for stimulating economic growth. The government intervenes directly in supply decisions by *regulating* employment and output behavior. In general, those

---

intervene 干预，介入。

regulations are intended to foster safety, security, competition, and environmental protection. But we also have to recognize that such regulations limit the flexibility of producers to respond to changes in demand. Government regulation also tends to raise production costs. The higher costs result not only from required changes in the production process but also from the expense of monitoring government regulations. The budget costs and the burden of red tape discourage production and so limit aggregate supply. From this perspective, deregulation would shift the AS curve rightward.

Factor Markets 要素市场

Minimum wage laws are one of the most familiar forms of factor market regulation. The Fair Labor Standards Act of 1938 required employers to pay workers a minimum of 25 cents per hour. Over time, Congress has increased the minimum wage repeatedly (see the News Wire "Minimum Wage Hikes" in Chapter 7), up to $7.25 as of July 2009. Democrats in Congress proposed in 2016 to raise that wage floor to $15 an hour. Many states and cities already have wage minimums far above the $7.25 threshold.

最低工资法的目的是确保工人能有一个体面的生活水平。但是这项法律也有其他方面的影响。通过禁止雇主雇用低工资的工人，它限制了雇主雇用更多工人的能力。这种雇用管制限制了移民、年轻人以及低技能工人的就业机会。如果没有这项限制政策，更多这样的工人将会找到工作，获得宝贵的经验并拿到更高的工资，从而使总供给曲线向右移动。

The goal of the minimum wage law is to ensure workers a decent standard of living. But the law has other effects as well. By prohibiting employers from using lower-paid workers, it limits the ability of employers to hire additional workers. This hiring constraint limits job opportunities for immigrants, teenagers, and low-skill workers. Without that constraint, more of these workers would find jobs, gain valuable experience, and attain higher wages—shifting the AS curve rightward.

The government also sets standards for workplace safety and health. The Occupational Safety and Health Administration (OSHA), for example, sets limits on the noise levels at worksites. If noise levels exceed these limits, the employer is required to adopt administrative or engineering controls to reduce the noise level. Personal protection of workers (e.g., earplugs or earmuffs), though much less costly, will suffice only if source controls are not feasible. All such regulations are intended to improve the welfare of workers. In the process, however, these regulations raise the costs of production and inhibit supply responses. As with so many policy issues, there are trade-offs to consider.

Product Markets 产品市场

The government's regulation of factor markets tends to raise production costs and inhibit supply. The same is true of regulations imposed directly on product markets. A few examples illustrate the impact of such regulations.

Transportation Costs 运输成本

At the federal level, various agencies regulate the output and prices of transportation services. Until 1984 the Civil Aeronautics Board (CAB) determined which routes airlines could fly and how much they could charge. The Interstate Commerce Commission (ICC) has had the same kind of power over trucking, interstate bus lines, and railroads. The routes, services, and prices for ships (in U.S. coastal waters and foreign commerce) have been established by the Federal Maritime Commission. In all these cases, the regulations constrained the ability of producers to respond to increases in demand. Existing producers could not increase output at will, and new producers were excluded from the market. The easing of these restrictive regulations spurred more output, lower prices, and innovation in air travel, telecommunications, and land transportation. In the process, the AS curve shifted to the right.

Food and Drug Standards 食品和药品标准

The Food and Drug Administration (FDA) has a broad mandate to protect consumers from dangerous products. In fulfilling this responsibility, the FDA sets health standards for the content of specific foods. A hot dog, for example, can be labeled as such only if it contains specific mixtures of skeletal meat, pig lips, snouts, and ears. By the same token, the FDA requires that

---

threshold 门槛，界限值。OSHA 美国职业安全与健康管理局。mandate 指令。

chocolate bars must contain no more than 60 microscopic insect fragments per 100 grams of chocolate. The FDA also sets standards for the testing of new drugs and evaluates the test results. In all three cases, the goal of regulation is to minimize health risks to consumers.

Like all regulation, the FDA standards entail real costs. The tests required for new drugs are expensive and time-consuming. Getting a new drug approved for sale can take years of effort and require a huge investment. The net results are that (1) fewer new drugs are brought to market and (2) those that do reach the market are more expensive than they would be in the absence of regulation. In other words, the aggregate supply of goods is shifted to the left.

Financial Markets 金融市场

The Great Recession of 2008–2009 prompted a huge increase in federal regulation of financial markets. In the quest to avoid another financial crisis, Congress in 2010 approved sweeping new powers for federal regulators of banks, credit card companies, and other financial institutions (the Dodd-Frank Wall Street Reform and Consumer Protection Act). The act was so complex that it took federal regulators five years just to spell out the new regulations that would affect financial institutions. The uncertainties associated with that process made banks less willing to make new loans; excess reserves of the banking system skyrocketed (Figure 14.3), while new loan activity stagnated. That kept recovery from the recession in check. In 2018, Congress voted to roll back most of the Dodd-Frank regulations for smaller lenders and community banks, hoping to encourage more mortgage and small-business lending.

Many—perhaps most—of these regulatory activities are beneficial. In fact, all were originally designed to serve specific public purposes. As a result of such regulation, we get safer drugs, cleaner air, less deceptive advertising, and more secure loans. We must also consider the costs involved, however. All regulatory activities impose direct and indirect costs. These costs must be compared to the benefits received. ***The basic contention of supply-side economists is that regulatory costs are too high.*** To improve our economic performance, they assert, we must *deregulate* the production process, thereby shifting the aggregate supply curve to the right again. At a minimum, ***we should at least consider potential trade-offs between increased regulation and increased growth.***

这些监管措施很多（或者是大多数）都是有益的。实际上，它们原本就是为特定的公众目的而设计的。有了这些管制，我们确实获得了更安全的食物、更清新的空气、更少具有欺骗性的广告和更安全的贷款。然而我们必须要考虑其中的成本。所有管制行为都会给我们带来直接和间接成本，这些成本必须与获得的收益相比较。供给学派经济学家的一个基本观点是，管制成本太高了。他们坚持认为，为了改善我们的经济状况，我们必须对生产过程放松管制，使总供给曲线再次向右移动。至少，我们应该对加强管制和促进经济增长之间的潜在成本和收益进行权衡比较。

Economic Freedom 经济自由

Regulation and taxes are just two forms of government intervention that affect production possibilities. Governments also establish and enforce property rights, legal rights, and political rights. One of the greatest obstacles to growth in Russia after 1990s was the absence of legal protection. Few people wanted to invest in businesses that could be stolen or confiscated, with little hope of judicial redress. Nor did producers want to ship goods without ironclad payment guarantees. By contrast, producers in the United States are willing to produce and ship goods without prepayment, knowing that the courts, collection agencies, and insurance companies can help ensure payment, if necessary.

It is difficult to identify all of the institutional features that make an economy business-friendly. The Heritage Foundation, a conservative think tank, has constructed an index of economic freedom, using 50 different measures of government policy. Each year it ranks the world's countries on this index, thereby identifying the most "free" economies (least government control) and the most "repressed" (most government control). According to Heritage, the nations with the most economic freedom not only have the highest GDP per capita but continue to grow the fastest. As the accompanying News Wire "Institutional Framework" illustrates, the countries that moved the furthest toward free markets also grew the fastest from 1997 to 2017. Their average annual GDP growth rate (3.57 percent) greatly exceeded that (2.14 percent) of nations that made little progress toward free markets—or that actually *increased* government regulation of resource and product markets (e.g., Venezuela, Republic of the Congo, Cuba, and the Central African Republic).

---

microscopic 极小的，微小的。obstacle 障碍。confiscate 没收。judicial redress 司法赔偿。

NEWS WIRE INSTITUTIONAL FRAMEWORK

IMPROVEMENT IN ECONOMIC FREEDOM AND ECONOMIC GROWTH

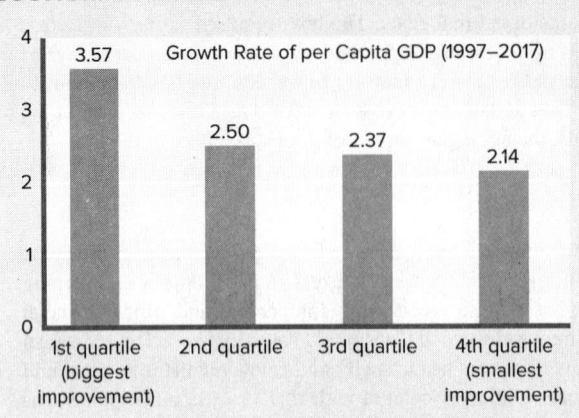

Growth Rate of per Capita GDP (1997–2017)

- 1st quartile (biggest improvement): 3.57
- 2nd quartile: 2.50
- 3rd quartile: 2.37
- 4th quartile (smallest improvement): 2.14

Improvement in Economic Freedom (1997–2017)

Source: Miller, Terry, Kim, Anthony B., and Roberts, James M., "2018 Index of Economic Freedom," The Heritage Foundation, 2018.

NOTE: As nations give more rein to market forces, they tend to grow faster. These data compare changes in the degree of market freedom (from government regulation) with GDP growth rates.

注：充分发挥市场力量的国家，其经济增长往往会更快。这些数据比较了市场自由度的变化（来自政府管制的变化）与 GDP 增长之间的关系。

The Heritage study doesn't imply that we should rely exclusively on private markets to resolve the WHAT, HOW, and FOR WHOM questions. But it does reinforce the notion that an economy's institutional framework—particularly the extent of market freedom—plays a critical role in its growth potential. We have to ask whether any specific government intervention promotes economic growth or slows it.

POLICY PERSPECTIVES

IS MORE GROWTH DESIRABLE?

The government clearly has a powerful set of levers for promoting faster economic growth. Many people wonder, though, whether more economic growth is really *desirable*. Those of us who commute on congested highways, worry about climate change, breathe foul air, and can't find a secluded camping site may raise a loud chorus of nos. But before reaching a conclusion, let us at least determine what it is people don't like about the prospect of continued growth. Is it really economic growth per se that people object to or, instead, the specific ways GDP has grown in the past?

First of all, let us distinguish clearly between economic growth and population growth. Congested neighborhoods, dining halls, and highways are the consequence of too many people, not of too many goods and services. And there's no indication that population growth will cease any time soon. The world's population of 7 billion people is likely to increase by another 2 billion people by the year 2050. The United States alone harbors another 3 million or so more people every year.

Who's going to feed, clothe, and house all these people? Are we going to redistribute the current level of output, leaving everyone with less? Or should we try to produce *more* output so living standards don't fall? If we had *more* goods and services—if we had more houses and transit systems—much of the population congestion we now experience might be relieved. Maybe if we had enough resources to meet our existing demands *and* to build a solar-generated "new town" in the middle of Montana, people might move out of the crowded neighborhoods of Chicago and St. Louis. Well, probably not, but at least one thing is certain: With fewer goods and services, more people will have to share any given quantity of output.

---

congest 拥挤。

Which brings us back to the really essential measure of growth: GDP per capita. Are there any serious grounds for desiring *less* GDP per capita—a reduced standard of living? Don't say yes just because you think we already have too many cars on our roads or calories in our bellies. That argument refers to the *mix* of output again and does not answer the question of whether we want *any* more goods or services per person. Increasing GDP per capita can take a million forms, including the educational services you are now consuming. The rejection of economic growth per se implies that none of those forms is desirable.

We could, of course, acquire more of the goods and services we consider beneficial simply by cutting back on the production of the things we consider unnecessary. But who is to say which mix of output is best? The present mix of output may be considered bad because it is based on a maldistribution of income, deceptive advertising, or failure of the market mechanism to account for external costs. If so, it would seem more efficient (and politically more feasible) to address those problems directly rather than to attempt to lower our standard of living.

CHAPTER 14 REVIEW

SUMMARY

- Economic growth refers to increases in real GDP. Short-run growth may result from increases in capacity utilization (e.g., less unemployment). In the long run, however, growth requires increases in capacity itself—rightward shifts of the long-run aggregate supply curve. **LO1**
- GDP per capita is a basic measure of living standards. By contrast, GDP per worker gauges our productivity. Over time, increases in productivity have been the primary cause of rising living standards. **LO2**
- Productivity gains can originate in a variety of ways. These sources include better labor quality, increased capital investment, research and development, and improved management. **LO3**
- The policy levers for increasing growth rates include education and training, immigration, investment and saving incentives, and the broader institutional framework. All of these levers may increase the quantity or quality of resources. **LO4**
- Budget deficits may inhibit economic growth by crowding out investment—that is, absorbing savings that would otherwise finance investment. **LO4**
- The goal of economic growth implies that macroeconomic policies must be assessed in terms of their long-run supply impact as well as their short-term demand effects. **LO4**
- Continued economic growth is desirable as long as it brings a higher standard of living for people and an increased ability to produce and consume socially desirable goods and services. **LO5**

TERMS TO REMEMBER

Define the following terms:

production possibilities
economic growth
nominal GDP
real GDP
growth rate
GDP per capita
labor force
employment rate
productivity
investment
saving
crowding out

QUESTIONS FOR DISCUSSION

1. In what specific ways (if any) does a college education increase a worker's productivity? **LO3**
2. What's wrong with a negative saving rate, as the United States had in 2006? **LO3**
3. Notice in the News Wire "Improved Living Standards" how the time spent working on the job and at home has declined. How are these changes indicative of economic growth? **LO5**

4. How would the following factors affect a nation's growth potential? **LO4**

   a. Legal protection of private property.
   b. High tax rates.
   c. Judicial corruption.
   d. Government price controls.
   e. Free trade.

5. Why do some nations grow so slowly and others so much faster? **LO4**

6. What role do immigrants play in economic growth? In what ways might immigrants accelerate or slow economic growth? **LO4**

7. How does easier bank lending contribute to economic growth? Are there any risks for growth with easier bank lending? **LO4**

8. Would a higher minimum wage accelerate or slow economic growth? **LO4**

9. **POLICY PERSPECTIVES** Suppose that economic growth could be achieved only by increasing inequality (e.g., via tax incentives for investment). Would economic growth still be desirable? **LO4**

10. **POLICY PERSPECTIVES** Is limitless growth really possible? What forces do you think will be most important is slowing or halting economic growth? **LO5**

PROBLEMS

1. a. Between 1500 and 1820, which areas of the world experienced zero economic growth in per capital GDP (Figure 14.4) **LO1**
   b. Between 1820 and 1995, which area of the world experienced the fastest growth in in per capita GDP?
   c. Between 1820 and 1995, which area of the world experienced the slowest growth in per capita GDP?

2. According to the Rule of 72 (Table 14.1), how many years will it take for GDP to double if GDP growth is **LO1**
   a. 3 percent?
   b. 2 percent?
   c. 1 percent?

3. China's output grew at an amazing rate of 6 percent in 2018. (See Table 14.1.) **LO2**
   a. At that rate, how long would it take for China's GDP to double?
   b. With its population increasing at 0.5 percent per year, how long will it take for *per capita* GDP to double?

4. In 2018, approximately 61 percent of the adult population (260 million) was employed. If the employment rate increased to the year 2000 level of 64 percent, **LO2**
   a. how many more people would be working?
   b. by how much would output increase if GDP per worker was $100,000?

5. According to the data in Figure 14.4, by what percent did world GDP per capita grow from **LO1**
   a. 1000 to 1500?
   b. 1500 to 1820?
   c. 1820 to 1995?

6. According to Figure 14.4, by what percentage did GDP per capita increase between 1820 and 1995 in **LO5**
   a. North America?
   b. Latin America?
   c. Africa?

7. a. According to the News Wire "Saving Rates," if a Swiss and an American both had $100, how many more dollars would the Swiss save in 2017? **LO5**
   b. Why are higher savings rates desirable?

8. Suppose that every additional 3 percentage points in the investment rate (I ÷ GDP) boosts GDP growth by 1 percentage point. Assume also that all investment must be financed with consumer saving. The economy is now characterized by

Consumption:	$ 10 trillion
Saving (= Investment):	2 trillion
GDP:	$ 12 trillion

If the goal is to raise the growth rate by 2 percentage points, **LO3**
   a. by how much must investment increase?
   b. by how much must consumption decline?
9. **POLICY PERSPECTIVES** The World Bank projects that the world's population will increase from 7.6 billion in 2019 to 8.6 billion in 2035. World output in 2019 was roughly $90 trillion. **LO5**
   a. What was the global income per capita in 2019?
   b. What will per capita income be in 2035 if the world's economy doesn't grow?
   c. By what percentage must the world economy grow by 2035 to maintain current living standards?

CHAPTER FIFTEEN

International Trade 国际贸易

©Roslan Rahman/AFP/Getty Images

LEARNING OBJECTIVES

After reading this chapter, you should be able to:

1. Describe U.S. trade patterns.
2. Explain how trade increases total output.
3. Tell how the terms of trade are established.
4. Discuss how trade barriers affect market outcomes.
5. Describe how currency exchange rates affect trade flows.

World travelers have discovered that Big Macs taste pretty much the same everywhere, but a Big Mac's price can vary tremendously. In 2018 a Big Mac was priced at 14,500 rupiah at the McDonald's in Jakarta, Indonesia. That sounds really expensive! The same Big Mac cost only 2.56 euros in Rome, 55 baht in Bangkok, and 9.9 yuan in Beijing. But what do all these foreign prices mean in American dollars? If you want a Big Mac in a foreign country, you need to figure out foreign prices.

Similar problems affect even consumers who stay at home. In 2018 American kids were clamoring for Sony's PlayStation 4 Pro game consoles produced in Japan. But how much would they have to pay? In Japan the machines were selling for 40,000 yen. What did that translate into in American dollars? In the same year, American steel, textile, and lumber companies were complaining that producers in some countries were selling their products too cheaply. They wanted the government to protect them from unfair foreign competition.

Why does life have to be so complicated? Why doesn't everyone just use American dollars? For that matter, why can't each nation simply produce for its own consumption so we don't have to worry about foreign competition?

This chapter provides a bird's-eye view of how America interacts with the rest of the world. Of particular interest are the following questions:

- Why do we trade so much?
- Who benefits and who loses from imports, exports, and changes in the value of the dollar?
- How is the international value of the dollar established?

As we'll see, international trade *does* diminish the job and income opportunities for specific industries and workers. But those individual losses are overwhelmed by the gains the average consumer gets from international trade. ∎

---

tremendously 非常地，惊人地。rupiah 卢比（印度尼西亚货币单位）。baht 铢（泰国货币单位）。

U.S. TRADE PATTERNS 美国贸易模式

To understand how international trade affects our standard of living, it's useful to have a sense of *how much* we actually trade.

Imports 进口

棒球通常被称为全美运动，但是在美国职业棒球赛中所使用的棒球却是在哥斯达黎加生产的。咖啡也一样。煮美式咖啡所用的咖啡豆只有少量产自美国（夏威夷）。所有的微软电脑和苹果手机也都是在美国以外制造的。实际上，美国消费的众多商品主要或完全是在其他国家或地区生产的。所有这些产品都是美国进口的一部分。

Baseball is often called the all-American sport. But the balls used in professional baseball are made in Costa Rica. The same is true of coffee. Only a tiny fraction of the beans used to brew American coffee are grown in the United States (in Hawaii). All our Microsoft Surface computers and Apple iPhones are also produced abroad. The fact is that many of the products we consume are produced primarily or exclusively in other nations or regions. All these products are part of America's **imports**.

All told, America imports $3 trillion worth of products from the rest of the world. Most of these products are *goods* like coffee, baseballs, and steel. The rest of the imports are *services*, like travel (on Air France or Aero Mexico), insurance (Lloyds of London), or entertainment (foreign movies). Together our imports account for about 15 percent of U.S. gross domestic product (GDP).

NEWS WIRE EXPORT RATIOS

Exports in Relation to GDP

Exports of goods and services account for 15 percent of total U.S. output. This export ratio is very low by international standards. China, for example, exports one-fifth of its total output, while Belgium exports more than 80 percent of its annual production (especially diamonds and chocolates). Myanmar, by contrast, is virtually a closed economy.

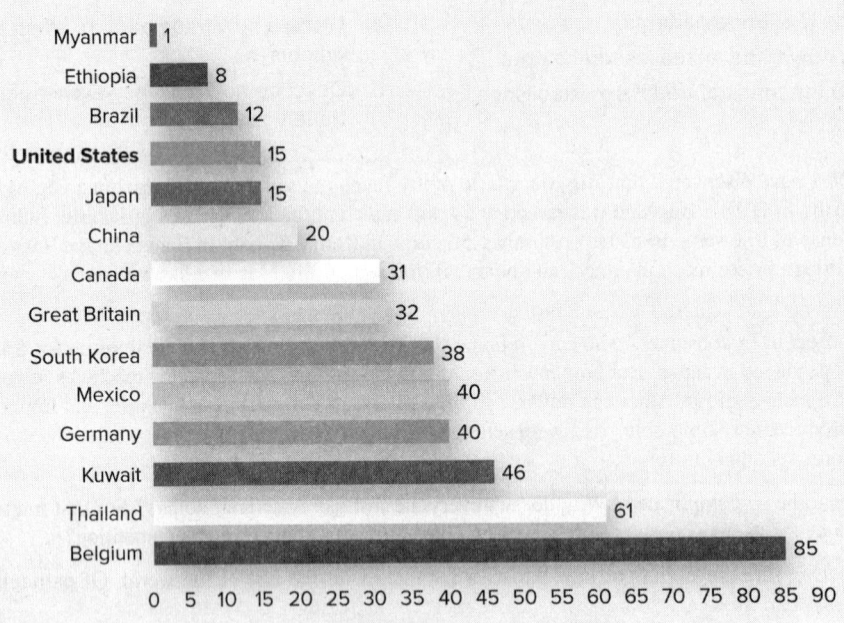

Country	Exports (% of GDP)
Myanmar	1
Ethiopia	8
Brazil	12
United States	15
Japan	15
China	20
Canada	31
Great Britain	32
South Korea	38
Mexico	40
Germany	40
Kuwait	46
Thailand	61
Belgium	85

EXPORTS (percentage of GDP)

Source: "Exports of Goods and Services (% of GDP)," *World Development Indicators*, World Bank, 2018.

NOTE: The ratio of exports to total output is a measure of trade dependence. Most countries are much more dependent on trade than is the United States.
注：出口与总产出的比率是衡量贸易依存度的指标。大多数国家比美国更依赖贸易。

Product Category	(In Billions of Dollars)		
	Exports	Imports	Surplus (Deficit)
Goods	$1,553	$2,361	$(808)
Services	798	542	256
Total trade	$2,351	$2,903	$(552)

Table 15.1 Trade Balances Both merchandise (goods) and services are traded between countries. The United States typically has a merchandise *deficit* and a services *surplus*. When combined, an overall trade deficit remained in 2017. ■

Source: U.S. Bureau of Economic Analysis, 2018.

Exports   出口

While we are buying baseballs, coffee, video game consoles, and oil from the rest of the world, foreigners are buying our **exports**. In 2018 we exported over $1.6 trillion of *goods*, including farm products (wheat, corn, soybeans, tobacco), machinery (computers, aircraft, automobiles, and auto parts), and raw materials (lumber, iron ore, and chemicals). We also exported over $800 billion of *services* such as tourism, insurance, and software.

As with our imports, our exports represent a relatively modest fraction of total GDP. Whereas we export 15 percent of total output, other developed countries export as much as 25–40 percent of their output (see the accompanying News Wire "Export Ratios"). Kuwait, for example, is considered a relatively prosperous nation, with a GDP per capita twice that of the world average. But how prosperous would it be if no one bought the oil exports that now account for nearly half of its output?

Even though the United States has a low export ratio, many American industries depend on export sales. We export 25 to 50 percent of our rice, corn, and wheat production each year and still more of our soybeans. Clearly a decision by foreigners to stop eating American agricultural products would devastate a lot of American farmers. Companies such as Boeing (planes), Caterpillar Tractor (construction and farm machinery), Weyerhaeuser (logs, lumber), Eastman Kodak (cameras), Dow (chemicals), and Sun Microsystems (computer workstations) sell more than one-fourth of their output in foreign markets. Pepsi and Coca-Cola are battling it out in the soft-drink markets of such unlikely places as Egypt, Abu Dhabi, Burundi, and Kazakhstan.

在美国从世界其他国家购买棒球、咖啡、电子游戏机以及石油的同时，外国人也在购买美国的出口产品。2018年美国出口了超过1.6万亿美元的商品，其中包括农产品（小麦、玉米、大豆、烟草）、机械设备（计算机、飞机、汽车及其零部件）和原材料（木材、铁矿石和化工材料）。美国还出口了超过8 000亿美元的服务，如旅游、保险和软件等。

Trade Balances   贸易余额

As the figures indicate, our imports and exports were not equal in 2017. Quite the contrary: We had a large imbalance in our trade flows, with many more imports than exports. The trade balance is computed simply as the difference between exports and imports:

$$\text{Trade balance} = \text{exports} - \text{imports}$$

During 2017 we imported more than we exported and so had a *negative* trade balance. A negative trade balance is called a **trade deficit**. In 2017 the United States had a negative trade balance of $552 billion. As Table 15.1 shows, this overall trade deficit reflected divergent patterns in goods and services. The United States had a large deficit in *merchandise* trade, mostly due to auto and oil imports. In *services* (e.g., travel, finance, consulting), however, the United States enjoyed a modest surplus. When the merchandise and services accounts are combined, the United States ends up with a trade deficit.

2017年美国进口大于出口，所以有一个负的贸易余额。负的贸易余额被称为**贸易逆差**。2017年美国的贸易逆差为5 520亿美元。如表15.1所示，总的贸易逆差反映了商品和服务贸易的不同表现。美国在商品贸易上有很大的逆差，这主要归因于汽车和石油的进口。然而，在服务贸易（如旅游、金融、咨询）上，美国却有适度的盈余。将商品贸易和服务贸易加总起来，美国最终存在贸易逆差。

---

prosperous 繁荣的，富足的。soybean 大豆，黄豆。devastate 摧毁，使伤心欲绝。

Country	Trade Balance (Billions of Dollars)
Top deficit countries	
China	−376
Mexico	−71
Japan	−69
Germany	−64
Vietnam	−38
Top surplus countries	
Netherlands	+25
United Arab Emirates	+16
Belgium	+15
Australia	+15

Table 15.2 Bilateral Trade Balances The U.S. trade deficit in 2017 was the net result of bilateral deficits and surpluses. We had a huge trade deficit with China but small trade surpluses with Australia and the Netherlands. International trade is *multi*national, with surpluses in some countries being offset by trade deficits elsewhere.

Source: "Top Trading Partners—December 2017," U.S. Census Bureau, 2017.

如果美国对其他国家或地区有贸易逆差，那么其他国家或地区就必定有可抵消这个赤字的**贸易顺差**。从全球角度看，进口一定与出口相等，因为一个国家或地区出口的任何一件商品必定被另外一个国家或地区进口。因此，美国贸易的任何不平衡必定被其他国家和地区的反向不平衡所抵消。

If the United States has a trade deficit with the rest of the world, then other countries or regions must have an offsetting **trade surplus**. On a global scale, imports must equal exports because every good exported by one country or regions must be imported by another. Hence, *any imbalance in America's trade must be offset by reverse imbalances elsewhere.*

Whatever the overall balance in our trade accounts, bilateral balances vary greatly. For example, our trade deficit incorporated a huge bilateral trade deficit with China and also large deficits with Mexico, Germany, and Japan. As Table 15.2 shows, however, we had trade surpluses with Australia, the Netherlands, and the United Arab Emirates.

MOTIVATION TO TRADE   贸易动机

Many people wonder why we trade so much, particularly since (1) we import many of the things we also export (e.g., computers, airplanes, clothes), (2) we *could* produce many of the other things we import, and (3) we seem to worry so much about imports and trade deficits. Why not just import those few things that we cannot produce ourselves and export just enough to balance that trade?

Although it might seem strange to be importing goods we could produce ourselves, such trade is entirely rational. Indeed, our decision to trade with other countries arises from the same considerations that motivate individuals to specialize in production. Why don't you grow your own food, build your own shelter, and record your own songs? Presumably because you have found that you can enjoy a much higher standard of living (and better music) by working at just one job and then buying other goods in the marketplace. When you do so, you're no longer self-sufficient. Instead you are *specializing* in production, relying on others to produce the array of goods and services you want. When countries trade goods and services, they are doing the same thing—*specializing* in production and then *trading* for other desired goods. Why do they do this? Because **specialization increases total output.**

---

multinational 多国的。specialization 专业化，专门化。

To demonstrate the economic gains from international trade, we examine the production possibilities of two countries. We want to demonstrate that two countries that trade can together produce *more* total output than they could in the absence of trade. If they can produce more, *the gain from trade will be increased world output and thus a higher standard of living in both countries.*

无贸易时的生产和消费
Production and Consumption without Trade

Consider the production possibilities of just two countries—say, the United States and France. For the sake of illustration, we assume that both countries produce only two goods, bread and wine. To keep things simple, we also transform the familiar **production possibilities** curve into a straight line, as shown in Figure 15.1.

为证明国际贸易的经济效益，我们将考察两个国家的生产可能性。我们想说明两个互相贸易的国家能够共同生产比没有贸易时更多的总产出。如果它们能生产更多，贸易带来的好处是世界总产出增加，从而使两国的生活水平都得到了提高。

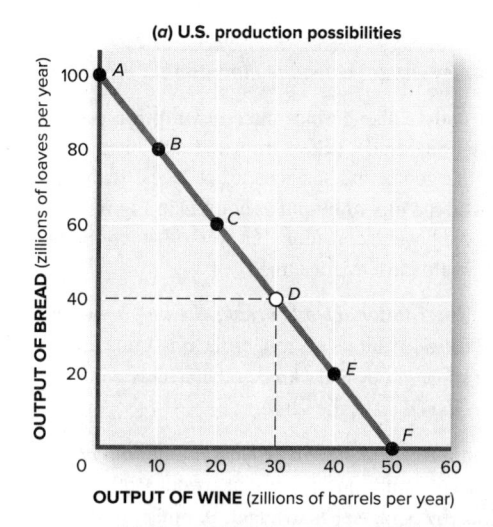

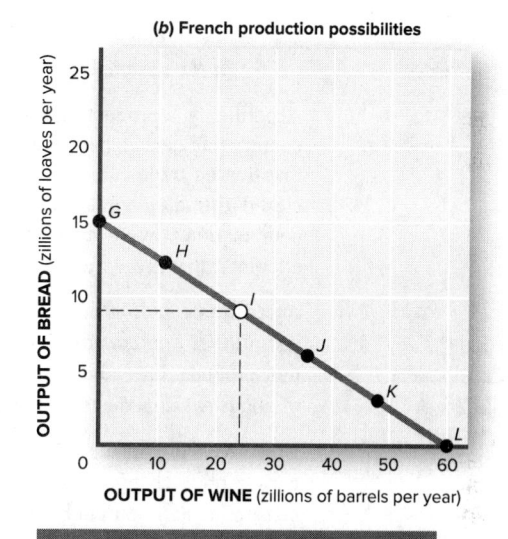

U.S. Production Possibilities	Bread (Zillions of Loaves)	Wine (Zillions of Barrels)
A	100	0
B	80	10
C	60	20
D	40	30
E	20	40
F	0	50

French Production Possibilities	Bread (Zillions of Loaves)	Wine (Zillions of Barrels)
G	15	0
H	12	12
I	9	24
J	6	36
K	3	48
L	0	60

Figure 15.1 Consumption Possibilities without Trade In the absence of trade, a country's *consumption* possibilities are identical to its *production* possibilities. The assumed production possibilities of the United States and France are illustrated in the graphs and the corresponding schedules. Before entering into trade, the United States chose to produce and consume at point *D*, with 40 zillion loaves of bread and 30 zillion barrels of wine. France chose point *I* on its own production possibilities curve. By trading, each country hopes to increase its consumption beyond these levels. ∎

The curves in Figure 15.1 suggest that the United States is capable of producing much more bread than France is. After all, we have a greater abundance of land, labor, and other factors of production. With these resources, we assume the United States is capable of producing up to 100 zillion loaves of bread per year if we devote *all* of our resources to that purpose. This capability is indicated by point A in Figure 15.1a and row A in the accompanying production possibilities schedule. France (Figure 15.1b), on the other hand, confronts a *maximum* bread production of only 15 zillion loaves per year (point G) because it has little available land, less fuel, and fewer potential workers.

The assumed capacities for wine production are also illustrated in Figure 15.1. The United States can produce *at most* 50 zillion barrels (point F), while France can produce a maximum of 60 zillion (point L), reflecting France's greater experience in tending vines. Both countries are also capable of producing alternative *combinations* of bread and wine, as evidenced by their respective production possibilities curves (points B–E for the United States and H–K for France).

We have seen production possibilities curves (PPCs) before. We are looking at them again to emphasize that

- 生产可能性曲线界定了一个国家的生产极限。
- 在没有贸易的情况下，一个国家的消费不能超过其产出。

- The production possibilities curve defines the limits to what a country can produce.
- ***In the absence of trade, a country cannot consume more than it produces.***

Accordingly, a production possibilities curve also defines the **consumption possibilities** for a country that does not engage in international trade. Like a truly self-sufficient person, a nation that doesn't trade can consume only the goods and services it produces. If the United States closed its trading windows and produced the mix of output at point D in Figure 15.1, that is the combination of wine and bread we would have to consume. If a self-sufficient France produced at point I, that is the mix of output it would have to consume.

国际贸易开启了全新的选择权。国际贸易打破了生产可能性和消费可能性之间的界线。各个国家不必完全消费它们自己生产的产品，相反，它们可以出口一些商品，进口其他商品。即使产出组合不变，这也可以改变商品的消费组合。

International trade opens new options. ***International trade breaks the link between production possibilities and consumption possibilities.*** Nations no longer have to consume exactly what they produce. Instead they can *export* some goods and *import* others. This will change the mix of goods *consumed* even if the mix *produced* stays the same.

Now here's the real surprise. When nations specialize in production, not only does the *mix* of consumption change—the *quantity* of consumption *increases* as well. Both countries end up consuming *more* output by trading than by being self-sufficient. In other words,

- ***With trade, a country's consumption possibilities exceed its production possibilities.***

To see how this startling outcome emerges, we'll examine how countries operate without trade and then with trade.

Initial Conditions 初始条件

Assume we start without any trade. The United States is producing at point D, and France is at point I (Figure 15.1). These output mixes have no special significance; they are just one of many possible production choices each nation could make. Our focus here is on the *combined* output of the two countries. Given their assumed production choices, their combined output is:

	Bread Output (Zillions of Loaves)	**Wine Output** (Zillions of Barrels)
U.S. (at point D)	40	30
France (at point I)	<u>9</u>	<u>24</u>
World total	**49**	**54**

---

loaf 一块（面包）（复数 loaves）。combination 组合。

	Pretrade Mix of Output		New Mix of Output	
	Bread	Wine	Bread	Wine
United States	40	30	60	20
	(point D)		(point C)	
France	9	24	3	48
	(point I)		(point K)	
World total	49	54	63	68
World gain			**+14**	**+14**

Table 15.3 Gains from Specialization The combined total output of two countries can be increased by simply altering the mix of output in each country. Here world output increases by 14 zillion loaves of bread and 14 zillion barrels of wine when nations specialize in production.

贸易促进专业化并增加世界产出
Trade Increases Specialization and World Output

Now comes the tricky part. We are about to increase total (combined) output of these two countries by trading. Watch closely.

At first blush, increasing total output might seem like an impossible task. Both countries, after all, are already fully using their limited production possibilities. But look at America's PPC. Suppose the United States were to produce at point *C* rather than point *D* in Figure 15.1a. At point *C* we could produce 60 zillion loaves of bread and 20 zillion barrels of wine. That combination is clearly possible since it lies on the U.S. production possibilities curve. We didn't start at point *C* earlier because consumers preferred the output mix at point *D*. Now, however, ***we can use trade to break the link between production and consumption.***

Suppose the French also change their mix of output. The French earlier produced at point *I*. Now we will move them to point *K*, where they can produce 48 zillion barrels of wine and 3 zillion loaves of bread. France might not want to consume this mix of output, but it clearly can produce it.

Now consider the consequences of these changes in each nation's *production* for combined (total) output. Like magic, total output of both goods has increased. This is illustrated in Table 15.3. Both the old (pretrade) and new output mixes in each country are shown, along with their combined totals. The combined output of bread has increased from 49 to 63 zillion loaves. And combined output of wine has increased from 54 to 68 zillion barrels. Just by changing the mix of output produced in each country, we have increased *total* world output. Nice trick, isn't it?

The reason the United States and France weren't producing at points *C* and *K* before is that they simply didn't want to *consume* those particular combinations of output. The United States wanted a slightly more liquid combination than point *C*, and the French could not survive long at point *K*. Hence they chose points *D* and *I*. Nevertheless, our discovery that points *C* and *K* result in greater *total* output suggests that everybody can be happier if we all cooperate. The obvious thing to do is to *specialize* in production and then start exchanging wine for bread in international trade. In this case, the United States specializes in bread production when it moves from point *D* to point *C*. France specializes in wine production when it moves from point *I* to point *K*.

The increase in the combined output of both countries is the gain from trading. In this case the net gain is 14 zillion loaves of bread and 14 zillion barrels of wine (Table 15.3). By trading, the United States and France can divide up this increase in output and end up consuming *more* goods than they did before.

---

pretrade 贸易前。trick 策略。

There is no sleight of hand going on here. Rather, *the gains from trade are due to specialization in production.* When each country goes it alone, it is a prisoner of its own production possibilities curve; it must make its production decisions on the basis of its own consumption desires. When international trade is permitted, however, each country can concentrate on those goods it makes best. Then the countries trade with each other to acquire the goods they desire to consume.

COMPARATIVE ADVANTAGE   比较优势

By now it should be apparent that international trade *can* generate increased output. But how do we get from here to there? Which products should countries specialize in? How much should they trade?

Opportunity Costs   机会成本

In the previous example, the United States specialized in bread production and France specialized in wine production. This wasn't an arbitrary decision. Rather, those decisions were based on the relative costs of producing both products in each nation. Bread production was relatively cheap in the United States but expensive in France. Wine production was more costly in the United States but relatively cheap in France.

How did we reach such conclusions? There is nothing in Figure 15.1 that reveals actual production costs, as measured in dollars or euros. That doesn't matter, however, because economists measure costs not in *dollars* but in terms of *goods* given up.

Reexamine America's PPC (Figure 15.1) from this basic economic perspective. Notice again that the United States can produce a maximum of 100 zillion loaves of bread. To do so, however, we must sacrifice the opportunity of producing 50 zillion barrels of wine. Hence the true cost—the **opportunity cost**—of 100 zillion bread loaves is 50 zillion barrels of wine. In other words, we're paying half a barrel of wine for every loaf of bread. Again, a loaf of bread produced in the U.S. costs us half a barrel of wine.

Although the opportunity costs of bread production in the United States might appear outrageous, the opportunity cost of bread is even higher in France. According to Figure 15.1*b*, the opportunity cost of producing a loaf of bread in France is a staggering four barrels of wine. To produce a loaf of bread, the French must use factors of production that could be used to produce four barrels of wine. That is very expensive bread!

A comparison of opportunity costs exposes the nature of what we call **comparative advantage**. The United States has a *comparative* advantage in bread production because less wine has to be given up to produce bread in the United States than in France. In other words, the opportunity costs of bread production are lower in the United States than in France. *Comparative advantage refers to the relative (opportunity) costs of producing particular goods.*

Why do we bother to compute relative opportunity costs? Because they tell us what products a country should produce and *export*—and what products it should *import*. In this case, the United States should produce bread because its opportunity cost (a half barrel of wine) is less than France's (four barrels of wine). Were you the production manager for the whole world, you would certainly want each country to exploit its relative abilities, thus maximizing world output. Each country can arrive at that same decision itself by comparing its own opportunity costs to those prevailing elsewhere. *World output, and thus the potential gains from trade, will be maximized when each country pursues its comparative advantage.* It does so by exporting goods that entail low domestic opportunity costs and importing goods that involve higher domestic opportunity costs.

---

arbitrary 随意的，武断的。reexamine 重新审视。

Absolute Costs Don't Count 不考虑绝对成本

In assessing the nature of comparative advantage, notice that we needn't know anything about the actual costs involved in production. Have you seen any data suggesting how much labor, land, or capital is required to produce a loaf of bread in either France or the United States? For all you and I know, the French may be able to produce both goods with fewer resources than we are using. Such an **absolute advantage** in production might exist because of their much longer experience in cultivating both grapes and wheat or simply because they have more talent.

We can envy such productivity, but it should not alter our production and trade decisions. *All we really care about are opportunity costs—what we have to give up in order to get more of a desired good.* If we can get a barrel of imported wine for less bread than we have to give up to produce that wine ourselves, we should *import* it, not *produce* it. In other words, as long as we have a *comparative* advantage in bread production, we should exploit it. It doesn't matter to us whether France uses a lot of resources or very few to produce the wine. The absolute costs of production were omitted from the previous illustration because they are irrelevant.

To clarify the distinction between absolute advantage and comparative advantage, consider this example. When Charlie Osgood joined the Willamette Warriors' football team, he was the fastest runner ever to play football in Willamette. He could also throw the ball farther than most people could see. In other words, he had an *absolute advantage* in both throwing and running. Charlie would have made the greatest quarterback *or* the greatest tight end ever to play football. *Would have*. The problem was that he could play only one position at a time. Thus the Willamette coach had to play Charlie either as a quarterback or as a tight end. He reasoned that Charlie could throw only a bit farther than some of the other top quarterbacks but could far outdistance all the other tight ends. In other words, Charlie had a *comparative advantage* in running and was assigned to play as a tight end.

TERMS OF TRADE 贸易条件

The principle of comparative advantage tells nations how to specialize in production. In our example, the United States specialized in bread production, and France specialized in wine. We haven't yet determined, however, how much output each country should *trade*. How much bread should the United States export? How much wine should it expect to get in return? Is there any way to determine the **terms of trade**, that is, the quantity of good *A* that must be given up in exchange for good *B*?

Limits to the Terms of Trade 贸易条件的限制

Our first clue to the terms of trade lies in each country's domestic opportunity costs. *A country will not trade unless the terms of trade are superior to domestic opportunity costs.* In our example, the opportunity cost of a barrel of wine in the United States is two loaves of bread. Accordingly, we will not export bread unless we get at least one barrel of wine in exchange for every two loaves of bread we ship overseas. In other words, we will not play the game unless the terms of trade are superior to our own opportunity costs. Otherwise we get no benefit.

No country will trade unless the terms of exchange are better than its domestic opportunity costs. Hence we can predict that *the terms of trade between any two countries will lie somewhere between their respective opportunity costs in production.* That is to say, a loaf of bread in international trade will be worth at least a half-barrel of wine (the U.S. opportunity cost) but no more than four barrels (the French opportunity cost).

The Market Mechanism 市场机制

Exactly where the terms of trade end up in the range of 0.5–4.0 barrels of wine per loaf of bread will depend on how market participants behave. Suppose that Henri, an enterprising

---

quarterback 橄榄球的四分卫。

我们可以嫉妒这样的生产能力，不过它不应当动摇我们的生产和贸易决策。我们真正关心的是机会成本——为了得到更多合意的商品所必须放弃的东西。如果我们进口一桶葡萄酒所需要的面包比我们亲自生产同样多的葡萄酒所必须放弃的面包少，那么我们就应该进口葡萄酒，而不是自己生产它。换句话说，只要我们在面包生产上具有比较优势，我们就应当利用这个优势。法国使用更多的资源还是更少的资源生产葡萄酒，对我们来说并不重要。因为无关紧要，在前面的证明中我们忽略掉了生产的绝对成本。

确立贸易条件的第一个提示是每个国家国内的机会成本。除非贸易条件优于国内的机会成本，否则一个国家不会进行贸易。在我们的例子中，美国一桶葡萄酒的机会成本是两个面包。所以，除非我们运往海外的每两个面包至少能换得一桶葡萄酒，否则美国不会出口面包。换句话说，除非贸易条件优于美国的机会成本，否则它不会参与这一贸易活动，也不会得到任何好处。

Frenchman, visited the United States before the advent of international trade. He noticed that bread was relatively cheap, while wine was relatively expensive—the opposite of the price relationship prevailing in France. These price comparisons brought to his mind the opportunity for making an easy euro. All he had to do was bring over some French wine and trade it in the United States for a large quantity of bread. Then he could return to France and exchange the bread for a greater quantity of wine. Were he to do this a few times, he would amass substantial profits.

Our French entrepreneur's exploits will not only enrich him but will also move each country toward its comparative advantage. The United States ends up exporting bread to France, and France ends up exporting wine to the United States. The activating agent is not the Ministry of Trade and its 620 trained economists, however, but simply one enterprising French trader. He is aided and encouraged by the consumers and producers in each country. American consumers are happy to trade their bread for his wines. They thereby end up paying less for wine (in terms of bread) than they would otherwise have to. In other words, the terms of trade Henri offers are more attractive than prevailing (domestic) relative prices. On the other side of the Atlantic, Henri's welcome is equally warm. French consumers get a better deal by trading their wine for his imported bread than by trading with the local bakers.

Even some producers are happy. The wheat farmers and bakers in America are eager to deal with Henri. He is willing to buy a lot of bread and even to pay a premium price for it. Indeed, bread production has become so profitable that a lot of farmers who used to cultivate grapes are now starting to grow wheat. This alters the mix of U.S. output in the direction of more bread, exactly as suggested earlier in Figure 15.1.

In France, the opposite kind of production shift is taking place. French wheat farmers start to plant grapes so they can take advantage of Henri's generous purchases. Thus Henri is able to lead each country in the direction of its comparative advantage—raking in a substantial profit for himself along the way.

> 贸易条件的最终结果在一定程度上取决于像亨利这类交易商的水平，它也取决于千千万万参与市场交换的消费者和生产者的行为。也就是说，贸易流动取决于每个国家面包和葡萄酒的供给和需求。贸易条件，跟其他任何商品的价格一样，取决于市场参与者在各个价格水平上买卖的意愿。我们可以确定的就是，贸易条件最终介于两个国家的机会成本所设定的两个极限之间。

Where the terms of trade end up depends in part on how good a trader Henri is. It will also depend on the behavior of the thousands of consumers and producers who participate in the market exchanges. In other words, trade flows depend on both the supply of and the demand for bread and wine in each country. ***The terms of trade, like the price of any good, will depend on the willingness of market participants to buy or sell at various prices.*** All we know for sure is that the terms of trade will end up somewhere between the limits set by each country's opportunity costs.

来自保护主义者的压力
PROTECTIONIST PRESSURES

Although the potential gains from world trade are impressive, not everyone will be smiling at the Franco-American trade celebration. On the contrary, some people will be upset about the trade routes that Henri has established. They will seek to discourage us from continuing to trade with France.

Microeconomic Losers 微观经济的失败者

Consider, for example, the wine growers in western New York State. Do you think they are going to be happy about Henri's entrepreneurship? Americans can now buy wine more cheaply from France than they can from New York. Before long we may hear talk about unfair foreign competition or about the greater nutritional value of American grapes. The New York wine growers may also emphasize the importance of maintaining an adequate grape supply and a strong wine industry at home.

Joining with the growers will be the farmworkers and all the other workers, producers, and merchants whose livelihood depends on the New York wine industry. If they are aggressive and clever enough, the growers will also get the governor of the state to join their demonstration. After all, the governor must recognize the needs of his or her people, and

---

advent 到来，出现。 amass 积累。 prevailing 一般的，盛行的。

those people definitely don't include the wheat farmers in Kansas who are making a bundle from international trade. New York consumers are, of course, benefiting from lower wine prices, but they are unlikely to demonstrate over a few cents a bottle. On the other hand, those few extra pennies translate into millions of dollars for domestic wine producers.

The wheat farmers in France are no happier about international trade. They would love to sink all those boats bringing wheat from America, thereby protecting their own market position.

If we are to make sense of international trade policies, we must recognize one central fact of life: Some producers have a vested interest in restricting international trade. In particular, ***workers and producers who compete with imported products—who work in import-competing industries—have an economic interest in restricting trade.*** This helps explain why GM, Ford, and Chrysler are unhappy about auto imports and why workers in Massachusetts want to end the importation of Italian shoes. Last, but not least, it also explains why French winemakers—who did well in our story of bread/wine trade—violently protested French imports of cheaper Spanish wine (see the News Wire "Import Competition").

要弄懂国际贸易政策，我们就必须意识到现实中一个最核心的事实：某些生产者将由于限制国际贸易而保有既得利益，特别是与进口产品竞争的工人和生产商——他们从事与进口产品竞争的行业，都会在限制贸易中获得经济利益。

NEWS WIRE IMPORT COMPETITION

Angry French Winemakers Destroy Spanish Wine Stocks

Paris, France. Winemakers in the Languedoc wine-producing region have turned violent. They have raided supermarkets, ransacked warehouses, and burned the offices of wine distributors. The source of their fury is the flood of cheap bulk wine coming into France from Spain. The Languedoc winemakers—long known for producing low-cost table wines—are seeing their sales and prices decline as Spanish bulk wines gain sales. They want the French government to force new labeling requirements for Spanish wine so that French consumers will be able to identify "inferior" wines from Spain.

Source: News accounts of March–August 2017.

NOTE: Imports reduce sales, jobs, profits, and wages in import-competing industries. This is the source of micro resistance to international trade.
注：进口减少了与进口竞争之行业的销售、就业岗位、利润和工资，这是从微观上抵制国际贸易的原因。

Although imports typically mean fewer jobs and less income for some domestic industries, exports represent increased jobs and incomes for other industries. Producers and workers in export industries gain from trade. Thus on a microeconomic level, there are identifiable gainers and losers from international trade. ***Trade not only alters the mix of output, but also redistributes income from import-competing industries to export industries.*** This potential redistribution is the source of political and economic friction.

尽管进口对一些国内产业意味着就业以及收入的减少，但出口意味着一些国内产业就业和收入的增加。出口行业的生产商和工人能从贸易中获益。因此，在微观层面上，国际贸易的赢家和输家很好识别。贸易不仅改变了产出组合，而且将收入从进口竞争产业再分配到出口产业。这一潜在的收入再分配是产生政治和经济摩擦的根源。

The Net Gain 净收益

We must be careful to note, however, that the microeconomic gains from trade are greater than the microeconomic losses. It's not simply a question of robbing Peter to enrich Paul. On the contrary, consumers in general enjoy a higher standard of living as a result of international trade. As we saw earlier, trade increases world efficiency and total output. Accordingly, we end up slicing up a larger pie rather than just reslicing the same smaller pie.

BARRIERS TO TRADE 贸易壁垒

The microeconomic losses associated with imports give rise to a constant clamor for trade restrictions. People whose jobs and incomes are threatened by international trade tend to organize quickly and air their grievances. Moreover, they are assured of a reasonably receptive hearing, both because of the political implications of well-financed organizations and because the gains from trade are widely diffused. If successful, such efforts can lead to a variety of trade restrictions.

---

raid 袭击，抢劫。 ransack 洗劫。 slice up 把……切成片。 clamor 呼声，大声的要求。

Tariffs 关税

One of the most popular and visible restrictions on trade is a **tariff**, a special tax imposed on imported goods. Tariffs, also called *customs duties*, were once the principal source of revenue for governments. In the eighteenth century, tariffs on tea, glass, wine, lead, and paper were imposed on the American colonies to provide extra revenue for the British government. The tariff on tea led to the Boston Tea Party in 1773 and gave added momentum to the American independence movement. In modern times, tariffs have been used primarily as a means of import protection to satisfy specific microeconomic or macroeconomic interests. The current U.S. tariff code specifies tariffs on over 10,000 different products—nearly 50 percent of all U.S. imports. Although the average tariff is only 3 percent, individual tariffs vary widely. The tariff on cars, for example, is only 2.5 percent, while tariffs imposed on wool sweaters and canned tuna are 25 percent and 35 percent, respectively.

关税对进口竞争产业的吸引力是显而易见的。对进口商品征收的关税使国内消费者购买进口商品变得更昂贵，因此降低了进口商品对国内商品的竞争力。

The attraction of tariffs to import-competing industries should be obvious. ***A tariff on imported goods makes them more expensive to domestic consumers and thus less competitive with domestically produced goods.*** Among familiar tariffs in effect in 2019 were $0.20 per gallon on Scotch whiskey and $0.76 per gallon on imported champagne. These tariffs made American-produced spirits look like relatively good buys and thus contributed to higher sales and profits for domestic distillers and grape growers. In the same manner, imported baby food is taxed at 34.6 percent, imported footwear at 20 percent, and imported stereos at rates ranging from 4 to 6 percent. In 2018, President Trump imposed a 25 percent tariff on imported steel and a 10 percent tariff on imported aluminum (see the News Wire "Tariff Protection"). In each of these cases, domestic producers in import-competing industries were the winners. The losers were domestic consumers, who ended up paying higher prices; domestic producers, who incurred higher costs; foreign producers, who lost business; and world efficiency, as trade was reduced.

NEWS WIRE TARIFF PROTECTION

Winners and Losers from Trump Steel Tariff

WASHINGTON, DC—President Trump today announced a 25 percent tariff on steel imports and 10 percent on aluminum. Citing national security concerns, Trump said the tariffs would protect a vital domestic industry from destructive import competition. Executives of U.S. Steel and Nucor, the nation's largest steel companies, expressed gratitude for the move and pledged to increase both capital investment and jobs.

Steel and aluminum consumers weren't so happy. The tariffs will increase input costs for a broad range of metal-using industries, including automakers, aircraft companies, construction, and more. Harley-Davidson said the tariffs will add $15–$20 million to its production costs. The Beer Institute noted that the tariffs will increase the cost of aluminum cans, ultimately raising the price of beer and all other canned beverages and products. The CEO of the National Retail Federation called the tariffs "a tax on American families."

Source: News accounts of March–April 2018.

NOTE: Tariffs protect prices, profits, and jobs in some industries, but raise costs, lower profits, and reduce employment in other industries. They also invite retaliation by foreign nations, curbing export sales.
注：关税保护了某些行业的价格、利润和工作岗位，但是使其他行业的成本提高，利润降低，就业减少，并且还会招致外国报复，限制出口销售。

Quotas 配额

Tariffs reduce the flow of imports by raising import prices. As an alternative barrier to trade, a country can impose import **quotas**, numerical restrictions on the quantity of a particular good that may be imported. The United States maintains import quotas on sugar, meat, dairy products, textiles, cotton, peanuts, steel, cloth diapers, and even ice cream. According to the U.S. Department of State, approximately 12 percent of our imports are subject to import quotas.

---

customs duty 关税，进口税。 momentum 动力，势头。

Quotas, like all barriers to trade, reduce world efficiency and invite retaliatory action. Moreover, quotas are especially harmful because of their impact on competition and prices. Figure 15.2 shows how this works.

Figure 15.2a depicts the supply-and-demand relationships that would prevail in a closed (no-trade) economy. In this situation, the **equilibrium price** of textiles is completely determined by domestic demand and supply curves. The equilibrium price is p_1, and the quantity of textiles consumed is q_1.

Suppose now that trade begins and foreign producers are allowed to sell textiles in the American market. The immediate effect of this decision will be a rightward shift of the market supply curve as foreign supplies are added to domestic supplies (Figure 15.2b). If an unlimited quantity of textiles can be bought in world markets at a price of p_2, the new supply curve will look like S_2 (infinitely elastic at p_2). The new supply curve (S_2) intersects the old demand curve

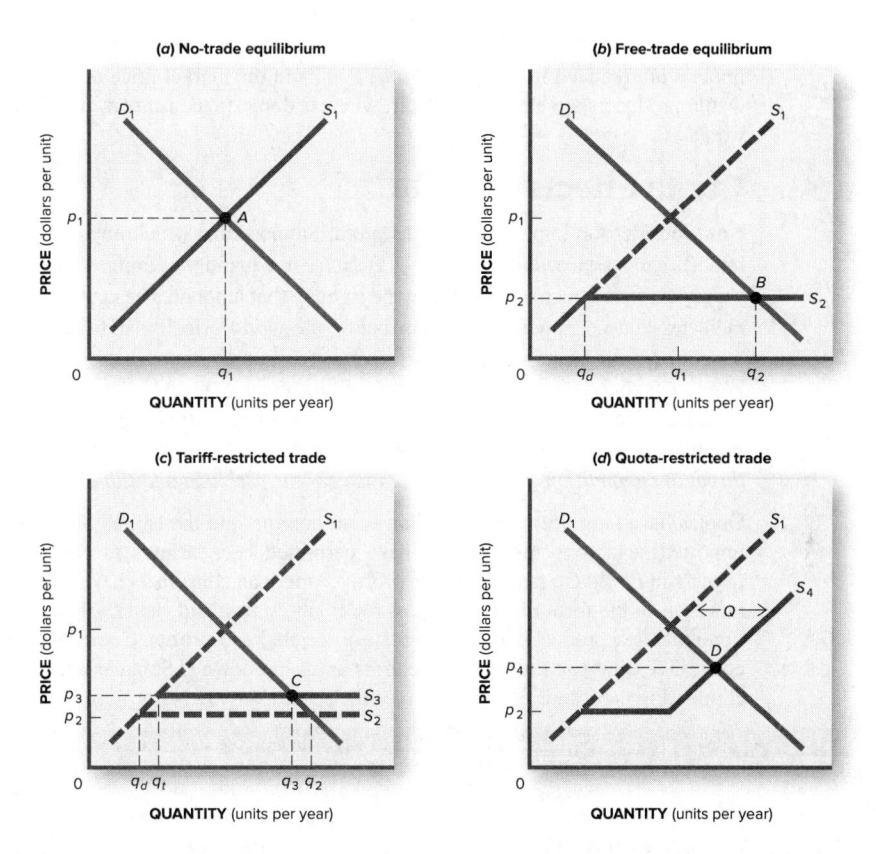

Figure 15.2 The Impact of Trade Restrictions In the *absence of trade,* the domestic price and sales of a good will be determined by domestic supply and demand curves (point A in graph [a]). Once trade is permitted, the market supply curve will be altered by the availability of imports. With *free trade* and unlimited availability of imports at price p_2, a new market equilibrium will be established at world prices (point B in graph [b]). At that equilibrium, domestic *consumption* is higher (q_2) but *production* is lower (q_d).

Tariffs raise domestic prices and reduce the quantity sold. In graph (c) a tariff that increases the import price from p_2 to p_3 reduces imports and increases domestic sales (from q_2 to q_t) and price.

Quotas put an absolute limit on imported sales and thus give domestic producers a great opportunity to raise the market price. In graph (d), the quota Q limits how far market supply can shift to the right, pushing the price up from P_2 to P_4. ∎

(D_1) at a new equilibrium price of p_2 and an expanded consumption of q_2. At this new equilibrium, domestic producers are supplying the quantity q_d, while foreign producers are supplying the rest ($q_2 - q_d$). Comparing the new equilibrium to the old one, we see that ***trade results in reduced prices and increased consumption.***

Domestic textile producers are unhappy, of course, with their foreign competition. In the absence of trade, the domestic producers would sell more output (q_1) and get higher prices (p_1). Once trade is opened up, the willingness of foreign producers to sell unlimited quantities of textiles at the price p_2 puts a limit on the price behavior of domestic producers. Accordingly, we can anticipate some lobbying for trade restrictions.

Tariff Effects 关税效应

Figure 15.2c illustrates what would happen to prices and sales if the United Textile Producers were successful in persuading the government to impose a tariff. Assume the tariff raises imported textile prices from p_2 to p_3. The higher price p_3 makes it more difficult for foreign producers to undersell domestic producers. Domestic production expands from q_d to q_t, imports are reduced from $q_2 - q_d$ to $q_3 - q_t$, and the market price of textiles rises. Domestic textile producers are clearly better off, whereas domestic consumers and foreign producers are worse off.

Quota Effects 配额效应

Now consider the impact of a textile *quota*. Suppose that we eliminate tariffs but decree that imports cannot exceed the quantity Q. Because the quantity of imports can never exceed Q, the supply curve is effectively shifted to the right by that amount. The new curve S_4 (Figure 15.2d) indicates that no imports will occur below the world price p_2 and that above that price the quantity Q will be imported. Thus the *domestic* supply curve determines subsequent prices. Foreign producers are precluded from selling greater quantities as prices rise further. This outcome is in marked contrast to that of tariff-restricted trade (Figure 15.2c), which at least permits foreign producers to respond to rising prices. Accordingly, ***quotas are a much greater threat to competition than tariffs because quotas preclude additional imports at any price.***

Quotas have long been maintained on sugar coming into the United States. By keeping cheap imported sugar out, these quotas have permitted beet farmers in Nebraska and sugarcane farmers in Florida to reap economic profits. American consumers have paid for that protection, however, in the form of higher prices for candy, sodas, and sugar—about $2 billion per year. Foreign sugar producers have also lost sales, jobs, and profits. Confronted with higher input costs, U.S. candy and soda manufacturers have shut down U.S. plants and relocated elsewhere, eliminating thousands of U.S. jobs (see the accompanying News Wire "Import Quotas").

现在来考虑一下纺织品配额的影响。假设我们取消了关税，但规定进口数量不能超过 Q。由于进口量不能超过 Q，供给曲线实际上只能右移到 Q。新的供给曲线 S_4（图 15.2d）表明，当价格低于世界价格 p_2 时，不会出现进口，在此价格之上，将有数量为 Q 的进口。于是国内的供给曲线决定了进口后的价格。即使价格进一步上涨，国外生产商也不能销售更多数量的产品。这一市场结果与关税限制下的贸易形成对比（图 15.2c），在关税限制下，至少还允许国外生产商对价格提高作出反应。所以，与关税相比，配额对竞争的威胁要严重得多，因为配额在任何价格上都能阻止进口增加。

NEWS WIRE IMPORT QUOTAS

Mexico Accepts Trump's Offer on Sugar Quotas

Washington, DC. Mexico has agreed to limit sugar exports to the United States to a maximum of 1.150 million metric tons a year and to further limit refined sugar shipments to 30 percent of that total (down from 53 percent last year). Commerce Secretary Wilbur Ross hailed the agreement as "fair to U.S. consumers and American sugar growers." But economists estimate that this and other sugar import quotas are keeping the U.S. price of sugar at roughly $0.28 per pound, far above the world price of $0.12. Those higher prices have already driven candy companies like Hershey's and Brach's to move candy production from the United States to Mexico.

Source: News accounts of June 2017.

NOTE: Import restrictions raise domestic prices, making both domestic consumers and foreign producers worse off. They enrich some domestic producers, however.
注：进口限制提高了国内的价格，使国内消费者和国外生产者的境况更差了，然而进口限制却使国内一些生产者变富了。

relocate 迁移，重新安置。hail 称赞。

Nontariff Barriers 非关税壁垒

Tariffs and quotas are the most visible barriers to trade, but they are only the tip of the iceberg. Indeed, the variety of protectionist measures that have been devised is testimony to human ingenuity. At the turn of the century, the Germans were officially committed to a policy of extending equal treatment to all trading partners. They wanted, however, to lower the tariff on cattle imports from Denmark without extending the same break to Switzerland. Accordingly, the Germans created a new and higher tariff on "brown and dappled cows reared at a level of at least 300 meters above sea level and passing at least one month in every summer at an altitude of at least 800 meters." The new tariff was, of course, applied equally to all countries. But Danish cows never climb that high, so they were not burdened with the new tariff.

With the decline in tariffs over the last 20 years, nontariff barriers have increased. The United States uses product standards, licensing restrictions, restrictive procurement practices, and other nontariff barriers to restrict roughly 15 percent of imports. Japan makes even greater use of nontariff barriers, restricting nearly 30 percent of imports in such ways.

In 1999–2000, the European Union banned imports of U.S. beef, arguing that the use of hormones on U.S. ranches created a health hazard for European consumers. Although both the U.S. government and the World Trade Organization disputed that claim, the ban was a highly effective nontariff trade barrier. The United States responded by slapping 100 percent tariffs on dozens of European products.

EXCHANGE RATES 汇率

Up until now, we've made no mention of how people *pay* for goods and services produced in other countries. In fact, the principle of comparative advantage is based only on opportunity costs; it makes no reference to monetary prices. Yet when France and the United States started specializing in production, market participants had to *purchase* wine and bread to get trade flows started. Remember Henri, the mythical French entrepreneur? He got trade started by buying bread in the United States for export to France. That meant he had to make purchases in *dollars* and sales in *euros*. *So long as each nation has its own currency, every trade will require use of two different currencies at some point.*

If you've ever traveled to a foreign country, you know the currency problem. Stores, hotels, vending machines, and restaurants price their products in local currency. So you've got to exchange your dollars for local currency when you travel (a service import). That's when you learn how important the **exchange rate** is. The exchange rate refers to the value of one currency in terms of another currency. If $1 exchanges for 2 euros, then a euro is worth 50 cents.

Global Pricing 全球定价

Exchange rates are a critical link in the global pricing of goods and services. Whether a bottle of French wine is expensive depends on two factors: (1) the French price of the wine, expressed in euros, and (2) the dollar–euro exchange rate. Specifically,

> Dollar price of imported good = foreign price of good × dollar price of foreign currency

Hence if French wine sells for 60 euros per bottle in France and the dollar price of a euro is $1.50, the American price of imported French wine is

$$= 60 \text{ euros} \times \$1.50 \text{ per euro}$$
$$= \$90.00$$

The same formula tells us how much a Big Mac costs at that McDonald's in Indonesia. As we noted at the beginning of this chapter, a Big Mac sold for 14,500 rupiah at the Jakarta

---

testimony 证明。 altitude 海拔。 procurement 采购。 hormone 激素。

McDonald's in mid-2018. A quick look at the foreign exchange market tells us that $1 was worth 13,907 rupiah at that time. Hence, the dollar price of the Big Mac was

$$14,500 \text{ rupiah} = \$1/13,904 \text{ rupiah} = \$1.04$$

Appreciation/Depreciation 升值/贬值

全球定价的公式突出了汇率对贸易流动的重要性。每当汇率发生变化时，所有进出口的全球价格也会发生变化。

The formula for global pricing highlights how important exchange rates are for trade flows. ***Whenever exchange rates change, so do the global prices of all imports and exports.***

Suppose the dollar were to get stronger against the euro. That means the dollar price of a euro would decline. Suppose the dollar price of a euro fell from $1.50 to only $1.20. That **currency appreciation** of the dollar would cut the dollar price of French wine by 20 percent. Americans would respond by buying more imported wine. In 2018 Americans took advantage of the dollar's appreciation to book more travel to Paris (see the accompanying News Wire "Currency Appreciation").

NEWS WIRE CURRENCY APPRECIATION

Paris Just Got Cheaper for American Tourists

Paris, France. Americans may discover some bargains in Paris this summer. Since the beginning of the year, the U.S. dollar has strengthened considerably, making everything in Paris a bit cheaper. In February a dollar bought 0.80 euro; today, the same dollar is worth 0.88 euro. What does that mean for American tourists? Admission to the Eiffel Tower still costs 10 euros, but the dollar price has dropped from $12.50 to $11.36. Tickets to the Louvre museum (15 euros) have fallen from $18.75 to $17.05 for American tourists. And for big spenders, the fixed price of the gourmet lunch at Le Cinq has fallen from $250 to a mere $227. Vive la Paris!

Source: Federal Reserve Board of Governors, August 2018.

©Aaron Roeth Photography

NOTE: When the dollar appreciates (rises in value), the euro simultaneously depreciates (falls in value). This makes European vacations cheaper for American college students.

注：当美元升值（价值上升）时，欧元自动贬值（价值下降）。对美国大学生来说，去欧洲度假更便宜了。

如果美元的价值上涨，那么另一种货币的价值必将下降。具体来说，美元的升值意味着欧元的**货币贬值**。如果1欧元的美元价值从1.50美元降至1.20美元，也就意味着1美元的欧元价值增加了（从0.67欧元增至0.83欧元）。因此法国消费者不得不为一个美国面包支付更多的欧元。受货币贬值之困，他们也许会减少购买进口面包。就如同上面的公式所表示的那样，如果一国货币贬值，

- 它的出口品变得更便宜；
- 它的进口品变得更昂贵。

If the dollar is *rising* in value, another currency must be *falling*. Specifically, the appreciation of the dollar implies a **currency depreciation** for the euro. If the dollar price of a euro declines from $1.50 to $1.20, that implies an *increase* in the *euro* price of a *dollar* (from 0.67 euro to 0.83 euro). Hence French consumers will have to pay more euros for an American loaf of bread. Stuck with a depreciated currency, they may decide to buy fewer imported loaves of bread. As the previous equation implies, ***if the value of a nation's currency declines,***

- ***Its exports become cheaper.***
- ***Its imports become more expensive.***

Imagine how Venezuelans felt in 2018 when their currency (the bolivar) collapsed. In January, Venezuelans needed 200,000 bolivars to buy a single U.S. dollar. That made all foreign-made products incredibly expensive for Venezuelan consumers. But that was only the beginning of an exchange-rate nightmare: By August, the bolivar had so massively depreciated that Venezuelans needed over *6 million* bolivars to buy a single U.S. dollar. Later that month, the Venezuelan government issued a new currency.

---

currency appreciation 货币升值。bolivar 玻利瓦尔（委内瑞拉货币单位）。

A Weaker Dollar 疲软的美元

The U.S. dollar had also experienced bouts of weakness, but nothing on the scale of the bolivar. From 2000 until 2009, the U.S. dollar lost about half its value relative to the European euro. This dollar depreciation dropped the *euro* price of a ticket to Disney World by 50 percent. Europeans responded by flocking to Florida. In 2018 the situation was reversed: The strong dollar hurt ticket sales at Disney World but increased ticket sales at the Eiffel Tower.

Foreign Exchange Markets 外汇市场

The changes in exchange rates that alter global prices are really no different in principle from other price changes. An exchange rate is, after all, simply the *price* of a currency. Like other market prices, an exchange rate is determined by supply and demand.

Figure 15.3 depicts a foreign exchange market. In this case, the supply and demand for euros is the focus. On the demand side of the market is everyone who has some use of euros, including U.S. travelers to Europe, U.S. importers of European products, and foreign investors who want to buy European stocks, bonds, and factories. The cheaper the euro, the greater the quantity of euros demanded.

The supply of euros comes from similar sources. German tourists visiting Disney World *supply* euros when they *demand* U.S. dollars. European consumers who buy American-made products set off a chain of transactions that *supplies* euros in exchange for dollars. The higher the price of the euro, the more they are willing to supply.

The intersection of the supply and demand curves in Figure 15.3 establishes the equilibrium price of the euro—that is, the prevailing exchange rate. As we have seen, however, exchange rates change. As with other prices, **exchange rates change when either the supply of or the demand for a currency shifts.** If American students suddenly decided to enroll in European colleges, the demand for euros would increase. This rightward shift of the euro demand curve would cause the euro to *appreciate* (go up), as shown in Figure 15.4. Such a euro appreciation would increase the cost of studying in Europe. But the euro appreciation would make it cheaper for European students to attend U.S. colleges. **There are always winners and losers when exchange rates change.**

图 15.3 中供给和需求曲线的交点确定了欧元的均衡价格，即现行汇率。不过，正如我们已经看到的，汇率是变化的。与其他价格一样，当货币供给和货币需求中任何一方发生移动时，汇率就会变化。如果美国的学生们突然决定去读欧洲的大学，欧元的需求将增加。欧元需求曲线的右移将促使欧元升值，如图 15.4。因此欧元升值会增加在欧洲求学的成本，但是欧元升值会降低欧洲学生到美国读大学的成本。当汇率变化时，总会有赢家和输家。

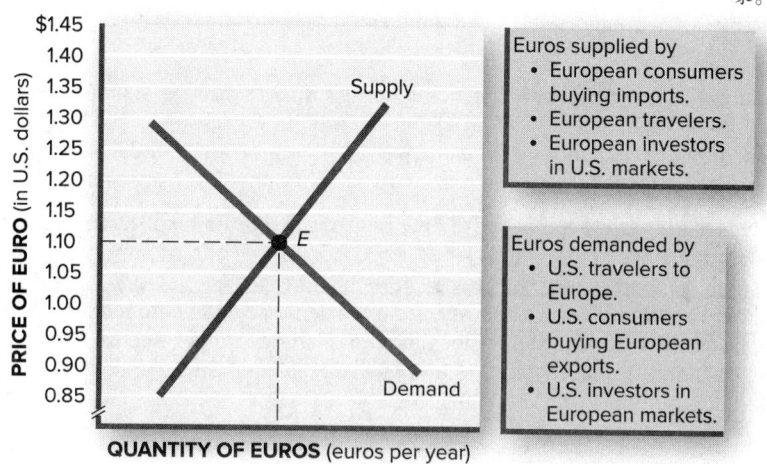

Figure 15.3 The Euro Market Exchange rates are set in foreign exchange markets by the international supply of and demand for a currency. In this case the equilibrium price is 110 U.S. cents for 1 euro.

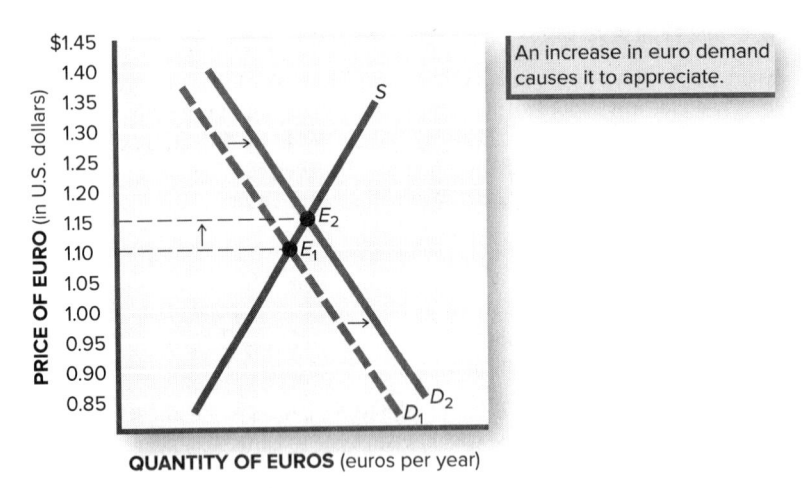

Figure 15.4 Currency Appreciation If the demand for a currency increases, its value will rise (appreciate). Shifts of a currency's demand or supply curve will alter exchange rates.

POLICY PERSPECTIVES

WHO ENFORCES WORLD TRADE RULES?

Trade policy is a continuing conflict between the benefits of comparative advantage and the pleadings of protectionists. Free trade promises more output, greater efficiency, and lower prices. At the same time, free trade threatens profits, jobs, and wealth in specific industries.

Politically, the battle over trade policy favors protectionist interests over consumer interests. Few consumers understand how free trade affects them. Moreover, consumers are unlikely to organize political protests just because the price of orange juice is 35 cents per gallon higher. By contrast, import-competing industries have a large economic stake in trade restrictions and can mobilize political support easily. After convincing Congress to pass new quotas on textiles in 1990, the Fiber Fabric Apparel Coalition for Trade (FFACT) mustered 250,000 signatures and 4,000 union members to march on the White House demanding that President Bush sign the legislation.

President Clinton faced similar political resistance when he sought congressional approval of NAFTA in 1993 and GATT in 1994. Indeed, the political resistance to free trade was so intense that Congress delayed a vote on GATT until after the November 1994 elections. This forced President Clinton to convene a special postelection session of Congress for the sole purpose of ratifying the GATT agreement.

President Trump was also keenly sensitive to the politics of international trade. Some of the states that were critical to his 2016 electoral victory had large concentrations of import-competing industries. In Pennsylvania, steel companies wanted more protection from steel imports. Florida sugar growers wanted tighter limits on imported sugar, especially from Mexico. Michigan auto manufacturers wanted less competition from imported cars. And Midwestern farmers wanted greater access to markets in Canada, Europe, and China. President Trump responded to these special interests by enacting a slew of new tariffs and renouncing trade agreements with other nations.

---

pleading 恳求，诉求。ratify 批准，正式签署。

GATT

The political resistance to free trade is not unique to the United States. International trade creates winners and losers in every trading nation. Recognizing this, the countries of the world decided long ago that multinational agreements were the most effective way to overcome domestic protectionism. Broad trade agreements can address the entire spectrum of trade restrictions rather than focusing on one industry at a time. Multinational agreements can also muster political support by offering greater *export* opportunities as *import* restrictions are lifted.

In 1947, 23 of the world's largest trading nations signed the General Agreement on Tariffs and Trade (GATT). The GATT pact committed these nations to pursue free trade policies and to extend equal access ("most favored nation" status) to domestic markets for all GATT members. This goal was pursued with periodic rounds of multilateral trade agreements. Because each round of negotiations entailed hundreds of industries and products, the negotiations typically dragged on for 6 to 10 years. At the end of each round, however, trade barriers were always lower. When GATT was first signed in 1947, tariff rates in developed countries averaged 40 percent. The first seven GATT rounds pushed tariffs down to an average of 6.3 percent, and the 1986–1994 Uruguay Round lowered them further to 3.9 percent. The Doha Round began in 2001 and focused on trade tools for promoting economic development.

WTO

The 117 nations that signed the 1994 Uruguay agreement also decided that a stronger mechanism was needed to enforce free trade agreements. To that end, the World Trade Organization (WTO) was created to replace GATT. If a nation feels its exports are being unfairly excluded from another country's market, it can file a complaint with the WTO. This is exactly what the United States did when the European Union (EU) banned U.S. beef imports. The WTO ruled in favor of the United States. When the EU failed to lift its import ban, the WTO authorized the United States to impose retaliatory tariffs on European exports.

The European Union turned the tables on the United States in 2003. It complained to the WTO that U.S. tariffs on steel violated trade rules. The WTO agreed and gave the EU permission to impose retaliatory tariffs on $2.2 billion of U.S. exports. That prompted the Bush administration to scale back the tariffs in December 2003.

In effect, the WTO is now the world's trade police force. It is empowered to cite nations that violate trade agreements and even to authorize remedial action when violations persist.

President Trump expressed frustration with the WTO, demanding that it take stronger action to curb unfair trade policies and block Europe from imposing retaliatory tariffs against the United States in the wake of his own tariff initiatives. He even threatened to pull the United States out of the WTO but didn't take steps to do so. Why do the United States and other sovereign nations cede any power to the WTO? Because they are convinced that free trade—based on comparative advantage—is the surest route to faster GDP growth and rising global living standards.

CHAPTER 15 REVIEW
SUMMARY

- International trade occurs when nations *export* goods and services to other nations and *import* goods and services from other nations. **LO1**
- A trade *deficit* arises when imports exceed exports; a trade *surplus* is the reverse. **LO1**
- Trade breaks the link between a nation's *consumption* possibilities and its *production* possibilities. With trade, nations don't have to consume exactly what they produce. **LO2**
- Trade permits each country to concentrate its resources on those goods it can produce most efficiently. This

---

remedial 补救的，纠正的。

kind of productive specialization increases world output. **LO2**
- In determining what to produce and offer in trade, each country will exploit its *comparative* advantage—its *relative* efficiency in producing various goods. One way to determine where comparative advantage lies is to compare the quantity of good *A* that must be given up in order to *produce* a given quantity of good *B*. If the same quantity of *B* can be obtained for less *A* by *trading*, we have a comparative advantage in the production of good *A*. Comparative advantage rests on a comparison of relative opportunity costs (domestic versus international). **LO2**
- The terms of trade—the rate at which goods are exchanged—are subject to the forces of international supply and demand. The terms of trade will lie somewhere between the opportunity costs of the trading partners. **LO3**
- Resistance to trade emanates from workers and firms that must compete with imports. Even though the country as a whole stands to benefit from trade, these individuals and companies may lose jobs and incomes in the process. **LO4**
- The means of restricting trade are many and diverse. Tariffs discourage imports by making them more expensive. Quotas limit the quantity of a good that may be imported. Nontariff barriers are less visible but also effective in curbing imports. **LO4**
- International trade requires converting one nation's currency into that of another. The exchange rate is the price of one currency in terms of another. **LO5**
- Changes in exchange rates (currency appreciation and depreciation) occur when supply or demand for a currency shifts. When a nation's currency appreciates, its exports become more expensive and its imports become cheaper. **LO5**
- The World Trade Organization (WTO) polices multilateral trade agreements to keep trade barriers low. **LO4**

TERMS TO REMEMBER

Define the following terms:

imports
exports
trade deficit
trade surplus
production possibilities
consumption possibilities
opportunity cost
comparative advantage
absolute advantage
terms of trade
tariff
quota
equilibrium price
exchange rate
currency appreciation
currency depreciation

QUESTIONS FOR DISCUSSION

1. Suppose a lawyer can type faster than any administrative assistant. Should the lawyer do her own typing? **LO2**
2. Can you identify three services Americans import? How about three exported services? **LO1**
3. If a nation exported much of its output but imported little, would it be better or worse off? How about the reverse—that is, exporting little but importing a lot? **LO1**
4. Are "Buy American" provisions good for (*a*) U.S. consumers, (*b*) U.S. producers? **LO4**
5. Why did Coors beer object to tariffs on imported aluminum? **LO2**
6. How would each of these events affect the supply or demand for Japanese yen? **LO5**
   a. Stronger U.S. economic growth.
   b. A decline in Japanese interest rates.
   c. Higher inflation in the United States.
7. Is a stronger dollar good or bad for America? Explain. **LO5**
8. **POLICY PERSPECTIVES** If another nation raises tariffs on U.S. products, should the United States retaliate with similar trade barriers? Who would gain? Who would lose? **LO4**
9. **POLICY PERSPECTIVES** If more jobs are lost in steel-using industries than are saved by tariffs in the steel industry, why are tariffs on steel ever imposed? **LO4**

PROBLEMS

1. Suppose the following table reflects the domestic supply and demand for T-shirts: **LO4**

Price ($)	15	13	11	9	7	5	3	1
Quantity supplied	8	7	6	5	4	3	2	1
Quantity demanded	2	4	6	8	10	12	14	16

    a. Graph these market conditions and identify when there is an absence of trade: (i) the market price, (ii) domestic consumption, and (iii) domestic production.
    b. Now suppose that foreigners enter the market, offering to sell an unlimited supply of T-shirts for $7 apiece. Now with free trade, identify (i) the market price, (ii) domestic consumption, and (iii) domestic production.
    c. If a tariff of $2 per T-shirt is imposed, with this trade barrier, identify (i) the market price, (ii) domestic consumption, and (iii) domestic production.

2. Alpha and Beta, two tiny islands off the east coast of Tricoli, produce pearls and pineapples. The production possibilities schedules in the table below describe their potential output in tons per year. **LO3**
    a. Graph the production possibilities confronting each island.
    b. What is the opportunity cost of one ton of pineapples on each island?
    c. Which island has a comparative advantage in pineapple production?

Alpha		Beta	
Pearls	Pineapples	Pearls	Pineapples
0	30	0	20
2	25	10	16
4	20	20	12
6	15	30	8
8	10	40	4
10	5	45	2
12	0	50	0

3. Suppose the two islands in problem 2 agree that the terms of trade will be 1 ton of pineapples for 1 ton of pearls and that trade soon results in an exchange of 10 tons of pineapples for 10 tons of pearls. **LO2**
    a. If Alpha produced 6 tons of pearls and 15 tons of pineapples and Beta produced 30 tons of pearls and 8 tons of pineapples before they decided to trade, how much would each be producing after trade became possible? Assume that the two countries specialize just enough to maintain their consumption of the item they export, and make sure each island trades the item for which it has a comparative advantage.
    b. How much would the combined production of pineapples increase for the two islands due to trade? How much would the combined production of pearls increase?
    c. How could both islands produce and consume even more?

4. What is the equilibrium euro price of the U.S. dollar **LO5**
    a. in Figure 15.3?
    b. in Figure 15.4?
    c. Did the dollar appreciate or depreciate in Figure 15.4?

5. In what country was the U.S. dollar price of a Big Mac the highest with the following exchange rates? **LO5**
    a. 13,907 rupiah = $1
    b. 0.85 euro = $1
    c. 33 baht = $1
    d. 6.61 yuan = $1
6. If a PlayStation 4 Pro costs 40,000 yen in Japan, how much will it cost in U.S. dollars if the exchange rate is as follows? **LO5**
    a. 120 yen = $1
    b. 1 yen = $0.00833
    c. 110 yen = $1
7. By what percent did the dollar price of a euro fall between February and August 2018 (see the News Wire "Currency Appreciation")? **LO5**
8. If an admission ticket to Disney World in Florida cost $116, what was the euro price of the ticket in (*a*) February 2018? (*b*) August 2018? (See the News Wire "Currency Appreciation.") **LO5**
9. According to the News Wire "Import Quotas," how much more are U.S. candy companies paying for sugar as a result of the import quota? **LO4**
10. **POLICY PERSPECTIVES** Using supply and demand, how would you illustrate the effect of a "Buy American" policy? **LO4**

CHAPTER SIXTEEN

Theory and Reality 理论与现实

©Comstock/Stockbyte/Getty Images

LEARNING OBJECTIVES

After reading this chapter, you should be able to:

1. Identify the major tools of macro policy.
2. Explain how macro tools can fix macro problems.
3. Depict the track record of macro outcomes.
4. Describe major impediments to policy success.
5. Discuss the pros and cons of discretionary policy.

Macroeconomic theory is supposed to explain the business cycle and show policymakers how to control it. But something is obviously wrong. Despite our relative prosperity, we have not consistently achieved the goals of full employment, price stability, and vigorous economic growth. All too often, either unemployment or inflation jumps unexpectedly or economic growth slows down. No matter how hard we try, the business cycle seems to persist.

What accounts for this gap between the promises of economic theory and the reality of economic performance? Are the theories inadequate? Or is sound economic advice being ignored? Many people blame the economists. They point to the conflicting theories and advice that economists offer and wonder what theory is supposed to be followed. If economists themselves can't agree, it is asked, why should anyone else listen to them?

Not surprisingly, economists see things a bit differently. First, they point out, the business cycle isn't as bad as it used to be. Since World War II, the economy has had many ups and downs, but none as severe as the Great Depression. In recent decades, the U.S. economy has enjoyed several long and robust economic expansions, even in the wake of recessions, terrorist attacks, and natural disasters. The recession and recovery of 2008–2010 was no exception. So the economic record contains more wins than losses.

Second, economists place most of the blame for occasional losses on the real world, not on their theories. They complain that politics takes precedence over good economic advice. Politicians are reluctant, for example, to raise taxes or cut spending to control inflation. Their concern is winning the next election, not solving the country's economic problems.

---

vigorous 强劲的。 sound 合理的。

Type of Policy	Policy Tools
Fiscal	Tax cuts and increases
	Changes in government spending
Monetary	Open market operations
	Reserve requirements
	Discount rates
Supply side	Tax incentives for investment and saving
	Deregulation
	Education and training
	Immigration
	Trade policy

Table 16.1 The Policy Tools Economic policymakers have access to a variety of policy instruments. The challenge is to choose the right tools at the right time. The mix of tools required may vary from problem to problem.

President Jimmy Carter anguished over another problem—the complexity of economic decision making. In the real world, neither theory nor politics can keep up with all our economic goals. As President Carter observed,

> We cannot concentrate just on inflation or just on unemployment or just on deficits in the federal budget or our international payments. Nor can we act in isolation from other countries. We must deal with all of these problems simultaneously and on a worldwide basis.

The purpose of this chapter is to confront these and other frustrations of the real world. In so doing, we will try to provide answers to the following questions:

- What is the ideal package of macro policies?
- How well does our macro performance live up to the promises of that package?
- What kinds of obstacles prevent us from doing better?

POLICY TOOLS 政策工具

表 16.1 总结了政策制定者可用来对抗**商业周期**和促进 GDP 增长的宏观经济工具。虽然这个列表很简短，但无需提醒我们就心知肚明：每一种工具都是强有力的。这些主要政策工具中的任何一个都能显著改变我们对基本经济问题（生产什么、如何生产以及为谁生产）的答案。

The macroeconomic tools available to policymakers for combating **business cycles** and fostering GDP growth are summarized in Table 16.1. Although this list is brief, we hardly need a reminder at this point of how powerful each instrument can be. Every one of these major policy instruments can significantly change our answers to the basic economic questions of WHAT, HOW, and FOR WHOM to produce.

Fiscal Policy 财政政策

The basic tools of **fiscal policy** are contained in the federal budget. Tax cuts are supposed to stimulate spending by putting more income in the hands of consumers and businesses. Tax increases are intended to curtail spending and thus reduce inflationary pressures. Some of the major tax changes implemented in recent years are summarized in Table 16.2.

The expenditure side of the federal budget provides another fiscal policy tool. Increases in government spending raise aggregate demand and so encourage more production. A slowdown in government spending restrains aggregate demand, lessening inflationary pressures. With federal spending approaching $4 trillion a year, changes in Uncle Sam's budget can influence aggregate demand significantly. That was the intent, of course, of President Obama's 2009 fiscal stimulus package—$787 billion of increased federal spending, income transfers, and tax cuts—and President Trump's $21 trillion 2017 tax cuts. Both initiatives were intended to give a big push to aggregate demand.

---

anguish 痛苦，苦恼。frustration 挫折。curtail 缩减。

Year	Act	Description
1981	Economic Recovery Tax Act	Three-year consumer tax cut of $213 billion plus $59 billion of business tax cuts.
1982	Tax Equity and Fiscal Responsibility Act	Raised business, excise, and income taxes by $100 billion over three years.
1985	Gramm-Rudman-Hollings Act	Required a balanced budget by 1991 and authorized automatic spending cuts.
1986	Tax Reform Act	Major reduction in tax rates coupled with broader tax base.
1990	Budget Enforcement Act	Imposed limits on discretionary spending; required PAYGO.
1993	Clinton's "New Direction"	Tax increases and spending cuts to reduce deficit, 1994–1997.
2001	Economic Growth and Tax Relief Reconciliation Act	$1.35 trillion in personal tax cuts spread over 10 years.
2003	Jobs and Growth Tax Relief Act	$350 billion tax cut, including reduced dividend and capital gains taxes.
2008	Tax rebates	$160 billion in $600 rebates and business tax cuts.
2009	American Recovery and Reinvestment Act	$787 billion package of increased spending and tax cuts.
2012	American Taxpayer Relief Act	Raised top tax rate to 39.6 percent; ended payroll tax cut.
2017	Tax Cuts and Jobs Act	Reduced corporate tax from 35 to 21 percent and reduced the top personal income tax rate from 39.6 to 37 percent.

Table 16.2 Fiscal Policy Milestones

Automatic Stabilizers 自动稳定器

Changes in the budget don't necessarily originate in presidential decisions or congressional legislation. Tax revenues and government outlays also respond to economic events. ***When the economy slows, tax revenues decline, and government spending increases automatically.*** The 2008–2009 recession, for example, displaced 8 million workers and reduced the incomes of millions more. As their incomes fell, so did their tax liabilities. As a consequence, government tax revenues fell.

The recession also caused government spending to *rise*. The swollen ranks of unemployed workers increased outlays for unemployment insurance benefits, welfare, food stamps, and other transfer payments. None of this budget activity required new legislation. Instead the benefits were increased *automatically* under laws already written. No *new* policy was required.

These recession-induced changes in tax receipts and budget outlays are referred to as **automatic stabilizers**. Such budget changes help stabilize the economy by increasing after-tax incomes and spending when the economy slows. Specifically, *recessions automatically*

- *Reduce tax revenues.*
- *Increase government outlays.*
- *Widen budget deficits.*

这些由经济衰退引发的税收收入和预算支出的变化被称为**自动稳定器**。在经济增长缓慢时通过增加税后收入和政府支出，这些预算变化有助于经济的稳定。具体说来，经济衰退会自动
- 减少税收收入。
- 增加政府支出。
- 加大预算赤字。

swollen 上涨的。

Economic expansions have the opposite effect on government budgets. When the economy booms, people have to pay more taxes on their rising incomes. They also have less need for government assistance. Hence tax receipts rise and government spending drops automatically when the economy heats up. These changes tend to shrink the budget deficit. This is exactly the kind of automatic deficit reduction that occurred in the late 1990s. While President Clinton and congressional Republicans were squabbling about how to reduce the federal deficit, the economy kept growing. Indeed, it grew so fast that the budget *deficit* turned into a budget *surplus* in 1998. Soon thereafter both the Democrats and the Republicans claimed credit for that turn of events.

Discretionary Policy 相机抉择的政策

To assess political claims for deficit reduction, we need to distinguish *automatic* changes in the budget from *policy-induced* changes. Automatic changes in taxes and spending do not reflect current fiscal policy decisions; they reflect laws already on the books. Discretionary fiscal policy entails only *new* tax and spending decisions. Specifically, **fiscal policy refers to deliberate changes in tax or spending legislation.** These changes can be made only by the U.S. Congress. Every year the president proposes specific budget and tax changes, negotiates with Congress, and then accepts or vetoes specific acts that Congress has passed. The resulting policy decisions represent discretionary fiscal policy. Policymakers deserve credit (or blame) only for the effects of the discretionary policy decisions they make (or fail to make).

The distinction between automatic stabilizers and discretionary spending helps explain why the federal budget deficit soared from $459 billion in **fiscal year (FY)** 2008 to over $1.4 trillion in 2009. President Obama blamed that trillion-dollar jump in the deficit on the 2008–2009 recession—that is, the automatic stabilizers. His critics blamed Obama's enormous spending plans—that is, policy decisions. The Congressional Budget Office studied the situation and concluded that only a quarter of the trillion-dollar deficit increase was caused by the recession, as Figure 16.1 illustrates. The remaining three-quarters was due to the federal government's fiscal policy.

The same kind of dual causes operate on *shrinking* deficits. When the economy started to recover from the Great Recession, the government's budget deficit shrank. Between 2011 and 2012, for example, the deficit shrank by approximately $200 billion. About a third of this deficit reduction was due to the growing economy, which reduced unemployment and welfare payments and increased tax revenues.

Monetary Policy 货币政策

The policy arsenal described in Table 16.1 also contains monetary tools. The tools of **monetary policy** include open market operations, discount rate changes, and reserve requirements. The Federal Reserve uses these tools to change the **money supply**. In so doing, the Fed strives to change interest rates and shift the aggregate demand curve in the desired direction.

The effectiveness of both fiscal policy and monetary policy depends on the shape of the aggregate supply (AS) curve. If the AS curve is horizontal, changes in the money supply (and related aggregate demand shifts) affect output only. If the AS curve is vertical, money supply changes will affect prices only. In the typical case of an upward-sloping AS curve, changes in the money supply affect both prices and output (review Figure 14.7).

Rules versus Discretion 固定规则与相机抉择

Disagreements about the actual shape of the AS curve raise questions about how to conduct monetary policy. As discussed in Chapter 13, some economists urge the Fed to play an active role in adjusting the money supply to changing economic conditions. Others suggest that we would be better served by fixed rules for money supply growth. Fixed rules would make the Fed more of a passive mechanic, as opposed to an active policymaker.

---

squabble 争论。

There are clear risks of error in discretionary policy. In 1979 and again in 1989, the Fed pursued restrictive policies that pushed the economy into recessions. In both cases, the Fed had to reverse its policies. (In Table 16.3, compare October 1982 to October 1979 and the year 1991 to 1989.) In 1999–2000 the Fed again raised interest rates substantially, in six separate steps. When the economy slowed abruptly at the end of 2000, critics said the Fed had again stepped too hard on the monetary brake. The Fed was forced to reverse course again in 2001.

Critics say the stimulative monetary policy (low interest rates) after 2001 fueled the rapid rise in home prices that proved to be excessive. When the Fed later started exercising some monetary restraint, the housing bubble burst, pushing the economy into the 2008–2009 recession.

Critics charge that these repeated U-turns in monetary policy have *destabilized* the economy rather than stabilizing it. They contend that strict rules for money management would be better than Fed discretion. It certainly looks that way at times, especially in hindsight. But fixed rules might not work better. The September 11 terrorist attacks and a subsequent plunge in consumer confidence forced the Fed to respond quickly and with more forcefulness than fixed policy rules would have permitted.

The September 2008 credit crisis required even more discretionary intervention. The Fed had to act quickly and boldly—more quickly than fixed rules would permit—to pump reserves into the banking system. Without such dramatic discretionary action by the Fed, the credit crisis could have brought the economy to a complete standstill.

批评人士指责货币政策中反复的 U 形大转弯不但没有稳定经济，反而破坏了经济的稳定。他们认为，严格的货币管理规则优于美联储的相机抉择。有时确实如此，尤其是事后来看。然而，固定规则也许不能有效实行。"9·11"恐怖袭击和随后的消费者信心大幅下降，迫使美联储不得不快速作出反应，其力度超出了固定政策规则所允许的范围。

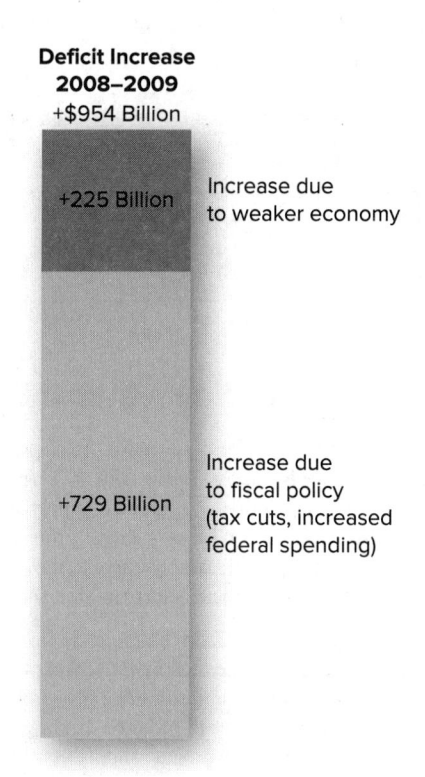

Deficit Increase 2008–2009
+$954 Billion

+225 Billion — Increase due to weaker economy

+729 Billion — Increase due to fiscal policy (tax cuts, increased federal spending)

FIGURE 16.1 Cyclical vs. Policy Effects on Deficits The budget deficit is affected by both deliberate fiscal policy and cyclical changes in the economy. A recession, combined with a huge fiscal stimulus, caused the deficit to soar in 2008–2009. ■

Source: Congressional Budget Office.

October 1979	Fed adopts monetarist approach, tightening money supply; interest rates soar.
October 1982	Fed abandons pure monetarist approach and expands money supply rapidly.
May 1987	Fed abandons money supply targets as policy guides.
June 1987	Alan Greenspan appointed chairman; money supply growth decreases; discount rate increased.
1989	Greenspan announces goal of zero inflation, slows money supply growth.
1991	In midst of recession Fed reverses monetary policy; interest rates fall to their lowest level in decades.
1994	As growth accelerates and unemployment dips, Fed raises interest rates substantially.
1995	Fed reduces interest rates slightly when economy stalls in first quarter.
1997	When unemployment rate drops below 5 percent, Fed nudges interest rates higher.
1998	Fed cuts interest rates to offset shock of Asian crisis.
1999–2000	Fed increases interest rates six times in one year.
2001–2003	Fed reverses policy, cuts interest rates; continues cutting interest rates repeatedly until mid-2003.
2004–2006	Fearing inflationary pressures, the Fed raises interest rates 17 times.
2006	Alan Greenspan retires; Ben Bernanke becomes Fed chairman.
2008–2009	Battling recession, Fed cuts interest rates sharply and repeatedly.
2010–2014	Fed engages in "quantitative easing" (QE), buying huge quantities of bonds and mortgage-backed securities.
February 2014	Janet Yellen becomes Fed chair, nudges interest rates higher in 2016–2017.
February 2018	Jerome Powell becomes Fed chair, accelerates interest rate hikes, and continues selling QE bonds.

Table 16.3 Monetary Policy Milestones

Supply-Side Policy 供给学派的政策

供给学派理论为我们提供了第三类重要的政策工具。我们已经看到，总供给曲线的形状如何限制财政政策和货币政策的有效性（图 13.7）。总供给曲线的移动也是经济增长的一个先决条件。**供给学派政策**直接关注这些约束条件。供给学派政策的目标是使总供给曲线向右移动。这种移动不但能促进长期的增长，而且还使短期需求方面的干预更成功。

Supply-side theory offers the third major set of policy tools. We have seen how *the shape of the aggregate supply curve limits the effectiveness of fiscal and monetary policies* (see Figure 13.7). Shifts of the aggregate supply curve are also a prerequisite for economic growth. **Supply-side policy** focuses directly on these constraints. The goal of supply-side policy is to shift the aggregate supply curve to the right. Such rightward shifts not only promote long-term growth, but also make short-run demand-side intervention more successful.

The supply-side toolbox is filled with tools. Tax cuts designed to stimulate work effort, saving, and investment are among the most popular and powerful supply-side tools. Deregulation may also reduce production costs and stimulate investment. Expenditure on education, training, and research expands our capacity to produce. Immigration policy alters the size and skills of the labor force and thus affects aggregate supply as well.

In the 1980s tax rates were reduced dramatically. The maximum marginal tax rate on individuals was cut from 70 percent to 50 percent in 1981, and then still further, to 28 percent, in 1987. The 1980s also witnessed major milestones in the deregulation of airlines, trucking, telephone service, and other industries (see Table 16.4). All of these policies helped shift the AS curve rightward.

---

milestone 里程碑。

1978	Airline Deregulation Act	Phased out federal regulations of airline routes, fares, and entry.
1980	Motor Carrier Act	Eliminated federal restrictions on entry, routes, and fares in the trucking industry.
1981	Economic Recovery Tax Act	Decreased marginal tax rates by 30 percent.
1986	Tax Reform Act	Eliminated most tax preferences for investment and saving but sharply reduced marginal tax rates.
1990	Social Security Act amendments	Increased payroll tax to 7.65 percent.
1990	Americans with Disabilities Act	Required employers to provide more universal access.
1990	Clean Air Act	Toughened pollution standards.
1993	Family Leave Act	Required employers to offer unpaid leave.
1994	NAFTA	Lowered North American trade barriers.
2001	Economic Growth and Tax Relief Reconciliation Act	Reduced marginal tax rates over 10 years.
2002	Job Creation and Worker Assistance Act	Provided business tax cuts and incentives.
2003	Jobs and Growth Tax Relief Act	Reduced taxes on dividends and capital gains.
2007–2009	Minimum wage	Increased minimum wage from $5.15 to $7.25 per hour.
2009	American Recovery and Reinvestment Act	Sharply increased infrastructure and energy development.
2010	Dodd-Frank Act	Increased regulation of banks.
2010	Affordable Care Act	Raised taxes and payroll costs to pay for expanded health care.
2012	American Taxpayer Relief Act	Raised tax rates on high incomes and investment income.
2017	Tax Cuts and Jobs Act	Reduced corporate tax rate and increased investment incentives.

Table 16.4 Supply-Side Milestones

Government policies can also shift the AS curve leftward. When the minimum wage jumped to $7.25 an hour in 2009, the cost of supplying goods and services went up. A 1990 increase in the payroll tax boosted production costs as well. In the early 1990s, private employers also incurred higher labor costs associated with government-mandated benefits (Family Leave Act of 1993) and accommodations for handicapped workers (Americans with Disabilities Act). In 2013 marginal tax rates were increased for wealthy individuals and many small businesses. All of these policies restrained aggregate supply.

Even welfare reform has supply-side implications. The 1996 Personal Responsibility and Work Opportunity Act established time limits for welfare dependence. When those limits were reached in 1998–1999, more welfare recipients had to enter the labor market. When they did, aggregate supply shifted rightward. The extension of unemployment benefits in 2009–2011 had the opposite effect.

甚至福利改革也与供给学派有关。1996年的《个人责任和工作机会法案》确立了福利依赖的时间限制。当在1998—1999年达到这些时限时，更多的福利接受者不得不进入劳动力市场。当他们进入劳动力市场时，总供给曲线就向右移动了。2009—2011年间延长失业救济金的发放却产生了相反的效果。

---

handicapped 残疾的，有生理缺陷的。

Because tax rates are a basic tool of supply-side policy, fiscal and supply-side policies are often intertwined. When Congress changes the tax laws, it almost always alters marginal tax rates and thus changes production incentives. Notice, for example, that tax legislation appears in Table 16.4 as well as in Table 16.2. The Tax Cuts and Jobs Act of 2017 not only changed total tax revenues (fiscal policy), but also restructured production and investment incentives (supply-side policy).

IDEALIZED USES 理想化的应用

These fiscal, monetary, and supply-side tools are potentially powerful levers for controlling the economy. In principle, they can cure the excesses of the business cycle. To see how, let us review their use in three distinct macroeconomic settings.

Case 1: Recession 情形 1：衰退

当产出和就业水平远远低于充分就业的潜力时，对公共政策的要求就很明确了。GDP 缺口必须弥补。总支出必须增加，这样生产者才能销售更多的商品，雇用更多的工人，并提高经济的生产能力。此时，最迫切的要求是让更多的人重返工作岗位。

When output and employment levels fall far short of the economy's full-employment potential, the mandate for public policy is clear. The **GDP gap** must be closed. Total spending must be increased so that producers can sell more goods, hire more workers, and move the economy toward its productive capacity. At such times the most urgent need is to get people back to work.

How can a recession be ended? Keynesians emphasize the need to stimulate aggregate demand. They seek to shift the aggregate demand curve rightward by cutting taxes or boosting government spending. The resulting stimulus will set off a **multiplier** reaction, propelling the economy to full employment.

Modern Keynesians acknowledge that monetary policy might also help. Specifically, increases in the money supply may lower interest rates and give investment spending a further boost. To give the economy a really powerful stimulus, we might want to do everything at the same time—that is, cut taxes, increase government spending, and expand the money supply simultaneously (as in 2001–2003 and again in 2008–2009). By taking such convincing action, we might also increase consumer confidence, raise investor expectations, and induce still greater spending and output.

Other economists offer different advice. So-called monetarists and other critics of government intervention see no point in these discretionary policies. As they see it, the aggregate supply curve is vertical at the natural rate of unemployment (see Figure 14.7). Quick fixes of monetary or fiscal policy may shift the aggregate demand curve but won't change the aggregate supply curve. Monetary or fiscal stimulus will only push the price level up (more inflation) without reducing unemployment. In this view, the appropriate policy response to a recession is patience. As sales and output slow, interest rates will decline, and new investment will be stimulated.

Supply-siders confront these objections head-on. In their view, policy initiatives should focus on changing the shape and position of the aggregate supply curve. Supply-siders emphasize the need to improve production incentives. They urge cuts in marginal tax rates on investment and labor. They also look for ways to reduce government regulation.

Case 2: Inflation 情形 2：通货膨胀

经济过热也要求类似的政策处方。在这种情形下，直接目标是抑制总需求，也就是说，使总需求曲线向左移动。凯恩斯主义者将通过增加税收、减少政府支出，利用乘数效应使经济降温，从而抑制总需求。

An overheated economy elicits a similar assortment of policy prescriptions. In this case the immediate goal is to restrain aggregate demand—that is, shift the aggregate demand curve to the left. Keynesians would do this by raising taxes and cutting government spending, relying on the multiplier to cool down the economy.

The monetary policy response to inflation would be a hike in interest rates. By making credit more expensive, the Fed would discourage some investment and consumption, shifting the AD curve leftward. Pure monetarists would simply cut the money supply, expecting the same outcome. The Fed might even seek to squeeze AD extra hard just to convince market participants that the inflation dragon was really slain.

---

set off 引发。multiplier reaction 乘数效应。head-on 正面地。

Supply-siders would point out that inflation implies both too much money and not enough goods. They would look at the supply side of the market for ways to expand productive capacity. In a highly inflationary setting, they would propose more incentives to save. The additional savings would automatically reduce consumption while creating a larger pool of investable funds. Supply-siders would also cut taxes and regulations, encourage more immigration, and lower import barriers that keep out cheaper foreign goods.

Case 3: Stagflation 情形 3：滞胀

Although serious inflations and recessions provide reasonably clear options for economic policy, there is a vast gray area between these extremes. Occasionally the economy suffers from both inflation and unemployment at the same time—a condition called **stagflation**. In 1975, for example, the unemployment rate (8.5 percent) and the inflation rate (9.1 percent) were both far too high. With an upward-sloping aggregate supply curve, there is no easy way to bring both rates down at the same time. Any demand-side stimulus to attain full employment worsens inflation. Likewise, restrictive demand policies increase unemployment. Although any upward-sloping AS curve poses such a trade-off, the position of the curve also determines how difficult the choices are. Figure 16.2 illustrates this stagflation problem.

There are no simple solutions for stagflation. Any demand-side initiatives must be designed with care, seeking to balance the competing threats of inflation and unemployment. This requires more attention to the specific nature of the supply constraints. Perhaps the early rise in the AS curve is due to **structural unemployment**. Prices may be rising in the auto industry, for example, while unemployed workers are abundant in the housing industry. The higher prices and wages in the auto industry function as a signal to transfer resources from the construction industry into autos. Such resource shifts, however, may not occur smoothly or quickly. In the interim, public policy can be developed to facilitate interindustry mobility or to alter the structure of supply or demand.

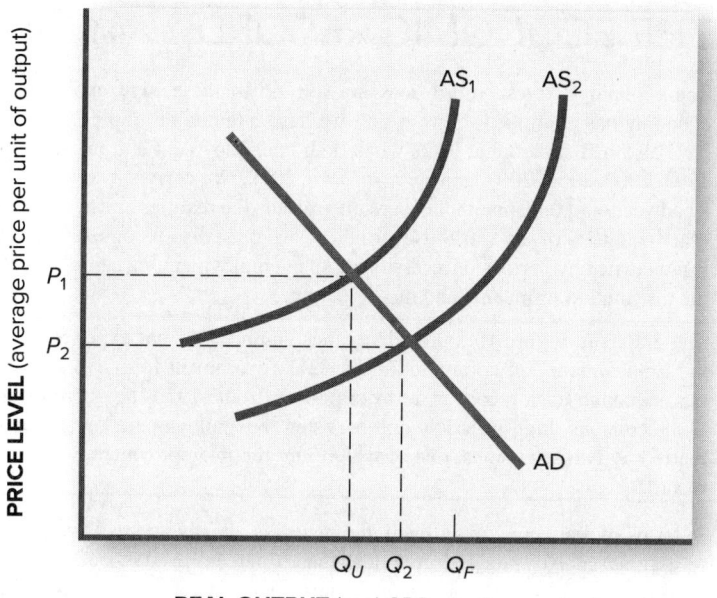

尽管严重的通货膨胀和衰退为经济政策提供了相当清晰的选择，但是，这两个极端之间还存在着巨大的灰色地带。有时，经济会同时受到通货膨胀和失业的冲击——这种情形就是所谓的**滞胀**。例如，1975 年的失业率（8.5%）和通货膨胀率（9.1%）都是很高的。由于总供给曲线向上倾斜，所以没有一个简单的方法让两者同时降低。任何以充分就业为目标的需求方面的刺激都会加剧通货膨胀，而限制需求的政策则会加剧失业。尽管任一向上倾斜的总供给曲线都会带来这种权衡，但是，曲线的位置也决定了选择的难易程度。图 16.2 说明了这种滞胀问题。

滞胀没有简单的解决办法。任何需求方面的刺激都应谨慎实施，力求平衡通货膨胀和失业的双重威胁。这就需要更多地注意供给约束的具体性质。也许，总供给曲线的早期上升是由**结构性失业**引起的。例如，当房地产业出现大量失业工人时，汽车产业的价格却在上涨。汽车产业较高的价格和工资就是资源由建筑业转移到汽车产业的信号。但是，这种资源转移可能不会平稳或迅速发生。在此期间，就需要制定公共政策来推动产业间的转移，或者改变供给或需求的结构。

Figure 16.2 Stagflation Both unemployment and inflation may occur at the same time. This is always a potential problem with an upward-sloping AS curve. The farther the AS curve is to the left, the worse the stagflation problem is likely to be. The curve AS_1 implies higher prices and more unemployment than AS_2 for any given level of aggregate demand. ∎

On the demand side, the government could reduce the demand for new cars by increasing interest rates. The government could also cut back on its fleet purchases. It could increase the demand for construction workers by offering larger tax deductions for new home purchases. On the supply side, the government could offer tax credits or skill classes, teach construction workers how to build cars, or speed up the job search process.

High tax rates or costly regulations might also contribute to stagflation. If either of these constraints exists, high prices (inflation) may not be a sufficient incentive for increased output. In this case, reductions in tax rates and regulation could shift the AS curve rightward, easing stagflation pressures.

Stagflation may have arisen from a temporary contraction (leftward shift) of aggregate supply that both reduces output and drives up prices. In this case, neither structural unemployment nor excessive demand is the culprit. Rather, an external shock (such as a natural disaster) or an abrupt change in world trade (such as higher oil prices) is the cause of stagflation. The high oil prices and supply disruptions caused by Hurricanes Katrina (2005) and Harvey (2017) illustrate this problem. In such circumstances, conventional policy tools are unlikely to provide a complete cure. In most cases the economy simply has to adjust to a temporary setback.

Fine-Tuning 微调

Everything looks easy on the blackboard. Indeed, economic theory seems to have all the answers for our macro problems. Some people even imagine that economic theory has the potential to fine-tune the economy—that is, to correct any and all macro problems that arise. Such **fine-tuning** would entail continual adjustments to policy levers. When unemployment is the problem, simply give the economy a jolt of fiscal or monetary stimulus; when inflation is worrisome, simply tap on the fiscal or monetary brakes. To fulfill our goals for content and distribution, we simply pick the right target for stimulus or restraint. With a little attention and experience, the right speed could be found and the economy guided successfully down the road to prosperity.

THE ECONOMIC RECORD 经济记录

The economy's track record does not live up to these high expectations. To be sure, the economy has continued to grow, and we have attained an impressive standard of living. We have also had some great years when both unemployment and inflation rates were low, as in 1994–2000, 2004–2007, and again in 2016–2018. Nor can we lose sight of the fact that even in a bad year our per capita income greatly exceeds the realities and even the expectations in most other countries of the world. Nevertheless, we must also recognize that our economic history is punctuated by periods of recession, high unemployment, inflation, and recurring concern for the distribution of income and mix of output.

The graphs in Figure 16.3 provide a quick summary of our experiences since 1946, the year the Employment Act committed the federal government to macro stability. It is evident that our economic track record is far from perfect. In the 1970s the record was particularly bleak: two recessions, high inflation, and persistent unemployment. The 1980s were better but still marred by two recessions, one of which sent the unemployment rate to a post–World War II record.

In terms of real economic growth, the record is equally spotty. Output actually declined (i.e., recessions) in 10 years and grew less than 3 percent in another 25. The Great Recession of 2008–2009 caused the largest annual contraction of GDP (−2.5 percent) in over 50 years.

The economic performance of the United States is similar to that of other Western nations. The economies of most developed countries did not grow as fast as the U.S. economy from 2000 to 2017. But as the accompanying News Wire "Comparative Performance" shows, some countries did a better job of restraining prices. And China registered spectacular growth rates.

---

culprit（造成问题或麻烦的）原因。conventional 传统的，常规的。spotty 时好时坏。

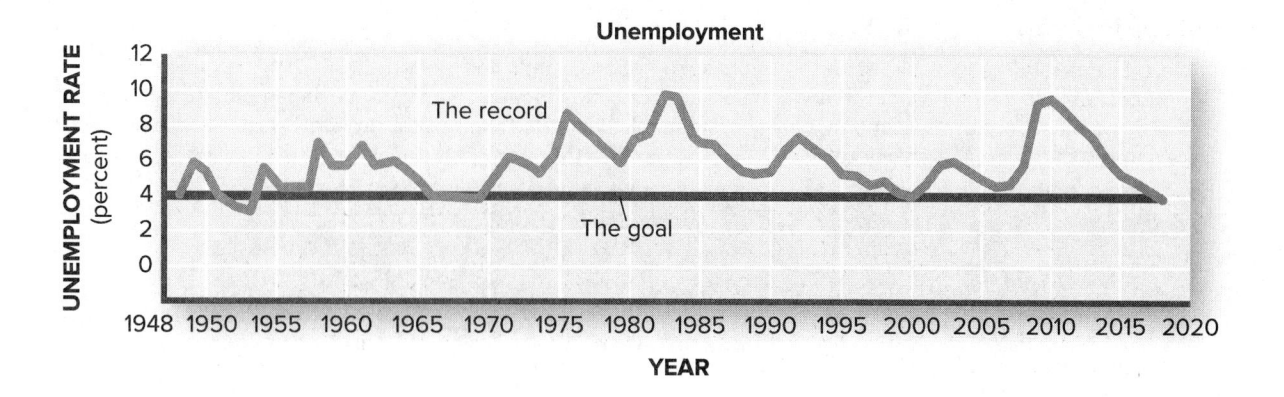

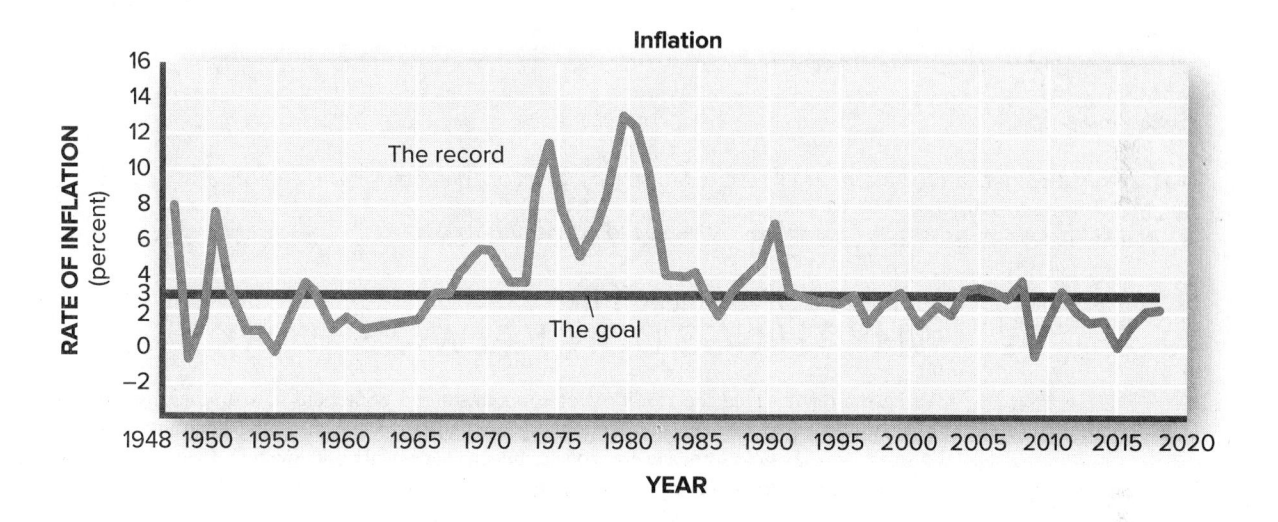

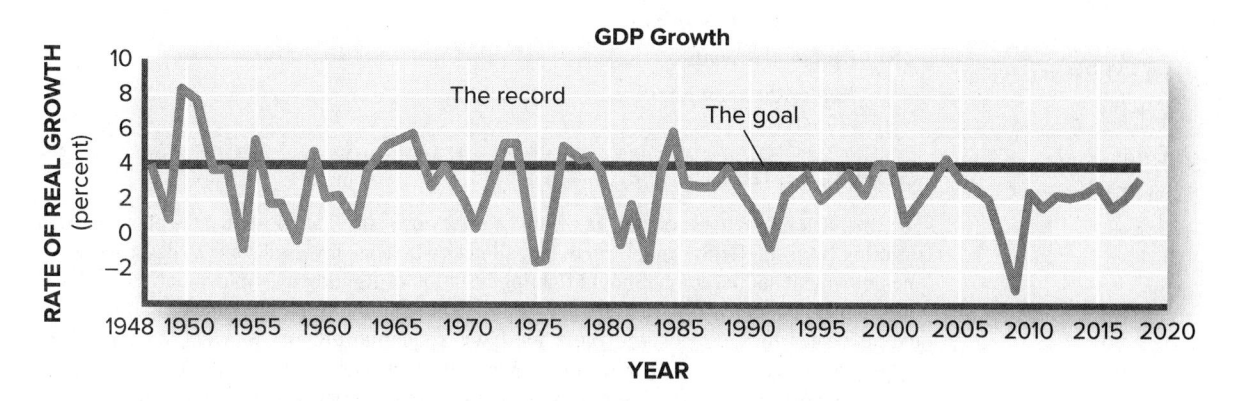

Figure 16.3 The Economic Record The Full Employment and Balanced Growth Act of 1978 established specific goals for unemployment (4 percent), inflation (3 percent), and economic growth (4 percent). We have rarely attained all those goals, however, as these graphs illustrate. Measurement, design, and policy implementation problems help explain these shortcomings.

Source: U.S. Commerce and Labor Departments.

NEWS WIRE COMPARATIVE PERFORMANCE

Macro Performance, 2000–2017

The U.S. economy grew a bit faster than European nations during the period 2000–2017; however, U.S. economic growth was far slower in comparison to economies in Mexico and China. Japan did a great job restraining inflation, but its economy barely grew at all. China had the fastest growth. Macro outcomes are a mixed bag almost everywhere.

Performance (Annual Average Percentage)	United States	Japan	Germany	United Kingdom	France	Canada	Mexico	China
Real growth	1.7	0.7	1.2	1.5	1.1	1.9	2.1	9.7
Inflation	1.7	0.2	1.3	2.4	1.4	1.6	4.1	2.6
Unemployment	6.1	4.3	7.3	5.8	9.0	6.2	3.8	4.4

Source: World Bank.

NOTE: No nation gets a gold medal in all macro dimensions. Inflation, unemployment, and growth records reveal uneven performance.
注：没有哪个国家能在所有宏观表现上都拿到金牌。通货膨胀、失业和经济增长记录揭示了实际经济表现的不均衡。

为什么办法并不总能起作用
WHY THINGS DON'T ALWAYS WORK

我们已经注意到，对于我们的经济目标和经济表现之间持续存在的差距，经济学家和政治家们总是互相指责。但是，不是偏袒哪一方，我们可能会注意到成功决策的一些普遍制约因素。在这方面，我们能够识别影响政策成功的四个障碍：

- 目标冲突
- 衡量问题
- 设计问题
- 实施问题

We have already noted the readiness of economists and politicians to blame each other for the continuing gap between our economic goals and performance. Rather than taking sides, however, we may note some general constraints on successful policymaking. In this regard, we can distinguish *four obstacles to policy success:*

- *Goal conflicts.*
- *Measurement problems.*
- *Design problems.*
- *Implementation problems.*

Goal Conflicts   目标冲突

The first factor to note is potential conflicts in policy priorities. Suppose that the economy was suffering from stagflation and, further, that all macro policies involved some trade-off between unemployment and inflation. Should fighting inflation or fighting unemployment get priority? Unemployed people will put the highest priority on attaining full employment. Labor unions and advocates for the poor will press for faster economic growth. Bankers, creditors, and people on fixed incomes will worry more about inflation. They will lobby for more restrictive fiscal and monetary policies. There is no way to satisfy everyone in such a situation.

In practice, these goal conflicts are often institutionalized in the decision-making process. The Fed is traditionally viewed as the guardian of price stability and tends to favor policy restraint. The president and Congress worry more about people's jobs and government programs, so they lean toward policy stimulus. The end result may entail a mix of contradictory policies.

---

guardian 守卫者，保护者。

Distributional goals may also conflict with macro objectives. Anti-inflationary policies may require cutbacks in programs for the poor, the elderly, or needy students. These cutbacks may be politically impossible. Likewise, tight money policies may be viewed as too great a burden for small businesses.

Although the policy levers listed in Table 16.1 are powerful, they cannot grant all our wishes. Since we still live in a world of scarce resources, **all policy decisions entail opportunity costs.** This means that we will always be confronted with trade-offs: The best we can hope for is a set of compromises that yields *optimal* outcomes, not ideal ones.

Even if we all agreed on policy priorities, success would not be assured. We would still have to confront the more mundane problems of measurement, design, and implementation.

Measurement Problems 衡量问题

One reason firefighters are pretty successful in putting out fires before whole cities burn down is that fires are highly visible phenomena. Economic problems are rarely so visible. An increase in the unemployment rate from 5 percent to 6 percent, for example, is not the kind of thing you notice while crossing the street. Unless you lose your own job, the increase in unemployment is not likely to attract your attention. The same is true of prices; small increases in product prices are unlikely to ring many alarms. Hence both inflation and unemployment may worsen considerably before anyone takes serious notice. Were we as slow and ill equipped to notice fires, whole neighborhoods would burn before someone rang the alarm.

To formulate good economic policy, we must be able to see the scope of our economic problems. To do so, we must measure employment changes, output changes, price changes, and other macro outcomes. Although the government spends vast sums of money to collect and process such data, the available information is always dated and incomplete. ***At best, we know what was happening in the economy last month or last week.*** The processes of data collection, assembly, and presentation take time, even in this age of high-speed computers. The average recession lasts about 11 months, but official data generally do not even confirm the existence of a recession until 8 months after a downturn starts! The recession of 2008–2009 was no exception, as the accompanying News Wire "Measurement Problems" shows. Notice that it took an entire year before the onset of that recession was officially recognized.

尽管表 16.1 列出的政策杠杆很强大，但是它们不能满足我们所有的愿望。由于我们仍然生活在资源稀缺的世界里，所以所有的政策决策都要承担机会成本。这就意味着我们将始终面临权衡问题：我们能够期望的是达成一系列的妥协以取得最佳结果，而不是理想结果。

要制定好的经济政策，我们必须首先确定经济问题的范围。为此，我们就必须衡量就业变化、产出变化、价格变化和其他宏观结果。尽管政府花了大量资金来收集和处理这些数据，然而可利用的信息总是过时的、不完整的。我们充其量是知道上个月或者上个星期经济发生了什么问题。即使是在这个拥有高速计算机的时代，数据收集、汇编和展示的过程也需要时间。经济衰退平均持续约 11 个月，但是官方的数据要到衰退开始 8 个月后才能确认衰退的存在！正如后文的新闻摘要表明的，2008—2009 年的经济衰退也不例外。我们注意到，直到发生了一整年后衰退才得到正式确认。

NEWS WIRE MEASUREMENT PROBLEMS

One Year Later, NBER Acknowledges Start of Recession

Cambridge, MA—The National Bureau of Economic Research (NBER) is the official scorekeeper of when recessions begin and end. Just today they announced that the peak of recent economic activity occurred a year ago, in December 2007. The peak refers to the end of an economic expansion and therewith the beginning of a recession. Economists use the term "recession" to refer to a significant decline in economic activity that lasts for at least several months and causes visible declines in production and employment. The NBER chose not to label last year's slowdown as a recession until it had more evidence of production cutbacks.

Source: "Business Cycle Dating Committee," National Bureau of Economic Research, December 1, 2008.

NOTE: Successful macro policy requires timely and accurate data on the economy. The measurement process is slow and imperfect, however.

注：成功的宏观经济政策需要及时、精确的经济数据。然而衡量过程却是缓慢的、有缺陷的。

Forecasts 预测

In an ideal world, policymakers would not only respond to economic problems that occur, but also *anticipate* their occurrence and act to avoid them. If we foresee an inflation emerging, for example, we want to take immediate action to restrain aggregate demand. That is to say, the successful firefighter not only responds to fires but also looks for hazards that might start one.

---

needy 贫困的。mundane 普通的。

Unfortunately, economic policymakers are again at a disadvantage. Their knowledge of future problems is even worse than their knowledge of current problems. ***In designing policy, policymakers must depend on economic forecasts***—informed guesses about what the economy will look like in future periods.

Macro Models

Those guesses are often based on complex computer models of how the economy works. These models—referred to as *econometric macro models*—are mathematical summaries of the economy's performance. The models try to identify the key determinants of macro performance and then show what happens to macro outcomes when they change.

An economist feeds the computer two essential inputs. One is a model of how the economy allegedly works. Such models are quantitative summaries of one or more macro theories. A Keynesian model, for example, will include equations that show multiplier spending responses to tax cuts. A monetarist model will show that tax cuts raise interest rates (crowding out), not total spending. And a supply-side model stipulates labor supply and production responses. The computer can't tell which theory is right; it just predicts what it is programmed to see. In other words, the computer sees the world through the eyes of its economic master.

The second essential input in a computer forecast is the assumed values for critical economic variables. A Keynesian model, for example, must specify how large a multiplier to expect. All the computer does is carry out the required mathematical routines once it is told that the multiplier is relevant and what its value is. It cannot discern the true multiplier any better than it can pick the right theory.

Given the dependence of computers on the theories and perceptions of their economic masters, it is not surprising that computer forecasts often differ greatly. It's also not surprising that they are often wrong.

Even policymakers who are familiar with both economic theory and computer models can make bad calls. In January 1990 Fed chairman Alan Greenspan assured Congress that the risk of a recession was as low as 20 percent. Although he said he "wouldn't bet the ranch" on such a low probability, he was confident that the odds of a recession were below 50 percent. Five months after his testimony, the 1990–1991 recession began.

Martin Baily, chairman of President Clinton's Council of Economic Advisers, made the same mistake in January 2001. "Let me be clear," he told the press, "we don't think that we're going into recession." President Clinton echoed this optimism, projecting growth of 2–3 percent in 2001. Two months later the U.S. economy fell into another recession.

President Obama made a similarly bad forecast. In January 2009 he predicted that his $787 billion fiscal stimulus would create so many jobs that the national unemployment rate, then at 7.7 percent, would not rise above 8 percent and would fall to 5 percent by 2012. In fact, the unemployment rate jumped to 10 percent in 2009 and was still at 7.8 percent at the beginning of 2013.

Design Problems

Forget all these bad forecasts for a moment and just pretend that we can somehow foresee where the economy is headed. The outlook, let us suppose, is bad. Now we are in the driver's seat, trying to steer the economy past looming dangers. What action should we take?

Suppose we adopt a Keynesian approach to fighting recession. Specifically, we cut income taxes to stimulate consumer spending. How do we know that consumers will respond as anticipated? Perhaps the marginal propensity to consume has changed. Maybe the level of consumer confidence has dropped. Any of these changes could frustrate even the best-intentioned policy, as Japanese policymakers learned in 1998–1999. Japanese consumers *saved* their tax cuts rather than *spending* them, nullifying the intended policy stimulus. Who would have foreseen such a response?

---

ranch 大农场，大牧场。

Implementation Problems 实施问题

Suppose our crystal ball foresees all these problems, allowing us to design a "perfect" policy package. How will we implement the package? To understand fully why things go wrong, we must also consider the difficulties of implementing a well-designed (and credible) policy initiative.

Congressional Deliberations 国会方面的考虑

Suppose the president and his Council of Economic Advisers (perhaps in conjunction with the secretary of the Treasury and the director of the Office of Management and Budget) correctly foresee that aggregate demand is slowing. A tax cut, they believe, is necessary to stimulate demand for goods and services. Can they simply cut tax rates? No, because all tax changes must be legislated by Congress. Once the president decides on the appropriate policy initiative, he must ask Congress for authority to take the required action. This means a delay in implementing policy, and possibly no policy at all.

At the very least, the president must convince Congress of the desirability of his suggested action. The tax proposal must work its way through separate committees of both the House of Representatives and the Senate, get on the congressional calendar, and be approved in each chamber. If there are important differences in Senate and House versions of the tax cut legislation, they must be compromised in a joint conference. The modified proposal must then be returned to each chamber for approval.

至少，总统必须要让国会相信他所建议的行动是可取的。税收提案必须经过如下几个步骤：经众议院和参议院各自的委员会同意，进入国会议程，然后在每个议院获得批准。如果两院对税收减免法案意见有重大分歧，他们必须在联合会议上协商。之后修改的建议还必须返回每个议院获得批准。

The same kind of process applies to the outlay side of the budget. Once the president has submitted his budget proposals (in January), Congress reviews them and then sets its own spending goals. After that the budget is broken down into 13 different categories, and a separate appropriations bill is written for each one. These bills spell out in detail how much can be spent and for what purposes. Once Congress passes them, they go to the president for acceptance or veto.

In theory, all of these budget deliberations are to be completed in nine months. Budget legislation requires Congress to finish the process by October 1 (the beginning of the federal fiscal year). Congress rarely meets this deadline, however. In most years the budget debate continues well into the fiscal year. In some years, the budget debate is not resolved until the fiscal year is nearly over! The final budget legislation is typically over 1,000 pages long and so complex that few people understand all its dimensions.

This description of congressional activity is not an outline for a civics course; rather, it explains why economic policy is not fully effective. ***Even if the right policy is formulated to solve an emerging economic problem, there is no assurance that it will be implemented. And if it is implemented, there is no assurance that it will take effect at the right time.*** One of the most frightening prospects for economic policy is that a policy design intended to serve a specific problem will be implemented much later, when economic conditions have changed. The policy's effect on the economy may then be the opposite of what was intended.

Figure 16.4 is a schematic view of why things don't always work out as well as economic theory suggests they might. There are always delays between the time a problem emerges and the time it is recognized. There are additional delays between recognition and response design, between design and implementation, and finally between implementation and impact. Not only may mistakes be made at each juncture, but even correct decisions may be overcome by changing economic conditions.

这种对国会活动的描述不是对公民学课程的概括，而是解释了为什么经济政策不是完全有效的。即使一项正确的政策明确阐述了如何解决出现的经济问题，也不能保证该项政策能得以实施。即使政策实施了，也同样不能确保它会在恰当的时机发挥作用。经济政策最可怕的前景之一是：原本打算解决某个特定问题的政策方案将延期实施，而实施时的经济状况已发生了变化。因此，该项政策对经济起到了适得其反的效果。

Politics versus Economics 政治与经济

Last but not least, we must confront the politics of economic policy. Tax hikes and budget cuts rarely win votes. On the other hand, tax cuts and pork-barrel spending are always popular. Accordingly, savvy politicians tend to stimulate the economy before elections, then tighten the fiscal restraints afterward. This creates a kind of *political* business cycle—a two-year pattern of short-run stops and starts. The conflict between the urgent need to get reelected and the necessity to manage the economy results in a seesaw kind of instability.

---

crystal ball（占卜用的）水晶球，预言未来的方法。submit 递交，提交。appropriation 拨款。schematic 图解的，概要的。savvy 精明的，聪慧的。seesaw 跷跷板似的。

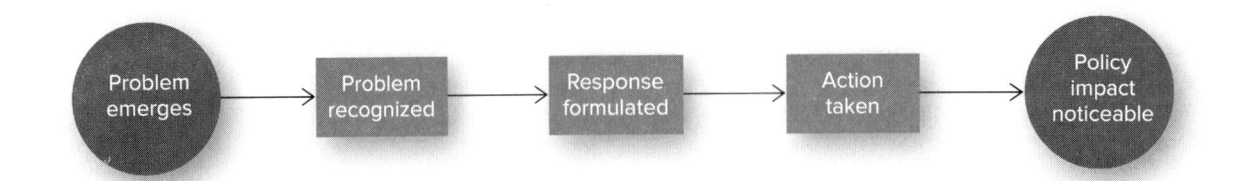

Problem emerges → Problem recognized → Response formulated → Action taken → Policy impact noticeable

Figure 16.4 Policy Response: A Series of Time Lags Even the best-intentioned economic policy can be frustrated by time lags. It takes time for a problem to be recognized, time to formulate a policy response, and still more time to implement that policy. By the time the policy begins to affect the economy, the underlying problem may have changed.

Fiscal Policy 财政政策

The politics of fiscal policy were clearly visible in the policy response to the 2008–2009 recession. Democrats preferred to rely on increases in government spending to stimulate aggregate demand. Republicans preferred tax cuts to expand the private sector while limiting the size of government. Democrats wanted more stimulus; Republicans worried that too much stimulus would widen the deficit and increase inflation. No Republican in the House of Representatives and only three Republicans in the Senate voted for President Obama's massive fiscal stimulus package. When the stimulus didn't deliver the promised AD shift, Republicans were quick to label the fiscal package wasteful and ineffective.

The tables were turned in 2017 when President Trump proposed a $1.5 trillion tax cut. Republicans emphasized that the tax cuts would jumpstart investment, accelerate growth, and create millions more jobs. Democrats responded that the tax cuts were unfairly targeted on wealthy individuals and corporations, with little benefit for the middle class. They also worried that the implied increase in the government's budget deficit would put a lid on government spending. In the end, not a single Democrat voted for the tax cuts, in either the Senate or the House of Representatives.

The increase in the federal budget deficit alarmed not just Democrats, but Republicans as well. Polls revealed that the public was concerned about growing deficits as well. But what could be done about it?

Republicans opposed any tax increases, and Democrats opposed any spending cuts. That didn't leave many tools in the fiscal policy toolbox. In the end, the president and the Congress made vague promises to reduce *future* deficits but adopted little immediate fiscal restraint.

Monetary Policy 货币政策

理论上，美联储理事会政治上的独立性提供了某种保护，使其免受一些不明智但在政治上有利的政策决策的影响。然而在实际中，美联储的相对沉默和独立性可能会适得其反。总统和国会都知道，如果不采取强有力的措施来抑制通货膨胀——通过提高税收或减少政府支出，那么美联储能够并且将会采取更加强硬的措施来抑制总需求。这是一个"鱼和熊掌都想兼得"的典型案例。当选者因为不加税或者不削减某些选民偏好的支出项目而赢得选票，他们还将美联储的政策带来的通货膨胀率下降归功于自己。最绝的是，国会和总统还会指责美联储提高了利率，或指责他们制定的货币政策过于严厉，从而导致了经济衰退。

In theory, the political independence of the Fed's Board of Governors provides some protection from ill-advised but politically advantageous policy decisions. In practice, however, the Fed's relative obscurity and independence may backfire. The president and the Congress know that if they don't take action against inflation—by raising taxes or cutting government spending—the Fed can and will take stronger action to restrain aggregate demand. This is a classic case of having one's cake and eating it too. Elected officials win votes for not raising taxes or not cutting some constituent's favorite spending program. They also take credit for any reduction in the rate of inflation brought about by Federal Reserve policies. To top it off, Congress and the president can also blame the Fed for driving up interest rates or starting a recession if monetary policy becomes too restrictive.

This was the tactic President Trump pursued in late 2018. In response to the strong economy and low unemployment, the Fed raised interest rates three times in the first nine months of 2018 and declared its intention to raise them further. President Trump worried that higher interest rates might slow the economy down, particularly just before the November midterm elections. He was quick to say that the Fed had "gone crazy" and was "making a mistake." If the economy did slow down, Trump could blame the Fed (including the Fed chair he appointed). If the economy continued to grow, he could take credit for stimulative tax cuts—a political win-win for the president. Fed defenders pointed out that the Fed's job was to foresee macro problems (like inflation) and step in early to try and avert them. To do that successfully, the Fed had to be immune to political pressure.

Finally, we must recognize that policy design is obstructed by a certain lack of will. Neither the person in the street nor the elected public official is constantly attuned to economic goals and activities. Even students enrolled in economics courses have a hard time keeping their minds on the economy and its problems. The executive and legislative branches of government, for their part, are likely to focus on economic concerns only when economic problems become serious or voters demand action. Otherwise policymakers are apt to be complacent about economic policy as long as economic performance is within a tolerable range of desired outcomes.

POLICY PERSPECTIVES

HANDS OFF OR HANDS ON?

In view of the goal conflicts and the measurement, design, and implementation problems that policymakers confront, it is less surprising that things sometimes go wrong than that things often work out right. The maze of obstacles through which theory must pass before it becomes policy explains many economic disappointments. On this basis alone, we may conclude that **consistent fine-tuning of the economy is not compatible with either our design capabilities or our decision-making procedures.**

HANDS-OFF POLICY

Some critics of economic policy take this argument a few steps further. If fine-tuning isn't really possible, they say, we should abandon discretionary policies altogether. Typically policymakers seek minor adjustments in interest rates, unemployment, inflation, and growth. The pressure to do something is particularly irresistible in election years. In so doing, however, policymakers are as likely to worsen the economic situation as to improve it. Moreover, the potential for such short-term discretion undermines people's confidence in the economy's future.

Critics of discretionary policies say we would be better off with fixed policy rules. They would require the Fed to increase the money supply at a constant rate. Congress would be required to maintain balanced budgets or at least to offset deficits in sluggish years with surpluses in years of high growth. Such rules would prevent policymakers from over- or understimulating the economy. They would also add a dose of certainty to the economic outlook.

Milton Friedman has been one of the most persistent advocates of fixed policy rules instead of discretionary policies. With discretionary authority, Friedman argues,

> the wrong decision is likely to be made in a large fraction of cases because the decision makers are examining only a limited area and not taking into account the cumulative consequences of the policy as a whole. On the other hand, if a general rule is adopted for a group of cases as a bundle, the existence of that rule has favorable effects on people's attitudes and beliefs and expectations that would not follow even from the discretionary adoption of precisely the same policy on a series of separate occasions.[1]

The case for a hands-off policy stance is based on practical, not theoretical, arguments. Everyone agrees that flexible, discretionary policies *could* result in better economic performance. But Friedman and others argue that the practical requirements of monetary and fiscal management are too demanding and thus prone to failure. Moreover, required policies may be compromised by political pressures.

---

[1] Friedman, Milton, and Friedman, Rose D., *Capitalism and Freedom*. Chicago, IL: The University of Chicago Press, 1962, 53.

attune 使协调，使一致。complacent 自满的，自鸣得意的。irresistible 不可抵抗的。sluggish 萧条的。

HANDS-ON POLICY

Critics of fixed rules acknowledge occasional policy blunders but emphasize that the historical record of prices, employment, and growth has improved since active fiscal and monetary policies were adopted. Without flexibility in the money supply and the budget, they argue, the economy would be less stable and our economic goals would remain unfulfilled. They say the government must maintain a hands-on policy of active intervention.

The historical evidence does not provide overwhelming support for either policy stance. Victor Zarnowitz showed that the U.S. economy has been much more stable since 1946 than it was in earlier periods (1875–1918 and 1919–1945). Recessions have gotten shorter and economic expansions longer. But a variety of factors—including a shift from manufacturing to services, a larger government sector, and automatic stabilizers—have contributed to this improved macro performance. The contribution of discretionary macro policy is less clear. It is easy to observe what actually happened but almost impossible to determine what would have occurred given other circumstances. It is also evident that there have been noteworthy occasions—the September 11 terrorist attacks, for example—when something more than fixed rules for monetary and fiscal policy was called for, a contingency even Professor Friedman acknowledges. Thus occasional flexibility is required, even if a nondiscretionary policy is appropriate in most situations.

Finally, one must contend with the difficulties inherent in adhering to any fixed rules. How is the Fed, for example, supposed to maintain a steady rate of growth in M1? The supply of money (M1) is not determined exclusively by the Fed. It also depends on the willingness of market participants to buy and sell bonds, maintain bank balances, and borrow money. Because all of this behavior is subject to change at any time, maintaining a steady rate of M1 growth is an impossible task.

The same is true of fiscal policy. Policymakers can't control deficits completely. Government spending and taxes are directly affected by the business cycle—by changes in unemployment, inflation, interest rates, and growth. These automatic stabilizers make it virtually impossible to maintain any fixed rule for budget balancing. Moreover, if we eliminated the automatic stabilizers, we would risk greater instability.

MODEST EXPECTATIONS

The clamor for fixed policy rules is more a rebuke of past policy than a viable policy alternative. We really have no choice but to pursue discretionary policies. Recognition of measurement, design, and implementation problems is important for an understanding of the way the economy functions. But even though it is impossible to reach all our goals, we cannot abandon the pursuit. If public policy can create a few more jobs, a better mix of output, a little more growth and price stability, or an improved distribution of income, those initiatives are worthwhile.

CHAPTER 16 REVIEW

SUMMARY

- The major options available for macro policy are fiscal policy, monetary policy, and supply-side policy. **LO1**
- Policy guidelines are clear: To end a recession, we can cut taxes, expand the money supply, or increase government spending. To curb inflation, we can reverse each of these policy levers. To overcome stagflation, we can combine fiscal and monetary levers with improved supply-side incentives. **LO2**
- Although the potential of economic theory is impressive, the economic record does not look as good. Persistent unemployment, recurring economic slowdowns, and nagging inflation suggest that the realities of policymaking are more difficult than theory implies. **LO3**
- To a large extent, the failures of economic policy are a reflection of scarce resources and competing goals. Even when consensus exists, however, serious obstacles to effective economic policy remain:
    a. *Measurement problems.* Our knowledge of economic performance is always dated and incomplete. We must rely on forecasts of future problems.

---

blunder 大错，失误。 stance 态度，立场。 rebuke 指责。

b. *Design problems.* We don't know exactly how the economy will respond to specific policies.

c. *Implementation problems.* It takes time for Congress and the president to agree on an appropriate plan of action. Moreover, the agreements reached may respond more to political needs than to economic needs.

For all these reasons, fine-tuning of economic performance rarely lives up to its theoretical potential. **LO4**

- Many people favor rules rather than discretionary macro policies. They argue that discretionary policies are unlikely to work and risk being wrong. Critics respond that discretionary policies are needed to cope with ever-changing economic circumstances. **LO5**

TERMS TO REMEMBER

Define the following terms:

business cycle
fiscal policy
automatic stabilizer
fiscal year (FY)
monetary policy
money supply (M1)

supply-side policy
GDP gap
multiplier
stagflation
structural unemployment
fine-tuning

QUESTIONS FOR DISCUSSION

1. What policies would Keynesians, monetarists, and supply-siders advocate for? **LO2**
   a. Restraining inflation.
   b. Reducing unemployment.
2. Suppose it is an election year and aggregate demand is growing so fast that it threatens to set off an inflationary movement. Why might Congress and the president hesitate to cut back on government spending or raise taxes, as economic theory suggests is appropriate? **LO4**
3. Should military spending be subject to macroeconomic constraints? What programs should be expanded or contracted to bring about needed changes in the budget? **LO4**
4. Why does it take so long to recognize that a recession has begun (see the News Wire "Measurement Problems")? **LO4**
5. Democrats opposed President Trump's 2017 tax cuts because the cuts favored corporations over middle-class families. If the tax cuts had favored families over corporations, what differences would it have made for macro outcomes? **LO2**
6. Outline a macro policy package for attaining full employment and price stability in the next 12 months. What obstacles, if any, will impede attainment of these goals? **LO2**
7. Which nation had the best macro performance in 2000–2017 (see the News Wire "Comparative Performance")? **LO3**
8. According to the News Wire "Comparative Performance," which country had (*a*) the fastest growth and highest inflation? (*b*) the slowest growth and the lowest inflation? (*c*) Why might these performance measures be correlated? **LO3**
9. President Trump said the Fed was making a mistake when it raised interest rates in 2018. Should the president have more control of the Fed? Should Congress? **LO5**
10. **POLICY PERSPECTIVES** Should economic policies respond immediately to any changes in reported unemployment or inflation rates? When should a response be undertaken? **LO5**

PROBLEMS

1. The 2008 fiscal policy package included roughly $100 billion in tax rebates that were mailed to taxpayers. By how much would aggregate demand shift (*a*) initially and (*b*) ultimately as a result of these rebates? Assume the MPC is 0.95. **LO2**

2. The expiration of the payroll tax cut of January 1, 2013 raised taxes by $110 billion per year. If the marginal propensity to save was 0.20, (*a*) by how much did consumer spending decrease initially? (*b*) what was the ultimate decline in aggregate demand? **LO2**

3. If every one-point reduction in the corporate tax rate increases business investment by $40 billion, by how much did the 2017 tax cut increase investment (refer to Table 16.2)? **LO2**

4. Suppose that for every 1 percentage point increase (decrease) in GDP growth, automatic stabilizers **LO4**

    a. increase (decrease) tax revenues by $80 billion and

    b. decrease (increase) transfer payments by $40 billion.

    Using this information, complete the table.

Change in GDP Growth Rate	Change in Tax Revenue (billions)	Change in Transfer Payments (billions)	Change in Budget Balance (billions)
−2%			
+1%			
+3%			

5. If automatic stabilizers increase the federal budget balance by $60 billion for every 1 percent increase in real GDP growth, what will happen to the federal budget balance if economic growth accelerates from 1 percent to 4 percent? **LO4**

6. The so-called misery index is computed as the sum of the unemployment and inflation rates. According to the News Wire "Comparative Performance," what was the most miserable nation from 2000 to 2017 by this measure? **LO3**

7. The following table presents hypothetical data on inflation, unemployment, and pollution associated with various levels of government expenditure and taxation. A government decision maker is trying to determine the optimal level of government expenditures and taxation with each of the three columns being a possible option (policy options A, B, or C). **LO4**

	Policy Option		
	A	B	C
Government expenditure	$700	$800	$ 900
Taxes	$600	$800	$1,000
Inflation (index)	1.00	1.04	1.15
Unemployment rate	10%	4%	3.5%
Pollution index	1.00	1.80	2.00

    a. Compute the federal budget balance for each policy option.

    b. What policy option would best accomplish each of the following goals?

    i. Lowest taxes.

    ii. Lowest pollution.

    iii. Lowest inflation rate.

    iv. Lowest unemployment rate.

    v. A balanced federal budget.

8. **POLICY PERSPECTIVES** Monetary stimulus in the form of lower interest rates is an alternative to fiscal stimulus. If a 0.1 percentage point change in interest rates has the stimulus impact of $10 billion in spending, what is the monetary equivalent (in terms of a change in the interest rate) of a $400 billion fiscal stimulus? **LO2**

图书在版编目（CIP）数据

经济学基础：第11版：双语教学通用版：英、汉／（美）布拉德利·希勒，（美）卡伦·格布哈特著；王福重，张志超译注.—北京：商务印书馆，2023
ISBN 978-7-100-21834-4

Ⅰ.①经… Ⅱ.①布… ②卡… ③王… ④张… Ⅲ.①经济学-双语教学-教材-英、汉 Ⅳ.①F0

中国版本图书馆CIP数据核字（2022）第245955号

版权所有。未经出版人事先书面许可，对本出版物的任何部分不得以任何方式或途径复制或传播，包括但不限于复印、录制、录音，或通过任何数据库、信息或可检索的系统。

此双语版本经授权仅限在中华人民共和国境内（不包括香港特别行政区、澳门特别行政区和台湾地区）销售。

翻译版权©2023由麦格劳-希尔教育（新加坡）有限公司与商务印书馆所有。

本书封面贴有McGraw-Hill Education公司防伪标签，无标签者不得销售。

权利保留，侵权必究。

经济学基础（第11版，双语教学通用版）
〔美〕布拉德利·希勒 卡伦·格布哈特 著
王福重 张志超 译注
王涧秋 责任编辑

商 务 印 书 馆 出 版
（北京王府井大街36号 邮政编码100710）
商 务 印 书 馆 发 行
人卫印务（北京）有限公司印刷
ISBN 978-7-100-21834-4

2023年1月第1版　　开本850×1092　1/16
2023年1月第1次印刷　　印张 23.25
定价：88.00元